Windows® Server 2008 TCP/IP Protocols and Services

Joseph Davies

PUBLISHED BY
Microsoft Press
A Division of Microsoft Corporation
One Microsoft Way
Redmond, Washington 98052-6399

Copyright © 2008 by Microsoft Corporation

All rights reserved. No part of the contents of this book may be reproduced or transmitted in any form or by any means without the written permission of the publisher.

Library of Congress Control Number: 2007940505

Printed and bound in the United States of America.

1 2 3 4 5 6 7 8 9   QWT   3 2 1 0 9 8

Distributed in Canada by H.B. Fenn and Company Ltd.

A CIP catalogue record for this book is available from the British Library.

Microsoft Press books are available through booksellers and distributors worldwide. For further information about international editions, contact your local Microsoft Corporation office or contact Microsoft Press International directly at fax (425) 936-7329. Visit our Web site at www.microsoft.com/mspress. Send comments to mspinput@microsoft.com.

Microsoft, Active Directory, DirectX, Excel, Internet Explorer, Microsoft Press, MS-DOS, Outlook, PowerPoint, Windows, Windows NT, Windows Server, and Windows Vista are either registered trademarks or trademarks of Microsoft Corporation in the United States and/or other countries. Other product and company names mentioned herein may be the trademarks of their respective owners.

The example companies, organizations, products, domain names, e-mail addresses, logos, people, places, and events depicted herein are fictitious. No association with any real company, organization, product, domain name, e-mail address, logo, person, place, or event is intended or should be inferred.

This book expresses the author's views and opinions. The information contained in this book is provided without any express, statutory, or implied warranties. Neither the authors, Microsoft Corporation, nor its resellers, or distributors will be held liable for any damages caused or alleged to be caused either directly or indirectly by this book.

Acquisitions Editor: Martin DelRe
Developmental Editor: Karen Szall
Project Editor: Maureen Zimmerman
Editorial Production: Abshier House
Technical Reviewer: Jim Johnson; Technical Review services provided by Content Master, a member of CM Group, Ltd.
Cover: Tom Draper Design

Body Part No. X14-31160

For Joe and Helga:

For setting an example and showing me the way.

Contents at a Glance

Part I　The Network Interface Layer
1　Local Area Network (LAN) Technologies 3
2　Wide Area Network (WAN) Technologies 31
3　Address Resolution Protocol (ARP). 43
4　Point-to-Point Protocol (PPP) 61

Part II　Internet Layer Protocols
5　Internet Protocol (IP). 89
6　Internet Control Message Protocol (ICMP) 125
7　Internet Group Management Protocol (IGMP) 157
8　Internet Protocol Version 6 (IPv6) 179

Part III　Transport Layer Protocols
9　User Datagram Protocol 191
10　Transmission Control Protocol (TCP) Basics. 199
11　Transmission Control Protocol (TCP) Connections. 223
12　Transmission Control Protocol (TCP) Data Flow 245
13　Transmission Control Protocol (TCP) Retransmission
　　and Time-Out 271

Part IV　Application Layer Protocols and Services
14　Dynamic Host Configuration Protocol (DHCP) 293
15　Domain Name System. 313
16　Windows Internet Name Service 333
17　Remote Authentication Dial-In User Service (RADIUS) 353
18　Internet Protocol Security (IPsec) 373
19　Virtual Private Networks (VPNs) 407

Appendix A: Internet Protocol (IP) Addressing. 421
Glossary. 455
Bibliography 461
Index　 463

Table of Contents

Acknowledgments xxv
Introduction xxxvii

Part I   The Network Interface Layer

1   Local Area Network (LAN) Technologies 3
    LAN Encapsulations 3
    Ethernet 4
        Ethernet II 5
        IEEE 802.3 9
        IEEE 802.3 SNAP 12
        Special Bits on Ethernet MAC Addresses 14
    Token Ring 15
        IEEE 802.5 16
        IEEE 802.5 SNAP 19
        Special Bits on Token Ring MAC Addresses 20
    FDDI 21
        FDDI Frame Format 22
        FDDI SNAP 24
        Special Bits on FDDI MAC Addresses 25
    IEEE 802.11 26
        IEEE 802.11 Frame Format 26
        IEEE 802.11 SNAP 30
    Summary 30

2   Wide Area Network (WAN) Technologies 31
    WAN Encapsulations 31
    Point-to-Point Protocol 32
        PPP on Asynchronous Links 34
        PPP on Synchronous Links 35
        PPP Maximum Receive Unit 36
        PPP Multilink Protocol 36
    Frame Relay 38
        Frame Relay Encapsulation 39
    Summary 41

3 Address Resolution Protocol (ARP) 43
Overview of ARP 43
    The ARP or Neighbor Cache 45
ARP Frame Structure 45
ARP in Windows Server 2008 and Windows Vista 48
    Address Resolution 48
    Duplicate Address Detection 51
    Neighbor Unreachability Detection 54
    ARP Registry Values 56
Inverse ARP (InARP) 57
Proxy ARP 58
Summary 60

4 Point-to-Point Protocol (PPP) 61
PPP Connection Process 62
    Phase 1: PPP Configuration Using LCP 62
    Phase 2: Authentication 62
    Phase 3: Callback 62
    Phase 4: Protocol Configuration Using NCPs 63
PPP Connection Termination 63
Link Control Protocol 63
    LCP Options 64
    LCP Negotiation Process 66
PPP Authentication Protocols 67
    PAP 68
    CHAP 70
    MS-CHAP v2 71
    EAP 73
Callback and the Callback Control Protocol 78
Network Control Protocols 79
    IPCP 79
    Compression Control Protocol 80
    Encryption Control Protocol 82
Network Monitor Example 82
PPP over Ethernet 83
    PPPoE Discovery Stage 84
    PPPoE Session Stage 85
Summary 85

Part II Internet Layer Protocols

5 Internet Protocol (IP) 89

Introduction to IP 89
    IP Services 90
    IP MTU 91
The IP Datagram 92
The IP Header 93
    Version 93
    Internet Header Length 94
    Type Of Service 94
    Total Length 98
    Identification 99
    Flags 99
    Fragment Offset 99
    Time-To-Live 99
    Protocol 101
    Header Checksum 101
    Source Address 102
    Destination Address 102
    Options and Padding 102
Fragmentation 103
    Fragmentation Fields 103
    Fragmentation Example 105
    Reassembly Example 107
    Fragmenting a Fragment 109
    Avoiding Fragmentation 109
    Fragmentation and TCP/IP for Windows Server 2008 and Windows Vista ...112
IP Options 112
    Copy 113
    Option Class 113
    Option Number 113
    Strict and Loose Source Routing 116
    IP Router Alert 120
    Internet Timestamp 121
Summary 123

6 Internet Control Message Protocol (ICMP) 125

ICMP Message Structure 126

Table of Contents

- ICMP Messages 127
  - ICMP Echo and Echo Reply 127
  - ICMP Destination Unreachable 129
  - PMTU Discovery 133
  - ICMP Source Quench 136
  - ICMP Redirect 137
  - ICMP Router Discovery 141
  - ICMP Time Exceeded 144
  - ICMP Parameter Problem 145
  - ICMP Address Mask Request and Address Mask Reply 146
- Ping.exe Tool 148
  - Ping Options 148
- Tracert.exe Tool 150
  - Tracert Options 152
- Pathping.exe Tool 153
  - Pathping Options 155
- Summary 155

7 Internet Group Management Protocol (IGMP) 157
- Introduction to IP Multicast and IGMP 157
  - IP Multicasting Overview 158
  - Host Support 158
  - Router Support 160
  - The Multicast-Enabled IP Internetwork 161
  - The Internet's Multicast-Enabled Backbone 162
- IGMP Message Structure 163
  - IGMP Version 1 (IGMPv1) 163
  - IGMP Version 2 (IGMPv2) 166
  - IGMP Version 3 (IGMPv3) 169
- IGMP in Windows Server 2008 and Windows Vista 173
  - TCP/IP Protocol 173
  - Routing And Remote Access Service 174
- Summary 176

8 Internet Protocol Version 6 (IPv6) 179
- The Disadvantages of IPv4 179
- IPv6 Addressing 181
  - Basics of IPv6 Address Syntax 182
  - Types of Addresses 182

		Types of Unicast Addresses 183
		IPv6 Interface Identifiers 183
		DNS Support 184
	Core Protocols of IPv6 184
		IPv6 184
		ICMPv6 185
		Neighbor Discovery 185
		Multicast Listener Discovery 186
	Differences Between IPv4 and IPv6 186
	Summary 187

Part III Transport Layer Protocols

9 User Datagram Protocol 191

Introduction to UDP 191
Uses for UDP 192
The UDP Message 193
The UDP Header 193
UDP Ports 195
The UDP Pseudo Header 196
Summary 197

10 Transmission Control Protocol (TCP) Basics 199

Introduction to TCP 199
The TCP Segment 200
The TCP Header 201
TCP Ports 204
TCP Flags 205
The TCP Pseudo Header 207
TCP Urgent Data 208
TCP Options 210
End Of Option List and No Operation 210
Maximum Segment Size Option 210
TCP Window Scale Option 213
Selective Acknowledgment Option 215
TCP Timestamps Option 218
Summary 221

11 Transmission Control Protocol (TCP) Connections 223

The TCP Connection 223

Table of Contents

TCP Connection Establishment 224
    Segment 1: The Synchronize (SYN) Segment 225
    Segment 2: The SYN-ACK Segment 227
    Segment 3: The ACK Segment 228
    Results of the TCP Connection 229
TCP Half-Open Connections 230
TCP Connection Maintenance 232
TCP Connection Termination 234
    Segment 1: The FIN-ACK from TCP Peer 1 234
    Segment 2: The ACK from TCP Peer 2 235
    Segment 3: The FIN-ACK from TCP Peer 2 236
    Segment 4: The ACK from TCP Peer 1 237
TCP Connection Reset 238
TCP Connection States 240
    Controlling the TIME WAIT state in Windows Server 2008 and
    Windows Vista 242
Summary 243

12 Transmission Control Protocol (TCP) Data Flow 245

Basic TCP Data Flow Behavior 245
TCP Acknowledgments 246
    Delayed Acknowledgments 246
    Cumulative for Contiguous Data 247
    Selective for Noncontiguous Data 248
TCP Sliding Windows 249
    Send Window 249
    Receive Window 252
    Receive Window Auto-Tuning 255
Small Segments 257
    The Nagle Algorithm 257
    Silly Window Syndrome 258
Sender-Side Flow Control 259
    Slow Start Algorithm 260
    Congestion Avoidance Algorithm 262
    Compound TCP 264
    Explicit Congestion Notification 265
    Limited Transmit 268
Summary 268

13 Transmission Control Protocol (TCP) Retransmission and Time-Out 271
Retransmission Time-Out and Round-Trip Time............................271
Congestion Collapse 273
Retransmission Behavior...273
Retransmission Behavior for New Connections 275
Dead Gateway Detection 275
Forward RTO-Recovery..277
Using the Selective Acknowledgment (SACK) TCP Option 278
Calculating the RTO...279
Using the TCP Timestamps Option 280
Karn's Algorithm 284
Karn's Algorithm and the Timestamps Option 285
Fast Retransmit and Fast Recovery 286
Fast Recovery 288
Summary 289

Part IV Application Layer Protocols and Services

14 Dynamic Host Configuration Protocol (DHCP).................. 293
DHCP Messages 293
DHCP Message Format..294
DHCP Options 297
DHCP Message Exchanges 301
Obtaining an Initial Lease..301
Renewing a Lease...308
Changing Subnets 308
Detecting Unauthorized DHCP Servers 309
Updating DNS Entries 310
Summary 311

15 Domain Name System.................................... 313
Sample of an AA (section1, H1, heading1) Heading Entry 000
DNS Messages..313
DNS Name Query Request and Name Query Response Messages..........314
DNS Update and Update Response Messages 319
DNS Message Exchanges...323
Resolving Names to Addresses 323
Resolving Addresses to Names 325
Resolving Aliases 326

		Dynamically Updating DNS 327
		Transferring Zone Information Between DNS Servers 330
	Summary 331
16	**Windows Internet Name Service** 333
	NetBT Name Service Messages 333
		NetBIOS Name Service Messages 334
		NetBIOS Name Representation 338
		Question RR Format 340
	WINS Client and Server Message Exchanges 344
		Resolving NetBIOS Names to IPv4 Addresses 344
		Registering NetBIOS Names 346
		Refreshing NetBIOS Names 349
		Releasing NetBIOS Names 351
	Summary 352
17	**Remote Authentication Dial-In User Service (RADIUS)** 353
	RADIUS Messages 353
		RADIUS Message Structure 355
		RADIUS Attributes 356
		Vendor-Specific Attributes 362
	RADIUS Message Exchanges 364
		Authentication of Network Access 364
		Accounting of Network Access 367
		RADIUS Proxy Forwarding 370
	Summary 372
18	**Internet Protocol Security (IPsec)** 373
	IPsec Headers 373
		Authentication Header 374
		Encapsulating Security Payload (ESP) 378
	IPsec and Security Associations 383
	Internet Key Exchange 385
	ISAKMP Message Structure 385
		ISAKMP Header 385
		SA Payload 388
		Proposal Payload 389
		Transform Payload 390
		Vendor ID Payload 392
		Nonce Payload 393

Table of Contents

        Key Exchange Payload 393
        Notification Payload 394
        Delete Payload 395
        Identification Payload 396
        Hash Payload 396
        Certificate Request Payload 397
        Certificate Payload 398
        Signature Payload 398
    Main Mode Negotiation 399
    Quick Mode Negotiation 399
    Authenticated Internet Protocol (AuthIP) 401
        AuthIP Messages 401
        AuthIP and IKE Coexistence 401
    IPsec NAT Traversal 404
    Summary 406

19 Virtual Private Networks (VPNs) 407
    PPTP 407
        PPTP Data Encapsulation 408
        PPTP Control Connection 411
    L2TP/IPsec 413
        L2TP/IPsec Data Encapsulation 413
        L2TP Control Connection 416
    SSTP 418
        SSTP-based VPN Connection Creation Process 419
    Summary 420

Appendix A: Internet Protocol (IP) Addressing 421
    Types of IP Addresses 421
    Expressing IP Addresses 421
        Converting from Binary to Decimal 422
        Converting from Decimal to Binary 423
        IP Addresses in the IP Header 423
    Unicast IP Addresses 423
        A History Lesson: IP Address Classes 424
        Rules for Enumerating Address Prefixes 426
        Rules for Enumerating Usable Host IDs 426

      Subnets and the Subnet Mask 427
      How to Subnet 431
      Variable-Length Subnetting 440
      Supernetting and CIDR 443
      Public and Private Addresses 446
      Automatic Private IP Addressing 448
  IP Broadcast Addresses 450
      Network Broadcast 450
      Subnet Broadcast 451
      All-Subnets-Directed Broadcast 451
      Limited Broadcast 451
  IP Multicast Addresses 452
      Mapping IP Multicast Addresses to MAC Addresses 453
  Summary 454

Glossary 455

Bibliography 461

Index 463

List of Figures

Figure 1-1: The Ethernet II frame format showing the Ethernet II header and trailer 5
Figure 1-2: The maximum-extent Ethernet network and the slot time. 8
Figure 1-3: The IEEE 802.3 frame format showing the IEEE 802.3 header and trailer and the IEEE 802.2 LLC header. 9
Figure 1-4: IEEE 802.3 SNAP frame format showing the SNAP header and an IP datagram. 12
Figure 1-5: The special bits defined for Ethernet source and destination MAC addresses. 14
Figure 1-6: The IEEE 802.5 frame format showing the IEEE 802.5 header and trailer and the IEEE 802.2 LLC header. 16
Figure 1-7: The IEEE 802.5 SNAP frame format showing the SNAP header and an IP datagram. 20
Figure 1-8: The special bits defined on Token Ring source and destination MAC addresses. 21
Figure 1-9: The FDDI frame format showing the FDDI header and trailer and IEEE 802.2 LLC header. 22
Figure 1-10: The FDDI SNAP frame format showing the SNAP header and an IP datagram 25
Figure 1-11: The IEEE 802.11 frame format showing the IEEE 802.11 header and trailer and the IEEE 802.2 LLC header. 27
Figure 1-12: The Frame Control field in the IEEE 802.11 header 29
Figure 1-13: The IEEE 802.11 SNAP frame format showing the SNAP header and an IP datagram. 30
Figure 2-1: PPP encapsulation using HDLC framing for an IP datagram 33
Figure 2-2: Typical PPP encapsulation for an IP datagram 34
Figure 2-3: The Multilink Protocol header, using the long sequence number format . . 37
Figure 2-4: The Multilink Protocol header, using the short sequence number format . . 38
Figure 2-5: Frame Relay encapsulation for IP datagrams, showing the Frame Relay header and trailer 39
Figure 2-6: A 2-byte Frame Relay Address field 40
Figure 3-1: The structure of an ARP frame. 46
Figure 3-2: An example of address resolution. 48
Figure 3-3: A single subnet configuration, using a proxy ARP device. 59
Figure 3-4: A remote access server running Windows Server 2008 and configured with an on-subnet address range using Proxy ARP 60
Figure 4-1: The structure of an LCP frame. 63
Figure 4-2: The structure of an LCP frame containing LCP options. 65
Figure 4-3: The structure of the PAP Authenticate-Request message 69

Figure 4-4: The structure of the PAP Authenticate-Ack and Authenticate-Nak messages 69
Figure 4-5: The structure of the CHAP Challenge and CHAP Response messages...... 70
Figure 4-6: The CHAP Success and CHAP Failure message structure 71
Figure 4-7: The MS-CHAP v2 Response message structure 73
Figure 4-8: EAP-Request and EAP-Response message structure 74
Figure 4-9: EAP-Success and EAP-Failure message structure....................... 76
Figure 4-10: The structure of a PPPoE frame 83
Figure 4-11: The structure of a PPPoE frame that contains a PPP frame.............. 85
Figure 5-1: The structure of the IP datagram at the Network Interface layer.......... 93
Figure 5-2: The structure of the IP header 93
Figure 5-3: The structure of the RFC 791 IP Type Of Service field................... 94
Figure 5-4: The structure of the RFC 2474 IP TOS field............................ 97
Figure 5-5: The structure of the RFC 3168 IP TOS field............................ 98
Figure 5-6: The fields in the IP header used for fragmentation..................... 103
Figure 5-7: An example of a network where IP fragmentation can occur............ 105
Figure 5-8: The IP fragmentation process when fragmenting from a 4482-byte IP MTU link to a 1500-byte IP MTU link 106
Figure 5-9: The IP reassembly process for the four fragments of the original IP datagram 108
Figure 5-10: An MTU problem in a translational bridging environment caused by two FDDI hosts connected to two Ethernet switches......................... 111
Figure 5-11: The structure of the first byte in an IP option 113
Figure 6-1: ICMP message encapsulation showing the IP header and Network Interface Layer header and trailer 126
Figure 6-2: The structure of an ICMP message showing the fields common to all types of ICMP messages.. 126
Figure 6-3: The structure of the ICMP Echo message 128
Figure 6-4: The structure of the ICMP Echo Reply message 128
Figure 6-5: The structure of the ICMP Destination Unreachable message 129
Figure 6-6: A PMTU-compliant ICMP Destination Unreachable-Fragmentation Needed And DF Set message showing the Next Hop MTU field 134
Figure 6-7: The structure of the ICMP Source Quench message.................... 137
Figure 6-8: An ICMP Redirect scenario in which a host with a configured default gateway must forward an IP datagram using another router 138
Figure 6-9: The structure of the ICMP Redirect message 139
Figure 6-10: The structure of the ICMP Router Advertisement message............. 142
Figure 6-11: The structure of the ICMP Router Solicitation message 143

Table of Contents   xix

Figure 6-12: The structure of the ICMP Time Exceeded message 145
Figure 6-13: The structure of the ICMP Parameter Problem message 145
Figure 6-14: The structure of the ICMP Address Mask Request and Reply messages. . . 147
Figure 7-1: A multicast-enabled intranet showing multicast-enabled hosts
and routers 162
Figure 7-2: IGMP message structure showing the IP header and Network
Interface Layer header and trailer 163
Figure 7-3: The structure of an IGMPv1 message 164
Figure 7-4: The structure of an IGMPv2 message 168
Figure 7-5: The structure of the IGMPv3 Host Membership Query message 171
Figure 7-6: The structure of the IGMPv3 Host Membership Report message 171
Figure 7-7: The structure of the IGMPv3 Host Membership Report message
group record 172
Figure 7-8: The use of IGMP router mode and proxy mode 175
Figure 9-1: UDP message encapsulation showing the IP header and Network
Interface Layer header and trailer 193
Figure 9-2: The structure of the UDP header 193
Figure 9-3: The demultiplexing of a UDP message to the appropriate
Application Layer protocol using the IP Protocol field and the UDP Destination
Port field 196
Figure 9-4: The structure of the UDP pseudo header 197
Figure 9-5: The resulting quantity used for the UDP checksum calculation 197
Figure 10-1: TCP segment encapsulation showing the IP header and
Network Interface Layer header and trailer 201
Figure 10-2: The structure of the TCP header 201
Figure 10-3: The demultiplexing of a TCP segment to the appropriate
Application Layer protocol using the IP Protocol field and the TCP Destination
Port field 205
Figure 10-4: The eight TCP flags in the Flags field of the TCP header 206
Figure 10-5: The structure of the TCP pseudo header 207
Figure 10-6: The resulting quantity used for the TCP checksum calculation 208
Figure 10-7: The location of TCP urgent data within a TCP segment 209
Figure 10-8: The structure of multiple-byte TCP options 210
Figure 10-9: The TCP MSS defined in terms of the IP MTU and the TCP and IP
header sizes 211
Figure 10-10: The structure of the TCP MSS option 211
Figure 10-11: Hosts connected to two wireless APs that are connected by
an Ethernet backbone 213
Figure 10-12: The structure of the TCP Window Scale option 214

Figure 10-13: The structure of the TCP SACK-Permitted option 216
Figure 10-14: The structure of the TCP SACK option. 217
Figure 10-15: The structure of the TCP Timestamps option. 219
Figure 10-16: An example of the use of the TCP Timestamps option. 219
Figure 11-1: A TCP connection showing both inbound and outbound logical pipes . . 224
Figure 11-2: The TCP connection establishment process, showing the exchange of three TCP segments. 225
Figure 11-3: A TCP half-open connection showing the SYN segment and retransmissions of the SYN-ACK segment. 230
Figure 11-4: A TCP keepalive showing the sending of an exchange of ACK segments to confirm both ends of the connection are still present. 233
Figure 11-5: A TCP connection termination showing the exchange of four TCP segments 234
Figure 11-6: A TCP connection reset showing the SYN and RST segments. 239
Figure 11-7: The states of a TCP connection. 241
Figure 11-8: The states of a TCP connection during TCP connection establishment. . . 242
Figure 11-9: The states of a TCP connection during TCP connection termination. 242
Figure 12-1: The cumulative acknowledgment scheme of TCP. 247
Figure 12-2: The selective acknowledgment scheme of TCP 248
Figure 12-3: The types of data for the TCP send window. 249
Figure 12-4: The sliding of the send window showing window closing and opening . . 251
Figure 12-5: The types of data for the TCP receive window. 253
Figure 12-6: Sliding the receive window 255
Figure 12-7: An example of ECN for a TCP connection 267
Figure 13-1: The behavior of TCP timestamps with pauses in data 281
Figure 13-2: The behavior of TCP timestamps for delayed acknowledgments. 282
Figure 13-3: The behavior of TCP timestamps for out-of-order segments 283
Figure 13-4: The behavior of TCP timestamps for retransmitted segments 283
Figure 13-5: Fast retransmit behavior when the first of five segments is dropped. 287
Figure 13-6: Fast retransmit behavior when combined with limited transmit. 287
Figure 14-1: DHCP message format. 295
Figure 14-2: DHCP option format. 297
Figure 14-3: DHCP messages exchanged during initial lease acquisition 301
Figure 14-4: DHCP message exchange when a DHCP client moves to a different subnet. 309
Figure 14-5: A DHCP server performing rogue server detection. 310
Figure 15-1: DNS Name Query Request and Name Query Response message structure. 314

Figure 15-2: DNS Name Query Request and Name Query Response message header . 315
Figure 15-3: The Flags field 315
Figure 15-4: Question entry format 316
Figure 15-5: DNS RR format in a DNS name query response 317
Figure 15-6: The RR Name as a pointer to a name stored elsewhere in the
DNS message 319
Figure 15-7: Example of a pointer value in the RR Name field in Network
Monitor 3.1 319
Figure 15-8: DNS Update and Update Response message structure 320
Figure 15-9: DNS Update and Update Response message header 320
Figure 15-10: The Flags field for DNS Update and Update Response messages 320
Figure 15-11: Zone entry format 321
Figure 16-1: NetBIOS name service message structure 335
Figure 16-2: Name Service header 335
Figure 16-3: The Flags field in the Name Service header 336
Figure 16-4: Example of a NetBIOS name in Network Monitor 3.1 340
Figure 16-5: Question entry format 340
Figure 16-6: RR format in NetBIOS name service messages 341
Figure 16-7: Format for General Name Service RRs 342
Figure 16-8: Format of the RDATA flags field 342
Figure 16-9: The RR Name as a pointer to a name stored elsewhere in the message . . 343
Figure 16-10: Example of a pointer value in the RR Name field in Network
Monitor 3.1 343
Figure 17-1: RADIUS message structure 355
Figure 17-2: RADIUS attribute structure 356
Figure 17-3: General VSA structure 363
Figure 17-4: Recommended VSA structure 363
Figure 18-1: The IPsec Authentication header 374
Figure 18-2: AH Transport mode 376
Figure 18-3: AH Tunnel mode 377
Figure 18-4: The IPsec Encapsulating Security Payload header and trailer 378
Figure 18-5: ESP Transport mode 380
Figure 18-6: Using both AH and ESP to protect an IP packet 381
Figure 18-7: ESP Tunnel mode 382
Figure 18-8: An ISAKMP message 385
Figure 18-9: The ISAKMP header 386
Figure 18-10: The SA payload 388

Figure 18-11: The Proposal payload. 389
Figure 18-12: The Transform payload 390
Figure 18-13: The Vendor ID payload 392
Figure 18-14: The Nonce payload. 393
Figure 18-15: The Key Exchange payload 393
Figure 18-16: The Notification payload... 394
Figure 18-17: The Delete payload.. 395
Figure 18-18: The Identification payload... 396
Figure 18-19: The Hash payload 397
Figure 18-20: The Certificate Request payload..................................... 397
Figure 18-21: The Certificate payload 398
Figure 18-22: The Signature payload... 399
Figure 18-23: AuthIP messages containing the Crypto payload 401
Figure 19-1: PPTP data packet structure 408
Figure 19-2: GRE header for PPTP data encapsulation 409
Figure 19-3: L2TP encapsulation without IPsec encryption 414
Figure 19-4: L2TP encapsulation with IPsec encryption 414
Figure 19-5: The L2TP header for encapsulated data 415
Figure 19-6: The structure of SSTP packets....................................... 419
Figure A-1: The generalized IP address consisting of 32 bits expressed in dotted decimal notation. 422
Figure A-2: An 8-bit number showing bit positions and their decimal equivalents. 422
Figure A-3: The structure of an example IP address showing the subnet prefix and host ID. 424
Figure A-4: The class A address showing the address prefix and the host ID. 425
Figure A-5: The class B address showing the address prefix and the host ID. 425
Figure A-6: The class C address showing the address prefix and the host ID. 425
Figure A-7: The class B address prefix 131.107.0.0 before subnetting. 427
Figure A-8: The class B network 131.107.0.0 after subnetting. 428
Figure A-9: The relationship between the number of subnets and hosts per subnet when subnetting the class B address prefix 131.107.0.0. 433
Figure A-10: The variable-length subnetting of 131.107.0.0/16 into address prefixes of different sizes. 442
Figure A-11: The mapping of IP multicast addresses to Ethernet MAC addresses. 454

List of Tables

Table 2-1: Defined Values for the Frame Relay DLCI 40
Table 3-1: ARP Hardware Type Values 46
Table 3-2: ARP Operation Values 47
Table 4-1: LCP Frame Types 64
Table 4-2: LCP Options 65
Table 4-3: EAP Types 75
Table 4-4: CBCP Options 78
Table 4-5: IPCP Options 79
Table 4-6: CCP Options 80
Table 5-1: IP MTUs for Common Network Interface Layer Technologies 91
Table 5-2: Values of the IP Precedence Field 95
Table 5-3: Values of the IP Protocol Field 101
Table 5-4: Original IP Datagram 105
Table 5-5: Fragments of the Original IP Datagram 106
Table 5-6: Option Classes 113
Table 5-7: Option Classes and Numbers 113
Table 6-1: Common ICMP Types 127
Table 6-2: Code Values for ICMP Destination Unreachable Messages 130
Table 6-3: Plateau Values for PMTU 135
Table 6-4: Values of the Code Field in an ICMP Redirect Message 140
Table 6-5: ICMP Parameter Problem Code Values 146
Table 6-6: Ping Tool Options 148
Table 6-7: Tracert Tool Options 152
Table 6-8: Pathping Tool Options 155
Table 7-1: Recommended Values of the TTL for IP Multicast Traffic 159
Table 7-2: Addresses Used in IGMPv1 Messages 165
Table 7-3: Values of the IGMPv2 Type Field 168
Table 7-4: Addresses Used in IGMPv2 Messages 168
Table 8-1: Differences Between IPv4 and IPv6 186
Table 9-1: Well-Known UDP Port Numbers 195
Table 10-1: Well-Known TCP Port Numbers 204
Table 11-1: TCP Connection States 240
Table 14-4: DHCP Options for Windows-based DHCP Clients and Servers 298
Table 15-1: The Most Common Values of the Question Type Field 317
Table 15-2: Return Code Values for Update Response Messages 321
Table 16-1: NetBIOS Name Service Operation Codes 337

Table 16-2:	Converting the Hexadecimal Digit to an ASCII Character	338
Table 16-3:	Values for the Record Type Field	341
Table 16-4:	Return Code Values for Name Registration Errors	348
Table 17-1:	Values for the RADIUS Code Field	356
Table 17-2:	Common RADIUS Attributes	357
Table 17-3:	Common Vendor-Specific Attributes	363
Table 18-1:	Values of the Next Payload Field	386
Table 18-2:	Values of the Exchange Type Field	387
Table 18-3:	Notification Error Messages	395
Table 18-4:	Notification Status Messages	395
Table 18-5:	Certificate Type Values	397
Table 19-1:	PPTP Control Messages	411
Table 19-2:	L2TP Control Messages	417
Table A-1:	Address Class Ranges of Address Prefixes	426
Table A-2:	Address Class Ranges of Host IDs	427
Table A-3:	Dotted Decimal Notation for Default Subnet Masks	429
Table A-4:	Prefix Length Notation for Default Subnet Masks	430
Table A-5:	Subnetting of a Class A Address Prefix	433
Table A-6:	Subnetting of a Class B Address Prefix	434
Table A-7:	Subnetting of a Class C Address Prefix	435
Table A-8:	A 3-Bit Subnetting of 131.107.0.0 (Binary)	436
Table A-9:	Enumeration of IP Addresses for the 3-Bit Subnetting of 131.107.0.0 (Binary)	436
Table A-10:	A 3-Bit Subnetting of 131.107.0.0 (Decimal)	438
Table A-11:	Enumeration of IP Addresses for the 3-Bit Subnetting of 131.107.0.0 (Decimal)	439
Table A-12:	The Eight Subnets for the 3-Bit Subnetting of 131.107.0.0/16	441
Table A-13:	A Block of Eight Class C Address Prefixes Starting with 223.1.184.0	444
Table A-14:	The Aggregated Block of Class C Address Prefixes	444
Table A-15:	Supernetting and Class C Addresses	444
Table A-16:	Reserved Local Subnet IP Multicast Addresses	453

Acknowledgments

I would like to the thank the following people at Microsoft for participating in the technical reviews of the chapters and appendices of this book: Boyd Benson, Lee Gibson, Philippe Joubert, Jason Popp, Katarzyna Puchala, Aaron Schrader, Ben Schultz, Murari Sridharan, Brian Swander, Mark Swift, and Jeff Westhead. I would like to give honorable mention to Dmitry Anipko, a Software Development Engineer on the Windows Networking Core development team, who gave me very detailed feedback on multiple chapters for both standards-based IPv4 and the implementation details of IPv4 in Windows Server 2008 and Windows Vista.

I would also like to thank Maureen Zimmerman (content project manager at Microsoft Press), Kelly D. Henthorne (project manager for Abshier House), Jim Johnson (technical reviewer), Kim Heusel (copy editor), Debbie Berman (compositor), and Johnna VanHoose Dinse (indexer).

And lastly, I would like to express my thanks and appreciation to my wife, Kara, and daughter, Katie, for their patience and tolerance for the preoccupation and time away.

Introduction

This book is a straightforward discussion of the concepts, principles, and processes of many protocols in the TCP/IP protocol suite and how they are supported by Windows Server 2008 and Windows Vista. The focus of this book is on Internet Protocol version 4 (IPv4), referred to as Internet Protocol (IP), and associated transport and network infrastructure support protocols. This book provides an overview of Internet Protocol version 6 (IPv6), but not in-depth technical details. For more information about IPv6 and its implementation in Windows Server 2008 and Windows Vista, see *Understanding IPv6, Second Edition* by Joseph Davies (Redmond, Wash.: Microsoft Press, 2008; ISBN 978-0735624467).

This book is primarily a discussion of protocols (what you might see on the wire during communication) and processes (how things work under the covers), rather than a discussion of planning, configuration, deployment, management, or application development. For a discussion of TCP/IP planning, configuration, deployment, and management, see *Windows Server® 2008 Networking and Network Access Protection (NAP)* (Redmond, Wash.: Microsoft Press, 2008; ISBN 978-0735624221), Help And Support for Windows Server 2008, and the Windows Server 2008 TechCenter at *http://technet.microsoft.com/windowsserver/2008*. For a discussion of TCP/IP application development using Windows Sockets, see the Microsoft Developer Network at *http://msdn.microsoft.com*.

This book does not contain code-level details of the Microsoft implementation of TCP/IP in Windows Server 2008 and Windows Vista, such as internal structures, tables, buffers and their use, or coding logic. These details are only of interest to a relative handful of readers and are not published for security reasons and to protect Microsoft intellectual property. However, this book does contain details of how the Microsoft implementation of TCP/IP in Windows Server 2008 and Windows Vista works for described TCP/IP processes and how to modify default behaviors with registry values and Netsh.exe tool commands.

Note Except where noted, changes to registry values require a system restart to become effective.

The purpose of this book is to both provide an educational vehicle to learn TCP/IP to a fair amount of technical depth and serve as a detailed technical reference. This book is not intended to be a TCP/IP or networking technology primer.

Who Should Read This Book

This book is intended for the following audiences:

- **Windows networking consultants and planners**   This includes anyone planning for or deploying a network containing computers running Windows Server 2008 or Windows Vista.

- **Windows network administrators**   This includes anyone who is currently managing a Windows network and wants to gain additional technical knowledge about TCP/IP and its implementation for Windows Server 2008 and Windows Vista.

- **Microsoft Certified Systems Engineers (MCSEs) and Microsoft Certified Trainers (MCTs)**   This book can be a standard reference for MCSEs and MCTs for the TCP/IP protocol suite.

- **General technical staff**   Because this book is mostly about TCP/IP protocols and processes, independent of its implementation in Windows Server 2008 or Windows Vista, general technical staff can use this book as an in-depth reference on TCP/IP protocols.

- **Information technology (IT) students**   This book, using the training slides included on the companion CD-ROM, can serve as an excellent textbook for a comprehensive intermediate or advanced-level TCP/IP course taught at an educational institution or inside your organization.

What You Should Know Before Reading This Book

This book assumes a foundation of networking knowledge that includes basic networking concepts and widely used networking technologies. For example, although the book explains in detail how IP packets are encapsulated when sent over an Ethernet network segment, it does not explain the history of Ethernet or its technical details, such as signal encoding, cabling, topologies, or configuration options. This knowledge is assumed.

This book also assumes a basic understanding of the TCP/IP protocol suite and its set of support protocols for Windows-based network. This includes an understanding of the architecture of the TCP/IP protocol suite, IP addressing, IP routing, name resolution, and the role of network infrastructure protocols such as Dynamic Host Configuration Protocol (DHCP) and Internet Protocol security (IPsec). To obtain a basic understanding of TCP/IP for Windows, see the *TCP/IP Fundamentals for Microsoft Windows* book in the \Fundamentals folder on the companion CD-ROM.

> **Note**   The *TCP/IP Fundamentals for Microsoft Windows* online book on the companion CD-ROM is the version that was available in November 2007, which is focused on TCP/IP in Windows Server 2003 and Windows XP. This online book will be updated to include information about Windows Server 2008 and Windows Vista in 2008. The most current version of the *TCP/IP Fundamentals for Microsoft Windows* online book is available at *http://technet.microsoft.com/en-us/library/bb726983.aspx*.

Organization of This Book

This book is divided into four parts, corresponding to the four layers of the Department of Defense (DoD) Advanced Research Projects Agency (DARPA) model:

- **The Network Interface Layer**   This part contains two chapters describing the local area network (LAN) and wide area network (WAN) technologies supported by Windows Server 2008 and Windows Vista, and, in particular, how they encapsulate IP datagrams. This section also includes a chapter describing Address Resolution Protocol (ARP), a simple protocol that resolves the hardware address (typically a media access control [MAC] address) for a specific next-hop IP address. This section also includes a chapter describing the Point-to-Point Protocol (PPP) suite of protocols, which provides encapsulation, link negotiation, and protocol configuration services for point-to-point links.

- **Internet Layer Protocols**   This part includes chapters describing IP, Internet Control Message Protocol (ICMP), and Internet Group Management Protocol (IGMP). A chapter on IPv6 is also included to provide an overview and to describe how it compares with IPv4, the current version of IP used on the Internet.

- **Transport Layer Protocols**   This part contains chapters describing User Datagram Protocol (UDP), a simple Transport Layer protocol for sending unreliable messages, and Transmission Control Protocol (TCP), a complex Transport Layer protocol for sending reliable data.

- **Application Layer Protocols and Services**   This part contains chapters describing key TCP/IP-related infrastructure protocols and network infrastructure services, including DHCP, the Domain Name System (DNS), the Windows Internet Name Service (WINS), Remote Authentication Dial-In User Service (RADIUS), IPsec, and virtual private networks (VPNs).

Network Monitor Traces

Throughout this book, packet structure and protocol processes are illustrated with packet captures as displayed with Network Monitor 3.1. These show the actual behavior of a protocol or service as seen on the wire. All of the traces referenced in this book are included in the \Captures folder on the companion CD-ROM.

> **Note**   Different versions of Network Monitor can display packet structure differently. You might not be able to open all of the capture files in the \Captures folder on the companion CD-ROM with a version of Network Monitor prior to Network Monitor 3.1.

About the Companion CD-ROM

The companion CD-ROM included with this book contains the following:

- **Electronic version of this book (eBook)**   An Adobe Portable Document Format (PDF) version of the book allows you to view it online and perform text searches. If you do not already have the Adobe Reader installed, you can install it from *http://www.adobe.com*. You can get the latest version of this online book at *http://technet.microsoft.com/en-us/library/bb726983.aspx*.

- **Network Monitor 3.1**   A link to the installation site for Network Monitor 3.1. The Network Monitor allows you to capture and view network traffic and view capture files. You can also install Network Monitor 3.1 from *http://go.microsoft.com/fwlink/?LinkID=92844*. For the latest information about Network Monitor, see the Network Monitor blog at *http://blogs.technet.com/netmon/*.

- **Network Monitor captures**   The Network Monitor capture files for all the captures displayed or mentioned in the book are included.

- **Internet Engineering Task Force (IETF) standards**   The set of IETF RFCs and Internet drafts that are either mentioned or relevant for each chapter of the book are stored in separate folders based on the chapter number.

- **TCP/IP Fundamentals for Microsoft Windows**   The *TCP/IP Fundamentals for Microsoft Windows* online book published on Microsoft TechNet in November of 2007, in PDF format.

- **Microsoft PowerPoint Viewer**   A link to the installation site for the Microsoft PowerPoint Viewer 2003, which enables you to read the training slides on the CD-ROM. If you already have PowerPoint installed, you do not need to install this viewer. You can also install the PowerPoint Viewer 2003 from *http://go.microsoft.com/fwlink/?LinkID=59771*.

- **Training slides**   The \TrainingSlides folder contains a set of Microsoft PowerPoint files that can be used to teach TCP/IP with this book. For more information, see "A Special Note to Teachers and Instructors" in this Introduction.

> **Note** **Digital Content for Digital Book Readers**
> If you bought a digital-only edition of this book, you can enjoy select content from the print edition's companion CD. Visit *http://go.microsoft.com/fwlink/?LinkId=104977* to get your downloadable content. This content is always up to date and available to all readers.

Disclaimer: Third-Party Sites

For the user's convenience, this CD-ROM includes links to third-party sites. Please note that these products and links are not under the control of Microsoft Corporation and Microsoft is therefore not responsible for their content, nor should their inclusion on the CD-ROM be construed as an endorsement of the products or the sites. Please check third-party Web sites for the latest version of their software.

System Requirements

For detailed system requirements for the contents of the companion CD-ROM, see "System Requirements" at the back of this book.

A Special Note to Teachers and Instructors

If you are a teacher or instructor whose task it is to inculcate an advanced understanding of the TCP/IP protocol suite in others, it is strongly urged that you consider using this book and its slides as a basis for your own TCP/IP course. Obviously, it can be used for courses that supplement TCP/IP knowledge for Windows network administrators and systems engineers. However, because the content is mostly about the details of TCP/IP protocol suite packet structure and protocol processes, this book can also be used for an implementation-independent TCP/IP course.

The slides are included to provide a foundation for your own slide presentation and contain either bulleted text or drawings that are synchronized with their chapter content. Because the slides are based on my original figures and were completed after the final book pages were done, there are some minor differences between the slides and the chapter content. Some changes were made to enhance the ability to teach a TCP/IP course based on this book.

The template that I chose for the included slides is intentionally simple so that there are minimal issues with text and drawing color translations when you switch to a different template. Please feel free to customize the slides as you see fit.

As a fellow instructor, I wish you success in your efforts to teach this interesting and important technology to others.

What Is New in This Edition

This book is an update of *Microsoft® Windows® Server 2003 TCP/IP Protocols and Services Technical Reference* by Joseph Davies and Thomas Lee. The changes and updates are the following:

- **Chapter 2: Wide Area Network (WAN) Technologies**   Coverage of the Serial Line Internet Protocol (SLIP), X.25, and Asynchronous Transfer Mode (ATM) has been removed
- **Chapter 3: Address Resolution Protocol (ARP)**   Includes coverage of new duplicate address detection and neighbor unreachability detection behavior in Windows Server 2008 and Windows Vista
- **Chapter 4: Point-to-Point Protocol (PPP)**   Coverage of the Shiva Password Authentication Protocol (SPAP), Microsoft Challenge Handshake Authentication Protocol

(MS-CHAP) (also known as MS-CHAP v1), and Extensible Authentication Protocol-Message Digest 5 (EAP-MD5) authentication protocols has been removed and coverage of the Protected EAP (PEAP) authentication protocol has been added

- **Chapter 5: Internet Protocol (IP)** Now includes a discussion of the Explicit Congestion Notification (ECN) field in the IP Type of Service (TOS) field defined in RFC 3168

- **Chapter 10 (formerly Chapter 12): Transmission Control Protocol (TCP) Basics** Now includes a discussion of the ECN flags in the TCP header defined in RFC 3168

- **Chapter 12 (formerly Chapter 14): Transmission Control Protocol (TCP) Data Flow** Now includes discussion of receive window auto-tuning, compound TCP, ECN, and limited transmit

- **Chapter 13 (formerly Chapter 15): Transmission Control Protocol (TCP) Retransmission and Time-Out** Now includes discussion of the new dead gateway detection algorithm, Forward RTO-Recovery, and new loss recovery methods

- **Chapter 14 (formerly Chapter 16): Dynamic Host Configuration Protocol (DHCP)** Restructured and rewritten to focus on DHCP protocol details and message exchanges

- **Chapter 15 (formerly Chapter 17): Domain Name System (DNS)** Restructured and rewritten to focus on DNS protocol details and message exchanges

- **Chapter 16 (formerly Chapter 18): Windows Internet Name Service (WINS)** Restructured and rewritten to focus on network basic input/output system (NetBIOS) over TCP/IP protocol details and WINS message exchanges

- **Chapter 17 (formerly Chapter 20): Remote Authentication Dial-In User Service (RADIUS)** Restructured and rewritten to focus on RADIUS protocol details and message exchanges

- **Chapter 18 (formerly Chapter 22): Internet Protocol Security (IPsec)** Updated to include information about Authenticated IP (Auth IP)

- **Chapter 19 (formerly Chapter 23): Virtual Private Networks (VPNs)** Restructured and rewritten to focus on Point-to-Point Tunneling Protocol (PPTP), Layer Two Tunneling Protocol (L2TP) details and message exchanges, and updated to include information about the Secure Socket Tunneling Protocol (SSTP)

- **Appendix A (formerly Chapter 6): IP Internet Protocol (IP) Addressing** Updated for new terminology and for Windows Server 2008 and Windows Vista

The chapters not listed were updated for new features, behaviors, and settings in Windows Server 2008 and Windows Vista.

The following chapters were removed:

- **Chapter 7: Internet Protocol (IP) Routing** The information in this chapter can be found in Chapter 5 of the *TCP/IP Fundamentals for Microsoft Windows* book in the \Fundamentals folder on the companion CD-ROM.

- **Chapter 19: File and Printer Sharing** For information about the Internet Printing Protocol (IPP), see RFCs 2567, 2568, 2569, 2910, and 2911; for information about the Common Internet File System (CIFS), see the "Common Internet File System (CIFS) File Access Protocol" document at *http://www.microsoft.com/downloads /details.aspx?FamilyID=c4adb584-7ff0-4acf-bd91-5f7708adb23c&displaylang=en*.

- **Chapter 21: Internet Information Services (IIS) and the Internet Protocols** For information about the Hypertext Transfer Protocol (HTTP), see RFC 2616; for information about the File Transfer Protocol (FTP), see RFC 959; for information about the Network News Transfer Protocol (NNTP), see RFCs 977 and 2980; for information about the Simple Mail Transfer Protocol (SMTP), see RFC 821.

Find Additional Content Online

As new or updated material becomes available that complements your book, it will be posted online on the Microsoft Press Online Windows Server And Client Web site. Based on the final build of Windows Server 2008, the type of material you might find includes updates to book content, articles, links to companion content, errata, sample chapters, and more. This Web site will be available soon at *www.microsoft.com/learning/books/online/serverclient* and will be updated periodically.

Support

This book represents a best-effort snapshot of information at the time of its publication for the implementation of many protocols in the TCP/IP suite provided in Windows Server 2008 and Windows Vista, as of the Release Candidate 0 version of Windows Server 2008 and the Beta 1 release version of Windows Vista Service Pack 1. Changes to Windows Server 2008 and Windows Vista with Service Pack 1 that were made after these versions or to IETF standards after November 15, 2007, are not reflected in this book.

To obtain the latest information about IETF standards for TCP/IP, see the IETF Web site at *http://www.ietf.org/*.

Every effort has been made to ensure the accuracy of this book and the contents of the companion CD-ROM. Microsoft Press provides corrections for books in the Microsoft Knowledge Base. To connect directly to the Microsoft Knowledge Base and enter a query regarding a question or issue that you might have concerning this book, visit *http://support.microsoft.com/ search/?adv=1*, type **978-0735624474** in the search box, and then click Search.

If you have comments, questions, or ideas regarding this book or the companion CD-ROM, please send them to Microsoft Press using either postal mail or e-mail. The postal mail address is:

Microsoft Press
Attn: *Windows Server 2008 TCP/IP Protocols and Services* Editor
One Microsoft Way
Redmond, WA 98052-6399

The e-mail address is:

MSPInput@microsoft.com.

Please note that product support is not offered through these addresses. For Windows product support information, please visit the Microsoft Support Web site at *http://support.microsoft.com/default.aspx.*

Part I
The Network Interface Layer

In this part:
Chapter 1: Local Area Network (LAN) Technologies....................3
Chapter 2: Wide Area Network (WAN) Technologies.................31
Chapter 3: Address Resolution Protocol (ARP).......................43
Chapter 4: Point-to-Point Protocol (PPP)...........................61

Chapter 1
Local Area Network (LAN) Technologies

In this chapter:
LAN Encapsulations... 3
Ethernet.. 4
Token Ring 15
FDDI... 21
IEEE 802.11 26
Summary.. 30

To successfully troubleshoot Transmission Control Protocol/Internet Protocol (TCP/IP) problems on a local area network (LAN), it is important to understand how IP datagrams and Address Resolution Protocol (ARP) messages are encapsulated when sent by a computer running Windows Server 2008 or Windows Vista on LAN technology links such as Ethernet, Token Ring, Fiber Distributed Data Interface (FDDI), and Institute of Electrical and Electronics Engineers (IEEE) 802.11. For example, IP datagrams sent over an Ethernet network segment can be encapsulated two different ways. If two hosts are not using the same encapsulation, communication cannot occur. It is also important to understand LAN technology encapsulations to correctly interpret the Ethernet, Token Ring, FDDI, and IEEE 802.11 portions of the frame when using Microsoft Network Monitor.

LAN Encapsulations

Because IP datagrams are an Open Systems Interconnection (OSI) Network Layer entity, IP datagrams must be encapsulated with a Data Link Layer header and trailer before being sent on the physical medium. The Data Link Layer header and trailer provide the following services:

- **Delimitation** Frames at the Data Link Layer must be distinguished from each other. For each frame, the start and end of the frame are indicated, and the frame's payload is distinguished from the Data Link Layer header and trailer.

- **Protocol identification** Because many organizations use multiple protocol suites such as TCP/IP or AppleTalk, the protocols must be distinguished from each other.

- **Addressing** For shared-access LAN technologies such as Ethernet, the source node and destination node must be identified.
- **Bit-level integrity** To detect bit-level errors in the entire frame received by the hardware, a bit-level integrity check in the form of a checksum is needed. The checksum is computed by the source node and included in the frame header or trailer. The destination recalculates the checksum and checks it against the included checksum. If the checksums match, the frame is considered free of bit-level errors. If the checksums do not match, the frame is silently discarded. This frame checksum is in addition to the checksums provided by upper layer protocols such as IP or TCP.

The particular way a network type (such as Ethernet or Token Ring) encapsulates data to be transmitted is called a *frame format*. The frame format corresponds to the information placed on the frame at the Logical Link Control (LLC) and Media Access Control (MAC) sublayers of the OSI Data Link Layer, and the frame format manifests itself as a header and trailer. If multiple frame formats exist for a given network type (such as Ethernet), the frame formats represent different header and trailer structures and are, therefore, incompatible with each other. In other words, all the nodes on the same network segment (bounded by routers) must use the same frame format to communicate.

This chapter is a discussion of Ethernet, Token Ring, FDDI, and IEEE 802.11 LAN technologies and their frame formats for IP datagrams and ARP messages. Attached Resources Computer Network (ARCnet) is not discussed, as it is not a widely used networking technology.

Ethernet

Ethernet evolved from a 9.6 kilobit-per-second (Kbps) radio transmission system developed at the University of Hawaii called ALOHA. A key feature of ALOHA was that all transmitters shared the same channel and contended for access to the channel to transmit. This became the basis for the contention-based Ethernet that we know today.

In 1972, the Xerox Corporation created a 2.94-megabit-per-second (Mbps) network based on the principles of the ALOHA system. This new network, called Ethernet, featured carrier sense, in which the transmitter listens before attempting to transmit. In 1979, Digital, Intel, and Xerox (DIX) created an industry standard 10-Mbps Ethernet known as Ethernet II. In 1981, the IEEE Project 802 formed the 802.3 subcommittee to make 10-Mbps Ethernet an international standard. In 1995, the IEEE approved a 100-Mbps version of Ethernet called Fast Ethernet. Additional standards define even higher speeds for Ethernet including 1 Gigabit per second (Gbps), 10 Gbps, and 100 Gbps.

Ethernet existed before the IEEE 802.3 specification and, because there are multiple Ethernet standards, there are multiple ways of encapsulating data to be transmitted on an Ethernet network. This can be very confusing when two hosts on an Ethernet network segment cannot communicate, even though they are using the correct communication protocol (such as TCP/IP) and Application Layer protocol (such as File Transfer Protocol [FTP]).

IP datagrams and ARP messages sent on an Ethernet network segment use either Ethernet II encapsulation (described in RFC 894) or IEEE 802.3 Sub-Network Access Protocol (SNAP) encapsulation (described in RFC 1042).

> **More Info** All of the RFCs referenced in this chapter can be found in the \Standards\Chap01_LAN folder on the companion CD-ROM.

Ethernet II

The Ethernet II frame format was defined by the Ethernet specification created by Digital, Intel, and Xerox before the IEEE 802.3 specification. The Ethernet II frame format is also known as the DIX frame format. Figure 1-1 shows Ethernet II encapsulation for an IP datagram.

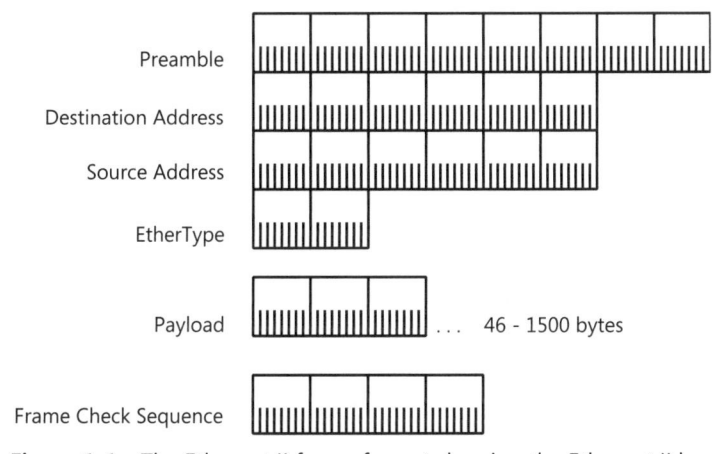

Figure 1-1 The Ethernet II frame format showing the Ethernet II header and trailer

Ethernet II Header and Trailer

The fields in the Ethernet II header and trailer are defined as follows:

- **Preamble** The Preamble field is 8 bytes long and consists of 7 bytes of alternating 1s and 0s (each byte is the bit sequence 10101010) to synchronize a receiving station and a 1-byte 10101011 sequence that indicates the start of a frame. The Preamble provides receiver synchronization and frame delimitation services.

> **Note** The Preamble field is not visible with Network Monitor.

- **Destination Address** The Destination Address field is 6 bytes long and indicates the destination's address. The destination can be a unicast, a multicast, or the Ethernet broadcast address. The unicast address is also known as an individual, physical, hardware, or MAC address. For the Ethernet broadcast address, all 48 bits are set to 1 to create the address 0xFF-FF-FF-FF-FF-FF.

- **Source Address**   The Source Address field is 6 bytes long and indicates the sending node's unicast address.

- **EtherType**   The EtherType field is 2 bytes long and indicates the upper layer protocol contained within the Ethernet frame. After the network adapter passes the frame to the host's network operating system, the EtherType field's value is used to pass the Ethernet payload to the appropriate upper layer protocol. If no upper layer protocols have registered interest in receiving the payload at the frame's EtherType field value, it is silently discarded.

  The EtherType field acts as the protocol identifier for the Ethernet II frame format. For an IP datagram, the field is set to 0x0800. For an ARP message, the EtherType field is set to 0x0806. The current list of defined EtherType field values can be found at *http://standards.ieee.org/regauth/ethertype/eth.txt*.

- **Payload**   The Payload field for an Ethernet II frame consists of a protocol data unit (PDU) of an upper layer protocol. Ethernet II can send a maximum-sized payload of 1500 bytes. Because of Ethernet's collision detection facility, Ethernet II frames must send a minimum payload size of 46 bytes. If an upper layer PDU is less than 46 bytes long, it must be padded so that it is at least 46 bytes long. The Ethernet minimum frame size is discussed in greater detail in the section titled "Ethernet Minimum Frame Size," later in this chapter.

- **Frame Check Sequence**   The Frame Check Sequence (FCS) field is 4 bytes long and provides bit-level integrity verification on the bits in the Ethernet II frame. The FCS is also called a cyclical redundancy check (CRC). The source node calculates the FCS and places the result in this field. When the destination receives the FCS, it runs the same CRC algorithm and compares its own value with the one placed in the FCS field by the source node. If the two values match, the frame is considered valid, and the destination node processes it. If the two values do not match, the frame is silently discarded.

  The FCS calculation consists of dividing a 33-bit prime number into the number consisting of the bits in the frame (not including the Preamble and FCS fields). The result of the division is a quotient and a remainder. The 4-byte FCS field is set to the remainder, which is always a 32-bit value. The FCS can detect 100 percent of all single-bit errors. Although it is mathematically possible to selectively change multiple bits in the frame without invalidating the value of the FCS field, it is highly improbable that the type of random noise and damage that occurs on networks will result in a frame with bits that are changed but retains a valid FCS.

  The FCS calculation provides only a bit-level integrity service, not a data integrity or authentication service. A valid FCS does not imply that only the node with the unicast address stored in the Source Address field could have sent it and that it was not modified in transit. The FCS calculation is well known, and an intermediate node could easily intercept the frame, alter its contents, perform the FCS calculation, and place the new value in the FCS field before forwarding the frame. The receiver of the frame could not detect that the frame contents were altered using just the FCS field. For data integrity and authentication services, use Internet Protocol Security (IPsec). For more information on IPsec, see Chapter 18, "Internet Protocol Security (IPsec)."

The FCS field provides only bit-level error detection, not error recovery. When the receiver-calculated FCS value does not match the value of the FCS stored in the frame, the only conclusion that can be reached is that, somewhere in the frame, a bit or bits were changed. The FCS calculation does not produce any information on where the error occurred or how to correct it, but other types of CRC calculations do provide this information. An example of such a CRC calculation is the 1-byte Header Checksum field in the Asynchronous Transfer Mode (ATM) cell header, which provides error detection and limited error recovery services for the bits in the ATM header.

Note The FCS field is not visible with Network Monitor.

The following is an example of the Ethernet II frame format for an IP datagram from Capture 01-01, included in the \Captures folder on the companion CD-ROM, as displayed with Network Monitor 3.1:

```
  Frame:
- Ethernet: Etype = Internet IP (IPv4)
  - DestinationAddress: 001054 CAE140
     IG:   (0.......) Individual address
     UL:   (.0......) Universally Administered Address
     Rsv:  (..000000)
  - SourceAddress: 006008 52F9D8
     UL:   .0...... Universally Administered Address
    EthernetType: Internet IP (IPv4), 2048(0x800)
+ Ipv4: Next Protocol = ICMP, Packet ID = 44553, Total IP Length = 60
+ Icmp: Echo Request Message, From 192.168.160.186 To 192.168.160.1
```

The Ethernet Interframe Gap

Unlike Token Ring and FDDI, Ethernet frame formats do not have a way to explicitly indicate the end of the frame. Rather, Ethernet frames use an implied postamble by leaving a gap between each Ethernet frame. This gap, known as the Ethernet interframe gap, is used to space Ethernet frames. The Ethernet interframe gap is a specific measure of the time required to send 96 bits of data (9.6 μs on a 10-Mbps Ethernet network segment).

The Ethernet interframe gap is used as a postamble; after receiving bits of a frame, if the wire falls silent for 96 bit times, the last bit in the received frame occurred 96 bit-times ago.

Ethernet Minimum Frame Size

All Ethernet frames must carry a minimum payload of 46 bytes. The Ethernet minimum frame size is a result of the Ethernet collision detection scheme applied to a maximum-extent Ethernet network. To detect a collision, Ethernet nodes must be transmitting long enough for the signal indicating the collision to be propagated back to the sending node. The maximum-extent Ethernet network consists of Ethernet segments configured using 10Base5 cabling and the IEEE 802.3 Baseband 5-4-3 rule.

The IEEE 802.3 Baseband 5-4-3 rule states that there can be a maximum of five physical segments between any two nodes, with four repeaters between the nodes. However, only three of these physical segments can have connected nodes (populated physical segments). The other two physical segments can be used only to link physical segments to extend the network length. Repeaters count as a node on the physical segment. When using 10Base5 cabling, each physical segment can be up to 500 meters long. Therefore, an Ethernet network's maximum linear length is 2500 meters.

Figure 1-2 shows Ethernet Node A and Ethernet Node B at the farthest ends of a 5-4-3 network using 10Base5 cabling.

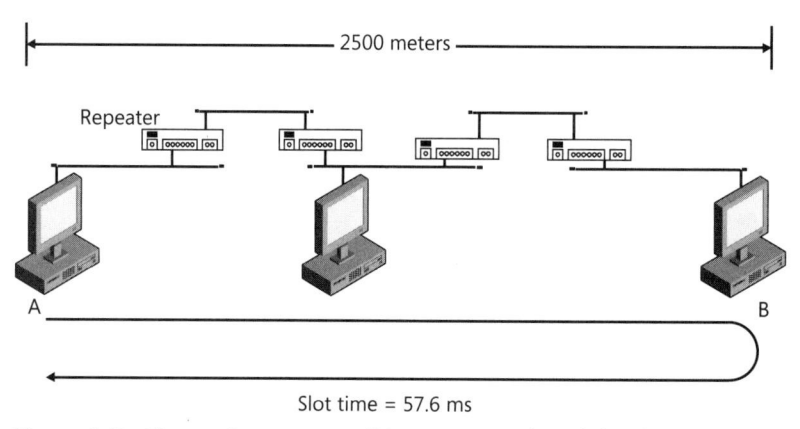

Figure 1-2 The maximum-extent Ethernet network and the slot time

When Node A begins transmitting, the signal must propagate the network length. In the worst-case collision scenario, Node B begins to transmit just before the signal for Node A's frame reaches it. The collision signal of Node A and Node B's frame must travel back to Node A for Node A to detect that a collision has occurred.

The time it takes for a signal to propagate from one end of the network to the other is known as the *propagation delay*. In this worst-case collision scenario, the time that it takes for Node A to detect that its frame has been collided with is twice the propagation delay. Node A's frame must travel all the way to Node B, and then the collision signal must travel all the way from Node B back to Node A. This time is known as the *slot time*. An Ethernet node must be transmitting a frame for the slot time for a collision with that frame to be detected. This is the reason for the minimum Ethernet frame size.

The propagation delay for this maximum-extent Ethernet network is 28.8 μs. Therefore, the slot time is 57.6 μs. To transmit for 57.6 μs with a 10 Mbps bit rate, an Ethernet node must transmit 576 bits. Therefore, the entire Ethernet frame, including the Preamble field, must be a minimum size of 576 bits, or 72 bytes long. Subtracting the Preamble (8 bytes), Source Address (6 bytes), Destination Address (6 bytes), EtherType (2 bytes), and FCS (4 bytes) fields, the minimum Ethernet payload size is 46 bytes.

Upper-layer PDUs smaller than 46 bytes are padded to 46 bytes, ensuring the minimum Ethernet frame size. This padding is not part of the IP datagram or the ARP message and is not included in any length indicator fields within the IP datagram or ARP message. For example, this padding is not included in the IP header's Total Length field, which indicates only the size of the IP datagram, and is used to discard the padding bytes.

IEEE 802.3

The IEEE 802.3 frame format is the result of the IEEE 802.2 and 802.3 specifications and consists of an IEEE 802.3 header and trailer and an IEEE 802.2 LLC header. Figure 1-3 shows the IEEE 802.3 frame format.

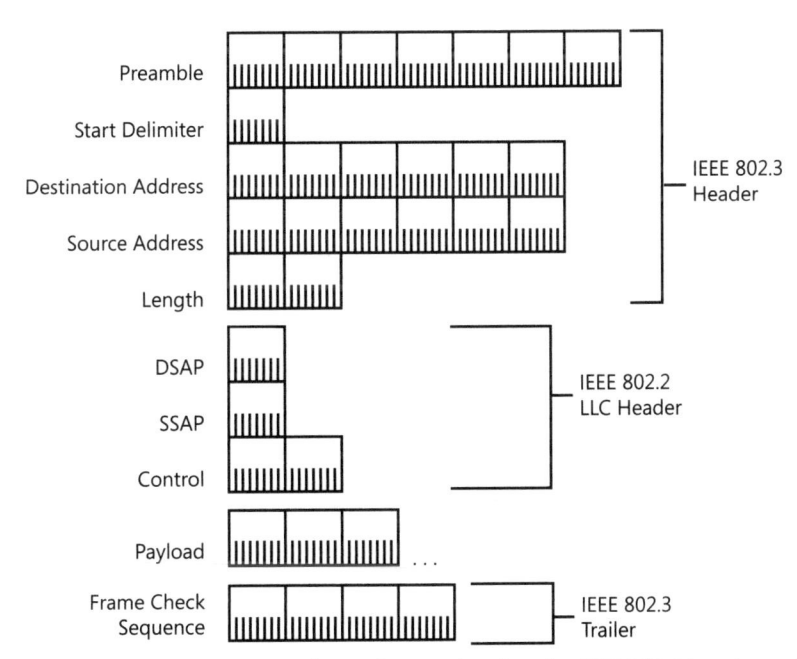

Figure 1-3 The IEEE 802.3 frame format showing the IEEE 802.3 header and trailer and the IEEE 802.2 LLC header

IEEE 802.3 Header and Trailer

The fields in the IEEE 802.3 header and trailer are defined as follows:

- **Preamble** The Preamble field is 7 bytes long and consists of alternating 1s and 0s that synchronize a receiving station. Each byte is the bit sequence 10101010.

- **Start Delimiter** The Start Delimiter field is the 1-byte bit sequence 10101011, which indicates the start of a frame. The combination of the IEEE 802.3 Preamble and Start Delimiter fields is the exact same bit sequence as the Ethernet II Preamble field.

> **Note** The Preamble and Start Delimiter fields are not visible with Network Monitor.

- **Destination Address** The Destination Address field is the same as the Ethernet II Destination Address field except that IEEE 802.3 allows both 6-byte and 2-byte addresses. IEEE 802.3 2-byte addresses are not commonly used.

- **Source Address** The Source Address field is the same as the Ethernet II Source Address field except that IEEE 802.3 allows both 6-byte and 2-byte addresses.

- **Length** The Length field is 2 bytes long and indicates the number of bytes from the LLC header's first byte to the payload's last byte. The Length field does not include the IEEE 802.3 header or the FCS field. This field's minimum value is 46 (0x002E), and its maximum value is 1500 (0x05DC).

- **Frame Check Sequence** The FCS field is 4 bytes long and is identical to the Ethernet II FCS field.

IEEE 802.2 LLC Header

The fields in the IEEE 802.2 LLC header are defined as follows:

- **DSAP** The Destination Service Access Point (DSAP) field is 1 byte long and indicates the destination upper layer protocol for the frame.

- **SSAP** The Source Service Access Point (SSAP) field is 1 byte long and indicates the source upper layer protocol for the frame.

  The DSAP and SSAP fields act as protocol identifiers for the IEEE 802.3 frame format. The defined value for the DSAP and SSAP fields for IP is 0x06. However, it is not used in the industry. Instead, the SNAP header is used to encapsulate IP datagrams with an IEEE 802.3 header. The SNAP header is discussed in greater detail in the section titled "IEEE 802.3 SNAP," later in this chapter. The current list of defined link service access point values, which are used for the values of the DSAP and SSAP fields, can be found at *http://www.iana.org/assignments/ieee-802-numbers*.

- **Control** The Control field can be 1 or 2 bytes long depending on whether the LLC-encapsulated data is an LLC datagram, known as a Type 1 LLC operation, or part of an LLC session, known as a Type 2 LLC operation.

  A Type 1 LLC operation (a 1-byte Control field) is a connectionless, unreliable LLC datagram. With an LLC datagram, LLC is not providing reliable delivery service on behalf of the upper layer protocol. A Type 1 LLC datagram is known as an Unnumbered Information (UI) frame and is indicated by setting the Control field to the value 0x03.

  A Type 2 LLC operation (a 2-byte Control field) is a connection-oriented, reliable LLC session. Type 2 LLC frames are used when LLC is providing reliable delivery service for the upper layer protocol.

  For IP datagrams and ARP messages, reliable LLC services are never used. Therefore, IP datagrams and ARP messages are always sent as a Type 1 LLC datagram with the Control field set to 0x03 to indicate a UI frame.

Differentiating an Ethernet II Frame from an IEEE 802.3 Frame

It is common for a network operating system to support multiple frame formats simultaneously. TCP/IP for Windows Server 2008 and Windows Vista supports both Ethernet II and IEEE 802.3 frame formats for IP datagrams and ARP messages. There are many similarities between the Ethernet II and IEEE 802.3 frame formats, such as the following:

- The Ethernet II Preamble field is identical to the IEEE 802.3 Preamble and Start Delimiter fields.
- With the exception of the 2-byte address allowed by IEEE 802.3, the Source Address and Destination Address fields are identical.
- The FCS is identical.

The ability to differentiate between the Ethernet II and the IEEE 802.3 frame formats lies in the first 2 bytes past the Source Address field. For the Ethernet II frame format, these 2 bytes are the EtherType field. For the IEEE 802.3 frame format, these 2 bytes are the Length field. The following algorithm is used to determine whether these 2 bytes are an EtherType field or a Length field:

- If the value of these 2 bytes is greater than 1500 (0x05DC), it is an EtherType field and an Ethernet II frame format.
- If the value of these 2 bytes is less than or equal to 1500 (0x05DC), it is a Length field and an IEEE 802.3 frame.

This comparison can be made because there are no defined EtherType values less than 0x05DC. The lowest EtherType value is 0x0600, used to indicate the Xerox Network Systems (XNS) protocol.

IEEE 802.3 SNAP

Although there is a defined value of 0x06 for the Service Access Point (SAP) for IP, it is not used in the industry. RFC 1042 states that IP datagrams and ARP frames sent over IEEE 802.3, 802.4, and 802.5 networks must use the SNAP encapsulation.

The IEEE 802.3 SNAP was created as an extension to the IEEE 802.3 specification to allow protocols that were designed to operate with an Ethernet II header to be used in an IEEE 802.3–compliant environment. Figure 1-4 shows the IEEE 802.3 SNAP frame format.

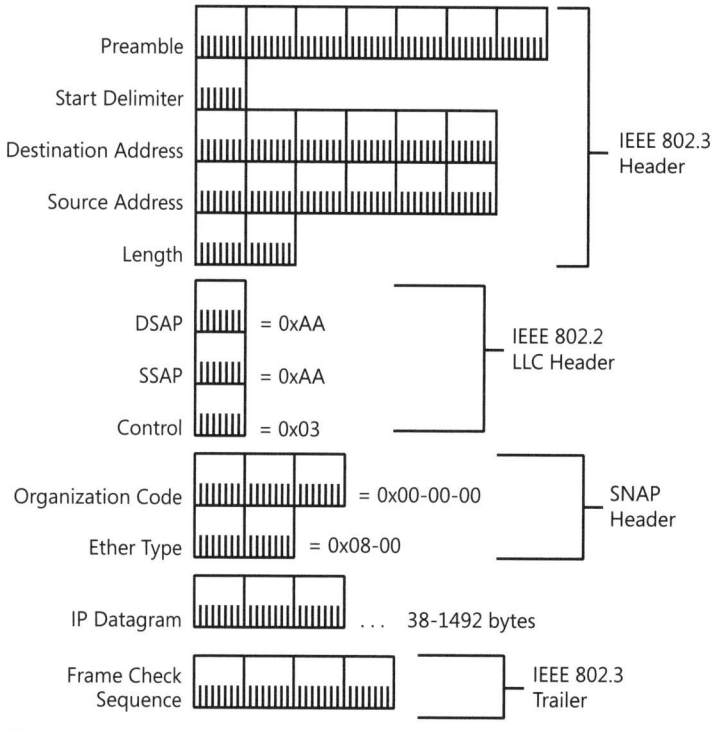

Figure 1-4 The IEEE 802.3 SNAP frame format showing the SNAP header and an IP datagram

To denote a SNAP frame, the DSAP and SSAP fields are set to the SNAP-defined value of 0xAA within the LLC header. Because all SNAP-encapsulated payloads are not using reliable LLC services, every SNAP frame is an LLC datagram. Therefore, the Control field is set to 0x03 to indicate a UI frame. The SNAP header consists of the following two fields:

- The Organization Code field is 3 bytes long and is used to indicate the organization that maintains the meaning of the 2 bytes that follow. For IP datagrams and ARP messages, the Organization Code field is set to 0x00-00-00.

- For the Organization Code field set to 0x00-00-00, the next 2 bytes of the SNAP header are the 2-byte EtherType field. The same values for IP (0x0800) and ARP (0x0806) are used.

Because of the increased overhead of the LLC header (3 bytes total) and the SNAP header (5 bytes), the payload for an IEEE 802.3 SNAP frame has a maximum size of 1492 bytes and a minimum size of 38 bytes. Padding is added when needed to ensure that the payload is at least 38 bytes long.

The following is an example of the IEEE 802.3 SNAP frame format for an ARP Request from Capture 01-02, included in the \Captures folder on the companion CD-ROM , as displayed with Network Monitor 3.1:

```
Frame:
- Ethernet: 802.3, DataLength = 36 bytes
  - DestinationAddress: *BROADCAST
     IG:  (1.......) Group address
     UL:  (.1......) Locally Administered Address
     Rsv: (..111111)
  - SourceAddress: 00AA00 4BB147
     UL:  .0...... Universally Administered Address
    DataLength: 36 (0x24)
- Llc: Unnumbered(U) Frame, Command Frame, SSAP = SNAP(Sub-
Network Access Protocol), DSAP = SNAP(Sub-Network Access Protocol)
  + DSAP: SNAP(Sub-Network Access Protocol), Individual DSAP
  + SSAP: SNAP(Sub-Network Access Protocol), Command
  + Unnumbered: UI - Unnumbered Information
+ Snap: EtherType = ARP, OrgCode = XEROX CORPORATION
+ Arp: Request, 192.168.50.1 asks for 192.168.50.2
```

By default, TCP/IP for Windows Server 2008 and Windows Vista uses Ethernet II encapsulation when sending and receiving frames on an Ethernet network. TCP/IP for Windows Server 2008 and Windows Vista receives both types of frame formats but, by default, only responds with Ethernet II encapsulated frames. To send IEEE 802.3 SNAP encapsulated IP and ARP messages, use the following registry value:

ArpUseEtherSNAP
```
Location: HKEY_LOCAL_MACHINE\SYSTEM\CurrentControlSet\Services\
Tcpip\Parameters
Data type: REG_DWORD
Valid range: 0-1
Default value: 0
Present by default: No
```

ArpUseEtherSNAP either enables (when set to 1) or disables (when set to 0) the use of the IEEE 802.3 SNAP frame format when sending IP and ARP frames. ArpUseEtherSNAP is disabled by default, meaning that IP and ARP frames are sent with Ethernet II encapsulation. Regardless of the ArpUseEtherSNAP setting, both types of frame formats are received.

With ArpUseEtherSNAP disabled, TCP/IP for Windows Server 2008 and Windows Vista recognizes a SNAP-encapsulated ARP Request message and responds with an Ethernet II–encapsulated ARP Reply frame. The assumption is that the node sending the ARP Request message will recognize the Ethernet II encapsulation on the ARP Reply and use Ethernet II encapsulation for subsequent communications. If the node sending the ARP Request does not switch, IP communication between the node sending the ARP Request and the node sending the ARP Reply is impossible.

With ArpUseEtherSNAP enabled, TCP/IP for Windows Server 2008 and Windows Vista switches to Ethernet II encapsulation if one of the following two scenarios occurs: a SNAP-encapsulated ARP Request frame is responded to with an Ethernet II–encapsulated ARP Reply frame, or an Ethernet II–encapsulated ARP Request is received.

Special Bits on Ethernet MAC Addresses

Within the Source Address and Destination Address fields of the Ethernet II and IEEE 802.3 frame formats, special bits are defined, as Figure 1-5 shows.

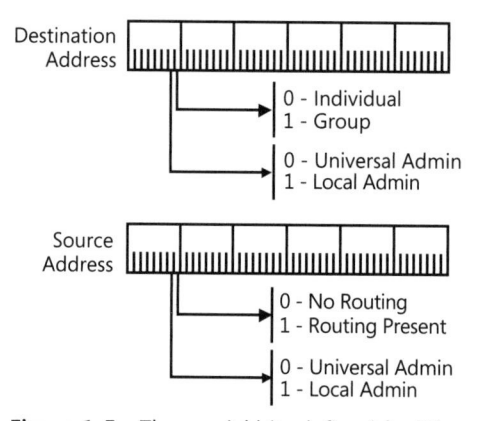

Figure 1-5 The special bits defined for Ethernet source and destination MAC addresses

The Individual/Group Bit

The Individual/Group (I/G) bit is used to indicate whether the destination address is a unicast (individual) or multicast (group) address. For a unicast address, the I/G bit is set to 0. For a multicast address, the I/G bit is set to 1. The broadcast address is a special case of multicast, and its I/G bit is set to 1. The I/G bit is also known as the multicast bit.

The Universal/Locally Administered Bit

The Universal/Locally (U/L) Administered bit is used to indicate whether the IEEE allocated the address. For a universal address allocated by the IEEE, the U/L bit is set to 0. Universal addresses are guaranteed to be universally unique because network adapter manufacturers obtain universally unique vendor identifiers from the IEEE and assign unique 3-byte serial numbers to each network adapter. The 6-byte physical address of a network adapter, as programmed into the adapter during the manufacturing process, is a universally administered address.

For a locally administered address, the U/L bit is set to 1. Some network adapters allow you to override the network adapter's physical address and specify a new physical address. In this case, the new address must have the U/L bit set to 1 to indicate that it is locally administered.

The U/L bit is significant only for unicast addresses (the I/G bit is set to 0). When the I/G bit is set to 1, this bit does not imply either a locally or a universally administered address. The U/L bit is relevant for both the Source Address and Destination Address.

Routing Information Indicator Bit

The Routing Information Indicator bit, the low-order bit of the first byte of the source address, indicates whether MAC-level routing information is present. This bit is meaningful only for Token Ring addresses. Token Ring has a MAC-level routing mechanism known as Token Ring source routing. Even though this bit is meaningless for Ethernet addresses, it is still reserved and set to 0 to prevent problems when employing a translating bridge or Layer 2 switch between an Ethernet segment and a Token Ring ring.

For example, suppose the Routing Information Indicator bit is not reserved at the value of 0 for Ethernet addresses, and this bit is set to 1 through a universal or locally administered address. Then, when the address is translated to a Token Ring address, the Routing Information Indicator bit remains set to 1 even though there is no source routing information present, which can cause the Token Ring node to drop the frame.

The following is an example of the special bits for Ethernet MAC addresses from Capture 01-03, included in the \Captures folder on the companion CD-ROM, as displayed with Network Monitor 3.1:

```
  Frame:
- Ethernet: Etype = Internet IP (IPv4)
  - DestinationAddress: 01005E 400009
     IG:  (0.......) Individual address
     UL:  (.0......) Universally Administered Address
     Rsv: (..000001)
  - SourceAddress: 00E034 C0A060
     UL:  .0...... Universally Administered Address
     EthernetType: Internet IP (IPv4), 2048(0x800)
+ Ipv4: Next Protocol = UDP, Packet ID = 56274, Total IP Length = 577
+ Udp: SrcPort = 3985, DstPort = 20441, Length = 557
```

Note Network Monitor 3.1 does not display the Routing Information Indicator bit.

Token Ring

Token Ring is a ring access network technology originally proposed by Olaf Soderblum in 1969. IBM purchased the rights to the original design and created and released its Token Ring product in 1984. Key elements of the original IBM design were the use of proprietary connectors, twisted-pair cable out to the network node, and structured wiring systems using centralized active hubs.

In 1985, the IEEE Project 802 created the 802.5 subcommittee and Token Ring became an international standard. IBM created Token Ring to replace Ethernet as the most popular LAN technology. Although Token Ring is in many ways a superior technology to Ethernet, a combination of cost issues and marketing has made it less popular than Ethernet.

The original specification was for a 4 Mbps transmission rate, but that was followed by an additional specification at 16 Mbps. On the same ring, all nodes must operate at the same speed. Common implementations use 4-Mbps rings connected together, using 16-Mbps rings as a high-speed backbone.

IP and ARP encapsulation over Token Ring networks are described in RFC 1042.

IEEE 802.5

The IEEE 802.5 frame format is the result of the IEEE 802.2 and 802.5 specifications and consists of an IEEE 802.5 header and trailer and an IEEE 802.2 LLC header. The IEEE 802.5 frame format is shown in Figure 1-6.

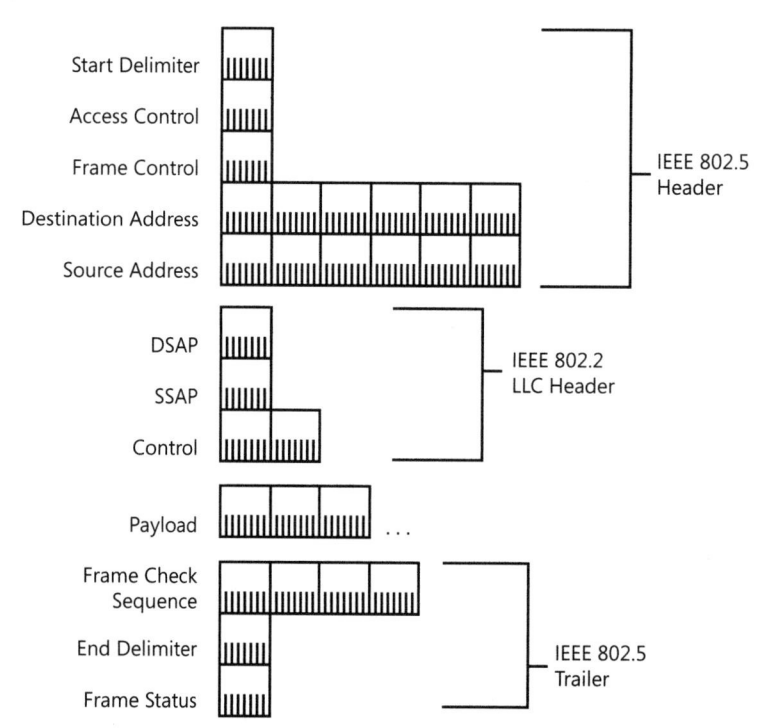

Figure 1-6 The IEEE 802.5 frame format showing the IEEE 802.5 header and trailer and the IEEE 802.2 LLC header

IEEE 802.5 Header and Trailer

The fields in the IEEE 802.5 header and trailer are defined as follows:

- **Start Delimiter**   The Start Delimiter field is 1 byte long and identifies the start of the frame. The Start Delimiter field contains nondata symbols known as J and K symbols that are deliberate violations of the Token Ring signal encoding scheme. The J symbol is an encoding violation of a 1 and the K symbol is an encoding violation of a 0. The Start Delimiter field provides a very explicit preamble. Unlike Ethernet, Token Ring frames do not have an interframe gap to separate frames on the wire. The Start Delimiter field also provides synchronization for the receiver.

> **Note**   The Start Delimiter field is not visible with Network Monitor.

- **Access Control**   The Access Control field is 1 byte long and contains bits for the following:
    - Setting the current priority of the token (3 bits). An interesting facility of Token Ring is its ability to prioritize access to the token and, therefore, the right to transmit data based on seven priority levels.
    - Setting the token reservation level (3 bits). The token reservation bits set the priority of the token once the station that is currently transmitting releases it.
    - Indicating whether the frame has passed the ring monitor station (1 bit). As the frame passes the ring monitor station, this Monitor bit is set to 1. If the ring monitor station sees a frame with the Monitor bit set to 1, the frame has already been sent on the ring. The ring monitor station removes the frame from the ring and then purges the ring.
    - Indicating whether the frame that follows is a token or a frame (1 bit). If set to 0, what follows is a token. If set to 1, what follows is a frame.
- **Frame Control**   The Frame Control field is 1 byte long and contains bits for the following:
    - Indicating whether the frame that follows is a Token Ring MAC management frame or an LLC frame (2 bits).
    - Indicating the type of Token Ring MAC management frame such as Purge, Claim Token, or Beacon (4 bits).
    - Two bits within the Frame Control field are reserved.
- **Destination Address**   The Destination Address field is 6 bytes long and indicates the address of the destination. For Token Ring, the Destination Address field can be the following:
    - A universal or locally administered unicast address.
    - The universal broadcast address (0xFF-FF-FF-FF-FF-FF).

- The Token Ring broadcast address (0xC0-00-FF-FF-FF-FF). A frame using the Token Ring broadcast address is designed to remain on a single ring and is not forwarded by Token Ring source-route bridges.
- A multicast address.
- A Token Ring functional address. A functional address is a type of multicast address that is specific to Token Ring and is typically used by Token Ring MAC management frames.

- **Source Address**   The Source Address field is 6 bytes long and indicates the sending node's unicast address.

- **Payload**   The Payload field for a Token Ring frame consists of a PDU of an upper layer protocol. Unlike Ethernet, there is no minimum frame size and the maximum transmission unit (MTU) for Token Ring is not a defined number, but dependent on factors such as the bit rate and the token holding time. Token Ring MTUs are further complicated by the presence of Token Ring source-routing bridges. More information on Token Ring MTUs for IP datagrams can be found in the section titled "IEEE 802.5 SNAP," later in this chapter.

- **Frame Check Sequence**   The FCS field is a 4-byte CRC that uses the same algorithm as Ethernet to provide a bit-level integrity check of all fields in the Token Ring frame, from the Frame Control field to the Payload field. The FCS does not provide bit-level integrity for the Access Control or Frame Status fields. This allows bits in these fields, such as the Monitor bit, to be set without forcing a recalculation of the FCS.

  The FCS is checked as it passes each node on the ring. If the FCS fails at any node, the Error Detected indicator in the End Delimiter field is set to 1 and the receiving node does not copy the frame.

- **End Delimiter**   The End Delimiter is a 1-byte field that identifies the end of the frame. Like the Start Delimiter, the End Delimiter contains J and K nondata symbols to provide an explicit postamble. The End Delimiter field also contains the following:
  - An Intermediate Frame indicator (1 bit), used to indicate whether this frame is the last frame in the sequence (when set to 0) or more frames are to follow (when set to 1).
  - An Error Detected indicator (1 bit), used to indicate whether this frame has failed the FCS calculation.
  - Because there is no Length field in the IEEE 802.5 frame, the End Delimiter is used to locate the end of the payload and the position of the FCS and Frame Status fields.

- **Frame Status** The Frame Status field is a 1-byte field that contains the following:

    Two copies of the Address Recognized indicator. The destination node sets the Address Recognized indicators to indicate that the address in the Destination Address field was recognized.

    Two copies of the Frame Copied indicator. The destination node sets the Frame Copied indicators to indicate that the frame was successfully copied into a buffer on the network adapter.

    - ❑ Two copies of each indicator are needed because the FCS field does not protect the Frame Status field.
    - ❑ The Address Recognized and Frame Copied indicators are not used as acknowledgments for reliable data delivery. The sending Token Ring network adapter uses these indicators to retransmit the frame, if necessary.

> **Note** The FCS, End Delimiter, and Frame Status fields are not visible with Network Monitor.

IEEE 802.2 LLC Header

The fields in the IEEE 802.2 LLC header are defined and used in the same way as the IEEE 802.2 LLC header for the IEEE 802.3 frame format, as discussed in the section titled "IEEE 802.3," earlier in this chapter.

IEEE 802.5 SNAP

As described earlier in this chapter, the value of 0x06 is defined as the DSAP and SSAP for IP. However, it is not defined for use in RFC 1042 and not used in the industry. Therefore, similar to the case of IEEE 802.3 frames, to send an IP datagram over an IEEE 802.5 network, the IP datagram must be encapsulated using SNAP, as Figure 1-7 shows.

For a 10-millisecond (ms) token-holding time, the maximum sizes for IP datagrams are 4464 bytes for 4-Mbps Token Ring network adapters and 17,914 bytes for 16-Mbps Token Ring network adapters. If Token Ring source-routing bridges are present, the maximum size of IP datagrams can be 508, 1020, 2044, 4092, and 8188 bytes. For more information on Token Ring MTUs, see RFC 1042.

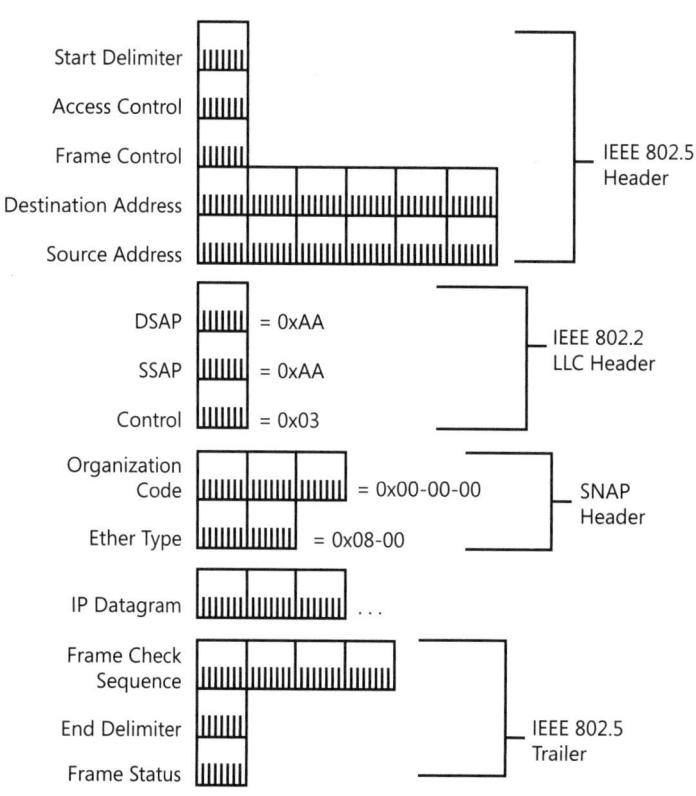

Figure 1-7 The IEEE 802.5 SNAP frame format showing the SNAP header and an IP datagram

Special Bits on Token Ring MAC Addresses

Within the Source Address and Destination Address fields of the IEEE 802.5 frame format, special bits are defined, as Figure 1-8 shows.

The Individual/Group Bit

Identical to Ethernet, the I/G bit for Token Ring addresses is used to indicate whether the address is a unicast (individual) or multicast (group) address. For unicast addresses, the I/G bit is set to 0. For multicast addresses, the I/G bit is set to 1.

The Universal/Locally Administered Bit

Identical to Ethernet, the U/L Administered bit for Token Ring addresses is used to indicate whether the IEEE has allocated the address. For universal addresses allocated by the IEEE, the U/L bit is set to 0. For locally administered addresses, the U/L bit is set to 1. The U/L bit is relevant for both the Source Address and Destination Address fields.

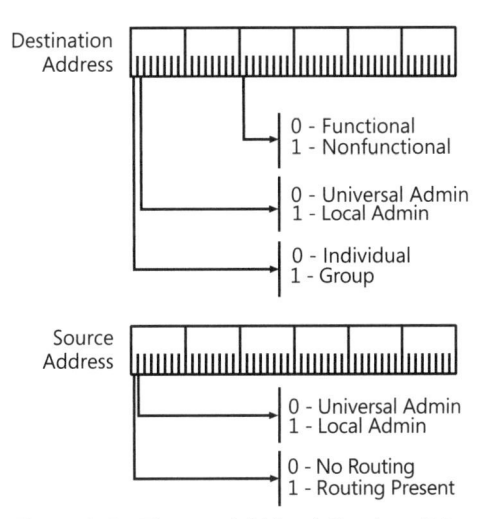

Figure 1-8 The special bits defined on Token Ring source and destination MAC addresses

Functional Address Bit

The Functional Address bit indicates whether the destination address is a functional address (when set to 0) or a nonfunctional address (when set to 1). Token Ring defines the following two types of multicast addresses:

- **Functional addresses**   Multicast addresses that are specific to Token Ring. There are specific functional addresses for identifying the ring monitor, the ring-parameter server, and a source-routing bridge.
- **Nonfunctional addresses**   General multicast addresses that are not specific to Token Ring.

The Functional Address bit is significant only if the I/G bit is set to 1.

Routing Information Indicator Bit

The Routing Information Indicator bit indicates whether MAC-level routing information is present. In the case of Token Ring, the Routing Information Indicator bit indicates the presence of a source-routing header between the IEEE 802.5 header and the IEEE 802.2 LLC header. Token Ring source routing is not OSI Network Layer routing, but rather a MAC sublayer routing scheme that allows a sending node to discover and specify a route through a defined series of rings and bridges within a Token Ring network segment.

FDDI

FDDI is a network technology developed by the American National Standards Institute (ANSI). FDDI is an optical fiber-based token passing ring with a bit rate of 100 Mbps. It was designed to span long distances and, in most implementations, it acts as a campus-wide high-speed backbone. FDDI offers advanced features beyond Token Ring, such as the ability to self-heal a break in the ring and the use of guaranteed bandwidth.

Although not developed by the IEEE as part of the 802 standards, the FDDI specification is quite similar to the IEEE 802.3 and 802.5 specifications; it defines the MAC sublayer of the OSI Data Link Layer and the Physical Layer, and it uses the IEEE 802.2 LLC sublayer. Copper Data Distributed Interface (CDDI) is a version of FDDI that operates over twisted-pair copper wire.

RFC 1188 describes IP encapsulation over FDDI networks.

FDDI Frame Format

The FDDI frame format is the result of the IEEE 802.2 and ANSI FDDI specifications, and consists of an FDDI header and trailer and an IEEE 802.2 LLC header. Figure 1-9 shows the FDDI frame format.

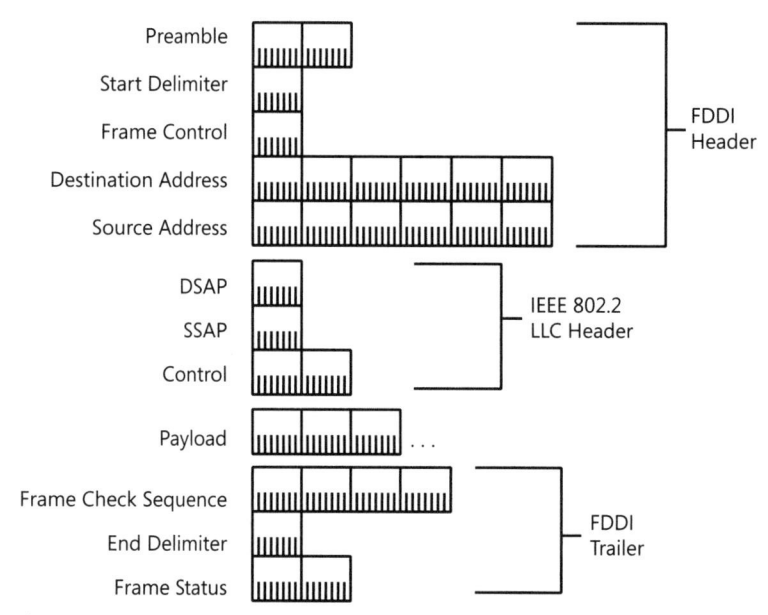

Figure 1-9 The FDDI frame format showing the FDDI header and trailer and IEEE 802.2 LLC header

FDDI Header and Trailer

The fields in the FDDI header and trailer are defined as follows:

- **Preamble** The Preamble field is 2 bytes long and provides receiver synchronization.
- **Start Delimiter** The Start Delimiter field is 1 byte long and identifies the start of the frame. Like Token Ring, the Start Delimiter field contains nondata symbols known as J

and K symbols that are deliberate violations of the FDDI signal encoding scheme. The J symbol is an encoding violation of a 1 and the K symbol is an encoding violation of a 0.

> **Note** The Preamble and Start Delimiter fields are not visible with Network Monitor.

- **Frame Control**   The Frame Control field is 1 byte long and contains bits for the following:
    - Setting the class of the frame (1 bit). FDDI frames can be sent as synchronous or asynchronous frames. Synchronous frames are used for guaranteed bandwidth and response time. Asynchronous frames are used for dynamic bandwidth sharing. This Class bit is set to 1 for synchronous frames and 0 for asynchronous frames.
    - Setting the length of the Destination Address and the Source Address fields (1 bit). Like IEEE 802.3, FDDI supports 2-byte and 6-byte addresses. The Address bit is set to 1 for 6-byte addresses and 0 for 2-byte addresses.
    - Indicating that what follows is a token (either nonrestricted or restricted), a station management frame, a MAC frame, an LLC frame, or an LLC frame with a specific priority (6 bits).
- **Destination Address**   The Destination Address field is either 2 bytes or 6 bytes long and indicates the address of the destination (2-byte addresses are seldom used). For 6-byte addresses, FDDI Destination Address fields are defined the same as Ethernet Destination Address fields to provide easy interoperability between bridged or Layer 2 switched Ethernet and FDDI segments. The destination address is a unicast, multicast, or broadcast address.
- **Source Address**   The Source Address field is either 2 bytes or 6 bytes long and indicates the unicast address of the sending node (2-byte addresses are seldom used).
- **Frame Check Sequence**   The FCS field is a 4-byte CRC that uses the same algorithm as Ethernet to provide a bit-level integrity check of all fields in the FDDI frame, from the Frame Control field to the Payload field. The FCS is checked as it passes each node on the ring. If the FCS fails at any node, the Error bit in the Frame Status field is set to 1 and the receiving node does not copy the frame.
- **End Delimiter**   The End Delimiter field is 1 byte long and identifies the end of the frame. Like the Start Delimiter field, the End Delimiter field contains J and K nondata symbols to provide an explicit postamble. Because there is no Length field in the FDDI frame, the End Delimiter field is also used to locate the end of the payload, and the position of the FCS and Frame Status fields.

- **Frame Status** The Frame Status field is typically 2 bytes long and contains bits for the following:

    The Address Recognized indicator

    - ❏ The destination node sets the Address Recognized indicator to show that the address in the Destination Address field was recognized.

    The Frame Copied indicator

    - ❏ The destination node sets the Frame Copied indicator to show that the frame was successfully copied into a buffer on the network adapter.

    The Error indicator

    - ❏ Any FDDI station sets the Error indicator to 1 when the FCS field is invalid.
    - ❏ Similar to Token Ring, the Address Recognized and Frame Copied indicators are not used as acknowledgments for reliable data delivery. Rather, the sending FDDI network adapter uses these indicators to retransmit the frame if necessary.

IEEE 802.2 LLC Header

The fields in the IEEE 802.2 LLC header are defined and used in the same way as the IEEE 802.2 LLC header for the IEEE 802.3 and IEEE 802.5 frame format discussed earlier in this chapter.

Payload

The payload for an FDDI frame consists of a PDU of an upper layer protocol. The entire FDDI frame from the Preamble field to the Frame Status field can be a maximum size of 4500 bytes. Once you subtract the FDDI and IEEE 802.2 LLC headers, the maximum payload size is 4474 bytes with a 3-byte LLC header, and 4473 bytes with a 4-byte LLC header.

FDDI SNAP

As described earlier in this chapter, the value of 0x06 is defined as the SAP for IP. However, it is not defined for use in RFC 1188 and not used in the industry. Therefore, similar to the case of IEEE 802.3 frames and IEEE 802.5 frames, to send an IP datagram over an FDDI network, the IP datagram must be encapsulated using the SNAP header, as shown in Figure 1-10.

The maximum-sized IP datagram that can be sent on an FDDI network is 4352 bytes. This number of bytes is the result of taking the maximum FDDI frame size of 4500 bytes and subtracting the FDDI header and trailer (23 bytes), the LLC header (3 bytes), and the SNAP header (5 bytes) and reserving 117 bytes for future purposes.

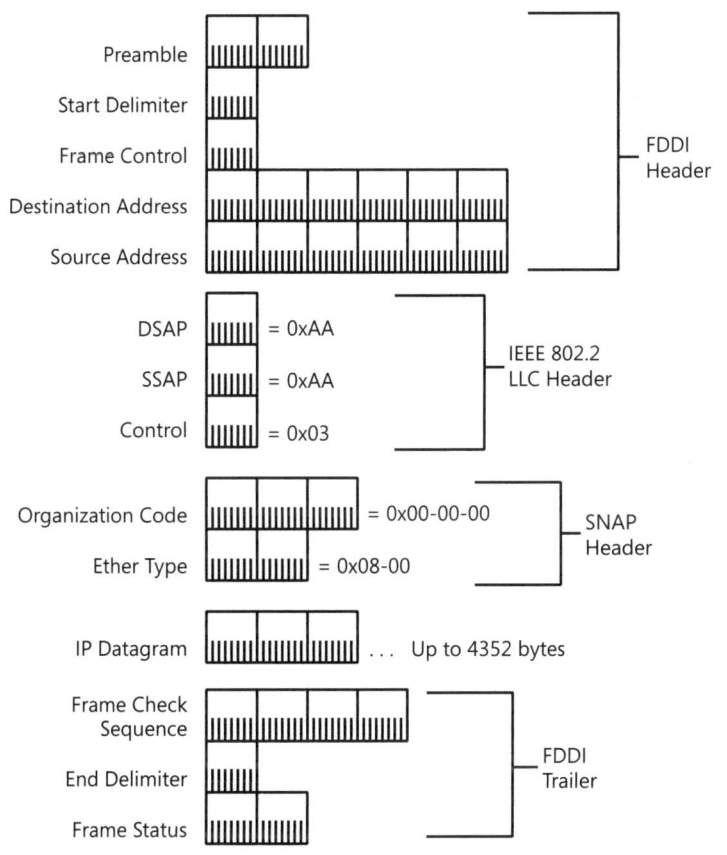

Figure 1-10 The FDDI SNAP frame format showing the SNAP header and an IP datagram

IP datagrams and ARP messages sent over FDDI networks also have the following constraints:

- Only 6-byte FDDI source and destination addresses can be used.
- All IP and ARP frames are transmitted as asynchronous class LLC frames using unrestricted tokens.

RFC 1188 does not define how frame priorities are used or how the FDDI node deals with the values of the Address Recognized and Frame Copied indicators.

FDDI nodes send ARP Requests using the Ethernet ARP Hardware Type value of 0x00-01, but can receive ARP Requests using the ARP Hardware Types of 0x00-01 and 0x00-06 (IEEE networks). The use of the Ethernet ARP Hardware Type value is designed to allow FDDI hosts and Ethernet hosts in a bridged or Layer 2 switched environment to send and receive ARP messages.

Special Bits on FDDI MAC Addresses

Because FDDI MAC addresses are defined in the same way as Ethernet MAC addresses, the special bits on FDDI MAC addresses are the same as those defined for Ethernet MAC addresses.

IEEE 802.11

IEEE 802.11 is a set of standards for wireless LAN technologies. The original 802.11 standard defines wireless networking using either 1-Mbps or 2-Mbps bit rates in the Industrial, Scientific, and Medical (ISM) 2.54-gigahertz (GHz) frequency band. IEEE 802.11b defines a maximum bit rate of 11 Mbps in the 2.54-GHz ISM band. IEEE 802.11a defines a maximum bit rate of 54 Mbps in the 5.8-GHz band. 802.11g defines a maximum bit rate of 54 Mbps in the 2.54-GHz band. IEEE 802.11b is the most widely deployed of the IEEE 802.11 standards.

At the MAC sublayer, IEEE 802.11 (all versions) uses a combination of congestion avoidance and Request to Send (RTS), Clear to Send (CTS), and Acknowledgment (ACK) frames to ensure that only one wireless node is transmitting at a time and that the sent frame is successfully received.

IEEE 802.11 wireless nodes can communicate in the following ways:

- Directly with each other using an operating mode known as ad hoc mode.
- With a wireless access point (AP) using an operating mode known as infrastructure mode. In infrastructure mode, the wireless AP acts as a transparent bridge connecting wireless nodes to a wired network.

To identify a wireless network in either operating mode, IEEE 802.11 uses a Service Set Identifier (SSID), also known as a wireless network name.

Because wireless networking uses broadcast radio waves, a wireless node within range of a transmitting wireless node can capture IEEE 802.11 frames and interpret the data. To provide data confidentiality (encryption) for IEEE 802.11 payloads, IEEE 802.11 networks can use Wi-Fi Protected Access 2 (WPA2), Wi-Fi Protected Access (WPA), or Wired Equivalent Privacy (WEP).

IEEE 802.11 Frame Format

The IEEE 802.11 frame format consists of an IEEE 802.11 header and trailer and an IEEE 802.2 LLC header. Figure 1-11 shows the IEEE 802.11 frame format.

IEEE 802.11 Header and Trailer

The fields in the IEEE 802.11 header and trailer for a data frame sent by wireless nodes or by a wireless AP to a wireless node are defined as follows:

- **Frame Control**   A 2-byte field that contains control information that defines the type of frame and how to process the frame. For more information, see the section titled "Frame Control Field," later in this chapter.
- **Duration/ID Field**   A 2-byte field that is used to indicate the duration of time in microseconds needed to transmit the frame and the acknowledgment.

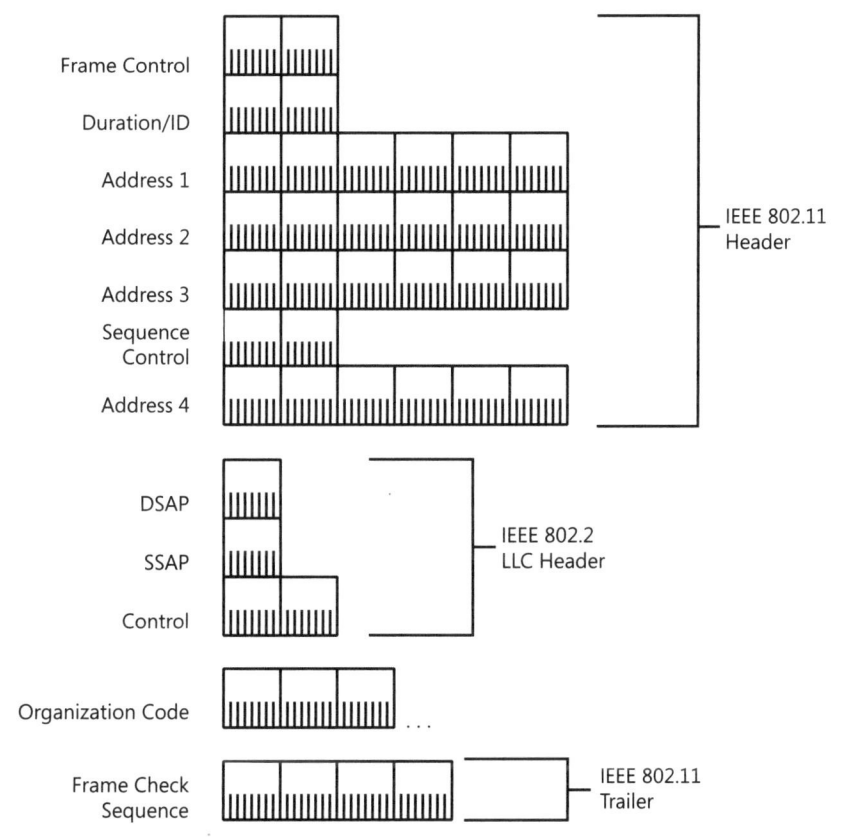

Figure 1-11 The IEEE 802.11 frame format showing the IEEE 802.11 header and trailer and the IEEE 802.2 LLC header

- **Address 1** A 6-byte field that contains either the destination MAC address of a wireless node (when sent by a wireless node to another wireless node in ad hoc mode or sent by the wireless AP to the wireless node) or the SSID (when sent by a wireless node to a wireless AP).

- **Address 2** A 6-byte field that contains either the MAC address of the sending node (when sent to another wireless node in ad hoc mode or sent to the wireless AP) or the SSID (when sent by the wireless AP to a wireless node).

- **Address 3** A 6-byte field that contains the SSID for frames sent to another wireless node in ad hoc mode, the source address for frames sent from the wireless AP to a wireless node, or the destination address for frames sent from a wireless node to a wireless AP.

- **Sequence Control** A 2-byte field that contains a 4-bit Fragment Number field and a 12-bit Sequence Number field that, when used together, allow the receiver to discard duplicate frames. When a frame is fragmented, the Fragment Number field is used to indicate the number of the fragment. Otherwise, the Fragment Number field is set to 0. The Sequence Number field indicates the number of the frame starting at 0, incrementing to 4095, and then starting again at 0. All fragments of a frame have the same sequence number.

- **Address 4** A 6-byte field that contains the MAC address of the originating wireless node. This field is typically present only in frames in which both the To DS and From DS flags in the Frame Control field are set to 1, indicating inter-wireless AP communication.
- **Frame Check Sequence** A 4-byte CRC that uses the same algorithm as Ethernet to provide a bit-level integrity check of all fields in the IEEE 802.11 frame, from the Frame Control field to the Payload field.

IEEE 802.2 LLC Header

The fields in the IEEE 802.2 LLC header are defined and used in the same way as the IEEE 802.2 LLC header for the IEEE 802.3, IEEE 802.5, and FDDI frame formats discussed earlier in this chapter.

Payload

The payload for an IEEE 802.11 frame can be a maximum size of 2312 bytes. IEEE 802.11 payloads can be MAC management frames (such as beacon frames sent by wireless APs), control fames (such as RTS, CTS, and ACK frames), or data frames containing the PDU of an upper layer protocol (such as an IP datagram).

If the payload of a data frame is encrypted with WEP, the upper layer PDU is preceded by a plain-text 4-byte field containing an Initialization Vector (IV) field and followed with an encrypted 4-byte Integrity Check Value (ICV) field, lowering the maximum upper layer PDU size to 2304 bytes.

If the payload of a data frame is encrypted with WPA and the Temporal Key Integrity Protocol (TKIP), the upper layer PDU is preceded by a plain-text 8-byte field containing the IV and followed with an encrypted 8-byte Message Integrity Code (MIC) and 4-byte ICV field, lowering the maximum upper layer PDU size to 2292 bytes.

If the payload of a data frame is encrypted with WPA2 and the Advanced Encryption Standard (AES), the upper layer PDU is preceded by a plaintext 8-byte field containing the Packet Number field and followed with an encrypted 8-byte Message Integrity Code (MIC), lowering the maximum upper layer PDU size to 2296 bytes.

The header and trailer fields for the various encryption methods are not shown in Figure 1-11.

Frame Control Field

Figure 1-12 shows the Frame Control field.

The Frame Control field contains the following subfields:

- **Protocol Version** A 2-bit field that indicates the version of the 802.11 protocol used to construct the frame. This field is set to 0 for the current version of IEEE 802.11. If the Protocol Version field is set to a value that is not supported by the receiving wireless node, the frame is silently discarded.

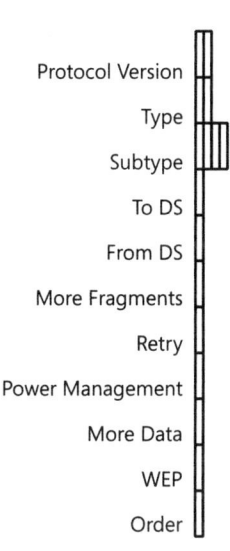

Figure 1-12 The Frame Control field in the IEEE 802.11 header

- **Type** A 2-bit field that indicates the type of IEEE 802.11 frame. There are three defined values: 00 for management frames, 01 for control frames, and 10 for data frames. The value of 11 is currently reserved.
- **Subtype** A 4-bit field that indicates the specific type of management, control, or data frame.
- **To DS** A 1-bit flag that indicates (when set to 1) that the frame is destined for the distribution system (DS), the wired network that connects wireless APs and provides access to wired network nodes. Only wireless nodes that are operating in infrastructure mode set this flag.
- **From DS** A 1-bit flag that indicates (when set to 1) that the frame is originating from the wired network. This flag is only set by the wireless AP when forwarding a frame to a wireless node operating in infrastructure mode.
- **More Fragments** A 1-bit flag that indicates (when set to 1) that there are more fragments of the frame for which this frame is also a fragment. If the frame is not fragmented or is the last fragment of a fragmented frame, the More Fragments flag is set to 0.
- **Retry** A 1-bit flag that indicates (when set to 1) that this frame is a retransmission of a previously transmitted frame.
- **Power Management** A 1-bit flag that indicates (when set to 1) that the transmitting wireless node is operating in a power-saving mode.
- **More Data** A 1-bit flag that indicates (when set to 1) that the wireless AP has at least one frame buffered to send to the wireless node.
- **WEP** A 1-bit flag that indicates (when set to 1) that the payload is encrypted.
- **Order** A 1-bit flag that indicates (when set to 1) that the frames must be processed in order.

IEEE 802.11 SNAP

An IP datagram sent over an IEEE 802.11 network must be encapsulated with a SNAP header. Figure 1-13 shows SNAP encapsulation for IP datagrams sent over an IEEE 802.11 link (rather than between wireless APs).

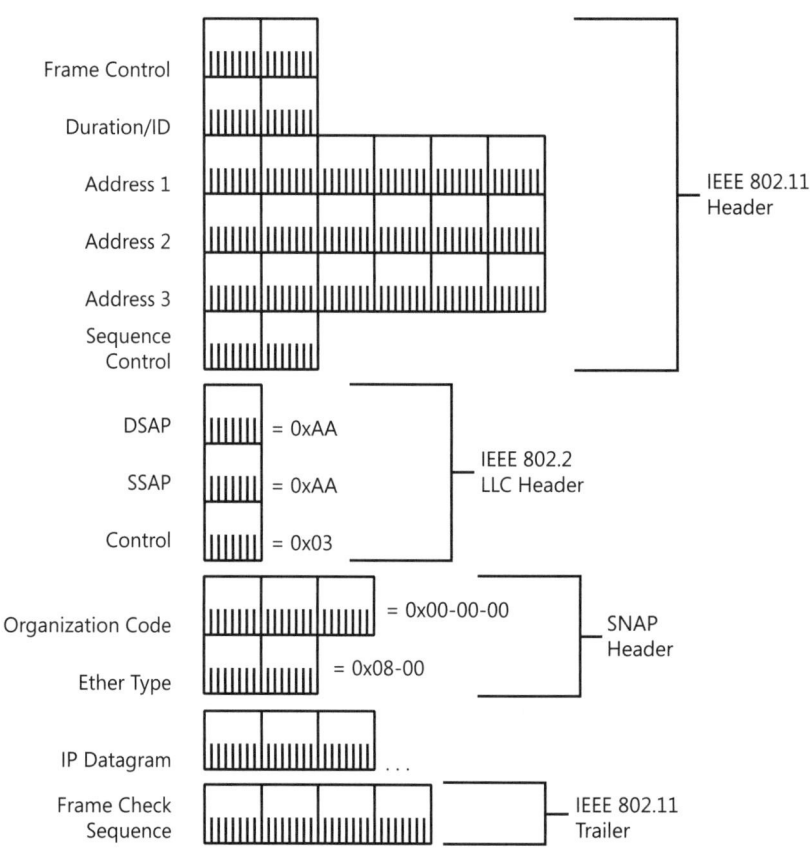

Figure 1-13 The IEEE 802.11 SNAP frame format showing the SNAP header and an IP datagram

Summary

LAN technology encapsulations provide delimitation, addressing, protocol identification, and bit-level integrity services. IP datagrams and ARP messages sent over Ethernet links are encapsulated using either the Ethernet II or IEEE 802.3 SNAP frame formats. IP datagrams and ARP messages sent over Token Ring links are encapsulated using the IEEE 802.5 SNAP frame format. IP datagrams and ARP messages sent over FDDI links are encapsulated using the FDDI SNAP frame format. IP datagrams and ARP messages sent over IEEE 802.11 links are encapsulated using the IEEE 802.11 SNAP frame format.

Chapter 2

Wide Area Network (WAN) Technologies

In this chapter:
WAN Encapsulations 31
Point-to-Point Protocol. 32
Frame Relay. 38
Summary. 41

To successfully troubleshoot TCP/IP problems on a wide area network (WAN), it is important to understand how IP datagrams and Address Resolution Protocol (ARP) messages are encapsulated by a computer running Windows Server 2008 or Windows Vista that uses a WAN technology such as T-carrier, Public Switched Telephone Network (PSTN), Integrated Services Digital Network (ISDN), or Frame Relay. It is also important to understand WAN technology encapsulations to interpret the WAN encapsulation portions of a frame when using Microsoft Network Monitor or other types of WAN frame capture programs or facilities.

Note Support for Serial Line Internet Protocol (SLIP), X.25, and Asynchronous Transfer Mode (ATM) has been removed from Windows Server 2008 and Windows Vista.

WAN Encapsulations

As discussed in Chapter 1, "Local Area Network (LAN) Technologies," IP datagrams are an Open Systems Interconnection (OSI) Network Layer entity that require a Data Link Layer encapsulation before being sent on a physical medium. For WAN technologies, the Data Link Layer encapsulation provides the following services:

- **Delimitation**   Frames at the Data Link Layer must be distinguished from each other, and the frame's payload must be distinguished from the Data Link Layer header and trailer.

- **Protocol identification**   On a multiprotocol WAN link, protocols such as TCP/IP or AppleTalk must be distinguished from each other.

- **Addressing**   For WAN technologies that support multiple possible destinations using the same physical link, the destination must be identified.

- **Bit-level integrity check** A checksum provides a bit-level integrity check between either the peer nodes on the link or forwarding nodes on a packet-switching network.

This chapter discusses WAN technologies and their encapsulations for IP datagrams and ARP messages. WAN encapsulations are divided into two categories based on the types of IP networks of the WAN link:

- Point-to-point links support an IP network segment with a maximum of two nodes. These links include analog phone lines, ISDN lines, Digital Subscriber Line (DSL) lines, and T-carrier links such as T-1, T-3, Fractional T-1, E-1, and E-3. Point-to-point links do not require Data Link Layer addressing.

- Non-broadcast multiple access (NBMA) links support an IP network segment with more than two nodes; however, there is no facility to broadcast a single IP datagram to multiple locations. NBMA links include packet-switching WAN technologies such as Frame Relay. NBMA links require Data Link Layer addressing.

Point-to-Point Protocol

The Point-to-Point Protocol (PPP) is a standardized point-to-point network encapsulation method that provides Data Link Layer functionality comparable to LAN encapsulations. PPP provides frame delimitation, protocol identification, and bit-level integrity services. PPP is defined in RFC 1661.

> **More Info** All of the RFCs referenced in this chapter can be found in the \Standards\Chap02_WAN folder on the companion CD-ROM.

RFC 1661 describes PPP as a suite of protocols that provide the following:

- A Data Link Layer encapsulation method that supports multiple protocols simultaneously on the same link.

- A protocol for negotiating the Data Link Layer characteristics of the point-to-point connection named the Link Control Protocol (LCP).

- A series of protocols for negotiating the Network Layer properties of Network Layer protocols over the point-to-point connection named Network Control Protocols (NCPs). For example, RFCs 1332 and 1877 describe the NCP for IP called Internet Protocol Control Protocol (IPCP). IPCP is used to negotiate an IP address, the addresses of name servers, and the use of the Van Jacobsen TCP compression protocol.

This chapter discusses only the Data Link Layer encapsulation. Chapter 4, "Point-to-Point Protocol (PPP)," describes LCP and the NCPs needed for IP connectivity.

PPP encapsulation and framing is based on the International Organization for Standardization (ISO) High-Level Data Link Control (HDLC) protocol. HDLC was derived from the Synchronous Data Link Control (SDLC) protocol developed by IBM for the Systems Network Architecture (SNA) protocol suite. HDLC encapsulation for PPP frames is described in RFC 1662. Figure 2-1 shows HDLC encapsulation for PPP frames.

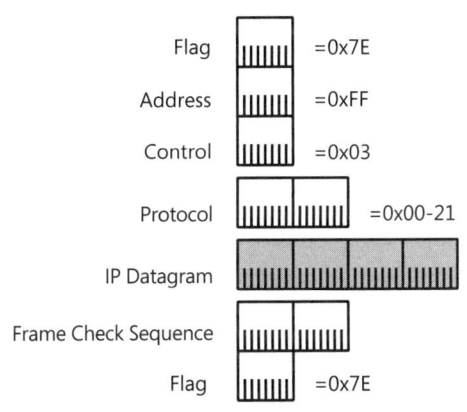

Figure 2-1 PPP encapsulation using HDLC framing for an IP datagram

The fields in the PPP header and trailer are defined as follows:

- **Flag** A 1-byte field set to the FLAG character, 0x7E (bit sequence 01111110), that indicates the start and end of a PPP frame.

- **Address** A 1-byte field that is a by-product of HDLC. In HDLC environments, the Address field is used as a destination address on a multipoint network. PPP links are point-to-point, and the destination node is always the other node on the point-to-point link. Therefore, the Address field for PPP encapsulation is set to 0xFF—the broadcast address.

- **Control** A 1-byte field that is also an HDLC by-product. In HDLC environments, the Control field is used to implement sequencing and acknowledgments to provide Data Link Layer reliability services. For session-based traffic, the Control field is more than 1 byte long. For datagram traffic, the Control field is 1 byte long and set to 0x03 to indicate an unnumbered information (UI) frame. Because PPP does not provide reliable Data Link Layer services, PPP frames are always UI frames. Therefore, PPP frames always use a 1-byte Control field set to 0x03.

- **Protocol** A 2-byte field used to identify the upper layer protocol of the PPP payload. For example, 0x00-21 indicates an IP datagram and 0x00-29 indicates an AppleTalk datagram.

    For the current list of PPP protocol numbers, see *http://www.iana.org/assignments/ppp-numbers*.

- **Frame Check Sequence (FCS)** A 2-byte field used to provide bit-level integrity services for the PPP frame. The sender calculates the FCS, which is then placed in the FCS field. The receiver performs the same FCS calculation and compares its result with the result stored in this field. If the two FCS values match, the PPP frame is considered valid and is processed further. If the two FCS values do not match, the PPP frame is silently discarded.

The HDLC encapsulation for PPP frames is also used for Asymmetric Digital Subscriber Line (ADSL) broadband Internet connections.

Figure 2-2 shows a typical PPP encapsulation for an IP datagram when using Address and Control field suppression and Protocol field compression.

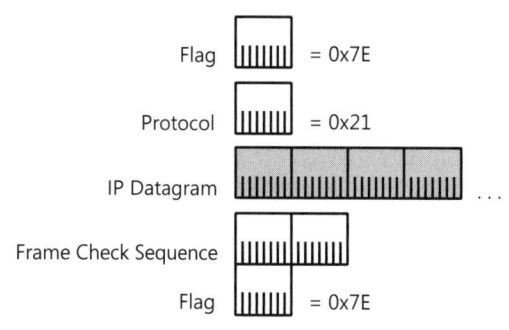

Flag	= 0x7E
Protocol	= 0x21
IP Datagram	...
Frame Check Sequence	
Flag	= 0x7E

Figure 2-2 Typical PPP encapsulation for an IP datagram

This abbreviated form of PPP encapsulation is a result of the following:

- Because the Address field is irrelevant for point-to-point links, in most cases the PPP peers agree during LCP negotiation to not include the Address field. This is done through the Address and Control Field Compression LCP option.

- Because the Control is always set to 0x03 and provides no other service, in most cases the PPP peers agree during LCP negotiation to not include the Control field. This, too, is done through the Address and Control Field Compression LCP option.

- Because the high-order byte of the PPP Protocol field for Network Layer protocols such as IP or AppleTalk is always set to 0x00, in most cases the PPP peers agree during LCP negotiation to use a 1-byte Control field. This is done through the Protocol Compression LCP option.

Note PPP frames captured with Network Monitor do not display the HDLC structure, as shown in Figures 2-1 and 2-2. PPP control frames contain simulated source and destination media access control (MAC) addresses and only the PPP Protocol field. PPP data frames contain a simulated Ethernet II header.

PPP on Asynchronous Links

PPP on asynchronous links such as analog phone lines uses character stuffing to prevent the occurrence of the FLAG (0x7E) character within the PPP payload. The FLAG character is escaped, or replaced, with a sequence beginning with another special character called the ESC (0x7D) character. The PPP ESC character has no relation to the ASCII ESC character.

If the FLAG character occurs within the original IP datagram, it is replaced with the sequence 0x7D-5E. To prevent the misinterpretation of the ESC character by the receiving node, if the ESC (0x7D) character occurs within the original IP datagram, it is replaced with the sequence 0x7D-5D. Therefore:

- FLAG characters can occur only at the beginning and end of the PPP frame.
- On the sending node, PPP replaces the FLAG character within the IP datagram with the sequence 0x7D-5E. On the receiving node, the 0x7D-5E sequence is translated back to 0x7E.
- On the sending node, PPP replaces the ESC character within the PPP frame with the sequence 0x7D-5D. On the receiving node, the 0x7D-5D sequence is translated back to 0x7D. If the IP datagram contains the sequence 0x7D-5E, the escaping of the ESC character turns this sequence into 0x7D-5D-5E to prevent the receiver from misinterpreting the 0x7D-5E sequence as 0x7E.

Additionally, character stuffing is used to stuff characters with values less than 0x20 (32 in decimal notation) to prevent these characters from being misinterpreted as control characters when software flow control is used over asynchronous links. The escape sequence for these characters is 0x7D-x, where x is the original character with the fifth bit set to 1. The fifth bit is defined as the third bit from the high-order bit using the bit position designation of 7-6-5-4-3-2-1-0. Therefore, the character 0x11 (bit sequence 0-0-0-1-0-0-0-1) would be escaped to the sequence 0x7D-31 (bit sequence 0-0-1-1-0-0-0-1).

The use of character stuffing for characters less than 0x20 is negotiated using the Asynchronous Control Character Map (ACCM) LCP option. This LCP option uses a 32-bit bitmap to indicate exactly which character values need to be escaped.

For more information on the ACCM LCP option, see RFCs 1661 and 1662.

PPP on Synchronous Links

Character stuffing is an inefficient method of escaping the FLAG character. If the PPP payload consists of a stream of 0x7E characters, character stuffing roughly doubles the size of the PPP frame as it is sent on the medium. For asynchronous, byte-boundary media such as analog phone lines, character stuffing is the only alternative.

On synchronous links such as T-carrier, ISDN, and Synchronous Optical Network (SONET), a technique called *bit stuffing* is used to mark the location of the FLAG character. Recall that the FLAG character is 0x7E, or the bit sequence 01111110. With bit stuffing, the only time six 1 bits in a row are allowed is for the FLAG character as it is used to mark the start and end of a PPP frame. Throughout the rest of the PPP frame, if there are five 1 bits in a row, a 0 bit is inserted into the bit stream by the synchronous link hardware. Therefore, the bit sequence

111110 is stuffed to produce 1111100 and the bit sequence 111111 is stuffed to become 1111101. Therefore, six 1 bits in a row cannot occur except for the FLAG character when it is used to mark the start and end of a PPP frame. If the FLAG character does occur within the PPP frame, it is bit stuffed to produce the bit sequence 011111010. Bit stuffing is much more efficient than character stuffing. If stuffed, a single byte becomes 9 bits, not 16 bits, as is the case with character stuffing. With synchronous links and bit stuffing, data sent no longer falls along bit boundaries. A single byte sent can be encoded as either 8 or 9 bits, depending on the presence of a 11111 bit sequence within the byte.

PPP Maximum Receive Unit

The maximum-sized PPP frame, the maximum transmission unit (MTU) for a PPP link, is known as the Maximum Receive Unit (MRU). The default value for the PPP MRU is 1500 bytes. The MRU for a PPP connection can be negotiated to a lower or higher value using the Maximum Receive Unit LCP option. If an MRU is negotiated to a value lower than 1500 bytes, a 1500-byte MRU must still be supported in case the link has to be resynchronized.

PPP Multilink Protocol

The PPP Multilink Protocol (MP) is an extension to PPP defined in RFC 1991 that allows you to bundle or aggregate the bandwidth of multiple physical connections. It is supported by Windows Server 2008 and Windows Vista Network Connections and the Windows Server 2008 Routing and Remote Access service. MP takes multiple physical connections and makes them appear as a single logical link. For example, with MP, two analog phone lines operating at 28.8 Kbps appear as a single connection operating at 57.6 Kbps. Another example is the aggregation of multiple channels of an ISDN Basic Rate Interface (BRI) or Primary Rate Interface (PRI) line. In the case of a BRI line, MP makes the two 64-Kbps BRI B-channels appear as a single connection operating at 128 Kbps.

MP is an extra layer of encapsulation that operates within a PPP payload. To identify an MP packet, the PPP Protocol field is set to 0x00-3D. The payload of an MP packet is a PPP frame or the fragment of a PPP frame. If the size of the PPP payload that would be sent on a single-link PPP connection, plus the additional MP header, is greater than the MRU for the specific physical link over which the MP packet is sent, MP fragments the PPP payload.

MP fragmentation divides the PPP payload along boundaries that will fit within the link's MRU. The fragments are sent in sequence using an incrementing sequence number, and flags are used to indicate the first and last fragments of an original PPP payload. A lost MP fragment causes the entire original PPP payload to be silently discarded.

MP encapsulation has two different forms: the long sequence number format (shown in Figure 2-3) and the short sequence number format. The long sequence number format adds 4 bytes of overhead to the PPP payload.

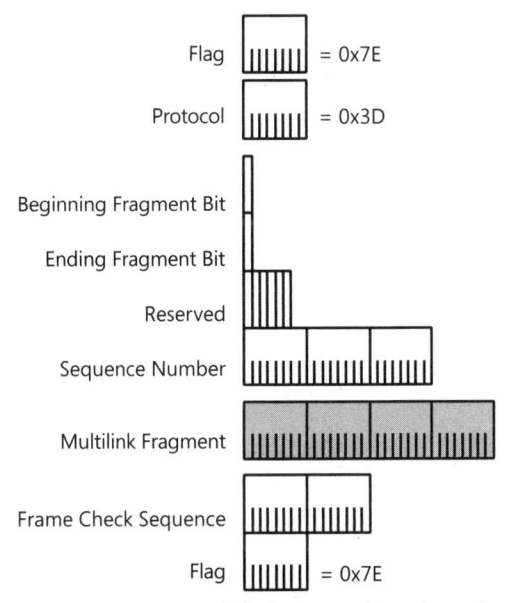

Figure 2-3 The Multilink Protocol header, using the long sequence number format

The fields in the MP long sequence number format header are defined as follows:

- **Beginning Fragment Bit**   Set to 1 on the first fragment of a PPP payload and to 0 on all other PPP payload fragments.

- **Ending Fragment Bit**   Set to 1 on the last fragment of a PPP payload and to 0 on all other PPP payload fragments. If a PPP payload is not fragmented, both the Beginning Fragment Bit and Ending Fragment Bit are set to 1.

- **Reserved**   Set to 0.

- **Sequence Number**   Set to an incrementally increasing number for each MP payload sent. For the long sequence number format, the Sequence Number field is 3 bytes long. The Sequence Number field is used to number successive PPP payloads that would normally be sent over a single-link PPP connection and is used by MP to preserve the packet sequence as sent by the PPP peer. Additionally, the Sequence Number field is used to number individual fragments of a PPP payload so that the receiving node can detect a fragment loss.

Figure 2-4 shows the short sequence number format, which adds 2 bytes of overhead to the PPP payload.

The short sequence format has only 2 reserved bits, and its Sequence Number field is only 12 bits long. The long sequence number format is used by default unless the Short Sequence Number Header Format LCP option is used during the LCP negotiation.

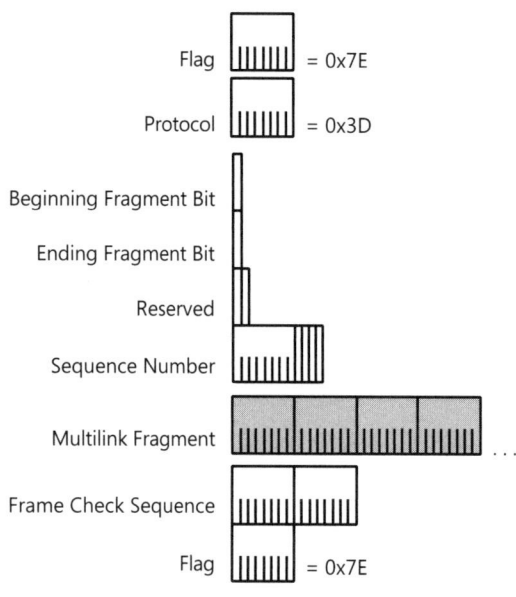

Figure 2-4 The Multilink Protocol header, using the short sequence number format

Frame Relay

When packet-switching networks were first introduced, they were based on existing analog copper lines that experienced a high number of errors. The X.25 packet-switched technology was designed to compensate for these errors and provide connection-oriented reliable data transfer. In these days of high-grade digital fiber-optic lines, there is no need for the overhead associated with X.25. Frame Relay is a packet-switched technology similar to X.25, but without the added framing and processing overhead to provide guaranteed data transfer. Unlike X.25, Frame Relay does not provide link-to-link reliability. If a frame in the Frame Relay network is corrupted in any way, it is silently discarded. Upper layer communication protocols such as TCP must detect and recover discarded frames.

A key advantage Frame Relay has over private-line facilities, such as T-Carrier, is that Frame Relay customers can be charged based on the amount of data transferred, instead of the distance between the endpoints. It is common, however, for the Frame Relay vendor to charge a fixed monthly cost. In either case Frame Relay is distance-insensitive. A local connection, such as a T-1 line, to the Frame Relay vendor's network is required. Frame Relay allows widely separated sites to exchange data without incurring long-haul telecommunications costs.

Frame Relay is a packet-switching technology defined in terms of a standardized interface between user devices (typically routers) and the switching equipment in the vendor's network (Frame Relay switches).

Typical Frame Relay service providers currently only offer permanent virtual circuits (PVCs). A PVC is a path through a packet-switching network that is statically programmed into the switches. The Frame Relay service provider establishes the PVC when the service is ordered. A new standard for a switched virtual circuit (SVC) version of Frame Relay uses the ISDN signaling protocol as the mechanism for establishing the virtual circuit. An SVC is a path through a packet-switching network that is negotiated using a signaling protocol each time a connection is initiated. This new standard is not widely used in production networks.

Frame Relay speeds range from 56 Kbps to 1.544 Mbps. The required throughput for a given link determines the committed information rate (CIR). The CIR is the throughput guaranteed by the Frame Relay service provider. Most Frame Relay service providers allow a customer to transmit bursts above the CIR for short periods of time. Depending on congestion, the bursted traffic can be delivered by the Frame Relay network. However, traffic that exceeds the CIR is delivered on a best-effort basis only. This flexibility allows for network traffic spikes without dropping frames.

Frame Relay Encapsulation

Frame Relay encapsulation of IP datagrams is based on HDLC, as RFC 2427 describes. Because Frame Relay was designed for multiple protocols, Frame Relay encapsulation uses a Network Layer Protocol Identifier (NLPID) field to identify the payload. IP datagrams are encapsulated with a NLPID field set to 0xCC and a Frame Relay header and trailer. Figure 2-5 shows the Frame Relay encapsulation for IP datagrams.

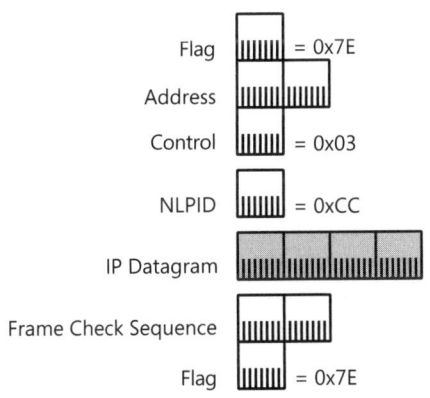

Figure 2-5 Frame Relay encapsulation for IP datagrams, showing the Frame Relay header and trailer

The fields in the Frame Relay header and trailer are defined as follows:

- **Flag** As in PPP frames, the Flag field is 1 byte long and is set to 0x7E to mark the beginning and end of the Frame Relay frame. Bit stuffing is used on synchronous links to prevent the occurrence of the Flag character within the Frame Relay payload.

- **Address** The Address field is multiple bytes long (typically 2 bytes) and contains the Frame Relay virtual circuit identifier called the Data Link Connection Identifier (DLCI) and congestion indicators. The Address field's structure is discussed in the section titled "Frame Relay Address Field," later in this chapter.

- **Control** A 1-byte field set to 0x03 to indicate a UI frame.
- **NLPID** A 1-byte field set to 0xCC to indicate an IP datagram.
- **Frame Check Sequence** A 2-byte CRC used for bit-level integrity verification in the Frame Relay frame. If a Frame Relay frame fails integrity verification, it is silently discarded.

Frame Relay Address Field

The Frame Relay Address field can be 1, 2, 3, or 4 bytes long. Typical Frame Relay implementations use a 2-byte Address field, as shown in Figure 2-6.

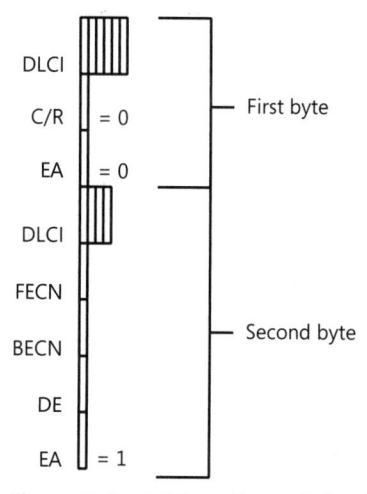

Figure 2-6 A 2-byte Frame Relay Address field

The fields within the 2-byte Address field are defined as follows:

- **DLCI** The first 6 bits of the first byte and the first 4 bits of the second byte comprise the 10-bit DLCI. The DLCI is used to identify the Frame Relay virtual circuit over which the Frame Relay frame is traveling. The DLCI is only locally significant. Each Frame Relay switch changes the DLCI value as it forwards the Frame Relay frame. The devices at each end of a virtual circuit use a different DLCI value to identify the same virtual circuit. Table 2-1 lists the defined values for the DLCI.

Table 2-1 Defined Values for the Frame Relay DLCI

DLCI Value	Use
0	In-channel signaling
1–15	Reserved
16–991	Assigned to user connections
992–1022	Reserved
1023	In-channel signaling

- **Command/Response (C/R)** The seventh bit in the first byte of the Address field is the C/R bit. It currently is not used for Frame Relay operations and is set to 0.

- **Extended Address (EA)** The last bit in each byte of the Address field is the EA bit. If this bit is set to 1, the current byte is the last byte in the Address field. For the 2-byte Address field, the value of the EA bit in the first byte of the Address field is 0, and the value of the EA bit in the second byte of the Address field is 1.

- **Forward Explicit Congestion Notification (FECN)** The fifth bit in the second byte of the Address field is the FECN bit. It is used to inform the destination Frame Relay node that congestion exists in the path from the source to the destination. The FECN bit is set to 0 by the source Frame Relay node and set to 1 by a Frame Relay switch if it is experiencing congestion in the forward path. If the destination Frame Relay node receives a Frame Relay frame with the FECN bit set, the node can indicate the congestion condition to upper layer protocols that can implement receiver-side flow control. The interpretation of the FECN bit for IP traffic is not defined.

- **Backward Explicit Congestion Notification (BECN)** The sixth bit in the second byte of the Address field is the BECN bit. The BECN bit is used to inform the destination Frame Relay node that congestion exists in the path from the destination to the source (in the opposite direction in which the frame was traveling). The BECN bit is set to 0 by the source Frame Relay node and set to 1 by a Frame Relay switch if it is experiencing congestion in the reverse path. If the destination Frame Relay node receives a Frame Relay frame with the BECN bit set, the node can indicate the congestion condition to upper layer protocols that can implement sender-side flow control. The interpretation of the BECN bit for IP traffic is not defined.

- **Discard Eligibility (DE)** The seventh bit in the second byte of the Address field is the DE bit. Frame Relay switches use the DE bit to decide which frames to discard during a period of congestion. Frame Relay switches consider the frames with the DE bit set to be a lower priority and discards them first. The initial Frame Relay switch sets the DE bit to 1 on a frame when a customer has exceeded the CIR for the virtual circuit.

The maximum-sized frame that can be sent across a Frame Relay network varies according to the Frame Relay provider. RFC 2427 requires all Frame Relay networks to support a minimum frame size of 262 bytes, and a maximum frame size of 1600 bytes, although maximum frame sizes of up to 4500 bytes are common. Using a maximum frame size of 1600 bytes and a 2-byte address field, the IP MTU for Frame Relay is 1592.

Summary

Typical WAN technology encapsulations used by Windows Server 2008 and Windows Vista provide delimitation, addressing, protocol identification, and bit-level integrity services. IP datagrams sent over point-to-point WAN links can be encapsulated using PPP or MP. IP datagrams and ARP messages sent over Frame Relay use an HDLC-based multiprotocol encapsulation.

Chapter 3

Address Resolution Protocol (ARP)

In this chapter:
Overview of ARP 43
ARP Frame Structure. 45
ARP in Windows Server 2008 and Windows Vista 48
Inverse ARP (InARP). 57
Proxy ARP 58
Summary. 60

To successfully troubleshoot problems forwarding IP datagrams on a local area network (LAN) link, it is important to understand how TCP/IP uses Address Resolution Protocol (ARP) to resolve a next-hop IP address to its corresponding Network Interface Layer address. TCP/IP for Windows Server 2008 and Windows Vista uses ARP for address resolution, duplicate address detection, and neighbor unreachability detection. The Network Bridge for Windows Server 2008 and Windows Vista and the Routing and Remote Access service for Windows Server 2008 uses a variation of ARP called proxy ARP to forward IP datagrams between nodes on separate segments of a subdivided subnet.

Note This chapter assumes prior knowledge of the route determination process for IP hosts and routers in Microsoft Windows. For more information, see Chapter 5, "IP Routing," of the "TCP/IP Fundamentals for Microsoft Windows" book, located in the \Fundamentals folder on the companion CD-ROM.

Overview of ARP

ARP is used by TCP/IP nodes on shared access, broadcast-based networking technologies such as Ethernet and Token Ring. ARP is used to resolve the next-hop IP address of a node to its corresponding media access control (MAC) address. The MAC address also is known as the physical, hardware, or network adapter address. The resolved MAC address becomes the destination MAC address in the Ethernet or Token Ring header to which an IP datagram is addressed when it is sent on the medium. ARP resolves an Internet Layer address (an IP address) to a Network Interface Layer address (a MAC address). ARP is defined in RFC 826.

> **More Info** The RFCs referenced in this chapter can be found in the \Standards\Chap03_ARP folder on the companion CD-ROM.

The next-hop IP address is not necessarily the same as the destination IP address of the IP datagram. The result of the route determination process for every outgoing IP datagram is a next-hop interface and a next-hop IP address. For direct deliveries to destinations on the same subnet, the next-hop IP address is the datagram's destination IP address. For indirect deliveries to remote destinations, the next-hop IP address is the IP address of a neighboring router on the same subnet as the forwarding host.

IP was designed to be independent of any specific Network Interface Layer technology. Therefore, there is no way to determine the destination Network Interface Layer address from the next-hop IP address. For example, Ethernet and Token Ring MAC addresses are 6 bytes long, and IP addresses are 4 bytes long. During the manufacturing process, the MAC address is assigned to the adapter. A network administrator assigns the IP address (either directly through manual configuration or indirectly through the administration of a Dynamic Host Configuration Protocol [DHCP] server). Because there is no correlation between the assignments of these two addresses for a given IP node, it is impossible to derive one address from the other. ARP is a request-reply protocol that provides a dynamic address resolution facility to map next-hop IP addresses to their corresponding MAC addresses.

As defined in RFC 826, ARP consists of the following messages:

- **ARP Request** The forwarding node uses the ARP Request message to request the MAC address for a specific next-hop IP address. The ARP Request is a MAC-level broadcast frame intended to reach all the nodes on the physical subnet to which the interface sending the ARP Request is attached. The node sending the ARP Request is known as the *ARP requester*.

- **ARP Reply** The ARP Reply message is used to reply to the ARP requester. The node whose IP address matches the requested IP address in the ARP Request message sends the ARP Reply. The ARP Reply is a unicast MAC frame sent to the destination MAC address of the ARP requester. The node sending the ARP Reply is known as the *ARP responder*.

Because the ARP Request message is a MAC-level broadcast, all next-hop IP addresses to be resolved must be directly reachable (on the same subnet) from the interface used to send the ARP Request. For proper routing table entries, this is always the case. If a routing table entry contains an invalid next-hop IP address and the address is not directly reachable for the interface, ARP will fail to resolve the next-hop IP address.

All nodes within the same broadcast domain receive the ARP Request. A broadcast domain is a portion of a network over which a broadcast frame is propagated. Hubs, bridges, and Layer 2 switches propagate the ARP Request. However, IP routers do not propagate ARP frames.

ARP for Windows Server 2008 and Windows Vista supports the broadcast ARP Request and unicast ARP Reply exchange described in RFC 826 to perform address resolution. As described in the "Duplicate Address Detection" and "Neighbor Unreachability Detection" sections of this chapter, Windows Server 2008 and Windows Vista also support a unicast ARP Request and unicast ARP Reply exchange and a broadcast ARP Reply.

The ARP or Neighbor Cache

As is common in many TCP/IP implementations, TCP/IP for Windows Server 2008 and Windows Vista maintains a RAM-based table of IP and MAC address mappings. Historically known as the ARP cache, in Windows Server 2008 and Windows Vista, it is also known as the neighbor cache. When an ARP exchange for address resolution is complete, both the ARP requester and the ARP responder have each other's IP address-to-MAC address mappings in their ARP caches. Subsequent packets forwarded to the previously resolved IP addresses use the ARP cache entry's MAC address. The ARP cache is always checked before an ARP Request is sent.

After the MAC address for a next-hop IP address is determined using an ARP Request–ARP Reply exchange, the resolved MAC address is used as the destination MAC address for subsequent packets. If the node whose IP address has already been resolved becomes unavailable on the subnet, the ARP requester node continues to use its ARP cache entry and send packets on the medium to the resolved MAC address. Because the next-hop IP address was mapped to a MAC address with the ARP cache entry, and the frame was sent on the medium, IP and ARP on the sending node consider the IP datagram to be successfully delivered.

This condition is known as a *network black hole*; packets sent on the subnet are dropped, and the sender or forwarder is unaware of the condition. The user at the ARP requester computer does not notice this condition until TCP connections or other types of session-oriented traffic begin to time out. This particular type of network black hole persists as long as the entry for the mapping remains in the ARP cache. After the entry is removed, an ARP Request–ARP Reply exchange is attempted again. Because the failed node does not respond to the ARP Request, the lack of an ARP Reply can be used to indicate an unsuccessful delivery of IP packets using the next-hop IP address.

To reduce the impact of a network black hole due to an incorrect entry in the ARP cache, ARP in Windows Server 2008 and Windows Vista uses neighbor unreachability detection to track the reachability of neighboring nodes on a subnet and remove or update entries in the ARP cache. For more information, see "Neighbor Unreachability Detection" in this chapter.

ARP Frame Structure

ARP frames use the EtherType of 0x0806. ARP is not a client protocol of IP, and ARP frames do not contain an IP header. Thus, ARP is useful only for resolving MAC addresses for IP addresses that are on the same physical subnet, the boundaries of which are defined by IP routers. IP routers never forward an ARP Request or ARP Reply frame.

As RFC 826 describes, an ARP frame's structure suggests that ARP could be used for MAC address resolution for protocols other than IP. However, in practice, IP is the only protocol that uses the ARP frame format. Figure 3-1 shows the structure of the ARP frame for the IP protocol and for LAN technologies that use a 6-byte MAC address.

Hardware Type
Protocol Type = 0x00-80
Hardware Address Length = 6
Protocol Address Length = 4
Operation
Sender Hardware Address
Sender Protocol Address
Target Hardware Address
Target Protocol Address

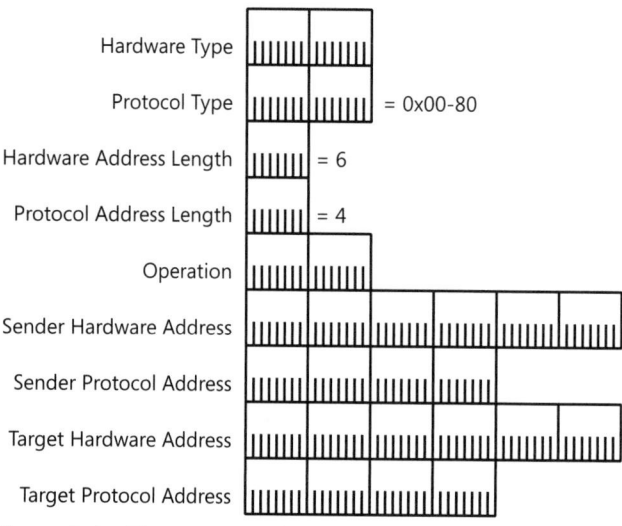

Figure 3-1 The structure of an ARP frame

> **More Info** ARP as a potential MAC address resolution method for non-IP protocols is discussed in RFC 826.

The fields in the ARP header are defined as follows:

- **Hardware Type** A 2-byte field that indicates the type of hardware being used at the Network Interface Layer. Table 3-1 lists some commonly used ARP Hardware Type values. After receipt of an ARP frame, an IP node verifies that the Hardware Type value of the ARP frame matches the Hardware Type value of the interface on which the ARP frame was received. If it does not match, the frame is silently discarded. For a complete list of ARP Hardware Type values, see *http://www.iana.org/assignments/arp-parameters*.

Table 3-1 ARP Hardware Type Values

Hardware Type Value	Data Link Layer Technology
1 (0x00-01)	Ethernet
6 (0x00-06)	IEEE 802.5 Networks (Token Ring)
15 (0x00-0F)	Frame Relay
16 (0x00-10)	Asynchronous Transfer Mode (ATM)

- **Protocol Type**   A 2-byte field that indicates the protocol for which ARP is providing address resolution. This field uses the same values as the Ethernet II EtherType field. For IP address resolution, the Protocol Type field is set to the EtherType for IP, 0x0800. After receipt of an ARP frame, an IP node verifies that the ARP Protocol Type is set to 0x0800. If it is not set to 0x0800, the frame is silently discarded.

- **Hardware Address Length**   A 1-byte field that indicates the length in bytes of the hardware address in the Sender Hardware Address and Target Hardware Address fields. For Ethernet and Token Ring, the Hardware Address Length field is set to 6. For frame relay, the Hardware Address Length typically is set to 2 (for the commonly used 2-byte Frame Relay Address field).

- **Protocol Address Length**   A 1-byte field that indicates the length in bytes of the protocol address in the Sender Protocol Address and Target Protocol Address fields. For the IP protocol, the length of IP addresses is 4 bytes.

- **Operation (Opcode)**   A 2-byte field that indicates the type of ARP frame. Table 3-2 lists the commonly used ARP Operation values. For a complete list of ARP Operation values, see *http://www.iana.org/assignments/arp-parameters*.

Table 3-2 **ARP Operation Values**

Operation Value	Type of ARP Frame
1 (0x00-01)	ARP Request
2 (0x00-02)	ARP Reply
8 (0x00-08)	Inverse ARP Request
9 (0x00-09)	Inverse ARP Reply

- **Sender Hardware Address (SHA)**   A field that is the length of the value of the Hardware Address Length field and contains the hardware or Data Link Layer address of the ARP frame's sender. For Ethernet and Token Ring, the SHA field contains the MAC address of the node sending the ARP frame.

- **Sender Protocol Address (SPA)**   A field that is the length of the value of the Protocol Address Length field and contains the protocol address of the ARP frame's sender. For IP, the SPA field contains the IP address of the node sending the ARP frame.

- **Target Hardware Address (THA)**   A field that is the length of the value of the Hardware Address Length field and contains the hardware or Data Link Layer address of the ARP frame's target (destination). For Ethernet and Token Ring, the THA field is set to 0x00-00-00-00-00-00 for ARP Request frames, and it is set to the MAC address of the ARP requester for ARP Reply frames.

- **Target Protocol Address (TPA)**   A field that is the length of the value of the Protocol Address Length field and contains the protocol address of the ARP frame's target (destination). For IP, the TPA field is set to the IP address being resolved in the ARP Request frame, and it is set to the IP address of the ARP requester in the ARP Reply frame.

ARP in Windows Server 2008 and Windows Vista

Unlike ARP in previous versions of Windows, ARP in Windows Server 2008 and Windows Vista is designed to work in the same way as Neighbor Discovery in IP version 6 (IPv6), as described in RFC 4861. Neighbor Discovery in IPv6 is the replacement for ARP, router discovery, and the redirect function in IP version 4 (IPv4). IPv6 nodes use a neighbor cache to store the MAC addresses of recently resolved IPv6 addresses, rather than an ARP cache. Neighbor Discovery in IPv6 also provides additional capabilities that are not present in IPv4, such as neighbor unreachability detection.

The following sections describe how ARP in Windows Server 2008 and Windows Vista works for the following processes:

- Address resolution
- Duplicate address detection
- Neighbor unreachability detection

Address Resolution

ARP in Windows Server 2008 and Windows Vista supports the broadcast ARP Request and unicast ARP Reply exchange to perform address resolution, as described in RFC 826. The ARP Request and ARP Reply exchange contains all the information for the ARP requester to determine the IP address and MAC address of the ARP responder, and for the ARP responder to determine the IP address and MAC address of the ARP requester. Figure 3-2 shows an ARP Request and ARP Reply exchange.

Node 1
IP Address: 10.0.0.99
MAC Address: 00-60-08-52-F9-D8

Node 2
IP Address: 10.0.0.1
MAC Address: 00-10-54-CA-E1-40

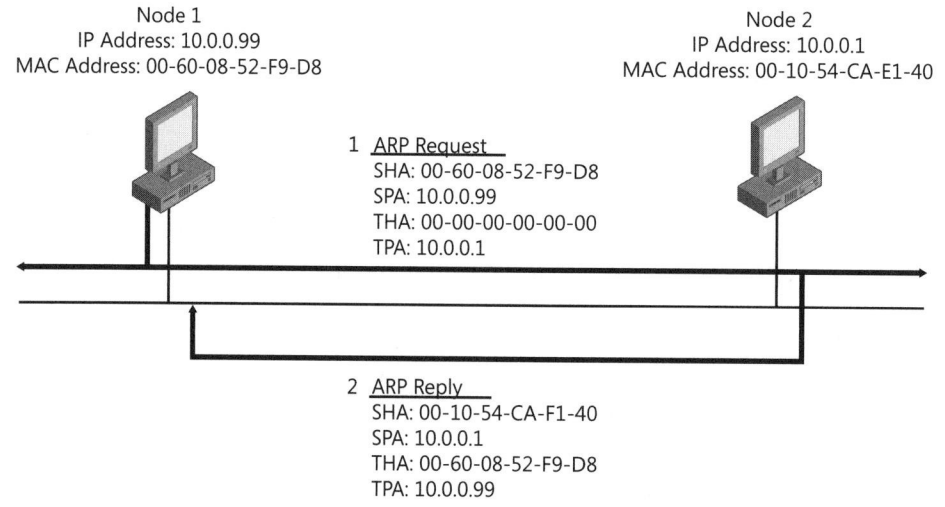

1 ARP Request
SHA: 00-60-08-52-F9-D8
SPA: 10.0.0.99
THA: 00-00-00-00-00-00
TPA: 10.0.0.1

2 ARP Reply
SHA: 00-10-54-CA-F1-40
SPA: 10.0.0.1
THA: 00-60-08-52-F9-D8
TPA: 10.0.0.99

Figure 3-2 An example of address resolution

Node 1, with the IP address of 10.0.0.99 and the MAC address of 0x00-60-08-52-F9-D8, needs to forward an IP datagram to Node 2 at the IP address of 10.0.0.1. Based on information in Node 1's routing table, the next-hop IP address to reach Node 2 is 10.0.0.1, using the Ethernet interface. Node 1 constructs an ARP Request frame and sends it as a MAC-level broadcast using the Ethernet interface.

The following Network Monitor 3.1 trace (Frame 1 of Capture 03-01 in the \Captures folder on the companion CD-ROM) is for the ARP Request frame sent by Node 1:

```
Frame:
- Ethernet: Etype = ARP
  + DestinationAddress: *BROADCAST
  + SourceAddress: 006008 52F9D8
    EthernetType: ARP, 2054(0x806)
- Arp: Request, 10.0.0.99 asks for 10.0.0.1
    HardwareType: Ethernet
    ProtocolType: Internet IP (IPv4)
    HardwareAddressLen: 6 (0x6)
    ProtocolAddressLen: 4 (0x4)
    OpCode: Request, 1(0x1)
    SendersMacAddress: 00-60-08-52-F9-D8
    SendersIp4Address: 10.0.0.99
    TargetMacAddress: 00-00-00-00-00-00
    TargetIp4Address: 10.0.0.1
```

The known quantity—the IP address of Node 2 (10.0.0.1)—is set to the TPA field. The unknown quantity—the hardware address of Node 2—is the THA field in the ARP Request frame, which is set to 00-00-00-00-00-00. Included in the ARP Request are the IP and MAC addresses of Node 1 so that Node 2 can add an entry for Node 1 to its own neighbor cache.

After receipt of the ARP Request frame at Node 2, the node checks the values of the ARP Hardware Type and Protocol Type fields. Node 2 then examines the value of the TPA. Because the TPA is the same as Node 2's IP address, Node 2 adds a neighbor cache entry consisting of [SPA, SHA, Interface] to its neighbor cache. It then checks the ARP Operation field. Because the received ARP frame is an ARP Request, Node 2 constructs an ARP Reply to send back to Node 1.

The following Network Monitor 3.1 trace (Frame 2 of Capture 03-01 in the \Captures folder on the companion CD-ROM) is for the ARP Reply frame sent by Node 2:

```
Frame:
- Ethernet: Etype = ARP
  + DestinationAddress: 006008 52F9D8
  + SourceAddress: 001054 CAE140
    EthernetType: ARP, 2054(0x806)
    UnkownData: Binary Large Object (18 Bytes)
- Arp: Response, 10.0.0.1 at 00-10-54-CA-E1-40
    HardwareType: Ethernet
    ProtocolType: Internet IP (IPv4)
```

```
HardwareAddressLen: 6 (0x6)
ProtocolAddressLen: 4 (0x4)
OpCode: Response, 2(0x2)
SendersMacAddress: 00-10-54-CA-E1-40
SendersIp4Address: 10.0.0.1
TargetMacAddress: 00-60-08-52-F9-D8
TargetIp4Address: 10.0.0.99
```

In the ARP Reply, all quantities are known and the frame is addressed at the MAC level using Node 1's unicast MAC address. The quantity that Node 1 needs—Node 2's MAC address—is the value of the SHA field (SendersMacAddress).

Upon receipt of the ARP Reply frame, Node 1 checks the values of the ARP Hardware Type and Protocol Type fields. Node 1 then examines the value of the TPA field. Because the TPA is the same as Node 1's IP address, Node 1 adds a neighbor cache entry consisting of [SPA, SHA, Interface] to its neighbor cache.

Frame Padding and Ethernet

ARP frames can contain padding bytes. This is not an ARP field, but the consequence of sending an ARP frame on an Ethernet network. As discussed in Chapter 1, Ethernet payloads using the Ethernet II encapsulation must be a minimum length of 46 bytes to adhere to the minimum Ethernet frame size. The ARP frame is only 28 bytes long. Therefore, to send the ARP frame on an Ethernet network, it must be padded with 18 padding bytes.

> **Note** When using Network Monitor, you might notice that sometimes the padding bytes do not appear on either the ARP Request or the ARP Reply frames. Does this mean that the ARP frame was sent as a runt—an Ethernet frame with a length below the minimum frame size? No. This is due to the implementation of Network Monitor within Windows. Network Monitor receives frames by acting as a Network Driver Interface Specification (NDIS) protocol. When any frame is sent or received, Network Monitor receives a copy. However, when frames are sent, Network Monitor receives a copy of the frame before the frame padding is added. When the frame is received, Network Monitor receives a full copy of the frame. Therefore, you do not see a frame padding bytes on an ARP frame if it was captured on the node sending the ARP frame. The example Network Monitor trace Capture 03-01 displayed in this chapter was taken on Node 1. Therefore, the frame padding is only seen on the ARP Reply frame.

The Neighbor Cache

Similar to IPv6 nodes, ARP in Windows Server 2008 and Windows Vista use a neighbor cache to store recently resolved IP address-to-MAC address mappings. This was known as an ARP cache in previous versions of Windows. You can view the neighbor cache in Windows Server 2008 and Windows Vista with the following commands:

- **`netsh interface ipv4 show neighbors`** Shows the contents of the neighbor cache for each interface, including the loopback interface. For each entry, the command displays the IP address, the resolved MAC address, and the neighbor unreachability detection state of the entry. For more information, see "Neighbor Unreachability Detection" in this chapter.

- **`arp -a`** Shows the contents of the neighbor cache for each LAN or PPP interface that has an IP address assigned, but does not include the loopback interface. For each entry, the command displays the IP address, the resolved MAC address, and the state of the entry (which is either "static" for a permanent cache entry or "dynamic" for an entry obtained through an ARP message exchange).

You can add permanent neighbor cache entries (also known as static entries) to the neighbor cache with the following commands:

- **`netsh interface ipv4 add neighbors InterfaceNameorIndex IPAddress MACAddress store=active|persistent`** Creates a permanent neighbor cache entry for an interface (*InterfaceNameorIndex*) that maps an IP address (*IPAddress*) to a MAC address (*MACAddress*). The `store=` option allows you to specify that the permanent entry is maintained (`persistent`, the default) or removed (`active`) when the computer is restarted.

- **`arp -s IPAddress MACAddress InterfaceAddress`** Creates a permanent neighbor cache entry for an interface identified by an IP address (*InterfaceAddress*) that maps an IP address to a MAC address. Entries added with `arp -s` are removed when the computer is restarted.

You can flush the neighbor cache of nonpermanent entries with the following commands:

- **`netsh interface ipv4 delete neighbors`**
- **`arp -d *`**

Updating the Neighbor Cache

Unlike previous versions of Windows, ARP in Windows Server 2008 and Windows Vista does not update a neighbor cache entry with a different MAC address when it receives an ARP Request with the SPA field that matches a neighbor cache entry's IP address. This new behavior is consistent with Neighbor Discovery for IPv6 and prevents the neighbor cache from being updated with incorrect information.

If a node on a subnet changes its MAC address, the corresponding entry in the neighbor cache of its neighbors is not changed until there is a new exchange of broadcast ARP Request and unicast ARP Reply messages.

Duplicate Address Detection

ARP also is used to perform duplicate address detection by sending an ARP Request in which the TPA is set to the IP address for which duplication is being detected. In other words, to detect whether other nodes on the subnet are using the same address, a node sends an ARP Request for its own IP address. For example, when a node is assigned the IP address 10.0.23.89, it sends an ARP Request with the TPA set 10.0.23.89.

If a node sends an ARP Request for its own IP address and no ARP Reply frames are received, the IP address is unique on the subnet and is not a duplicate. If a node sends an ARP Request for its own IP address and receives an ARP Reply, the IP address is a duplicate. In an IP address conflict, the node that sends the ARP Request is the *offending node*. The node that has already verified the uniqueness of its address and sends the ARP Reply is the *defending node*.

In Windows Server 2008 and Windows Vista, the number of broadcast ARP Requests sent during duplicate address detection by default is 3. You can change the number with the `netsh interface ipv4 set interface InterfaceNameOrIndex dadtransmits=Number`.

In previous versions of Windows, the ARP Request for duplicate address detection sent by the offending node set both the SPA and TPA to the IP address for which duplication is being detected. This type of ARP Request caused the receivers with an entry for the conflicted IP address in the SPA field to update their ARP caches with the MAC address of the offending node. To correct the ARP caches with the MAC address of the defending node, the offending node sent an additional broadcast ARP Request with the MAC address of the defending node.

To prevent incorrect entries in neighbor caches during duplicate address detection, the behavior of ARP in Windows Server 2008 and Windows Vista has been changed in the following ways:

- The initial ARP Request just has the TPA set to the address for which uniqueness is being verified. The SPA field is set to 0.0.0.0. This new ARP Request message does not update the ARP or neighbor caches of neighboring nodes and, therefore, does not have to be corrected with an additional broadcast ARP Request.

- If ARP receives an ARP Request with both the SPA and TPA set to an existing entry in the neighbor cache (as sent by previous versions of Windows), ARP does not update the entry with the offending node's MAC address.

With Windows Server 2008 and Windows Vista, there are two different exchanges when there is an IP address conflict, depending on the version of Windows running on the offending node.

Offending Node Runs Windows Server 2008 or Windows Vista

If the offending node is running Windows Server 2008 or Windows Vista, it sends the ARP Request with the SPA field to 0.0.0.0, which does not modify the neighbor or ARP caches of the receiving nodes. The defending node sends a unicast ARP Reply to the offending node, informing it of the address conflict. Therefore, this ARP exchange consists of the following:

1. A broadcast ARP Request sent by the offending node
2. A unicast ARP Reply sent by the defending node

For an example of this exchange, see the Network Monitor trace in Capture 03-02 in the \Captures folder on the companion CD-ROM.

Offending Node Runs a Previous Version of Windows

If the offending node is running a previous version of Windows, it sends the ARP Request with both the TPA and SPA fields set to the duplicate address, which can modify the ARP caches of the neighboring nodes that are running a previous version of Windows. If the defending node is running a previous version of Windows, it sends a unicast ARP Reply to the offending node, informing it of the address conflict. If the defending node is running a Windows Server 2008 or Windows Vista, it sends a broadcast ARP Reply, informing all nodes on the subnet of the address conflict. The offending node then sends an additional broadcast ARP Request message with the MAC address of the defending node to correct the ARP caches of the neighboring nodes that are running a previous version of Windows.

Therefore, this ARP exchange consists of the following:

1. A broadcast ARP Request sent by the offending node
2. A unicast ARP Reply (previous versions of Windows) or a broadcast ARP Reply (Windows Server 2008 or Windows Vista) sent by the defending node
3. A broadcast ARP Request sent by the offending node with the MAC address of the defending node

For an example of this exchange with a broadcast ARP Reply, see the Network Monitor trace in Capture 03-03 in the \Captures folder on the companion CD-ROM.

Note Duplicate address detection attempts to detect the use of a duplicate IP address on the same subnet. Because routers do not propagate ARP frames, duplicate address detection does not detect an IP address conflict between two nodes that are located on different subnets.

Duplicate Address Detection and DHCP

If the offending node is a computer running Windows Server 2008 or Windows Vista that is manually configured with a conflicting IP address, the receipt of an ARP Reply during duplicate address detection causes TCP/IP to select an IPv4 link-local address, also known as an Automatic Private IP Addressing (APIPA) address, from the 169.254.0.0/16 address range. Windows displays an error message and logs an event in the system event log.

A computer running Windows Server 2008 or Windows Vista and using automatic configuration with DHCP performs duplicate address detection for the IP address received in the DHCPOFFER message. If there is an IP address conflict, the DHCP client sends a DHCPDECLINE message to the DHCP server. If the DHCP server is running Windows Server 2008, the IP address sent in the DHCPOFFER is flagged as a bad IP address and is not allocated to any other DHCP clients. The DHCP client starts the DHCP lease allocation process by sending a new DHCPDISCOVER message. For more information about DHCP messages, see Chapter 14, "Dynamic Host Configuration Protocol (DHCP)."

Duplicate Address Detection and the Defending Node

The defending node detects an address conflict whenever the SPA of the incoming ARP Request is the same as an IP address configured on the interface receiving the ARP Request. For ARP Requests sent by an offending node running a previous version of Windows, both the SPA and TPA are set to the conflicting address. However, ARP Requests sent during duplicate address detection are not the only ARP Requests that can have the SPA set to a conflicting address.

For example, if a node using a conflicting address is started without being connected to its subnet, no replies to the initial ARP Requests are received, and the node initializes TCP/IP using the conflicting address. If the node is then placed on the same subnet as the defending node, no additional ARP Requests for duplicate address detection are sent. However, each time either node using the conflicting address sends an ARP Request to perform address resolution, the SPA is set to the conflicting address. In this case, an error message is displayed and an event is logged in the system event log. Both nodes continue to use the conflicting IP address, but each displays an error message and logs an event every time the other node sends an ARP Request.

Neighbor Unreachability Detection

ARP in previous versions of Windows added entries to the ARP cache and refreshed their lifetime when they were used without regard to whether the neighboring node was actually reachable, was receiving the packets sent to it, and was able to respond. Neighbor unreachability detection in Windows Server 2008 and Windows Vista is the process by which a node determines that the IP layer of a neighbor is no longer receiving packets.

A neighboring node is reachable if there has been a recent confirmation that IP packets sent to the neighboring node were received and processed by the neighboring node. Neighbor unreachability does not necessarily verify the end-to-end reachability of the destination. Because a neighboring node can be a host or router, the neighboring node might not be the final destination of the packet. Neighbor unreachability verifies only the reachability of the first hop to the destination.

One of the ways that reachability is confirmed after the initial address resolution exchange of messages is through the sending of a unicast ARP Request and the receipt of a unicast ARP Reply message. The exchange of ARP Request and ARP Reply messages confirms only the reachability of the node that sent the ARP Reply from the node that sent the ARP Request. It does not confirm the reachability of the node that sent the ARP Request from the node that sent the ARP Reply.

For example, if Host A sends a unicast ARP Request to Host B and Host B sends a unicast ARP Reply to Host A, Host A considers Host B reachable. Because there is no confirmation in this exchange that Host A actually received the ARP Reply, Host B does not consider Host A reachable. To confirm reachability of Host A from Host B, Host B must send its own unicast ARP Request to Host A and receive a unicast ARP Reply from Host A.

Another method of determining reachability is when upper-layer protocols indicate that the communication using the next-hop address is making forward progress. For TCP traffic, forward progress is determined when acknowledgment segments for sent data are received. The end-to-end reachability confirmed by the receipt of TCP acknowledgments implies the reachability of the first hop to the destination. The TCP component of the TCP/IP stack provides these indications to the IP component on an ongoing basis.

Other protocols, such as UDP, might not have a method of determining or indicating the forward progress of communication. In this case, the exchange of unicast ARP Request and ARP Reply messages is used to confirm reachability.

Neighbor unreachability detection for IPv4 is enabled by default for TCP/IP in Windows Server 2008 and Windows Vista. To disable neighbor unreachability detection for IPv4 on an interface, use the `netsh interface ipv4 set interface InterfaceNameOrIndex nud=disabled` command.

Neighbor Cache Entry States

The reachability of a neighboring node is determined by monitoring the state of the neighboring node's entry in the neighbor cache. RFC 4861 defines the following states for a neighbor cache entry:

- **INCOMPLETE**   Address resolution is in progress. The INCOMPLETE state is entered when a new neighbor cache entry is created but does not yet have the node's corresponding MAC address. By default, ARP in Windows Server 2008 and Windows Vista sends up to three ARP Requests before abandoning address resolution. The number of ARP Requests that are sent is controlled by the ArpRetryCount registry value, which is described later in this chapter.

- **REACHABLE**   Reachability has been confirmed by receipt of an ARP Reply. The neighbor cache entry stays in the REACHABLE state until the number of milliseconds of the Reachable Time for the interface. The Reachable Time is randomly calculated based on the Base Reachable Time, which is 30 seconds by default. You can view the Base Reachable Time and calculated Reachable Time from the display of the `netsh interface ipv4 show interface InterfaceNameOrIndex` command. You can specify the value of the Base Reachable Time with the `netsh interface ipv4 set interface InterfaceNameOrIndex basereachabletime=Milliseconds` command. As long as upper layer protocols such as TCP indicate that communication is making forward progress, the entry stays in the REACHABLE state. Each time an indication of forward progress is made, the reachable time for the entry is refreshed.

- **STALE** Reachable time (the duration since the last reachability confirmation was received) has elapsed. The neighbor cache entry goes into the STALE state after the reachable time elapses and remains in this state until a packet is sent to the neighbor.

- **DELAY** To allow time for upper-layer protocols to provide reachability confirmation before sending ARP Request messages, the state of the neighbor cache entry enters the DELAY state and waits 5 seconds. If no reachability confirmation is received by the delay time, then the entry enters the PROBE state and a unicast ARP Request message is sent. ARP in Windows Server 2008 and Windows Vista does not use this state, but goes from the STALE state to either the UNREACHABLE or PROBE state directly.

- **PROBE** Reachability confirmation is in progress for a neighbor cache entry that was in either the STALE state or the DELAY state. Unicast ARP Request messages are sent at intervals corresponding to the Retransmission Interval, which is 1000 milliseconds, or 1 second. You can specify the value of the Retransmission Interval with the `netsh interface ipv4 set interface InterfaceNameOrIndex retransmittime=Milliseconds` command. ARP in Windows Server 2008 and Windows Vista probes for up to 5 seconds.

If an incoming ARP Request message is for duplicate address detection and it matches an entry in the neighbor cache that is in the REACHABLE state, ARP in Windows Server 2008 and Windows Vista changes the state of the entry to STALE. This will allow the host to confirm the MAC address through a unicast ARP Request and ARP Reply exchange more quickly for better failover when communicating with clustered servers.

ARP Registry Values

By default, TCP/IP for Windows Server 2008 and Windows Vista use the Ethernet II encapsulation described in Chapter 1, "Local Area Network (LAN) Technologies," when sending both IP and ARP frames. The TCP/IP protocol for Windows Server 2008 and Windows Vista receives both Ethernet II and IEEE 802.3 Sub-Network Access Protocol (SNAP)–encapsulated frames, but, by default, they respond only with Ethernet II–encapsulated frames. To send IEEE 802.3 SNAP-encapsulated IP and ARP frames, use the ArpUseEtherSNAP registry value.

ArpUseEtherSNAP
```
Location: HKEY_LOCAL_MACHINE\SYSTEM\CurrentControlSet\Services\Tcpip\Parameters
Data type: REG_DWORD
Valid range: 0-1
Default value: 0
Present by default: No
```

ArpUseEtherSNAP either enables (when set to 1) or disables (when set to 0) the use of the IEEE 802.3 SNAP frame format when sending IP and ARP frames. ArpUseEtherSNAP is disabled by default, meaning that IP and ARP frames are sent with Ethernet II encapsulation. Regardless of the ArpUseEtherSNAP setting, both types of frame formats are received.

To enable communication with a Network Load Balancing (NLB) cluster that is operating in multicast mode, use the EnableBcastArpReply registry value.

EnableBcastArpReply
Location: HKEY_LOCAL_MACHINE\SYSTEM\CurrentControlSet\Services\Tcpip\Parameters
Data type: REG_DWORD
Valid range: 0-1
Default value: 1
Present by default: No

EnableBcastArpReply either enables (when set to 1) or disables (when set to 0) the use of a multicast MAC address in the Sender Hardware Address (SHA) field in an ARP Reply message. NLB clusters that are operating in multicast mode use a multicast MAC address for their hardware address. This multicast address is the value of the SHA field in an ARP Reply sent by a cluster member when responding to an ARP Request for the IP address of the cluster. If a host on the same subnet as the NLB cluster does not support the use of a multicast MAC address in the SHA field of an ARP Reply, communication with the cluster is not possible. EnableBcastArpReply is enabled by default.

To set the number of ARP Requests that are sent during name resolution, use the ArpRetryCount registry value.

ArpRetryCount
Location: HKEY_LOCAL_MACHINE\SYSTEM\CurrentControlSet\Services\Tcpip\Parameters
Data type: REG_DWORD
Valid range: 0-3
Default value: 3
Present by default: No

> **Note** The ArpCacheLife and ArpCacheMinReferencedLife registry values used by TCP/IP in Windows XP and Windows Server 2003 are no longer supported by TCP/IP in Windows Server 2008 and Windows Vista.

Inverse ARP (InARP)

For non-broadcast multiple access (NBMA)–based WAN technologies such as X.25, frame relay, and ATM, the Network Interface Layer address is not a MAC address but a virtual circuit identifier. For example, for frame relay, the virtual circuit identifier is the Frame Relay Data Link Connection Identifier (DLCI). To address frames for a given destination, the Frame Relay header's DLCI is set to the value that corresponds to the virtual circuit over which the frame is traveling. With NMBA technologies, the virtual circuit identifier is known but the IP address of the interface on the other end of the virtual circuit is not.

InARP is used to resolve the IP address on the other end of a virtual circuit based on a known Frame Relay DLCI. As RFC 2390 describes, InARP was designed specifically for frame relay virtual circuits. Frame relay link management protocols such as Local Management Interface

(LMI) determine which virtual circuits are in use over the physical connection to the frame relay service provider. Once the DLCIs are determined, InARP is used to query each virtual circuit to determine the IP address of the interface on the other end. The responses are used to build a table of entries consisting of [DLCI, next-hop IP address].

Because the DLCI values are only locally significant, the SHA and THA are irrelevant. In both the InARP Request and InARP Reply, the SHA field is typically set to 0 and the TPA field is set to the local DLCI value. The relevant information is the value of the SPA field in the InARP Request and the InARP Reply. The InARP responder uses the InARP Request's SPA to add an entry to its table consisting of [local DLCI, SPA of InARP Request]. The InARP requester uses the InARP Reply's SPA to add an entry to its table consisting of [local DLCI, SPA of InARP Reply].

The InARP Request and Reply have the same structure as the ARP Request and Reply, except 2-byte hardware addresses are used. The ARP Operation field is set to 0x0008 for an InARP Request and 0x0009 for an InARP Reply.

Proxy ARP

Proxy ARP is the answering of ARP Requests on behalf of another node. As RFC 925 describes, Proxy ARP is used in situations in which a subnet is divided without the use of a router. A proxy ARP device is placed between nodes on the same subnet. The proxy ARP device is aware of which nodes are available on which segment. The proxy ARP device also answers ARP Requests and facilitates the forwarding of unicast IP packets for communication between nodes on separate segments. The existence of the proxy ARP device is transparent to the nodes on the subnet. A proxy ARP device is often physically a router device; however, it is not acting as an IP router, forwarding IP datagrams between two IP subnets. Figure 3-3 shows an example of a proxy ARP configuration.

When Node 1 wants to send an IP datagram to Node 2 on the other side of the proxy ARP device, because Node 1 and Node 2 are on the same logical IP subnet, Node 1 sends an ARP Request with Node 2's IP address as the TPA. The proxy ARP device receives the ARP Request and, even though the TPA is not its own address, the proxy ARP device sends an ARP Reply to Node 1 with the proxy ARP device's MAC address as the SHA. Node 1 then sends the IP datagram to the proxy ARP device's MAC address. As far as Node 1 is concerned, it has resolved Node 2's MAC address and delivered the IP datagram to Node 2. The proxy ARP device next delivers the IP datagram to Node 2, using ARP if necessary to resolve Node 2's MAC address.

The Network Bridge feature of the Network Connections folder in Windows Server 2008 and Windows Vista acts as a proxy ARP device when performing Layer 3 bridging between segments for which the Network Bridge cannot perform Layer 2 transparent bridging.

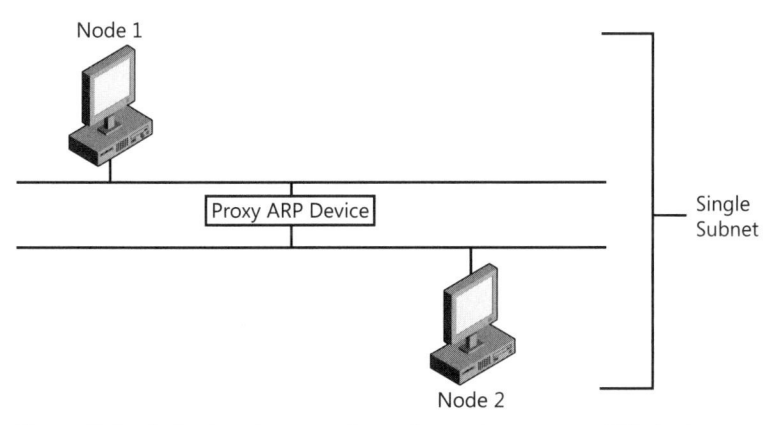

Figure 3-3 A single subnet configuration, using a proxy ARP device

For Windows Server 2008, the Routing and Remote Access service also uses proxy ARP to facilitate communications between remote access clients and nodes on the subnet to which the remote access server is attached. When IP-based remote access clients connect, the remote access server assigns them an IP address. The IP address assigned can either be from the address range of a subnet to which the remote access server is attached (an on-subnet address) or from the address range of a separate subnet (an off-subnet address). Proxy ARP is used when the remote access server assigns an on-subnet address. An on-subnet address range is used when either the Routing and Remote Access service is configured to use DHCP to obtain addresses, or a range of addresses from a directly attached subnet is manually configured. Figure 3-4 shows an example of a remote access server manually configured with an on-subnet address range.

The subnet to which the remote access server is attached is 10.1.1.0/24, implying a range of usable addresses from 10.1.1.1 through 10.1.1.254. In this case, the network administrator is using the high end of the range (10.1.1.200 through 10.1.1.254) for assignment to remote access clients.

When an IP-based remote access client successfully connects and is assigned an IP address, the Routing and Remote Access service tracks the assigned address in a connection table. When a host on the network to which the remote access server is attached sends an ARP Request for the remote access client's assigned on-subnet IP address, the remote access server answers with an ARP Reply and receives the IP datagram. The Routing and Remote Access service then forwards the IP datagram addressed to the remote access client over the appropriate remote access connection.

If the remote access server is manually configured with a range of addresses that represents a different subnet (an off-subnet address range), the remote access server acts as an IP router forwarding IP datagrams between separate subnets and proxy ARP is not used.

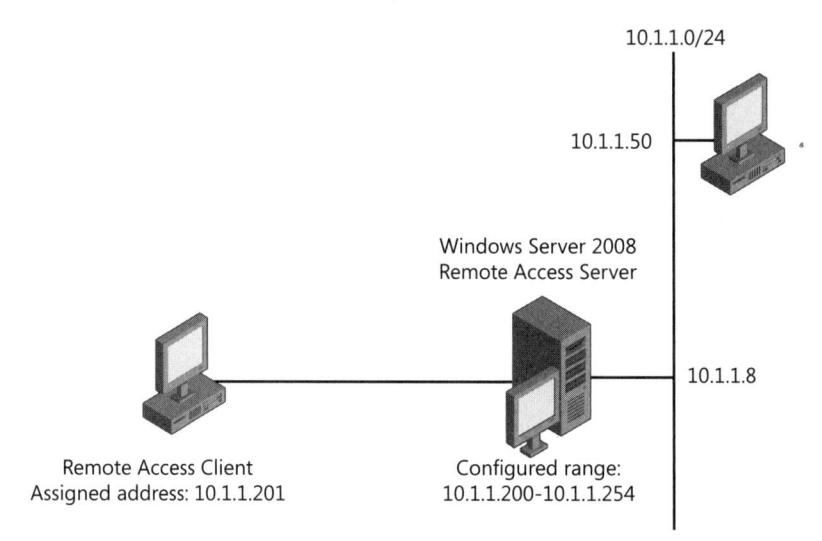

Figure 3-4 A remote access server running Windows Server 2008 and configured with an on-subnet address range using Proxy ARP

Summary

ARP is used as a translation layer between Internet Layer addresses and Network Interface Layer addresses. ARP on LAN links is used to resolve the next-hop IP address of a node to its corresponding MAC address, to detect IP address conflicts, and to determine neighbor reachability. InARP on Frame Relay links is used to map a DLCI value to the IP address of the node on the other end of the virtual circuit. Proxy ARP is used to subdivide an IP subnet and provide transparent communication without using an IP router.

Chapter 4

Point-to-Point Protocol (PPP)

In this chapter:

PPP Connection Process 62
PPP Connection Termination 63
Link Control Protocol 63
PPP Authentication Protocols 67
Callback and the Callback Control Protocol 78
Network Control Protocols 79
Network Monitor Example 82
PPP over Ethernet 83
Summary 85

As first introduced in Chapter 2, "Wide Area Network (WAN) Technologies," PPP is a standard for using point-to-point network links that provides the following:

- A Data Link Layer encapsulation method that supports multiple protocols simultaneously on the same link.

- A protocol for negotiating the Data Link Layer characteristics of the point-to-point connection named the Link Control Protocol (LCP).

- A series of protocols for negotiating the Network Layer properties of Network Layer protocols over the point-to-point connection named Network Control Protocols (NCPs). For example, RFCs 1332 and 1877 describe the Internet Protocol Control Protocol (IPCP), the NCP for IP. IPCP is used to negotiate an IP address, the addresses of name servers, and the use of the Van Jacobsen TCP compression protocol.

Chapter 2 discusses only the Data Link Layer encapsulation. This chapter describes LCP and the set of NCPs needed for PPP and IP connectivity.

More Info All of the RFCs and Internet drafts referenced in this chapter can be found in the \Standards\Chap04_PPP folder on the companion CD-ROM.

PPP Connection Process

There are four phases to a PPP connection, all of which must be completed before data can be sent on the connection. The four phases are the following:

1. PPP configuration using LCP
2. Authentication using a PPP authentication protocol (optional)
3. Callback
4. Protocol configuration using NCPs

Phase 1: PPP Configuration Using LCP

In the first phase of the PPP connection process, PPP connection parameters are configured using LCP. With LCP, the PPP peers negotiate a common set of parameters that are used for all subsequent phases of the PPP connection and for sending data. Some of the communication parameters that are negotiated are the following:

- The maximum receive unit (MRU), the largest PPP frame that can be sent on the connection
- Whether the Address and Control fields in the PPP header are used (for links that use the High-Level Data Link Control [HDLC] encapsulation that is described in RFC 1662)
- Whether the Protocol field in the PPP header can be compressed from 2 bytes to 1 byte
- The PPP authentication protocol to be used during the authentication phase
- Whether Multilink PPP (MP) is used

For more information, see the section titled "Link Control Protocol," later in this chapter.

Phase 2: Authentication

After LCP negotiation, the authentication process using the PPP authentication protocol negotiated during phase 1 is performed. This process is specific to the PPP authentication protocol used. For more information, see the section titled "PPP Authentication Protocols" later in this chapter.

Phase 3: Callback

If the authentication process succeeds and callback behavior is configured, the answering PPP peer terminates the connection and initiates a connection to the original calling PPP peer, a feature of PPP implementations known as *callback*. The PPP implementation in Windows Server 2008 and Windows Vista uses the Callback Control Protocol (CBCP) to complete the callback phase. For more information, see the section titled "Callback and the Callback Control Protocol," later in this chapter.

Phase 4: Protocol Configuration Using NCPs

After PPP is configured, the original initiating PPP peer is authenticated, and callback is done (optional and only if configured), individual data protocols and ancillary PPP services such as encryption and compression are configured using NCPs. For more information, see the section titled "Network Control Protocols," later in this chapter.

PPP Connection Termination

After a PPP connection is established, it can be terminated at any time by either the connection-initiating or connection-receiving PPP peer. PPP connections can be terminated by user action, connection policy action (such as terminating the connection after a specific amount of idle time), or link failure. When the PPP connection terminates, PPP informs the data protocols that were operating over it that the point-to-point interface is no longer available.

Link Control Protocol

LCP, described in RFC 1661, is a simple protocol to configure a common set of PPP connection parameters (for phase 1 of the PPP connection). It is also used by NCPs to configure specific data protocol configuration parameters (for phase 2 of the PPP connection). LCP uses the PPP Protocol ID 0xC0-21. Figure 4-1 shows an LCP frame.

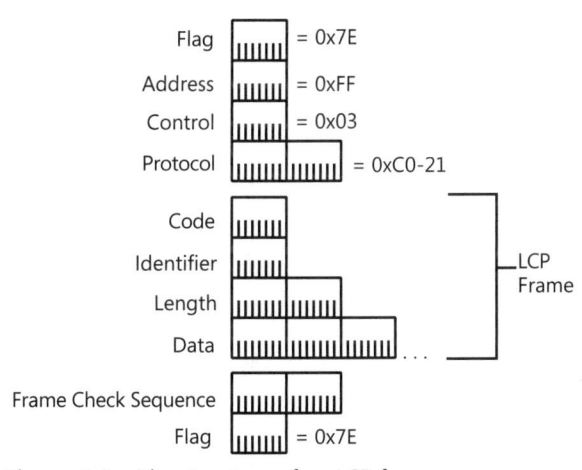

Figure 4-1 The structure of an LCP frame

The fields in the LCP frame are defined as follows:

- **Code**   A 1-byte field that identifies the type of LCP message
- **Identifier**   A 1-byte field that identifies a specific pair of LCP messages: the request and the response

- **Length** A 2-byte length field that indicates the size of the LCP message in bytes
- **Data** A variable-sized field that contains the LCP frame type-specific data

Table 4-1 lists the LCP frame types described in RFC 1661.

Table 4-1 LCP Frame Types

Code	Frame Type	Description
1	Configure-Request	Sent to open or reset a PPP connection.
2	Configure-Ack	Sent to indicate when the last Configure-Request frame contains options with acceptable values. The LCP negotiation is complete when each PPP peer both sends and receives Configure-Ack frames.
3	Configure-Nak	Sent to indicate that the LCP options in the Configure- Request are recognized, but some option values are not acceptable.
4	Configure-Reject	Sent to indicate that the LCP options in the Configure- Request frame are either not recognized or not acceptable.
5	Terminate-Request	Sent to close the PPP connection.
6	Terminate-Ack	Sent to respond to the Terminate-Request message.
7	Code-Reject	Sent when the LCP Code field of a received LCP frame is unknown.
8	Protocol-Reject	Sent when the PPP Protocol field of a received PPP frame is unknown.
9	Echo-Request	Sent to test the PPP connection.
10	Echo-Reply	Sent in response to an Echo-Request frame.
11	Discard-Request	Sent to test outbound data on the link.

Note The LCP Echo-Request and Echo-Reply messages are not related to the Internet Control Message Protocol (ICMP) Echo and Echo Reply messages.

LCP Options

The data portion of an LCP message consists of one or more LCP options for the Configure-Request, Configure-Ack, Configure-Nak, and Configure-Reject LCP frames. An LCP option is formatted in type-length-value (TLV) format. A 1-byte Type field indicates the option type, a 1-byte Length field indicates the length in bytes of the entire option, and the Option Data field contains the data of the option. Figure 4-2 shows an LCP message that contains LCP options.

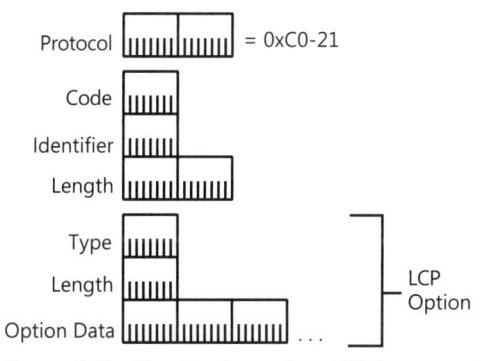

Figure 4-2 The structure of an LCP frame containing LCP options

Table 4-2 lists common LCP options used by PPP peers that run Windows.

Table 4-2 LCP Options

Option Name	Type	Length	Description
Maximum Receive Unit (MRU)	1	4	Used to indicate the maximum size of the PPP frame that can be supported on the connection. The maximum size is 65,535. The default MRU is 1500.
Asynchronous Control Character Map (ACCM)	2	6	Contains a 4-byte bitmap indicating which ASCII control characters from 0x0 to 0x20 use character escapes for asynchronous links. Character escapes are used to distinguish data from control characters sent on the connection. By default, character escapes are used for all 32 control characters.
Authentication Protocol	3	5 or 6	Used to indicate the PPP authentication protocol for the authentication phase to verify the identity. For Windows Server 2008-based or Windows Vista-based PPP peers, the values are 0xC2-27 for Extensible Authentication Protocol (EAP), 0xC2-23-81 for MS-CHAP version 2, 0xC2-23-05 for Message Digest version 5 Challenge Handshake Authentication Protocol (MD5-CHAP), and 0xC0-23 for Password Authentication Protocol (PAP).
Magic Number	5	6	Contains a random number to distinguish a PPP peer and detect looped back lines.
Protocol Compression	7	2	A flag option that indicates that the sender wants to use a 1-byte Protocol field for PPP data frames. PPP control frames using LCP or NCPs still use a 2-byte Protocol field.
Address and Control Field Compression	8	2	A flag option that indicates that the sender wants to remove the Address and Control fields from the HDLC-based PPP header.
Callback	13	3	Used to determine the callback behavior for the connection. For PPP clients and servers running a modern 32-bit or 64-bit Windows operating system, CBCP is used to determine callback behavior.

Additional LCP options are defined in RFC 1661.

LCP Negotiation Process

LCP is used to negotiate the parameters of PPP when sending data in a single direction on the PPP connection. Different PPP parameters could be negotiated in the two different directions of data travel on a PPP connection. Therefore, each PPP peer must perform a separate LCP negotiation. An LCP negotiation is used by a PPP peer to establish how the other PPP peer should send data to it. Each LCP negotiation is a series of LCP frames to negotiate the use of a common set of parameters for data sent by the PPP peer on the other side of the PPP connection from the LCP negotiation initiator. For two PPP peers, Peer A and Peer B, Peer A initiates an LCP negotiation for the data to be sent by Peer B and Peer B initiates a separate LCP negotiation for the data to be sent by Peer A.

An individual LCP negotiation consists of an initial set of LCP options using the LCP Configure-Request message. The specific set of LCP options is negotiated using Configure-Nak and Configure-Reject messages and finally confirmed with a Configure-Ack message. Both negotiations occur simultaneously, making it more difficult to read the captures of PPP connection establishments.

When a PPP peer sends a Configure-Request message, the response is one of the following:

- **Configure-Nak message**   Sent because one or more options in the Configure-Request message have unacceptable values
- **Configure-Reject message**   Sent because one or more of the options are either unknown or non-negotiable
- **Configure-Ack message**   Sent because all of the options have acceptable values

When the Configure-Reject message is received, the unknown or non-negotiable options are removed from the list of LCP options being configured by the initiating PPP peer and a new Configure-Request message is sent. When the Configure-Nak message is received, the included options are set to their indicated values and a new Configure-Request message is sent. When the Configure-Ack message is received, the LCP negotiation is complete. For each new Configure-Request message, the Identifier field in the LCP header is changed to a new value to match a sent Configure-Request message with its response.

For example, the following is a sample LCP negotiation using fictional options:

1. Peer 1 sends a Configure-Request message requesting that options A and B (both flag options) be used, that option C be set to 5000, and that option D be set to 1.
2. Because Peer 2 does not understand option B, it sends a Configure-Reject message containing option B.
3. Peer 1 sends a new Configure-Request message requesting that option A be used, that option C be set to 5000, and that option D be set to 1.
4. Because Peer 2 prefers that option C be set to 1500 and option D be set to 3, it sends a Configure-Nak message containing option C set to 1500 and option D set to 3.

5. Peer 1 sends a new Configure-Request message requesting that option A be used, that option C be set to 1500, and that option D be set to 3.

6. Because all the options in the Configure-Request message contain known options with preferred values, Peer 2 sends a Configure-Ack message.

The following is a summary of frames 1 through 8 of Capture 04-01 in the \Captures folder on the companion CD-ROM, which show an LCP negotiation between a remote access client and a remote access server.

```
Frame   Source   Dest    Description
1       RECV     RECV    Configure-Request, ID = 0
2       SEND     SEND    Configure-Request, ID = 0
3       SEND     SEND    Configure-Ack, ID = 0
4       RECV     RECV    Configure-Reject, ID = 0
5       SEND     SEND    Configure-Request, ID = 1
6       RECV     RECV    Configure-Nak, ID = 1
7       SEND     SEND    Configure-Request, ID = 2
8       RECV     RECV    Configure-Ack, ID = 2
```

Due to the architecture of PPP in Windows Vista and the Windows Server 2008, PPP frames captured by Network Monitor are displayed as an Ethernet frame with the PPP Protocol ID field taking the place of the EtherType field. The source and destination media access control (MAC) addresses are set to either SEND or RECV, depending on whether the frame was sent to (set to SEND) or received from (set to RECV) the computer on which the Network Monitor capture was taken. In this instance, the Network Monitor capture was taken on the remote access server. Therefore, the RECV frames were sent by the remote access client and the SEND frames were sent by the remote access server.

For this trace, Frames 1 and 3 correspond to the LCP negotiation initiated by the remote access client for the frames sent by the remote access server. Frame 2 and frames 4 through 8 correspond to the LCP negotiation initiated by the remote access server for the frames sent by the remote access client.

PPP Authentication Protocols

After LCP negotiation is complete, the authentication protocol agreed on during LCP negotiation using LCP option 3 is used to establish the identity and credentials of the PPP peer that is requesting the PPP connection, typically a remote access client (for remote access dial-up or virtual private network [VPN] connections) or a calling router (for router-to-router dial-up or VPN connections). The authentication process is phase 2 of the PPP connection establishment.

Windows Server 2008 and Windows Vista support the following PPP authentication protocols:

- Password Authentication Protocol (PAP)
- Challenge Handshake Authentication Protocol (CHAP)

- Microsoft Challenge Handshake Authentication Protocol version 2 (MS-CHAP v2)
- Extensible Authentication Protocol (EAP)

Note Windows Server 2008 and Windows Vista no longer support the Shiva Password Authentication Protocol (SPAP) or Microsoft Challenge Handshake Authentication Protocol (MS-CHAP) (also known as MS-CHAP v1) authentication protocols.

PAP

PAP is a very simple, plain-text authentication protocol described in RFC 1334. The entire PAP negotiation consists of the following messages:

1. The connection-initiating PPP peer (the calling peer) sends a PAP Authenticate-Request message to the authenticating PPP peer (the answering peer), which contains the calling peer's user name and password in plain-text.

2. The answering peer validates the user name and password. If the user name and password are correct, the answering peer sends a PAP Authenticate-Ack message. If not, the answering peer sends a PAP Authenticate-Nak message.

Obviously, PAP is not a secure authentication protocol. A malicious user that can capture the PAP frames sent between the calling peer and answering peer can view the contents of the PAP Authenticate-Request message to determine the user name and password of a valid user account. The use of PAP is highly discouraged and is only included in Windows Server 2008 and Windows Vista for troubleshooting and compatibility with PPP peers that do not support more secure authentication protocols.

PPP peers negotiate the use of PAP during phase 1 by specifying LCP option 3 (authentication protocol) and the authentication protocol 0xC0-23. After phase 1 negotiation is complete, PAP messages use the PPP protocol ID 0xC0-23.

Figure 4-3 shows the PAP Authenticate-Request message.

The following are the fields in the PAP Authenticate-Request message:

- **Code** A 1-byte field that identifies the type of PAP message. For Authenticate-Request messages, the value of the Code field is set to 1.
- **Identifier** A 1-byte field that is used to identify a pair of PAP messages: the request and the response. The calling peer sets the value of the Identifier field.
- **Length** A 2-byte field that indicates the size of the PAP message in bytes.
- **Peer ID Length** A 1-byte field that indicates the size of the Peer ID field in bytes.
- **Peer ID** A variable-sized field that contains the user name of the calling peer.

Chapter 4: Point-to-Point Protocol (PPP) 69

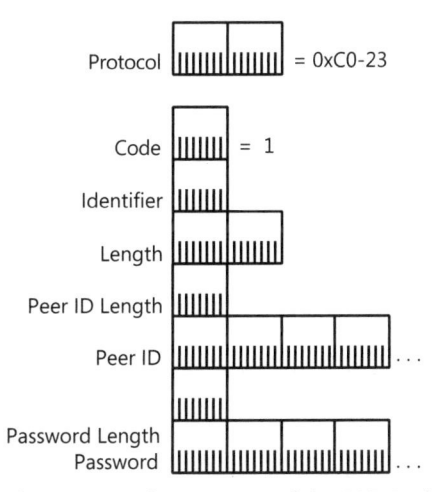

Figure 4-3 The structure of the PAP Authenticate-Request message

- **Password Length**   A 1-byte field that indicates the size of the Password field in bytes.
- **Password**   A variable-sized field that contains the password of the calling peer.

Figure 4-4 shows the PAP Authenticate-Ack and Authenticate-Nak messages.

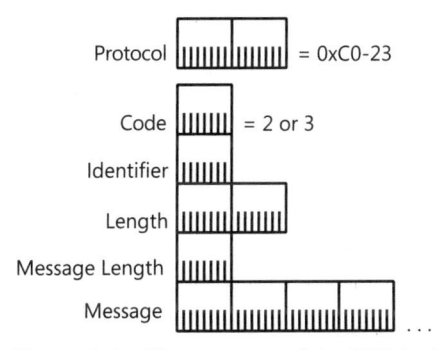

Figure 4-4 The structure of the PAP Authenticate-Ack and Authenticate-Nak messages

The following are the fields in the Authenticate-Ack and Authenticate-Nak messages:

- **Code**   For an Authenticate-Ack message, the value of the Code field is set to 2. For an Authenticate-Nak message, the value of the Code field is set to 3.
- **Identifier**   A 1-byte field that is set to the value of the Identifier field in the corresponding Authenticate-Request message.
- **Length**   A 2-byte field that indicates the size of the PAP message in bytes.
- **Message Length**   A 1-byte field that indicates the size of the Message field in bytes.
- **Message**   A variable-sized field that contains a message for the calling peer. The Message field is not used by Windows. Some PPP implementations display the message text to the user who is connecting.

Capture 04-02 in the \Captures folder on the companion CD-ROM contains an example of a PAP authentication.

CHAP

CHAP is a more secure authentication protocol, described in RFC 1994, which uses a challenge–response exchange of messages to validate that the calling peer has knowledge of the user's password. The password itself is never sent. Although more secure than PAP, CHAP does not provide mutual authentication. The calling peer authenticates to the answering peer but the answering peer does not authenticate to the calling peer. Without mutual authentication, a calling peer is unable to determine whether it is calling a valid answering peer.

When the use of CHAP is negotiated during phase 1, an algorithm that is used to provide proof of knowledge of the user password is also specified. For the Message Digest-5 (MD5) algorithm, the LCP option data for the authentication protocol contains the CHAP authentication protocol (0xC2-23) and the MD-5 algorithm (0x05). CHAP messages use the PPP Protocol ID 0xC2-23.

CHAP authentication using MD5 consists of the following three messages:

1. The answering peer sends a CHAP Challenge message that contains a CHAP session ID (the value of the Identifier field), a challenge string, and the name of the answering peer.

2. The calling peer sends a CHAP Response message that contains the user name of the calling peer and an MD5 hash of the CHAP session ID, the challenge string, and the user's password.

3. The answering peer calculates its own MD5 hash of the CHAP session ID, the challenge string, and user password and compares the result with the MD5 hash in the CHAP Response message. If the two hashes are identical, the answering peer sends a CHAP Success message. If not, the answering peer sends a CHAP Failure message and the connection is terminated.

Figure 4-5 shows the CHAP Challenge and CHAP Response messages.

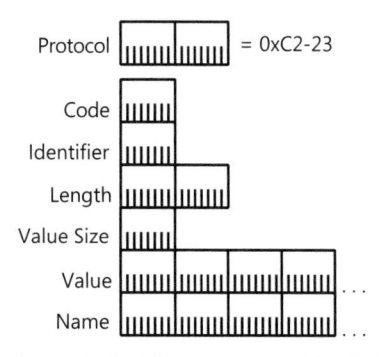

Figure 4-5 The structure of the CHAP Challenge and CHAP Response messages.

The following are the fields in the CHAP Challenge and CHAP Response messages:

- **Code** A 1-byte field that identifies the type of CHAP message. For a CHAP Challenge message, the value of the Code field is set to 1. For a CHAP Response message, the value of the Code field is set to 2.
- **Identifier** A 1-byte field that is used to identify a pair or sequence of CHAP messages (the CHAP session ID). The calling peer sets the value of the Identifier field.
- **Length** A 2-byte field that indicates the size of the CHAP message in bytes.
- **Value Size** A 1-byte field that indicates the size of the Value field.
- **Value** A variable-sized field that contains either the challenge string for the CHAP Challenge message or the MD5 hash for the CHAP Response message.
- **Name** A variable-sized field that contains the name of either the answering peer for the CHAP Challenge message or the calling peer for the CHAP Response message.

Figure 4-6 shows the structure of the CHAP Success and CHAP Failure messages.

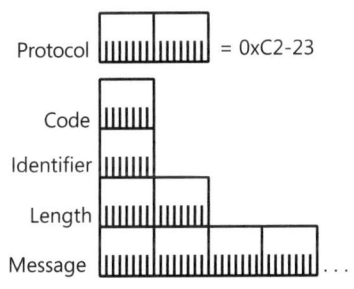

Figure 4-6 The CHAP Success and CHAP Failure message structure

The following are the fields in the CHAP Success and CHAP Failure messages:

- **Code** For a CHAP Success message, the value of the Code field is set to 3. For a CHAP Failure message, the value of the Code field is set to 4.
- **Identifier** A 1-byte field that is used to indicate the CHAP session ID.
- **Length** A 2-byte field that indicates the size of the CHAP message in bytes.
- **Message** A variable-sized field that contains a message for the calling peer. The Message field is optional and is not used by Windows.

Capture 04-03 in the \Captures folder on the companion CD-ROM contains an example of an MD5-CHAP authentication.

MS-CHAP v2

MS-CHAP v2 is a CHAP-based authentication protocol described in RFC 2759 that, unlike CHAP, provides mutual authentication. With MS-CHAP v2, the answering peer receives confirmation that the calling peer has knowledge of the user account's password and the calling peer receives confirmation that the answering peer has knowledge of the user account's password. To provide for this mutual authentication, both peers issue a challenge and must receive a valid response or the connection is terminated.

When MS-CHAP v2 is negotiated during phase 1, the LCP option data for the authentication protocol contains the CHAP authentication protocol (0xC2-23) and the MS-CHAP v2 algorithm (0x81). MS-CHAP v2 messages use the PPP Protocol ID 0xC2-23.

MS-CHAP v2 authentication consists of the following four steps:

1. The answering peer sends a CHAP Challenge message that contains a challenge string and the name of the answering peer.

2. The calling peer sends an MS-CHAP v2 Response message that contains the user name of the calling peer, a challenge string for the answering peer, and an encrypted response based on the answering peer's challenge string and the MD4 hash of the user's password.

3. The answering peer calculates its own encrypted result based on its challenge string and the MD4 hash of the user's password and compares it to the version in the MS-CHAP v2 Response message. If the two results are identical, the answering peer sends a CHAP Success message with a Message field that contains an encrypted response based on the calling peer's challenge string, the answering peer's challenge string, the calling peer's response, the calling peer's user name, and the calling peer's password. If the two results are not identical, the answering peer sends a CHAP Failure message.

4. The calling peer calculates its own encrypted result to validate the answering peer's encrypted response. If the results match, the calling peer continues with the next phase of the PPP connection. If not, the calling peer terminates the connection.

Figure 4-7 shows the structure of the MS-CHAP v2 Response message.

The following are the fields in the MS-CHAP v2 Response message:

- **Code**   For an MS-CHAP v2 Response message, the value of the Code field is set to 2.
- **Identifier**   A 1-byte field that is set to the value of the Identifier field in the original CHAP Challenge message.
- **Length**   A 2-byte field that indicates the size of the MS-CHAP v2 Response message in bytes.
- **Value Size**   A 1-byte field that indicates the size of the CHAP Value field. For the MS-CHAP v2 Response message, the CHAP Value field consists of the Peer Challenge, Reserved, Windows NT Response, and Flags fields and is a fixed size of 49 bytes.
- **Peer Challenge**   A 16-byte field that contains the challenge string for the answering peer as set by the calling peer.

Chapter 4: Point-to-Point Protocol (PPP)

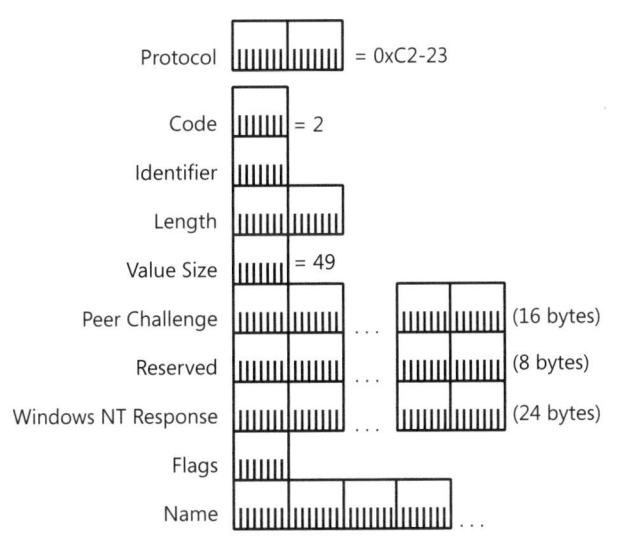

Figure 4-7 The MS-CHAP v2 Response message structure

- **Reserved** An 8-byte field that should be set to 0.
- **Windows NT Response** A 24-byte field that contains the Windows NT–encoded response.
- **Flags** A 1-byte field that is reserved for future use and should be set to 0.
- **Name** A variable-sized field that contains the name of the calling peer.

Capture 04-04 in the \Captures folder on the companion CD-ROM contains an example of an MS-CHAP v2 authentication.

MS-CHAP v2 allows the answering peer to indicate specific error conditions in the Message field of the CHAP Failure message. One of the errors is ERROR_PASSWD_EXPIRED. When the calling peer receives this error indication, it can submit an MS-CHAP v2 Change Password message to submit a new password for the account corresponding to the user name. For more information about the MS-CHAP v2 Change Password message, see RFC 2759.

EAP

EAP was designed as an extension to PPP to allow for more extensibility and flexibility in the implementation of authentication methods for PPP connections. For PAP, CHAP, and MS-CHAP v2, the authentication process is a fixed exchange of messages. With EAP, the authentication process can consist of an open-ended conversation, in which messages are sent by either PPP peer on an as-needed basis. In addition, unlike the PPP authentication protocols discussed so far in this chapter, EAP does not select a specific authentication method during phase 1 of the connection. Rather, the selection of a specific EAP authentication method, known as an EAP type, is done during phase 3 of the connection. EAP is described in RFC 3748.

When EAP is negotiated during phase 1, the LCP option data for the authentication protocol indicates EAP (0xC2-27). EAP messages use the PPP Protocol ID 0xC2-27.

Because EAP is architecturally designed to support multiple EAP types, additional types can be added by creating an EAP type dynamic-link library (DLL) file using the EAP Software Development Kit (SDK), which is part of the Windows Server Platform SDK, and installing the DLL file on the calling peer and the authenticating server (the server requiring authentication of the calling peer). The authenticating server is the computer that actually performs the validation of the calling peer's credentials and is typically either the answering peer or a central authentication server, such as a Remote Authentication Dial-In User Service (RADIUS) server.

Note Windows Server 2008 and Windows Vista no longer support the EAP-MD5-CHAP authentication protocol.

EAP defines four types of messages:

1. An EAP-Request message is sent by the authentication server to request information from the calling peer. There can be multiple EAP-Request messages for an EAP authentication session.

2. An EAP-Response message is sent by the calling peer to indicate information requested by the authentication server in an EAP-Request message.

3. An EAP-Success message is sent by the authentication server when the calling peer has successfully responded to all of the EAP-Request messages for the EAP session.

4. An EAP-Failure message is sent by the authentication server when the calling peer has not successfully responded to all of the EAP-Request messages for the EAP session.

Figure 4-8 shows the structure of EAP-Request and EAP-Response messages.

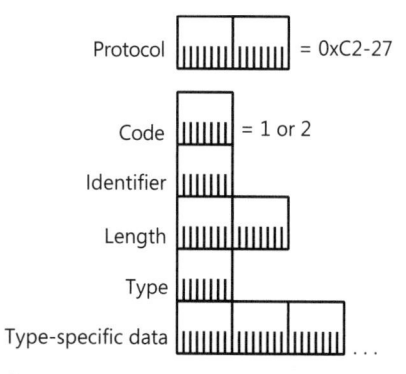

Figure 4-8 EAP-Request and EAP-Response message structure

The following are the fields in an EAP-Request or EAP-Response message:

- **Code** A 1-byte field that identifies the type of EAP message. For an EAP-Request message, the value of the Code field is set to 1. For an EAP-Response message, the value of the Code field is set to 2.
- **Identifier** A 1-byte field that is used to match an EAP-Request message with an EAP-Response message.
- **Length** A 2-byte field that indicates the size of the EAP message in bytes.
- **Type** A 1-byte field that indicates the EAP type. For EAP-MS-CHAP v2, the value of the Type field is 29.
- **Type-Specific Data** A variable-sized field that contains data for the specific EAP message. For example, in the EAP-Response/Identity message, the type-specific data is a string that identifies the calling PPP peer.

Table 4-3 lists EAP types.

Table 4-3 **EAP Types**

Type Value	Type	Description
1	Identity	Used by the authenticating server to request the identity of the calling client (in the EAP-Request/Identity message) and used by the calling client to indicate its identity to the authenticating server (in the EAP-Response/Identity message).
2	Notification	Used by the authentication server to indicate a displayable message to the calling peer.
3	Nak	Used by a calling peer in a response message to indicate that the calling peer does not support the authentication type proposed by the authenticating server. The Nak message also includes a proposed authentication type that is supported by the calling peer.
13	EAP-TLS	Used for the messages of the TLS authentication method.
25	PEAP	Used for the messages of the PEAP method.
29	EAP-MS-CHAP-V2	Used for the messages of the MS-CHAP v2 method.

For a current listing of the defined EAP types, see *http://www.iana.org/assignments/eap-numbers*.

Windows Server 2008 and Windows Vista provide the following EAP types:

- EAP-TLS (displayed as **Smart Card Or Other Certificate** when selecting an EAP type)
- PEAP (displayed as **Protected EAP (PEAP)** when selecting an EAP type)

Figure 4-9 shows the structure of EAP-Success and EAP-Failure messages.

```
Protocol  |||||||||||||||  = 0xC2-27
Code      ||||||||  = 3 or 4
Identifier ||||||||
Length    |||||||||||||||| = 4
```

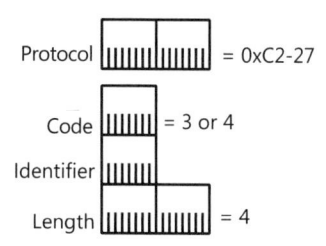

Figure 4-9 EAP-Success and EAP-Failure message structure

The following are the fields in an EAP-Success and EAP-Failure message:

- **Code** For an EAP-Success message, the value of the Code field is set to 3. For an EAP-Failure message, the value of the Code field is set to 4.
- **Identifier** Set to the value of the last EAP-Response message.
- **Length** For the EAP-Success and EAP-Failure messages, the Length field is set to 4.

EAP-MS-CHAP v2

The EAP-MS-CHAP v2 type is the MS-CHAP v2 authentication protocol performed using EAP messages, rather than a set of MS-CHAP v2 messages. In Windows Server 2008 and Windows Vista, EAP-MS-CHAP v2 is available as an authentication method for PEAP, rather than as an EAP type like EAP-TLS.

EAP-MS-CHAP v2 authentication consists of the following process:

1. The authenticating server sends an EAP-Request/Identity message to the calling peer.
2. The calling peer sends an EAP-Response/Identity message to the authenticating server.
3. The authenticating server sends an EAP-Request/MS-CHAP v2 Challenge message to the calling peer that contains a challenge string and the name of the authenticating server.
4. The calling peer sends an EAP-Response/MS-CHAP v2 Response message that contains the user name of the calling peer, a challenge string for the authenticating server, and an encrypted response based on the authenticating server's challenge string and the MD4 hash of the user's password.
5. The authenticating server calculates its own encrypted result based on its challenge string and the MD4 hash of the user's password and compares it to the version in the MS-CHAP v2 Response message. If the two results are identical, the authenticating server sends an EAP-Response/MS-CHAP v2 Success message with a Message field that contains an encrypted response based on the calling peer's challenge string, the authenticating server's challenge string, the calling peer's response, the calling peer's user name, and the calling peer's password. If the two results are not identical, the authenticating server sends an EAP-Response/MS-CHAP v2 Failure message.

6. The calling peer calculates its own encrypted result to validate the authenticating server's encrypted response. If the results match, the calling peer continues with the next phase of the PPP connection. If not, the calling peer terminates the connection.

> **More Info** EAP-MS-CHAP v2 is described in the Internet draft named draft-kamath-pppext-eap-mschapv2-01.txt.

EAP-TLS

EAP-TLS is the use of TLS to provide authentication for the establishment of a PPP connection. TLS is described in RFC 2246 and EAP-TLS is described in RFC 2716. EAP-TLS can provide mutual authentication (the calling PPP peer authenticates to the authenticating server and the authenticating server answers to the calling PPP peer), protected negotiation of the set of cryptographic services used for the connection, and mutual determination of encryption and signing key material. EAP-TLS uses digital certificates rather than passwords for authentication, resulting in a highly protected authentication method.

By default in Windows Server 2008 and Windows Vista, EAP-TLS provides two-way, or mutual authentication. The authenticating server verifies the PPP peer's certificate and the PPP peer verifies the certificate of the authenticating server. It is possible to configure the calling peer to not verify the certificate of the authenticating server, but this is not recommended for security reasons.

The details of EAP-TLS negotiation are beyond the scope of this book. For more details, see RFCs 2716 and 2246.

PEAP

Although EAP provides authentication flexibility through the use of EAP types, the entire EAP conversation might be sent as clear text (unencrypted). A malicious user with access to the path between the negotiating PPP peers can inject packets into the conversation or capture the EAP messages from a successful authentication for later analysis. For example, an attacker can capture a successful password-based authentication exchange with MS-CHAP v2, and then begin attacking the user's password with an offline dictionary attack.

Protected EAP (PEAP) is an EAP type that addresses this security issue by first creating a session that is both encrypted and integrity-protected with TLS. Then a new EAP negotiation with another EAP type occurs, authenticating the user credentials of the PPP client. Because the TLS session protects EAP negotiation and authentication for the network access attempt, password-based authentication protocols that are normally susceptible to an offline dictionary attack can be used for authentication even in environments where the path between the PPP peers might be subject to eavesdropping.

Therefore, PEAP is not an EAP type for authenticating the credentials of PPP peers. PEAP is an EAP type to create a protected TLS session so that another EAP type can be used to authenticate the credentials of PPP peers.

> **More Info** The PEAP implementation in Windows is described in the Internet draft named draft-kamath-pppext-peapv0-00.txt.

By default in Windows Server 2008 and Windows Vista, PEAP provides one-way authentication for the TLS session. The PPP peer verifies the certificate of the authenticating server. It is possible to configure the calling peer to not verify the certificate of the authenticating server, but this is not recommended for security reasons.

Windows Server 2008 and Windows Vista provide the following authentication methods when you select the PEAP EAP type:

- EAP-MS-CHAP v2 (displayed as **Secured Password (EAP-MSCHAP v2)** when selecting a PEAP authentication method)
- EAP-TLS (displayed as **Smart Card Or Other Certificate** when selecting a PEAP authentication method)

Callback and the Callback Control Protocol

After the authentication phase of the PPP connection process, CBCP negotiates the use of callback. If callback is negotiated, the answering PPP peer terminates the PPP connection, and then calls the original calling PPP peer at a specified phone number. CBCP messages use the PPP Protocol ID 0xC0-29 and have the same structure as LCP messages. However, only the first seven LCP message types are used, corresponding to LCP Codes 1 through 3. For the Callback-Request (Code set to 1), Callback-Response (Code set to 2), and Callback-Ack (Code set to 3) messages, the data portion of the CBCP message contains one or more CBCP options.

Table 4-4 lists the CBCP options used by Windows-based PPP peers.

Table 4-4 **CBCP Options**

Option Name	Type	Length	Description
No Callback	1	2	Used to specify that callback is not used
Callback to a User- Specified Number	2	Variable	Used to specify that the calling PPP peer determines the callback number
Callback to an Administrator- Defined Number	3	Variable	Used to specify that the answering PPP peer determines the callback number
Callback to Any of a List of Numbers	4	Variable	Used to specify that the answering PPP peer calls the calling PPP peer back at one of a list of phone numbers

Network Control Protocols

After the callback phase of the PPP connection process, individual NCPs are used to negotiate the configuration of networking protocols, such as TCP/IP, and the additional PPP facilities of compression and encryption.

IPCP

IPCP is used to automatically configure TCP/IP configuration for a calling PPP peer. IPCP as used by Windows-based PPP peers is described in RFCs 1332 and 1877. RFC 1332 defines the original set of IPCP options and RFC 1877 defines an additional set of options to automatically configure the IP address of name servers such as Domain Name System (DNS) and Windows Internet Name Service (WINS) servers.

IPCP messages use the PPP Protocol ID 0x80-21 and have the same structure as LCP messages. However, only the first seven LCP message types are used, corresponding to LCP Codes 1 through 7. For the Configure-Request (Code set to 1), Configure-Ack (Code set to 2), Configure-Nak (Code set to 3), and Configure-Reject (Code set to 4) IPCP messages, the data portion of the IPCP message contains one or more IPCP options.

Table 4-5 lists the IPCP options defined in RFCs 1332 and 1877 that are used by Windows-based PPP peers.

Table 4-5 IPCP Options

Option Name	Type	Length	Description
IP Compression Protocol	2	4	Negotiates the use of Van Jacobsen compression
IP Address	3	6	Used to assign an IP address to the point-to-point interface of the calling PPP peer
Primary DNS Server Address	129	6	Used to assign a primary DNS server to the point-to-point interface of the calling PPP peer
Primary NBNS Server Address	130	6	Used to assign a primary NetBIOS Name Server (NBNS) server, a WINS server, to the point-to-point interface of the calling PPP peer
Secondary DNS Server Address	131	6	Used to assign a secondary DNS server to the point-to-point interface of the calling PPP peer
Secondary NBNS Server Address	132	6	Used to assign a secondary NBNS server, a WINS server, to the point-to-point interface of the calling PPP peer

A typical TCP/IP configuration for a local area network (LAN) interface includes an IP address, a subnet mask, and a default gateway. A PPP interface configured with IPCP does not include a subnet mask or a default gateway. Computers running Windows Server 2008 or Windows Vista automatically configure the subnet mask of 255.255.255.255.

By default, a new default route is added to the routing table. This new default route has the gateway and interface addresses set to the IP address of the PPP interface and has the lowest routing metric of all the default routes. The routing metric of the existing default route is increased for the duration of the PPP connection. To prevent this behavior, you can clear the Use Default Gateway On Remote Network check box on the IP Settings tab in the advanced TCP/IP settings for the Internet Protocol Version 4 (TCP/IPv4) component for a dial-up or VPN connection in the Network Connections folder. You can also disable this behavior with the Connection Manager Administration Kit, provided with Windows Server 2008.

Although DNS server IP addresses are assigned, a DNS domain name is not. To automatically configure a DNS domain name, PPP calling peers running Windows Server 2008 or Windows Vista send a Dynamic Host Configuration Protocol (DHCP) DHCPINFORM message on the PPP link after the PPP connection is established. If the answering peer supports the relaying of DHCP messages, the answering peer relays the DHCPINFORM message to a DHCP server and relays the response back to the PPP calling peer. Based on the DNS domain name DHCP option (Option 15) in the response, the PPP peer automatically configures a DNS domain name on the point-to-point interface.

Compression Control Protocol

Compression Control Protocol (CCP), described in RFC 1962, allows PPP peers to negotiate the use of a data compression algorithm. CCP messages use the PPP Protocol 0x80-FD and have the same structure as LCP messages. However, only the first seven LCP message types are used, corresponding to LCP Codes 1 through 7. For the Configure-Request (Code set to 1), Configure-Ack (Code set to 2), Configure-Nak (Code set to 3), and Configure-Reject (Code set to 4) CCP messages, the data portion of the CCP message contains one or more CCP options. Table 4-6 lists these CCP options.

Table 4-6 CCP Options

Option Name	Type	Length	Description
Organization Unique Identifier	0	6 or larger	Used to identify a proprietary compression protocol
Microsoft Point-to-Point Compression (MPPC)	18	6	Used to indicate the use of MPPC, Microsoft Point-to-Point Encryption (MPPE), and MPPE encryption options

MPPE and MPPC

CCP option 18 for MPPC is used to negotiate the use of both MPPC and MPPE, as described in RFC 3078. The data for CCP option is a 4-byte (32-bit) Supported Bits field that contains bits to indicate the use of CCP and the use of MPPE and MPPE encryption options. Within the 32-bit Supported Bits field, the following bits are defined:

- The low-order bit enables (when set to 1) or disables (when set to 0) the use of MPPC.

- The fifth low-order bit (starting from 1) enables (when set to 1) or disables (when set to 0) the use of 40-bit encryption keys for MPPE that are derived from the LAN Manager encoding of the user's password. This bit is obsolete and its use should be rejected.

- The sixth low-order bit (starting from 1) enables (when set to 1) or disables (when set to 0) the use of 40-bit encryption keys for MPPE that are derived from the Windows NT encoding of the user's password.

- The seventh low-order bit (starting from 1) enables (when set to 1) or disables (when set to 0) the use of 128-bit encryption keys for MPPE that are derived from the Windows NT encoding of the user's password.

- The eighth low-order bit (starting from 1) enables (when set to 1) or disables (when set to 0) the use of 56-bit encryption keys that are derived from the Windows NT encoding of the user's password.

- The 25th low-order bit (starting from 1) enables (when set to 1) or disables (when set to 0) the use of stateless encryption mode, in which the MPPE encryption key is changed with every message sent or received.

When negotiating MPPC and MPPE, the PPP peers determine a common setting for MPPC (enabled or disabled), a common highest MPPE encryption strength (the use of 40-bit, 56-bit, or 128-bit encryption keys), and whether to use stateless MPPE.

MPPE is only possible if the authentication protocol used during the authentication phase is MS-CHAP v2, EAP-MS-CHAP v2, or EAP-TLS. Only these authentication methods provide mutually determined keying material that is used as the initial MPPE encryption key.

Both MPPC and MPPE use the same PPP Protocol ID, 0x00-FD. However, each PPP peer knows whether MPPC, MPPE, or both are being used for frames sent on the PPP connection. Therefore, for the following cases:

- If MPPC is used and MPPE is not, the PPP Protocol ID is 0x00-FD and the PPP payload is decompressed using the MPPC decompression algorithm.

- If MPPE is used and MPPC is not, the PPP Protocol ID is 0x00-FD and the PPP payload is decrypted using the MPPE decryption algorithm.

- If both MPPC and MPPE are used, the PPP payload is always compressed before it is encrypted. Therefore, the PPP Protocol ID 0x00-FD identifies an MPPE-encrypted payload. The payload is first decrypted using MPPE. The resulting MPPE payload consists of a PPP header with the PPP Protocol ID set to 0x00-FD and a payload compressed with MPPC. MPPC decompresses the payload. The resulting MPPC payload consists of a PPP header with the PPP Protocol ID set to 0x00-21 (assuming an IP datagram).

If the PPP payload is compressed with MPPC or encrypted with MPPE, the PPP payload is not parsed by Network Monitor. To view PPP payloads with Network Monitor after the PPP connection is created, disable compression and encryption for the PPP connection.

Encryption Control Protocol

Encryption Control Protocol (ECP), described in RFC 1968, allows PPP peers to negotiate the use of a data encryption algorithm. ECP messages use the PPP Protocol IDs 0x80-53 or 0x80-55 and have the same structure as LCP messages. However, because Windows-based PPP peers only support the use of MPPE for encryption of PPP payloads, ECP is not supported or used. For more information, see RFC 1968.

Network Monitor Example

The following summary of Capture 04-01 in the \Captures folder on the companion CD-ROM is an example of a successful PPP connection using the MS-CHAP v2 authentication protocol:

```
Frame  Source  Dest   Protocol   Description
1      RECV    RECV   LCP        Configure-Request, ID = 0
2      SEND    SEND   LCP        Configure-Request, ID = 0
3      SEND    SEND   LCP        Configure-Ack, ID = 0
4      RECV    RECV   LCP        Configure-Reject, ID = 0
5      SEND    SEND   LCP        Configure-Request, ID = 1
6      RECV    RECV   LCP        Configure-Nak, ID = 1
7      SEND    SEND   LCP        Configure-Request, ID = 2
8      RECV    RECV   LCP        Configure-Ack, ID = 2
9      SEND    SEND   CHAP       Challenge, ID =0
10     RECV    RECV   LCP        Identification, ID = 1
11     RECV    RECV   LCP        Identification, ID = 2
12     RECV    RECV   CHAP       Response, ID = 0
13     SEND    SEND   CHAP       Success, ID = 0
14     SEND    SEND   CBCP       Callback Request, ID = 1
15     RECV    RECV   CBCP       Callback Response, ID = 1
16     SEND    SEND   CBCP       Callback Ack, ID = 1
17     SEND    SEND   CCP        Configure-Request, ID = 4
18     SEND    SEND   IPCP       Configure-Request, ID = 5
19     RECV    RECV   CCP        Configure-Request, ID = 3
20     SEND    SEND   CCP        Configure-Ack, ID = 3
21     RECV    RECV   IPCP       Configure-Request, ID = 4
22     SEND    SEND   IPCP       Configure-Reject, ID = 4
23     RECV    RECV   CCP        Configure-Ack, ID = 4
24     RECV    RECV   IPCP       Configure-Ack, ID = 5
25     RECV    RECV   IPCP       Configure-Request, ID = 5
26     SEND    SEND   IPCP       Configure-Nak, ID = 5
27     RECV    RECV   IPCP       Configure-Request, ID = 6
28     SEND    SEND   IPCP       Configure-Ack, ID = 6
```

In this example, the following frames show the four phases of the PPP connection:

- Frames 1 through 8 and frames 10 and 11 are for phase 1, the LCP negotiation.
- Frames 9, 12, and 13 are for phase 2, authentication.
- Frames 14 through 16 are for phase 3, callback.

- Frames 16, 19, 20, and 23 are for CCP negotiation (in phase 4).
- Frames 18, 21, 22, and 24 through 28 are for IPCP negotiation (in phase 4).

PPP over Ethernet

PPP over Ethernet (PPPoE) is a method of encapsulating PPP frames so that they can be sent over an Ethernet network. PPPoE was created so that Internet service providers (ISPs) that deploy a broadband Internet access technology in a bridged Ethernet topology, such as cable modems or Digital Subscriber Line (DSL), can use the per-user authentication and connection identification facilities of PPP to identify individual customer connections for accounting and billing purposes. PPPoE is described in RFC 2516.

PPPoE connections have the following two phases:

1. A discovery phase in which a client computer uses PPPoE frames to discover the presence of an access concentrator (AC), a device that terminates the cable modem or DSL connection and provides access to the Internet, and to determine a PPPoE session ID
2. A PPP session phase, in which a PPP connection is established and used for data transfer in the same way as a dial-up or VPN-based PPP connection

Figure 4-10 shows a PPPoE frame.

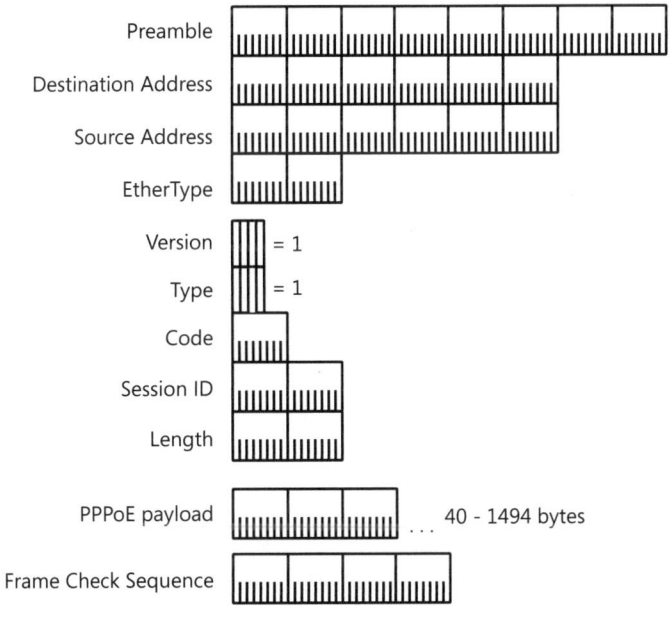

Figure 4-10 The structure of a PPPoE frame

The following are the fields in the PPPoE frame:

- **Version**   A 4-bit field that is set to the value of 1.
- **Type**   A 4-bit field that is set to the value of 1.
- **Code**   A 1-byte field that is used to identify the type of PPPoE message. There are defined values for the PPPoE frames exchanged during the discovery phase. For PPP frames, the Code field is set to 0.
- **Session_ID**   A 2-byte field that identifies the PPPoE session ID. This field is set to 0 until a session ID is negotiated with the AC during the discovery phase of the PPPoE connection.
- **Length**   A 2-byte field that is used to indicate the size in bytes of the PPPoE payload.
- **PPPoE Payload**   A variable-sized payload that can contain either one or more PPPoE tags for PPPoE frames sent during the discovery phase or PPP frames for the PPP session phase. PPPoE tags are information elements in TLV format. Typical PPPoE tags used during the discovery phase are Service-Name (the name of the ISP or service offered by the AC) and AC-Name (the name of the AC). For a complete list of PPPoE tags and their structure, see RFC 2516. The EtherType value in the Ethernet II header for PPPoE frames is set to 0x88-63 for PPPoE discovery frames and 0x88-64 for PPP session frames. For more information about the Ethernet II header, see Chapter 1, "Local Area Network (LAN) Technologies."

PPPoE Discovery Stage

The PPPoE discovery process consists of the following four PPPoE frames:

1. The PPPoE Active Discovery Initiation (PADI) frame is sent by the PPPoE client to the Ethernet broadcast address (0xFF-FF-FF-FF-FF-FF). Within the Ethernet payload, the Code field is set to 9, the Session ID is set to 0, and there is a single Service-Name PPPoE tag, as well as other tags as needed. If the network connection in the Network Connections folder corresponding to the broadband Internet adapter has been configured with a service name, that service name is sent. Otherwise, the PADI frame is sent with a null service name.

2. The PPPoE Active Discovery Offer (PADO) frame is sent by the AC to the unicast MAC address of the PPPoE client. Within the Ethernet payload, the Code field is set to 7, the Session ID is set to 0, there are the AC-Name and Service-Name tags, and other tags as needed. If the network connection in the Network Connections folder corresponding to the broadband Internet adapter has not been configured with a service name, it is automatically set to the value of the Service-Name tag in the PADO frame.

3. The PPPoE Active Discovery Request (PADR) frame is sent by the PPPoE client to the unicast MAC address of the AC. Within the Ethernet payload, the Code field is set to 25, the Session ID is set to 0, and there is a Service-Name tag and other tags as needed.

4. The PPPoE Active Discovery Session-confirmation (PADS) frame is sent by the AC to the unicast MAC address of the PPPoE client. Within the Ethernet payload, the Code field is set to 101, the Session ID field is set to the session ID for the PPP session of the PPPoE client, and there is a Service-Name tag, as well as other tags as needed.

To terminate the PPPoE session, either the PPPoE client or the AC can send a PPPoE Active Discovery Terminate (PADT) frame, which contains the Code field set to 167 and the session ID set to the session being terminated.

PPPoE Session Stage

After the PPPoE discovery process is complete, a PPP connection is negotiated and network protocol data such as IP datagrams are sent over the PPPoE connection. Figure 4-11 shows a PPPoE frame that contains a PPP frame.

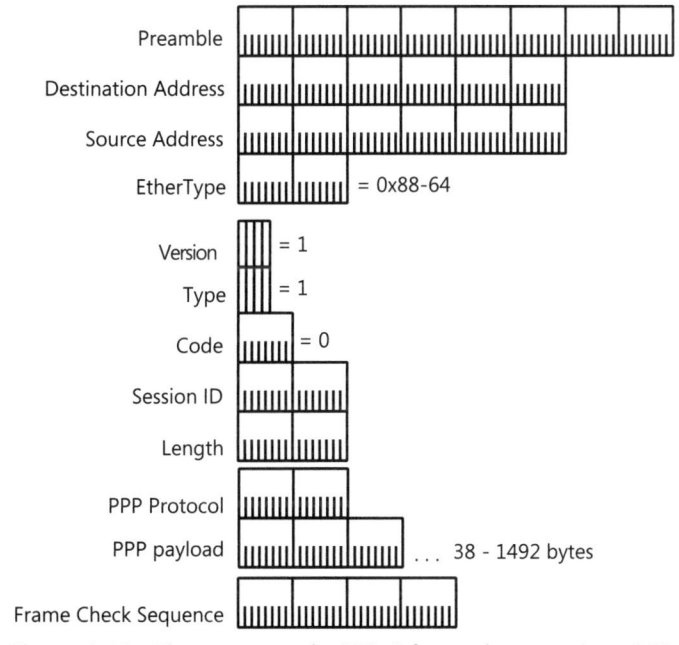

Figure 4-11 The structure of a PPPoE frame that contains a PPP frame

Because of the additional PPPoE overhead, the maximum size of PPP frames that can be sent over a PPPoE connection is 1494 bytes.

Summary

PPP is used for encapsulation, link negotiation, and network protocol negotiation for network protocol packets that are sent over a point-to-point link. The PPP connection process has four phases: link negotiation, authentication, callback negotiation, and network protocol negotiation.

During link negotiation, each PPP peer determines how it will send PPP frames. During authentication, PPP authentication protocols such as MS-CHAP v2 or EAP-TLS are used to verify the credentials of the calling or answering PPP peer. During callback negotiation, the calling and answering PPP peers determine whether the answering PPP peer will call the calling peer back and at which phone number. During network protocol negotiation, NCPs such as IPCP, CCP, and ECP are used to determine the use and configuration of TCP/IP, compression, and encryption.

PPPoE is a method of encapsulating PPP frames so that they can be sent over an Ethernet link. A PPPoE connection consists of two phases: a PPPoE discovery phase and a PPPoE session phase. After a PPPoE connection is negotiated during the discovery phase, PPP is used to negotiate a connection and send network protocol frames during the PPPoE session phase.

Part II
Internet Layer Protocols

> **In this part:**
> Chapter 5: Internet Protocol (IP) 89
> Chapter 6: Internet Control Message Protocol (ICMP) 125
> Chapter 7: Internet Group Management Protocol (IGMP) 157
> Chapter 8: Internet Protocol Version 6 (IPv6) 179

Chapter 5

Internet Protocol (IP)

In this chapter:
Introduction to IP 89
The IP Datagram 92
The IP Header... 93
Fragmentation 103
IP Options... 112
Summary... 123

IP is the internetworking building block of all the other protocols at the Internet Layer and above. IP is a datagram protocol primarily responsible for addressing and routing packets between hosts. This chapter describes the details of the fields in the IP header and their role in IP packet delivery.

Note This chapter uses the term *IP* to refer to version 4 of IP (IPv4), which is in widespread use today. IP version 6 is denoted as IPv6.

Introduction to IP

IP is the primary protocol for the Internet Layer of the Department of Defense (DoD) Advanced Research Projects Agency (DARPA) model and provides the internetworking functionality that makes large-scale internetworks such as the Internet possible. IP has lasted since it was formalized in 1981 with RFC 791 and will continue to be used on the Internet for years to come. Only relatively recently have IP's shortcomings been addressed in a new version known as IPv6. For more information about IPv6, see Chapter 8, "Internet Protocol Version 6 (IPv6)." IP's amazing longevity is a tribute to its original design.

More Info All of the RFCs referenced in this chapter can be found in the \Standards\Chap05_IP folder on the companion CD-ROM.

IP Services

IP offers the following services to upper layer protocols:

- **Internetworking protocol**   IP is an internetworking protocol, also known as a routable protocol. The IP header contains information necessary for routing the packet, including source and destination IP addresses. An IP address is composed of two components: a network address and a node address. Internetwork delivery, or routing, is possible because of the existence of a destination network address. IP allows the creation of an IP internetwork, which consists of two or more networks interconnected by IP router(s). The IP header also contains a link count, which is used to limit the number of links on which the packet can travel before being discarded.

- **Multiple client protocols**   IP is an internetwork carrier for upper layer protocols. IP can carry several different upper layer protocols, but each IP packet can contain data from only one upper layer protocol at a time. Because each packet can carry one of several protocols, there must be a way to indicate the upper layer protocol of the packet payload so that it can be forwarded to the appropriate upper layer protocol at the destination. Both the client and the server always use the same protocol for a given exchange of data. Therefore, the packet does not need to indicate separate source and destination protocols.

  Examples of upper-layer protocols include other Internet Layer protocols such as Internet Control Message Protocol (ICMP) and Internet Group Management Protocol (IGMP) and Transport Layer protocols such as Transmission Control Protocol (TCP) and User Datagram Protocol (UDP).

- **Datagram delivery**   IP is a datagram protocol that provides a connectionless, unreliable delivery service for upper layer protocols. Connectionless means that no handshaking occurs between IP nodes prior to sending data, and no logical connection is created or maintained at the Internet Layer. Unreliable means that IP sends a packet without sequencing and without an acknowledgment that the destination was reached. IP makes a best effort to deliver packets to the next hop or the final destination. End-to-end reliability is the responsibility of upper-layer protocols such as TCP.

- **Independence from Network Interface Layer**   At the Internet Layer, IP is designed to be independent of the network technology present at the Network Interface Layer of the DARPA model, which encompasses the Open Systems Interconnection (OSI) Physical and Data Link Layers. IP is independent of OSI Physical Layer attributes such as cabling, signaling, and bit rate. It also is independent of OSI Data Link Layer attributes such as media access control (MAC) scheme, addressing, and maximum frame size. IP uses a 32-bit address that is independent of the addressing scheme used at the Network Interface Layer.

- **Fragmentation and reassembly**   To support the maximum frame sizes of different Network Interface Layer technologies, IP allows for the fragmentation of a payload when forwarding onto a link that has a lower maximum transmission unit (MTU) than the IP datagram size. Routers or sending hosts fragment an IP payload, and fragmentation can occur multiple times. The destination host then reassembles the fragments into the originally sent IP payload. More information on fragmentation and reassembly are provided later in this chapter in the section titled "Fragmentation."

- **Extensible through IP options**   When features are required that are not available using the standard IP header, IP options can be used. IP options are appended to the standard IP header and provide custom functionality, such as the ability to specify a path that an IP datagram follows through the IP internetwork.

- **Datagram packet-switching technology**   IP is an example of a datagram packet-switching technology: Each packet is a datagram, an unacknowledged and nonsequenced message that is forwarded by the switches of the switching network using a globally significant address. In the case of IP, each switch in the switching network is an IP router, and the globally significant address is the destination IP address. This address is examined at each router, which makes an independent routing decision and forwards the packet. Because each router decides independently where to forward a packet, a packet's path from Node 1 to Node 2 is not necessarily a packet's path from Node 2 to Node 1. Because each packet is separately switched, each can take a different path between the source and destination. Because of various transit delays, each packet can arrive in a different order from which it was sent. Additionally, packets can be duplicated by intermediate routers.

> **Note**   The term *switch* is used here for a generalized forwarding device and is not meant to imply a Layer 2 switch. A Layer 2 switch is typically used in Ethernet environments to segment traffic.

IP MTU

Each Network Interface Layer technology imposes a maximum-sized frame that can be sent. This frame typically consists of the framing header and trailer and a payload. The maximum size of a frame for a given Network Interface Layer technology is called the MTU. For an IP packet, the Network Interface Layer payload is an IP datagram. Therefore, the maximum-sized payload becomes the maximum-sized IP datagram. This is known as the IP MTU.

Table 5-1 lists the IP MTUs for the various Network Interface Layer technologies that are described in Chapter 1, "Local Area Network (LAN) Technologies," and Chapter 2, "Wide Area Network (WAN) Technologies."

In an environment with mixed Network Interface Layer protocols, fragmentation can occur when crossing a router from a link with a higher IP MTU to a link with a lower IP MTU. IP fragmentation is discussed in more detail later in this chapter in the section titled "Fragmentation."

Table 5-1   IP MTUs for Common Network Interface Layer Technologies

Network Interface Layer Technology	IP MTU
Ethernet (Ethernet II encapsulation)	1500
Ethernet (IEEE 802.3 Sub-Network Access Protocol [SNAP] encapsulation)	1492

Table 5-1 IP MTUs for Common Network Interface Layer Technologies

Network Interface Layer Technology	IP MTU
Token Ring (4 and 16 Mbps)	Varies based on token holding time
Fiber Distributed Data Interface (FDDI)	4352
Frame relay	1592 (with a 2-byte Address field in the Frame Relay header)

In Windows Server 2008 and Windows Vista, it is possible to override the MTU as reported to the Network Driver Interface Specification (NDIS) interface by the network adapter driver with the following command:

```
netsh interface ipv4 set interface InterfaceNameOrIndex mtu=MtuSize
```

InterfaceNameOrIndex is the name of the interface from the Network Connections folder or its interface index. *MtuSize* is the IP MTU.

You can also use the following registry value:

MTU
```
Key: HKEY_LOCAL_MACHINE\SYSTEM\CurrentControlSet\Services\Tcpip\
Parameters\Interfaces\InterfaceGUID
Data type: REG_DWORD
Valid range: 576 - <the MTU reported by the network adapter>
Default: 0xFFFFFFFF (the MTU reported by the network adapter)
Present by default: No
```

When TCP/IP initializes, it queries its bound NDIS network adapter driver and receives the MTU. The MTU registry value is used to set an MTU that is lower than the default MTU, as reported by the NDIS driver, and greater than the minimum value of 576. Values in the MTU registry value that are greater than the default MTU are ignored. If the MTU registry value is set to a value less than 576, 576 is used.

It is useful to change the default MTU size for testing or for solving MTU issues in translational bridge environments.

The IP Datagram

Figure 5-1 shows the structure of an IP datagram.

The IP datagram consists of the following:

- **IP header** The IP header is of variable size, between 20 and 60 bytes, in 4-byte increments. It provides routing support, payload identification, IP header and datagram size indication, fragmentation support, and options.

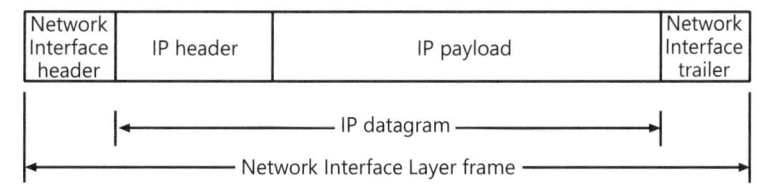

Figure 5-1 The structure of the IP datagram at the Network Interface layer

- **IP payload** The IP payload is of variable size, ranging from 0 bytes (a 20-byte IP datagram with a 20-byte IP header) to 65,515 bytes (a 65,535-byte IP datagram with a 20-byte header).

As sent on a link, the IP datagram is wrapped with a Network Interface Layer header and trailer to create a Network Interface Layer frame.

The IP Header

Figure 5-2 shows the IP header's structure. The following sections discuss the fields of the IP header.

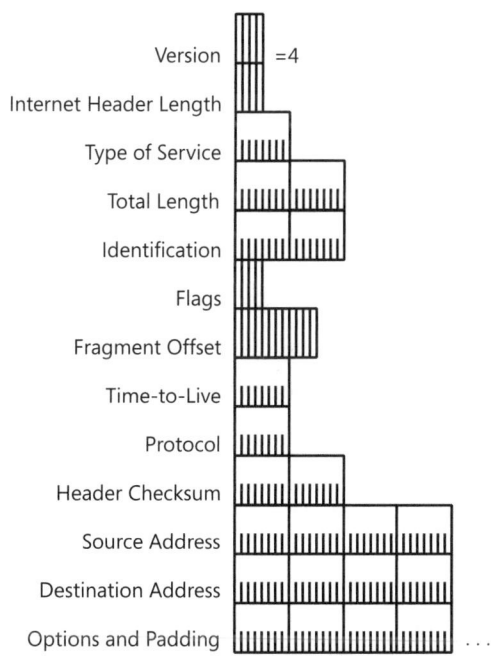

Figure 5-2 The structure of the IP header

Version

The Version field is 4 bits long and is used to indicate the IP header version. A 4-bit field can have values from 0 through 15. The most prevalent IP version used today on organization intranets and the Internet is version 4, sometimes referred to as IPv4. The next version of IP is IPv6. All other values for the Version field are either undefined or not in use. For the latest list of the defined values of the IP Version field, see *http://www.iana.org/assignments/version-numbers*.

Internet Header Length

The Internet Header Length (IHL) field is 4 bits long and is used to indicate the IP header size. The maximum number that can be represented with 4 bits is 15. Therefore, the IHL field cannot possibly be a byte counter. Rather, the IHL field indicates the number of 32-bit words (4-byte blocks) in the IP header. The typical IP header does not contain any options and is 20 bytes long. The smallest possible IHL value is 5 (0x5). With the maximum amount of IP options, the largest IP header can be 60 bytes long, indicated with a IHL value of 15 (0xF).

Using a 4-byte block counter to indicate the IP header size means that the IP header size must always be a multiple of 4. If a set of IP options extend the IP header, they must do so in 4-byte increments. If the set of IP options is not a multiple of 4 bytes long, option padding bytes must be used so that the IP header an each option is always on a 4-byte boundary.

Type Of Service

The Type Of Service (TOS) field is 8 bits long and is used to indicate the quality of service with which this datagram is to be delivered by the internetwork routers. The TOS field has two definitions: the original RFC 791 definition and the newer definition based on RFCs 2474 and 3168. The RFC 791 definition has been deprecated by RFCs 2474 and 3168.

RFC 791 Definition of the TOS Field

As defined in RFC 791, the TOS field contains subfields and flags to indicate desired precedence, delay, throughput, reliability, and cost characteristics.

Within the 8 bits of the TOS field, there are five fields that indicate a different quality of the datagram delivery, as shown in Figure 5-3. The TOS field is set by the sending host and is not modified by routers. All IP fragments contain the same TOS setting as the original IP datagram.

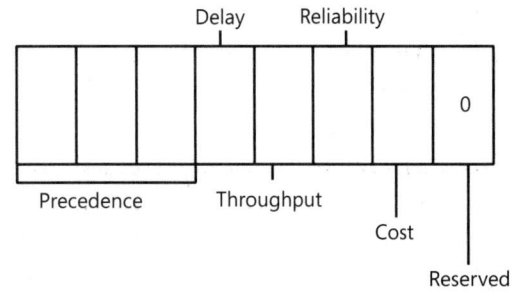

Figure 5-3 The structure of the RFC 791 IP Type Of Service field

Normally, a sending host sends an IP datagram with the TOS field set to the value of 0x00: routine precedence, normal delay, normal throughput, normal reliability, and normal cost. Routers normally ignore the values in the TOS field and forward all datagrams as if the fields are not set. This is known as TOS0 routing. However, modern routing protocols such as Open Shortest Path First (OSPF) and Integrated Intermediate System-Intermediate System (Integrated IS-IS) now support the calculation of routes for each value of the TOS field.

The routers and the routing protocol determine how the various values in the TOS field are interpreted. In a properly configured network, packets with specific TOS values are forwarded over different paths. This can improve routing and delivery efficiency in a multipath IP internetwork. For example, an IP internetwork could have one path for general traffic, one for low-delay traffic, and another path for high-reliability traffic. When sending hosts set various combinations of TOS values, routers can choose among those paths. The TOS field is used for prioritized delivery, sometimes referred to as quality of service (QoS), in IP internetworks.

Precedence

The Precedence field is 3 bits long and is used to indicate the importance of the datagram. Table 5-2 lists the defined values of the Precedence field.

Table 5-2 Values of the IP Precedence Field

Precedence Value	Precedence
000	Routine
001	Priority
010	Immediate
011	Flash
100	Flash Override
101	CRITIC/ECP
110	Internetwork Control
111	Network Control

The Precedence field is set to 000 (Routine) by default.

Delay

The Delay field is a flag indicating either Normal Delay (when set to 0) or Low Delay (when set to 1). If Delay is set to 1, the IP router forwards the IP datagram along the path that has the lowest delay characteristics. An application can request the low delay path when sending either time-sensitive data, such as digitized voice or video, or interactive traffic, such as Telnet sessions. Based on the Delay flag, the router might choose the lower delay terrestrial wide area network (WAN) link over the higher delay satellite link, even if the satellite link has a higher bandwidth.

Throughput

The Throughput field is a flag indicating either Normal Throughput (when set to 0) or High Throughput (when set to 1). If the Throughput field is set to 1, the IP router forwards the IP datagram along the path that has the highest throughput characteristics. An application can request the high throughput path when sending bulk data. Based on the Throughput flag, the router can choose the higher throughput satellite link over the lower throughput terrestrial WAN link, even if the terrestrial link has a lower delay.

Reliability

The Reliability field is a flag indicating either Normal Reliability (when set to 0) or High Reliability (when set to 1). During periods of congestion at an IP router, the Reliability field is used to decide which IP datagrams to discard first. If the Reliability field is set to 1, the IP router discards these datagrams last. An application can request the high reliability path when sending time-sensitive data, so that it cannot be discarded. For example, with some methods of sending digital video, the digitized video is sent as two types of packets: The primary type is used to reconstruct the basic video image, and a secondary type is used to provide a higher resolution image. In this case, the primary packets are sent with the Reliability field set to 1 and the secondary packets are sent with the Reliability field set to 0. If congestion occurs at the router, the router discards the secondary packets first.

Cost

The Cost field is a flag indicating either Normal Cost (when set to 0) or Low Cost (when set to 1), where cost indicates monetary cost. If the Cost field is set to 1, the IP router forwards the IP datagram along the path that has the lowest cost characteristics. An application can request the low cost path when sending noncritical data. Based on the Cost flag, the router can choose a lower cost terrestrial link over a higher cost satellite link, even if the terrestrial link has a lower bandwidth.

Reserved

The Reserved field is the last bit and must be set to 0. Routers ignore this field when forwarding IP datagrams.

RFC 2474 Definition of the TOS Field

To accommodate prioritized delivery of IP packets over an IP internetwork, RFC 2474 redefines the 8 bits in the TOS field in terms of a 6-bit Differentiated Services Code Point (DSCP) field and 2 unused bits. The DSCP value identifies the per-hop behavior that the receiving routers use to determine the special delivery handling for the packet. DSCP values are defined by network policy.

The RFC 2474–defined TOS field is shown in Figure 5-4.

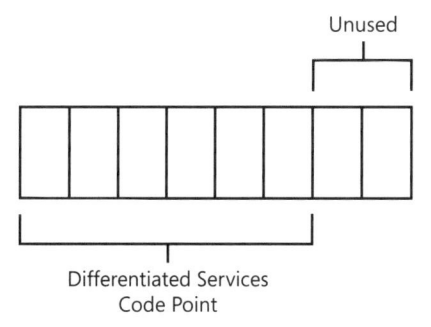

Figure 5-4 The structure of the RFC 2474 IP TOS field

Differentiated services are an alternative to prioritized delivery mechanisms that use the Resource ReSerVation Protocol (RSVP). RSVP requires that communicating nodes use an initial signaling process and that intermediate routers maintain a flow state. With differentiated services, network policy determines the DSCP values and their corresponding delivery and queuing parameters. The network policy is propagated to both the routers and the communicating hosts. When a host needs prioritized delivery for a packet, it selects the appropriate DSCP value and places it in the TOS field in the IP header. The intermediate routers note the DSCP value and provide the corresponding prioritized delivery service.

TCP/IP for Windows Server 2008 and Windows Vista uses the RFC 2474 definition of the TOS field by default. Because the IP_TOS Winsock option has been removed, you can set its value with the QoS components of Windows Server 2008 and Windows Vista. You can use Group Policy-based QoS settings to set DSCP values and control application sending rates without having to use application programming interfaces (APIs) or modify existing applications. You can use the Generic QoS (GQoS) and Traffic Control (TC) APIs to set the DSCP value or the new QoS2 API, also known as Quality Windows Audio-Video Experience (qWAVE).

Note IP for Windows Server 2008 and Windows Vista does not support the DisableUserTOSSetting registry value.

Explicit Congestion Notification and the TOS Field

To prevent the problems associated with dropped packets due to congested routers, the designers of TCP/IP created a new set of standards for both hosts and routers. These standards describe active queue management (AQM) on IP routers (RFC 2309) to allow the router to monitor that state of its forwarding queues and provide a mechanism to enable routers to report to sending hosts that congestion is occurring, allowing the sending hosts to lower their transmission rate before the router begins dropping packets. The router reporting and host response mechanism is known as Explicit Congestion Notification (ECN) and is defined in RFC 3168.

ECN support in IP uses the two unused bits of the RFC 2474-defined TOS field. Figure 5-5 shows the new definition of the TOS field with ECN.

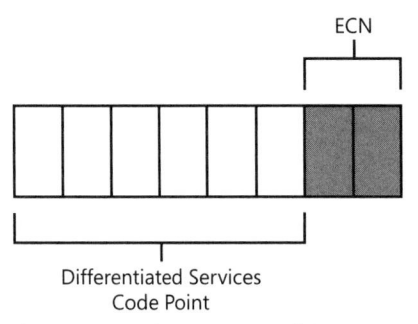

Figure 5-5 The structure of the RFC 3168 IP TOS field

The two unused bits in the RFC 2474-defined TOS field are defined in RFC 3168 as the ECN field, which has the following values:

- **00** The sending host does not support ECN.
- **01 or 10** The sending host supports ECN.
- **11** Congestion has been experienced by a router.

An ECN-capable host sends its packets with the ECN field set to 01 or 10. For packets sent by ECN-capable hosts, if a router in the path is ECN-capable and is experiencing congestion, it sets the ECN field to 11. If the ECN field has been set to 11, downstream routers in the path to the destination do not modify its value.

TCP/IP in Windows Server 2008 and Window Vista supports ECN but it is disabled by default. To enable ECN support, use the `netsh interface tcp set global ecncapability=enabled` command. Because ECN is using bits in the IP and TCP headers that were previously defined as unused or reserved, intermediate network devices such as routers and firewalls might silently discard packets when the ECN fields are set to nonzero values. To ensure that ECN-marked TCP/IP traffic will not be dropped from your network, survey your networking equipment and perform the appropriate configuration or upgrades to ensure that ECN-marked packets are not discarded.

Total Length

As Figure 5-2 shows, the Total Length field is 2 bytes long and is used to indicate the size of the IP datagram (IP header and IP payload) in bytes. With 16 bits, the maximum total length that can be indicated is 65,535 bytes. For typical maximum-sized IP datagrams, the total length is the same as the IP MTU for that Network Interface Layer technology.

Between the header length and the total length, the IP payload length can be determined from the following formula:

IP payload length (bytes) = Total Length value (bytes) − (4 × IHL value (32-bit words))

Identification

The Identification field is 2 bytes long and is used to identify a specific IP packet sent between a source and destination node. The sending host sets the field's value, and the field is incremented for successive IP datagrams. The Identification field is used to identify the fragments of an original IP datagram.

Flags

The Flags field is 3 bits long and contains two flags for fragmentation. One flag is used to indicate whether the IP payload is eligible for fragmentation, and the other indicates whether or not there are more fragments to follow for this fragmented IP datagram.

More information on these flags and their uses can be found in the section titled "Fragmentation," later in this chapter.

Fragment Offset

The Fragment Offset field is 13 bits long and is used to indicate the offset of where this fragment begins relative to the original unfragmented IP payload.

More information on the Fragment Offset field can be found in the section titled "Fragmentation," later in this chapter.

Time-To-Live

The Time-To-Live (TTL) field is 1 byte long and is used to indicate how many links on which this IP datagram can travel before an IP router discards it. The TTL field was originally intended for use as a time counter, to indicate the number of seconds that the IP datagram could exist on the Internet. An IP router was intended to keep track of the time that it received the IP datagram and the time that it forwarded the IP datagram. The TTL was then decreased by the number of seconds that the packet resided at the router.

However, the latest modern standard (RFC 1812) specifies that IP routers decrement the TTL by 1 when forwarding an IP datagram. Therefore, the TTL is an inverse link count. The sending host sets the initial TTL, which acts as a maximum link count. The maximum value limits the number of links on which the datagram can travel and prevents a datagram from indefinitely looping.

Some additional aspects of the TTL field include the following:

- Routers decrement the TTL in received packets to be routed before consulting the routing table. If the TTL is less than 1, the packet is discarded and an ICMP Time Expired-TTL Expired In Transit message is sent back to the sending host.

- Unicast destination hosts do not check the TTL field.

- Sending hosts must send IP datagrams with a TTL greater than 0. The exact value of the TTL for sent IP datagrams is either an operating system default or is specified by the application. The maximum value of the TTL is 255.

- A recommended value of the TTL is twice the diameter of your internetwork. The diameter is the number of links between the farthest two nodes on the IP internetwork.

- The TTL is independent of routing protocol metrics such as the Routing Information Protocol (RIP) hop count and the OSPF cost.

> **Note** The TTL can be mistakenly referred to as a hop count when in fact it is a link count. The difference is subtle but important. The hop count is the number of routers to cross to reach a given destination. Link count is the number of Network Interface Layer links to cross to reach a given destination. The difference between hop count and link count is 1. For example, if Host A and Host B are separated by five routers, the hop count is 5, but the link count is 6. An IP datagram sent from Host A to Host B with a TTL of 5 is discarded by the fifth router. An IP datagram sent from Host A to Host B with a TTL of 6 will arrive at Host B.

The default TTL for Windows Server 2008 and Windows Vista is 128. You can change the default value of the TTL field for sent packets with the following command:

```
netsh interface ipv4 set global defaultcurhoplimit=TTL
```

You can also use the following registry value:

DefaultTTL
```
Key: HKEY_LOCAL_MACHINE\SYSTEM\CurrentControlSet\Services\Tcpip\Parameters
Value type: REG_DWORD
Valid range: 0 - 255
Default: 128
Present by default: No
```

The default value of DefaultTTL is set to 128 so that IP packets sent by a Windows Server 2008 or Windows Vista–based computer can reach locations on the Internet that might need to traverse many links. Changing the value of DefaultTTL is necessary only when the diameter of your network changes. Windows Sockets applications can override this default value.

Setting the TTL with Ping

The Windows Server 2008 and Windows Vista Ping.exe tool with the `-i` option can be used to set the TTL value in ICMP Echo messages. The syntax is:

```
ping -i TTLValue Destination
```

For example, to ping 10.0.0.1 with a TTL field that is set to 7, use the following command:

```
ping -i 7 10.0.0.1
```

The default TTL for ICMP Echo messages sent by the Ping.exe tool is 128.

Protocol

The Protocol field is 1 byte long and is used to indicate the upper layer protocol contained within the IP payload. Some common values of the IP Protocol field are 1 for ICMP, 6 for TCP, and 17 (0x11) for UDP. The Protocol field acts as a multiplex identifier so that the payload can be passed to the proper upper layer protocol on receipt at the destination node.

Windows Sockets applications can refer to protocols by name. Protocol names are resolved to protocol numbers through the Protocol file stored in the *%SystemRoot%*\System32\Drivers\Etc directory.

Table 5-3 lists some of the values of the IP Protocol field for protocols that Windows Server 2008 and Windows Vista support.

Table 5-3 Values of the IP Protocol Field

Value	Protocol
1	ICMP
2	IGMP
6	TCP
17	UDP
41	IPv6
47	Generic Routing Encapsulation (GRE)
50	IP security Encapsulating Security Payload (ESP)
51	IP security Authentication Header (AH)

For a complete list of IP Protocol field values, see *http://www.iana.org/assignments/protocol-numbers*.

Header Checksum

The Header Checksum field is 2 bytes long and performs a bit-level integrity check on the IP header only. The IP payload is not included, and IP payloads must include their own checksums to check for bit-level integrity. The sending host performs an initial checksum in the sent IP datagram. Each router in the path between the source and destination verifies the Header Checksum field before processing the packet. If the verification fails, the router silently discards the IP datagram.

Because each router in the path between the source and destination decrements the TTL, the header checksum changes at each router.

To compute the header checksum, each 16-bit quantity in the IP header is ones-complemented; bits within the 16-bit quantity that are set to 0 are changed to 1, bits within the 16-bit quantity that are set to 1 are changed to 0. The ones-complemented 16-bit quantities are added together and the sum is ones-complemented. The result is placed in the Header Checksum field.

For the purposes of computing the header checksum over all the fields in the IP header, the value of the Header Checksum field is set to 0.

Source Address

The Source Address field is 4 bytes long and contains the IP address of the source host, unless a network address translator (NAT) is translating the IP datagram. A NAT is used to translate between public and private addresses when connecting to the Internet. NAT is defined in RFC 1631.

Destination Address

The Destination Address field is 4 bytes long and contains the IP address of the destination host, unless the IP datagram is being translated by a NAT or being loose-or strict-source routed. More information on IP source routing can be found in the section titled "IP Options," later in this chapter.

Options and Padding

Options and padding can be added to the IP header, but must be done in 4-byte increments so that the size of the IP header can be indicated using the Header Length field.

For an example of the structure of the IP header, the following is frame 1 of Capture 05-01, a Network Monitor trace that is included in the \Captures folder on the companion CD-ROM, as displayed with Network Monitor 3.1:

```
Frame:
+ Ethernet: Etype = Internet IP (IPv4)
- Ipv4: Next Protocol = ICMP, Packet ID = 13517, Total IP Length = 60
  - Versions: IPv4, Internet Protocol; Header Length = 20
    Version:        (0100....) IPv4, Internet Protocol
    HeaderLength: (....0101) 20 bytes (0x5)  - DifferentiatedServicesField: DSCP: 0, ECN: 0
    DSCP: (000000..) Differentiated services codepoint 0
    ECT:  (......0.) ECN-Capable Transport not set
    CE:   (.......0) ECN-CE not set
    TotalLength: 60 (0x3C)
    Identification: 13517 (0x34CD)
  - FragmentFlags: 0 (0x0)
    Reserved: (0..............)
    DF:       (.0.............) Fragment if necessary
    MF:       (..0............) This is the last fragment
    Offset:   (...0000000000000) 0
```

```
    TimeToLive: 128 (0x80)
    NextProtocol: ICMP, 1(0x1)
    Checksum: 47209 (0xB869)
    SourceAddress: 157.59.11.19
    DestinationAddress: 157.59.8.1
+ Icmp: Echo Request Message, From 157.59.11.19 To 157.59.8.1
```

Fragmentation

When a source host or a router must transmit an IP datagram on a link and the MTU of the link is less than the IP datagram's size, the IP datagram must be fragmented. When IP fragmentation occurs, the IP payload is segmented and each segment is sent with its own IP header.

The IP header contains information required to reassemble the original IP payload at the destination host. Because IP is a datagram packet-switching technology and the fragments can arrive in a different order from which they were sent, the fragments must be grouped (using the Identification field), sequenced (using the Fragment Offset field), and delimited (using the More Fragments flag).

Fragmentation Fields

Figure 5-6 shows the fragmentation fields in the IP header, which are described in the following sections.

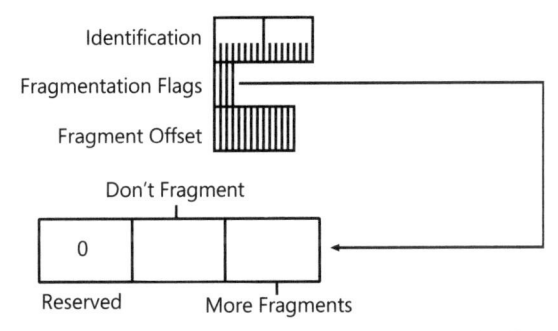

Figure 5-6 The fields in the IP header used for fragmentation

Identification

The IP Identification field is used to group all the fragments of the payload of an original IP datagram together. The sending host sets the value of the Identification field, and this value is not changed during the fragmentation process. The Identification field is set even when fragmentation of the IP payload is not allowed by setting the Don't Fragment (DF) flag.

Don't Fragment Flag

The DF flag is set to 0 to allow fragmentation and set to 1 to prohibit fragmentation, so fragmentation occurs only if the DF flag is set to 0. If fragmentation is needed to forward the IP datagram and the DF flag is set to 1, the router should send an ICMP Destination Unreachable-Fragmentation Needed And DF Set message back to the source host and discards the IP datagram.

Fragmentation and reassembly is an expensive process at the routers and the destination host. The DF flag and the ICMP Destination Unreachable-Fragmentation Needed And DF Set message are the mechanisms by which a sending host discovers the MTU of the path between the source and the destination, or Path MTU Discovery. For more information, see Chapter 6, "Internet Control Message Protocol (ICMP)."

More Fragments Flag

The More Fragments (MF) flag is set to 0 if there are no more fragments that follow this fragment (this is the last fragment), and set to 1 if there are more fragments that follow this fragment (this is not the last fragment).

Fragment Offset

The Fragment Offset field is set to indicate the position of the fragment relative to the original IP payload. The Fragment Offset is an offset used for sequencing during reassembly, putting the incoming fragments in proper order to reconstruct the original payload. The Fragment Offset field is 13 bits long. With a maximum IP payload size of 65,515 bytes (the maximum IP MTU of 65,535 minus a minimum-sized IP header of 20 bytes), the Fragment Offset field cannot possibly indicate a byte offset. At 13 bits, the maximum value is 8191. The fragment offset must be 16 bits long to be a byte offset.

Because 16 bits are required to indicate a maximum-sized IP payload and only 13 bits are available in the Fragment Offset field, each value of the fragment offset must represent 3 bits. Therefore, the Fragment Offset field is defined in terms of 8-byte blocks, called *fragment blocks*.

During fragmentation, the payload is fragmented along 8-byte boundaries and the maximum number of 8-byte fragment blocks is placed in each fragment. The Fragment Offset field is set to indicate the starting fragment block for the fragment relative to the original IP payload.

For each fragment being fragmented by a router, the original IP header is copied and the following fields are changed:

- **Header Length** Might or might not change depending on whether IP options are present and whether the options are copied to all fragments or just the first fragment. IP options are discussed in the section titled "IP Options," later in this chapter.
- **TTL** Decremented by 1.
- **Total Length** Changed to reflect the new IP header and payload size.
- **MF** Set to 1 for the first or middle fragments. Set to 0 for the last fragment.

- **Fragment Offset**   Set to indicate the position of the fragment in fragment blocks relative to the start of the original unfragmented payload.
- **Header Checksum**   Recalculated based on the changed fields in the IP header.

The Identification field does not change for any fragment.

Fragmentation Example

As an example of the fragmentation process, a node on a Token Ring network sends a fragmentable IP datagram with the IP Identification field set to 9999 to a node on an Ethernet network, as shown in Figure 5-7.

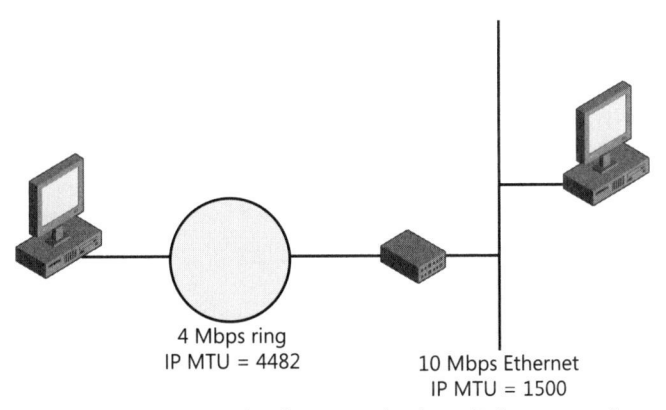

Figure 5-7   An example of a network where IP fragmentation can occur

Assuming a 9-ms token holding time, a 4-Mbps ring, and no Token Ring source routing header, the IP MTU for the Token Ring network is 4482 bytes. The Ethernet IP MTU is 1500 bytes using Ethernet II encapsulation. Table 5-4 shows the fields relevant to fragmentation in the IP header and their values for the original IP datagram.

Table 5-4   Original IP Datagram

IP Header Field	Value
Total Length	4482
Identification	9999
DF	0
MF	0
Fragment Offset	0

The IP router connecting the two networks receives the IP datagram, checks its routing table, and notes that the interface on which to forward the datagram has a lower IP MTU than the datagram's size. The router then checks the DF flag. If set to 1, the router discards the IP datagram and then might send an ICMP Destination Unreachable-Fragmentation Needed And DF Set message back to the source host. If set to 0, the IP router fragments the 4462-byte IP payload (assuming no IP options are present) into four fragments, each of which can be sent on the 1500-byte Ethernet network.

IP payloads on an Ethernet network can be 1480 bytes long, assuming no IP options are present. Each 1480-byte payload is 185 fragment blocks (1480 8 = 185). Therefore, the four fragments are three fragments each with payloads of 1480 bytes and the last fragment with a payload of 22 bytes (4462 = 1480 + 1480 + 1480 + 22). Figure 5-8 shows the fragmentation process.

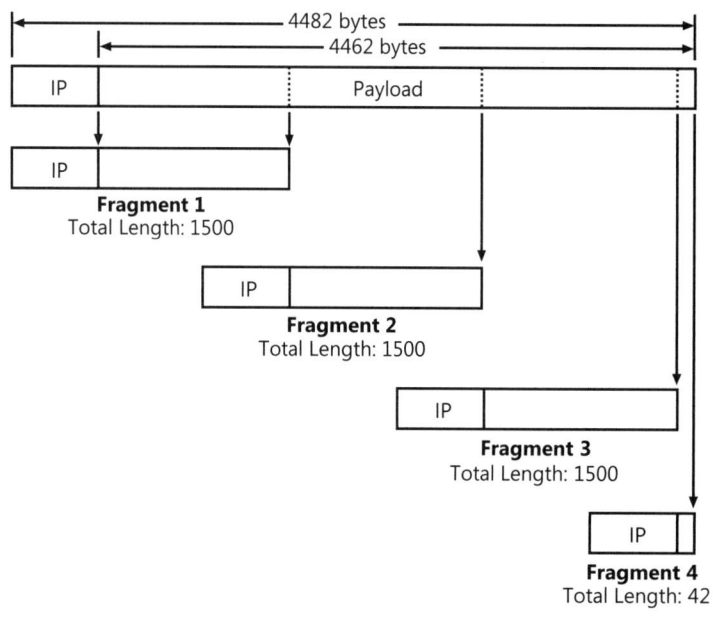

Figure 5-8 The IP fragmentation process when fragmenting from a 4482-byte IP MTU link to a 1500-byte IP MTU link

Table 5-5 shows the fields relevant to fragmentation in the IP header of the four fragments.

Table 5-5 Fragments of the Original IP Datagram

IP Header Field	Value
Fragment 1	
Total Length	1500
Identification	9999
DF	0
MF	1
Fragment Offset	0

Table 5-5 Fragments of the Original IP Datagram

IP Header Field	Value
Fragment 2	
Total Length	1500
Identification	9999
DF	0
MF	1
Fragment Offset	185
Fragment 3	
Total Length	1500
Identification	9999
DF	0
MF	1
Fragment Offset	370
Fragment 4	
Total Length	42
Identification	9999
DF	0
MF	0
Fragment Offset	555

Note Token Ring is an older technology this is not in wide use today. This configuration is uncommon on modern networks and serves only as an example of a mixed-media network.

Reassembly Example

The fragments are forwarded by the intermediate IP router(s) to the destination host. Because IP is a datagram-based packet-switching technology, the fragments can take different paths to the destination and arrive in a different order from which the fragmenting router forwarded them. IP uses the Identification and Source IP Address fields to group the arriving fragments together.

After receiving a fragment (not necessarily the first fragment of the original IP payload), an IP implementation can allocate reassembly resources comprised of the following:

- A data buffer to contain the IP payload (65,515 bytes)
- A header buffer to contain the IP header (60 bytes)

- A fragment block bit table (1024 bytes or 8192 bits)
- A total length data variable
- A timer

IP can determine that a fragment arrived because either the MF flag or the Fragment Offset field has a nonzero value. An unfragmented IP datagram has the MF flag set to 0 and the Fragment Offset field set to 0. When the first fragment arrives (the Fragment Offset field is 0), its IP header is placed in the header buffer. When the last fragment arrives (the MF flag is 0), the total data length is computed.

For each arriving fragment, the IP payload is placed in the data buffer according to the values of the Fragment Offset and Total Length fields; the bits corresponding to the arriving fragment blocks are set in the fragment block bit table. When the final fragment arrives (which might not be the last fragment), all the bits in the fragment block bit table are set and reassembly of the original IP datagram is complete. IP delivers the IP payload to the appropriate upper layer protocol based on the Protocol field's value.

The reassembly timer is used to abandon the reassembly process within a certain amount of time. If all the fragments do not arrive before the reassembly timer expires, the IP datagram is discarded and the destination host can send an ICMP Time Exceeded-Fragmentation Time Expired message to the source host. RFC 791 recommends a default reassembly timer of 15 seconds; as fragments arrive, the reassembly timer is set to the maximum of the current value and the value of the arriving fragment's TTL field.

Figure 5-9 shows the reassembly process for our example fragmentation.

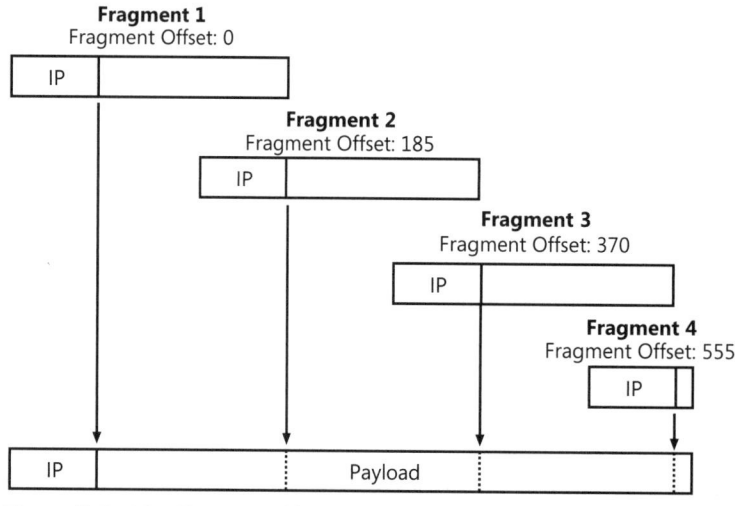

Figure 5-9 The IP reassembly process for the four fragments of the original IP datagram

Fragmenting a Fragment

It is possible for fragments to become further fragmented. In this case, each fragmented payload is fragmented to fit the MTU of the link onto which it is being forwarded. The process of fragmenting a fragmented payload is slightly different from fragmenting an original IP payload in how the MF flag is set.

When fragmenting a previously fragmented payload, the MF flag is always set to 1, except when the fragment of the fragmented payload is the last fragment of the original payload.

- If an IP router fragments a previously fragmented first or middle fragment, all of the fragments have the MF flag set to 1.
- If an IP router fragments a previously fragmented last fragment, all of the fragments except the last fragment have the MF flag set to 1.

Therefore, regardless of how many times the IP datagram is fragmented, only one fragment has the MF flag set to 0, indicating the last fragment of the original IP payload.

Network Monitor Capture 05-02 (in the \Captures folder on the companion CD-ROM) provides an example of source-based IP fragmentation. The capture is the fragmentation of a 5008-byte ICMP Echo message so that it fits on an Ethernet network.

Avoiding Fragmentation

Although fragmentation allows IP nodes to communicate regardless of differing MTUs in intermediate subnets and without user intervention, IP fragmentation and reassembly is a relatively expensive process—both at the routers (or sending hosts) and at the destination host. On the modern Internet, fragmentation is highly discouraged; Internet routers are busy enough with the forwarding of IP traffic.

Fragmentation can be avoided by taking the following two measures:

- Discover the IP MTU that is supported by all of the links in the path between the source and the destination (the path MTU).
- Set the DF flag to 1 on all IP datagrams sent.

For more information on the Path MTU Discovery process, see Chapter 6, "Internet Control Message Protocol (ICMP)."

Setting the DF Flag with Ping

The Windows Server 2008 and Windows Vista Ping.exe tool with the -f option can be used to set the DF flag to 1 in ICMP Echo messages. The syntax is

```
ping -f Destination
```

For example, to ping 10.0.0.1 and set the DF flag to 1, use the following command:

```
ping -f 10.0.0.1
```

By default, ICMP Echo messages sent by the Ping.exe tool have the DF flag set to 0 (fragmentation allowed).

Setting the IP Payload Size with Ping

The Windows Server 2008 and Windows Vista Ping.exe tool with the -l option can be used to send IP packets with an arbitrary size by specifying the size of the Optional Data field in an ICMP Echo message. The syntax is:

```
ping -l OptionalDataFieldSize Destination
```

OptionalDataFieldSize is the size of the Optional Data field in an ICMP Echo message in bytes.

For example, to ping 10.0.0.1 with an Optional Data field size of 5000, use the following command:

```
ping -l 5000 10.0.0.1
```

The default Optional Data field size for Ping is 32 bytes.

The Optional Data field size is not the same as the IP payload size because ICMP Echo messages include an 8-byte ICMP header. Therefore, to calculate the IP payload's size, add 8 to the Optional Data field size. To calculate the IP datagram's size, add 20 to the size of the IP payload (or 28 to the size of the Optional Data field size). To ping with an ICMP Echo message at the maximum size allowed by the Network Interface technology, subtract 28 from the IP MTU. For example, to ping the address 10.0.0.1 with a maximum-sized ICMP Echo message on an Ethernet network (with an IP MTU of 1500), use the following Ping command:

```
ping -l 1472 10.0.0.1
```

Using Ping to Do Source Fragmentation

The Windows Server 2008 and Windows Vista Ping.exe tool with the -l option can be used to do source fragmentation. Pinging with an Optional Data field size that is greater than (IP MTU – 28) bytes produces source-fragmented packets. For example, pinging from an Ethernet node with an Optional Data field size of 1472 or less does not produce fragmented packets. Pinging from an Ethernet node with an Optional Data field size greater than 1472 does produce fragmented packets.

Fragmentation and Translational Bridging Environments

Translational bridging is the interconnection of two different Network Interface Layer technologies on the same network by a Layer 2 device such as a bridge or switch. Translational bridges were used to connect an Ethernet segment to a Token Ring segment. In modern networks, switches use translational bridging to connect 10-Mbps or 100-Mbps Ethernet nodes to servers on high-speed ports. Common high-speed port technologies include FDDI, Gigabit Ethernet (GbE), and ATM.

The most serious obstacle to translational bridging is the difference in MTU between various Network Interface Layer technologies. Because there is no router involved, we cannot rely on either fragmentation or Path MTU Discovery processes to account for the differing MTUs. A translational bridge does not have the capability to fragment. Frames larger than the MTU of the link onto which they are to be forwarded are silently discarded by the bridge. As discussed in Chapter 10, "Transmission Control Protocol (TCP) Basics," when a TCP connection is established, both nodes communicate MTU information in the form of the TCP Maximum Segment Size (MSS) option. However, despite this indication, proper communication between all nodes in a translational bridging environment might require the modification of the IP MTU of specific nodes.

For example, Figure 5-10 shows two Ethernet switches connected on an Ethernet backbone. On each Ethernet switch is an FDDI port connected to an FDDI ring containing application servers. When the servers on the same FDDI ring communicate with each other, they can send packets with the FDDI MTU of 4352 bytes. When an Ethernet node on one of the switches uses TCP to connect to an application server on either FDDI ring, the TCP MSS option lowers the maximum size of TCP segments for IP datagrams of 1500 bytes.

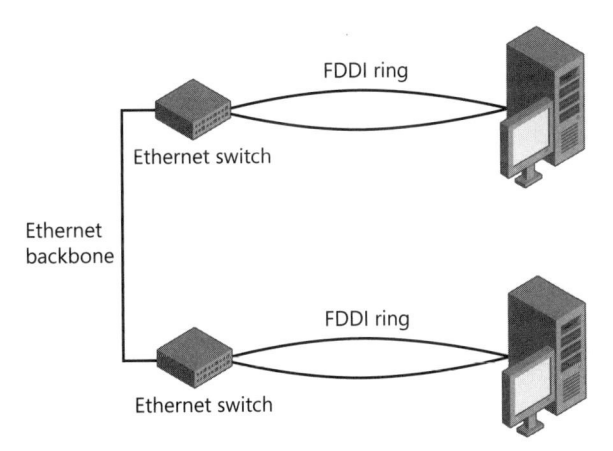

Figure 5-10 An MTU problem in a translational bridging environment caused by two FDDI hosts connected to two Ethernet switches

However, consider the communication between application servers on different FDDI rings. In creating the TCP connection, each server indicates an FDDI-based TCP MSS. Therefore, Ethernet switches silently discard TCP-based IP datagrams sent between servers on different rings that have an IP total length greater than 1500.

The solution to this problem is to manually configure the application servers' IP MTU for the smallest IP MTU of all the links within the translational bridged network.

Using our example, the IP MTU of the application servers on the FDDI rings are set to 1500, so translational bridges can forward IP datagrams between FDDI rings. Changing the application servers' MTU means that when sending packets to application servers on the same ring, the packets are sent at the lower MTU of 1500, a lower efficiency than the default FDDI MTU of 4352. However, it is better to have lower efficiency between servers on the same ring than zero efficiency between servers on different rings. For nodes running Windows Server 2008 or Windows Vista, use the netsh interface ipv4 set interface `InterfaceNameOrIndex mtu= MtuSize` command or the MTU registry value to override the default MTU setting reported by NDIS.

Note FDDI is an older technology whose use has been made obsolete by 100 Mbps Ethernet. This configuration is unlikely on modern networks and serves only as an example of a mixed-media subnet.

Fragmentation and TCP/IP for Windows Server 2008 and Windows Vista

TCP/IP for Windows Server 2008 and Windows Vista supports IP fragmentation and reassembly with the following additional behaviors:

- IP can handle irregular fragments, which overlap either fully or partially, with already received fragments for the same payload.

- When forwarding fragments, IP can forward the individual fragments separately or hold all of the fragments and then send all of them when the last one arrives. The default behavior is to forward individual fragments. You can change this behavior with the `netsh interface ipv4 set global groupforwardedfragments=enabled` command.

- The maximum amount of memory that can be allocated for reassembly for all incoming IP packets is controlled by the `netsh interface ipv4 set global reassemblylimit=MemorySize` command. You can view the current size of the reassembly buffer with the `netsh interface ipv4 show global` command.

IP Options

IP options are additional fields appended to the standard 20-byte IP header. Although IP options are not required on each IP header, the ability to process IP option fields is required. IP options are used infrequently and mostly for network testing purposes.

The IP options portion size of the IP header varies in length based on the IP options that are being used. The individual IP options also vary in length from a single byte to multiple four-byte quantities. Recall that the maximum-sized IP header that can be indicated with the Header Length field is 60 bytes. With a standard IP header size of 20 bytes, 40 bytes are left for IP options.

The first byte of each IP option has the format shown in Figure 5-11.

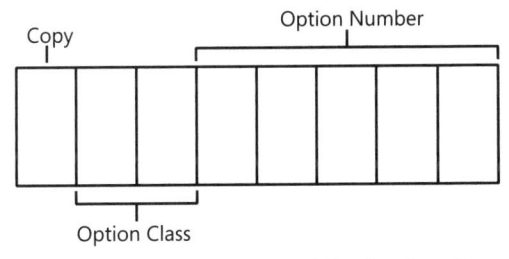

Figure 5-11 The structure of the first byte in an IP option

Copy

The Copy field is 1 bit long and is used when a router or a sending host must fragment the IP datagram. When the Copy field is set to 0, the IP option should be copied only into the first fragment. When the Copy field is set to 1, the IP option should be copied into all fragments.

Option Class

The Option Class field is 2 bits long and is used to indicate the general class of the option. Table 5-6 lists the defined option classes.

Table 5-6   Option Classes

Option Class	Description
0	Network control
1	Reserved for future use
2	Debugging and measurement
3	Reserved for future use

Option Number

The Option Number field is 5 bits long and is used to indicate a specific option within the option class. Each option class can have up to 32 different option numbers.

Table 5-7 lists the defined option classes and numbers for nonmilitary computing.

Table 5-7   Option Classes and Numbers

Option Class	Option Number	Description
0	0	**End Of Option List** A one-byte option used to indicate the end of an option list
0	1	**No Operation** A one-byte option used to align bytes in a list of options

Table 5-7 Option Classes and Numbers

Option Class	Option Number	Description
0	3	**Loose Source Routing** A variable-length option used to route a datagram through a specified path where alternate routes can be taken
0	7	**Record Route** A variable-length option used to trace a route through an IP internetwork
0	9	**Strict Source Routing** A variable-length option used to route a datagram through a specified path where alternate routes cannot be taken
0	20	**IP Router Alert** A fixed-length option used to inform the router that additional processing of the datagram is required
2	4	**Internet Timestamp** A variable-length option used to record a series of timestamps at each hop

End Of Option List

Option Code ▯ = 0

The End Of Option List option is always a single byte in length and is used at the end of the IP options when they do not fall on a 4-byte boundary. This option is used only at the end of all the IP options, not at the end of each option.

No Operation

Option Code ▯ = 1

The No Operation option is always a single byte in length and is used between IP options when an IP option does not fall on a 4-byte boundary.

Record Route

Option Code = 7
Option Length
Next Slot Pointer
First IP Address
Second IP Address
...

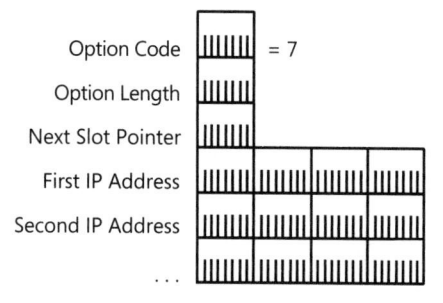

The Record Route option is a variable-length option that is used to record the IP addresses of the far side interfaces of IP routers as it traverses the IP internetwork. The far side interface is the interface on the router on which the IP datagram is forwarded, presumed to be farthest from the sending host.

As the IP datagram is forwarded from router to router, each router adds its IP address to the list; each router also modifies the Next Slot Pointer field. The route from the source host to the destination host is recorded. To get the complete route, there must be enough room in the Record Route option. Unlike Token Ring source routing, the number of IP address slots is specified by the sending host and is fixed in the IP header.

The Record Route option contains the following fields:

- **Option Code**   Set to 7 (Copy Bit=0, Option Class=0, Option Number=7).
- **Option Length**   Set by the sending host to the number of bytes in the Record Route option.
- **Next Slot Pointer**   Set to the byte offset (starting at 1) within the Record Route option of the next available IP address. The minimum value of the Next Slot Pointer field is 4.
- **First IP Address, Second IP Address**   Set to the IP address of the far side interface by routers. With a maximum of 40 bytes in the IP options portion of the IP header, there is enough room for a maximum of nine IP addresses.

Record Route Processing

An IP router receiving an IP datagram with the Record Route option compares the Option Length and Next Slot Pointer fields. If the Next Slot Pointer field is less than the Option Length field, there are open IP address fields. The router records the IP address of the interface that is forwarding the datagram in the next available IP address field; the router also updates the Next Slot Pointer field by adding 4. If the value of the Next Slot Pointer field is greater than the Option Length field, routers have used all of the available IP address fields. The router then forwards the IP datagram without modifying the Record Route option.

Because the Record Route option size is not a multiple of 4 bytes, either an End Of Options option (if there are no more options) or a No Operation option (if there are more options) must be added to ensure that the IP header is an integral multiple of 4 bytes.

Setting the Record Route Option with Ping

The Windows Server 2008 and Windows Vista Ping.exe tool with the -r option can be used to add the Record Route option and set the number of IP address slots in the Record Route option within an ICMP Echo message. The syntax is:

```
ping -r IPAddressSlots Destination
```

For example, to ping 10.0.0.1 with seven IP address slots, use the following command:

```
ping -r 7 10.0.0.1
```

When both hosts are computers running Windows Server 2008 or Windows Vista, the Record Route option records the IP addresses of the far side interfaces of forwarding routers in the ICMP Echo message. When the Echo message is received, the IP addresses recorded are maintained and the Echo Reply message is sent with the same Record Route option. The Echo Reply message contains the recorded route for the Echo message and the recorded route for the Echo Reply message.

Therefore, with the Ping -r option, it is possible to record the far side router interfaces for the Echo message (the path from Host A to Host B) and the far side router interfaces for the Echo Reply message (the path from Host B to Host A). However, because there is only room for nine IP address slots, this is possible only if there are no more than four routers between hosts.

Network Monitor Capture 05-03 (in the \Captures folder on the companion CD-ROM) provides an example of Ping.exe tool traffic and the use of the Record Route option.

Note The Tracert.exe tool does not use the Record Route option.

Strict and Loose Source Routing

The IP routing process at IP routers is performed through a comparison of the destination IP address with entries in a local routing table. Each router makes a forwarding decision. However, it is sometimes necessary to specify a path that an IP datagram is to take regardless of the router's routing table entries. The path is specified before the source host sends the datagram; this is known as *source routing*.

For example, in a multipath IP internetwork (where there is more than one path between IP networks), routers choose the best path based on a lowest cost metric. Once a router determines all of the best paths, the higher cost paths are not used unless the topology of the internetwork changes. To check that higher cost paths contain valid links, you must do source routing.

Source routing in IP is done by specifying the IP addresses of the near side interfaces of the desired routers between the source and its destination. At each leg of the journey, the destination IP address in the IP header is set to the IP address of the next near side router interface. IP supports both loose and strict source routing. In loose source routing, the next router's IP address does not have to be a neighboring router; it can be multiple hops away. In strict source routing, the next router's IP address must be a neighboring router (a single hop away).

IP source routing also records the path taken in the same way as the Record Route option. For each intermediate destination, the IP address of the interface on the router that forwarded the IP datagram is recorded.

> **Note** To use IP source routing, it must be enabled on all the routers in the path between the source and destination hosts. It is a common practice to disable source routing on routers, especially those connected to the Internet.

Strict Source Route Option

```
Option Code       [       ] = 137
Option Length     [       ]
Next Slot Pointer [       ]
First IP Address  [                         ]
Second IP Address [                         ]
              ... [                         ]
```

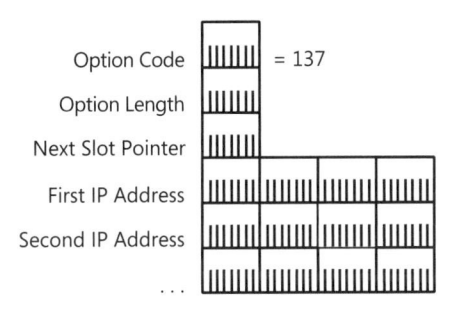

The Strict Source Route option contains the following fields:

- **Option Code**   Set to 137 (Copy Bit=1, Option Class=0, Option Number=9).
- **Option Length**   Set by the sending host to the number of bytes in the Strict Source Route option.
- **Next Slot Pointer**   Set to the byte offset (starting at 1) within the Strict Source Route option for the next router. The Next Slot Pointer field's minimum value is 4. This field is used also in the same manner as the Record Route option to determine the location of the next IP address slot for recording the route.
- **First IP Address, Second IP Address**   Set by the sending host for the series of IP addresses for successive router destinations in the strict source route; set also by IP routers to the IP address of the forwarding interface. With a maximum of 40 bytes in the IP options portion of the IP header, there is enough room for a maximum of nine IP addresses.

When a sending host sends an IP datagram with the Strict Source Route option, the sending host does the following:

1. Sets the Next Slot Pointer field's value to 4.
2. Places the first IP address in the strict source route in the IP header's Destination IP Address field.

When an IP router receives an IP datagram as the destination with the Strict Source Route option, it compares the Option Length and Next Slot Pointer fields. If the Next Slot Pointer field is less than the Option Length field, the router does the following:

1. Adds 4 to the Next Slot Pointer field's value.

2. Replaces the IP header's destination IP address with the IP address that is recorded in the next slot (based on the Next Slot Pointer field's new value).

3. Records the IP address of the forwarding interface in the previous slot.

If the next destination IP address is not reachable using a directly attached network (the IP address of a neighboring router or host), the IP datagram is discarded and an ICMP Destination Unreachable-Source Route Failed message is sent back to the source host.

If the Next Slot Pointer field's value is greater than the Option Length field's value, the IP datagram has reached its final destination.

Because the size of the Strict Source Route option is not a multiple of 4 bytes, either an End Of Options option (if there are no more options) or a No Operation option (if there are more options after the Strict Source Route option) must be added to ensure that the IP header is an integral multiple of 4 bytes. In Windows Server 2008 and Windows Vista, TCP/IP places the Strict Source Route option as the last option in the list and uses an End Of Options option to specify the end of the list of options.

Setting the Strict Source Route Option with Ping

The Windows Server 2008 and Windows Vista Ping.exe tool with the -k option can be used to add the Strict Source Route option. The Ping.exe tool with the -k option also can be used to set the IP addresses of successive routers and the final destination in ICMP Echo messages. The syntax is:

```
ping -k FirstHopIPAddress SecondHopIPAddress … Destination
```

For example, to ping 10.0.0.1 through neighboring router interfaces 192.168.1.1 and 192.168.2.1, use the following command:

```
ping -k 192.168.1.1 192.168.2.1 10.0.0.1
```

Network Monitor Capture 05-04 (in the \Captures folder on the companion CD-ROM) provides an example of Ping.exe tool traffic and the use of the Strict Source Route option.

Loose Source Route Option

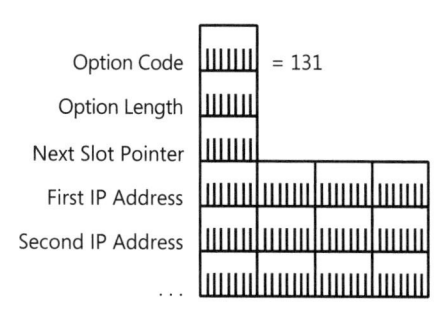

The Loose Source Route option contains the following fields:

- **Option Code**   Set to 131 (Copy Bit=1, Option Class=0, Option Number=3).
- **Option Length**   Set by the sending host to the number of bytes in the Loose Source Route option.
- **Next Slot Pointer**   Set to the byte offset (starting at 1) within the Loose Source Route option for the next router. The Next Slot Pointer field's minimum value is 4. The Next Slot Pointer field also is used in the same manner as the Record Route option to determine the location of the next IP address slot for recording the route.
- **First IP Address, Second IP Address**   Set by the sending host for the series of IP addresses for successive router destinations in the loose source route, and set by IP routers to the forwarding interface's IP address. With a maximum of 40 bytes in the IP options portion of the IP header, there is enough room for a maximum of nine IP addresses.

When a sending host sends an IP datagram with the Loose Source Route option, the sending host does the following:

1. Sets the Next Slot Pointer field's value to 4.
2. Places the first IP address in the loose source route in the IP header's Destination IP Address field.

When an IP router receives an IP datagram as the destination with the Loose Source Route option, it compares the Option Length and Next Slot Pointer fields. If the Next Slot Pointer field's value is less than the Option Length field's value, the router does the following:

1. Adds 4 to the Next Slot Pointer field's value.
2. Replaces the IP header's destination IP address with the IP address that is recorded in the next slot (based on the Next Slot Pointer field's new value).
3. Records the IP address of the forwarding interface in the previous slot.

If the Next Slot Pointer field's value is greater than the Option Length field's value, the IP datagram has reached its final destination.

Because the size of the Loose Source Route option is not a multiple of 4 bytes, either an End Of Options option (if there are no more options) or a No Operation option (if there are more options) must be added to ensure that the IP header is an integral multiple of 4 bytes.

Setting the Loose Source Route Option with Ping

The Windows Server 2008 and Windows Vista Ping.exe tool with the -j option can be used to add the Loose Source Route option. Additionally, it is used to set the IP addresses of successive routers and the final destination in ICMP Echo messages. The syntax is:

```
ping -j FirstHopIPAddress SecondHopIPAddress … Destination
```

For example, to ping 10.0.0.1 through neighboring router interfaces 192.168.1.1 and 192.168.2.1, use the following command:

```
ping -j 192.168.1.1 192.168.2.1 10.0.0.1
```

Network Monitor Capture 05-05 (in the \Captures folder on the companion CD-ROM) provides an example of Ping.exe tool traffic and the use of the Loose Source Route option.

By default, an IP router running Windows Server 2008 or Windows Vista does not forward source-routed IP packets. You can change the behavior of IP for source-routed IP packets with the following command:

```
netsh interface ipv4 set global sourceroutingbehavior=drop|forward|dontforward
```

You can also use the following registry value:

DisableIPSourceRouting
```
Key: HKEY_LOCAL_MACHINE\SYSTEM\CurrentControlSet\Services\Tcpip\Parameters
Value type: REG_DWORD
Valid range: 0 - 2
Default: 1
Present by default: No
```

Set the DisableIPSourceRouting registry value to 0 to forward source-routed packets, to 1 to not forward source-routed packets (for packets being forwarded), or to 2 to drop all incoming source-routed packets (for packets being forwarded and for packets destined to the node).

IP Router Alert

Option Code = 148
Option Length
Value = 0

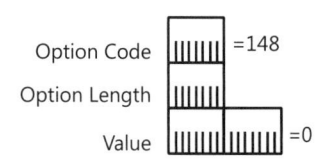

The IP Router Alert option is used to indicate to IP routers that additional processing of the IP datagram is required even when the IP datagram is not addressed to the router. The IP Router Alert option is used for the Resource Reservation Protocol (RSVP), IGMP version 2, and IGMP version 3. For example, when a router receives an IP datagram with the IP Router Alert option, it looks at the IP Protocol field to see if the IP payload requires additional processing before making a forwarding decision. RFC 2113 describes the IP Router Alert option.

The IP Router Alert option contains the following fields:

- **Option Code** Set to 148 (Copy Bit=1, Option Class=0, Option Number=20).
- **Option Length** Set to the fixed length of 4.
- **Value** A 2-byte field set to 0. All other values are reserved. The value of 0 indicates that the router must examine the packet.

Internet Timestamp

```
Option Code       |||||||| =68
Option Length     ||||||||
Next Slot Pointer ||||||||
Overflow          ||||
Flags             ||||
First IP Address  ||||||||||||||||||||||||||||||||
First Timestamp   ||||||||||||||||||||||||||||||||
...               ||||||||||||||||||||||||||||||||
```

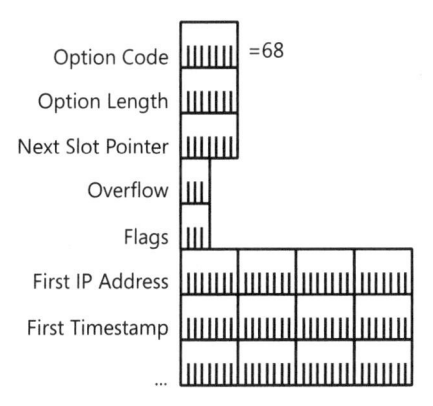

The Internet Timestamp option is used to record the time that an IP datagram arrived at each IP router in the path between the source and destination host. The Internet Timestamp option is similar to the Record Route option in that the sending node creates blank entries in the IP header that routers fill out as the packet travels through the IP internetwork. Each entry consists of the router's IP address and a 32-bit integer timestamp that indicates the number of milliseconds since midnight, Universal Time. If Universal Time is not being used, the high-order bit of the timestamp field is set to 1.

> **Note** To use Internet timestamps, Internet timestamping must be enabled on all the routers in the path between the source and destination hosts. It is common for routers to either not support Internet timestamping or have it disabled.

The Internet Timestamp option contains the following fields:

- **Option Code** Set to 68 (Copy Bit=0, Option Class=2, Option Number=4).
- **Option Length** Set by the sending host to the number of bytes in the Internet Timestamp option.
- **Next Slot Pointer** Set to the byte offset (starting at 1) within the Internet Timestamp option of the next slot for the recording of the IP address and timestamp. The Next Slot Pointer field's minimum value is 5.
- **Overflow** Set by routers to indicate the number of routers that were unable to record their IP address and timestamp.
- **Flags** Set by the sending host to indicate the format of the IP Address/Timestamp slots. When Flags is set to 0, the IP address is omitted. This allows up to nine timestamps to be recorded. When Flags is set to 1, the IP address is recorded, allowing up to four IP address/timestamp pairs to be recorded. The Internet Timestamp option format shown assumes Flags is set to 1. When Flags is set to 3, the sending node specifies the IP

addresses of successive routers: A timestamp is recorded only if the IP address in the slot matches the router's IP address.

- **First IP Address/First Timestamp** Set by routers to record the IP address and timestamp of the routers encountered (when Flags is set to 1) or specified (when Flags is set to 3).

When a sending host sends an IP datagram with the Internet Timestamp option, the sending host does the following:

1. Sets the Next Slot Pointer field's value to 5.
2. For a specified route (when Flags is set to 3), places the series of IP addresses in the Internet Timestamp option.

When an IP router receives an IP datagram with the Internet Timestamp option, it compares the Option Length and Next Slot Pointer fields. If the Next Slot Pointer field's value is less than the Option Length field's value, it does the following:

- If Flags is set to 3, the router replaces the IP header's destination IP address with the IP address that is recorded in the next slot (based on the Next Slot Pointer field).
- If Flags is set to 1 or 3, the router records the IP address of the interface on which the IP datagram was received in the same slot.
- If Flags is set to 0, the router records the timestamp and adds 4 to the Next Slot Pointer field. If Flags is set to 1, the router records the timestamp after the IP address and adds 8 to the Next Slot Pointer field. If Flags is set to 3, the router replaces the IP address and adds 4 to the Next Slot Pointer field.

If the Next Slot Pointer field's value is greater than the Option Length field's value, the router increments the Overflow field. If the Overflow field is 15 before incrementing, an ICMP Parameter Problem is sent back to the source host.

Setting the Internet Timestamp Option with Ping

The Windows Server 2008 and Windows Vista Ping.exe tool and the -s option can be used to send ICMP Echo messages with the Internet timestamp. The syntax is the following:

```
ping -s Slots Destination
```

For example, to ping the IP address of 10.9.1.1 using Internet timestamps with three slots, use the following command:

```
ping -s 3 10.9.1.1
```

Network Monitor Capture 05-06 (in the \Captures folder on the companion CD-ROM) provides an example of Ping.exe tool traffic and the use of the Internet Timestamp option.

Summary

IP provides the internetworking building block for all other Internet Layer and higher protocols in the TCP/IP suite. IP provides a best effort, unreliable, connectionless datagram delivery service between networks of an IP internetwork. The IP header provides addressing, type of delivery, maximum link count, fragmentation, and checksum services. IP fragmentation provides a way for IP datagrams to travel over links with a lower IP MTU than the original IP datagram. The basic services of the IP header are extended through IP options, the most common of which provide source routing, path recording, router alert, and timestamping functions.

Chapter 6
Internet Control Message Protocol (ICMP)

In this chapter:
ICMP Message Structure. 126
ICMP Messages 127
Ping.exe Tool 148
Tracert.exe Tool 150
Pathping.exe Tool 153
Summary. 155

IP provides end-to-end datagram delivery capabilities for IP datagrams. However, IP does not provide any facilities for reporting routing or delivery errors encountered by an IP datagram in its journey from the source to the destination. The Internet Control Message Protocol (ICMP) reports error and control conditions on behalf of IP.

When a protocol encounters an error that cannot be recovered in the processing of a packet, it can do one of the following:

- Discard the offending packet without sending an error notification to the sending host. This is known as a *silent discard*. For example, an Ethernet network adapter checks each Ethernet frame for bit-level errors by performing a checksum and comparing its own result with the Frame Check Sequence value stored in the frame. If the two checksums do not match, the adapter considers the frame invalid and silently discards it.

- Discard the offending packet and send an error notification to the sending host. This is known as an *informed discard*. ICMP provides an informed discard service for specific types of IP routing and delivery errors.

ICMP is an extensible protocol that also provides functions to check IP connectivity and aid in the automatic configuration of hosts.

ICMP does not make IP reliable. There are no facilities within IP or ICMP to provide sequencing or retransmission of IP datagrams that encounter errors. ICMP messages are unreliably sent as IP datagrams, and although ICMP reports an error, there are no requirements for how the sending host treats the error. It is up to the TCP/IP implementation to interpret the error and adjust its behavior accordingly.

ICMP messages are sent only for the first fragment of an IP datagram. ICMP messages are not sent for problems encountered by ICMP error messages or for problems encountered by broadcast or multicast datagrams.

ICMP is defined in RFCs 792, 950, 1812, 1122, 1191, and 1256.

More Info All of the RFCs referenced in this chapter can be found in the \Standards\Chap06_ICMP folder on the companion CD-ROM.

ICMP Message Structure

ICMP messages are sent as IP datagrams. Therefore, an ICMP message consisting of an ICMP header and ICMP message data is encapsulated with an IP header using IP Protocol number 1. The resulting IP datagram is then encapsulated with the appropriate Network Interface Layer header and trailer. Figure 6-1 shows the resulting frame.

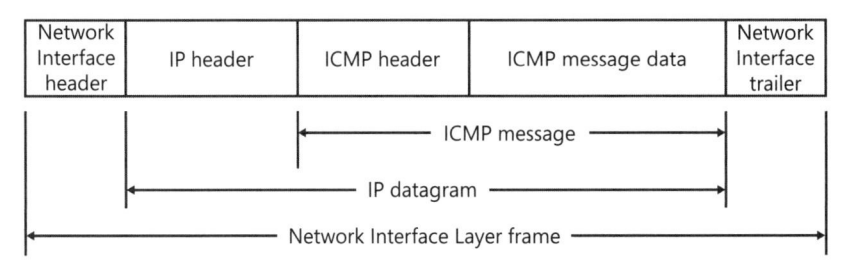

Figure 6-1 ICMP message encapsulation showing the IP header and Network Interface Layer header and trailer

In the IP header of ICMP messages, the Source IP Address field is set to the router or host interface that sent the ICMP message. The Destination IP Address field is set to the sending host of the offending packet (in the case of ICMP error messages), a specific host, an IP broadcast, or IP multicast address. Every ICMP message has the same structure, as Figure 6-2 shows.

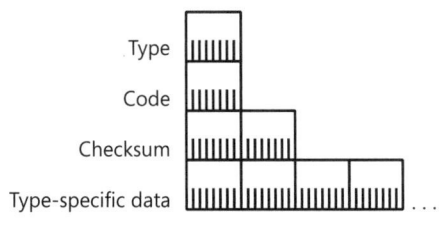

Figure 6-2 The structure of an ICMP message showing the fields common to all types of ICMP messages

The common fields in the ICMP message are defined as follows:

- **Type** A 1-byte field that indicates the type of ICMP message (Echo vs. Echo Reply, and so on). Table 6-1 lists the most commonly used ICMP types.

- **Code** A 1-byte field that indicates a specific ICMP message within an ICMP message type. If there is only one ICMP message within an ICMP type, the Code field is set to 0. The combination of ICMP Type and Code determines a specific ICMP message.
- **Checksum** A 2-byte field for a 16-bit checksum covering the ICMP message. ICMP uses the same checksum algorithm as IP for the IP header checksum.
- **Type-Specific Data** Optional data for each ICMP type.

ICMP Messages

Table 6-1 lists the most commonly used ICMP types.

Table 6-1 Common ICMP Types

ICMP Type	Description
0	Echo Reply
3	Destination Unreachable
4	Source Quench
5	Redirect
8	Echo (also known as an Echo Request)
9	Router Advertisement
10	Router Solicitation
11	Time Exceeded
12	Parameter Problem

For a complete list of ICMP types, see *http://www.iana.org/assignments/icmp-parameters*.

The following sections discuss the ICMP messages supported by TCP/IP for Windows Server 2008 and Windows Vista.

ICMP Echo and Echo Reply

One of the most heavily used ICMP facilities is the ability to send a simple message to an IP node and have the message echoed back to the sender. This facility is useful for network troubleshooting and debugging. The simple message sent is an ICMP Echo, and the message echoed back to the sender is an ICMP Echo Reply. For Windows Server 2008 and Windows Vista, the Ping.exe, Tracert.exe, and Pathping.exe tools use Echo and Echo Reply messages to provide information about reachability and the path taken to reach a destination node. Figure 6-3 shows the ICMP Echo message structure.

The fields in the ICMP Echo message are defined as follows:

- **Type** Set to 8.
- **Code** Set to 0.

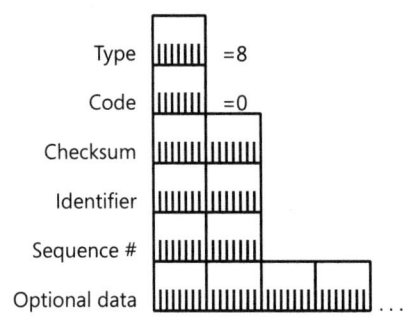

Figure 6-3 The structure of the ICMP Echo message

- **Identifier** A 2-byte field that stores a number generated by the sender that is used to match the ICMP Echo with its corresponding Echo Reply.
- **Sequence Number** A 2-byte field that stores an additional number that is used to match the ICMP Echo with its corresponding Echo Reply. The combination of the values of the Identifier and Sequence Number fields identifies a specific Echo message.
- **Optional Data** Optionally, data can be added at the end of the ICMP packet.

For information on how Windows Server 2008 and Windows Vista determine Identifier, Sequence Number, and Optional Data fields, see the sections "Ping.exe Tool" and "Tracert.exe Tool," later in this chapter.

Frame 1 of the Network Monitor Capture 06-01 (in the \Captures folder on the companion CD-ROM) shows the structure of an ICMP Echo message.

Figure 6-4 shows the ICMP Echo Reply message structure.

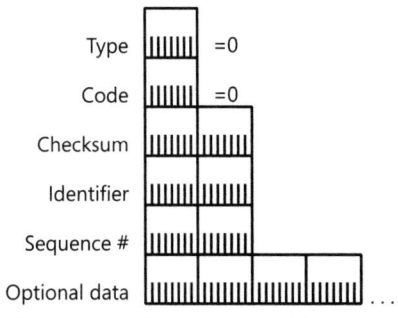

Figure 6-4 The structure of the ICMP Echo Reply message

The fields in the ICMP Echo Reply message are defined as follows:

- **Type** Set to 0.
- **Code** Set to 0.
- **Identifier** Set to the value of the Identifier field of the Echo message being echoed.

- **Sequence Number** Set to the value of the Sequence Number field of the Echo message being echoed.

- **Optional Data** Set to the value of the Optional Data field of the Echo message being echoed.

Echoed in the Echo Reply message are the Identifier, Sequence Number, and Optional Data fields. The host that sent the original Echo message can verify these fields on receipt. If the fields are not correctly echoed, the Echo Reply message can be ignored.

Frame 2 of the Network Monitor Capture 06-01 (in the \Captures folder on the companion CD-ROM) shows the structure of an ICMP Echo Reply message sent in response to an ICMP Echo message.

Sending ICMP Echo messages and receiving ICMP Echo Reply messages checks for the following:

- The host sending the Echo message can forward the Echo message to either the destination (direct delivery) or to a neighboring router (indirect delivery).

- The routing infrastructure between the host sending the Echo message and the destination can forward the Echo message to the destination.

- The host sending the Echo Reply message can forward the Echo Reply message to either the destination (the sender of the Echo message) or to a neighboring router.

- The routing infrastructure between the host sending the Echo Reply message and the destination can forward the Echo Reply message to the destination.

ICMP Destination Unreachable

IP attempts a best-effort delivery of datagrams to their destination. Routing or delivery errors can occur along the path or at the destination. When a routing or delivery error occurs, a router or the destination discards the offending datagram and attempts to report the error by sending an ICMP Destination Unreachable message to the source IP address of the offending packet. Figure 6-5 shows the ICMP Destination Unreachable message structure.

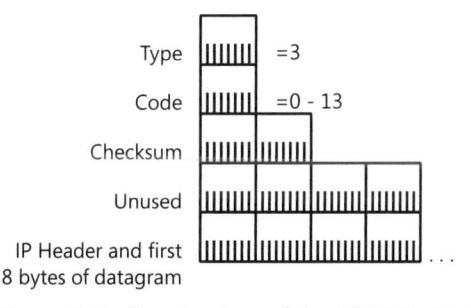

Figure 6-5 The structure of the ICMP Destination Unreachable message

The fields in the ICMP Destination Unreachable message are defined as follows:

- **Type** Set to 3.
- **Code** Set to a value from 0 to 13. Table 6-2 lists and discusses the different ICMP Destination Unreachable Code values.
- **Unused** A 4-byte field that is set to 0.
- **IP Header + First 8 Bytes Of Offending Datagram** To provide meaningful information to the sender of the offending datagram, the ICMP Destination Unreachable message contains the IP header and the first 8 bytes of the discarded datagram. The IP header contains the IP Identification field. For Transmission Control Protocol (TCP) segments, the first 8 bytes of the IP payload contain the source and destination port numbers and the sequence number. For User Datagram Protocol (UDP) messages, the first 8 bytes contain the entire UDP header including the source and destination port numbers.

Table 6-2 Code Values for ICMP Destination Unreachable Messages

Code Value	Meaning
0 – Network Unreachable	Sent by an IP router when a route for the destination IP address cannot be found in the routing table. The source IP address of this message identifies the router that could not find a route. This message is largely obsolete in today's classless Internet due to the inability of the router to determine the subnet prefix (also known as the network ID) of the destination.
1 – Host Unreachable	Sent by an IP router when a route to the destination was not found in the routing table. In today's classless Internet, this is the more appropriate message to send when a router cannot determine the next hop for an IP datagram. This message's source IP address identifies the router that could not deliver the datagram to the destination host.
2 – Protocol Unreachable	Sent by the destination host when the Protocol field in the datagram's IP header does not match a client protocol of IP that is being used by the destination. For example, if a host is sent an Open Shortest Path First (OSPF) packet (IP protocol 89), it sends a Protocol Unreachable message back to the sender.
3 – Port Unreachable	Sent by the destination host when the destination port in the UDP or TCP header does not match an application running on the destination. In practice, however, when TCP ports cannot be found, TCP sends a Connection Reset segment. Therefore, Port Unreachable messages are sent only for UDP messages.
4 – Fragmentation Needed And DF Set	Sent by an IP router when fragmentation is needed to forward the IP datagram but the Don't Fragment (DF) flag is set in the IP header. The Fragmentation Needed And DF Set message is an important part of the Path Maximum Transmission Unit (PMTU) Discovery process discussed in the "PMTU Discovery" section of this chapter. This message's source IP address identifies the router that could not fragment the IP datagram.

Chapter 6: Internet Control Message Protocol (ICMP) **131**

Table 6-2 Code Values for ICMP Destination Unreachable Messages

Code Value	Meaning
5 – Source Route Failed	Sent by an IP router when it cannot forward an IP datagram using information stored in the Source Route option in the IP header. For example, this ICMP Destination Unreachable message is sent if the sending host is using a strict source route and the next router is not directly reachable. The Source Route Failed message contains source route options of the same type as the offending datagram and includes the path back to the sending host. This message's source IP address identifies the router that could not forward the source-routed IP datagram. For more information on IP source routing, see Chapter 5, "Internet Protocol (IP)."
6 – Destination Network Unknown	Sent by an IP router when the destination network for the destination IP address is indicated in the routing table as an unknown network. In practice, the Destination Network Unknown message is obsolete; IP routers send a Host Unreachable message instead.
7 – Destination Host Unknown	Sent by an IP router when the destination host does not exist as detected through Network Interface Layer mechanisms. In practice, the Destination Host Unknown message is sent only when the router cannot deliver to a host that is connected to the router by a point-to-point link. This message's source IP address identifies the router that could not deliver the IP datagram.
8 – Source Host Isolated	A message sent by an IP router when it can detect that the source host is isolated from the rest of the network. This message is obsolete.
9 – Communication with Destination Network Administratively Prohibited	Sent by an IP router when a route to the destination IP address was found but the router cannot forward the IP datagram because of a prohibitive network policy. This message's source IP address identifies the router that could not forward the IP datagram.
10 – Communication with Destination Host Administratively Prohibited	Sent by an IP router when it cannot deliver to the destination host because of a prohibitive network policy. This message's source IP address identifies the router that could not deliver the IP datagram.
11 – Network Unreachable for the Type Of Service (TOS)	Sent by an IP router when a route to the destination IP address indicated in the IP header of the IP Type of Service datagram was not found. Only routers that use the TOS field when forwarding IP datagrams send this message. This message's source IP address identifies the router that could not forward the IP datagram.
12 – Host Unreachable for Type of Service	Sent by an IP router when it cannot deliver to the destination host for the TOS indicated in the IP header of the IP datagram. Only routers that use the TOS field when forwarding IP datagrams send this message. This message's source IP address identifies the router that could not forward the IP datagram.
13 – Communication Administratively Prohibited	Sent by an IP router when it cannot forward or deliver the IP datagram because of administratively configured packet filters on the router. This message's source IP address identifies the router that could not forward or deliver the IP datagram.

Network Monitor Example

Network Monitor Capture 06-02 (in the \Captures folder on the companion CD-ROM) is an example of a Destination Unreachable message. Frame 1 is an ICMP Echo message sent to a private address while on the Internet. Because private addresses are not reachable on the Internet, Frame 2 is the ICMP Destination Unreachable-Host Unreachable message sent by an Internet router.

Frame 1: The ICMP Echo Message

```
Frame:
+ Ethernet: Etype = Internet IP (IPv4)
- Ipv4: Next Protocol = ICMP, Packet ID = 35331, Total IP Length = 60
  + Versions: IPv4, Internet Protocol; Header Length = 20
  + DifferentiatedServicesField: DSCP: 0, ECN: 0
    TotalLength: 60 (0x3C)
    Identification: 35331 (0x8A03)
  + FragmentFlags: 0 (0x0)
    TimeToLive: 32 (0x20)
    NextProtocol: ICMP, 1(0x1)
    Checksum: 9898 (0x26AA)
    SourceAddress: 134.39.89.236
    DestinationAddress: 10.0.0.1
- Icmp: Echo Request Message, From 134.39.89.236 To 10.0.0.1
    Type: Echo Request Message, 8(0x8)
  - EchoReplyRequest:
    Code: 0 (0x0)
    Checksum: 7004 (0x1B5C)
    ID: 256 (0x100)
    SequenceNumber: 12544 (0x3100)
    ImplementationSpecificData: Binary Large Object (32 Bytes)
```

Frame 2: The ICMP Destination Unreachable-Host Unreachable Message

```
Frame:
+ Ethernet: Etype = Internet IP (IPv4)
- Ipv4: Next Protocol = ICMP, Packet ID = 31401, Total IP Length = 56
  + Versions: IPv4, Internet Protocol; Header Length = 20
  + DifferentiatedServicesField: DSCP: 0, ECN: 0
    TotalLength: 56 (0x38)
    Identification: 31401 (0x7AA9)
  + FragmentFlags: 0 (0x0)
    TimeToLive: 252 (0xFC)
    NextProtocol: ICMP, 1(0x1)
    Checksum: 47690 (0xBA4A)
    SourceAddress: 168.156.1.33
    DestinationAddress: 134.39.89.236
- Icmp: Destination Unreachable Message, 134.39.89.236
    Type: Destination Unreachable Message, 3(0x3)
  - DestinationUnreachable:
    Code: Host Unreachable 1(0x1)
    Checksum: 42914 (0xA7A2)
    Unused: 0 (0x0)
   - Data: Next Protocol = ICMP, Packet ID = 35331, Total IP Length = 60
    + Versions: IPv4, Internet Protocol; Header Length = 20
    + DifferentiatedServicesField: DSCP: 0, ECN: 0
```

```
    TotalLength: 60 (0x3C)
    Identification: 35331 (0x8A03)
  + FragmentFlags: 0 (0x0)
    TimeToLive: 28 (0x1C)
    NextProtocol: ICMP, 1(0x1)
    Checksum: 10922 (0x2AAA)
    SourceAddress: 134.39.89.236
    DestinationAddress: 10.0.0.1
    OriginalIPPayload: Binary Large Object (8 Bytes)
```

The ICMP Destination Unreachable-Host Unreachable message contains the discarded version of the IP header and the first 8 bytes (the ICMP header) of Frame 1.

PMTU Discovery

As discussed in Chapter 5, "Internet Protocol (IP)," IP fragmentation is an expensive process for both routers and the destination host and should be avoided. An early solution to avoiding fragmentation was the use of a 576-byte IP maximum transmission unit (MTU) to send data to a location on another network. However, this solution is inefficient; two Ethernet nodes separated by routers send each other 576-byte IP datagrams rather than 1500-byte IP datagrams.

The current solution to avoiding fragmentation is known as PMTU Discovery, and is described in RFC 1191. With PMTU Discovery, hosts send all IP datagrams with the DF flag set to 1. If a router cannot forward an IP datagram onto a link because the datagram's size exceeds the link's MTU, it sends an ICMP Destination Unreachable-Fragmentation Needed And DF Set message (ICMP Type 3, Code 4) back to the sender. Although this has been the behavior since the inception of IP and ICMP, PMTU Discovery support on the router modifies the ICMP message to include the IP MTU of the link onto which the forwarding of the IP datagram failed.

Figure 6-6 shows the modified ICMP Destination Unreachable message. The previous 4-byte Unused field is now a 2-byte Unused field and a 2-byte Next Hop MTU field. The router sets the Next Hop MTU field to the next-hop network segment's IP MTU. After receiving this message, the sending host adjusts the size of the IP datagram to the Next Hop MTU size and retransmits the IP datagram. Sending hosts and all the IP routers in your internetwork must support PMTU.

To discover the initial PMTU, a sending host that supports PMTU sets the initial PMTU to the IP MTU of the directly attached network. The host then sends an IP datagram with the DF flag set to 1 at the PMTU size.

After receipt of an ICMP Destination Unreachable-Fragmentation Needed And DF Set message with the Next Hop MTU indicated, the sending host sets the PMTU to the value of the Next Hop MTU and resends the adjusted IP datagram (if needed).

The PMTU is determined when no more ICMP Destination Unreachable-Fragmentation Needed And DF Set messages are received and the destination is responding.

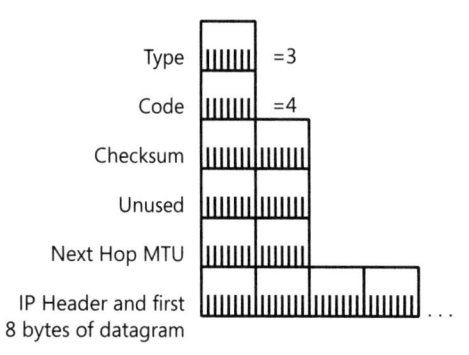

Figure 6-6 A PMTU-compliant ICMP Destination Unreachable-Fragmentation Needed And DF Set message showing the Next Hop MTU field

In Network Monitor Capture 06-03 (in the \Captures folder on the companion CD-ROM), Frame 1 shows an ICMP Echo message with the DF set to 1 and a 1000-byte Optional Data field. This packet is being forwarded across a router interface that supports only a 576-byte IP MTU. Frame 2 is an ICMP Destination Unreachable-Fragmentation Needed And DF Set message indicating the Next Hop MTU of 576.

Adjusting the PMTU

In a single-path internetwork, the PMTU remains the same once discovered. In a multipath internetwork, the PMTU can change based on the paths that the IP datagrams travel because of changing conditions in the routing infrastructure. The PMTU can change to be either higher or lower than the currently known PMTU.

- For a lower PMTU, the sending host is immediately informed through a Destination Unreachable-Fragmentation Needed And DF Set message.

- For a higher PMTU, because there is no mechanism on the routers to inform the sending host that larger datagrams can now be sent, it is up to the host to rediscover the new larger PMTU. If the host's PMTU is smaller than the IP MTU of the locally attached network, the sending host attempts to send larger IP datagrams five minutes after receiving the last ICMP Destination Unreachable-Fragmentation Needed And DF Set message and at one-minute intervals thereafter.

Routers That Do Not Support PMTU

PMTU Discovery relies on PMTU support on the sending host and all of the internetwork's routers. TCP/IP for Windows Server 2008 and Windows Vista supports PMTU Discovery for both hosts and routers. However, what happens when an intermediate router does not support PMTU Discovery?

The lack of support for PMTU Discovery on IP routers can occur on the following two levels:

- The router sends back ICMP Destination Unreachable-Fragmentation Needed And DF Set messages without the Next Hop MTU field.

- The router does not send back ICMP Destination Unreachable-Fragmentation Needed And DF Set messages.

In the first case, the router is not RFC 1191–compliant and according to the sending host, the Destination Unreachable-Fragmentation Needed And DF Set message contains a 0 Next Hop MTU. The sending host assumes that PMTU Discovery is not possible and uses either the minimum PMTU of 576 bytes or a series of diminishing plateau values for the PMTU until Destination Unreachable-Fragmentation Needed And DF Set messages are no longer received. Table 6-3 lists the plateau values, which correspond to the IP MTUs of common Network Interface Layer technologies. PMTU behavior for TCP/IP in Windows Server 2008 and Windows Vista is described later in this chapter.

Table 6-3 Plateau Values for PMTU

Plateau Value	Representing
65,535	Maximum IP MTU
32,000	Just in case
17,914	16-Mbps IBM Token Ring
8166	IEEE 802.4
4352	IEEE 802.5 (4 Mbps) and Fiber Distributed Data Interface (FDDI)
2002	Wideband Network and IEEE 802.5 (4 Mbps)
1492	Ethernet/IEEE 802.3 (Sub-Network Access Protocol [SNAP])
1006	Serial Line Internet Protocol (SLIP)
508	X.25 and Attached Resource Computer Network (ARCnet)
296	Point-to-Point (low delay)
68	Minimum IP MTU

When a router does not send back Destination Unreachable-Fragmentation Needed And DF Set messages, it is called a PMTU black hole router. PMTU black hole routers perform silent discards for datagrams that cannot be fragmented. Because IP is unreliable, it is the responsibility of an upper layer protocol to recover from the discarded packet. For example, TCP segments are retransmitted when their retransmission timer expires.

To successfully detect a PMTU black hole router, discarded packets with the DF flag set to 1 are retransmitted with the DF flag set to 0. If an acknowledgment is received, the TCP maximum segment size (MSS) is lowered to the next lowest plateau value and the DF flag for subsequent IP datagrams is set to 1. This process repeats until the PMTU is found.

PMTU behavior for TCP/IP in Windows Server 2008 and Windows Vista is controlled by the following registry values:

EnablePMTUDiscovery

Location: HKEY_LOCAL_MACHINE\SYSTEM\CurrentControlSet\Services\Tcpip\Parameters
Data type: REG_DWORD
Valid range: 0-1
Default: 1
Present by default: No

When this value is set to 1 (enabled), TCP attempts to discover the PMTU to a remote host. Setting this value to 0 (disabled) causes an MTU of 576 bytes to be used for all connections that are not to destinations on a locally attached subnet. Disabling path MTU discovery is not recommended.

EnablePMTUBHDetect

Location: HKEY_LOCAL_MACHINE\SYSTEM\CurrentControlSet\Services\Tcpip\Parameters
Data type: REG_DWORD
Valid range: 0-1
Default: 1
Present by default: No

EnablePMTUBHDetect enables (when set to 1) or disables (set to 0) PMTU black hole router detection while doing PMTU discovery. When enabled, TCP tries to send segments with the Don't Fragment flag set to 0 when it begins retransmitting full-sized segments with the DF flag set to 1. If the segment is then acknowledged, the TCP MSS for the connection is decreased and the Don't Fragment flag is set to 1 for subsequent segments. Enabling PMTU black hole detection increases the maximum number of retransmissions that are performed for a given segment.

Another problem with PMTU discovery is intermediate routers that drop ICMP messages because of configured packet filtering rules. The result is that TCP connections can time out and terminate because intermediate routers silently discard large TCP segments, their retransmissions, and the ICMP error messages for PMTU discovery. For this reason, PMTU black hole router detection is enabled by default for Windows Server 2008 and Windows Vista.

ICMP Source Quench

When a router becomes congested because of a sudden increase in traffic, a slow link, or inadequate processor and memory resources, the router begins to discard incoming IP datagrams. When a router discards an IP datagram because of congestion, it might send an ICMP Source Quench message back to the sending host. The Source IP Address field of the ICMP Source Quench message identifies the congested router. The destination host can also send ICMP Source Quench messages when IP datagrams are arriving too quickly to be buffered.

RFC 792 does not document the specific implementation details of when a router or destination host sends ICMP Source Quench messages. A router can begin sending Source Quench messages when its memory buffer for storing incoming packets is approaching its maximum capacity, rather than waiting for the buffer to fill. A router does not have to send a Source Quench message for every packet discarded. In fact, RFC 1812 states that routers should not send ICMP Source Quench messages because creating more traffic on a congested internetwork only aggravates the congestion.

The ICMP Source Quench message is an Internet Layer notification. However, the Internet Layer has no mechanism for flow control. IP is unaware of when to increase or decrease its transmission rate. Similarly, UDP has no mechanism for flow control.

TCP is an upper layer protocol that has flow control mechanisms to lower the transmission rate. Therefore, after receipt of the ICMP Source Quench message for a discarded TCP segment, a notification is made to TCP. TCP treats the receipt of the ICMP Source Quench message for a specific TCP segment as a lost TCP segment that needs to be retransmitted. TCP then adjusts its transmission rate for the connection according to the slow start and congestion avoidance algorithms. The sending host gradually increases its transmission rate, giving time for the routers to clear their buffers. For more information, see Chapter 12, "Transmission Control Protocol (TCP) Data Flow." Figure 6-7 shows the ICMP Source Quench message structure.

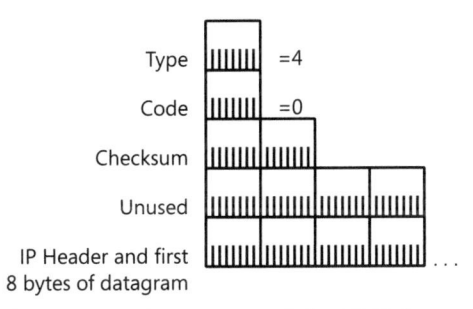

Figure 6-7 The structure of the ICMP Source Quench message

The fields in the ICMP Source Quench message are defined as follows:

- **Type** Set to 4.
- **Code** Set to 0.
- **Unused** A 4-byte field that is set to 0.
- **IP Header + First 8 Bytes Of Discarded Datagram** The ICMP Source Quench message contains the IP header and the first 8 bytes of the discarded datagram.

In Windows Server 2008 and Windows Vista, TCP/IP does not implement TCP flow control if an ICMP Source Quench message is received. When acting as a router, TCP/IP for Windows Server 2008 and Windows Vista does not send ICMP Source Quench messages when the router buffers fill and packets are discarded.

ICMP Redirect

It is common for hosts to have minimal routing tables. A typical host has a route to the locally attached network and a default route corresponding to the host's configured default gateway.

The routers keep all other knowledge of the internetwork's topology—the entire list of reachable address prefixes and the best next-hop IP addresses to reach them. For network segments containing a single router and hosts configured with the IP address of the single router as their default gateway, all routing from hosts to remote networks occurs through the optimal path—the single router.

However, if there are multiple routers on a network segment with hosts configured with a default gateway of a single router, the possibility exists for nonoptimal routing. Consider the IP internetwork in Figure 6-8.

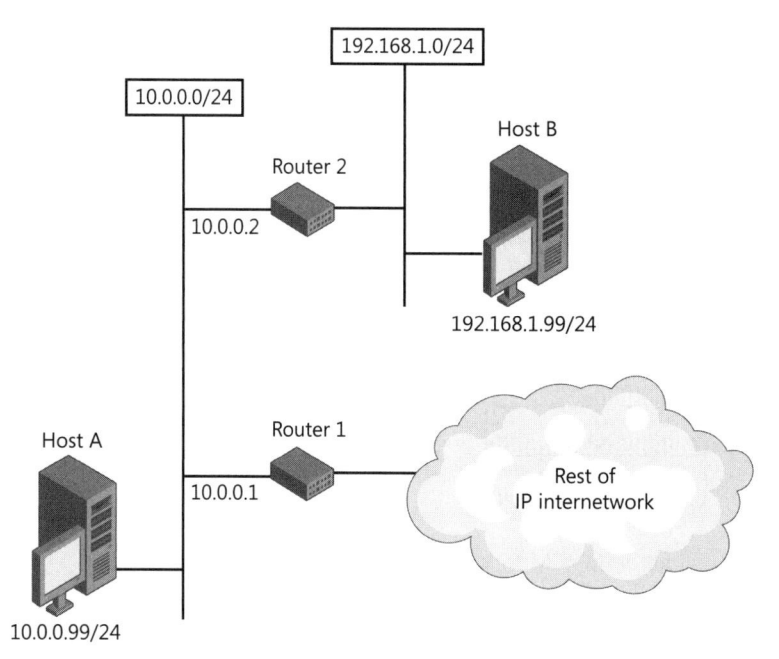

Figure 6-8 An ICMP Redirect scenario in which a host with a configured default gateway must forward an IP datagram using another router

Host A, 10.0.0.99/24, is configured with the default gateway of 10.0.0.1. Host A sends an IP datagram to Host B at 192.168.1.99. Router 1 is attached to network 10.0.0.0/24 and the rest of the IP internetwork. Router 2 is attached to network 10.0.0.0/24 and 192.168.1.0/24. According to the default route in Host A's IP routing table, the next-hop address to reach the destination 192.168.1.99 is 10.0.0.1. This is not the optimal path, however. For the optimal path, the datagram must be forwarded to 10.0.0.2.

To inform Host A of the more optimal route for traffic to Host B at 192.168.1.99, Router 1 uses an ICMP Redirect message. Host A uses the contents of the ICMP Redirect message to create a host route in its routing table so that subsequent IP datagrams to Host B take the more optimal route through Router 2 at 10.0.0.2.

The following is the ICMP Redirect process in detail:

1. Host A forwards the IP datagram destined for Host B to its default gateway, Router 1, at the IP address of 10.0.0.1.
2. Router 1 receives the IP datagram. Because the IP datagram is not destined for an IP address assigned to Router 1, Router 1 checks the contents of its routing table for a route to Host B. A route is found for 192.168.1.0/24 at the next-hop IP address of 10.0.0.2.
3. Before forwarding the IP datagram to Router 2 at 10.0.0.2, Router 1 notices that the sending host's IP address, the IP address of the interface on which the IP datagram was received, and the next-hop IP address are all on the same network, 10.0.0.0/24.
4. Router 1 forwards the IP datagram to Router 2.
5. Router 1 sends an ICMP Redirect message to Host A. The Redirect message contains the next-hop IP address for Router 2, 10.0.0.2, and the IP header of the discarded IP datagram.
6. Based on the contents of the Redirect message, Host A creates a host route for the IP address of Host B, 192.168.1.99, at the next-hop IP address of 10.0.0.2.
7. Subsequent packets from Host A to Host B are forwarded to Router 2 at the IP address of 10.0.0.2.

ICMP Redirect messages are never sent for IP datagrams using source route options. The presence of source route options means that a specific path must be followed without regard to whether it is optimal. Source route options are sometimes used to test connectivity along non-optimal paths.

Figure 6-9 shows the ICMP Redirect message structure.

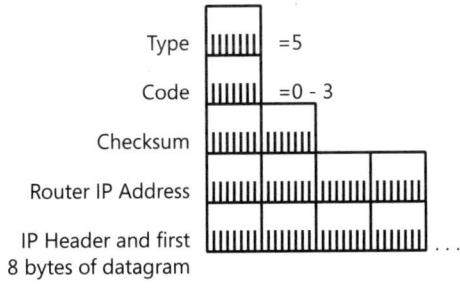

```
Type                =5
Code                =0 - 3
Checksum
Router IP Address
IP Header and first
8 bytes of datagram
```

Figure 6-9 The structure of the ICMP Redirect message

The fields in the ICMP Redirect message are defined as follows:

- **Type** Set to 5.
- **Code** Set to 0–3 (see Table 6-4).

- **Router IP Address**   A 4-byte field set to the next-hop IP address for the more optimal route to the destination of the offending IP datagram. This IP address becomes the next-hop address for the host route created in the IP routing table.

- **IP Header + First 8 Bytes Of Forwarded Datagram**   To identify the forwarded IP datagram, the IP header and the first 8 bytes of the IP payload are encapsulated and sent back to the sending host. Included in the encapsulated IP header is the destination IP address for the host route.

Table 6-4   Values of the Code Field in an ICMP Redirect Message

Code Value	Meaning
0	Redirected datagrams for the network (obsolete)
1	Redirected datagrams for the host
2	Redirected datagrams for the TOS and the network
3	Redirected datagrams for the TOS and the host

> **Note**   ICMP Redirect messages are sent only when the sending host forwards an IP datagram using a nonoptimal route. ICMP Redirect messages are never sent when routers forward IP datagrams using nonoptimal routes.

Network Monitor Capture 06-04 (in the \Captures folder on the companion CD-ROM) shows an ICMP Echo message and the ICMP Redirect message for the example previously discussed.

Rather than adding a host route to the IP routing table, IP in Windows Server 2008 and Windows Vista updates the route cache entry (RCE) for the destination with the Router IP Address field as the next-hop address. The route cache stores the next-hop IP address for a destination address, as determined by an initial routing table lookup. When sending a packet, IP checks the route cache first, before performing a routing table lookup.

In Windows Server 2008 and Windows Vista, TCP/IP behavior for ICMP Redirect messages can be controlled by the `netsh interface ipv4 set global icmpredirects=enabled|disabled` command. By default, support for ICMP Redirect messages is enabled. When enabled, when a host running TCP/IP for Windows Server 2008 and Windows Vista receives an ICMP Redirect message, it first checks the source IP address to ensure that it was sent from the router indicated by the Gateway column for the route to the destination in the IP routing table. TCP/IP for Windows Server 2008 and Windows Vista also ensures that the source IP address of the ICMP Redirect is directly reachable. If the ICMP Redirect did not come from the directly reachable indicated router, the ICMP Redirect is ignored.

You can also use the following registry value:

EnableICMPRedirect
```
Location: HKEY_LOCAL_MACHINE\SYSTEM\CurrentControlSet\Services\Tcpip\Parameters
Data type: REG_DWORD
Valid range: 0-1
```

```
Default: 1
Present by default: Yes
```

EnableICMPRedirect enables (when set to 1) and disables (when set to 0) the updating of RCEs when an ICMP Redirect message is received. EnableICMPRedirect is enabled by default.

ICMP Router Discovery

ICMP Router Discovery is a set of ICMP messages documented in RFC 1256 that are used by routers to advertise their presence and by hosts to discover their network segment's routers, and choose which router will be the host's default gateway. ICMP Router Discovery provides a fault-tolerance mechanism for downed routers. Hosts eventually realize that their current default gateway has become unavailable and switch their default gateway to the next most preferred router.

ICMP Router Discovery uses the following two different ICMP messages:

- **ICMP Router Advertisement** The ICMP Router Advertisement message is sent pseudo-periodically (at a random interval between a minimum and maximum value) by a router to advertise its continued existence, a preference level, and a time after which it can be considered unavailable.

- **ICMP Router Solicitation** Hosts send an ICMP Router Solicitation message whenever they need to discover the most preferred router to use as their default gateway. ICMP Router Discovery–capable hosts that have not been configured with a default gateway send an ICMP Router Solicitation message on startup. Additionally, hosts send an ICMP Router Solicitation message when the availability time of their current default gateway (discovered through ICMP Router Discovery) expires.

ICMP Router Discovery is not a routing protocol; it provides information only on a preferred default gateway for hosts on a network segment. ICMP Router Discovery does not provide any information on address prefixes or optimal paths.

ICMP Router Advertisement

Routers send the ICMP Router Advertisement message to either the all-hosts multicast IP address (224.0.0.1), the subnet (or network) broadcast address, or the limited broadcast address. ICMP Router Advertisements are sent pseudo-periodically and in response to an ICMP Router Solicitation. The default interval for ICMP Router Advertisements is between 7 and 10 minutes. The Routing and Remote Access service implementation of ICMP Router Discovery sends ICMP Router Advertisements to the all-hosts multicast IP address. Figure 6-10 shows the ICMP Router Advertisement message structure.

The fields in the ICMP Router Advertisement message are defined as follows:

- **Type** Set to 9.
- **Code** Set to 0.

```
              Type  ||||||||  =9
              Code  ||||||||  =0
          Checksum  ||||||||||||||||
Number of Addresses ||||||||
 Address Entry Size ||||||||  =2
           Lifetime ||||||||||||||||
   Router IP Address 1 ||||||||||||||||||||||||||||||||
    Preference Level 1 ||||||||||||||||||||||||||||||||
                ...
   Router IP Address n ||||||||||||||||||||||||||||||||
    Preference Level n ||||||||||||||||||||||||||||||||
```

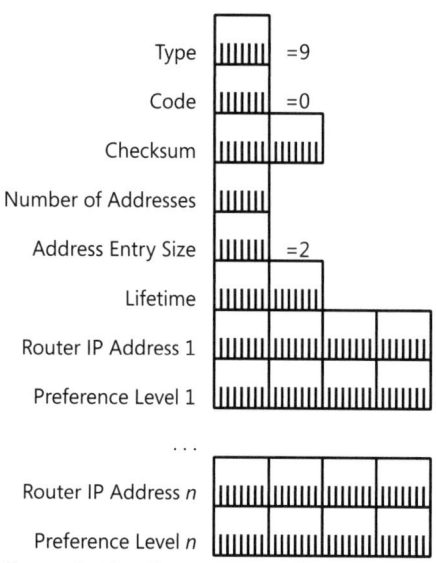

Figure 6-10 The structure of the ICMP Router Advertisement message

- **Number Of Addresses** A 1-byte field that indicates how many IP addresses are being advertised. Normally, only a single IP address is advertised. For a router with multiple interfaces on the same network segment, multiple IP addresses are advertised.

- **Address Entry Size** A 1-byte field that indicates how many 32-bit words (4-byte quantities) are contained in a Router Advertisement entry. A Router Advertisement entry consists of an IP address (32 bits) and a preference level (32 bits). Therefore, the Address Entry Size field is always set to 2.

- **Lifetime** A 2-byte field that indicates the time in seconds after the last received Router Advertisement that the router can be considered down. This is equivalent to the Dead Interval for the OSPF routing protocol.

- **Router IP Address** A 4-byte field that indicates the IP address of the network segment's router interface on which the advertisement was sent.

- **Preference Level** A 4-byte field that indicates the level of preference for using the Router Address as the IP address of your default gateway. The router advertising the highest preference level is the most preferred router. If there are two or more routers with the same preference level, the router with the numerically smallest router address becomes the default gateway. Router Advertisement behavior for the Routing and Remote Access service is configured per interface through the properties of an interface in the IPv4\General node in the Routing and Remote Access snap-in.

ICMP Router Solicitation

Hosts send the ICMP Router Solicitation message to the all-routers multicast IP address (224.0.0.2), the subnet (or network) broadcast address, or the limited broadcast address.

TCP/IP for Windows Server 2008 and Windows Vista listens for ICMP Router Advertisements that are sent to the all-hosts multicast address of 224.0.0.1 and sends up to three ICMP Router Solicitation messages spaced 600 milliseconds apart to the all-routers multicast IP address. Figure 6-11 shows the ICMP Router Solicitation message structure.

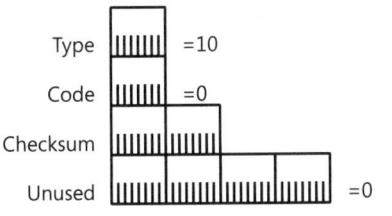

```
Type       ||||||  =10
Code       ||||||  =0
Checksum   ||||||||||||
Unused     |||||||||||||||||||||||||  =0
```

Figure 6-11 The structure of the ICMP Router Solicitation message

The fields in the ICMP Router Solicitation message are defined as follows:

- **Type** Set to 10.
- **Code** Set to 0.
- **Reserved** A 4-byte field that is set to 0

In Windows Server 2008 and Windows Vista, you can control TCP/IP host Router Discovery behavior with the following command:

```
netsh interface ipv4 set interface InterfaceNameOrIndex
routerdiscovery=enabled|disabled|dhcp
```

With the **dhcp** option (the default), Router Discovery is disabled but can be enabled if the computer is a Dynamic Host Configuration Protocol (DHCP) client and the Perform Router Discovery option (option code 31) is sent by the DHCP server.

You can also use the following registry value:

PerformRouterDiscovery
```
Location: HKEY_LOCAL_MACHINE\SYSTEM\CurrentControlSet\Services\ Tcpip\Parameters\Interfaces\
InterfaceGUID
Data type: REG_DWORD
Valid range: 0-2
Default: 2
Present by default: No
```

Set the PerformRouterDiscovery registry value to 0 to disable Router Discovery, to 1 to enable Router Discovery, or to 2 to enable based on the Perform Router Discovery option (option code 31) sent by the DHCP server.

The following registry value controls how TCP/IP in Windows Server 2008 and Windows Vista sends ICMP Router Solicitation messages.

SolicitationAddressBCast
Location: `HKEY_LOCAL_MACHINE\SYSTEM\CurrentControlSet\Services\Tcpip\Parameters\Interfaces\`*InterfaceGUID*
Data type: `REG_DWORD`
Valid range: 0-1
Default: 0 (disabled)
Present by default: No

SolicitationAddressBCast enables (when set to 1) or disables (when set to 0) the use of the subnet (or network) broadcast address as the destination IP address of ICMP Router Solicitation messages. When disabled (the default), TCP/IP for Windows Server 2008 and Windows Vista uses the all-routers IP multicast address (224.0.0.2).

ICMP Time Exceeded

The ICMP Time Exceeded message is sent in the following instances:

- When a router decrements the IP header's TTL field to 0 (the ICMP Time Exceeded-TTL Exceeded in Transit message)

- When the reassembly timer for a fragmented IP datagram expires (the ICMP Time Exceeded-Fragment Reassembly Time Exceeded message)

When the TTL goes to 0 for an IP datagram, it can mean one of two things:

- The IP datagram was sent with an inadequate TTL that does not reflect the current number of links between the source and destination nodes. In this case, the TTL should be increased.

- A routing loop exists in the internetwork. A routing loop occurs when IP routers have incorrect routing information and forward an IP datagram in a loop that never reaches the destination. To test for a routing loop, send an IP datagram with a TTL of 255, the maximum value. If an ICMP Time Exceeded-TTL Exceeded in Transit message is still received, a routing loop exists in your internetwork.

Destination hosts receiving a fragmented IP datagram use a reassembly timer as a maximum time to wait before discarding the incomplete IP datagram. If all of an IP datagram's fragments arrive within the time allotted in the reassembly timer, the IP datagram is successfully reassembled. If the reassembly timer expires before all of an IP datagram's fragments have been received, the destination host discards the incomplete payload and can send an ICMP Time Exceeded-Fragment Reassembly Time Exceeded message back to the source. Figure 6-12 shows the ICMP Time Exceeded message structure.

The fields in the ICMP Time Exceeded message are defined as follows:

- **Type** Set to 11.

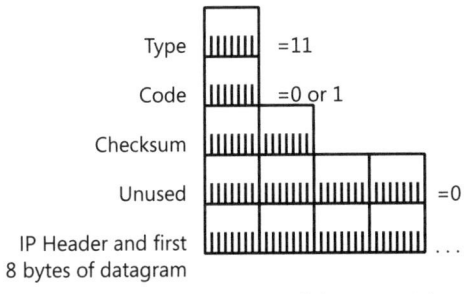

```
         Type  ▏▏▏▏▏▏▏  =11
         Code  ▏▏▏▏▏▏▏  =0 or 1
     Checksum  ▏▏▏▏▏▏▏▏▏▏▏▏▏▏
       Unused  ▏▏▏▏▏▏▏▏▏▏▏▏▏▏▏▏▏▏▏▏▏▏▏▏▏▏▏▏  =0
IP Header and first ▏▏▏▏▏▏▏▏▏▏▏▏▏▏▏▏▏▏▏▏▏▏▏▏▏▏▏▏ ...
8 bytes of datagram
```

Figure 6-12 The structure of the ICMP Time Exceeded message

- **Code** Set to 0 or 1. Set to 0 by a router to indicate a TTL expiration (the ICMP Time Exceeded-TTL Exceeded in Transit message). Set to 1 by a destination host to indicate a reassembly expiration (the ICMP Time Exceeded-Fragment Reassembly Time Exceeded message).
- **Unused** A 4-byte field that is set to 0.
- **IP Header + First 8 Bytes Of Discarded Datagram** To identify the discarded IP datagram, the ICMP Time Exceeded message contains the IP header and the first 8 bytes of the IP payload.

Network Monitor Capture 06-05 (in the \Captures folder on the companion CD-ROM) shows an ICMP Echo message from an Internet host sent to an Internet Web site with an insufficient TTL.

ICMP Parameter Problem

A router or a destination host sends an ICMP Parameter Problem message when an error occurs in the processing of the IP header that causes the IP datagram to be discarded, and there are no other ICMP messages that can be used to indicate the error. ICMP Parameter Problem messages can be sent because of errors in TCP/IP implementations causing incorrect formatting of IP header fields. Typically, ICMP Parameter Problem messages are sent because of incorrect arguments in IP option fields. Figure 6-13 shows the ICMP Parameter Problem message structure.

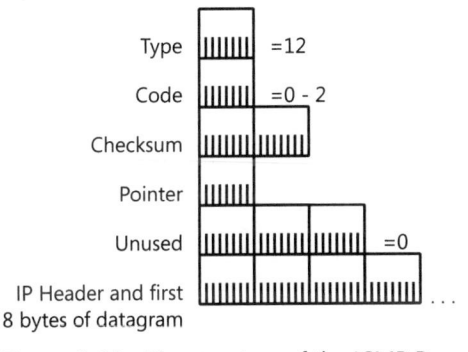

```
         Type  ▏▏▏▏▏▏▏  =12
         Code  ▏▏▏▏▏▏▏  =0 - 2
     Checksum  ▏▏▏▏▏▏▏▏▏▏▏▏▏▏
      Pointer  ▏▏▏▏▏▏▏
       Unused  ▏▏▏▏▏▏▏▏▏▏▏▏▏▏▏▏▏▏▏▏▏  =0
IP Header and first ▏▏▏▏▏▏▏▏▏▏▏▏▏▏▏▏▏▏▏▏▏▏▏▏▏▏▏▏ ...
8 bytes of datagram
```

Figure 6-13 The structure of the ICMP Parameter Problem message

The fields in the ICMP Parameter Problem message are defined as follows:

- **Type** Set to 12.
- **Code** Set to 0–2. See Table 6-5.
- **Pointer** A 1-byte field set to the byte offset (starting at 0) in the encapsulated IP header where the error was detected (applies only to Parameter Problem messages with the Code field set to 0).
- **Unused** A 3-byte field that is set to 0.
- **IP Header + First 8 Bytes Of Discarded Datagram** To identify the discarded IP datagram, the ICMP Parameter Problem message contains the IP header and the first 8 bytes of the IP payload.

Table 6-5 ICMP Parameter Problem Code Values

Code Value	Meaning
0	Pointer indicates error
1	Missing a required option
2	Bad length

Note ICMP Parameter Problem messages are never sent for IP datagrams with an invalid checksum. IP datagrams that fail the checksum are silently discarded.

ICMP Address Mask Request and Address Mask Reply

The ICMP Address Mask Request and Address Mask Reply messages were introduced in RFC 950 as a method for an IP node to discover its subnet mask. When subnetting, a class-based subnet mask based on the first three bits of the IP address can no longer be assumed. An IP node can send an ICMP Address Mask Request as directed traffic to a known router or as a broadcast using either the all-subnets-directed broadcast or the limited broadcast IP address. If an IP node does not know its IP address, it can send the ICMP Address Mask Request with a source IP address of 0.0.0.0. The subsequent ICMP Address Mask Reply must then be sent as a broadcast.

The ICMP Address Mask Reply is sent by a router and contains the 32-bit subnet mask for the network segment on which the Address Mask Request was received. If no Address Mask Reply is received, the IP node assumes a class-based subnet mask.

The ICMP Address Mask Request and Address Mask Reply messages have the structure shown in Figure 6-14.

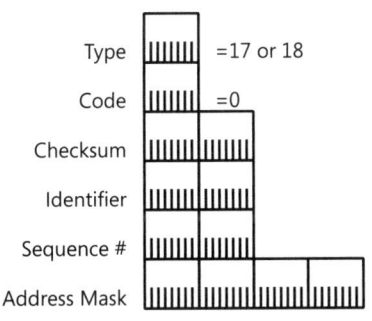

```
     Type    ||||||||   =17 or 18
     Code    ||||||||   =0
 Checksum    ||||||||||||||||
  Identifier ||||||||||||||||
 Sequence #  ||||||||||||||||
Address Mask ||||||||||||||||||||||||||||||||
```

Figure 6-14 The structure of the ICMP Address Mask Request and Reply messages

The fields in the ICMP Address Mask Request and Address Mask Reply messages are defined as follows:

- **Type**   Set to 17 for the Address Mask Request and 18 for the Address Mask Reply.
- **Code**   Set to 0.
- **Identifier**   Optionally used to match an Address Mask Reply with its original Address Mask Request.
- **Sequence Number**   Also optionally used to match an Address Mask Reply with its original Address Mask Request.
- **Address Mask**   The 32-bit subnet mask corresponding to the IP host's network or subnet. The Address Mask field is set to 0.0.0.0 in the Address Mask Request and to the 32-bit subnet mask of the network segment in the Address Mask Reply.

In TCP/IP for Windows Server 2008 and Windows Vista, you can control ICMP Address Mask Reply message behavior with the following command:

```
netsh interface ipv4 set global addressmaskreply=enabled|disabled
```

This command enables or disables the sending of an Address Mask Reply message after the receipt of an Address Mask Request message. By default, the sending of Address Mask Reply messages is disabled.

You can also use the following registry value:

EnableAddrMaskReply
```
Location: HKEY_LOCAL_MACHINE\SYSTEM\CurrentControlSet\Services\ Tcpip\Parameters
Data type: REG_DWORD
Valid range: 0-1
Default: 0
Present by default: No
```

Set EnableAddrMaskReply to 1 to enable and to 0 to disable.

Ping.exe Tool

The Ping.exe command-line tool for Windows Server 2008 and Windows Vista is the primary network tool for troubleshooting IP connectivity. The Ping tool tests reachability, name resolution, source routing, network latency, and other issues for both IP version 4 (IPv4) and IP version 6 (IPv6). For IPv4, Ping sends an ICMP Echo message to a specified destination and records the round-trip time, the number of bytes sent, and the corresponding Echo Reply's TTL. When Ping finishes sending ICMP Echo messages, it displays statistics on the average number of replies and round-trip time. For IPv6, Ping works the same way and performs the same functions only using Internet Control Message Protocol version 6 (ICMPv6) Echo Request messages.

When you ping an IPv4 destination address, the default behavior is to send four fragmentable, non-source-routed ICMP Echo messages with an Optional Data field of 32 bytes and wait four seconds for the corresponding ICMP Echo Reply. When you ping a name, Windows name resolution mechanisms resolve the name to an IPv4 or IPv6 address before the ICMP Echo or ICMPv6 Echo Request messages are sent. If TCP/IP for Windows Server 2008 and Windows Vista is unable to resolve the name to an address, the Ping tool displays an error message. If a corresponding Echo Reply is not received within four seconds (and no other ICMP error messages are received), Ping displays the error message "Request Timed Out."

In the ICMP header of Ping-generated ICMP Echo messages in Windows Server 2008 and Windows Vista:

- The Identifier field is set to 1.
- The Sequence Number field uses an internal counter and is incremented by 1 for subsequent Echo messages.
- The Optional Data field is 32 bytes (by default), consisting of the string "abcdefghijklmnopqrstuvwabcdefghi."

Ping Options

Table 6-6 lists the use and default values of Ping tool options.

Table 6-6 **Ping Tool Options**

Option	Use	Default
-t	Sends Echo messages until interrupted.	Not used
-a	Performs a Domain Name System (DNS) reverse query to resolve the DNS host name of the specified address.	Not used
-n *count*	The number of Echo messages to send.	4
-l *size*	The size of the Optional Data field up to a maximum of 65,500.	32

Table 6-6 Ping Tool Options

Option	Use	Default
-f	Sets the DF flag to 1. This option is only valid for IPv4 traffic.	Not used
-i *TTL*	Sets the value of the TTL field in the IPv4 header or the Hop Limit field in the IPv6 header.	128
-v *TOS*	Sets the value of the TOS field in the IPv4 header. The TOS value is in decimal notation. This option is only valid for IPv4 traffic.	0
-r *count*	Sends the ICMP Echo messages using the IP Record Route option and sets the value of the number of slots. Count has a maximum value of 9. This option is only valid for IPv4 traffic.	Not used
-s *count*	Sends the ICMP Echo messages using the IP Internet Timestamp option and sets the value of the number of slots. Count has a maximum value of 4. In Windows Server 2008 and Windows Vista, Ping uses the Internet Timestamp flag set to 1 (records both the IP addresses of each hop and the timestamp). This option is only valid for IPv4 traffic.	Not used
-j *host-list*	Sends the ICMP Echo messages using the Loose Source Route option and sets the next-hop addresses to the IP addresses in the host list. The host list is made up of IP addresses separated by spaces corresponding to the loose source route. There can be up to nine IP addresses in the host list. This option is valid only for IPv4 traffic.	Not used
-k *host-list*	Sends the ICMP Echo messages using the Strict Source Route option and sets the next-hop addresses to the IP addresses in the host list. The host list is made of IP addresses separated by spaces corresponding to the strict source route. There can be up to nine IP addresses in the host list. This option is only valid for IPv4 traffic	Not used
-w *timeout*	Waits the specified amount of time, in milliseconds, for the corresponding Echo Reply before displaying a Request Timed Out message.	4000
-R	Forces Ping to trace the round-trip path by sending the ICMPv6 Echo Request message to the destination and including an IPv6 Routing extension header with the next destination of the sending node. This option is only valid for IPv6 traffic.	Not used
-S *sourceaddr*	Forces Ping to use a specified source address. This option is only valid for IPv6 traffic.	Not used
-4	Forces Ping to use an IPv4 address when the DNS name query for a host name returns both IPv4 and IPv6 addresses.	Not used
-6	Forces Ping to use an IPv6 address when the DNS name query for a host name returns both IPv4 and IPv6 addresses.	Not used

Note For more information about the Record Route, Strict Source Route, Loose Source Route, and Internet Timestamps IP header options, see Chapter 5.

Network Monitor Example

Network Monitor Capture 06-01 (in the \Captures folder on the companion CD-ROM) is an example of a typical use of the Ping tool to ping a destination IPv4 address. Four ICMP Echo messages are sent and four ICMP Echo Reply messages are received. The following is a summary of Capture 06-01.

```
Frame  Source          Destination     Protocol    Description
1      157.59.11.19    157.59.8.1      ICMPICMP    Echo Request
2      157.59.8.1      157.59.11.19    ICMPICMP    Time Reply
3      157.59.11.19    157.59.8.1      ICMPICMP    Echo Request
4      157.59.8.1      157.59.11.19    ICMPICMP    Time Reply
5      157.59.11.19    157.59.8.1      ICMPICMP    Echo Request
6      157.59.8.1      157.59.11.19    ICMPICMP    Time Reply
7      157.59.11.19    157.59.8.1      ICMPICMP    Echo Request
8      157.59.8.1      157.59.11.19    ICMPICMP    Time Reply
```

Tracert.exe Tool

The Tracert.exe tool uses ICMP Echo or ICMPv6 Echo Request messages to determine the path—the series of routers—that unicast IPv4 and IPv6 traffic takes from a source host to a destination host. Tracert tests reachability, name resolution, network latency, routing loops, and other issues.

When you tracert a destination IP address, the default behavior is to trace the route and report the round-trip time, the near-side router IP address, and the DNS name corresponding to the near-side router IP address. When you tracert a name, normal name resolution techniques resolve the name to an IP address before the ICMP Echo messages are sent. If TCP/IP for Windows Server 2008 and Windows Vista is unable to resolve the name to an IP address, the Tracert tool displays an error message.

Tracert for IPv4 destinations works in the following manner:

1. An ICMP Echo message is sent to the destination with the TTL in the IP header set to 1. If the destination is on a directly attached network, the destination responds with a corresponding Echo Reply message and Tracert is done.

2. If the destination is not in a directly attached network, the ICMP Echo message is forwarded to an IP router.

3. The IP router determines that the IP datagram is transit traffic (not destined for the router) and decrements the TTL. Because the TTL is now 0, the IP router discards the IP datagram and sends back an ICMP Time Exceeded-TTL Exceeded in Transit message to the sending host with the source IP address set to the IP address of the interface on which the ICMP Echo message was received. The interface on which the ICMP Echo message was received is the near-side interface, the interface that is the smallest number of hops from the sending host.

4. After receipt of the ICMP Time Exceeded-TTL Exceeded in Transit message, the Tracert tool records the round-trip time and the source IP address.

5. Tracert sends two more ICMP Echo messages and records their round-trip time.

6. An ICMP Echo message is sent to the destination with the IP header's TTL set to 2. The Echo is forwarded to a neighboring IP router.

7. The neighboring IP router determines that the IP datagram is transit traffic, decrements the TTL to 1, and forwards it to the next hop or the final destination.

8. If the destination is on a directly attached network, the destination responds with a corresponding Echo Reply and Tracert is done.

9. If the destination is not on a directly attached network, the IP router determines that the IP datagram is transit traffic and decrements the TTL. Because the TTL is now 0, the IP router discards the IP datagram and sends back an ICMP Time Exceeded-TTL Exceeded in Transit message to the sending host with the source IP address set to the IP address of the interface on which the ICMP Echo was received. The interface on which the ICMP Echo was received is the near-side interface, the interface that is the smallest number of hops from the sending host.

10. After receipt of the ICMP Time Exceeded-TTL Exceeded in Transit message, the Tracert tool records the round-trip time and the source IP address.

11. Tracert sends two more ICMP Echo messages and records their round-trip time.

The process of incrementing the TTL and sending three ICMP Echo messages continues until the destination is reached and replies with ICMP Echo Reply messages.

The Tracert tool records the series of near-side router interfaces in the path from the sending host to a destination. By default, Tracert also performs a DNS reverse query on each near-side router interface and displays the host name corresponding to the IP address. You can prevent this behavior and speed up the completion of Tracert by using the -d option.

Note If a router silently discards packets with an expired TTL, Tracert shows a series of * characters for that hop. If ICMP packet filtering is occurring on a near-side router interface, that router and all subsequent routers show the * character until 30 hops are attempted (the default).

Network Monitor Example

Network Monitor Capture 06-06 (in the \Captures folder on the companion CD-ROM) is an example of a typical use of the Tracert tool to trace the route to a destination IP address. In this capture, Tracert is used to trace the path across two routers, and the -d option is used to simplify the process and the display. The following is a summary of Capture 06-06.

Frame	Source	Destination	Protocol	Description
1	157.59.11.19	157.54.224.33	ICMP	ICMP Echo Request
2	157.59.8.1	157.59.11.19	ICMP	ICMP Time Exceeded
3	157.59.11.19	157.54.224.33	ICMP	ICMP Echo Request
4	157.59.8.1	157.54.11.19	ICMP	ICMP Time Exceeded
5	157.59.11.19	157.54.224.33	ICMP	ICMP Echo Request
6	157.59.8.1	157.59.11.19	ICMP	ICMP Time Exceeded
7	157.59.11.19	157.54.224.33	ICMP	ICMP Echo Request
8	157.54.231.130	157.59.11.19	ICMP	ICMP Time Exceeded
9	157.59.11.19	157.54.224.33	ICMP	ICMP Echo Request
10	157.54.231.130	157.59.11.19	ICMP	ICMP Time Exceeded
11	157.59.11.19	157.54.224.33	ICMP	ICMP Echo Request
12	157.54.231.130	157.59.11.19	ICMP	ICMP Time Exceeded
13	157.59.11.19	157.54.224.33	ICMP	ICMP Echo Request
14	157.54.224.33	157.59.11.19	ICMP	ICMP Time Reply
15	157.59.11.19	157.59.224.33	ICMP	ICMP Echo Request
16	157.54.224.33	157.59.11.19	ICMP	ICMP Time Reply
17	157.59.11.19	157.54.224.33	ICMP	ICMP Echo Request
18	157.54.224.33	157.59.11.19	ICMP	ICMP Time Reply

Frames 1 through 6 are the first hop. In Frames 1, 3, and 5, the IP header's TTL is set to 1. The local router decrements the TTL to 0 and sends back ICMP Time Exceeded-TTL Exceeded in Transit messages (Frames 2, 4, and 6).

Frames 7 through 12 are the second hop. In Frames 7, 9, and 11, the IP header's TTL is set to 2. The second router in the path decrements the TTL to 0 and sends back the ICMP Time Exceeded-TTL Exceeded in Transit messages (Frames 8, 10, and 12).

Frames 13 through 18 reach the destination. In Frames 13, 15, and 17, the IP header's TTL is set to 3, which is an adequate TTL to reach a destination two routers away. The destination sends back the appropriate Echo Reply messages (Frames 14, 16, and 18).

Note The round-trip times reflected in the Tracert display are not necessarily the same round-trip times for normal traffic. Most routers process ICMP errors and messages at a lower priority. Therefore, the round-trip times reflected in the Tracert display might be larger than the round-trip times for normal traffic. Additionally, it is possible for network conditions and the path to change during the route-tracing process, giving misleading results.

Tracert Options

Table 6-7 lists the use and default values of Tracert tool options.

Table 6-7 Tracert Tool Options

Option	Use	Default
-d	Instructs Tracert to not perform a DNS reverse query on every router IP address. If the host name of each router is unimportant, using the -d option speeds up the Tracert display of the path.	Performs DNS reverse queries on each router IP address

Table 6-7 Tracert Tool Options

Option	Use	Default
-h max_hops	Instructs Tracert to increment the TTL up to max_hops.	30
-j host-list	Sends the ICMP Echo messages using the loose source route specified in the host-list. The host list is up to nine IP addresses separated by spaces, corresponding to the loose source route to the destination. This option is valid only for IPv4 traffic.	Not used
-w timeout	Waits the specified amount of time in milliseconds for the response before displaying a *.	4000
-R	Forces Tracert to trace the round-trip path by sending the ICMPv6 Echo Request message to the destination and including an IPv6 Routing extension header with the next destination of the sending node. This option is valid only for IPv6 traffic.	Not used
-S sourceaddr	Forces Tracert to use a specified source address. This option is valid only for IPv6 traffic.	Not used
-4	Forces Tracert to use an IPv4 address when the DNS name query for a host name returns both IPv4 and IPv6 addresses.	Not used
-6	Forces Tracert to use an IPv6 address when the DNS name query for a host name returns both IPv4 and IPv6 addresses.	Not used

Pathping.exe Tool

The Pathping command-line tool for Windows Server 2008 and Windows Vista is used to test router and link latency and packet losses for both IPv4 and IPv6. For IPv4, Pathping works by sending successive ICMP Echo messages to each point in the path and recording the following: the average round-trip time, the packet loss when sending ICMP Echo messages to each router, and the packet loss when sending ICMP Echo messages across the links between each router.

The following is an example of the display of the Pathping tool:

```
C:\>pathping 10.10.2.99
Tracing route to 10.10.2.99 over a maximum of 30 hops
  0  10.0.1.100
  1  10.0.1.1
  2  192.168.1.2
  3  172.16.1.2
  4  10.10.2.99
Computing statistics for 100 seconds...
            Source to Here   This Node/Link
Hop  RTT    Lost/Sent = Pct  Lost/Sent = Pct  Address
  0                                           10.0.1.100
                              0/ 100 =  0%    |
  1   0ms   0/ 100 =  0%      0/ 100 =  0%    10.0.1.1
                              0/ 100 =  0%    |
  2   0ms   0/ 100 =  0%      0/ 100 =  0%    192.168.1.2
                              0/ 100 =  0%    |
```

```
3       0ms      0/ 100 =  0%    0/ 100 =  0%   172.16.1.2
                                 0/ 100 =  0%   |
4       1ms      0/ 100 =  0%    0/ 100 =  0%   10.10.2.99
Trace complete.
```

In this example, Pathping is sending ICMP Echo messages from a sending host (10.0.1.100) to a destination host (10.10.2.99) across three routers (10.0.1.1, 192.168.1.2, and 172.16.1.2). Pathping first resolves the path using the same method as Tracert. Next, Pathping sends ICMP Echo messages to each near-side router interface and to the destination (in the path order), and repeats this process 99 times. In this example, the Tracert tool sends an ICMP Echo message to 10.0.1.1, then to 192.168.1.2, then to 172.16.1.2, then to the destination, 10.10.2.99. This process is repeated 99 times so that 100 ICMP Echo messages are sent to each near-side router interface in the path and the destination. From the responses (and lack of responses), Pathping accumulates statistics for the following:

- Packet losses for packets sent on the link between the source host (10.0.1.100) and the first router (10.0.1.1)
- Packet losses and average round-trip times for packets sent from the source host to the first router in the path (with the near-side interface of 10.0.1.1)
- Packet losses for packets sent on the link between the first router (10.0.1.1) and the second router in the path (with the near-side interface of 192.168.1.2)
- Packet losses and average round-trip times for packets sent from the source host to the second router in the path (192.168.1.2)
- Packet losses for packets sent on the link between the second router (192.168.1.2) and the third router in the path (with the near-side interface of 172.16.1.2)
- Packet losses and average round-trip times for packets sent from the source host to the third router in the path (172.16.1.2)
- Packet losses for packets sent on the link between the third router (172.16.1.2) and the destination (10.10.2.99)
- Packet losses and average round-trip times for packets sent to the destination (10.10.2.99)

The Source To Here column displays the average round-trip time and packet loss for packets destined to a specific IP address. These packets must be processed by the destination and an ICMP Echo Reply message must be constructed and sent. The This Node/Link column displays the packet loss for packets that are either traveling across a link (as indicated by | in the Address column), across a router (as indicated by an intermediate router IP address in the Address column), or to the destination (as indicated by the destination IP address in the Address column). Packets sent across a router are typically forwarded using an optimized forwarding process that is much faster than responding as the destination of an ICMP Echo Reply message.

Network Monitor Capture 06-07 (in the \Captures folder on the companion CD-ROM) contains the traffic of the Pathping tool for this example.

Pathping Options

Table 6-8 lists the use and default values of Pathping tool options.

Table 6-8 Pathping Tool Options

Option	Use	Default
-n	Instructs Pathping to not perform a DNS reverse query on every router IP address. If the host name of each router is unimportant, the -n option accelerates the Pathping display of the path.	Performs DNS reverse queries on each router IP address
-h *max_hops*	Instructs Pathping to increment the TTL up to *max_hops*.	30
-g *host-list*	Sends the ICMP Echo messages using the loose source route specified in the *host-list*. The host list is up to nine IP addresses separated by spaces, corresponding to the loose source route to the destination.	Not used
-p *period*	Waits the specified amount of time in milliseconds between successive Echo messages.	250
-q *num_queries*	Sends the *num_queries* number of queries for each hop.	100
-i *address*	Sends the Pathping traffic from a specified address.	Not used
-w *timeout*	Waits the specified amount of time in milliseconds for the response.	3000
-4	Forces Pathping to use an IPv4 address when the DNS name query for a host name returns both IPv4 and IPv6 addresses.	Not used
-6	Forces Pathping to use an IPv6 address when the DNS name query for a host name returns both IPv4 and IPv6 addresses.	Not used

Summary

ICMP is a set of messages that provides services that are not part of IP. ICMP includes the following services: diagnostic (Echo and Echo Reply messages), delivery error reporting (Destination Unreachable, Time Exceeded, Source Quench, and Redirect messages), router discovery (Router Advertisement and Router Solicitation messages), IP header problems (Parameter Problem message), and address mask discovery (Address Mask Request and Address Mask Reply messages).The ICMP Destination Unreachable-Fragmentation Needed And DF Set message is used for PTMU Discovery. The Ping, Tracert, and Pathping tools provided with Windows Server 2008 and Windows Vista use ICMP messages for diagnostic functions.

Chapter 7
Internet Group Management Protocol (IGMP)

In this chapter:
Introduction to IP Multicast and IGMP 157
IGMP Message Structure 163
IGMP in Windows Server 2008 and Windows Vista. 173
Summary. 176

Data transfer services typically use one-to-one delivery with unicast addressing and routing across an IP internetwork. However, one-to-many delivery with multicast addressing across an IP internetwork is a bandwidth-efficient way to deliver audio, video, and other types of content to multiple destinations. One-to-many delivery service requires hosts to inform local routers of their interest in receiving the traffic so that routers can forward the traffic to the subnets of the listening hosts. This chapter describes how IP multicast works and the role of the Internet Group Management Protocol (IGMP).

Introduction to IP Multicast and IGMP

IP multicast provides an efficient one-to-many delivery service. To achieve one-to-many delivery using IP unicast traffic, each datagram needs to be sent multiple times. To achieve one-to-many delivery using IP broadcast traffic, a single datagram is sent, but all nodes process it, even those that are not interested. Broadcast delivery service is unsuitable for internetworks, as routers are designed to prevent the spread of broadcast traffic. With IP multicast, a single datagram is sent and forwarded across routers only to the subnets containing nodes that are interested in receiving it.

Historically, IP multicast traffic has been little utilized. However, recent developments in audio and video teleconferencing, distance learning, and data transfer to a large number of hosts have made IP multicast traffic more important.

RFCs 1112 and 2236 describe IP multicast and the Internet Group Management Protocol (IGMP).

More Info All of the RFCs referenced in this chapter can be found in the \Standards\Chap07_IGMP folder on the companion CD-ROM.

IP Multicasting Overview

The following are the essential facets of IP multicast operation:

- All multicast traffic is sent to a class D address in the range 224.0.0.0 through 239.255.255.255 (224.0.0.0/4). All traffic in the range 224.0.0.0 through 224.0.0.255 (224.0.0.0/24) is for the local subnet and is not forwarded by routers. Multicast-enabled routers forward multicast traffic in the range 224.0.1.0 through 239.255.255.255 with an appropriate Time to Live (TTL).
- A specific multicast address is called a *group address*.
- The set of hosts that listen for multicast traffic at a specific group address is called a *multicast group* or *host group*. Multicast group members can receive traffic to their unicast address and the group address. Multicast groups can be permanent or transient. A *permanent group* is assigned a well-known group address. An example of a permanent group is the all-hosts multicast group, listening for traffic on the well-known multicast address of 224.0.0.1. The membership of a permanent group is transient; only the group address is permanent.
- There are no limits on a multicast group's size.
- A host can send multicast traffic to the group address without belonging to the multicast group.
- There are no limits to how many multicast groups to which a host can belong.
- There are no limits on when members of a multicast group can join and leave a multicast group.
- There are no limits on the location of multicast group members.

IP multicast must be supported by the hosts and the routers of an IP internetwork.

Host Support

To support IP multicast, hosts must be able to send and receive IP multicast traffic. RFC 1112 defines the following three levels of IP multicast support for hosts:

- **Level 0** No support for sending or receiving IP multicast traffic
- **Level 1** Support for sending IP multicast traffic
- **Level 2** Support for sending and receiving IP multicast traffic

In Windows Server 2008 and Windows Vista, the IP multicast level can be controlled by the `netsh interface ipv4 set global mldlevel=none|sendonly|all` command. By default, Windows Server 2008 and Windows Vista support both sending and receiving IP multicast traffic (the `all` option).

You can also use the following registry value:

IGMPLevel
```
Location: HKEY_LOCAL_MACHINE\SYSTEM\CurrentControlSet\Services\Tcpip\Parameters
Value Type: REG_DWORD
Valid Range: 0-2
Default: 2
Present by Default: No
```

By default, TCP/IP for Windows Server 2008 and Windows Vista supports Level 2 IP multicasting.

Sending IP Multicast Traffic

A host sending an IP multicast packet must first determine the IP multicast address. The IP multicast address is determined by either the application or protocol (a well-known or reserved IP multicast address), or obtained from a server allocating unique IP multicast addresses. Multicast Address Dynamic Client Allocation Protocol (MADCAP) is defined in RFC 2730 and used by a multicast host to obtain a unique IP multicast address. Multicast scopes configured on the DHCP server define ranges of IP multicast addresses. Similar to allocating unicast IP addresses, unique IP multicast addresses are allocated to a single DHCP client. If multiple hosts use the same IP multicast address for different applications, the wrong traffic could be forwarded to host group members. The DHCP Server service in Windows Server 2008 supports MADCAP. For more information, see Help a+nd Support in Windows Server 2008.

After determining the destination IP multicast address, the sending host must construct the IP datagram with its own IP address as the source IP address, the intended IP multicast address as the destination IP address, and an appropriate TTL value. For local subnet IP multicast traffic destined for addresses in the range 224.0.0.0 through 224.0.0.255 (224.0.0.0/24), the TTL is set to 1. Routers do not forward IP multicast traffic in this range even if the TTL is greater than 1. For nonlocal subnet traffic, the TTL should be set to a value that is high enough to reach all host group members. Table 7-1 lists the recommended values of the TTL for IP multicast traffic and their scope.

Table 7-1 Recommended Values of the TTL for IP Multicast Traffic

TTL Value	Description
0	Restricted to the same host
1	Restricted to the same subnet
15	Restricted to the same site
63	Restricted to the same region
127	Worldwide
191	Worldwide; limited bandwidth
255	Unrestricted

IP on the sending host constructs the IP multicast packet and uses the IP sending process to determine the next-hop address and interface to send the packet. The destination address matches the multicast entry in the IP routing table (the route with the destination of 224.0.0.0 and the network mask of 240.0.0.0). IP determines that the packet must be forwarded to the destination IP address using the appropriate network interface. IP then submits the IP datagram, the next-hop IP address, and the interface to the Address Resolution Protocol (ARP) module.

The ARP module checks the next-hop IP address. Because the forwarding IP address is in the range 224.0.0.0 through 239.255.255.255 (224.0.0.0/4), ARP bypasses the process of checking the ARP cache and sending a broadcast ARP Request frame. For Ethernet hosts, the destination IP address is mapped to the destination media access control (MAC) address by combining the fixed high-order 25 bits of 0000001 00000000 01011110 0 and the low-order 23 bits of the destination IP multicast address to create the MAC-level 48-bit multicast address. For example, for the IP multicast address 224.0.0.1, the corresponding MAC-level 48-bit address is the concatenation of 0000001 00000000 01011110 0 and 0000000 00000000 00000001, or 0x01-00-5E-00-00-01.

Receiving IP Multicast Traffic

To receive IP multicast traffic, a host informs the IP layer to process incoming traffic for a specific group address. To facilitate the request, the IP module does the following:

- Informs the Network Interface Layer technology to add the MAC-level multicast address that corresponds to the group address to the list of interesting destination MAC addresses.

- If the group address is not in the range 224.0.0.1 through 224.0.0.255 (224.0.0.0/24), the IP module sends an IGMP Host Membership Report message to inform local routers to forward the host group traffic to the subnet of the listening host.

If there are multiple applications on the host using the same group address, IP tracks application group membership and passes a copy of the received IP multicast datagram to each listening application. For a multihomed host, IP tracks group membership for each subnet.

Router Support

To support IP multicast forwarding and routing, a router must be able to do the following:

- Listen for IGMP Host Membership Report messages sent from hosts on local subnets.

- Track and maintain group membership for hosts on local subnets. Routers maintain host group membership through the receipt of IGMP Host Membership Report messages and the sending of IGMP Host Membership Query messages.

- On a multicast-enabled intranet with more than two routers, a router must be able to communicate host group membership information to neighboring routers. IP multicast routers use a multicast routing protocol such as Distance Vector Multicast Routing Protocol (DVMRP), Multicast Extensions to Open Shortest Path First (MOSPF), or Protocol Independent Multicast (PIM).

- Listen for all IP multicast traffic on all attached subnets. To do this, the router must put the network interface into either promiscuous listening mode or multicast promiscuous listening mode. In promiscuous mode, all incoming frames are considered interesting and passed to upper layers for processing. Promiscuous mode is a processor and interrupt-intensive listening mode typically used only for protocol analysis or network sniffing.

    Multicast promiscuous mode is a special listening mode in which all packets with the Individual/Group (I/G) bit set in the destination MAC address are considered interesting. The I/G bit is also known as the multicast bit. For Ethernet frames, the multicast bit is the last bit of the first byte in the destination MAC address. In multicast promiscuous mode, all frames with the multicast bit set and a valid Frame Check Sequence (FCS) field are passed up to the operating system for processing. See Chapter 1, "Local Area Network (LAN) Technologies," for more information on the multicast bit. In multicast promiscuous mode, an IP multicast router receives a copy of every IP multicast packet for processing or forwarding. Not all network adapters support multicast promiscuous mode. A network adapter that supports promiscuous mode might not support multicast promiscuous mode.

- Forward IP multicast traffic with a valid TTL on appropriate subnets where there are host group members or where there are downstream routers that have host group members. The IP multicast forwarding capability is provided by the TCP/IP protocol. Similar to unicast forwarding, when IP multicast forwarding is enabled, IP decrements the TTL of the packet being forwarded, and then forwards the packet over the appropriate interfaces based on the entries in a local multicast forwarding table. IP silently discards multicast traffic with a TTL of 0.

    IP multicast routers forward IP multicast traffic to subnets that have either a listening host or a router that has informed the router forwarding the IP multicast traffic that there are host group members downstream. The entries in the IP multicast forwarding table do not indicate which hosts are listening or how many group members there are on a subnet—only that at least one host member is present on the subnet (or a downstream subnet).

The Multicast-Enabled IP Internetwork

Figure 7-1 shows a multicast-enabled intranet.

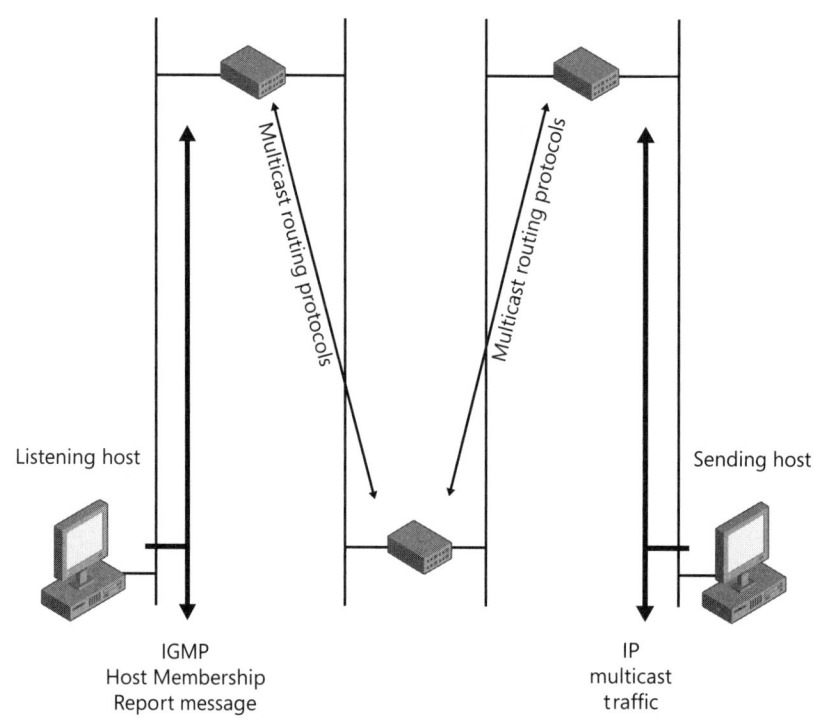

Figure 7-1 A multicast-enabled intranet showing multicast-enabled hosts and routers

To support the forwarding of IP multicast traffic from any host to any group member, hosts and routers must support the following criteria:

- Any host receiving IP multicast traffic joins the multicast group by sending IGMP Host Membership Report messages on the local subnet.

- Any host sending IP multicast traffic constructs the IP multicast frame and sends it on the local subnet.

- IP multicast routers forward the IP multicast traffic from the originating subnet to all subnets that contain group members. IGMP Host Membership Report messages inform the routers about group members on locally attached subnets. For downstream host members, IP multicast routers communicate downstream host member information using multicast routing protocols. In both cases, IGMP and multicast routing protocols update the router's local TCP/IP multicast forwarding tables.

The Internet's Multicast-Enabled Backbone

The portion of the Internet that is IP-multicast-enabled is known as the multicast backbone (MBONE). The MBONE was originally created to multicast the audio for Internet Engineering Task Force (IETF) meetings for members who could not attend. Today, the MBONE is used for the audio and video of IETF meetings, launches of the National Aeronautic and Space

Administration (NASA) space shuttle, and teleconferences of all kinds. The MBONE is also the test bed for the development of IP multicast applications, tools, and routing protocols.

The MBONE is a logical IP multicast topology overlaid on the Internet's physical unicast topology. Not all Internet service providers (ISPs) support the forwarding of IP multicast traffic. To connect two portions of the Internet that support IP multicast traffic, IP multicast traffic is tunneled or wrapped with another IP header addressed from one router to another router. The typical tunneling is called IP-in-IP tunneling and is described in RFC 1853. The MBONE is a series of multicast-enabled islands connected together with IP-in-IP tunnels.

IGMP Message Structure

Hosts and routers use IGMP to maintain local subnet host group membership and it is required for hosts that support Level 2 IP multicasting. IGMP messages are sent as IP datagrams with the IP Protocol field set to 2. The resulting IP datagram is then encapsulated with the appropriate Network Interface Layer header and trailer. Figure 7-2 shows the resulting frame.

Network Interface header	IP header	IGMP message	Network Interface trailer

IP datagram spans IP header through IGMP message. Network Interface Layer frame spans the entire structure.

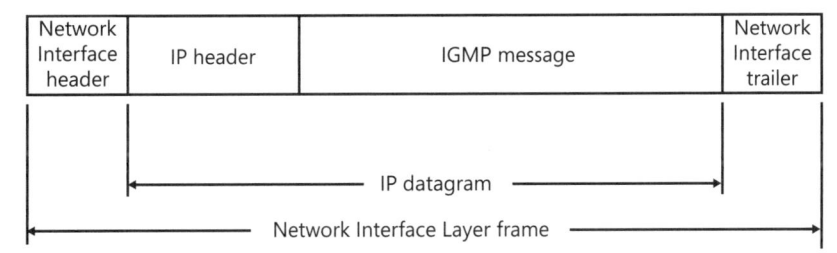

Figure 7-2 IGMP message structure showing the IP header and Network Interface Layer header and trailer

In the IP header of IGMP messages, the Source IP Address field is set to the router or host interface that sent the IGMP message and the Destination IP Address field depends on the type of IGMP message.

IGMP Version 1 (IGMPv1)

IGMPv1 is described in Appendix I of RFC 1112. IGMPv1 defines two types of IGMP messages: the Host Membership Report and the Host Membership Query.

Host Membership Report

A host sends a Host Membership Report message to inform local routers that the host wants to receive IP multicast traffic at a specified group address. A host also sends a Host Membership Report in response to a Host Membership Query message sent by a router. Hosts send Host Membership Report messages to the destination IP address of the multicast group with a TTL of 1.

Host Membership Query

A router sends a Host Membership Query message to poll a subnet and verify that there are hosts still listening for IP multicast traffic. Routers send Host Membership Query messages to the destination IP address of the all-hosts IP multicast address (224.0.0.1) with a TTL of 1. An IGMPv1 Host Membership Query is a general query, attempting to identify all multicast groups being listened to by hosts on a subnet.

Hosts that receive the Host Membership Query message send a Host Membership Report message for all the host groups in which they are members. To prevent an avalanche of response traffic, host group members choose a random report delay time for each host group and wait to hear from other host group members on the subnet. If another host group member sends a Host Membership Report message, the waiting host does not send a reply.

This behavior is consistent with the information kept by multicast routers. A multicast router does not track which hosts on a subnet are members of a host group, only that there is at least one host group member.

If no hosts respond with a Host Membership Report to a group address that the multicast router is tracking for the subnet, the multicast router can remove that entry from the multicast forwarding table and inform other multicast routers through multicast routing protocols. Upstream routers no longer forward multicast traffic for the removed group address to the subnet.

IGMPv1 Message Structure

Figure 7-3 shows the structure of an IGMPv1 message.

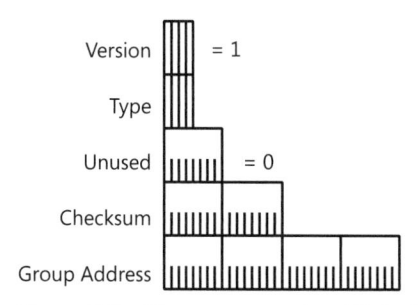

Figure 7-3 The structure of an IGMPv1 message

The fields in an IGMPv1 message are defined as follows:

- **Version**   A 4-bit field set to 1 to indicate IGMPv1.
- **Type**   A 4-bit field that indicates the type of IGMP message. Set to 1 for a Host Membership Query message. Set to 2 for a Host Membership Report message.
- **Unused**   A 1-byte field zeroed by the sender and ignored by the receiver.
- **Checksum**   A 2-byte field that stores the checksum on the 8-byte IGMP message.

- **Group Address** A 4-byte field that for a Host Membership Report message stores the multicast group address being joined by the listening host. In a Host Membership Query message, the Group Address field is 0.0.0.0.

Table 7-2 summarizes the addresses used in IGMPv1 Host Membership Report and Host Membership Query messages.

Table 7-2 Addresses Used in IGMPv1 Messages

	Host Membership Report	Host Membership Query
Source IP Address (IP header)	Host IP Address	Router IP Address
Destination IP Address (IP header)	Group IP Address	224.0.0.1
Group Address	Group IP Address	0.0.0.0

Network Monitor Examples

The following Network Monitor trace (Capture 07-01 in the \Captures folder on the companion CD-ROM) is an IGMPv1 Host Membership Report message for a host joining the host group 224.0.1.41:

```
Frame:
- Ethernet: Etype = Internet IP (IPv4)
  - DestinationAddress: 01005E 000129
     IG:   (0.......) Individual address
     UL:   (.0......) Universally Administered Address
     Rsv:  (..000001)
  + SourceAddress: 00C04F D7BAEC
    EthernetType: Internet IP (IPv4), 2048(0x800)
    UnkownData: Binary Large Object (18 Bytes)
- Ipv4: Next Protocol = IGMP, Packet ID = 45569, Total IP Length = 28
  + Versions: IPv4, Internet Protocol; Header Length = 20
  + DifferentiatedServicesField: DSCP: 0, ECN: 0
    TotalLength: 28 (0x1C)
    Identification: 45569 (0xB201)
  + FragmentFlags: 0 (0x0)
    TimeToLive: 1 (0x1)
    NextProtocol: IGAP/IGMP/RGMP, 2(0x2)
    Checksum: 4494 (0x118E)
    SourceAddress: 10.0.11.40
    DestinationAddress: 224.0.1.41
- Igmp: IGMPv1 membership report
    Type: IGMPv1 membership report, 18(0x12)
  - Igmpv1:
    Unused: 0 (0x0)
    CheckSum: 3286 (0xCD6)
    MulticastAddress: 224.0.1.41
```

Note that the group address of 224.0.1.41 is being mapped to the Ethernet destination address of 01-00-5E-00-01-29 (41 in hexadecimal is 0x29). Also note that IGMP messages must be padded with 18 padding bytes on Ethernet networks to adhere to the Ethernet minimum payload size of 46 bytes (padding bytes not shown).

The following Network Monitor trace (Capture 07-02 in the \Captures folder on the companion CD-ROM) is an IGMPv1 Host Membership Query message:

```
Frame:
- Ethernet: Etype = Internet IP (IPv4)
  - DestinationAddress: 01005E 000001
      IG:  (0.......) Individual address
      UL:  (.0......) Universally Administered Address
      Rsv: (..000001)
  + SourceAddress: 00E034 C0A060
    EthernetType: Internet IP (IPv4), 2048(0x800)
    UnkownData: Binary Large Object (18 Bytes)
- Ipv4: Next Protocol = IGMP, Packet ID = 0, Total IP Length = 28
  + Versions: IPv4, Internet Protocol; Header Length = 20
  + DifferentiatedServicesField: DSCP: 48, ECN: 0
    TotalLength: 28 (0x1C)
    Identification: 0 (0x0)
  + FragmentFlags: 0 (0x0)
    TimeToLive: 1 (0x1)
    NextProtocol: IGAP/IGMP/RGMP, 2(0x2)
    Checksum: 50974 (0xC71E)
    SourceAddress: 10.0.8.1
    DestinationAddress: 224.0.0.1
- Igmp: IGMP Membership query
    Type: IGMP Membership query, 17(0x11)
  - Igmpv2:
    + MaxResqCode: Max Resp Time is 10.0 seconds
      CheckSum: 61083 (0xEE9B)
      MulticastAddress: 0.0.0.0
```

Notice that for both traces, the IP header's TTL field is set to 1.

IGMP Version 2 (IGMPv2)

IGMPv2 provides additional capabilities to help multicast routers converge a multicast group to the set of hosts listening for traffic. IGMPv2 is described in RFC 2236 and is backward compatible with IGMPv1.

The additional features of IGMPv2 are the following:

- The Leave Group message
- The Group-Specific Query message
- The election of a multicast querier
- The IGMPv2 Host Membership Report message

The Leave Group Message

With IGMPv1, if a host leaves a specific multicast group and it is the last member of the multicast group for that subnet, the local router is not explicitly informed. The router maintains the entry in its multicast forwarding table and continues to forward multicast traffic for the group to the host's subnet. Only after the router sends a Host Membership Query message and receives no response for the multicast group does the router recognize that there are no more group members on that subnet for that group address. The router then updates its multicast forwarding table, discontinues forwarding IP multicast traffic to the subnet, and informs neighboring routers of the new state. This can lead to long leave latency times. During the leave latency time, multicast routers can forward multicast traffic to subnets that do not contain group members.

During the periodic polling process, when an IGMPv2 host responds to a membership query, it assumes that it is potentially the last member in the group for that subnet because no other hosts responded before it. If that host leaves the group, it sends an IGMPv2 Leave Group message to the all-routers IP multicast address (224.0.0.2). To ensure that the host leaving is truly the last host in the group for the subnet, the multicast router sends a series of group-specific membership queries. If the multicast router receives a response from another host for that group, the router maintains the group membership state for that group on that subnet. If the multicast router does not receive any responses, it can prevent the forwarding of traffic to that group to the subnet. If there are host members on downstream subnets available across subnet routers, multicast traffic for the group is still forwarded to the subnet.

The Group-Specific Query Message

In the case of IGMPv2, two different types of Host Membership Query messages are defined: the General Query and the Group-Specific Query. The General Query is the same as the IGMPv1 Host Membership Query. The Group-Specific Query is designed to check for host membership in a specific group. In the Group-Specific Query, the IP header's destination IP address and the IGMP header's group address are set to the group address being queried.

The Multicast Querier

IGMPv2 supports the election of a multicast querier, a single router per subnet that sends Host Membership Query messages. With IGMPv1, the designation of a single multicast router to perform queries is a function of the multicast routing protocol. Because all IGMP traffic is sent to multicast addresses, every multicast router on a subnet receives all IGMP messages. Therefore, only a single router is needed to send queries.

The IGMPv2 multicast querier election is simple: A router assumes that it is the multicast querier until it receives a Host Membership Query message (either General or Group-Specific) from another router with a numerically lower IP address. If it is the only router on a subnet and it does not receive a query from another router in an interval called the Other Querier Present Interval (by default set for 255 seconds), the router becomes the querier for that network.

IGMPv2 Message Structure

Figure 7-4 shows the structure of an IGMPv2 message.

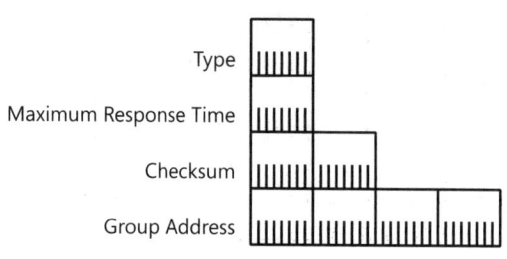

Figure 7-4 The structure of an IGMPv2 message

The fields in an IGMPv2 message are defined as follows:

- **Type** IGMPv2 combines the IGMPv1 4-bit Version field and IGMPv1 4-bit Type field into a single 8-bit Type field. Table 7-3 lists the Type field values.

Table 7-3 Values of the IGMPv2 Type Field

Type	Message
17 (0x11)	**Host Membership Query** The previous Version 0x1 and Type 0x1 are combined to form 0x11, or 17.
18 (0x12)	**IGMPv1 Host Membership Report** The previous Version 0x1 and Type 0x2 are combined to form 0x12, or 18.
22 (0x16)	**IGMPv2 Host Membership Report** The IGMPv2 Host Membership Report has the same function as the IGMPv1 Host Membership Report and is intended to be received by only IGMPv2-capable multicast routers.
23 (0x17)	**Leave Group Message**

- **Maximum Response Time** The IGMPv1 Unused field is used in IGMPv2 Membership Query messages (either General or Group-Specific) to store a maximum time in tenths of a second within which a host must respond to the query. The maximum response time becomes the maximum value of the report delay timer for subnet host members.
- **Checksum** A 2-byte field that stores a checksum on the 8-byte IGMP message.
- **Group Address** Set to 0.0.0.0 for the general Host Membership Query and set to the specific group address for all other IGMPv2 message types.

Table 7-4 summarizes the addresses used in IGMPv2 Group-Specific Host Membership Query and Group Leave messages.

Table 7-4 Addresses Used in IGMPv2 Messages

	Group-Specific Query	**Group Leave**
Source IP Address (IP header)	Router IP Address	Host IP Address
Destination IP Address (IP header)	Group IP Address	224.0.0.2
Group Address (IGMPv2 header)	Group IP Address	Group IP Address

Network Monitor Example

The following Network Monitor trace (Capture 07-03 in the \Captures folder on the companion CD-ROM) shows an IGMPv2 Host Membership Report message for a host registering the group address 239.255.255.252:

```
Frame:
- Ethernet: Etype = Internet IP (IPv4)
  + DestinationAddress: 01005E 7FFFFC
  + SourceAddress: 006008 3E4607
    EthernetType: Internet IP (IPv4), 2048(0x800)
    UnkownData: Binary Large Object (14 Bytes)
- Ipv4: Next Protocol = IGMP, Packet ID = 6694, Total IP Length = 32
  + Versions: IPv4, Internet Protocol; Header Length = 24
  + DifferentiatedServicesField: DSCP: 0, ECN: 0
    TotalLength: 32 (0x20)
    Identification: 6694 (0x1A26)
  + FragmentFlags: 0 (0x0)
    TimeToLive: 1 (0x1)
    NextProtocol: IGAP/IGMP/RGMP, 2(0x2)
    Checksum: 2029 (0x7ED)
    SourceAddress: 10.1.8.200
    DestinationAddress: 239.255.255.252
  - routerAlert:
    - option: RTRALT - Router Alert.
        C:       (1.......) Copy this option to all fragments
        Class:   (.00.....) Datagram or Network Control
        Option:  (...10100) RTRALT - Router Alert.
      Length: 4 (0x4)
      RouterAlertValue: Router shall examine packet (0)
- Igmp: IGMPv2 Membership Report
    Type: IGMPv2 Membership Report, 22(0x16)
  - Igmpv2:
    + MaxResqCode: Max Resp Time is 0.0 seconds
      CheckSum: 64002 (0xFA02)
      MulticastAddress: 239.255.255.252
```

Notice the existence of the IP Router Alert option (Option Type 0x94) that is used to inform the router that further processing of the IP header is required. For more information about the IP Router Alert option, see Chapter 5, "Internet Protocol (IP)."

IGMP Version 3 (IGMPv3)

IGMPv3, described in RFC 3376, supports multicast source-specific reports and queries. With IGMPv1 and IGMPv2, multicast group members report membership and routers query for membership without regard to the source of the multicast traffic. IGMPv3 allows you to have multiple sources for multicast traffic, which can be beneficial when you are multicasting a video session across an enterprise organization. Rather than having a single source of the multicast packets that comprise the video broadcast, you can have multiple sources distributed regionally. Multicast hosts can then join the group and specify a multicast source that is topologically closest to them (a regional source).

When an IGMPv3 host sends a Host Membership Report message, it can specify the multicast group and either the list of multicast sources from which the host can receive the multicast packets (an include list) or a list of the multicast sources from which the host must not receive multicast packets (an exclude list). Multicast routers and multicast routing protocols use the list of sources to include or exclude in the IGMPv3 Host Membership Report message to promote the forwarding of multicast packets from included sources and prevent the forwarding and delivery of multicast packets from excluded sources.

In IGMPv3, the Host Membership Query message has been modified to allow an IGMPv3 router to send source- and-group-specific queries. An IGMPv3 host uses a new Host Membership Report message to send source-specific reports.

IGMPv3 Host Membership Query

The IGMPv3 Host Membership Query message is a group- and source-specific query that is sent by an IGMPv3 router to determine if there are any group members in the indicated group address for traffic from one of the sources in the source list. The IGMPv3 Host Membership Query message uses the same IGMP Type number (0x11) and has the same format as the IGMPv2 Host Membership Query message. However, there are additional fields after the Group Address field that allow the router to specify querying parameters and list the sources of the multicast group being queried. These additional fields are only included for an IGMPv3 group- and source-specific query. The receiver of a Host Membership Query message can determine the version of IGMP from the length of the message. IGMPv2 Host Membership Query messages are 8 bytes long. IGMPv3 Host Membership Query messages are at least 12 bytes long.

Figure 7-5 shows the structure of the IGMPv3 Host Membership Query message.

Beyond the Group Address field, the IGMPv3 Host Membership Query message contains the following fields:

- **Reserved**   A 4-bit field set to 0 by the sender that is ignored by the receiver.
- **Suppress Router-Side Processing**   A 1-bit field that indicates, when set to 1, that receiving routers are to suppress normal processing when receiving a query message.
- **Querier's Robustness Variable**   A 3-bit field that indicates the robustness variable of the sending router. The robustness variable is a measure of how many IGMP packets can be lost without recovery. IGMP can recover from Querier's Robustness Variable - 1 lost IGMP packets.
- **Querier's Query Interval**   A 1-byte field that indicates the number of seconds between query messages of the sending router.
- **Number Of Sources**   A 2-byte field that indicates the number of source addresses included in the message.
- **Source Address**   A 4-byte field that indicates the unicast IP address of a multicast source.

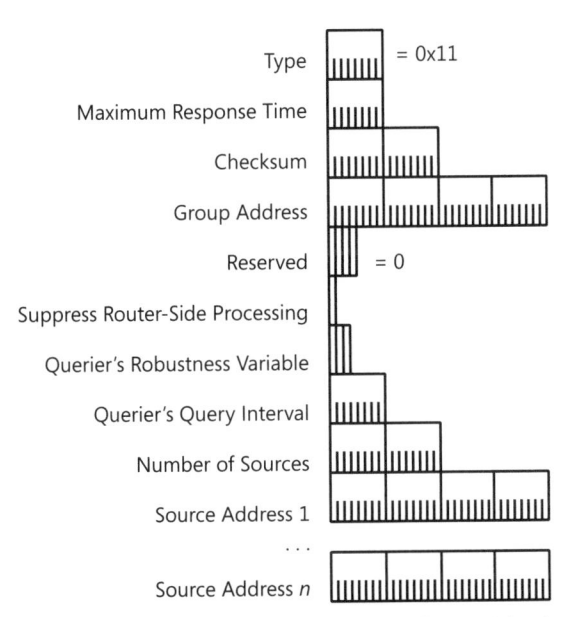

Chapter 7: Internet Group Management Protocol (IGMP)

Figure 7-5 The structure of the IGMPv3 Host Membership Query message

For more information about the operation of an IGMPv3 router, see RFC 3376.

IGMPv3 Host Membership Report

The IGMPv3 Host Membership Report message contains one or more group records. Hosts send IGMPv3 Host Membership Report messages to the multicast address 224.0.0.22, a reserved multicast address for all IGMPv3-capable multicast routers. Each group record contains the group address and the list of sources to either include or exclude.

Figure 7-6 shows the structure of the IGMPv3 Host Membership Report message.

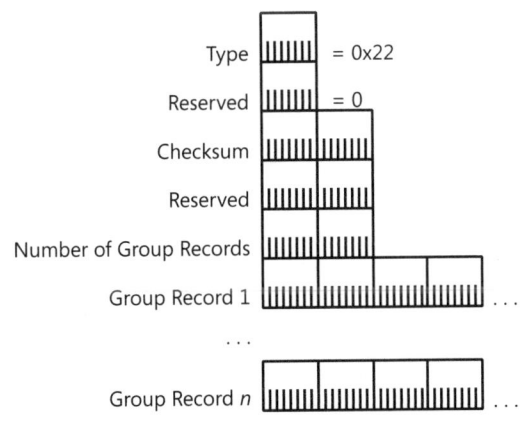

Figure 7-6 The structure of the IGMPv3 Host Membership Report message

The IGMPv3 Host Membership Report message contains the following fields:

- **Type**   A 1-byte field set to 0x22 to indicate an IGMPv3 Host Membership Report message.
- **Reserved**   A 1-byte field set to 0 by the sender and ignored by the receiver.
- **Checksum**   A 2-byte field that stores a checksum on the IGMPv3 message.
- **Reserved**   A 2-byte field set to 0 by the sender and ignored by the receiver.
- **Number Of Group Records**   A 2-byte field that indicates the number of group records contained in the message.
- **Group Record**   A variable-sized field that contains a multicast address on which the sending host is listening and either an include list or exclude list of sources.

Figure 7-7 shows the structure of an IGMPv3 Host Membership Report message group record.

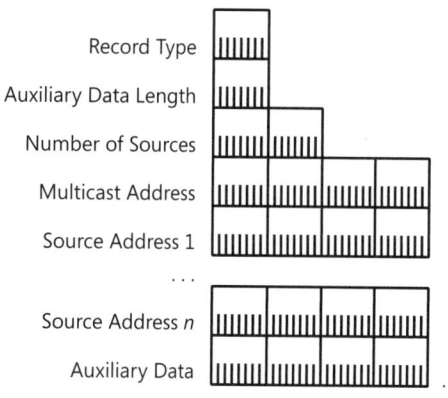

Figure 7-7   The structure of the IGMPv3 Host Membership Report message group record

The IGMPv3 Host Membership Report message group record contains the following fields:

- **Record Type**   A 1-byte field that indicates the type of group record and whether the list of sources is an inclusion or exclusion list.
- **Auxiliary Data Length**   A 1-byte field that indicates the number of bytes of auxiliary data included in the group record.
- **Number Of Sources**   A 2-byte field that indicates the number of multicast sources contained in the group record.
- **Multicast Address**   A 4-byte field that indicates the IP address of the group that the host is joining.
- **Source Address**   A 4-byte field that indicates the unicast IP address of a multicast source.
- **Auxiliary Data**   A variable-sized field that contains additional data for this group record.

IGMP in Windows Server 2008 and Windows Vista

Windows Server 2008 and Windows Vista support IP multicast sending, receiving, and forwarding through the TCP/IP protocol and, for Windows Server 2008, the Routing and Remote Access service.

TCP/IP Protocol

TCP/IP for Windows Server 2008 and Windows Vista supports IP multicast traffic in the following ways:

- To support host reception of IP multicast traffic, TCP/IP for Windows Server 2008 and Windows Vista is an IGMPv1, IGMPv2, and IGMPv3-capable host.

- To support host transmission and reception of IP multicast traffic, TCP/IP for Windows Server 2008 and Windows Vista supports the mapping of IP multicast addresses to MAC addresses for Ethernet network adapters as described in this chapter. For Token Ring network adapters, all IP multicast traffic is mapped to the Token Ring functional address of 0x-C0-00-00-04-00-00.

- To support the forwarding of IP multicast traffic, TCP/IP for Windows Server 2008 and Windows Vista supports multicast forwarding based on the setting of the EnableMulticastForwarding registry value and the entries in the TCP/IP multicast forwarding table. You can view the contents of the TCP/IP multicast forwarding table on a computer running Windows Server 2008 from the Routing and Remote Access snap-in or from the display of the `netsh routing ip show mfe` command.

In Windows Server 2008 and Windows Vista, IP multicast forwarding is controlled by the following registry value:

EnableMulticastForwarding
```
Location: HKEY_LOCAL_MACHINE\SYSTEM\CurrentControlSet\Services\Tcpip\Parameters
Data Type: REG_DWORD
Valid Range: 0-1
Default: 0
Present by Default: No
```

EnableMulticastForwarding enables (when set to 1) or disables (when set to 0) the forwarding of IP multicast traffic. By default, multicast forwarding is disabled.

In Windows Server 2008 and Windows Vista, the maximum version of IGMP can be controlled by the `netsh interface ipv4 set global mldversion=version1|version2|version3` command. By default, Windows Server 2008 and Windows Vista support IGMPv3 as the maximum version of IGMP.

Routing And Remote Access Service

In Windows Server 2008, the Routing and Remote Access service functions as a limited multicast forwarder using IGMPv1, IGMPv2, or IGMPv3 to track local group membership. Because IGMP is not a true multicast routing protocol, routers running Windows Server 2008 can support only limited multicast configurations.

In the Routing and Remote Access service, IGMP is a routing protocol component that is typically added by the Routing and Remote Access Server Setup wizard. Alternatively, you can add IGMP as an IPv4 routing protocol from the Routing and Remote Access snap-in. Depending on your choices in the wizard, you might need to add individual routing interfaces to the IGMP routing protocol and configure them for either IGMP router mode or IGMP proxy mode.

Interfaces in IGMP Router Mode

An interface in IGMP router mode acts as an IGMP-capable IP multicast forwarder and performs the following actions:

- **Places the network adapter in multicast promiscuous mode** If the network interface is a broadcast network type such as Ethernet, the network adapter is placed in multicast promiscuous mode. If the network adapter does not support multicast promiscuous mode, an event is logged in the system event log.

- **Manages local subnet multicast group membership** The routing interface uses IGMP to listen for IGMP Host Membership Report and Leave Group messages, to elect an IGMP querier, and to send General and Group-Specific Host Membership Query messages.

- **Updates the TCP/IP multicast forwarding table** Based on ongoing group membership for the interface, IGMP in conjunction with other components of the Routing and Remote Access service maintains the TCP/IP multicast forwarding table.

Interfaces in IGMP Proxy Mode

An interface in IGMP proxy mode acts as an IGMP-capable IP multicast proxy host for hosts on IGMP router mode interfaces and performs the following functions:

- **Forwards IGMP Host Membership Report messages** IGMP Host Membership Report messages received on IGMP router mode interfaces are forwarded on the IGMP proxy mode interface. The forwarded Host Membership Report messages have a TTL of 1. The received Host Membership Report messages are not forwarded using the entries in the TCP/IP multicast forwarding table.

- **Adds multicast MAC addresses to the network adapter table** For each group address registered by proxy, the corresponding multicast MAC address is added to the table of interesting MAC addresses on the network adapter (for local area network [LAN] technologies such as Ethernet). The network adapter is not placed in promiscuous mode unless the network card cannot support listening to all required multicast MAC addresses. Nonlocal IP multicast traffic received on the IGMP proxy mode interface is passed to the TCP/IP protocol for multicast forwarding.

- **Updates the TCP/IP multicast forwarding table**   To facilitate the forwarding of multicast traffic from a multicast source on an IGMP router mode interface to a group member downstream from the IGMP proxy mode interface, the IGMP routing protocol adds entries to the TCP/IP multicast forwarding table so that all nonlocal IP multicast traffic received on IGMP router mode interfaces is forwarded over the IGMP proxy mode interface. The IGMP proxy mode interface forwards all nonlocal multicast traffic received from IGMP router mode interfaces regardless of whether or not there are group members present downstream from the IGMP proxy mode interface.

IGMP proxy mode is designed to connect a Windows Server 2008-based router to a fully capable IP multicast internetwork. As Figure 7-8 shows, IGMP proxy mode is enabled on the interface that is connected to the multicast-enabled internetwork.

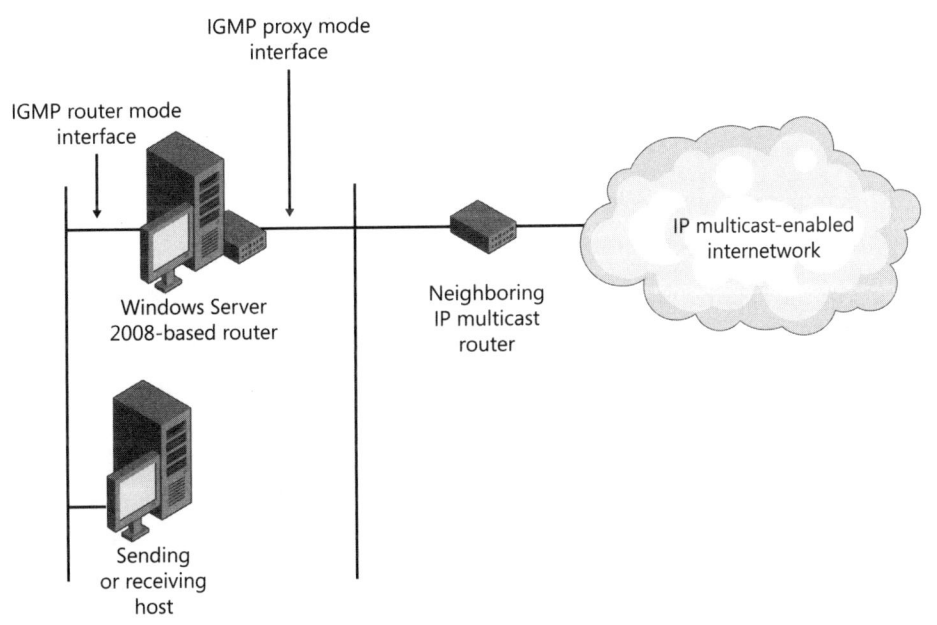

Figure 7-8   The use of IGMP router mode and proxy mode

The combination of IGMP router mode interfaces and the IGMP proxy mode interface allows the sending and receiving of IP multicast traffic for hosts on a peripheral subnet using a router running Windows Server 2008.

Multicast Group Members on IGMP Router Mode Interfaces   Host members on IGMP router mode interfaces receive host group traffic through the following process:

1. A host sends an IGMP Host Membership Report message on the local subnet.

2. The router updates its multicast forwarding table with the appropriate entry.

3. The IGMP routing protocol adds the multicast MAC address corresponding to the IP multicast address to the table of interesting MAC addresses on the network adapter on which IGMP proxy mode is enabled.

4. The router forwards the IGMP Host Membership Report message on the IGMP proxy mode interface.

5. The neighboring IP multicast-enabled router receives the IGMP Host Membership Report message, makes the appropriate changes to its multicast forwarding table, and informs downstream IP multicast-enabled routers using multicast routing protocols that a host member exists on the IGMP proxy mode interface subnet.

Routers of the IP multicast-enabled internetwork forward IP multicast traffic sent to the host group to the neighboring IP multicast-enabled router, which forwards the traffic on the IGMP proxy mode interface subnet. The IGMP proxy mode interface receives the multicast traffic and submits it to the TCP/IP multicast forwarding process. Based on the entries in the multicast forwarding table, the IP multicast traffic is forwarded on the IGMP router mode interface connected to the subnet containing the host member.

Multicast Sources on IGMP Router Mode Interfaces The multicast traffic of multicast sources on IGMP router mode interfaces is forwarded through the following process:

1. A multicast source host sends nonlocal IP multicast traffic to a specific group address.

2. The IGMP router mode interface receives the multicast traffic.

3. For the first multicast packet, the IGMP routing protocol adds an entry to the TCP/IP multicast forwarding table, indicating that there are host members present on the IGMP proxy mode interface.

4. The multicast traffic is passed to the multicast forwarding process. Based on the entries in the multicast forwarding table, the multicast traffic is forwarded on the IGMP proxy mode interface.

5. The neighboring IP multicast-enabled router receives the IP multicast traffic and passes it to the multicast forwarding process. Based on the entries in the multicast forwarding table of the IP multicast-enabled router, the multicast packet is either forwarded to host members (local or downstream) or silently discarded.

Summary

IGMP provides a mechanism for hosts to register their interest in receiving IP multicast traffic sent to a specific group address (the Host Membership Report message), for hosts to indicate that they are no longer interested in receiving IP multicast traffic sent to a specific group address (the Leave Group message), and for routers to query the membership of all host groups (the General Host Membership Query) or a single host group (the Group-Specific Host Membership Query). TCP/IP for Windows Server 2008 and Windows Vista supports IGMPv1, IGMPv2, and IGMPv3, as well as IP multicast forwarding. In Windows Server 2008, the Routing and Remote Access service uses the IGMP routing protocol component and interfaces in IGMP router and proxy mode to maintain the IP multicast forwarding table and provide multicast forwarding in limited configurations.

Chapter 8

Internet Protocol Version 6 (IPv6)

In this chapter:

The Disadvantages of IPv4 179
IPv6 Addressing 181
Core Protocols of IPv6. 184
Differences Between IPv4 and IPv6 186
Summary. 187

After decades of faithful service, the current version of IP, also known as IP version 4 (IPv4), is showing signs of age. The growth of the Internet and the inclusion of a variety of unanticipated technologies are putting a strain on the original design. Before we begin to discuss IPv4's pitfalls, we must take a moment to reflect on the design of IPv4. This protocol was designed in the late 1970s (roughly the Bronze Age of computing) and has risen above all other networking protocols to become the de facto world standard for data communications. There are not many computer technologies that were designed in 1978 that are still in use today, much less as the cornerstone of a global communications infrastructure.

Note Because this book is primarily about IPv4, the coverage of IPv6 in this chapter is deliberately written to provide an overview and how it compares with IPv4. Throughout the rest of this book, when IP is used, it denotes IPv4. For more information about IPv6 and its implementation in Microsoft Windows Server 2008 and Windows Vista, see the book *Understanding IPv6, 2nd Edition* (Redmond, Wash: Microsoft Press, 2008) by Joseph Davies or the resources on *http://www.microsoft.com/ipv6*.

More Info All of the RFCs referenced in this chapter can be found in the \Standards\Chap08_IPv6 folder on the companion CD-ROM.

The Disadvantages of IPv4

On today's Internet, IPv4 has the following disadvantages:

- **Limited address space** The most visible and urgent problem with using IPv4 on the modern Internet is the rapid depletion of public addresses. Due to the initial address class allocation practices of the early Internet, public IPv4 addresses are becoming scarce. Organizations in the United States hold most public IPv4 address space worldwide.

This limited address space has forced the wide deployment of network address translators (NATs), which can share one public IPv4 address among several privately addressed computers. NATs have the side effect of acting as a barrier for server, listener, and peer-to-peer applications running on computers that are located behind the NAT. Although there are workarounds for NAT issues, they only add complexity to what should be an end-to-end addressable global network.

- **Flat routing infrastructure**   In the early Internet, address prefixes were not allocated to create a summarizable, hierarchical routing infrastructure. Instead, individual address prefixes were assigned and each address prefix became a new route in the routing tables of the Internet backbone routers. Today's Internet is a mixture of flat and hierarchical routing, but there are still more than 85,000 routes in the routing tables of Internet backbone routers.

- **Configuration**   IPv4 must be configured, either manually or through the Dynamic Host Configuration Protocol (DHCP). DHCP allows IPv4 configuration administration to scale to large networks, but you must also configure and manage a DHCP infrastructure.

- **Security**   Security for IPv4 is specified by the use of Internet Protocol security (IPsec). However, IPsec is optional for IPv4 implementations. Because an application cannot rely on IPsec being present to secure traffic, an application might resort to other security standards or a proprietary security scheme. The need for built-in security is even more important today, when we face an increasingly hostile environment on the Internet.

- **Prioritized delivery**   Prioritized packet delivery, such as special handling parameters for low delay and low variance in delay for voice or video traffic, is possible with IPv4. However, it relies on a new interpretation of the IPv4 Type Of Service (TOS) field, which is not supported for all the devices on the network. Additionally, identification of the packet flow must be done using an upper layer protocol identifier such as a TCP or User Datagram Protocol (UDP) port. This additional processing of the packet by intermediate routers makes forwarding less efficient.

- **Mobility**   Mobility is a new requirement for Internet-connected devices, in which a node can change its address as it changes its physical attachment to the Internet and still maintain existing connections. Although there is a specification for IPv4 mobility, due to a lack of infrastructure, communications with an IPv4 mobile node are inefficient.

All of these issues and others prompted the Internet Engineering Task Force (IETF) to begin the development of a replacement protocol for IPv4 that would solve the problems of IPv4 and be extensible to solve additional problems in the future. The replacement for IPv4 is IPv6.

> **Note**   The version number 5 was reserved for a different replacement protocol for IPv4 that was never implemented.

IPv6 solves the problems of IPv4 in the following ways:

- **Huge address space** IPv6 addresses are 128 bits long, creating an address space with 3.4×10^{38} possible addresses. This is plenty of address space for the foreseeable future and allows all manner of devices to connect to the Internet without the use of NATs. Address space can also be allocated internationally in a more equitable manner.

- **Hierarchical routing infrastructure** IPv6 addresses that are reachable on the IPv6 portion of the Internet, known as *global addresses*, have enough address space for the hierarchy of Internet service providers (ISPs) that typically exist between an organization or home and the backbone of the Internet. Global addresses are designed to be summarizable and hierarchical, resulting in relatively few routing entries in the routing tables of Internet backbone routers.

- **Automatic configuration** IPv6 hosts can automatically configure their own IPv6 addresses and other configuration parameters, even in the absence of an address configuration infrastructure such as DHCP.

- **Required support for IPsec headers** Unlike IPv4, IPv6 support for IPsec protocol headers is required. Applications can always rely on industry standard security services for data sent and received. However, the requirement to process IPsec headers does not make IPv6 inherently more secure. IPv6 packets are not required to be protected with Authentication Header (AH) or Encapsulating Security Payload (ESP). For more information about IPsec, AH, and ESP, see Chapter 18, "Internet Protocol Security (IPsec)."

- **Better support for prioritized delivery** IPv6 has an equivalent to the IPv4 TOS field that has a single interpretation for nonstandard delivery. Additionally, a Flow Label field in the IPv6 header indicates the packet flow, making the determination of forwarding for nondefault delivery services more efficient at intermediate routers.

- **Support for mobility** Rather than attempting to add mobility to an established protocol with an established infrastructure (as with IPv4), IPv6 can support mobility more efficiently.

Note IPv6 is not designed to be a superset of IPv4 functionality and is not backward compatible with IPv4.

IPv6 Addressing

The IPv6 address is 128 bits long, creating an address space of almost inconceivable size. With 128 bits you can express more than 3.4×10^{38} combinations. Unlike IPv4 unicast addresses, the structure of an IPv6 unicast address is very simple: The first 64 bits are for a subnet prefix and the last 64 bits are for an interface identifier. Although you can perform variable-length subnetting within the 64 bits of the subnet prefix, the host ID equivalent for IPv6 is always the same size. The 64 bits of subnet prefix provide enough addressing space to enumerate networks from the Internet backbone to the individual subnets within an organization's site. The 64 bits of interface identifier can be used to map 48-bit media access control (MAC) addresses used by today's network adapters and 64-bit MAC addresses used by tomorrow's network adapters.

Basics of IPv6 Address Syntax

With such a large address space, expressing an individual IPv6 address became problematic. The designers of IPv6 settled on colon-hexadecimal notation, which divides the 128-bit address into eight 16-bit blocks separated by colons. Each 16-bit block is expressed in hexadecimal format (rather than decimal format for IPv4). The result is the IPv6 address.

The following are some examples of IPv6 unicast addresses:

- 2001:DB8:2A:41CD:2AA:FF:FE5F:47D1
- FE80:0:0:0:2AA:FF:FE5F:47D1
- FD47:2AD1:494E:41CD:2AA:FF:FE5F:47D1

Notice that the leading zeros within each block are suppressed, as long as each block contains at least one hexadecimal digit. A fully expressed block is always four hexadecimal digits.

There are many IPv6 addresses that have a sequence of blocks set to 0. To further compress IPv6 addresses, a single contiguous set of 0 blocks can be expressed as "::", a notation known as *double-colon*. For example:

- FE80:0:0:0:2AA:FF:FE5F:47D1 becomes FE80::2AA:FF:FE5F:47D1
- FF02:0:0:0:0:0:0:1 (a multicast address) becomes FF02::1

To express a subnet prefix, a route, or an address range, IPv6 uses the network prefix length notation (also used for Classless Inter-Domain Routing [CIDR] for IPv4). There are no subnet masks in IPv6. For example, 2001:DB8:2A:41CD::/64 is a subnet prefix; 2001:DB8:2A::/48 is a summarized route; and FF00::/8 is an address range (the range of all IPv6 multicast addresses).

Types of Addresses

IPv6 defines three types of addresses: unicast, multicast, and anycast. Unicast and multicast addresses work in the same way as they do for IPv4. An anycast address, however, is a strange mixture of unicast and multicast. Whereas a unicast address is used for one-to-one delivery and a multicast address is used for one-to-many delivery, an anycast address is used for one-to-one-of-many delivery. A set of interfaces, known as an anycast group, listens on the anycast address. When a sending host sends packets to an anycast address, the packets are delivered to the anycast group member that is topologically closest to the sending host. This delivery to the closest anycast group member is facilitated by host routes in the routing infrastructure that indicate with routing metrics where the closest group member is located. This new type of address allows some types of network resources to be scattered across an organization's network. For example, when a host sends a query to a server using a reserved anycast address, the routing infrastructure delivers the query to the server that is closest to the querying host.

Types of Unicast Addresses

Just as there are different types of IPv4 unicast addresses (such as public and private), there are different types of IPv6 unicast addresses.

Global

Global addresses are the equivalent of IPv4 public addresses. Global addresses are globally reachable on the IPv6 Internet. Unlike public IPv4 address prefixes, which are a combination of flat and summarizable address spaces, IPv6 global addresses are easier to aggregate and summarize at address space boundaries. This results in fewer routes in the various routing domains of the Internet.

Link-Local Addresses

Link-local addresses, which are used on the same link, are equivalent to Automatic Private IP Addressing (APIPA) IPv4 addresses used by current Microsoft desktop and server operating systems. Link-local addresses are automatically configured and can be used to provide automatic addressing for nodes connected to the same network segment when there is no router present. Link-local addresses always begin with "FE80".

Unique Local Addresses

Unique local addresses are defined to be used within the sites of an organization but not on the IPv6 Internet. Unique local addresses are roughly equivalent to private IPv4 addresses except that part of a unique local address prefix is randomly generated to prevent address duplication between sites of an organization and between organizations. Unique local addresses begin with "FD" or "FC".

IPv6 Interface Identifiers

The interface identifier, the last 64 bits of an IPv6 unicast address, can be determined in the following ways:

- Randomly generated to prevent address scans on a link
- Derived from the MAC address of the network adapter to which the address is assigned
- Randomly generated to provide IPv4-equivalent anonymity for client-initiated traffic
- Assigned during a Point-to-Point Protocol (PPP) connection
- Assigned during DHCP for IPv6 (DHCPv6) configuration

DNS Support

To resolve domain names to IPv6 addresses, RFC 1886 defines the use of the AAAA (or quad-A) Domain Name System (DNS) resource record to resolve a DNS name to an IPv6 address. The AAAA record is analogous to the address (A) record that exists for resolving a DNS name to an IPv4 address. To obtain an AAAA record in a DNS query response, a querying host must specify either AAAA records or all records in its DNS query.

For reverse name resolution, RFC 1886 also describes the use of pointer (PTR) records to determine the name of an IPv6 node from its address. The IP6.ARPA reverse name domain is used as the root of the reverse namespace rather than IN-ADDR.ARPA. To create the reverse query name, the IPv6 address is fully expressed as a sequence of hexadecimal digits (including all 0 digits), and then each hexadecimal digit in reverse order becomes a separate level in the reverse domain namespace.

For example, for the IPv6 address 2001:DB8:0:41CD:2AA:FF:FE5F:47D1 (fully expressed as 2001:0DB8:0000:41CD:02AA:00FF:FE5F:47D1), the name in the reverse domain namespace is 1.D.7.4.F.5.E.F.F.F.0.0.A.A.2.0.D.C.1.4.0.0.0.0.8.B.D.0.1.0.0.2.IP6.ARPA.

Core Protocols of IPv6

The core protocols of the IPv6 protocol suite consist of the following:

- IPv6
- Internet Control Message Protocol for IPv6 (ICMPv6)
- Neighbor Discovery (ND)
- Multicast Listener Discovery (MLD)

IPv6

The IPv6 header is described in RFC 2460. It has a new, streamlined design that removes unneeded fields and moves seldom-used fields to extension headers. Even with addresses that are four times larger than IPv4 addresses, the size of the IPv6 header is only twice as large as the IPv4 header, with a 40-byte fixed size. Although larger, the IPv6 header contains fewer fields and is more efficiently processed by routers. Like IPv4, IPv6 is connectionless and provides a best-effort delivery to the destination.

The IPv6 header is not compatible with the IPv4 header. An IPv4-only node silently discards IPv6 packets and an IPv6-only node silently discards IPv4 packets.

ICMPv6

ICMPv6, defined in RFC 4443, provides error reporting and diagnostic functions for IPv6. Additionally, ICMPv6 provides a common packet structure for the messages of ND and MLD. Analogous to ICMP for IPv4, ICMPv6 provides the following types of messages:

- Echo Request
- Echo Reply
- Destination Unreachable
- Time Exceeded
- Parameter Problem

ICMPv6 also includes a Packet Too Big message that is equivalent to the RFC 1191–defined Destination Unreachable-Fragmentation Needed and DF Set message for ICMP. The ICMPv6 Packet Too Big message is used for IPv6-based path maximum transmission unit (PMTU) discovery.

Neighbor Discovery

ND, defined in RFC 4861, consists of a set of ICMPv6 messages, message options, and defined processes that allow neighboring nodes to discover each other, discover the routers on the link, and provide support for host redirection. ND replaces the following facilities in IPv4:

- Address Resolution Protocol (ARP)
- ICMP Router Discovery
- ICMP Redirect

The five ND messages are as follows:

- Neighbor Solicitation
- Neighbor Advertisement
- Router Solicitation
- Router Advertisement
- Redirect

ND defines the following processes:

- **Address resolution** Instead of sending a broadcast ARP Request message and receiving a unicast ARP Reply message, an IPv6 node sends a multicast Neighbor Solicitation and receives a unicast Neighbor Advertisement.

- **Duplicate address detection** Just like the sending of gratuitous ARP frames in IPv4, an IPv6 node performs address resolution on addresses it attempts to use before initializing them on an interface.

- **Router discovery** When nodes start up on a link, they send a multicast Router Solicitation message. Routers on the link send a unicast or multicast Router Advertisement message that contains address prefixes and other configuration options so that the host can automatically configure global and unique local addresses. With proper configuration of routers, a DHCPv6 infrastructure is not required for IPv6 unicast address configuration.

- **Redirect** Just as in IPv4, if an IPv6 host sends traffic to the wrong first-hop router, the router forwards the packet and sends the sending host a Redirect message, informing the host of the better next-hop address of the optimal first-hop router.

- **Neighbor unreachability detection** IPv6 tracks whether neighboring nodes are reachable. If a neighboring node becomes unreachable, an IPv6 node detects the problem and makes adjustments, such as automatically choosing a new default router, or indicating the error to upper layer protocols.

Multicast Listener Discovery

MLD, defined in RFC 2710, is the IPv6 equivalent to Internet Group Management Protocol (IGMP) version 2 for IPv4. MLD defines ICMPv6 messages that are used by hosts to register group membership, by hosts to leave a group, and by routers to query the subnet for group membership.

MLD version 2 (MLDv2), defined in RFC 3810, is the IPv6 equivalent of IGMP version 3 (IGMPv3) for IPv4. MLDv2 performs the same functions as MLD, but allows IPv6 hosts to register interest in source-specific multicast traffic with local multicast routers. An MLDv2-capable host can register interest in receiving IPv6 multicast traffic from only specific source addresses (an include list) or from any source except specific source addresses (an exclude list).

Differences Between IPv4 and IPv6

Table 8-1 lists some of the differences between IPv4 and IPv6.

Table 8-1 Differences Between IPv4 and IPv6

Category	IPv4	IPv6
Address length	32 bits	128 bits
Header size	20–60 bytes	40 bytes
IPsec header support	Optional	Required
Prioritized delivery support	Limited	Better
Fragmentation	Done by hosts and routers	Done by hosts only
Is a header checksum present?	Yes	No

Table 8-1 Differences Between IPv4 and IPv6

Category	IPv4	IPv6
Does the header include options?	Yes	No
Link-layer address resolution	Broadcast ARP Request frames	Multicast Neighbor Solicitation messages
Error reporting and diagnostic protocol	ICMP (for IPv4)	ICMPv6
Multicast group membership protocol	IGMPv1, IGMPv2, IGMPv3	MLD, MLDv2
Router discovery support	Optional	Required
Network layer broadcast addresses?	Yes	No
Host configuration	DHCP or manual	Automatic, DHCPv6, or manual
DNS record type for name resolution	A record	AAAA record
DNS record type and location	PTR records in IN-ADDR.ARPA domain	PTR records in IP6.ARPA domain

Summary

The IPv6 suite of protocols is a revision of the Internet Layer protocols of the current TCP/IP protocol suite and replaces IP, ICMP, IGMP, and ARP. IPv6 attempts to solve the problems of IPv4 with efficient and plentiful addressing, a streamlined Internet Layer header that is easier for routers to process, and more efficient neighboring node interaction.

Part III
Transport Layer Protocols

In this part:

Chapter 9: User Datagram Protocol 191

Chapter 10: Transmission Control Protocol (TCP) Basics 199

Chapter 11: Transmission Control Protocol (TCP) Connections 223

Chapter 12: Transmission Control Protocol (TCP) Data Flow 245

Chapter 13: Transmission Control Protocol (TCP) Retransmission
and Time-Out 271

Chapter 9
User Datagram Protocol

> **In this chapter:**
> Introduction to UDP 191
> Uses for UDP. 192
> The UDP Message 193
> The UDP Header 193
> UDP Ports 195
> The UDP Pseudo Header 196
> Summary. 197

There are two protocols at the Transport Layer that TCP/IP applications typically use for transporting data: Transmission Control Protocol (TCP) and User Datagram Protocol (UDP). This chapter describes the characteristics of UDP and the fields in the UDP header.

Introduction to UDP

UDP, defined in RFC 768, has the following characteristics:

- **Connectionless**   Nodes send UDP messages, consisting of a UDP header and a message, without having to negotiate a connection between communicating peers.

- **Unreliable**   Nodes send UDP messages as datagrams without sequencing or acknowledgment. The Application Layer protocol must reorder and recover lost messages. Typical UDP-based Application Layer protocols either provide their own reliable service or retransmit UDP messages periodically or after a defined time-out value.

- **Provides identification of Application Layer protocols**   UDP provides a mechanism to send messages to a specific Application Layer protocol or process on an internetwork host. The UDP header provides both source and destination process identification.

- **Provides checksum of UDP message**   The UDP header provides a 16-bit checksum of the entire UDP message.

> **More Info**   All of the RFCs referenced in this chapter can be found in the \Standards\Chap09_UDP folder on the companion CD-ROM.

UDP is a direct reflection of the datagram services of IP, except that UDP provides a method to pass data to an Application Layer protocol.

UDP does not provide the following delivery services:

- **Buffering**   UDP does not provide any buffering of incoming or outgoing data. The Application Layer protocol must provide all buffering.

- **Segmentation**   UDP does not provide any segmentation of large blocks of data. Therefore, the application must send data in small enough blocks so that the IP datagrams for the UDP messages are no larger than the Maximum Transmission Unit (MTU) of the interface on which they are sent. Otherwise, IP on the sending host fragments the UDP message.

- **Flow control**   UDP does not provide any sender-side or receiver-side flow control. UDP message senders can react to the receipt of an Internet Control Message Protocol (ICMP) Source Quench message, but it is not required.

Uses for UDP

Although UDP does not provide any services beyond Application Layer protocol identification and a checksum, there are uses for sending data using UDP, including the following:

- **Lightweight protocol**   To conserve memory and processor resources, some Application Layer protocols require the use of a lightweight protocol that performs a specific function using a simple exchange of messages. A good example is Domain Name System (DNS) name queries. Typically, a DNS client sends a DNS Name Query Request message to a DNS server. The DNS server responds with a DNS Name Query Response message. If the DNS server does not respond, the DNS client retransmits the DNS Name Query Request message.

    If all the DNS clients used TCP rather than UDP, all DNS name queries would be sent reliably, but the DNS server would have to support hundreds or, on the Internet, thousands of TCP connections. The low-overhead solution of using UDP is the best choice for simple request-reply-based Application Layer protocols.

- **Reliability provided by the Application Layer protocol**   If the Application Layer protocol provides its own reliable data delivery services, there is no need for the Transport Layer protocol to provide them. Examples of reliable Application Layer protocols are Trivial File Transfer Protocol (TFTP) and Network File System (NFS).

- **Reliability not required due to periodic advertisement process**   If the Application Layer protocol periodically advertises information, reliable delivery is not required. If an advertisement is lost, it is announced again at the period interval. An example of an Application Layer protocol that uses periodic advertisements is the Routing Information Protocol (RIP).

- **One-to-many delivery** UDP can be used as the Transport Layer protocol whenever Application Layer data must be sent to multiple destinations using an IP multicast or broadcast address. TCP can be used only for one-to-one delivery. For example, a host sends a broadcast NetBIOS Name Query Request message using UDP.

The UDP Message

A UDP message, consisting of a UDP header and its payload (a message), is identified in the IP header with IP Protocol number 17 (0x11). The message can be a maximum size of 65,507 bytes: 65,535 minus the minimum-size IP header (20 bytes) and the UDP header (8 bytes). The resulting IP datagram is then encapsulated with the appropriate Network Interface Layer header and trailer. Figure 9-1 shows the resulting frame.

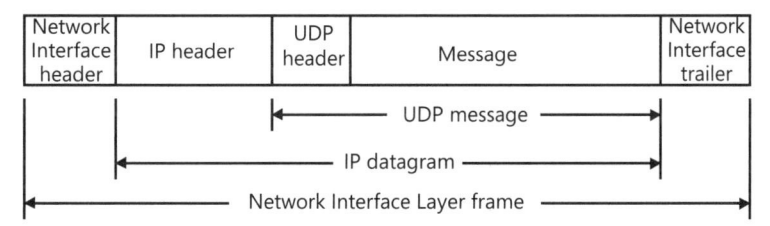

Figure 9-1 UDP message encapsulation showing the IP header and Network Interface Layer header and trailer

In the IP header of UDP messages, the Source IP Address field indicates the host interface that sent the UDP message. The Destination IP Address field indicates the unicast address of the destination host (or intermediate router if the packet is source routed), an IP broadcast address, or an IP multicast address.

The UDP Header

The UDP header is a fixed-length size of 8 bytes consisting of four fields, as Figure 9-2 shows.

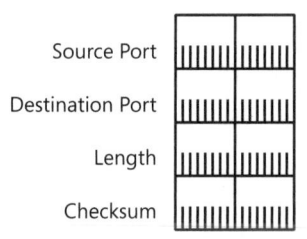

Figure 9-2 The structure of the UDP header

The fields in the UDP header are defined as follows:

- **Source Port** A 2-byte field that identifies the source Application Layer protocol sending the UDP message. The use of a source port is optional and, when not used, is set to 0. IP multicast traffic, such as videocasts sent using UDP, can use 0 because no reply to the video traffic is expected. Typical Application Layer protocols use the source port of an incoming UDP message as the destination port for replies. The combination of the IP header's source IP address and the UDP header's source port provides a unique, globally significant address for the process from which the message was sent.

- **Destination Port** A 2-byte field that identifies the destination Application Layer protocol. The combination of the IP header's destination IP address and the UDP header's destination port provides a unique, globally significant address for the process to which the message is sent.

- **Length** A 2-byte field indicates the length in bytes of the UDP message, including both the UDP header and the message. The minimum length is 8 bytes (the UDP header's size), and the maximum is 65,515 bytes (maximum-sized IP datagram of 65,535 bytes minus the minimum-sized IP header of 20 bytes). The actual maximum length is confined by the MTU of the link on which the UDP message is sent. In the absence of extension headers between the IP header and the UDP header, the Length field is redundant. The UDP length is the IP payload length, which can always be calculated from the Total Length and the IP Header Length fields in the IP header (UDP length = payload length = total length − 4 × IP header length [in 32-bit words]).

- **Checksum** A 2-byte field that provides a bit-level integrity check for the UDP message. The UDP checksum calculation uses the same method as the IP header checksum over the UDP pseudo header, the UDP header, the message, and, if needed, a padding byte of 0x00. The padding byte is used only if the message's length is an odd number of bytes. For more information about the UDP pseudo header, see "The UDP Pseudo Header" later in this chapter. The use of the UDP Checksum field is optional. If not used, the UDP Checksum field is set to 0. For more information about the checksum calculation, see Chapter 5, "Internet Protocol (IP)."

Note TCP/IP for Windows Server 2008 and Windows Vista always calculates a value for the UDP checksum.

The following Network Monitor trace (Capture 9-01 in the \Captures folder on the companion CD-ROM) shows the structure of the UDP header for a DNS Name Query Request message:

```
Frame:
+ Ethernet: Etype = Internet IP (IPv4)
+ Ipv4: Next Protocol = UDP, Packet ID = 16385, Total IP Length = 58
- Udp: SrcPort = DNS(53), DstPort = DNS(53), Length = 38
    SourcePort: DNS(53), 53(0x35)
    DestinationPort: DNS(53), 53(0x35)
    TotalLength: 38 (0x26)
    Checksum: 27297 (0x6AA1)
+ Dns: QueryId = 0x2, QUERY (Standard query), Query for www.acme.com of type Host Addr on class Internet
```

UDP Ports

A UDP port defines a location or message queue for the delivery of messages for Application Layer protocols using UDP services. Included in each UDP message is the source port (the message queue from which the message was sent) and a destination port (the message queue to which the message was sent). The Internet Assigned Numbers Authority (IANA) assigns port numbers, known as *well-known port numbers*, to specific Application Layer protocols. Table 9-1 shows well-known UDP port numbers used by Windows Server 2008 and Windows Vista-based components.

Table 9-1 Well-Known UDP Port Numbers

Port Number	Application Layer Protocol
53	DNS
67	BOOTP server (Dynamic Host Configuration Protocol [DHCP])
68	BOOTP client (DHCP)
69	TFTP
137	NetBIOS Name Service
138	NetBIOS Datagram Service
161	Simple Network Management Protocol (SNMP)
445	Direct hosting of Server Message Block (SMB) datagrams over TCP/IP (also known as Microsoft-DS)
520	RIP
1812, 1813	Remote Authentication Dial-In User Service (RADIUS)

See *http://www.iana.org/assignments/port-numbers* for the most current list of IANA-assigned UDP port numbers.

Typically, the server side of an Application Layer protocol listens on the well-known port number. The client side of an Application Layer protocol uses either the well-known port number or, more commonly, a dynamically allocated port number. These dynamically allocated port numbers are used for the duration of the process and are also known as *ephemeral* or *short-lived ports*.

A UDP port number can be referenced by name by a Microsoft Windows Sockets application using the `GetServByName()` function. The name is resolved to a UDP port number through the Services file stored in the *%SystemRoot%*\System32\Drivers\Etc folder.

A sending node determines the destination port (using either a specified value or the `GetServByName()` function) and the source port (using either a specified value or by obtaining a dynamically allocated port through Windows Sockets). The sending node then indicates the source IP address, destination IP address, source port, destination port, and the message to be sent to TCP/IP. The UDP component calculates the length and the checksum and indicates the UDP message with the appropriate source IP address and destination IP address to the IP component.

When receiving a UDP message at the destination, IP verifies the IP header and, based on the value of 17 (0x11) in the Protocol field, passes the UDP message, the source IP address, and the destination IP address to the UDP component. After verifying the UDP checksum, the UDP component verifies the destination port. If a process is listening on the port, UDP passes the message to the application. If no process is listening on the port, UDP uses the ICMP component to send an ICMP Destination Unreachable-Port Unreachable message to the sender, and then discards the UDP message.

Figure 9-3 shows the process of demultiplexing an incoming UDP message.

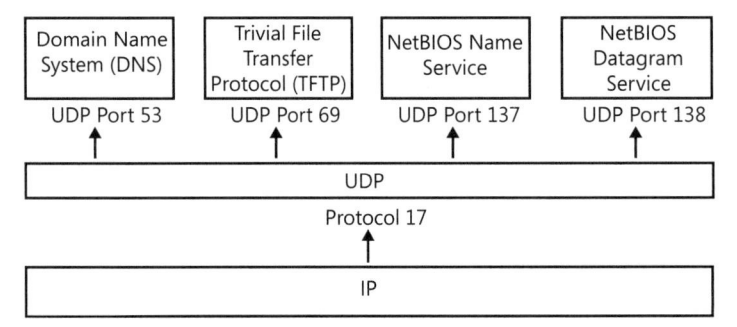

```
┌──────────────┐  ┌──────────────┐  ┌──────────────┐  ┌──────────────┐
│ Domain Name  │  │ Trivial File │  │ NetBIOS Name │  │   NetBIOS    │
│ System (DNS) │  │   Transfer   │  │   Service    │  │   Datagram   │
│              │  │Protocol(TFTP)│  │              │  │   Service    │
└──────────────┘  └──────────────┘  └──────────────┘  └──────────────┘
  UDP Port 53       UDP Port 69      UDP Port 137      UDP Port 138
       ↑                 ↑                 ↑                 ↑
┌─────────────────────────────────────────────────────────────────────┐
│                               UDP                                   │
└─────────────────────────────────────────────────────────────────────┘
                            Protocol 17
                                ↑
┌─────────────────────────────────────────────────────────────────────┐
│                                IP                                   │
└─────────────────────────────────────────────────────────────────────┘
```

Figure 9-3   The demultiplexing of a UDP message to the appropriate Application Layer protocol using the IP Protocol field and the UDP Destination Port field

Best Practices   UDP ports are separate from TCP ports, even for the same port number. A UDP port represents a UDP message queue for an Application Layer protocol. A TCP port represents one side of a TCP connection for an Application Layer protocol. The Application Layer protocol using the UDP port is not necessarily the same Application Layer protocol using the TCP port. A good example of the differentiation between TCP and UDP Application Layer protocols is the Extended Filename Server (EFS) protocol, which uses TCP port 520, and RIP, which uses UDP port 520. Clearly these are separate Application Layer protocols. Therefore, it is not good practice to refer to a port by just its port number because the port number alone is ambiguous. Always refer to either a TCP port number or a UDP port number.

The UDP Pseudo Header

The UDP pseudo header associates the UDP message with its IP header. UDP adds the UDP pseudo header to the beginning of the UDP message only for the checksum calculation; it is not sent as part of the UDP message. The UDP pseudo header assures the receiver that a routing or fragmentation process did not improperly modify key fields in the IP header.

Figure 9-4 shows the UDP pseudo header.

The UDP pseudo header consists of the Source IP Address field, the Destination IP Address field, an Unused field set to 0, the Protocol field for UDP (17 or 0x11), and the UDP Length field. When sending a UDP message, UDP is aware of all of these values. When receiving a UDP message, IP indicates all of these values to UDP.

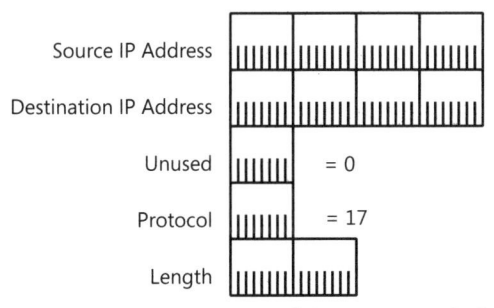

Figure 9-4 The structure of the UDP pseudo header

UDP calculates the UDP checksum over the combination of the UDP pseudo header, the UDP message, and a 0x00 padding byte if needed. The checksum calculation relies on summing 16-bit words. Therefore, the checksum quantity must be an even number of bytes. The padding byte is used only if the length of the message is an odd number of bytes. The padding byte is not included in the UDP length and is not sent as part of the UDP message. Figure 9-5 shows the resulting quantity for the calculation of the UDP Checksum field.

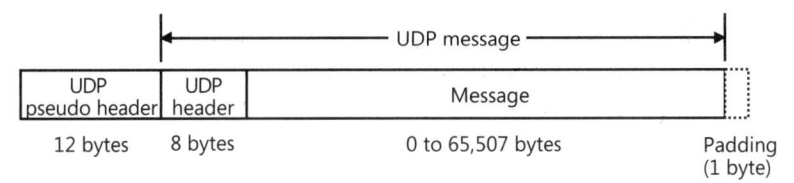

Figure 9-5 The resulting quantity used for the UDP checksum calculation

Note Unlike the IP security (IPsec) Authentication header, the UDP pseudo header and Checksum field are not providing data authentication or data integrity for fields in the IP header and the UDP message. IP header and UDP port fields can be modified as long as the UDP Checksum field is updated. This is how a Network Address Translator (NAT) works. An NAT is a router that translates public and private addresses during the forwarding process. For example, when translating a source IP address from a private address to a public address, the NAT also recalculates the UDP checksum.

Summary

UDP provides a connectionless and unreliable delivery service for applications that do not require the guaranteed delivery service of TCP. Application Layer protocols use UDP for lightweight interaction, for broadcast or multicast traffic, or when the Application Layer protocol provides its own reliable delivery service. The UDP header provides a checksum and source and destination port numbers to multiplex UDP message data to the proper Application Layer protocol.

Chapter 10

Transmission Control Protocol (TCP) Basics

In this chapter:
Introduction to TCP..199
The TCP Segment...200
The TCP Header..201
TCP Ports..204
TCP Flags..205
The TCP Pseudo Header...207
TCP Urgent Data...208
TCP Options...210
Summary..221

There are two protocols at the Transport Layer that TCP/IP applications typically use for transporting data: Transmission Control Protocol (TCP) and User Datagram Protocol (UDP). This chapter describes the characteristics of TCP and the fields in the TCP header.

Introduction to TCP

TCP, defined in RFC 793, is the Transport Layer protocol that provides a reliable data-transfer service and a method to pass TCP-encapsulated data to an Application Layer protocol. TCP has the following characteristics:

- **Connection-oriented** Before data can be transferred, two Application Layer processes must formally negotiate a TCP connection using the TCP connection establishment process. TCP connections are formally closed using the TCP connection termination process. For more information about TCP connection processes, see Chapter 11, "Transmission Control Protocol (TCP) Connections."

- **Full duplex** For each TCP peer, the TCP connection consists of two logical pipes: an outgoing pipe and an incoming pipe. With the appropriate Network Interface Layer technology, data can be flowing out of the outgoing pipe and into the incoming pipe simultaneously. The TCP header contains both the sequence number of the outgoing data and an acknowledgment of the incoming data.

- **Reliable** Data sent on a TCP connection is sequenced and a positive acknowledgment is expected from the receiver. If no acknowledgment is received, the segment is retransmitted. At the receiver, duplicate segments are discarded and segments arriving out of sequence are placed back in the proper sequence. A TCP checksum is always used to verify the bit-level integrity of the TCP segment.

- **Byte stream** TCP views the data sent over the incoming and outgoing logical pipes as a continuous stream of bytes. The sequence number and acknowledgment number in each TCP header are defined along byte boundaries. TCP is not aware of record or message boundaries within the byte stream. The Application Layer protocol must provide the proper parsing of the incoming byte stream.

- **Sender- and receiver-side flow control** To avoid sending too much data at one time and congesting the routers of the network, TCP implements sender-side flow control that gradually scales the amount of data sent at one time. To avoid having the sender send data that the receiver cannot buffer, TCP implements receiver-side flow control that indicates the number of bytes that the receiver can receive. For more information on how TCP implements sender- and receiver-side flow control, see Chapter 12, "Transmission Control Protocol (TCP) Data Flow."

- **Segmentation of Application Layer data** TCP segments data obtained from the Application Layer process so that it will fit within an IP datagram sent on the Network Interface Layer link. TCP peers inform each other of the maximum-sized segment that they can receive and adjust the maximum size using Path Maximum Transmission Unit (PMTU) discovery.

- **One-to-one delivery** TCP connections are a logical point-to-point circuit between two Application Layer protocols. TCP does not provide a one-to-many delivery service.

TCP is typically used when an Application Layer protocol requires a reliable data transfer service.

> **More Info** All of the RFCs referenced in this chapter can be found in the \Standards\Chap10_TCP folder on the companion CD-ROM.

The TCP Segment

A TCP segment, consisting of a TCP header and its optional payload (a segment), is identified in the IP header with IP Protocol number 6. The segment can be a maximum size of 65,495 bytes: 65,535 minus the minimum-size IP header (20 bytes) and the minimum-size TCP header (20 bytes). The resulting IP datagram is then encapsulated with the appropriate Network Interface Layer header and trailer. Figure 10-1 displays the resulting frame.

In the IP header of TCP segments, the Source Address field indicates the unicast address of the host interface that sent the TCP segment. The Destination Address field indicates the unicast address of the destination host (or intermediate router if the packet is source routed).

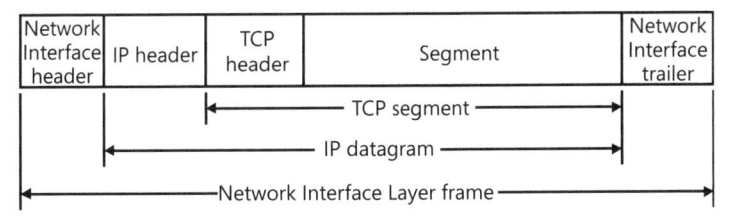

Figure 10-1 TCP segment encapsulation showing the IP header and Network Interface Layer header and trailer

The TCP Header

The TCP header is of variable length, consisting of the fields shown in Figure 10-2. When TCP options are not present, the TCP header is 20 bytes long.

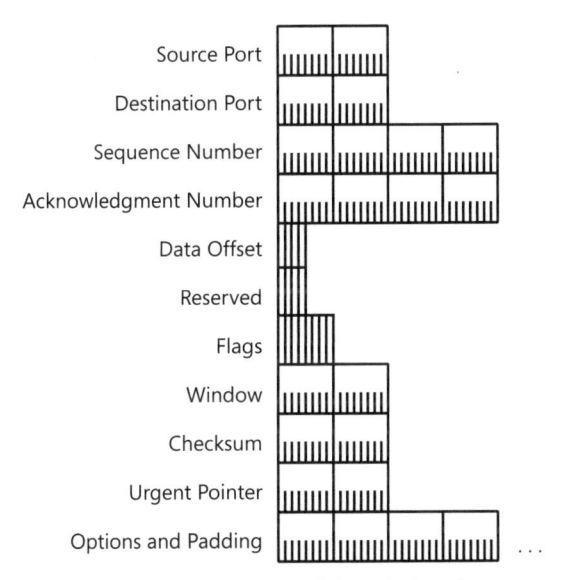

Figure 10-2 The structure of the TCP header

The fields in the TCP header are defined as follows:

- **Source Port** A 2-byte field that indicates the source Application Layer protocol sending the TCP segment. The combination of the source IP address in the IP header and the source port in the TCP header indicates a *source socket*—a unique, globally significant address from which the segment was sent.

- **Destination Port** A 2-byte field that indicates the destination Application Layer protocol. The combination of the destination IP address in the IP header and the destination port in the TCP header indicates a *destination socket*—a unique, globally significant address to which the segment is sent.

- **Sequence Number** A 4-byte field that indicates the outgoing byte-stream-based sequence number of the segment's first byte. The Sequence Number field is always set, even when there is no data in the segment. In this case, the Sequence Number field is set to the number of the outgoing byte stream's next byte. When establishing a TCP connection, TCP segments with a SYN (Synchronization) flag value of 1 set the Sequence Number field to the Initial Sequence Number (ISN). This indicates that the first byte in the outgoing byte stream sent on the connection is ISN + 1.

- **Acknowledgment Number** A 4-byte field that indicates the sequence number of the next byte in the incoming byte stream that the receiver of the incoming byte stream expects to receive. The acknowledgment number provides a positive acknowledgment that all bytes in the incoming byte stream up to, but not including, the acknowledgment number were received. The acknowledgment number is significant in all TCP segments with the ACK (Acknowledgment) flag set.

- **Data Offset** A 4-bit field that indicates where the TCP segment data begins. The Data Offset field is also the TCP header's size. Just as in the IP header's Header Length field, the Data Offset field is the number of 32-bit words (4-byte blocks) in the TCP header. For the smallest TCP header (no options), the Data Offset field is set to 5 (0x5), indicating that the segment data begins in the twentieth byte offset starting from the beginning of the TCP segment (the offset starts its count at 0). With a Data Offset field set to its maximum value of 15 (0xF), the largest TCP header, including TCP options, can be 60 bytes long.

- **Reserved** A 4-bit field that is reserved for future use. The sender sets these bits to 0.

- **Flags** An 8-bit field that indicates the eight TCP flags defined in RFCs 793 and 3168. The eight TCP flags, known as CWR (Congestion Window Reduced), ECE (Explicit Congestion Notification [ECN]-Echo), URG (Urgent), ACK, PSH (Push), RST (Reset), SYN, and FIN (Finish), are discussed in greater detail in the "TCP Flags" section of this chapter.

- **Window** A 2-byte field that indicates the number of bytes that the receiver of the incoming byte stream allows the other TCP peer to send. By advertising the window size with each segment, a TCP receiver is telling the sender how much data can be sent and successfully received and stored. The sender should not be sending more data than the receiver can receive. If the receiver cannot receive any more data, it advertises a window size of 0 bytes. With a window size of 0, the sender cannot send any more data until the window size is a nonzero value. The advertisement of the window size is an implementation of receiver-side flow control. The use of this field is extended to larger window sizes with the TCP Window Scale option, discussed in the "TCP Options" section of this chapter.

- **Checksum** A 2-byte field that provides a bit-level integrity check for the TCP segment (TCP header and segment). The Checksum field's value is calculated in the same way as the IP header checksum, over all the 16-bit words in a TCP pseudo header, the TCP header, the segment, and, if needed, a padding byte of 0x00. The padding byte is used only if the segment length is an odd number of bytes. The value of the Checksum field is set to 0 during the checksum calculation. For more information, see "The TCP Pseudo Header" section in this chapter.

- **Urgent Pointer**   A 2-byte field that indicates the location of urgent data in the segment. The Urgent Pointer field and urgent data are discussed in the "TCP Urgent Data" section of this chapter.

- **Options**   One or more TCP options can be added to the TCP header but must be done in 4-byte increments so that the TCP header size can be indicated with the Data Offset field. TCP options are discussed in the "TCP Options" section of this chapter.

An example of a TCP segment is Capture 10-01, a Network Monitor trace that is included in the \Captures folder on the companion CD-ROM. The following is frame 1 from Capture 10-01, as displayed with Network Monitor 3.1:

```
Frame:
+ Ethernet: Etype = Internet IP (IPv4)
+ Ipv4: Next Protocol = TCP, Packet ID = 57288, Total IP Length = 1500
- Tcp: Flags=....A..., SrcPort=FTP data(20), DstPort=1163, Len=1460, Seq=1038577021 -
 1038578481, Ack=3930983524, Win=17520 (scale factor not found)
    SrcPort: FTP data(20)
    DstPort: 1163
    SequenceNumber: 1038577021 (0x3DE76D7D)
    AcknowledgementNumber: 3930983524 (0xEA4E0C64)
  - DataOffset: 80 (0x50)
    DataOffset: (0101....) (20 bytes)
    Reserved:   (....000.)
    NS:         (.......0) Nonce Sum not significant
  - Flags: ....A...
    CWR:    (0.......) CWR not significant
    ECE:    (.0......) ECN-Echo not significant
    Urgent: (..0.....) Not Urgent Data
    Ack:    (...1....) Acknowledgement field significant
    Push:   (....0...) No Push Function
    Reset:  (.....0..) No Reset
    Syn:    (......0.) Not Synchronize sequence numbers
    Fin:    (.......0) Not End of data
    Window: 17520 (scale factor not found)
    Checksum: 46217 (0xB489)
    UrgentPointer: 0 (0x0)
    TCPPayload:
+ Ftp: Data Transfer To Client,DstPort = 1163,size = 1460 bytes
```

Note   Network Monitor 3.1 parses the last bit of the Reserved field of the TCP header as the Nonce Sum field, which is defined in RFC 3540. TCP/IP in Windows Server 2008 and Windows Vista does not support RFC 3540.

TCP Ports

A TCP port defines a location for the delivery of TCP connection data. Included in each TCP segment is the source port that indicates the Application Layer process from which the segment was sent, and a destination port that indicates the Application Layer process to which the segment was sent. There are port numbers that are assigned by the Internet Assigned Numbers Authority (IANA) to specific Application Layer protocols.

Table 10-1 shows assigned TCP port numbers used by components of Windows Server 2008 and Windows Vista.

Table 10-1 Well-Known TCP Port Numbers

Port Number	Application Layer Protocol
20	FTP Server (data channel)
21	FTP Server (control channel)
23	Telnet Server
25	Simple Mail Transfer Protocol (SMTP)
69	Trivial File Transfer Protocol (TFTP)
80	Hypertext Transfer Protocol (HTTP; Web server)
139	NetBIOS Session Service
443	HTTP protocol over Transport Layer Security (TLS)
445	Direct-Hosted Server Message Block (SMB) (also known as Microsoft-DS)

See *http://www.iana.org/assignments/port-numbers* for the most current list of IANA-assigned TCP port numbers.

Typically, the server side of an Application Layer protocol listens on the well-known port number. The client side of an Application Layer protocol uses either the well-known port number or, more commonly, a dynamically allocated port number. These dynamically allocated port numbers are used for the duration of the process and are known also as *ephemeral* or *short-lived ports*.

A Windows Sockets application using the `GetServByName()` function can refer to a TCP port number by name. The name is resolved to a TCP port number through the Services file stored in the *%SystemRoot%\System32\Drivers\Etc* folder.

A sending node determines the destination port (using either a specified value or the `GetServByName()` function) and the source port (using either a specified value, or by obtaining a dynamically allocated port through Windows Sockets). The sending node then passes the source IP address, destination IP address, source port, destination port, and the data to be sent to TCP/IP. The TCP component segments the data as needed. The TCP component calculates the Checksum field and indicates the TCP segment with the appropriate source IP address and destination IP address to the IP component.

When receiving a TCP segment at the destination, IP verifies the IP header. Then, based on the value of 6 in the Protocol field, IP passes the TCP segment, the source IP address, and the destination IP address to the TCP component. After verifying the TCP Checksum field, the TCP component verifies the destination port. If a process is listening on the port, the TCP segment is passed to the application. If no process is listening on the port, TCP sends a TCP Connection Reset segment to the sender. For more information about the TCP Connection Reset segment, see Chapter 11, "Transmission Control Protocol (TCP) Connections."

Figure 10-3 shows the demultiplexing of received TCP connection data based on the TCP destination port.

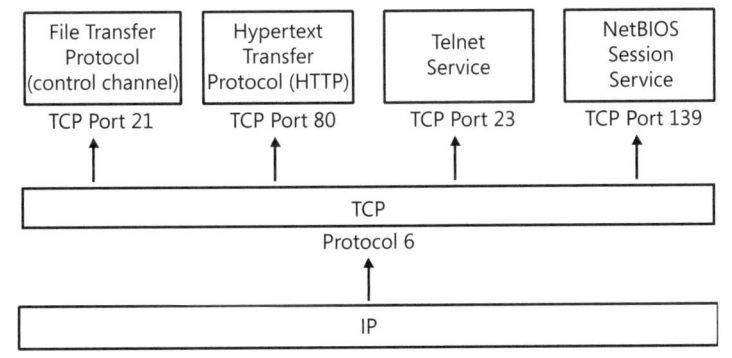

Figure 10-3 The demultiplexing of a TCP segment to the appropriate Application Layer protocol using the IP Protocol field and the TCP Destination Port field

Best Practices TCP ports are separate from UDP ports, even for the same port number. A TCP port represents one side of a TCP connection for an Application Layer protocol. A UDP port represents a UDP message queue for an Application Layer protocol. The Application Layer protocol using the TCP port is not necessarily the same Application Layer protocol using the UDP port. For example, the Extended Filename Server (EFS) protocol uses TCP port 520, and the Routing Information Protocol (RIP) uses UDP port 520. Clearly these are separate Application Layer protocols. Therefore, it is not good practice to refer to a port by just its port number, which is ambiguous. Always refer to either a TCP port number or a UDP port number.

TCP Flags

Figure 10-4 shows the eight TCP flags in the TCP header that are defined in RFCs 793 and 3168.

```
CWR
ECE
URG
ACK
PSH
RST
SYN
FIN
```

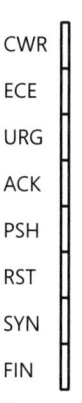

Figure 10-4 The eight TCP flags in the TCP header

The TCP flags are defined as follows:

- **CWR (congestion window has been reduced)**   Indicates that the sending host has received a TCP segment with the ECE flag set. The congestion window is an internal variable maintained by TCP to manage the size of the send window. For more information, see Chapter 12, "Transmission Control Protocol (TCP) Data Flow."

- **ECE (TCP peer is ECN-capable)**   Indicates that a TCP peer is ECN-capable during the TCP 3-way handshake and to indicate that a TCP segment was received on the connection with the ECN field in the IP header set to 11. For more information about ECN, see Chapter 12.

- **URG (Urgent Pointer field is significant)**   Indicates that the segment portion of the TCP segment contains urgent data and the Urgent Pointer field should be used to determine the location of the urgent data in the segment. Urgent data is discussed in more detail in the section "TCP Urgent Data," later in this chapter.

- **ACK (Acknowledgment field is significant)**   Indicates that the Acknowledgment field contains the next byte expected on the connection. The ACK flag is always set, except for the first segment of a TCP connection establishment.

- **PSH (the Push function)**   Indicates that the contents of the TCP receive buffer should be passed to the Application Layer protocol. The data in the receive buffer must consist of a contiguous block of data from the left edge of the buffer. In other words, there cannot be any missing segments of the byte stream up to the segment containing the PSH flag; the data cannot be passed to the Application Layer protocol until missing segments arrive. Normally, the TCP receive buffer is flushed (the contents are passed to the Application Layer protocol) when the receive buffer fills with contiguous data or during normal TCP connection maintenance processes. The PSH flag overrides this default behavior and immediately flushes the TCP receive buffer. The PSH flag is used also for interactive Application Layer protocols such as Telnet, in which each keystroke in the virtual terminal session is sent with the PSH flag set. Another example is the setting of the PSH flag on the last segment of a file transferred with FTP. Data sent with the PSH flag does not have to be immediately acknowledged.

- **RST (Reset the connection)** Indicates that the connection is being aborted. For active connections, a node sends a TCP segment with the RST flag in response to a TCP segment received on the connection that is incorrect, causing the connection to fail. The sending of an RST segment for an active connection forcibly terminates the connection, causing data stored in send and receive buffers or in transit to be lost. For TCP connections being established, a node sends an RST segment in response to a connection establishment request to deny the connection attempt.

- **SYN (Synchronize sequence number)** Indicates that the segment contains an ISN. During the TCP connection establishment process, TCP sends a TCP segment with the SYN flag set. Each TCP peer acknowledges the receipt of the SYN flag by treating the SYN flag as if it were a single byte of data. The Acknowledgment Number field for the acknowledgment of the SYN segment is set to ISN + 1.

- **FIN (Finish sending data)** Indicates that the TCP segment sender is finished sending data on the connection. When a TCP connection is gracefully terminated, each TCP peer sends a TCP segment with the FIN flag set. A TCP peer does not send a TCP segment with the FIN flag set until all outstanding data to the other TCP peer has been sent and acknowledged. Each peer acknowledges receipt of the FIN flag by treating it as if it were a single byte of data. When both TCP peers have sent segments with the FIN flag set and received acknowledgment of their receipt, the TCP connection is terminated.

The TCP Pseudo Header

The TCP pseudo header is used to associate the TCP segment with the IP header. The TCP pseudo header is added to the beginning of the TCP segment only during the checksum calculation and is not sent as part of the TCP segment. The use of the TCP pseudo header assures the receiver that a routing or fragmentation process did not improperly modify key fields in the IP header.

Figure 10-5 illustrates the TCP pseudo header.

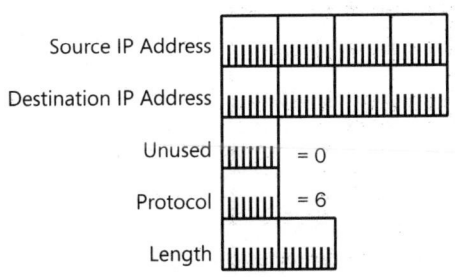

Figure 10-5 The structure of the TCP pseudo header

The TCP pseudo header consists of the Source IP Address field, the Destination IP Address field, an Unused field set to 0x00, the Protocol field for TCP (set to 6), and the length of the TCP segment. When sending a TCP segment, TCP knows all of these values. When receiving a TCP segment, IP indicates all of these values to TCP.

TCP calculates the TCP checksum over the combination of the TCP pseudo header, the TCP segment, and, if needed, a 0x00 padding byte. The checksum calculation relies on summing 16-bit words. Therefore, the quantity over which the checksum is calculated must be an even number of bytes. The padding byte is used only if the segment length is an odd number of bytes. The padding byte is not included in the IP length and is not sent as part of the TCP segment. Figure 10-6 shows the resulting quantity for the calculation of the TCP Checksum field.

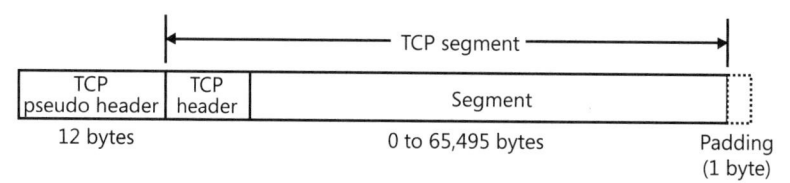

Figure 10-6 The resulting quantity used for the TCP checksum calculation

Note Unlike the IP security (IPsec) Authentication header, the TCP pseudo header and Checksum field are not providing data authentication or data integrity for the fields in the IP header and the TCP segment. IP header and TCP port number fields can be modified as long as the TCP checksum is updated. This is how a Network Address Translator (NAT) works. A NAT is a router that translates public and private addresses during the forwarding process. For example, when translating a source IP address from a private address to a public address, the NAT also recalculates the TCP Checksum field.

TCP Urgent Data

Normal data sent on a TCP connection is data corresponding to the incoming and outgoing byte stream data. In some data-transfer situations, there must be a method of sending control data to interrupt a process or inform the Application Layer protocol of asynchronous events. This control data is known as *out of band data*—data that is not part of the TCP byte stream but is needed to control the data flow. Out of band data for TCP connections can be implemented in the following ways:

- **Use a separate TCP connection for the out of band data.** The separate TCP connection sends control commands and status information without being combined on the data stream of the data connection. This is the method used by FTP. FTP uses a TCP connection on port 21 for control commands such as logins, gets (downloading files to the FTP client), and puts (uploading files to the FTP server), and a separate TCP connection on port 20 for the sending or receiving of file data.

- **Use TCP urgent data.** TCP urgent data is sent on the same TCP connection as the data. TCP urgent data is indicated by setting the URG flag, and the urgent data is distinguished from the nonurgent data using the Urgent Pointer field. Urgent data within the TCP segment must be processed before the nonurgent data. Urgent data is used by the Telnet protocol to send control commands, even though the advertised receive window of the Telnet server is 0.

The interpretation of the Urgent Pointer value depends on the TCP implementation's adherence to either RFC 793, the original TCP RFC, or RFC 1122, which defines requirements for Internet hosts. The difference between the two interpretations is the following:

- RFC 793 defines the value of the Urgent Pointer field as the positive offset from the beginning of the TCP segment to the first byte of nonurgent data.
- RFC 1122 defines the value of the Urgent Pointer field as the positive offset from the beginning of the TCP segment to the last byte of urgent data.

These two definitions of the Urgent Pointer field differ by one byte. Both hosts on a TCP connection must use the same interpretation, otherwise data corruption could occur. There is no interoperability of these two interpretations, nor is there a mechanism to negotiate the interpretation during the TCP connection establishment process.

The definition of the Urgent Pointer field in RFC 793 was made in error (the correct interpretation is actually given later in the RFC during the discussion of event processing in Section 3.9). The correct use of the Urgent Pointer field is the RFC 1122 version, but numerous implementations of TCP use the RFC 793 definition.

Figure 10-7 shows the placement of urgent data within the TCP segment and the RFC 793 and RFC 1122 interpretation of the Urgent Pointer field.

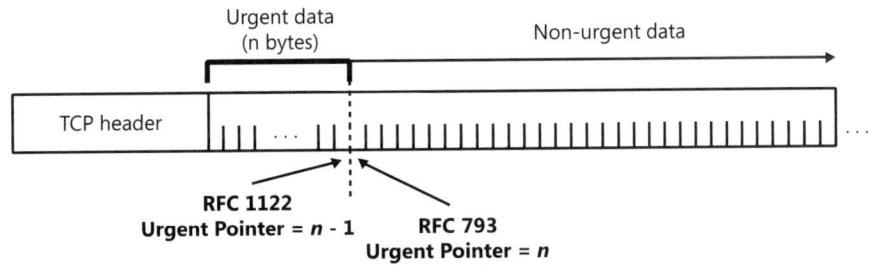

Figure 10-7 The location of TCP urgent data within a TCP segment

To configure the interpretation of the TCP Urgent Pointer field for TCP in Windows Server 2008 and Windows Vista, use the following registry value:

TcpUseRFC1122UrgentPointer
```
Key: HKEY_LOCAL_MACHINE\SYSTEM\CurrentControlSet\Services\Tcpip\Parameters
Value type: REG_DWORD
```

```
Valid range: 0-1
Default: 0
Present by default: No
```

Set this registry value to 1 to use the RFC 1122 interpretation of the Urgent Pointer field or to 0 to use the RFC 793 interpretation (the default).

TCP Options

Just like options in the IP header extend IP functionality, TCP options extend TCP functionality. There are a variety of defined TCP options that are used for negotiating maximum segment sizes, window scaling factors, performing selective acknowledgments, recording timestamps, and providing padding for 4-byte boundaries. A node is not required to support all TCP options; however, the support for processing TCP options is required. The presence of TCP options is indicated by a Data Offset field with a value greater than 5 (0x5) (the TCP header is longer than 20 bytes).

A TCP option is either a single byte or multiple bytes. For multiple-byte options, the TCP option is in type-length-value format, where the length is the length in bytes of the entire option. Figure 10-8 shows the structure of multiple-byte TCP options. A TCP option type is known as an *option kind*.

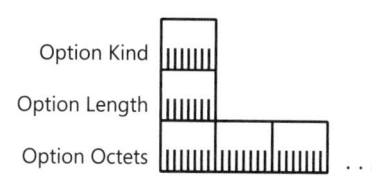

Figure 10-8 The structure of multiple-byte TCP options

End Of Option List and No Operation

To implement 4-byte boundary support for TCP options, RFC 793 defines the following single-byte TCP options:

- **The End Of Option List** The option kind set to 0 (0x00), which indicates that no other options follow. The End Of Option List option is not used to delimit TCP options. If the set of TCP options falls along a 4-byte boundary, this option is not needed.

- **The No Operation** The option kind set to 1 (0x01), which is used between TCP options for 4-byte alignment. The No Operation option is not required, so TCP implementations must be able to correctly interpret TCP options that are not on 4-byte boundaries.

Maximum Segment Size Option

The TCP maximum segment size (MSS) is the largest segment that can be sent on the connection. To obtain the MSS value, take the IP Maximum Transmission Unit (MTU) and subtract the IP header size and the TCP header size. Figure 10-9 shows the relationship between the IP MTU and the TCP MSS. For a typical IP header (without options) and a typical TCP header (without options), the MSS is 40 bytes less than the IP MTU.

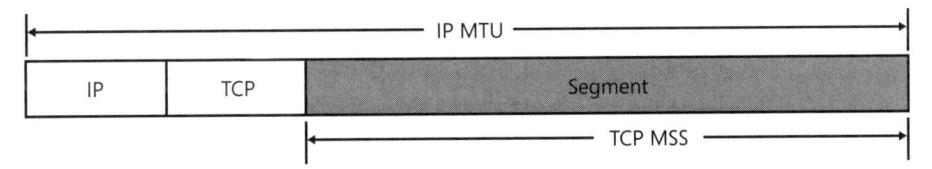

Figure 10-9 The TCP MSS defined in terms of the IP MTU and the TCP and IP header sizes

A TCP peer uses the TCP MSS option to indicate the MSS that it can receive. The TCP MSS option is included only in TCP segments with the SYN flag set during the TCP connection establishment process. Figure 10-10 shows the TCP MSS option structure.

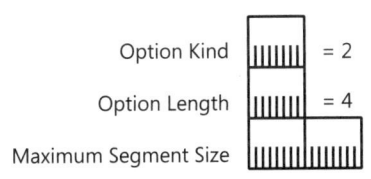

Figure 10-10 The structure of the TCP MSS option

The fields in the TCP MSS option are defined as follows:

- **Option Kind**   Set to 2 (0x02) to indicate the MSS option kind.
- **Option Length**   Set to 4 (0x04) to indicate that the size of the entire MSS option is 4 bytes.
- **Maximum Segment Size**   Two bytes that indicate the MSS of received segments. For IP datagrams sent on an Ethernet network segment using Ethernet II encapsulation, the MSS is 1460 (an IP MTU of 1500 minus 40 bytes for minimum-sized IP and TCP headers).

An example of the TCP MSS option is Capture 10-02, a Network Monitor trace that is included in the \Captures folder on the companion CD-ROM. The following is the TCP SYN segment from Capture 10-02 (frame 1), as displayed with Network Monitor 3.1:

```
Frame:
+ Ethernet: Etype = Internet IP (IPv4)
+ Ipv4: Next Protocol = TCP, Packet ID = 10474, Total IP Length = 48
- Tcp: Flags=.S......, SrcPort=1162, DstPort=FTP control(21), Len=0, Seq=3928116524, Ack=0, win=16384 (scale factor not found)
    SrcPort: 1162
    DstPort: FTP control(21)
    SequenceNumber: 3928116524 (0xEA224D2C)
    AcknowledgementNumber: 0 (0x0)
  - DataOffset: 112 (0x70)
    DataOffset: (0111....) (28 bytes)
    Reserved:   (....000.)
```

```
    NS:            (.......0) Nonce Sum not significant
- Flags: .S......
    CWR:    (0.......) CWR not significant
    ECE:    (.0......) ECN-Echo not significant
    Urgent: (..0.....) Not Urgent Data
    Ack:    (...0....) Acknowledgement field not significant
    Push:   (....0...) No Push Function
    Reset:  (.....0..) No Reset
    Syn:    (......1.) Synchronize sequence numbers
    Fin:    (.......0) Not End of data
    Window: 16384 (scale factor not found)
    Checksum: 34126 (0x854E)
    UrgentPointer: 0 (0x0)
 - TCPOptions:
  - MaxSegmentSize:
      type: Maximum Segment Size. 2(0x2)
      OptionLength: 4 (0x4)
      MaxSegmentSize: 1460 (0x5B4)
  + NoOption:
  + NoOption:
  + SACKPermitted:
```

When two TCP peers exchange their MSS during the connection establishment process, both peers adjust their initial MSS to the minimum value reported by both. For example, when an Ethernet node sends an MSS of 1460 and an 802.11 wireless node sends an MSS of 2272 (the 802.11 IP MTU of 2312, minus 40 bytes), both nodes agree to send maximum-sized TCP segments of 1460 bytes. The initial MSS is adjusted on an ongoing basis through PMTU discovery. For example, two 802.11 wireless nodes on two separate network segments—connected by routers over Ethernet network segments—exchange a TCP MSS of 2272. However, the wireless nodes begin sending 2272-byte TCP segments, and PMTU discovery messages adjust the MSS for the connection to 1460. For more information about PMTU, see Chapter 6, "Internet Control Message Protocol (ICMP)."

The TCP MSS option does not prevent problems that could occur between two hosts on the same network segment (subnet) that are separated by a Network Interface Layer technology with a lower IP MTU size. For example, Host A and Host B in Figure 10-11 are 802.11 wireless nodes connected to separate wireless access points (APs) that are connected by an Ethernet backbone.

Both wireless APs and their connected wireless clients and the Ethernet backbone are on the same network segment as the router. Therefore, when Hosts A and B exchange their MSSs, both agree to send maximum-sized TCP segments with a size of 2272 bytes. However, when they begin to send bulk data with maximum-sized segments, the wireless APs, acting as Layer 2 translating bridges, have no facilities for translating 2272-byte 802.11 payloads to 1500-byte Ethernet payloads. Therefore, the wireless APs silently discard the maximum-sized TCP segments. The wireless AP is not an IP router and does not send PMTU discovery messages to the TCP peers to lower their MSS. Maximum-sized TCP segments cannot be sent between the two TCP peers.

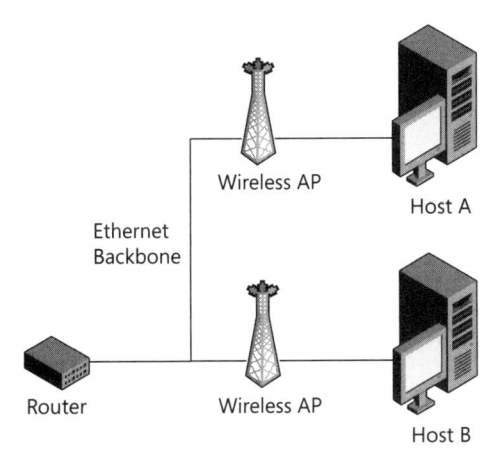

Figure 10-11 Hosts connected to two wireless APs that are connected by an Ethernet backbone

If Host A were an FTP server and Host B were an FTP client, the user at Host B would be able to connect and log in to the FTP server. However, when the user issued a get or put instruction to send a file, TCP segments at the maximum size would be dropped by the wireless APs.

The only solution to this problem is to adjust the IP MTU on the wireless nodes to the lowest value supported by all the Network Interface Layer technologies on the network segment. For example, you could use the `netsh interface ipv4 set interface mtu` command or the MTU registry value described in Chapter 5, "Internet Protocol (IP)," to lower the IP MTU of the two wireless adapters to 1500.

TCP Window Scale Option

The TCP window size defined in RFC 793 is a 16-bit field for a maximum receive window size of 65,535 bytes. This means that a sender can have only 65,535 bytes of data in transit before having to wait for an acknowledgment. This is not an issue on typical local area network (LAN) and wide area network (WAN) links, but it is possible on newer LAN and WAN technologies operating at gigabit-per-second speeds with a sizable transit delay to have more than 65,535 bytes in transit. If TCP cannot fill the logical pipe between the sender and receiver and keep it filled, it is operating at lower efficiency.

The TCP Window Scale option described in RFC 1323 allows the receiver to advertise a larger window size than 65,535 bytes. The Window Scale option includes a window scaling factor that, when exponentially combined with the 16-bit window size in the TCP header, increases the receive window size to a maximum of 1,073,741,824 bytes, or 1 gigabyte (GB). The Window Size option is sent only in a SYN segment during the connection establishment process. TCP peers can indicate different window scaling factors used for their receive window sizes. The receiver of the TCP connection establishment request (the SYN segment) cannot send a Window Scale option unless the initial SYN segment contains it.

Figure 10-12 illustrates the TCP Window Scale option structure.

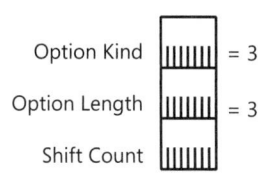

Figure 10-12 The structure of the TCP Window Scale option

The fields in the TCP Window Scale option are defined as follows:

- **Option Kind**   Set to 3 (0x03) to indicate the Window Scale option kind.

- **Option Length**   Set to 3 (0x03) to indicate that the size of the entire TCP option is 3 bytes.

- **Shift Count**   One byte that indicates the scaling factor as the exponent of 2. For example, for a Shift Count of 5, the scaling factor is 2^5, or 32. The exponent is used rather than a whole number so that implementations can take advantage of binary shift programming techniques to quickly calculate the actual window size. For example, for a Shift Count of 5, the actual window size is the binary value of the Window field with five zeros added (the Window field is left-shifted by 5). The maximum value of the Shift Count is 14 for a window scaling factor of 2^{14}, or 16,384. Combined with the original window size of 2^{16}, the maximum window size is $2^{16} \times 2^{14} = 2^{30}$, or 1,073,741,824 bytes.

An example of a TCP Window Scale option is Capture 10-03, a Network Monitor trace that is included in the \Captures folder on the companion CD-ROM. The following is the TCP SYN segment from Capture 10-03 (frame 1), as displayed with Network Monitor 3.1:

```
Frame:
+ Ethernet: Etype = Internet IP (IPv4)
+ Ipv4: Next Protocol = TCP, Packet ID = 594, Total IP Length = 52
- Tcp: Flags=.S......, SrcPort=49786, DstPort=NETBIOS Session Service(139), Len=0,
Seq=2626199192, Ack=0, Win=8192 (scale factor not found)
    SrcPort: 49786
    DstPort: NETBIOS Session Service(139)
    SequenceNumber: 2626199192 (0x9C889E98)
    AcknowledgementNumber: 0 (0x0)
  + DataOffset: 128 (0x80)
  + Flags: .S......
    Window: 8192 (scale factor not found)
    Checksum: 15591 (0x3CE7)
    UrgentPointer: 0 (0x0)
  - TCPOptions:
   + MaxSegmentSize:
   + NoOption:
   - WindowsScaleFactor:
      type: Window scale factor. 3(0x3)
      Length: 3 (0x3)
      ShiftCount: 8 (0x8)
   + NoOption:
   + NoOption:
   + SACKPermitted:
```

Notice the use of the TCP No Operation option (NoOption) preceding the Window Scale option to align the Window Scale option on a 4-byte boundary.

When the Window Scale option is used, the window size advertised in each TCP segment for the connection is scaled by the factor indicated in the peer's SYN segment. Therefore, the TCP header's Window field is no longer a byte counter of the amount of space left in the receive buffer. Rather, the Window field is a block counter in which the block size in bytes is the scaling factor. For example, for a TCP peer using a Shift Count of 3, the Window field in outgoing TCP segments is actually indicating the number of 8-byte blocks remaining in the receive buffer.

By default, TCP for Windows Server 2008 and Windows Vista always uses window scaling with a scaling factor of 8, for a 16-megabyte (MB) receive window. To disable window scaling, use the `netsh interface tcp set global autotuninglevel=disabled` command. When window scaling is disabled, TCP uses a window size based on the link speed of the sending interface. For more information about how TCP for Windows Server 2008 and Windows Vista uses the receive window to maximize incoming data, see Chapter 12, "Transmission Control Protocol (TCP) Data Flow."

Note When tracing TCP connection data, make sure that you also look at the connection establishment process to determine whether window scaling is being used. Otherwise, you might misinterpret the Window field value during the connection.

Selective Acknowledgment Option

The acknowledgment scheme for TCP was originally designed as a positive cumulative acknowledgment scheme in which the receiver sends a segment with the ACK flag set and the Acknowledgment field set to the next byte the receiver expects to receive. This use of the Acknowledgment field provides an acknowledgment of all bytes up to, but not including, the sequence number in the Acknowledgment field. This scheme provides reliable byte-stream data transfer, but can result in lower TCP throughput in environments with high packet losses.

If a segment at the beginning of the current send window is not received and all other segments are, the data received cannot be acknowledged until the missing segment arrives. The sender begins to retransmit the segments of the current send window until the acknowledgment for all the segments received has arrived. The sender needlessly retransmits some segments, consequently wasting network bandwidth. This problem is exacerbated in environments such as satellite links, with high bandwidth and high delay, when TCP has a large window size. The more segments in the send window, the more segments can be retransmitted unnecessarily when segments are lost.

RFC 2018 describes a method of selective acknowledgment using TCP options that selectively acknowledges the noncontiguous data blocks that have been received. A sender that receives a selective acknowledgment can retransmit just the missing blocks, preventing the sender from waiting for the retransmission time-out for the unacknowledged segments and retransmitting segments that have successfully arrived.

The selective acknowledgment scheme defines the following two different TCP options:

- The Selective Acknowledgment (SACK)-Permitted option to negotiate the use of selective acknowledgments during the connection establishment process
- The SACK option to indicate the noncontiguous data blocks that have been received

The SACK-Permitted Option

The SACK-Permitted option is sent in segments with the SYN flag set and indicates that the TCP peer can receive and interpret the TCP SACK option when data is flowing on the connection. The SACK-Permitted option is 2 bytes consisting of an Option Kind set to 4 (0x04) and an Option Length set to 2 (0x02), as shown in Figure 10-13.

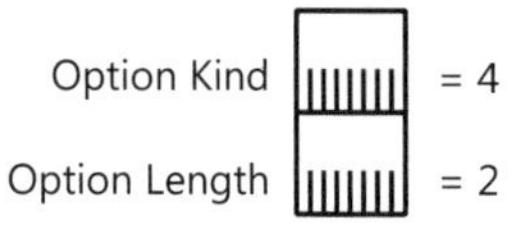

Option Kind ▦ = 4
Option Length ▦ = 2

Figure 10-13 The structure of the TCP SACK-Permitted option

An example of a TCP SACK-Permitted option is Capture 10-04, a Network Monitor trace that is included in the \Captures folder on the companion CD-ROM. The following is the TCP SYN segment from Capture 10-04 (frame 1), as displayed with Network Monitor 3.1:

```
Frame:
+ Ethernet: Etype = Internet IP (IPv4)
+ Ipv4: Next Protocol = TCP, Packet ID = 10474, Total IP Length = 48
- Tcp: Flags=.S......, SrcPort=1162, DstPort=FTP control(21), Len=0, Seq=3928116524, Ack=0,
Win=16384 (scale factor not found)
    SrcPort: 1162
    DstPort: FTP control(21)
    SequenceNumber: 3928116524 (0xEA224D2C)
    AcknowledgementNumber: 0 (0x0)
  + DataOffset: 112 (0x70)
  + Flags: .S......
    Window: 16384 (scale factor not found)
    Checksum: 34126 (0x854E)
    UrgentPointer: 0 (0x0)
  - TCPOptions:
   + MaxSegmentSize:
   + NoOption:
   + NoOption:
   - SACKPermitted:
      type: SACK permitted. 4(0x4)
      OptionLength: 2 (0x2)
```

Notice the use of the two TCP No Operation option (NoOption) fields preceding the SACK-Permitted option to align the SACK-Permitted option on a 4-byte boundary.

The SACK Option

The SACK option is sent as needed in segments of the open connection with the ACK flag set. As Figure 10-14 shows, the SACK option is a variable-size option, depending on how many contiguous blocks are being acknowledged.

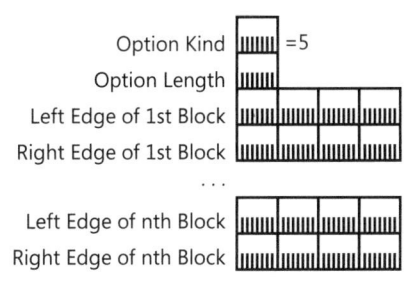

Figure 10-14 The structure of the TCP SACK option

The fields in the TCP SACK option are defined as follows:

- **Option Kind** Set to 5 (0x05) to indicate the SACK option kind.

- **Option Length** Set to 10 (a single noncontiguous block), 18 (two noncontiguous blocks), 26 (three noncontiguous blocks), or 34 (four noncontiguous blocks) bytes to indicate the size of the entire TCP option.

- **Left Edge of nth Block** A 4-byte field that indicates the sequence number of this block's first byte.

- **Right Edge of nth Block** A 4-byte field that indicates the next sequence number expected to be received immediately following this block.

An example of a TCP SACK option is Capture 10-05, a Network Monitor trace that is included in the \Captures folder on the companion CD-ROM. The following is the TCP segment from Capture 10-05 (frame 1), as displayed with Network Monitor 3.1:

```
Frame:
+ Ethernet: Etype = Internet IP (IPv4)
+ Ipv4: Next Protocol = TCP, Packet ID = 64013, Total IP Length = 64
- Tcp: Flags=....A..., SrcPort=1242, DstPort=NETBIOS Session Service(139), Len=0,
Seq=925293, Ack=55053434, Win=32767 (scale factor not found)
    SrcPort: 1242
    DstPort: NETBIOS Session Service(139)
    SequenceNumber: 925293 (0xE1E6D)
    AcknowledgementNumber: 55053434 (0x3480C7A)
  + DataOffset: 176 (0xB0)
  + Flags: ....A...
    Window: 32767 (scale factor not found)
    Checksum: 17262 (0x436E)
    UrgentPointer: 0 (0x0)
  - TCPOptions:
   + NoOption:
```

```
+ NoOption:
+ TimeStamp:
+ NoOption:
+ NoOption:
- SACK:
    type: SACK. 5(0x5)
    Length: 10 (0xA)
  - Blocks:
      LeftEdge: 55054882 (0x3481222)
      RightEdge: 55059226 (0x348231A)
```

In the trace, the sender of this segment is acknowledging the receipt of all contiguous bytes in the byte stream up to, but not including, byte 55053434, and the receipt of the block of contiguous data from bytes 55054882 through 55059225. There is a missing segment consisting of the bytes 55053434 through 55054881. Notice the use of the Nop options (NoOption) to align the SACK option on a 4-byte boundary.

TCP in Windows Server 2008 and Windows Vista always uses selective acknowledgments and the SACK options.

For more information on the use of selective acknowledgments to retransmit data, see Chapter 13, "Transmission Control Protocol (TCP) Retransmission and Time-Out."

Note TCP in Windows Server 2008 and Windows Vista no longer supports the SackOpts registry value.

TCP Timestamps Option

To set the retransmission time-out (RTO) on TCP segments sent, TCP monitors the round-trip time (RTT) on an ongoing basis. Normally, TCP calculates the RTT of a TCP segment and its acknowledgment once for every full send window of data. Although this works well in many environments, for high-bandwidth and high-delay environments such as satellite links with large window sizes, the sampling rate of one segment for each window size cannot monitor the RTT to determine the current RTO and prevent unnecessary retransmissions.

To calculate the RTT on any TCP segment, the segment is sent with the TCP Timestamps option described in RFC 1323. This option places a timestamp value based on a local clock on an outgoing TCP segment. The acknowledgment for the data in the TCP segment echoes back the timestamp, and the RTT can be calculated from the segment's echoed timestamp and the time (relative to the local clock) that the segment's acknowledgment arrived.

Including the Timestamps option in the SYN segment during the connection establishment process indicates its use for the connection. Both sides of the TCP connection can selectively use timestamps. Once indicated during connection establishment, the timestamp can be included in TCP segments at the discretion of the sending TCP peer.

Figure 10-15 shows the TCP Timestamps option structure.

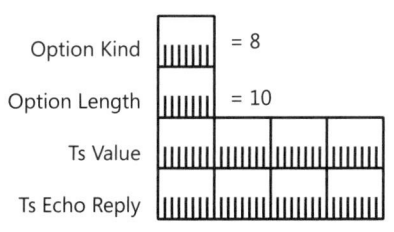

Figure 10-15 The structure of the TCP Timestamps option

The fields in the TCP Timestamps option are defined as follows:

- **Option Kind** Set to 8 (0x08) to indicate the Timestamps option kind.
- **Option Length** Set to 10 (0x0A) to indicate that the size of the entire TCP option is 10 bytes.
- **TS Value** A 4-byte field that indicates the timestamp value of this TCP segment. The TS Value is calculated from an internal clock that is based on real time. The TS Value increases over time and wraps around when needed.
- **TS Echo Reply** A 4-byte field set on a TCP segment that acknowledges data received (with the ACK flag set) that is set to the same value as the TS Value for the received segment being acknowledged. In other words, the TS Echo Reply is an echo of the TS Value of the acknowledged segment.

Figure 10-16 illustrates an example of the values of the TS Value and TS Echo Reply for an exchange of data between two hosts.

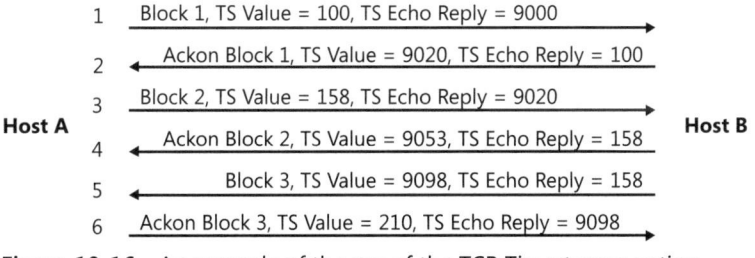

Figure 10-16 An example of the use of the TCP Timestamps option.

Host A's internal clock starts its TS Value at 100. Host B's internal clock starts its TS Value at 9000. Segments 1 through 4 are for two data blocks sent by Host A. Segments 5 and 6 are for a data block sent by Host B. Notice how the TS Echo Reply value for the acknowledgments is set to the TS Value of the segments they are acknowledging. To prevent gaps in the sending of data from increasing the RTT, the TS Echo Reply is used for RTT measurement only if the segment is an acknowledgment of new data sent.

An example of the use of the TCP Timestamps option is Capture 10-06, a Network Monitor trace that is included in the \Captures folder on the companion CD-ROM. The following is frame 1 containing the TCP Timestamps option and frame 2 containing the corresponding acknowledgment, as displayed with Network Monitor 3.1:

```
  Frame:
+ Ethernet: Etype = Internet IP (IPv4)
+ Ipv4: Next Protocol = TCP, Packet ID = 6677, Total IP Length = 1500
- Tcp: Flags=....A..., SrcPort=NETBIOS Session Service(139), DstPort=1242, Len=1448,
Seq=55050538 - 55051986, Ack=925293, Win=16564 (scale factor not found)
    SrcPort: NETBIOS Session Service(139)
    DstPort: 1242
    SequenceNumber: 55050538 (0x348012A)
    AcknowledgementNumber: 925293 (0xE1E6D)
  + DataOffset: 128 (0x80)
  + Flags: ....A...
    Window: 16564 (scale factor not found)
    Checksum: 48513 (0xBD81)
    UrgentPointer: 0 (0x0)
  - TCPOptions:
   + NoOption:
   + NoOption:
   - TimeStamp:
      type: Timestamp. 8(0x8)
      Length: 10 (0xA)
      TimestampValue: 4677 (0x1245)
      TimestampEchoReply: 7114 (0x1BCA)
    TCPPayload:
+ Nbtss: NbtSS Continue payload, Length = 1448
```

```
  Frame:
+ Ethernet: Etype = Internet IP (IPv4)
+ Ipv4: Next Protocol = TCP, Packet ID = 62989, Total IP Length = 52
- Tcp: Flags=....A..., SrcPort=1242, DstPort=NETBIOS Session Service(139), Len=0,
Seq=925293, Ack=55051986, Win=32722 (scale factor not found)
    SrcPort: 1242
    DstPort: NETBIOS Session Service(139)
    SequenceNumber: 925293 (0xE1E6D)
    AcknowledgementNumber: 55051986 (0x34806D2)
  + DataOffset: 128 (0x80)
  + Flags: ....A...
    Window: 32722 (scale factor not found)
    Checksum: 47929 (0xBB39)
    UrgentPointer: 0 (0x0)
  - TCPOptions:
   + NoOption:
   + NoOption:
   - TimeStamp:
      type: Timestamp. 8(0x8)
      Length: 10 (0xA)
      TimestampValue: 7126 (0x1BD6)
      TimestampEchoReply: 4677 (0x1245)
```

Notice that in the second frame the TS Echo Reply field (TimestampEchoReply) is set to 4677, echoing the TS Value field (TimestampValue) of the first frame.

In Windows Server 2008 and Windows Vista, the use of TCP timestamps can be controlled by the `netsh interface tcp set global timestamps=disabled|enabled|default` command. By default, TCP timestamps are disabled.

You can also use the following registry value:

Tcp1323Opts
```
Key:HKEY_LOCAL_MACHINE\SYSTEM\CurrentControlSet\Services\Tcpip\Parameters
Value type: REG_DWORD
Valid range: 0 or 2
Default value: 0
Present by default: No
```

Set this value to 0 to disable timestamps. Set this value to 2 to enable timestamps. The default behavior of TCP is to not use timestamps. For more information on RTT, RTO, and retransmission behavior, see Chapter 13, "Transmission Control Protocol (TCP) Retransmission and Time-Out."

Summary

TCP provides connection-oriented and reliable data transfer for applications that require end-to-end guaranteed delivery service. Application Layer protocols use TCP for one-to-one traffic. The TCP header provides sequencing, acknowledgment, a checksum, and the identification of source and destination port numbers to multiplex TCP segment data to the proper Application Layer protocol. TCP options are used to indicate maximum segment sizes and window scaling, indicate and provide selective acknowledgments, and provide timestamps for better RTT determination.

Chapter 11
Transmission Control Protocol (TCP) Connections

In this chapter:
The TCP Connection	223
TCP Connection Establishment	224
TCP Half-Open Connections	230
TCP Connection Maintenance	232
TCP Connection Termination	234
TCP Connection Reset	238
TCP Connection States	240
Summary	243

TCP is a connection-based protocol. Before data can flow on a TCP connection, the connection must be formally established through a handshake process. To gracefully stop the flow of data on a TCP connection and release the resources of the connection, it must be terminated through a similar handshake process. This chapter describes the details of TCP connection establishment and termination and the states of a TCP connection.

The TCP Connection

A TCP connection is a bidirectional, full-duplex logical circuit between two processes (Application Layer protocols) in an IP internetwork. The TCP connection's endpoints are identified by an [IP address, TCP port] pair. The connection is uniquely identified by both endpoints: [IP address 1, TCP port 1, IP address 2, TCP port 2]. TCP uses those four numbers to demultiplex the data portion of the TCP segment to the proper Application Layer process.

A TCP connection can be visualized as a bidirectional data pipe containing two logical pipes between the two TCP peers, as Figure 11-1 illustrates. One logical pipe is used for outbound data and the other logical pipe is used for inbound data (relative to the TCP peer). The outbound data pipe for one TCP peer is the inbound data pipe for the other TCP peer.

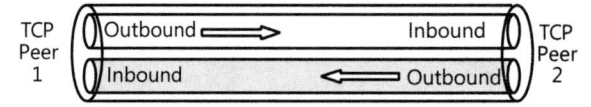

Figure 11-1 A TCP connection showing both inbound and outbound logical pipes

TCP connections are:

- Established through a handshake process in which both TCP peers agree to create a TCP connection.

- Optionally maintained through a periodic keepalive process that ensures that both TCP peers are active on the connection.

- Terminated through a handshake process in which both TCP peers agree to close the TCP connection.

TCP connections can also be reset by either TCP peer.

TCP Connection Establishment

To create a TCP connection over which full-duplex data can begin to flow, each TCP peer must obtain the following information from the other TCP peer:

- The starting sequence number for data sent on the inbound pipe

- The maximum amount of data that can be sent on the outbound pipe before waiting for an acknowledgment (the receive window size of the other TCP peer)

- The maximum segment size (MSS) that can be received

- The TCP options that are supported

This information is learned through an exchange of three TCP segments called the TCP connection establishment process, or the TCP three-way handshake.

To create a TCP connection, a listening TCP peer must allow a TCP connection, and an initiating TCP peer must initiate a TCP connection. The listening TCP peer issues a passive OPEN function call to permit incoming connection requests on a specific port number. This function call does not create any TCP traffic. The initiating TCP peer issues an active OPEN function call, which creates and sends the first segment of the TCP three-way handshake.

Figure 11-2 displays the TCP connection establishment process, showing the three TCP segments that are exchanged and the information in the TCP header that is vital to the connection establishment. Prior to segment 1, TCP Peer 2 issued a passive OPEN to receive TCP connection requests. TCP Peer 1 issues an active OPEN and creates segment 1. Segments 2 and 3 complete the connection establishment process. The vertical arrows show the passage of time during the connection establishment process.

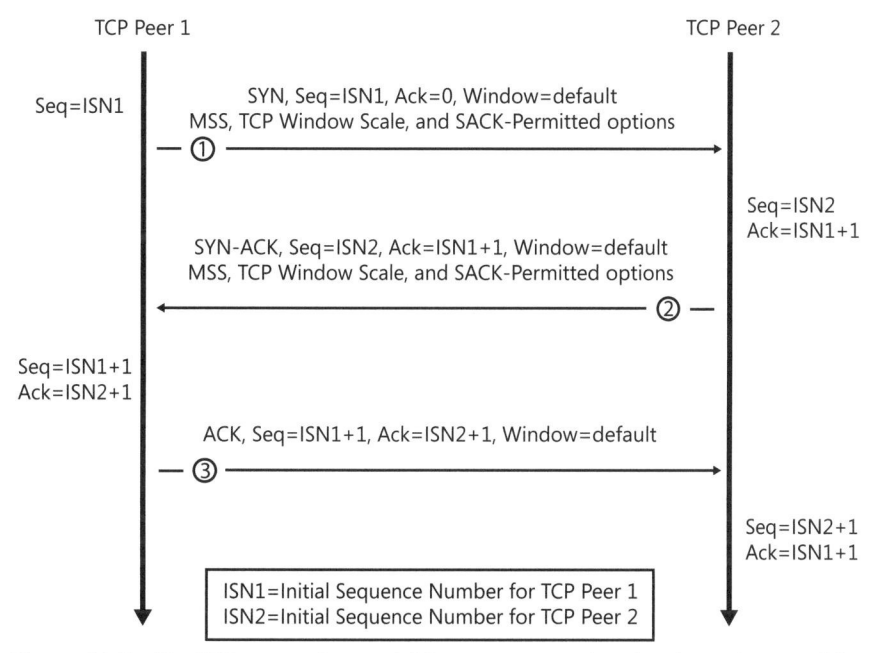

```
                              TCP Peer 1                                    TCP Peer 2
                                  │                                             │
                                  │    SYN, Seq=ISN1, Ack=0, Window=default    │
                   Seq=ISN1       │   MSS, TCP Window Scale, and SACK-Permitted options │
                                  │──①──────────────────────────────────────────▶│
                                  │                                             │   Seq=ISN2
                                  │                                             │   Ack=ISN1+1
                                  │  SYN-ACK, Seq=ISN2, Ack=ISN1+1, Window=default │
                                  │   MSS, TCP Window Scale, and SACK-Permitted options │
                                  │◀──────────────────────────────────────②─────│
                   Seq=ISN1+1     │                                             │
                   Ack=ISN2+1     │                                             │
                                  │   ACK, Seq=ISN1+1, Ack=ISN2+1, Window=default │
                                  │──③──────────────────────────────────────────▶│
                                  │                                             │   Seq=ISN2+1
                                  │                                             │   Ack=ISN1+1
                                  │   ┌─────────────────────────────────────┐   │
                                  │   │ ISN1=Initial Sequence Number for TCP Peer 1 │
                                  │   │ ISN2=Initial Sequence Number for TCP Peer 2 │
                                  ▼   └─────────────────────────────────────┘   ▼
```

Figure 11-2 The TCP connection establishment process, showing the exchange of three TCP segments

Segment 1: The Synchronize (SYN) Segment

TCP Peer 1 sends the first TCP segment, known as the SYN segment, to TCP Peer 2. The SYN segment establishes TCP connection parameters, such as the Initial Sequence Number (ISN) that TCP Peer 1 uses. The SYN segment as sent by a computer running Windows Server 2008 or Windows Vista contains the following fields in the TCP header:

- **Destination Port** Set to the TCP port number of the passive OPEN on TCP Peer 2. For typical TCP connections, the destination port in the SYN segment is a well-known TCP port in the range of 1 to 1023.

- **Source Port** Set to the local TCP port number of the active OPEN on TCP Peer 1. For typical TCP connections, the source port is a dynamically allocated port.

- **Sequence Number** Set to the ISN for data to be sent by TCP Peer 1 for the outbound data pipe (ISN1 in Figure 11-2). A TCP peer running Windows Server 2008 or Windows Vista chooses the ISN based on a startup-derived, 2048-bit random key and an RC4-based random number to reduce the predictability of the next TCP connection's ISN.

- **Acknowledgment Number** Set to 0. Because the Acknowledgment (ACK) flag is not set, the Acknowledgment Number field is not significant. Only after a TCP peer learns the sequence number for inbound data on the connection can the ACK flag be set and the Acknowledgment Number field set to the appropriate value.

- **SYN Flag** Indicates that the segment contains the ISN for data sent by TCP Peer 1.

- **Window** Set to an application-specified value or an operating system default value, indicating an initial value for the maximum amount of data that TCP Peer 1 can receive.
- **MSS in the MSS TCP Option** Set to the maximum-sized TCP segment that TCP Peer 1 can receive.
- **Window scaling factor in the TCP Window Scale TCP Option** Included to indicate that TCP Peer 1's advertised window size has a specified scaling factor.
- **Selective Acknowledgment (SACK)-Permitted TCP Option** Included to indicate that TCP Peer 1 can receive and interpret the SACK option included in TCP segments that TCP Peer 2 sends.

The following Network Monitor 3.1 trace (Frame 1 of Capture 11-01, included in the \Captures folder on the companion CD-ROM) shows a SYN segment for a Hypertext Transfer Protocol (HTTP) session:

```
Frame:
+ Ethernet: Etype = Internet IP (IPv4)
+ Ipv4: Next Protocol = TCP, Packet ID = 5779, Total IP Length = 52
- Tcp: Flags=.S......, SrcPort=49160, DstPort=HTTP(80), Len=0, Seq=1173532065, Ack=0, Win=8192 (scale factor not found)
    SrcPort: 49160
    DstPort: HTTP(80)
    SequenceNumber: 1173532065 (0x45F2ADA1)
    AcknowledgementNumber: 0 (0x0)
  + DataOffset: 128 (0x80)
  - Flags: .S......
    CWR:     (0.......) CWR not significant
    ECE:     (.0......) ECN-Echo not significant
    Urgent:  (..0.....) Not Urgent Data
    Ack:     (...0....) Acknowledgement field not significant
    Push:    (....0...) No Push Function
    Reset:   (.....0..) No Reset
    Syn:     (......1.) Synchronize sequence numbers
    Fin:     (.......0) Not End of data
    Window: 8192 (scale factor not found)
    Checksum: 34599 (0x8727)
    UrgentPointer: 0 (0x0)
  - TCPOptions:
    - MaxSegmentSize:
        type: Maximum Segment Size. 2(0x2)
        OptionLength: 4 (0x4)
        MaxSegmentSize: 1460 (0x5B4)
    + NoOption:
    - WindowsScaleFactor:
        type: Window scale factor. 3(0x3)
        Length: 3 (0x3)
        ShiftCount: 2 (0x2)
    + NoOption:
    + NoOption:
    + SACKPermitted:
        type: SACK permitted. 4(0x4)
        OptionLength: 2 (0x2)
```

Segment 2: The SYN-ACK Segment

After receipt of the SYN segment, TCP Peer 2 sends the second TCP segment known as the SYN-ACK segment to TCP Peer 1. The SYN-ACK segment establishes TCP connection parameters that TCP Peer 2 uses, such as the ISN, and acknowledges TCP connection parameters used by TCP Peer 1. The SYN-ACK segment as sent by a computer running Windows Server 2008 or Windows Vista contains the following fields in the TCP header:

- **Destination Port**   Set to the Source Port of the SYN segment.
- **Source Port**   Set to the local TCP port number of the passive OPEN on TCP Peer 2 as indicated by the Destination Port number of the SYN segment.
- **Sequence Number**   Set to the ISN for data to be sent by TCP Peer 2 for the outbound data pipe (ISN2 in Figure 11-2).
- **Acknowledgment Number**   Set to the value of the TCP Peer 1's ISN plus 1 (ISN1 + 1). To provide acknowledgement of the receipt of the SYN segment, TCP acts as if the SYN flag occupies a single byte of the sequence space of Peer 1. The acknowledgment number is the next byte in the byte stream that TCP Peer 2 expects to receive. If the SYN flag acts as a single byte of nondata, the next byte that TCP Peer 2 expects to receive is actual data, and must therefore begin with ISN1 + 1.
- **SYN Flag**   Indicates that the segment contains the ISN for data sent by TCP Peer 2.
- **ACK Flag**   Indicates that the Acknowledgment Number field is significant.
- **Window**   Set to an application-specified value or an operating system default value, indicating an initial value for the maximum amount of data that TCP Peer 2 can receive.
- **MSS in the MSS TCP Option**   Set to the maximum-sized TCP segment that TCP Peer 2 can receive.
- **Window scaling factor in the TCP Window Scale TCP Option**   Included to indicate that TCP Peer 2's advertised window size has a specified scaling factor.
- **SACK-Permitted TCP Option**   Indicates that TCP Peer 2 can receive and interpret the SACK option included in TCP segments that TCP Peer 1 sends.

The following Network Monitor 3.1 trace (Frame 2 of Capture 11-01, included in the \Captures folder on the companion CD-ROM) shows a SYN-ACK segment for an HTTP session (continued from the previous SYN segment):

```
  Frame:
+ Ethernet: Etype = Internet IP (IPv4)
+ Ipv4: Next Protocol = TCP, Packet ID = 1045, Total IP Length = 52
- Tcp: Flags=.S..A..., SrcPort=HTTP(80), DstPort=49160, Len=0, Seq=2269857730,
Ack=1173532066, Win=8192 (scale factor not found)
    SrcPort: HTTP(80)
    DstPort: 49160
    SequenceNumber: 2269857730 (0x874B47C2)
    AcknowledgementNumber: 1173532066 (0x45F2ADA2)
  + DataOffset: 128 (0x80)
```

```
- Flags: .S..A...
    CWR:    (0.......) CWR not significant
    ECE:    (.0......) ECN-Echo not significant
    Urgent: (..0.....) Not Urgent Data
    Ack:    (...1....) Acknowledgement field significant
    Push:   (....0...) No Push Function
    Reset:  (.....0..) No Reset
    Syn:    (......1.) Synchronize sequence numbers
    Fin:    (.......0) Not End of data
  Window: 8192 (scale factor not found)
  Checksum: 47106 (0xB802)
  UrgentPointer: 0 (0x0)
- TCPOptions:
  - MaxSegmentSize:
      type: Maximum Segment Size. 2(0x2)
      OptionLength: 4 (0x4)
      MaxSegmentSize: 1460 (0x5B4)
  + NoOption:
  - WindowsScaleFactor:
      type: Window scale factor. 3(0x3)
      Length: 3 (0x3)
      ShiftCount: 8 (0x8)
  + NoOption:
  + NoOption:
  - SACKPermitted:
      type: SACK permitted. 4(0x4)
      OptionLength: 2 (0x2)
```

Segment 3: The ACK Segment

After receipt of the SYN-ACK segment, TCP Peer 1 sends the third TCP segment, known as the ACK segment, to TCP Peer 2. The ACK segment establishes the final TCP connection parameters used by TCP Peer 1 and acknowledges TCP connection parameters that TCP Peer 2 uses. The ACK segment, as sent by a computer running Windows Server 2008 or Windows Vista, contains the following fields in the TCP header:

- **Destination Port** Set to the Source Port of the SYN-ACK segment.
- **Source Port** Set to the local TCP port number of the active OPEN on TCP Peer 1 as indicated by the Destination Port number of the SYN-ACK segment.
- **Sequence Number** Set to ISN1 + 1.
- **Acknowledgment Number** Set to the value of the TCP Peer 2's ISN plus 1 (ISN2 + 1). Similar to the SYN-ACK segment, TCP acts as if the SYN flag occupies a single byte of the sequence space of TCP Peer 2. The next byte that TCP Peer 1 expects to receive is actual data, and must therefore begin with ISN2 + 1.
- **ACK Flag** Indicates that the Acknowledgment Number field is significant.
- **Window** Set to an application-specified value or an operating system default value. This value indicates an initial value for the amount of data that TCP Peer 1 can receive.

The following Network Monitor 3.1 trace (Frame 3 of Capture 11-01, included in the \Captures folder on the companion CD-ROM) shows an ACK segment for an HTTP session (continued from the previous SYN-ACK segment):

```
Frame:
+ Ethernet: Etype = Internet IP (IPv4)
+ Ipv4: Next Protocol = TCP, Packet ID = 5780, Total IP Length = 40
- Tcp: Flags=....A..., SrcPort=49160, DstPort=HTTP(80), Len=0, Seq=1173532066,
Ack=2269857731, Win=4380 (scale factor not found)
    SrcPort: 49160
    DstPort: HTTP(80)
    SequenceNumber: 1173532066 (0x45F2ADA2)
    AcknowledgementNumber: 2269857731 (0x874B47C3)
  + DataOffset: 80 (0x50)
  - Flags: ....A...
    CWR:    (0.......) CWR not significant
    ECE:    (.0......) ECN-Echo not significant
    Urgent: (..0.....) Not Urgent Data
    Ack:    (...1....) Acknowledgement field significant
    Push:   (....0...) No Push Function
    Reset:  (.....0..) No Reset
    Syn:    (......0.) Not Synchronize sequence numbers
    Fin:    (.......0) Not End of data
    Window: 4380 (scale factor not found)
    Checksum: 1978 (0x7BA)
    UrgentPointer: 0 (0x0)
```

Results of the TCP Connection

The results of the TCP connection establishment process are as follows:

- Each TCP peer knows the sequence number of the first byte of data to be sent on the connection (TCP Peer 1's Acknowledgment Number field is set to TCP Peer 2's Sequence Number field; TCP Peer 2's Acknowledgment Number field is set to TCP Peer 1's Sequence Number field).

- Each TCP peer knows the MSS that can be sent on the connection. The connection's MSS is the minimum of the two MSSs advertised by TCP Peer 1 and TCP Peer 2. Path Maximum Transmission Unit (PMTU) Discovery adjusts the initial MSS for the duration of connection. For more information on PMTU Discovery, see Chapter 6, "Internet Control Message Protocol (ICMP)."

- Each TCP peer knows the other peer's window size and scaling factor, indicating the maximum amount of data that can be sent without waiting for an ACK and updated window size. Although a large amount of data can be initially sent, TCP peers use the slow start and congestion avoidance algorithms to slowly scale the amount of data sent to avoid congesting the internetwork. For more information, see Chapter 12, "Transmission Control Protocol (TCP) Data Flow."

- Each TCP peer is aware that the other peer is capable of receiving selective acknowledgments using the SACK TCP option. For more information on selective acknowledgment, see Chapter 12.

TCP sends three SYN segment retransmissions when attempting to establish a TCP connection. The retransmission time-out (RTO) is doubled between each retransmission. With the initial RTO of 3 seconds and two retransmissions of the SYN segment, it takes 21 seconds to time out a TCP connection attempt (initial SYN, wait 3 seconds, first retransmitted SYN, wait 6 seconds, second transmitted SYN, wait 12 seconds).

For an example of this behavior, see Network Monitor trace Capture 11-02, included in the \Captures folder on the companion CD-ROM.

Note TCP in Windows Server 2008 and Windows Vista no longer supports the TcpMaxConnectRetransmissions and TcpNumConnections registry values.

TCP Half-Open Connections

A TCP half-open connection, shown in Figure 11-3, is a TCP connection that has not completed the connection establishment process. A SYN segment has been received and a SYN-ACK has been sent, but the final ACK has not been received. Until the final ACK is received, data cannot be sent on the connection.

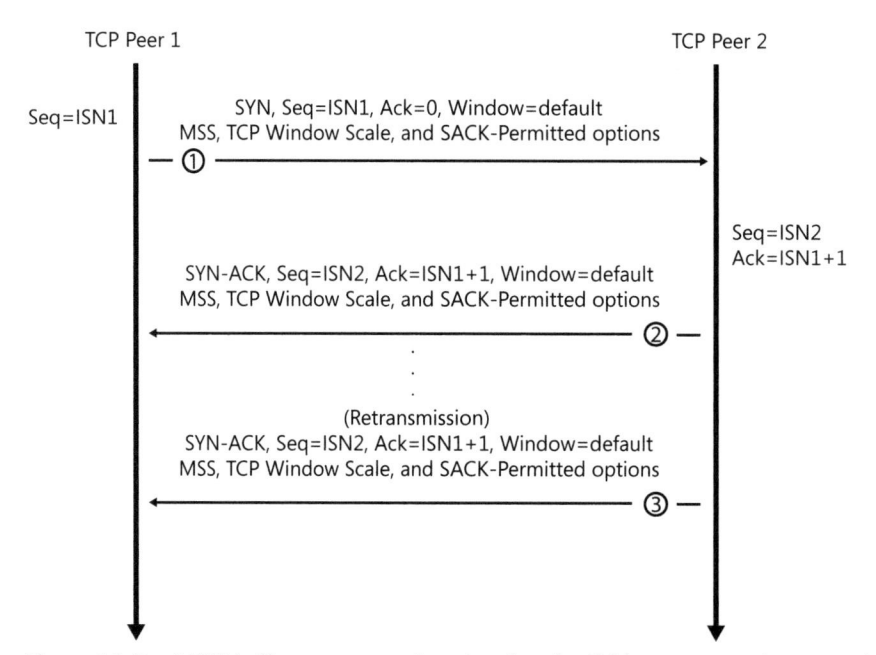

```
TCP Peer 1                                                         TCP Peer 2

Seq=ISN1        SYN, Seq=ISN1, Ack=0, Window=default
                MSS, TCP Window Scale, and SACK-Permitted options
                ──①──────────────────────────────────────────▶

                                                                   Seq=ISN2
                                                                   Ack=ISN1+1
                SYN-ACK, Seq=ISN2, Ack=ISN1+1, Window=default
                MSS, TCP Window Scale, and SACK-Permitted options
                ◀──────────────────────────────────────────②──

                              (Retransmission)
                SYN-ACK, Seq=ISN2, Ack=ISN1+1, Window=default
                MSS, TCP Window Scale, and SACK-Permitted options
                ◀──────────────────────────────────────────③──
```

Figure 11-3 A TCP half-open connection showing the SYN segment and retransmissions of the SYN-ACK segment

Although the SYN-ACK segment contains no data, TCP acts as if the SYN flag occupies a single byte of the sequence space and is treated as data. Therefore, TCP retransmission and time-out behaviors used for recovering from lost data are used to recover from a lost SYN-ACK segment. In the case of retransmitting a SYN-ACK segment, the default time-out is 3 seconds and the SYN-ACK is retransmitted twice, doubling the time-out period for each retransmission. Therefore, the first SYN-ACK is sent, 3 seconds later the first retransmission is sent, and 6 seconds later the second retransmission is sent. After waiting 12 seconds for a response to the final retransmission, the connection is abandoned and the memory and the connection's internal table entries are released. A total of 21 seconds elapse from the time the first SYN-ACK is sent until the connection is abandoned.

The SYN Attack

The SYN attack is a denial-of-service attack that exploits the retransmission and time-out behavior of the SYN-ACK to create a large number of half-open connections. Depending on the TCP/IP protocol implementation, a large number of half-open connections could do any of the following:

- Use all available memory.

- Use all possible entries in the TCP Transmission Control Block (TCB), an internal table used to track TCP connections. Once the half-open connections use all the entries, further connection attempts are responded to with a TCP connection reset. TCP connection resets are discussed in the section "TCP Connection Reset," later in this chapter.

- Use all available half-open connections. After all the half-open connections are used, further connection attempts are responded to with a TCP connection reset.

To create a large number of TCP half-open connections, malicious users send a large number of SYN segments from a spoofed IP address and TCP port number. The spoofed IP address and TCP port number are for a process that does not respond to the SYN-ACKs being sent by the attacked host. SYN attacks typically are used to render Internet servers inoperative.

To see a SYN attack in progress on a computer running Windows Server 2008 or Windows Vista, use the Netstat.exe tool at a command prompt to display the active TCP connections. For example:

```
c:\>netstat -n -p tcp
  Active Connections
      Proto      Local Address        Foreign Address      State
      TCP        127.0.0.1:1030       127.0.0.1:1032       ESTABLISHED
      TCP        127.0.0.1:1032       127.0.0.1:1030       ESTABLISHED
      TCP        131.107.1.5:21       192.168.0.1:1025     SYN_RECEIVED
      TCP        131.107.1.5:21       192.168.0.1:1026     SYN_RECEIVED
      TCP        131.107.1.5:21       192.168.0.1:1027     SYN_RECEIVED
```

```
TCP    131.107.1.5:21    192.168.0.1:1028    SYN_RECEIVED
TCP    131.107.1.5:21    192.168.0.1:1029    SYN_RECEIVED
TCP    131.107.1.5:21    192.168.0.1:1030    SYN_RECEIVED
TCP    131.107.1.5:21    192.168.0.1:1031    SYN_RECEIVED
TCP    131.107.1.5:21    192.168.0.1:1032    SYN_RECEIVED
TCP    131.107.1.5:21    192.168.0.1:1033    SYN_RECEIVED
TCP    131.107.1.5:21    192.168.0.1:1034    SYN_RECEIVED
TCP    131.107.1.5:21    192.168.0.1:1035    SYN_RECEIVED
```

This is an example of a SYN attack. There are a number of TCP connections in the SYN_RECEIVED state, and the foreign address is a spoofed private address with incrementally increasing TCP port numbers. The SYN_RECEIVED is the state of a TCP connection that has received a SYN, sent a SYN-ACK, and is waiting for the final ACK. TCP connection states are discussed in detail in the "TCP Connection States" section of this chapter.

TCP in Windows Server 2008 and Windows Vista use SYN attack protection to prevent a SYN attack from overwhelming the computer.

Note TCP in Windows Server 2008 and Windows Vista no longer supports the TcpMaxConnectResponseRetransmissions, SynAttackProtect, TcpMaxHalfOpen, and TcpMaxHalfOpenRetried registry values.

TCP Connection Maintenance

A TCP connection can optionally be maintained through the periodic exchange of a TCP keepalive segment, which is an ACK segment containing no data. The Sequence Number field in the TCP header of the keepalive segment is set to 1 less than the current sequence number for the outbound data stream. For example, if a TCP peer's next byte of data is 18745323, the TCP keepalive sent by the TCP peer has the Sequence Number field set to 18745322.

After receiving this ACK segment, the other TCP peer sends back an ACK segment with the Acknowledgment Number field set to the next byte that it expects to receive. In this example, the TCP peer sends an ACK segment with the Acknowledgment Number field set to 18745323. This simple exchange confirms that both TCP peers are still participating in the TCP connection.

Figure 11-4 shows the TCP keepalive.

TCP keepalives for TCP/IP for Windows Server 2008 and Windows Vista are disabled by default. If enabled through the use of the `setsockopt()` Windows Sockets function, a keepalive segment is sent every two hours by default, as controlled by the KeepAliveTime registry value. Even if enabled, other upper layer protocols such as NetBIOS send their own keepalive. If the keepalive interval that the upper layer protocol uses is less than the TCP keepalive interval, TCP keepalives are never sent. For example, NetBIOS sessions over TCP/IP send a NetBIOS keepalive every 60 minutes. Therefore, TCP keepalives enabled for a NetBIOS session are never used. The following registry values control TCP keepalive behavior:

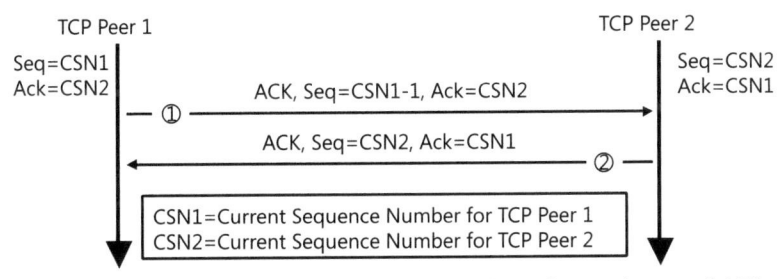

Figure 11-4 A TCP keepalive showing the sending of an exchange of ACK segments to confirm both ends of the connection are still present

KeepAliveTime
```
Location: HKEY_LOCAL_MACHINE\SYSTEM\CurrentControlSet\Services\Tcpip\Parameters
Data type: REG_DWORD
Valid range: 0-0xFFFFFFFF
Default value: 0x6DDD00 (7,200,000)
Present by default: No
```

KeepAliveTime sets the number of milliseconds between each TCP keepalive segment if no data has been sent on the connection and if keepalives have been enabled on the connection. The default value of 7,200,000 milliseconds corresponds to two hours.

KeepAliveInterval
```
Location: HKEY_LOCAL_MACHINE\SYSTEM\CurrentControlSet\Services\Tcpip\Parameters
Data type: REG_DWORD
Valid range: 0-0xFFFFFFFF
Default value: 0x3E8 (1000)
Present by default: No
```

KeepAliveInterval sets the number of milliseconds between successive retransmissions of the keepalive segment when a response to the initial keepalive is not received. The number of TCP keepalive retransmissions is controlled by the TcpMaxDataRetransmissions registry value, which has a default value of 5. After sending five TCP keepalive retransmissions, the connection is abandoned.

Therefore, with the default values of KeepAliveTime, KeepAliveInterval, and TcpMaxDataRetransmissions, a TCP connection on which keepalives have been enabled by the application is abandoned after two hours and six seconds.

Notice that for keepalives, the exponential backoff behavior between successive retransmissions is not done. For more information on the retransmission behavior of TCP, see Chapter 13, "Transmission Control Protocol (TCP) Retransmission and Time-Out."

TCP Connection Termination

Just as the TCP connection establishment process requires the sending of a SYN segment and its acknowledgment, the TCP connection termination process requires the sending of a FIN (Finish) segment, a TCP segment in which the FIN flag is set, and its acknowledgment. The FIN segment indicates that the FIN segment sender will send no more data on the connection. Because a TCP connection is made of two logical pipes (an outbound and inbound pipe for each TCP peer), both pipes must be closed and the closure must be acknowledged. Figure 11-5 shows a TCP connection termination.

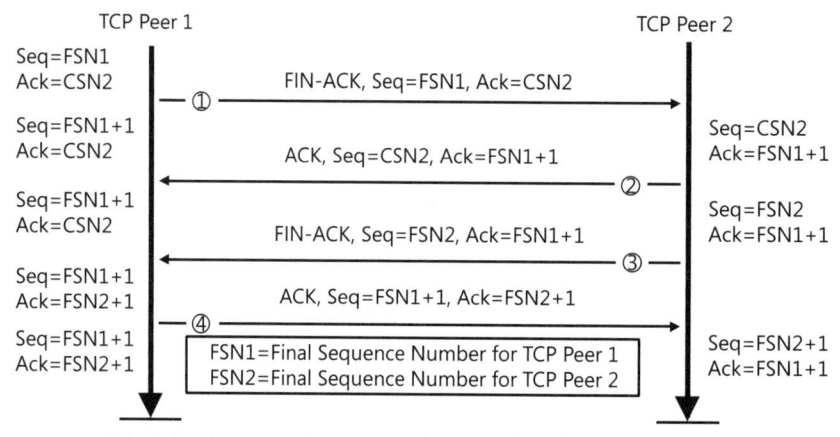

Figure 11-5 A TCP connection termination showing the exchange of four TCP segments

Typical TCP connection termination processes consist of the exchange of four TCP segments.

Segment 1: The FIN-ACK from TCP Peer 1

A TCP peer (TCP Peer 1) that wants to terminate outbound data flow sends a TCP segment that contains no data with the following:

- The Sequence Number field set to the current sequence number for outbound data. When closing the connection, the current sequence number is the final sequence number for outbound data (FSN1 in Figure 11-5).

- The Acknowledgment Number field set to the next byte of inbound data that the TCP peer expects to receive. This number also corresponds to the current sequence number of TCP Peer 2 (CSN2 in Figure 11-5).

- The ACK flag is set, indicating that the Acknowledgment Number field is significant.

- The FIN flag is set, indicating that no more data will be sent from this TCP peer on the connection.

The following Network Monitor 3.1 trace (Frame 1 of Capture 11-03, included in the \Captures folder on the companion CD-ROM) shows a FIN-ACK segment for an FTP session being closed by an FTP server:

```
Frame:
+ Ethernet: Etype = Internet IP (IPv4)
+ Ipv4: Next Protocol = TCP, Packet ID = 57337, Total IP Length = 40
- Tcp: Flags=F...A..., SrcPort=FTP control(21), DstPort=1162, Len=0, Seq=1035689055,
Ack=3928116597, Win=17448 (scale factor not found)
    SrcPort: FTP control(21)
    DstPort: 1162
    SequenceNumber: 1035689055 (0x3DBB5C5F)
    AcknowledgementNumber: 3928116597 (0xEA224D75)
  + DataOffset: 80 (0x50)
  - Flags: F...A...
    CWR:     (0.......) CWR not significant
    ECE:     (.0......) ECN-Echo not significant
    Urgent:  (..0.....) Not Urgent Data
    Ack:     (...1....) Acknowledgement field significant
    Push:    (....0...) No Push Function
    Reset:   (.....0..) No Reset
    Syn:     (......0.) Not Synchronize sequence numbers
    Fin:     (.......1) End of data
    Window: 17448 (scale factor not found)
    Checksum: 4983 (0x1377)
    UrgentPointer: 0 (0x0)
```

Segment 2: The ACK from TCP Peer 2

Similar to the SYN flag, TCP acts as if the FIN flag occupies a byte of the TCP sequence space and must be acknowledged as if it were a byte of data. Therefore, the TCP peer receiving the FIN-ACK segment (TCP Peer 2) sends an ACK with the following:

- The Sequence Number field set to the current sequence number for outbound data (CSN2 in Figure 11-5).

- The Acknowledgment Number field set to 1 more than the final sequence number for inbound data on the connection (FSN1 + 1).

- The ACK flag is set, indicating that the Acknowledgment Number field is significant.

The following Network Monitor 3.1 trace (Frame 2 of Capture 11-03, included in the \Captures folder on the companion CD-ROM) shows an ACK segment sent from the FTP client in response to a FIN-ACK sent by the FTP server:

```
Frame:
+ Ethernet: Etype = Internet IP (IPv4)
+ Ipv4: Next Protocol = TCP, Packet ID = 10526, Total IP Length = 40
- Tcp: Flags=....A..., SrcPort=1162, DstPort=FTP control(21), Len=0, Seq=3928116597,
Ack=1035689056, Win=17234 (scale factor not found)
    SrcPort: 1162
    DstPort: FTP control(21)
    SequenceNumber: 3928116597 (0xEA224D75)
    AcknowledgementNumber: 1035689056 (0x3DBB5C60)
  + DataOffset: 80 (0x50)
  - Flags: ....A...
    CWR:     (0.......) CWR not significant
```

```
    ECE:    (.0......) ECN-Echo not significant
    Urgent: (..0.....) Not Urgent Data
    Ack:    (...1....) Acknowledgement field significant
    Push:   (....0...) No Push Function
    Reset:  (.....0..) No Reset
    Syn:    (......0.) Not Synchronize sequence numbers
    Fin:    (.......0) Not End of data
  Window: 17234 (scale factor not found)
  Checksum: 5197 (0x144D)
  UrgentPointer: 0 (0x0)
```

Notice how the acknowledgment number is 1 more (1035689056) than the sequence number of the previous FIN-ACK (1035689055), explicitly acknowledging the receipt of the FIN-ACK segment.

Once the FIN is acknowledged, the TCP peer that sent the initial FIN-ACK segment cannot send data (TCP Peer 1). However, only one logical pipe has been terminated. The inbound data pipe for TCP Peer 1 is still open and data can still flow and be acknowledged with ACK segments that contain no data.

Segment 3: The FIN-ACK from TCP Peer 2

If the TCP peer with the open outbound data pipe (TCP Peer 2) still has data to send, data can be sent and acknowledged by TCP Peer 1. This is known as a TCP half-close. For example, a TCP half-close occurs when a client application sends the FIN-ACK segment and the server application still has data to send to the client before it can terminate its side of the connection.

Once all outstanding data from TCP Peer 2 is sent and acknowledged, TCP Peer 2 can close its outbound logical pipe to TCP Peer 1. TCP Peer 2 sends a segment with the following:

- The Sequence Number field set to the current sequence number for outbound data. When closing the connection, the current sequence number is the final sequence number for outbound data (FSN2 in Figure 11-5).

- The Acknowledgment Number field set to the next byte of inbound data that the TCP peer expects to receive. In this case, the acknowledgment number is the same as that acknowledged in Segment 2 (FSN1 + 1).

- The ACK flag is set, indicating that the Acknowledgment Number field is significant.

- The FIN flag is set, indicating that no more data will be sent from this TCP peer on the connection.

The following Network Monitor 3.1 trace (Frame 3 of Capture 11-03, included in the \Captures folder on the companion CD-ROM) shows a FIN-ACK segment for the FTP client closing its outbound pipe:

```
Frame:
+ Ethernet: Etype = Internet IP (IPv4)
+ Ipv4: Next Protocol = TCP, Packet ID = 10527, Total IP Length = 40
```

```
- Tcp: Flags=F...A..., SrcPort=1162, DstPort=FTP control(21), Len=0, Seq=3928116597,
Ack=1035689056, Win=17234 (scale factor not found)
    SrcPort: 1162
    DstPort: FTP control(21)
    SequenceNumber: 3928116597 (0xEA224D75)
    AcknowledgementNumber: 1035689056 (0x3DBB5C60)
  + DataOffset: 80 (0x50)
  - Flags: F...A...
    CWR:     (0.......) CWR not significant
    ECE:     (.0......) ECN-Echo not significant
    Urgent:  (..0.....) Not Urgent Data
    Ack:     (...1....) Acknowledgement field significant
    Push:    (....0...) No Push Function
    Reset:   (.....0..) No Reset
    Syn:     (......0.) Not Synchronize sequence numbers
    Fin:     (.......1) End of data
    Window: 17234 (scale factor not found)
    Checksum: 5196 (0x144C)
    UrgentPointer: 0 (0x0)
```

Segment 4: The ACK from TCP Peer 1

TCP acts as if the FIN flag of Segment 3 occupies a byte of the TCP sequence space and must be acknowledged as a byte of data. Therefore, the TCP peer receiving the FIN-ACK segment (TCP Peer 1) sends an ACK with the following:

- The Sequence Number field set to the current sequence number for outbound data (FSN1 + 1).

- The Acknowledgment Number field set to 1 more than the final sequence number for inbound data on the connection (FSN2 + 1).

- The ACK flag is set, indicating that the Acknowledgment Number field is significant.

The following Network Monitor 3.1 trace (Frame 4 of Capture 11-03, included in the \Captures folder on the companion CD-ROM) shows an ACK segment that the FTP server sent in response to a FIN-ACK sent by the FTP client:

```
Frame:
+ Ethernet: Etype = Internet IP (IPv4)
+ Ipv4: Next Protocol = TCP, Packet ID = 57338, Total IP Length = 40
- Tcp: Flags=....A..., SrcPort=FTP control(21), DstPort=1162, Len=0, Seq=1035689056,
Ack=3928116598, Win=17448 (scale factor not found)
    SrcPort: FTP control(21)
    DstPort: 1162
    SequenceNumber: 1035689056 (0x3DBB5C60)
    AcknowledgementNumber: 3928116598 (0xEA224D76)
  + DataOffset: 80 (0x50)
  - Flags: ....A...
    CWR:     (0.......) CWR not significant
    ECE:     (.0......) ECN-Echo not significant
    Urgent:  (..0.....) Not Urgent Data
    Ack:     (...1....) Acknowledgement field significant
    Push:    (....0...) No Push Function
```

```
Reset:       (.....0..) No Reset
Syn:         (......0.) Not Synchronize sequence numbers
Fin:         (.......0) Not End of data
Window: 17448 (scale factor not found)
Checksum: 4982 (0x1376)
UrgentPointer: 0 (0x0)
```

Notice how the acknowledgment number is 1 more (3928116598) than the sequence number of the previous FIN-ACK (3928116597), explicitly acknowledging the receipt of the FIN-ACK segment.

TCP Peer 2's outbound pipe is terminated when the ACK segment is received. The TCP connection, with both logical pipes gracefully terminated, is closed.

> **Note** TCP connection terminations do not have to use four segments. In some cases, Segments 2 and 3 are combined. The result is a FIN-ACK/FIN-ACK/ACK sequence.

TCP Connection Reset

The TCP connection termination process is for the graceful, mutually agreed closure of both pipes of a TCP connection. Both TCP peers exchange FIN segments that are acknowledged explicitly, indicating that all data on each outbound pipe has been sent and acknowledged. Another way to terminate a TCP connection is through a TCP connection reset—a TCP segment with the RST (Reset) flag set.

A TCP connection reset is sent when a parameter problem exists in the TCP header of an inbound TCP segment that cannot be reconciled. For example, an improper source or destination IP address or TCP port number could cause an established connection to be aborted.

Aborting an established TCP connection through a TCP reset also can be intentionally done through Windows Sockets. However, aborting a TCP connection causes the loss of all TCP data that is either in transit or in buffers waiting to be sent.

A TCP connection reset is used also to reject a TCP connection attempt in response to the receipt of a SYN segment. The most common reason a TCP peer denies a connection attempt with a connection reset is that the destination port in the SYN segment does not correspond to an Application Layer process running at the recipient of the SYN segment. Connection attempts also can be denied when the maximum number of allowed TCP connections is reached. Figure 11-6 shows a TCP connection reset.

> **Note** When a User Datagram Protocol (UDP) message arrives at a destination port that does not correspond to an Application Layer process, the receiving node sends an Internet Control Message Protocol (ICMP) Destination Unreachable-Port Unreachable message to the sender of the UDP message.

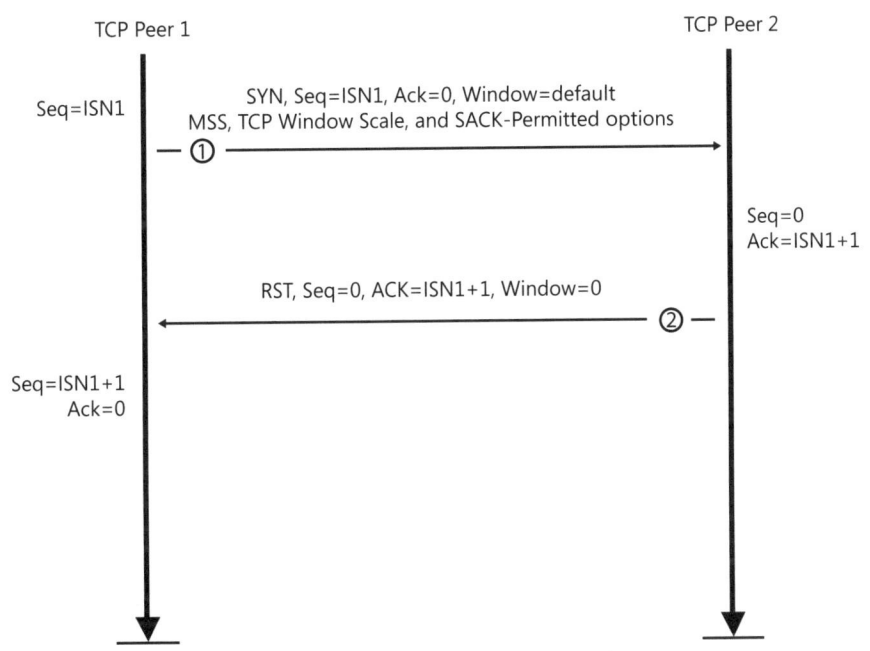

Chapter 11: Transmission Control Protocol (TCP) Connections 239

```
                TCP Peer 1                                                      TCP Peer 2
                    │                                                               │
   Seq=ISN1         │          SYN, Seq=ISN1, Ack=0, Window=default                 │
                    │       MSS, TCP Window Scale, and SACK-Permitted options       │
                    │───────────────────────①──────────────────────────────────────▶│
                    │                                                               │
                    │                                                               │ Seq=0
                    │                                                               │ Ack=ISN1+1
                    │                                                               │
                    │           RST, Seq=0, ACK=ISN1+1, Window=0                    │
                    │◀──────────────────────────────────────────②───────────────────│
                    │                                                               │
   Seq=ISN1+1       │                                                               │
   Ack=0            ▼                                                               ▼
```

Figure 11-6 A TCP connection reset showing the SYN and RST segments

The following Network Monitor 3.1 trace (Capture 11-04, included in the \Captures folder on the companion CD-ROM) shows the sequence of packets sent between a host running an FTP client application and a host that is not an FTP server. Frame 1 is a SYN segment to the FTP control port; Frame 2 is the connection reset.

```
Frame 1

    Frame:
+ Ethernet: Etype = Internet IP (IPv4)
+ Ipv4: Next Protocol = TCP, Packet ID = 10535, Total IP Length = 48
- Tcp: Flags=.S......, SrcPort=1164, DstPort=FTP control(21), Len=0, Seq=4065871748, Ack=0,
Win=16384 (scale factor not found)
    SrcPort: 1164
    DstPort: FTP control(21)
    SequenceNumber: 4065871748 (0xF2584784)
    AcknowledgementNumber: 0 (0x0)
  + DataOffset: 112 (0x70)
  + Flags: .S......
    Window: 16384 (scale factor not found)
    Checksum: 33470 (0x82BE)
    UrgentPointer: 0 (0x0)
  + TCPOptions:
```

```
Frame 2

    Frame:
+ Ethernet: Etype = Internet IP (IPv4)
```

```
+ Ipv4: Next Protocol = TCP, Packet ID = 57738, Total IP Length = 40
- Tcp: Flags=..R.A..., SrcPort=FTP control(21), DstPort=1164, Len=0, Seq=0, Ack=4065871749,
Win=0 (scale factor not found)
    SrcPort: FTP control(21)
    DstPort: 1164
    SequenceNumber: 0 (0x0)
    AcknowledgementNumber: 4065871749 (0xF2584785)
  + DataOffset: 80 (0x50)
  - Flags: ..R.A...
    CWR:     (0.......) CWR not significant
    ECE:     (.0......) ECN-Echo not significant
    Urgent:  (..0.....) Not Urgent Data
    Ack:     (...1....) Acknowledgement field significant
    Push:    (....0...) No Push Function
    Reset:   (.....1..) Reset
    Syn:     (......0.) Not Synchronize sequence numbers
    Fin:     (.......0) Not End of data
    Window: 0 (scale factor not found)
    Checksum: 61294 (0xEF6E)
    UrgentPointer: 0 (0x0)
```

In the connection reset segment:

- The RST and ACK flags are set.

- The sequence number is 0.

- The acknowledgment number is 1 more than the sequence number of the SYN segment (ISN1 + 1). As in the SYN-ACK segment of a connection establishment process, TCP acts as if the SYN flag occupies a byte of sequence space and is explicitly acknowledged

- The window size is 0.

After receipt of a connection reset, the initiating peer can either try again (in practice, three attempts are made) or abandon the connection attempt.

TCP Connection States

A TCP connection exists in one of the states listed in Table 11-1.

Table 11-1 TCP Connection States

State	Description
CLOSED	No TCP connection exists.
LISTEN	An Application Layer protocol has issued a passive open and is willing to accept TCP connection attempts.
SYN SENT	An Application Layer protocol has issued an active open and a SYN segment is sent.
SYN RCVD	A SYN segment is received and a SYN-ACK is sent.

Chapter 11: Transmission Control Protocol (TCP) Connections   241

Table 11-1 TCP Connection States

State	Description
ESTABLISHED	The final ACK for the TCP connection establishment process is sent and received. Data can now be transferred in both directions.
FIN WAIT-1	The initial FIN-ACK segment to close one side of the connection is sent.
FIN WAIT-2	The ACK in response to the initial FIN-ACK is received.
CLOSING	A FIN-ACK is received but the ACK is not for the FIN-ACK sent. This is known as a simultaneous close, when both TCP peers send FIN-ACKs at the same time.
TIME WAIT	FIN-ACKs have been sent and acknowledged by both TCP peers and the TCP connection termination process is completed. Once the TIME WAIT state is reached, TCP must wait twice the maximum segment lifetime (MSL) before the connection's TCP port number can be reused. The MSL is the maximum amount of time a TCP segment can exist in an internetwork, and its recommended value is 240 seconds. This delay prevents a new connection's TCP segments using the same port numbers from being confused with duplicated TCP segments of the old connection.
CLOSE WAIT	A FIN-ACK has been received and a FIN-ACK has been sent.
LAST ACK	The ACK in response to the FIN-ACK has been received.

The connection states that a TCP peer goes through depend on whether the TCP peer is the initiator of the TCP connection establishment or the initiator of the TCP connection termination.

Figure 11-7 shows the states of a TCP connection.

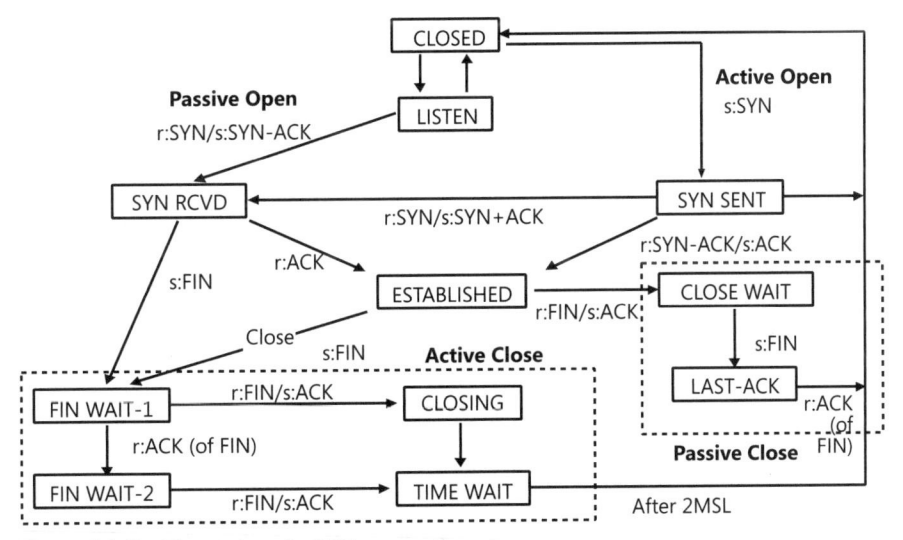

Figure 11-7 The states of a TCP connection

Figure 11-8 shows the connection states of two TCP peers during the connection establishment process.

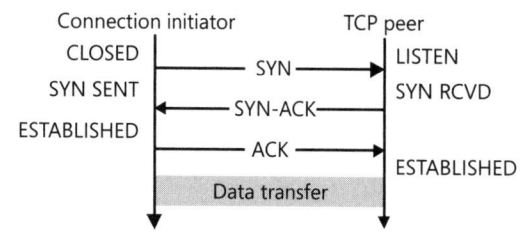

Figure 11-8 The states of a TCP connection during TCP connection establishment

Figure 11-9 shows the connection states of two TCP peers during the connection termination process.

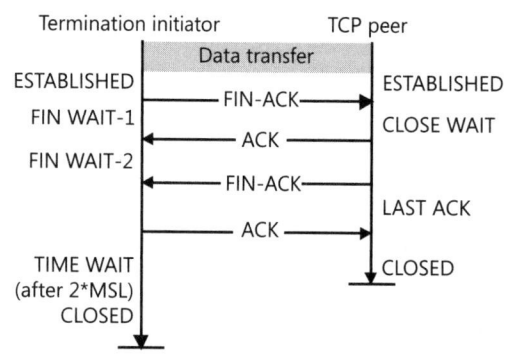

Figure 11-9 The states of a TCP connection during TCP connection termination

Controlling the TIME WAIT state in Windows Server 2008 and Windows Vista

The TIME WAIT state is used to delay the reuse of the same parameters for a TCP connection, ensuring that duplicates of the old connection's TCP segments in transit are not confused with a new connection's TCP segments. The RFC 793 recommended value for the MSL is two minutes. For Windows Server 2008 and Windows Vista with Service Pack 1, TCP connections in the TIME WAIT state are controlled by the following registry value:

TcpTimedWaitDelay
```
Location: HKEY_LOCAL_MACHINE\SYSTEM\CurrentControlSet\Services\Tcpip\Parameters
Data type: REG_DWORD
Valid range: 30-300
Default value: 120
Present by default: No
```

The value of TcpTimedWaitDelay is the number of seconds that a TCP connection remains in the TIME WAIT state. The default is 120 seconds (two minutes).

Summary

TCP connections are created through the TCP connection establishment process, where two TCP peers exchange SYN segments and determine starting sequence numbers, window sizes, window scaling factors, maximum segment sizes, and other TCP options. TCP connections can be maintained through the exchange of periodic keepalive segments, although this is not common. To terminate a TCP connection gracefully, each TCP peer must send a FIN segment and have it acknowledged. A TCP peer uses a TCP connection reset segment to either abort a current connection or refuse a connection attempt.

Chapter 12

Transmission Control Protocol (TCP) Data Flow

In this chapter:
Basic TCP Data Flow Behavior 245
TCP Acknowledgments. 246
TCP Sliding Windows 249
Small Segments 257
Sender-Side Flow Control. 259
Summary. 268

TCP provides reliable data transfer through the sequencing of outbound data and the acknowledgment of inbound data. Along with reliability, TCP includes behaviors to prevent inefficient use of the network and provide flow control for data sent and received. This chapter describes the details of the TCP send and receive windows, receiver-side flow control using the TCP receive window to prevent the sender overloading the receiver, and sender-side flow control using a variety of algorithms to prevent the sender from overloading the network.

Basic TCP Data Flow Behavior

The following mechanisms govern TCP data flow:

- **Acknowledgments** TCP acknowledgments are delayed and cumulative for contiguous data and selective for noncontiguous data.

- **Sliding send and receive windows** A send window for the sender and a receive window for the receiver control the amount of data that can be sent. Send and receive windows provide receiver-side flow control. As data is sent and acknowledged, the send and receive windows slide along the sequence space of the sender's byte stream.

- **Avoidance of small segments** Small segments—TCP segments that are not at the TCP maximum segment size (MSS)—are allowed but are governed to avoid inefficient internetwork use.

- **Sender-side flow control** TCP sliding windows provide a way for the receiver to determine flow control, but the sender also uses flow control algorithms to avoid sending too much data and congesting the internetwork.

These mechanisms work for interactive traffic, such as Telnet sessions, and for bulk data transfer, such as the downloading of a large file with the File Transfer Protocol (FTP).

TCP Acknowledgments

Recall that a TCP connection is a bidirectional, full-duplex logical circuit that consists of outbound and inbound logical pipes for the inbound and outbound byte streams. To account for data sent and received, each byte in the outbound and inbound byte streams is numbered. These numbers are used by TCP for reliable data transfer and are independent of the actual data in the byte streams.

A TCP acknowledgment (ACK) is a TCP segment with the ACK flag set. In an ACK, the Acknowledgment Number field indicates the number for the next byte in the contiguous byte stream that the ACK's sender expects to receive. Additionally, if the TCP Selective Acknowledgment (SACK) option is present, the ACK can indicate up to four blocks of noncontiguous data received.

Delayed Acknowledgments

When a TCP peer receives a segment, the acknowledgment for the segment (either cumulative or selective) is not sent immediately. The TCP peer delays the sending of the ACK segment for the following reasons:

- If, during the delay, additional TCP segments are received, a single ACK segment can acknowledge the receipt of multiple TCP segments.

- For full-duplex data flow, delaying the ACK makes it possible for the ACK segment to contain data. This is known as piggybacking the data on the ACK, or piggyback ACKs. If the incoming TCP segment contains data that requires a response from the receiver, the response can be sent along with the ACK. This is common for Telnet traffic, in which each keystroke of the Telnet client is sent to the Telnet server process. The received Telnet keystroke must be echoed back to the Telnet client. Rather than sending an ACK for the keystroke received and then sending the echoed keystroke, a single TCP segment containing the ACK and the echoed keystroke is sent.

- TCP has the time to perform general connection maintenance. The Application Layer protocol has additional time to retrieve data from TCP, and an updated window size can be sent with ACK.

RFC 1122 specifies that the acknowledgment delay should be no longer than 0.5 seconds. By default, TCP/IP for Windows Server 2008 and Windows Vista uses an acknowledgment delay of 200 ms (0.2 seconds), which can be configured per interface by the TcpDelAckTicks registry setting.

TcpDelAckTicks
Location:HKEY_LOCAL_MACHINE\SYSTEM
\CurrentControlSet\Services\Tcpip\Parameters

```
\Interfaces\InterfaceGUID
Data type: REG_DWORD
Valid range: 0-6
Default value: 2
Present by default: No
```

TcpDelAckTicks sets the delayed acknowledgment timer (in 100-ms intervals) of an interface. If you set this value to 0 or 1, the delayed-ACK time is 200 milliseconds. The default value of 2 specifies a 200-ms delayed acknowledgment timer.

> **More Info** All of the RFCs referenced in this chapter can be found in the \Standards\Chap12_TCPFlow folder on the companion CD-ROM.

Cumulative for Contiguous Data

As originally defined in RFC 793, the TCP acknowledgment scheme is cumulative. The presence of the ACK flag and the value of the Acknowledgment Number field explicitly acknowledge all bytes in the received byte stream numbered from the Initial Sequence Number (ISN) + 1 (the first byte of data sent on the connection), up to but not including the number in the Acknowledgment Number field (Acknowledgment Number – 1). Figure 12-1 illustrates the cumulative acknowledgment scheme of TCP.

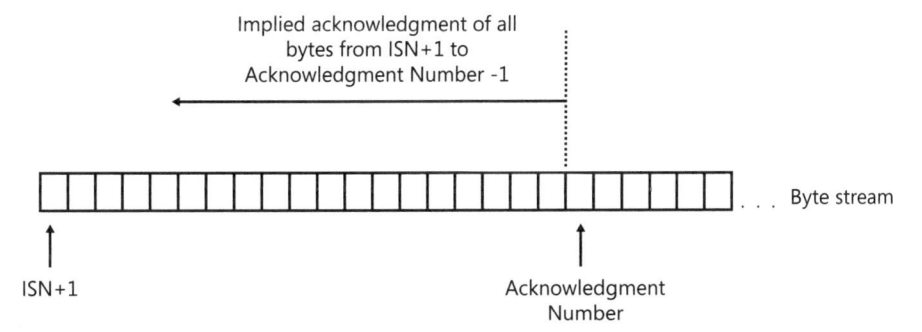

Figure 12-1 The cumulative acknowledgment scheme of TCP

A TCP peer sends an ACK with a new Acknowledgment Number field when a TCP segment is received containing data that is contiguous with previous data received. TCP segments received that are not contiguous with the previous segments received are not acknowledged. Only when the missing segments are retransmitted and received, creating a contiguous block of one or more TCP segments, does the receiver send an ACK segment with the new Acknowledgment Number field.

Although the original cumulative acknowledgment scheme for TCP works well and provides reliable data transfer, in high-loss environments this relatively simple acknowledgment scheme can slow throughput and use additional network bandwidth.

For example, a TCP peer sends six TCP segments. If the first of the six segments is dropped and the last five segments arrive, no ACK for the five received segments is sent. With normal TCP retransmission behavior, after the retransmission time-out (RTO), the sending TCP peer begins to retransmit all six segments. When the retransmission of the first TCP segment arrives, the receiving TCP peer sends an ACK segment confirming receipt of all six segments. Although the dropped first segment was successfully recovered, TCP on the sender needlessly sent duplicates of segments that successfully arrived.

Selective for Noncontiguous Data

With selective acknowledgments, the Acknowledgment Number field still indicates the number of the last contiguous byte received, but the TCP SACK option can acknowledge noncontiguous received segments. With the TCP SACK option, the left and right edges of the blocks of noncontiguous data received are explicitly acknowledged, preventing needless retransmission. Figure 12-2 illustrates TCP's selective acknowledgment scheme.

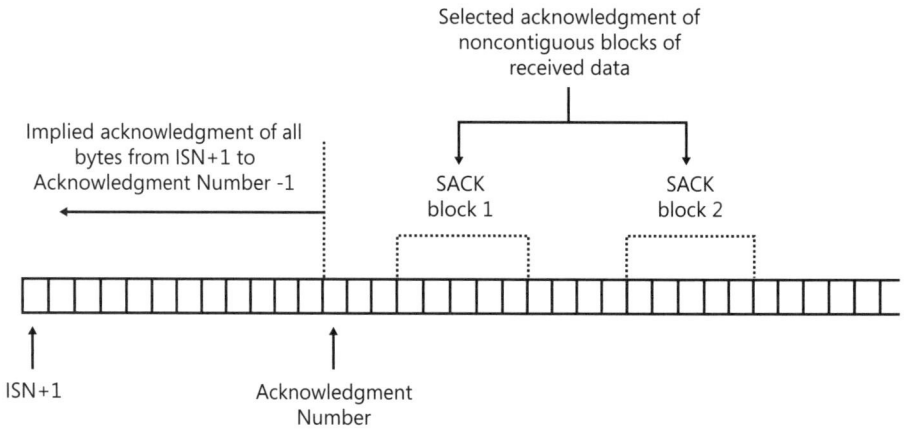

Figure 12-2 The selective acknowledgment scheme of TCP

Using the previous example, if six TCP segments are sent and the first segment is dropped, the receiving TCP peer sends an ACK segment with the following settings: the Acknowledgment Number field is set to the first byte of the missing TCP segment, and the TCP SACK option is set with the left and right edge of the block consisting of the second through the sixth received TCP segments. After receipt of the ACK with the TCP SACK option, the sender marks the selectively acknowledged TCP segments and does not retransmit them. The sending TCP peer retransmits the first TCP segment after its RTO. After receipt, the receiving TCP peer sends an ACK segment with the Acknowledgment Number field set to the number of the first byte past the sixth TCP segment.

Selective acknowledgments are especially important for the recovery of data on a TCP connection with a large window size. The previous example has a window size of six segments.

Imagine a high-bandwidth, high-delay link such as a satellite channel with a window size of 200 segments. The sender transmits 200 segments at a time. If cumulative acknowledgments are used and the first segment is dropped, the sender needlessly retransmits many of the successfully received segments before the dropped segment is recovered. Selective acknowledgments eliminate needless retransmissions of successfully received segments.

TCP Sliding Windows

To govern the amount of data that can be sent at any one time and to provide receiver-side flow control, data transfer between TCP peers is performed using a window. The window is the span of data on the byte stream that the receiver permits the sender to send. The sender can send only the bytes of the byte stream that lie within the window. New data can be sent only with the receiver's permission. The window slides along the sender's outbound byte stream and the receiver's inbound byte stream.

The values of the Acknowledgment Number and Window fields in ACKs that the receiver sends determine the actual numbered bytes within the window. The Acknowledgment Number field indicates the next byte of data that the receiver expects to receive. The Window field indicates the maximum amount of TCP data that the receiver can receive on this connection. The span of data within the window is from Acknowledgment Number through the value of Acknowledgment Number + Window − 1.

For a given logical pipe—one direction of the full-duplex TCP connection—the sender maintains a send window and the receiver maintains a receive window. When there are no data or ACK segments in transit, a logical pipe's send window and receive window are matched; the span of data that the sender is permitted to send is matched to the span of data that the receiver is able to receive.

Send Window

To maintain the send window, the sender must account for the bytes in the outbound byte stream that have been

- Sent and acknowledged (Sent/ACKed)
- Sent but not acknowledged (Sent/UnACKed)
- Unsent but fit within the current send window (Unsent/Inside)
- Unsent but lie beyond the current send window (Unsent/Outside)

Figure 12-3 illustrates the types of data that exist for the send window.

The span of data that lies within the send window is the Sent/UnACKed and Unsent/Inside data.

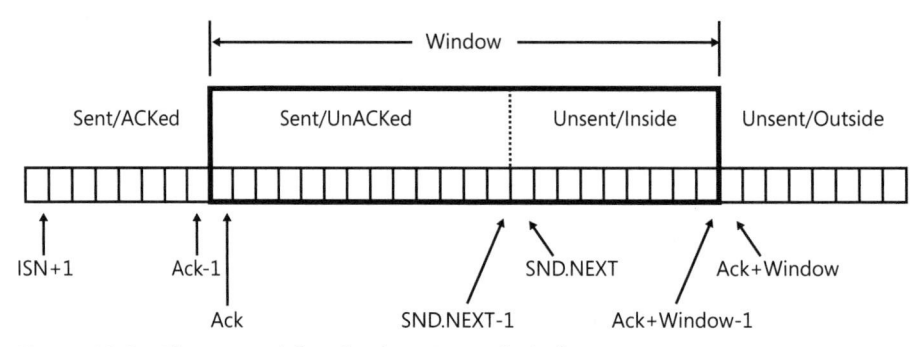

Figure 12-3 The types of data for the TCP send window

Sent/ACKed Data

Sent/ACKed data is data that has been sent and acknowledged as received. The first byte of Sent/ACKed data is numbered ISN + 1. Recall from the TCP connection establishment process that the TCP peer chooses an ISN in its SYN segment. The SYN flag is treated as if it was a byte of data and is explicitly acknowledged. Therefore, the first byte of user data sent on the connection is numbered ISN + 1. The acknowledgment number is the number of the next byte of data the receiver expects to receive, explicitly acknowledging all bytes received up to but not including the acknowledgment number. Therefore, the last byte of ACKed data is numbered Acknowledgment Number – 1.

Sent/UnACKed Data

Sent/UnACKed data is data that has been sent but for which no acknowledgments have been received. The Sent/UnACKed data is either in transit, dropped from the internetwork, has arrived at the receiver but no ACK has been sent (because of delayed acknowledgments), or the ACK for the Sent/UnACKed data is in transit.

To distinguish Sent/UnACKed data from Unsent/Inside data, TCP maintains a variable known as SND.NEXT, which is the number of the next byte to be sent. The value of SND.NEXT becomes the value of the Sequence Number field for the next TCP segment sent.

The first byte of Sent/UnACKed data is the Acknowledgment Number field's value of the last ACK segment received from the receiver. The last byte of Sent/UnACKed data is numbered as the value of SND.NEXT – 1.

Unsent/Inside Data

Unsent/Inside data is data that has not yet been sent but is within the current send window. Unsent/Inside data can be sent because the receiver has permitted it. It is natural to assume that if the data has been permitted, the sender will send all data within the send window before waiting for an acknowledgment and an updated window size from the receiver. In other words, there is no Unsent/Inside data when waiting for an acknowledgment.

However, as discussed later in this chapter, when starting the initial data flow and when encountering congestion, the sender-side flow control mechanisms of slow start and congestion avoidance prevent the sender from sending all the data that falls within the receiver's receive window. In such cases, these mechanisms govern the amount of data sent before waiting for an acknowledgment.

The first byte of Unsent/Inside data is numbered as the value of the SND.NEXT variable. The number of the last byte of Unsent/Inside data is the last byte of data within the send window, the value of Acknowledgment Number + Window − 1.

Unsent/Outside

Unsent/Outside data is data that is unsent and outside the current send window, representing future data to be sent. Unsent/Outside data relative to the current send window should never be sent because it falls outside the receive window. The receiver's receive window is a direct reflection of buffer space remaining to store incoming data. The receiver discards data that cannot be stored in the receive buffer for the connection and sends an ACK segment with the current acknowledgment number. The first byte of Unsent/Outside data is numbered as the value of Acknowledgment Number + Window.

Sliding the Send Window

The send window has a left edge (defined by the boundary between Sent/ACKed and Sent/UnACKed data) and a right edge (defined by the boundary between Unsent/Inside and Unsent/Outside data). When an ACK is received with a higher acknowledgment number, the left edge of the send window advances to the right (closes). When an ACK is received in which the value of Acknowledgment Number + Window is greater than the previous value of Acknowledgment Number + Window, the right edge of the send window advances to the right (opens). The sum of the Acknowledgment Number + Window fields is the value of the Acknowledgment Number field in the ACK for the last TCP segment that fits within the current send window. Figure 12-4 illustrates the sliding of the send window.

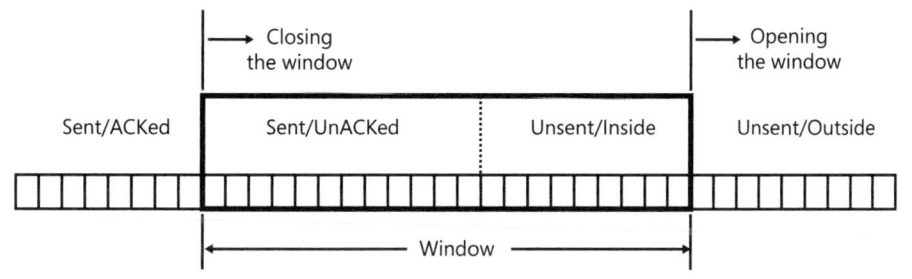

Figure 12-4 The sliding of the send window showing window closing and opening

It is possible for the send window to close but not open—for the left edge of the send window to advance while the right edge does not. For example, the sender receives an ACK with an increased acknowledgment number but a decreased window, such that the sum of

Acknowledgment Number + Window does not change. This can happen when the receiver receives the data, which is acknowledged, but the received data has not been passed to the Application Layer protocol on the receiver. Therefore, the value of the Acknowledgment Number field in the ACK increases because of the contiguous data arriving, but the window decreases by the same amount, keeping the value of Acknowledgment Number + Window the same.

Zero Send Window

When the receiver advertises a window size of zero, the left and right edges of the send window are at the same boundary—the boundary between Sent/ACKed data and Unsent/Outside data. A zero window size can occur when the receiver has received the maximum amount of acknowledged data but the data has not yet been retrieved by the Application Layer protocol. This can happen when TCP has not yet indicated the data to the Application Layer protocol or when the Application Layer protocol has not explicitly informed TCP that it is ready to receive the next block of data.

With a zero send window, no new data can be sent until an ACK with a nonzero window size is received. However, because no new data is sent, the receiver is not sending any new ACKs. This can produce a deadlock situation in which the sender waits to receive a new window size and the receiver does not send a new window size because there are no new ACKs to send. Consequently, receiver and sender behaviors are defined to prevent the deadlock.

To prevent the deadlock on the receiver side, when the received data is passed to the Application Layer protocol, the receiver sends an ACK segment with the current acknowledgment number and new nonzero window size. However, this segment is an ACK containing no data. ACK segments without data are not sent reliably; the receiving TCP peer does not acknowledge them, and the sending TCP peer cannot determine whether to retransmit the ACK segments. Therefore, if the ACK sent by the receiver to update the window size is lost, the sender would have no notification that new data can be sent. The TCP connection is indefinitely deadlocked; the receiver has informed the sender that new data can be sent, but the sender still considers the window size to be zero.

To prevent the deadlock caused by the dropped ACK that the receiver sent, the sender periodically sends a TCP segment containing 1 byte of new data for the connection. Because the data byte is Unsent/Outside data, the receiver discards the data and sends an ACK with the current acknowledgment number and window size. This sender-side mechanism is known as *probing the window*. The first window probe is sent after the current RTO, and the interval for successive probes is determined by doubling the timeout for the previous probe.

Receive Window

To maintain the receive window, the receiver must account for the bytes in the inbound byte stream that have been

- Received, acknowledged, and retrieved by the Application Layer protocol (Rcvd/ACKed/Retr)
- Received, acknowledged, and not retrieved by the Application Layer protocol (Rcvd/ACKed/NotRetr)
- Received, but not acknowledged (Rcvd/UnACKed)
- Not received, but inside the current receive window (NotRcvd/Inside)
- Not received, but outside the current receive window (NotRcvd/Outside)

Figure 12-5 illustrates the types of data that exist for the receive window.

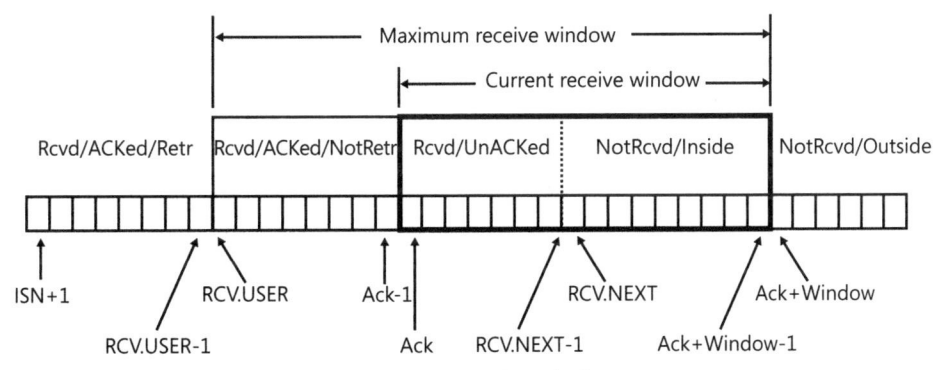

Figure 12-5 The types of data for the TCP receive window

The span of data that lies within the maximum receive window is Rcvd/ACKed/NotRetr, Rcvd/UnACKed, and NotRcvd/Inside. The span of data that lies within the current receive window is Rcvd/UnACKed and NotRcvd/Inside.

Notice the difference between the maximum receive window and the current receive window. The maximum receive window is a fixed size and corresponds to a maximum amount of data for inbound TCP segments. The current receive window is of variable size and is the number of bytes remaining from the maximum to store inbound TCP segments. The current receive window's size is the value of the Window field advertised in ACKs sent back to the sender and is the difference between the maximum receive window size (Rcvd/ACKed/NotRetr + Rcvd/UnACKed + NotRcvd/Inside) and the amount of data that has been received and acknowledged but not passed to the Application Layer protocol (Rcvd/ACKed/NotRetr).

Rcvd/ACKed/Retr Data

Rcvd/ACKed/Retr data is data that has been received, acknowledged, and retrieved by the Application Layer protocol. The first byte of Rcvd/ACKed/Retr data is numbered ISN + 1. To track the next byte to be passed to the Application Layer protocol, TCP maintains a variable called RCV.USER. Therefore, the last byte of Rcvd/ACKed/Retr data is numbered RCV.USER − 1.

Rcvd/ACKed/NotRetr Data

Rcvd/ACKed/NotRetr data is data that has been received and acknowledged but has not been passed up to the Application Layer protocol. This category of data is the difference between the fixed-size maximum receive window and the variable-size current receive window. The first byte of Rcvd/ACKed/NotRetr data is numbered RCV.USER. The last byte of Rcvd/ACKed/NotRetr data is numbered Acknowledgment Number − 1.

Rcvd/UnACKed Data

Rcvd/UnACKed data is data that has been received but not acknowledged. To keep track of the next contiguous byte to be received, TCP maintains a variable called RCV.NEXT. When an ACK segment is sent, the ACK segment's Acknowledgment Number field is set to the value of RCV.NEXT. The first byte of Rcvd/UnACKed data is the current acknowledgment number. The last byte of Rcvd/UnACKed data is numbered RCV.NEXT − 1.

If there are no TCP segments in transit and the receiver has not yet sent the ACK for TCP segments received, the send window's Sent/UnACKed data is the same as the receive window's Rcvd/UnACKed data. In this situation, the value of RCV.NEXT kept by the receiver is equal to the value of SND.NEXT kept by the sender.

NotRcvd/Inside Data

NotRcvd/Inside data is data that can be received and will fit within the current receive window. The first byte of NotRcvd/Inside data is numbered RCV.NEXT. The last byte of NotRcvd/Inside data within the receive window is numbered Acknowledgment Number + Window − 1.

NotRcvd/Outside Data

NotRcvd/Outside data is data that has not been received and is outside the current receive window, representing future data to be received. NotRcvd/Outside data relative to the current receive window should never be received because it falls outside the current receive window. The receiver discards data that cannot be stored in the current receive window and sends an ACK with the current acknowledgment number. The first byte of NotRcvd/Outside data is numbered Acknowledgment Number + Window.

Sliding the Receive Window

The current receive window has a left edge (defined by the boundary between Rcvd/ACKed/NotRetr and Rcvd/UnACKed data) and a right edge (defined by the boundary between NotRcvd/Inside and NotRcvd/Outside data). When an ACK segment is sent with an acknowledgment number set to RCV.NEXT, the left edge of the current receive window advances to the right (closes). When the Rcvd/ACKed/NotRetr data is passed up to the Application Layer protocol, the right edge of the maximum receive window advances to the right (opens). When this occurs, new data can be received. The maximum receive window slides to the right by the number of bytes passed to the Application Layer protocol. When the maximum receive window slides as a result of data being passed to the Application Layer protocol, the current receive window slides also, as the right edge of the maximum receive window and the right edge of the current receive window are the same. The next ACK that the receiver sends contains an updated window size. The increase in the sum of the acknowledgment number and the window size indicates to the sender that more data can be sent.

Figure 12-6 illustrates the sliding of the receive window.

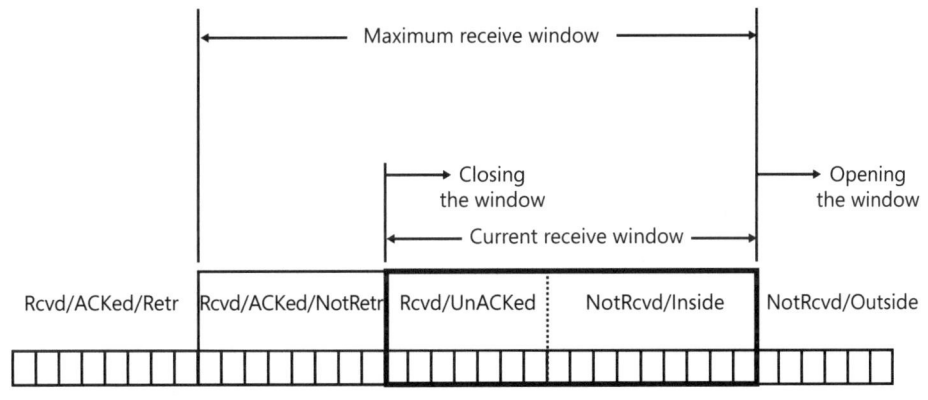

Figure 12-6 Sliding the receive window

If the Application Layer protocol does not receive the data in a timely fashion, the receive window closes instead of sliding. This is indicated to the sender by increasing the acknowledgment number for new data received and decreasing the value of the Window field by the same amount, thereby keeping the value of Acknowledgment Number + Window the same. In an extreme situation, the maximum receive window is filled with Rcvd/ACKed/NotRetr data and the left and right edges are the same (a zero receive window).

Shrinking the Window

Shrinking the window is the movement of the right edge of the receive window to the left. To shrink the receive window, an ACK segment is sent where the value of Acknowledgment Number + Window decreases. Normally, the value of Acknowledgment Number + Window either increases or remains the same. RFC 1122 discourages shrinking the window. However, a sending TCP peer must be prepared to adjust its send window accordingly. The receiver discards any data sent that is suddenly outside the shrunken receive window.

Receive Window Auto-Tuning

For optimal throughput, a sender should send enough packets to fill the logical pipe to the receiver. The capacity of this logical pipe can be calculated by multiplying the path bandwidth in bits per second by the round-trip time (RTT) in seconds. This capacity calculation is known as the bandwidth-delay product (BDP). The pipe can be fat (higher bandwidth), thin (lower bandwidth), short (lower RTT), or long (higher RTT). Pipes that are fat and long have the highest BDP. Examples of high BDP transmission paths are those across satellites or enterprise wide area networks (WANs) that include intercontinental optical fiber links.

To optimize TCP throughput, especially for transmission paths with a high BDP, TCP in Windows Server 2008 and Windows Vista supports Receive Window Auto-Tuning. Receive Window Auto-Tuning determines the optimal receive window size by measuring the BDP and the application retrieve rate and adapting the window size for ongoing transmission path and application conditions.

Receive Window Auto-Tuning enables TCP window scaling by default, allowing up to a 16-megabyte (MB) maximum receive window size. As the data flows over the connection, the TCP stack monitors the connection, measures its current BDP and application receive retrieve rate, and adjusts the receive window size to optimize throughput. TCP in Windows Server 2008 and Windows Vista no longer uses the TCPWindowSize registry value.

Receive Window Auto-Tuning automatically determines the optimal receive window size on a per-connection basis. In Windows XP, the TCPWindowSize registry value applied to all connections. Applications no longer need to specify TCP window sizes through Windows Sockets options to obtain optimal throughput. Additionally, IT administrators no longer need to determine the best TCP window size and manually configure a TCP receive window size for specific computers.

With Receive Window Auto-Tuning, a Windows Server 2008 or Windows Vista-based TCP peer will typically advertise much larger receive window sizes than a Windows XP or Windows Server 2003-based TCP peer. This allows the TCP peer sending data to the Windows Server 2008 or Windows Vista-based TCP peer to fill the pipe between the TCP peers by sending more TCP data segments without having to wait for an ACK (subject to TCP congestion control). For typical client-based networking traffic such as Web pages or e-mail, the Web server or e-mail server will be able to send more TCP data more quickly to the Windows Server 2008 or Windows Vista-based client computer, resulting in an overall increase in network performance. The higher the BDP and application retrieve rate for the connection, the better the performance increase.

The impact on the network is that a stream of TCP data packets that would normally be sent out at a lower, measured pace—based on a small and nonadaptive TCP receive window size—are sent much faster, resulting in a larger spike of network utilization during the data transfer. For example, for Windows XP and Windows Vista-based computers performing the same data transfer over a long, fat pipe, the same amount of data is transferred. However, the data transfer to the Windows Vista-based client computer is faster due to the larger receive window size and the server's ability to fill the pipe between the server and client.

Because Receive Window Auto-Tuning increases network utilization of high-BDP transmission paths, the use of Quality of Service (QoS) or application send rate throttling might become important for transmission paths that are operating at or near capacity. To address this possible need, Windows Server 2008 and Windows Vista support Group Policy-based QoS settings that allow you to define throttling rates for sent traffic on an IP address or TCP port basis. For more information, see the Quality of Service Web page at *http://go.microsoft.com/fwlink/?LinkID=82892*.

To disable window scaling and Receive Window Auto-Tuning, use the `netsh interface tcp set global autotuninglevel=disabled` command. To enable window scaling and Receive Window Auto-Tuning, use the `netsh interface tcp set global autotuninglevel=normal` command.

When Receive Window Auto-Tuning is disabled, the default advertised TCP receive window size is either specified by the application or is automatically determined based on the bit rate of the media as reported by the network adapter, according to the following rules:

- Below 1 megabits per second (Mbps): 8 kilobytes (KB)
- 1 Mbps to below 100 Mbps: 17 KB
- 100 Mbps to below 10 gigabits per second (Gbps): 64 KB
- 10 Gbps or higher: 128 KB

> **Note** Some firewall and network edge devices either do not properly handle the TCP window scaling option or must be configured to handle the TCP window scaling option. For information about specific devices, see the Microsoft Knowledge Base article at *http://support.microsoft.com/kb/934430/en-us*.

Small Segments

A small segment is a TCP segment that is smaller than the MSS. To increase the efficiency of sending data, TCP avoids sending and receiving small segments by using the Nagle algorithm and by avoiding silly window syndrome.

The Nagle Algorithm

For interactive data, such as the data of a Telnet or Rlogin session, much of the traffic is made up of individual keystrokes sent by the client and echoed by the server. For each keystroke, a single byte of data is sent. This is a network efficiency of 2.5 percent (the number of bytes of data [1 byte] divided by the number of bytes of overhead needed to send the data [40 bytes]). For interactive sessions, such as Telnet, each typed character must be sent and echoed back to the Telnet client application to be displayed on the user's screen. Therefore, sending small segments cannot be avoided for interactive sessions. Preventing the sending of a small segment would mean that the user would not see the keystroke as entered on the keyboard. In the case of Telnet and Rlogin, a single keystroke echoed back to the user generates the following three TCP segments:

1. The client application sends the keystroke byte as a small TCP segment with the Push (PSH) flag set.

2. The keystroke TCP segment is passed to the server application, which sends an echo of the keystroke back to the client application (along with an ACK of the keystroke byte) as a small TCP segment with the PSH flag set.

3. The echoed keystroke TCP segment is passed to the client application, which sends an ACK of the echoed keystroke segment.

Typical interactive sessions consist of multiple keystrokes in rapid succession.

To minimize the sending of small TCP segments, TCP is required to use the Nagle algorithm, named after John Nagle, the author of RFC 896, which describes the algorithm. The Nagle algorithm's premise is that a TCP connection can send only a single unacknowledged small segment. If a small segment is sent and not acknowledged, no other small segments can be sent.

In the case of interactive session traffic, such as Telnet and Rlogin, a keystroke segment is sent. Additional keystrokes entered by the user are accumulated in the TCP send buffer until the ACK for the outstanding small segment arrives. The next segment sent could contain multiple keystrokes. Depending on the average time to receive acknowledgments and the user's typing speed, this simple rule can decrease the number of TCP segments sent in the session by a factor of three or more.

The Nagle algorithm adapts itself to the environment in which the TCP segments are being sent. In a high-bandwidth, low-delay environment, such as a local area network (LAN), ACKs return more quickly and less accumulation occurs. However, in such an environment, lower efficiency can be tolerated because of the higher capacity of the LAN. In a low-bandwidth, high-delay environment, such as a wide area network (WAN), ACKs return less quickly, producing more accumulation. This results in more efficient data transfer for environments with less capacity.

TCP/IP for Windows Server 2008 and Windows Vista uses the Nagle algorithm by default. The Nagle algorithm is disabled through the TCP_NODELAY Windows Sockets option. Developers should disable the Nagle algorithm only when the immediate sending of multiple small segments is required. To improve performance of file locking and manipulation, a computer running Windows Server 2008 or Windows Vista disables the Nagle algorithm for NetBIOS over TCP/IP (NetBT) and non-NetBIOS–based file sharing traffic.

Silly Window Syndrome

Whenever data is passed to the receiver's Application Layer protocol, the receive window opens and a new window size is advertised. Depending on how much data is retrieved from the receive buffer, this mechanism can cause the following behavior:

1. The sender and receiver are in a zero window state. The sender has sent all the data it can. The receiver has acknowledged all the data in the receive buffer and is waiting for

the Application Layer protocol to retrieve the data before it is free to advertise a nonzero window size.

2. The Application Layer protocol retrieves a single byte of data from the receive buffer. The receive window advances by one byte.
3. The receiver sends an ACK with the window size set to 1.
4. The sender, realizing that the value of Acknowledgment Number + Window has increased, advances its send window by one byte. Because the receiver has permitted the sending of a single byte, the sender sends a single byte.

Each time the Application Layer protocol fetches a single byte of data from the buffer, the sender sends a single-byte TCP segment. The data sent on the TCP connection consists of a steady pattern of small segments. This behavior is known as the silly window syndrome (SWS). Both the sender and the receiver avoid SWS.

Receiver-Side SWS Avoidance

The receiver avoids SWS by not advertising a new window size unless it is at least either an MSS or half of the maximum receive window size. As data is passed to the application, the receive window advances. If the receive window advances *n* bytes, receiver-side SWS dictates that a new window size cannot be advertised unless *n* is at least MSS bytes or half the maximum receive window.

Sender-Side SWS Avoidance

The sender avoids SWS by not sending a TCP segment containing data unless the advertised receive window size is at least MSS bytes. However, as previously discussed, small segments must be allowed for interactive data. Therefore, small segments are allowed if either of the following is true:

- The data is being pushed and adheres to the Nagle algorithm. Interactive data typically sets the TCP header's PSH flag. A single small segment can be sent according to the Nagle algorithm.
- The data is at least half the size of the maximum receive window and adheres to the Nagle algorithm.

Sender-Side Flow Control

Receiver-side flow control is implemented through the send and receive windows. The receiver can inform the sender to stop sending data by reducing the advertised receive window to zero. However, once a non-zero receive window size is advertised, there is nothing in the TCP sliding window mechanism that prevents the sender from sending all possible segments in the send window. According to the TCP sliding window mechanism, the sender can immediately send all of the segments that fit within the receive window without waiting for any ACKs. Although this behavior is permitted, it also can lead to network congestion, especially when sending TCP segments across multiple routers.

To prevent the flooding of segments that fit within the advertised receive window, TCP implementations, including Windows Server 2008 and Windows Vista, use the following algorithms described in RFCs 2581 and 3465:

- **The slow start algorithm**   Increases the actual send window—the number of segments within the send window that the sender can send before waiting for an acknowledgment—when incoming ACKs acknowledge new data.
- **The congestion avoidance algorithm**   Increases the actual send window for each round-trip time.

Although the slow start and congestion avoidance algorithms were developed to solve separate problems, they are used together to provide sender-side flow control.

Both the slow start and congestion avoidance algorithms maintain an additional variable called the *congestion window* (*cwind*) to help define how much data can be sent. For both algorithms, the size of the actual send window is the minimum of the advertised receive window and the congestion window (the value of *cwind*).

Slow Start Algorithm

For the slow start algorithm defined in RFC 2581 and supported by TCP in Windows XP and Windows Server 2003, TCP increases the *cwind* by the MSS (or one segment size) for every ACK received that acknowledges new data. For this method, the increase in *cwind* over time depends on whether the receiver sends an ACK for each segment received or uses delayed ACKs. The congestion window grows faster if the receiver does not use delayed ACKs and sends an ACK segment for each segment received.

For the slow start algorithm defined in RFC 3465 and supported by TCP in Windows Server 2008 and Windows Vista, TCP increases the *cwind* by the number of bytes of previously unacknowledged data that are acknowledged with each incoming ACK. This makes the growth of *cwind* independent of whether the receiver is using delayed ACKs.

Every time *cwind* is updated, it is compared to the current advertised receive window size, and the minimum of both values is used to update the actual send window size.

When TCP data begins to flow on a connection after the connection establishment process or after a prolonged idle time, the following example for two Ethernet-based TCP peers running Windows Vista with a window size of 12 MSS shows how the slow start process defined in RFC 3465 increases the actual send window size:

1. Set *cwind*'s initial value to 2 MSS (two MSS-sized segments). Compare *cwind*'s value and the currently advertised receive window size (17,520 or 12 MSS). Set the actual send window

size to the minimum of *cwind* and the currently advertised receive window size. Result: *cwind* = 2 MSS, advertised receive window size = 12 MSS, actual send window = 2 MSS.

2. Two TCP segments are sent. The sender waits for ACKs.

3. When the sender receives an ACK for both segments that were received, *cwind* is set to 4 MSS. Compare *cwind*'s value and the currently advertised receive window size. Set the actual send window size to the minimum of *cwind* and the currently advertised receive window size. Result: *cwind* = 4 MSS, advertised receive window size = 12 MSS, actual send window = 4 MSS.

4. Four TCP segments are sent. The sender waits for ACKs.

5. When the sender receives an ACK for the four TCP segments that were received, *cwind* is set to 8 MSS. Compare *cwind*'s value and the currently advertised receive window size. Set the actual send window size to the minimum of *cwind* and the currently advertised receive window size. Result: *cwind* = 8 MSS, advertised receive window size = 12 MSS, actual send window = 8 MSS.

6. Eight TCP segments are sent. The sender waits for ACKs.

This process continues until *cwind* becomes greater than the currently advertised receive window (12 MSS), at which point the currently advertised receive window governs how much data can be sent at a time, and slow start is finished. There is no more sender-side flow control unless a TCP segment needs to be retransmitted or after a prolonged idle time.

The following summary of Network Monitor Capture 12-01, included in the \Captures folder on the companion CD-ROM, illustrates the slow start behavior for the downloading of a file using FTP up to 8 MSS:

```
Frame   Source     Dest       Description
1       10.0.0.1   10.0.0.2   Flags=.S......, Seq=2956468642, Ack=0
2       10.0.0.2   10.0.0.1   Flags=.S..A..., Seq=1990890983, Ack=2956468643
3       10.0.0.1   10.0.0.2   Flags=....A..., Seq=2956468643, Ack=1990890984
4       10.0.0.1   10.0.0.2   Flags=....A..., Seq=2956468643 - 2956470103, Ack=1990890984
5       10.0.0.1   10.0.0.2   Flags=....A..., Seq=2956470103 - 2956471563, Ack=1990890984
6       10.0.0.2   10.0.0.1   Flags=....A..., Seq=1990890984, Ack=2956471563
7       10.0.0.1   10.0.0.2   Flags=....A..., Seq=2956471563 - 2956473023, Ack=1990890984
8       10.0.0.1   10.0.0.2   Flags=....A..., Seq=2956473023 - 2956474483, Ack=1990890984
9       10.0.0.1   10.0.0.2   Flags=....A..., Seq=2956474483 - 2956475943, Ack=1990890984
10      10.0.0.1   10.0.0.2   Flags=....A..., Seq=2956475943 - 2956477403, Ack=1990890984
11      10.0.0.2   10.0.0.1   Flags=....A..., Seq=1990890984, Ack=2956474483
12      10.0.0.2   10.0.0.1   Flags=....A..., Seq=1990890984, Ack=2956477403
13      10.0.0.1   10.0.0.2   Flags=....A..., Seq=2956477403 - 2956478863, Ack=1990890984
14      10.0.0.1   10.0.0.2   Flags=....A..., Seq=2956478863 - 2956480323, Ack=1990890984
15      10.0.0.1   10.0.0.2   Flags=....A..., Seq=2956480323 - 2956481783, Ack=1990890984
16      10.0.0.1   10.0.0.2   Flags=....A..., Seq=2956481783 - 2956483243, Ack=1990890984
17      10.0.0.1   10.0.0.2   Flags=....A..., Seq=2956483243 - 2956484703, Ack=1990890984
18      10.0.0.1   10.0.0.2   Flags=....A..., Seq=2956484703 - 2956486163, Ack=1990890984
19      10.0.0.1   10.0.0.2   Flags=....A..., Seq=2956486163 - 2956487623, Ack=1990890984
20      10.0.0.1   10.0.0.2   Flags=....A..., Seq=2956487623 - 2956489083, Ack=1990890984
```

The slow start algorithm for this data transfer is as follows:

1. The TCP connection establishment process is done in Frames 1 through 3. *cwind* is set to 2 MSS.
2. Frames 4 and 5 are the two segments corresponding to the current actual send window size of 2 MSS.
3. Frame 6 is an ACK segment for Frames 4 and 5. *cwind* is set to 4 MSS.
4. Frames 7 through 10 are the four segments corresponding to the current send actual window size of 4 MSS.
5. Frame 11 is an ACK segment for Frames 7 and 8. Frame 12 is an ACK segment for Frames 9 and 10. *cwind* is set to 8 MSS.
6. Frames 13 through 20 are the eight segments corresponding to the current actual send window size of 8 MSS.

The rate at which the size of the actual send window increases depends on how quickly ACK segments are returned. In a high-bandwidth, low-delay environment such as a LAN, the actual send window opens quickly. In a low-bandwidth, high-delay environment such as a WAN, the actual send window opens more slowly.

Although called the slow start algorithm, the actual send window size can increase at an exponential rate based on the receipt of ACKs for multiple segments sent. In the example in Capture 12-01, when starting the actual send window at 2 MSS, two segments are sent. If an ACK for both segments is sent, the actual send window increases to 4 MSS; four segments are sent. If ACKs for all four segments are sent, the actual send window increases to 8 MSS. The actual send window has quickly grown from 2 MSS to 4 MSS, and then to 8 MSS.

Congestion Avoidance Algorithm

Once data is flowing on the TCP connection, the actual send window is governed by the currently advertised receive window, and receiver-side flow control is in effect. When a TCP segment must be retransmitted, the assumption is that the packet loss is a result of congestion at a router, rather than damage to the packet causing a checksum verification to fail. If the packet loss is a result of congestion at a router, the sender's transmission rate must be immediately lowered and then gradually increased back to the rate at which data was being sent before the congestion occurred. For TCP connections, the transmission rate is the amount of data that the sender can send before having to wait for an ACK.

When the congestion occurs, the slow start algorithm is used to increase the size of the actual window size to half of the value of the advertised receive window size when the congestion occurred. The congestion avoidance algorithm then takes over. To keep track of when to use slow start and when to use congestion avoidance, an additional variable called the slow start threshold (*ssthresh*) is used. When a connection is established, *ssthresh* is set to 65,535. As with slow start, during congestion avoidance, the actual send window is the minimum of *cwind* and the currently advertised receive window.

The premise of the congestion avoidance algorithm is to increase *cwind* by 1 MSS for each round-trip time, which is the time it takes for a TCP segment to be sent and acknowledged. The congestion avoidance algorithm provides a smooth, linear increase in *cwind,* thereby increasing the actual send window. There are different ways of implementing the change in *cwind* for congestion avoidance, as follows:

- One method is to increase *cwind* by MSSMSS/*cwind* (integer division) for each ACK segment that is received. For example, if *cwind* is set to 7 MSS, for each ACK segment that is received, *cwind* is incremented by MSSMSS/7MSS, or MSS/7. Therefore, after receiving seven ACK segments, *cwind* increases by 1 MSS. When *cwind* is incremented by a quantity that is not a full MSS, sender-side SWS prevents a small segment from being sent. Only after *cwind* is incremented to another MSS can another full segment be sent. If the receiver is using delayed ACKs, it can take more than one round-trip time to open the congestion window by one MSS.

- Another method is to track the current actual send window size in increments of the MSS. When the number of segments that correspond to the size of the current actual send window size are ACKed, increment *cwind* by an MSS. Thus, the actual send window grows by 1 MSS for each full window of data that has been acknowledged, regardless of whether the receiver is using delayed ACKs. This is the method described in RFC 3465 and supported by TCP in Windows Server 2008 and Windows Vista.

With slow start, the actual send window increases by an MSS for each segment acknowledged in a round-trip time. With congestion avoidance, the actual send window increases by an MSS for a full window of data that has been acknowledged in a round-trip time.

When congestion occurs (indicated when a TCP segment must be retransmitted or when a duplicate ACK is received), the combination of slow start and congestion avoidance for TCP/IP for Windows Server 2008 and Windows Vista works as follows:

1. Set *ssthresh* to half the value of the current send window with a minimum value of 2 MSS. Set *cwind* to the value of 2 MSS.
2. Set the actual send window to the minimum of the currently advertised receive window and *cwind*.
3. Send the appropriate number of TCP segments.
4. As ACKs are received, increment *cwind*. If *cwind* ≤ *ssthresh,* increment *cwind* using slow start. If *cwind* > *ssthresh,* increment *cwind* using congestion avoidance.
5. Return to step 2.

The result of using the combination of slow start and congestion avoidance is that when congestion occurs, the sender uses slow start to quickly increase the size of the actual send window size to half the size of the actual send window when the congestion occurred. Then, congestion avoidance is used to more slowly increase the size of the actual send window size up to the currently advertised receive window size. This gradual increase in the amount of data being sent allows the internetwork to clear its routing buffers and recover from the congestion.

Compound TCP

The slow start and congestion avoidance algorithms work well for LAN media speeds and smaller TCP window sizes. However, when you have a TCP connection with a large receive window size and a large BDP (high bandwidth and high delay), such as replicating data between two servers located across a high-speed WAN link with a 100-ms round-trip time, these algorithms do not increase the send window fast enough to fully utilize the bandwidth of the connection. For example, on a 1-Gbps WAN link with a 100-ms round-trip time (RTT), it can take up to an hour for the send window to initially increase to the large window size being advertised by the receiver and to recover when there are lost segments.

To better utilize the bandwidth of TCP connections in these situations, TCP in Windows Server 2008 and Windows Vista supports Compound TCP (CTCP). CTCP more aggressively increases the send window for connections with large receive window sizes and large BDPs. CTCP attempts to maximize throughput on these types of connections by monitoring delay variations and losses. CTCP also ensures that its behavior does not negatively impact other TCP connections.

To ensure that TCP is using the network fairly, CTCP incorporates a delay-based component in its algorithm to increase the actual send window. CTCP detects network utilization by measuring expected and actual RTTs to determine whether the network is experiencing congestion. If the network is underutilized, the delay-based component is aggressive in increasing the send window to get to full utilization as quickly as possible. If the network is utilized or the potential for congestion exists, the delay-based component scales back the send window accordingly.

In testing performed internally at Microsoft, large file backup times were reduced by almost half for a 1-Gbps connection with a 50ms RTT. Connections with a larger bandwidth delay product can have even better performance. CTCP and Receive Window Auto-Tuning work together for increased link utilization and can result in substantial performance gains for large BDP connections.

CTCP is enabled by default for computers running Windows Server 2008 and disabled by default in computers running Windows Vista. You can disable CTCP and use congestion avoidance for all types of links, including those with large BDPs, with the `netsh interface tcp set global congestionprovider=none` command. You can enable CTCP with the `netsh interface tcp set global congestionprovider=ctcp` command.

Explicit Congestion Notification

Modern implementations of TCP treat the intermediate network between TCP peers as an opaque box. Packets containing TCP segments go into and out of the box. Sometimes the packets that go into the box are dropped. Because bit-level errors on today's digital and optical media are relatively rare, modern implementations of TCP assume that a dropped packet is due to congestion at a router—a congested router's buffers for incoming packets have filled to capacity and the router is silently discarding incoming packets.

Although TCP detects that the packets containing TCP segments for a connection were dropped and retransmits them, recovering from dropped packets is an expensive process in terms of sending host TCP processing, retransmission of the dropped packets, and reduced throughput.

Although packet drops due to congested routers are an unfortunate occurrence, they do not negatively impact bulk data transfers other than the additional time required to retransmit the dropped segments and gradually increase the transmission rate. The slow start and congestion avoidance algorithms work well for time-insensitive, bulk data traffic. However, the TCP method for dealing with dropped packets does not work as well for interactive, loss-sensitive, or time-sensitive traffic.

Another issue with router congestion is the effect that congestion has on multiple data flows. When a router begins dropping incoming packets, it typically does not distinguish one data flow from another. When multiple TCP flows have packet drops, the senders of all of those flows reduce their transmission rate. Depending on how quickly the router clears its congested buffers, the multiple TCP data flows that had packet drops might still be gradually increasing their sending rate. This can result in the router and its links being underutilized until all of the TCP data flows are sending at their precongestion transmission rates. The router goes from a congested state to an underutilized state.

The issues of lowered throughput through retransmission and lower link utilization after congestion are the consequences of attempting to manage congestion only from the sending host, in which the only congestion indicator is dropped packets. To prevent the problems associated with dropped packets due to congested routers, the designers of TCP/IP have created a new set of standards for both hosts and routers. These standards describe active queue management (AQM) on IP routers (RFC 2309) to allow the router to monitor that state of its forwarding queues and provide a mechanism to allow routers to report to sending hosts that congestion is occurring, allowing the sending hosts to lower their transmission rate before the router begins dropping packets. The router reporting and host response mechanism is known as Explicit Congestion Notification (ECN), defined in RFC 3168.

When congestion occurs, sending hosts must still lower their transmission rates. However, by avoiding packet losses, sending hosts no longer incur the packet processing required to retransmit dropped packets and time, and loss-sensitive packet flows are not impacted as severely during congestion.

For ECN support at the Internet layer (for IP), a sending host must be able to indicate that it is capable of performing ECN, and a router must be able to indicate that it is experiencing congestion when forwarding a packet. ECN support in the IP header uses the ECN field, which are the two unused bits of the RFC 2474-defined Type of Service (TOS) field. The ECN field indicates whether the sending host supports ECN and whether congestion has been experienced by a forwarding router. For more information, see Chapter 5, "Internet Protocol (IP)."

For ECN support at the Transport layer (for TCP), TCP peers must indicate to each other that they are ECN-capable. A receiving peer must be able to inform the sending peer that it has received a packet from a router experiencing congestion. The sending peer must be able to inform the receiving peer that it has received the congestion indicator from the receiving peer and has reduced its transmission rate.

When a router sets the ECN field of an IP packet to 11 to indicate that the router is congested, the receiver is informed of the congestion in the path, but not the sender. ECN uses the TCP header to indicate to the sender that the network is experiencing congestion and to indicate to the receiver that the sender has received the congestion indication from the receiver and has lowered its transmission rate.

ECN support in TCP uses the ECN-Echo (ECE) and Congestion Window Reduced (CWR) flags in the TCP header. The ECE flag is used to indicate that a TCP peer is ECN-capable during the TCP 3-way handshake and to indicate that a TCP segment was received on the connection with the ECN field in the IP header set to 11. When two ECN-capable TCP peers establish a TCP connection, the SYN segment has both the ECE and CWR flags set and the SYN-ACK segment has the ECE flag set and the CWR flag cleared. The CWR flag is set by the sending host to indicate that it received a TCP segment with the ECE flag set.

An ECN-capable host sends TCP segments for an ECN-enabled TCP connection with the ECN field in the IP header set to either 10 or 01. An ECN-capable router that is experiencing congestion sets the ECN field in the IP header to 11. When a receiving TCP peer sends an ACK that includes the data of a received TCP segment that had the ECN field set to 11, it sets the ECE flag in the TCP header and continues setting the ECE flag in subsequent ACKs.

When the sending host receives the ACK with the ECE flag set, it behaves as though a packet was dropped and lowers its transmission rate using the slow start and congestion avoidance algorithms. For the next segment, the sender sets the CWR flag. Upon receipt of the new segment with the CWR flag set, the receiver stops setting the ECE flag in subsequent ACKs.

ECN Example

Figure 12-7 shows an example of a TCP connection between ECN-capable TCP peers that experiences congestion by an ECN-capable router.

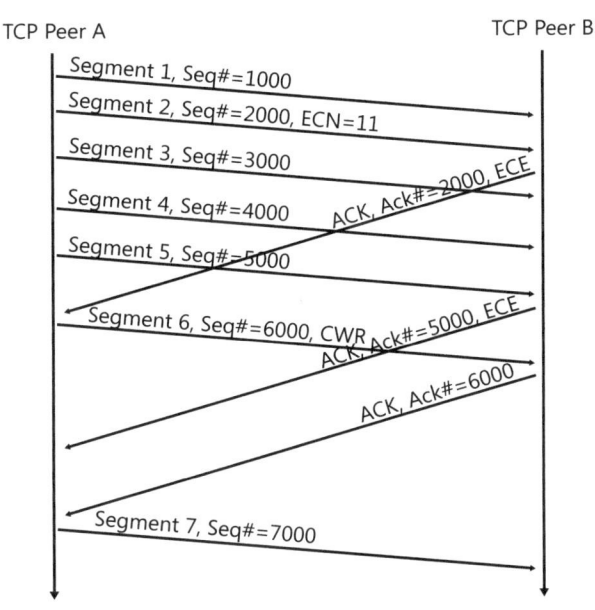

```
TCP Peer A                                    TCP Peer B
    |  Segment 1, Seq#=1000                        |
    |--------------------------------------------->|
    |  Segment 2, Seq#=2000, ECN=11                |
    |--------------------------------------------->|
    |  Segment 3, Seq#=3000                        |
    |--------------------------------------------->|
    |  Segment 4, Seq#=4000      ACK, Ack#=2000, ECE|
    |---------------------------\-----------------|
    |  Segment 5, Seq#=5000      \                 |
    |-----------------------\-----\---------------|
    |  Segment 6, Seq#=6000, CWR   Ack#=5000, ECE  |
    |<----------------------\\-------\------------|
    |                        \\       \            |
    |                     ACK, Ack#=6000           |
    |<---------------------------------------------|
    |                                              |
    |  Segment 7, Seq#=7000                        |
    |<---------------------------------------------|
```

Figure 12-7 An example of ECN for a TCP connection

In this example, TCP Peer A is sending data to TCP Peer B. TCP Peer A sends Segments 1 through 5. Segment 2 is forwarded by an ECN-capable router that is experiencing congestion, which sets the ECN field in the IP header to 11. When TCP Peer B receives this segment, it sends ACKs with the ECE flag set. When TCP Peer A receives the first ACK with the ECE flag set, it lowers its transmission rate and sends its next segment (Segment 6) with the CWR flag set. Upon receipt of Segment 6 with the CWR flag set, TCP Peer B sends subsequent ACKs with the ECE flag cleared.

For information about the behavior of ECN for different variations of TCP data flow, see RFC 3168.

ECN Support in Windows

TCP in Windows Server 2008 and Windows Vista supports ECN, but it is disabled by default. To enable ECN support, use the `netsh interface tcp set global ecncapability=enabled` command. To disable ECN support, use the `netsh interface tcp set global ecncapability=disabled` command.

Because ECN is using bits in the IP and TCP headers that were previously defined as unused or reserved, intermediate network devices such as routers and firewalls might silently discard packets when the ECN fields are set to nonzero values. To ensure that ECN-marked TCP/IP traffic will not be dropped from your network, survey your networking equipment and perform the appropriate configuration or upgrades to ensure that ECN-marked packets are not discarded.

Limited Transmit

Chapter 13, "Transmission Control Protocol (TCP) Retransmission and Timeout," describes how TCP typically uses either a retransmission timeout (RTO) or fast retransmit to detect a lost TCP segment. With a retransmission timeout, the RTO timer on a sent segment expires, and the segment is retransmitted. The RTO is typically on the order of seconds. With fast retransmit, when the sender receives three duplicate acknowledgments for a segment, it retransmits the segment before the RTO expires. Fast retransmit is a much faster way of detecting dropped segments. However, because fast retransmit relies on receiving three duplicate ACKs, it might not detect segment losses when the window size is very small or when a large number of segments are lost.

For example, if the window size only accommodates three MSS segments and the first segment is lost, then only two duplicate ACKs will be received. As another example, if the window size is 8 segments but only two arrive, then only two duplicate ACKs will be received. The lost segments are eventually detected when the RTO timer for the segment expires, but relying on the RTO expiration can dramatically decrease performance.

To address this problem, TCP in Windows Server 2008 and Windows Vista supports the Limited Transmit algorithm defined in RFC 3042. With Limited Transmit, when TCP has additional data to send on a connection and two consecutive duplicate ACKs have been received, TCP can send additional segments on the connection under the following conditions:

- The receiver's advertised window allows the transmission of the additional segments.
- The additional segments contain data that is within two segments beyond *cwind*.

The ability of TCP to send additional segments helps ensure that fast retransmit can be used to detect segment losses, rather than waiting for an RTO timer expiration.

Note The sender cannot send new segments in response to duplicate ACKs that contain no additional SACK information.

For the details of the algorithm, see RFC 3042.

Summary

TCP achieves reliable data transfer through the cumulative or selective acknowledgment of TCP segments received. Selective acknowledgments improve TCP performance in high-loss environments or for TCP connections with large window sizes. To provide receiver-side flow control, TCP uses sliding send and receive windows. With each ACK segment, the receiver indicates how much more data can be sent and successfully received. To avoid sending small segments, TCP uses the Nagle algorithm and SWS avoidance.

To provide sender-side flow control, TCP uses the slow start and congestion avoidance algorithms. Slow start increases the size of the actual send window by 1 MSS for each ACK segment received or each segment acknowledged. Congestion avoidance increases the size of the actual send window by 1 MSS for each round-trip time. Slow start and congestion avoidance are used to avoid congesting an IP internetwork when sending and retransmitting data.

CTCP increases the send window size more rapidly than slow start and congestion avoidance to optimize use of high-BDP connections. ECN attempts to detect a congested network and lower a TCP peer's transmission rate before a router begins discarding packets. Limited Transmit allows a TCP peer to send additional segments on a connection to ensure that fast retransmit can successfully detect dropped packets.

Chapter 13
Transmission Control Protocol (TCP) Retransmission and Time-Out

> **In this chapter:**
> Retransmission Time-Out and Round-Trip Time........................271
> Retransmission Behavior...273
> Calculating the RTO...279
> Fast Retransmit and Fast Recovery.................................286
> Summary...289

The reliable service of TCP requires that all segments containing data be acknowledged by the receiver. When an acknowledgment (ACK) for a segment is not received, the sender must retransmit the segment. The method by which the sender detects that a segment was not received can have a direct impact on performance. This chapter describes how TCP measures the expected time within which to receive an ACK and how it detects and recovers from lost segments.

Retransmission Time-Out and Round-Trip Time

For each connection, TCP maintains a variable called the retransmission time-out (RTO), which is the amount of time within which an ACK for the segment is expected. If TCP does not receive an ACK before the RTO expires, the segment is retransmitted.

The RTO must allow enough time for the following:

1. The initially sent TCP segment to traverse the internetwork (the transit time from source to destination).

2. The initially sent TCP segment to be received and processed by the destination node (the destination's inbound packet-processing time).

3. The generation of an ACK for the segment (the ACK generation time). One component of the ACK generation time is the delayed acknowledgment time of the destination node. Rather than sending an ACK segment for each TCP data segment received, TCP

delays ACKs. These delayed ACKs can contain data, include updated window sizes, and acknowledge multiple segments received.

4. The generated ACK to traverse the internetwork (the transit time from destination to source).

5. The generated ACK to be received and processed by the sending node (the source's inbound packet-processing time).

The sum of all these times is known as the round-trip time (RTT). The RTT varies over time and must be constantly measured throughout the TCP connection's life. The RTO is based on the currently known RTT and should always be greater than the currently known RTT to prevent unnecessary retransmissions.

The RTO should be neither too large nor too small to prevent the following behaviors:

- When the RTO is too large, the sending TCP peer must wait too long before retransmitting a lost segment. This lowers throughput for connections with some degree of packet loss.

- When the RTO is too small, segments are retransmitted unnecessarily. Retransmitted segments increase the load on the internetwork and waste internetwork capacity.

If the ACK for the initially sent segment does not arrive within the RTO, the ACK is either arriving late or not at all. The main causes of ACK segments arriving late are either an increase in the transit time from the source to the destination or an increase in the transit time from the destination to the source.

The following are reasons why the ACK is not received at all:

- The initially sent TCP segment is dropped at a router because of congestion.

- The initially sent TCP segment is dropped at a router or the destination because of damage to the packet, which occurs when electronic or optical errors corrupt the encoded signal, causing bits within the packet to change values. Damaged packets are silently discarded after failing checksum calculations.

- The ACK for the TCP segment is dropped at a router because of congestion.

- The ACK for the TCP segment is dropped at a router or the destination because of damage to the packet.

It is much more likely that the TCP segment or its ACK was discarded by a congested router rather than being damaged and silently discarded.

Note Unlike TCP segments containing data, ACKs that contain no data are not sent reliably. The ACK sender does not set an RTO for the ACK and does not retransmit the ACK segment. Therefore, a lost ACK is recovered by the sender retransmitting the segment(s) that the lost ACK is acknowledging, and not by the sender of the lost ACK retransmitting the ACK.

Congestion Collapse

The proper measurement of the RTT and determination of the RTO for sent TCP segments are important to prevent a phenomenon of routed internetworks known as *congestion collapse*. Congestion collapse occurs when the buffers of the internetwork routers fill to capacity and the routers begin to discard packets.

Congestion collapse begins with a steady increase in the load on the internetwork. As hosts send more data, more data is queued in the buffers of the internetwork routers. As this occurs, the transit time from the source to the destination and from the destination to the source increases. Therefore, the actual RTT grows larger than the currently known RTT of sending hosts.

The current RTO for sent segments is based on the currently known RTT. When the actual RTT increases to the extent that it is greater than the current RTO, sent TCP segments have ACKs that arrive late. When the ACKs do not arrive in the time based on the current RTO, the segments are retransmitted. There are then two copies of each retransmitted segment, effectively doubling the load on the internetwork at a time when the load needs to be decreased. As more TCP segments are retransmitted, eventually the buffers on the internetwork routers fill and the routers begin to discard packets.

Congestion collapse can be avoided through the ongoing determination of the current RTT, which is monitored on a per window or per segment basis. Changes in the current RTT are used to update the RTO.

The recurrence of congestion collapse is avoided through the combination of the slow start and congestion avoidance algorithms of the sending host, as discussed in Chapter 12, "Transmission Control Protocol (TCP) Data Flow." When the RTO for a segment expires, TCP assumes that RTO expiration is a result of the segment being discarded by a router experiencing congestion. Slow start and congestion avoidance are used to slowly scale the number of segments sent before waiting for an ACK up to the number of segments that fit in the receiver's advertised receive window.

Slow start and congestion avoidance are used together to prevent congestion collapse from recurring. Without slow start and congestion avoidance, once an internetwork becomes congested, it becomes congested again as the sending hosts begin transmitting new data, and the internetwork oscillates between congested and uncongested states.

Retransmission Behavior

TCP uses the following exponential backoff behavior to determine the RTO of successive retransmissions of the same segment:

1. When the TCP segment is initially sent, the RTO for the segment is set to the currently known RTO for the connection.

2. After RTO number of seconds, when the RTO expires, the segment RTO is set to twice the RTO for the segment's previous transmission and retransmitted.

Step 2 is repeated for the maximum number of retransmissions before the TCP connection is abandoned. The TcpMaxDataRetransmissions registry value controls the maximum number of retransmissions for TCP in Windows Server 2008 and Windows Vista.

TcpMaxDataRetransmissions
```
Location: HKEY_LOCAL_MACHINE\SYSTEM
\CurrentControlSet\Services\Tcpip\Parameters
Data type: REG_DWORD
Valid range: 0-0xFFFFFFFF
Default value: 5
Present by default: No
```

TcpMaxDataRetransmissions sets the maximum number of retransmissions of a TCP segment containing data before the connection is abandoned.

The following summary of Frames 5–12 of Network Monitor 3.1 Capture 13-01, included in the \Captures folder on the companion CD-ROM), shows the maximum number of retransmissions and the doubling of the RTO between successive retransmissions:

```
Frame   Time Offset   Time Delta   Description
5       3.464982      0.000000     FTP: Data Transfer To Server
6       3.464982      0.000000     FTP: Data Transfer To Server
7       3.464982      0.000000     FTP: Data Transfer To Server
8       3.965702      0.500720     FTP: Data Transfer To Server
9       4.967142      1.001440     FTP: Data Transfer To Server
10      6.970022      2.002880     FTP: Data Transfer To Server
11      10.975782     4.005760     FTP: Data Transfer To Server
12      18.987302     8.011520     FTP: Data Transfer To Server
```

This Network Monitor trace was captured from a File Transfer Protocol (FTP) client on which the uploading of a file was in progress and the cable connecting the network adapter of the FTP server was pulled. Frames 8 through 12 show the retransmission behavior of TCP. Notice how the initial RTO is 0.5 seconds, and successive retransmissions have RTOs that are doubled. After the last retransmission, the FTP server waits 16 seconds before abandoning the connection and recovering the connection's resources. It takes a total of 31.5 seconds to abandon the connection. The connection abandonment time is 63 times the RTO for the connection (the sum of RTO for the initial segment sent, 2*RTO for the first retransmission, 4*RTO for the second retransmission, 8*RTO for the third retransmission, 16*RTO for the fourth retransmission, and 32*RTO for the fifth retransmission).

Note The RTOs are doubled, but the elapsed time for sending the retransmitted segment might not be exactly doubled for other Network Monitor traces because of delays in processing, queuing, and the physical transmission of network frames.

Retransmission Behavior for New Connections

For new connections initiated by a TCP peer running Windows Server 2008 or Windows Vista, the maximum number of retransmissions of the synchronize (SYN) segment is two. TCP sends two retransmissions of a SYN segment before abandoning the connection attempt. Exponential backoff is used between successive retransmissions of the SYN segment. With an initial RTO value of 3 seconds, it takes 21 seconds to abandon a connection attempt (the sum of 3 seconds for the initial SYN, 6 seconds for the first retransmission, and 12 seconds for the second retransmission). The initial RTO's value is set to 3 seconds.

For new connections initiated with a TCP peer running Windows Server 2008 or Windows Vista, the maximum number of retransmissions for the SYN-ACK segment is two. TCP sends two retransmissions of a SYN-ACK segment in response to a SYN segment before abandoning the connection attempt. Exponential backoff is used between successive retransmissions of the SYN-ACK segment. With an initial RTO value of 3 seconds, it takes 21 seconds to abandon the connection (the sum of 3 seconds for the first SYN, 6 seconds for the first retransmission, and 12 seconds for the second retransmission).

Note TCP/IP in Windows Server 2008 and Windows Vista no longer supports the TcpMaxConnectRetransmissions and TcpMaxConnectResponseRetransmissions registry values.

Dead Gateway Detection

Dead gateway detection is an algorithm that detects the failure of the currently configured default gateway. If it detects a failure, dead gateway detection automatically switches to a new default gateway, provided there are multiple default gateways configured. Dead gateway detection uses TCP retransmission behavior to detect and recover from a downed router configured as the default gateway.

When an individual TCP connection retransmits a segment multiple times (half of TcpMaxDataRetransmissions), its next-hop IP address is changed to the next default gateway. When 25 percent of all TCP connections using the failed default gateway have been moved to the next default gateway, the default route in the IP routing table is updated with the next default gateway as the next-hop IP address.

If the new default gateway is unavailable, dead gateway detection is used to switch to the next default gateway in the configured list. When the last default gateway in the list is reached and becomes unavailable, the next default gateway is the first default gateway in the list. When the computer is restarted, the first default gateway in the list is used.

For a detailed example of how dead gateway detection works, consider a host with the following configuration:

- The IP address of 10.0.0.99/24.
- Two default gateways are configured: 10.0.0.1 and 10.0.0.2.
- The default route 0.0.0.0/0 has 10.0.0.1 as its next-hop IP address.
- There are currently 10 TCP connections for locations off the 10.0.0.0/24 subnet using 10.0.0.1 as their next-hop IP address.
- TcpMaxDataRetransmissions is set at its default value of 5.

When the router at 10.0.0.1 fails, dead gateway detection uses the following process to change the default route to use the next-hop IP address of 10.0.0.2:

1. A TCP connection (one of the 10 TCP connections at the host) sends a data segment. Because no ACK is received, the segment is retransmitted. After the third retransmission, the next-hop IP address for this specific TCP connection is changed to 10.0.0.2. At this point, 10 percent of the TCP connections using the next-hop IP address of 10.0.0.1 have been switched to 10.0.0.2.

2. Another TCP connection sends a data segment. Because no ACK is received, the segment is retransmitted. After the third retransmission, the next-hop IP address for this specific TCP connection is changed to 10.0.0.2. At this point, 20 percent of the TCP connections using the next-hop IP address of 10.0.0.1 have been switched to 10.0.0.2.

3. Another TCP connection sends a data segment. Because no ACK is received, the segment is retransmitted. After the third retransmission, the next-hop IP address for this specific TCP connection is changed to 10.0.0.2. At this point, 30 percent of the TCP connections using the next-hop IP address of 10.0.0.1 have been switched to 10.0.0.2.

4. Because more than 25 percent of the TCP connections using 10.0.0.1 as their next-hop IP address have had their next-hop IP addresses changed, the default route in the IP routing table is updated to use 10.0.0.2 as the next-hop IP address.

When dead gateway detection in Windows Server 2003 and Windows XP changes the default gateway, the new default gateway remains the primary gateway for default route traffic until dead gateway detection switches to the next one in the list (cycling through the list of default gateways) or until the computer is restarted. Therefore, dead gateway detection in TCP for Windows Server 2003 and Windows XP provides a fail-over function, but not a fail-back function.

The lack of fail-back for default gateways can cause throughput problems on a subnet containing two routers: a high-capacity primary router and a lower-capacity backup router. The hosts on the subnet have the high-capacity router as their first default gateway and the backup router as their second default gateway. If the high-capacity router has a temporary failure, hosts on the subnet switch over to the backup router. When the high-capacity router becomes available again, none of the hosts on the network use it because they have switched to the backup router.

TCP/IP in Windows Server 2008 and Windows Vista provides fail-back for default gateway changes by periodically attempting to send TCP traffic through the previous gateway. If the TCP traffic sent through the previous gateway is successful, TCP/IP in Windows Server 2008 and Windows Vista switches the default gateway to the previous gateway.

In our example with the high-capacity router and backup router, if the neighboring high-capacity router becomes unavailable, the hosts on the subnet use neighbor unreachability detection to switch their default gateways to the backup router. Neighbor unreachability detection for IPv4 is described in Chapter 3, "Address Resolution Protocol (ARP)." The hosts then periodically attempt to send TCP traffic through the high-capacity router. When the high-capacity router becomes available and the hosts determine that TCP traffic sent through the high-capacity router is successful, the hosts switch their default gateway back to the high-capacity router.

Support for fail-back to primary default gateways can provide faster throughput by sending traffic through the primary default gateway on the subnet.

Note Dead gateway detection can change the default gateway configuration even when the local default gateway is functioning and a remote router fails. If a remote router in the path of traffic for TCP connections fails, TCP retransmissions for multiple TCP connections can cause dead gateway detection to switch default gateways.

Note TCP/IP in Windows Server 2008 and Windows Vista no longer supports the EnableDeadGWDetect registry value.

Forward RTO-Recovery

Spurious retransmissions of TCP segments can occur when there is a sudden and temporary increase in the RTT. When the increase occurs, the RTOs of previously sent segments begin to expire and TCP starts retransmitting them. If the increase occurs just before sending a full window of data, a sender can retransmit the entire window of data. To prevent spurious retransmission of TCP segments, TCP in Windows Server 2008 and Windows Vista supports the Forward RTO-Recovery (F-RTO) algorithm defined in RFC 4138. F-RTO prevents spurious retransmission of TCP segments through the following behavior:

- When the RTO expires for multiple segments, TCP retransmits just the first segment. When the first acknowledgement is received, TCP begins sending new segments (if allowed by the advertised window size). If the next acknowledgment acknowledges the other segments that have timed out but have not been retransmitted, TCP determines that the time-out was spurious and does not retransmit the other segments that have timed out.

The result of this behavior is that for environments that have sudden and temporary increases in the RTT, such as when a wireless client roams from one wireless access point (AP) to another, F-RTO prevents unnecessary retransmission of segments and more quickly returns to its normal sending rate.

For the details of the F-RTO algorithm, see RFC 4138.

More Info All of the RFCs referenced in this chapter can be found in the \Standards\Chap13_TCPRetrans folder on the companion CD-ROM.

Using the Selective Acknowledgment (SACK) TCP Option

The SACK TCP option, defined in RFC 2018, allows the receiver to selectively acknowledge noncontiguous blocks of data received. However, the sender should not discard selectively acknowledged segments from its transmission queue until the segments are included in a cumulative acknowledgment.

RFC 2018 allows the data receiver to discard noncontiguous segments even though they have been selectively acknowledged. This is known as reneging on a selective acknowledgment, and its practice is discouraged. To keep reneged data from being lost on a connection, the sender must retransmit selectively acknowledged data until it is acknowledged by the Acknowledgment Number field in an ACK from the receiver. The retransmission behavior of selectively acknowledged segments is as follows:

1. For each segment, maintain a selective acknowledgment flag that is enabled when the segment is selectively acknowledged.

2. When initial RTO timers begin to expire, only retransmit the segments that have not been selectively acknowledged (segments for which the selective acknowledgment flag is disabled).

3. If an ACK is received that cumulatively acknowledges the retransmitted segment, the send window closes and opens depending on the new Acknowledgment Number + Window sum, and new segments can be sent. The selective acknowledgment flags on noncumulatively acknowledged segments are maintained.

4. If a retransmitted segment times out, indicating that the receiver might have reneged on the selectively acknowledged segments, disable the selective acknowledgment flags of all segments in the current window and retransmit them normally.

This mechanism recovers from the possibility that the receiver discarded the noncontiguous received segments. If necessary, the entire window of data is resent.

Using SACKs to Indicate Duplicate Received Packets

TCP in Windows Server 2008 and Windows Vista supports RFC 2883, which defines an additional use of the fields in the SACK TCP option to acknowledge duplicate packets. This allows the sender to determine when it has retransmitted a segment unnecessarily and adjust its behavior to prevent future retransmissions. The fewer retransmissions that are sent, the better the overall throughput.

Calculating the RTO

The determination of the RTO is an important function of TCP. The RTO must be adjusted to the internetwork's changing conditions. If the determined RTO is less than the RTT, segments are unnecessarily retransmitted.

In RFC 793, the suggested method of computing the RTO—known as the smoothed round-trip time (SRTT)—is based on the following formulas:

```
SRTT = (α*SRTT) + ((1-α)*RTT)
RTO = min[UpperBound, max[LowerBound,(β *SRTT)]]
```

Thus, the new RTO is based on the determination of the current RTT, the previous SRTT, a smoothing factor (α), and a variance factor (β) . In practice, this formula was found to be inadequate in determining the RTO in an environment in which the RTT changed suddenly. Instead, RFC 1122 states that TCP must use the following formulas as documented in "Congestion Avoidance and Control," a paper written by Van Jacobson and Michael J. Karels:

```
SRTT = RTT + 8*(New_RTT - RTT)
Dev = Dev + (|New_RTT - RTT| - Dev)/4
RTO = SRTT + Dev/4
```

This new way of calculating the RTO is based on the average and variance (Dev) of the RTT. The RTO is self-tuning for different environments (the low-delay local area network [LAN] and the high-delay wide area network [WAN]) and is sensitive to sudden changes in the RTT for environments such as the Internet.

RTO calculation is described in detail in RFCs 793 and 1122.

For TCP in Windows Server 2008 and Windows Vista, the RTO's initial value for establishing connections or sending data on new connections is 3 seconds for SYN segments, SYN-ACK segments, and initial data segments sent on a new connection for each interface.

As data segments are sent, the RTO is adjusted from 3 seconds to a value closer to the connection's RTT. By default, the connection's RTT is not sampled for each segment sent. Rather, the RTT is sampled once for every full send window of data sent. If the send window is 12*MSS (maximum segment size), the RTT is sampled once every 12 segments. For each sample of the RTT, the time that the sampled segment is sent is recorded based on the current value of an internal clock. When the ACK for the segment is received, the RTT is determined from the difference between the recorded value of when the segment was sent and the current value of the internal clock.

The RTT sampling rate is 1/(window size). For small window sizes, this sampling rate is adequate. However, for large windows, the sampling rate is inadequate and cannot keep up with rapid changes in the RTT. The result is increased network bandwidth utilization by unnecessary retransmissions when the currently known RTO is less than the current RTT. In these situations, the TCP Timestamps option is used to provide a sampling rate that is equal to the sending rate.

Note TCP/IP in Windows Server 2008 and Windows Vista no longer supports the TcpInitialRTT registry value.

Using the TCP Timestamps Option

As described in Chapter 10, "Transmission Control Protocol (TCP) Basics," the TCP Timestamps option allows TCP peers to place a timestamp value on each segment. The TCP Timestamps option contains two 32-bit fields to track timestamps: TS Value and TS Echo Reply. The TS Value field stores the current timestamp value. The TS Echo Reply field stores the timestamp echo, the value of the TS Value field of the segment being acknowledged.

The use of TCP timestamps allows an RTT to be calculated by subtracting the timestamp echo in the ACK from the current time value of the timestamp clock.

As an example, TCP Peer A sends a data segment to TCP Peer B, which sends an ACK back. The data segment's TS Value is 1285458 when it is sent and is echoed in the ACK segment's TS Echo Reply field. When the ACK is received and processed, the current value of TCP Peer A's timestamp clock is 1286506. Therefore, the RTT for this segment is based on the TCP timestamp value of 1048, or 1286506 − 1285458.

This basic method of RTT determination is complicated by the following factors:

- There might be pauses in sending data.
- ACKs are delayed and can acknowledge multiple TCP segments.
- Segments can arrive out of sequence.
- Segments can be dropped and must be retransmitted.

Figure 13-1 illustrates the problem with pauses in sending data. TCP Peer A sends TCP Peer B a series of segments and then pauses. Then TCP Peer A sends more segments. The new segment after the pause has the TS Echo Reply field set to the TS Value field of the last ACK received. If TCP Peer B now calculates the RTT for the last ACK sent, the RTT is inflated by the time of the pause in sending data.

Chapter 13: Transmission Control Protocol (TCP) Retransmission and Time-Out

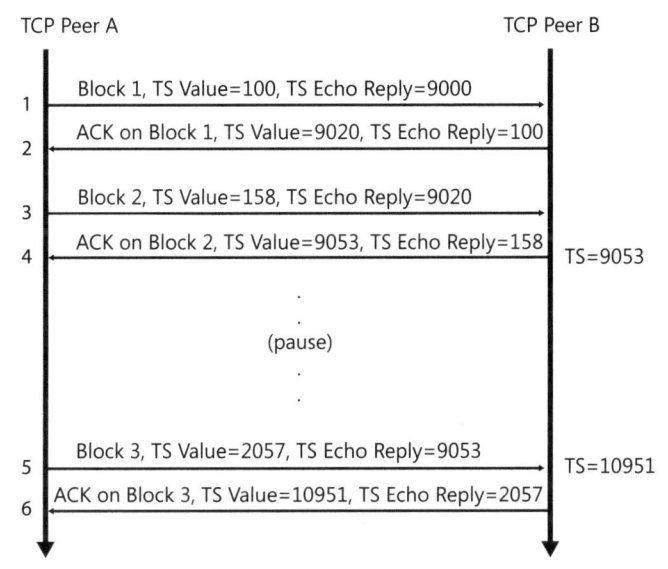

```
TCP Peer A                                                TCP Peer B
    |                                                          |
  1 |——— Block 1, TS Value=100, TS Echo Reply=9000 ————————————>|
    |                                                          |
  2 |<—— ACK on Block 1, TS Value=9020, TS Echo Reply=100 ——————|
    |                                                          |
  3 |——— Block 2, TS Value=158, TS Echo Reply=9020 ————————————>|
    |                                                          |
  4 |<—— ACK on Block 2, TS Value=9053, TS Echo Reply=158 ——————| TS=9053
    |                             .                            |
    |                             .                            |
    |                         (pause)                          |
    |                             .                            |
    |                             .                            |
  5 |——— Block 3, TS Value=2057, TS Echo Reply=9053 ———————————>| TS=10951
    |                                                          |
  6 |<—— ACK on Block 3, TS Value=10951, TS Echo Reply=2057 ————|
```

Figure 13-1 The behavior of TCP timestamps with pauses in data

From Figure 13-1, the TCP timestamp interval calculated from TCP segment 5 is 1898 (10951 − 9053), clearly the wrong value, as it includes the pause in sending data. With an RTO adjusted to this higher value of the RTT, throughput for data sent by TCP Peer 2 is not optimal because the RTO is too high. To prevent this behavior, the RTT is calculated only for TCP segments that acknowledge new data sent. Therefore, in the example shown in Figure 13-1, the RTT is calculated only by TCP Peer A. TCP Peer B does not calculate RTT because the segments received by TCP Peer B do not acknowledge data sent by TCP Peer B.

For delayed ACKs, segments that arrive out of order, and retransmitted segments, the value of TS Echo Reply for ACKs is based on the following algorithm:

1. For correct TCP timestamp behavior, TCP keeps track of two variables for each connection: *tsrecent* is the value of the TS Echo Reply that will be sent in the next ACK, and *lastack* is the value of the Acknowledgment Number field from the last ACK sent.

2. After receipt of a new segment, if the segment contains the byte numbered *lastack*, which means that a contiguous segment has arrived, update *tsrecent* with the value of the TS Value field from the arriving segment. If the segment does not contain *lastack*, ignore the value of the TS Value field of the arriving segment.

3. When sending a segment with the TCP Timestamp option, set the value of TS Echo Reply to the value of *tsrecent*.

4. When sending an ACK, set the value of *lastack* to the value of the Acknowledgment Number field in the ACK.

For delayed acknowledgments, the RTT determination must include the acknowledgment delay. Therefore, when sending a delayed acknowledgment, the TS Echo Reply of the delayed

ACK is set to the TS Value of the first segment being acknowledged. Figure 13-2 illustrates this behavior.

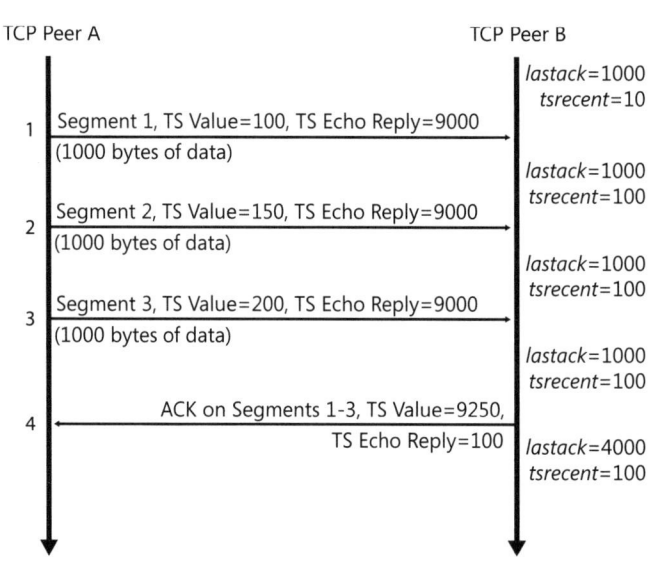

```
TCP Peer A                                          TCP Peer B
                                                    lastack=1000
                                                    tsrecent=10
   1   Segment 1, TS Value=100, TS Echo Reply=9000
       (1000 bytes of data)
                                                    lastack=1000
                                                    tsrecent=100
   2   Segment 2, TS Value=150, TS Echo Reply=9000
       (1000 bytes of data)
                                                    lastack=1000
                                                    tsrecent=100
   3   Segment 3, TS Value=200, TS Echo Reply=9000
       (1000 bytes of data)
                                                    lastack=1000
                                                    tsrecent=100
   4         ACK on Segments 1-3, TS Value=9250,
                         TS Echo Reply=100          lastack=4000
                                                    tsrecent=100
```

Figure 13-2 The behavior of TCP timestamps for delayed acknowledgments

Prior to receiving any TCP segments, the value of *tsrecent* is 10 and the value of *lastack* is 1000. When TCP segment 1 arrives, it contains the *lastack* byte, and therefore, *tsrecent* is updated with the TS Value of 100. When TCP segment 2 arrives, it does not contain the *lastack* byte, and *tsrecent* remains at the value of 100. When TCP segment 3 arrives, it does not contain the *lastack* byte, and *tsrecent* remains at the value of 100. When the delayed ACK is sent, the value of TS Echo Reply is set to *tsrecent*, and *lastack* is set to the value of the Acknowledgment Number field.

When segments arrive out of sequence, the value of *tsrecent*, and therefore the value of TS Echo Reply, is not updated. TS Echo Reply and *tsrecent* are updated only when the missing segment(s) arrives. Figure 13-3 illustrates this behavior.

Prior to receiving any TCP segments, the value of *tsrecent* is 10 and the value of *lastack* is 1000. When TCP segment 1 arrives, it contains the *lastack* byte, and therefore, *tsrecent* is updated with the TS Value field value of 100. When the ACK on segment 1 is sent, the value of TS Echo Reply field is set to *tsrecent*, and *lastack* is set to the Acknowledgment Number field's value.

When TCP segment 3 arrives, it does not contain the *lastack* byte, and *tsrecent* remains at the value of 100. When TCP segment 2 arrives, it does contain the *lastack* byte, and the value of *tsrecent* is updated.

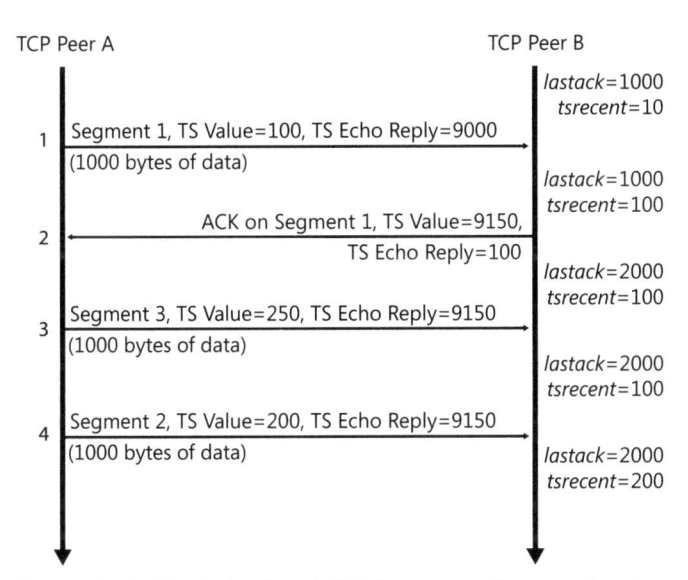

Chapter 13: Transmission Control Protocol (TCP) Retransmission and Time-Out 283

```
TCP Peer A                                              TCP Peer B
                                                        lastack=1000
                                                        tsrecent=10
  1   Segment 1, TS Value=100, TS Echo Reply=9000
      (1000 bytes of data)
                                                        lastack=1000
                                                        tsrecent=100
             ACK on Segment 1, TS Value=9150,
  2                        TS Echo Reply=100
                                                        lastack=2000
                                                        tsrecent=100
      Segment 3, TS Value=250, TS Echo Reply=9150
  3   (1000 bytes of data)
                                                        lastack=2000
                                                        tsrecent=100
  4   Segment 2, TS Value=200, TS Echo Reply=9150
      (1000 bytes of data)
                                                        lastack=2000
                                                        tsrecent=200
```

Figure 13-3 The behavior of TCP timestamps for out-of-order segments

When a segment is dropped and must be retransmitted and the segments arrive out of sequence, the value of *tsrecent*, and therefore the value of the TS Echo Reply field, is not updated. Because the RTT does not include the RTO for the retransmitted segment, *tsrecent* and TS Echo Reply are updated only when the missing retransmitted segment arrives. Figure 13-4 illustrates this behavior.

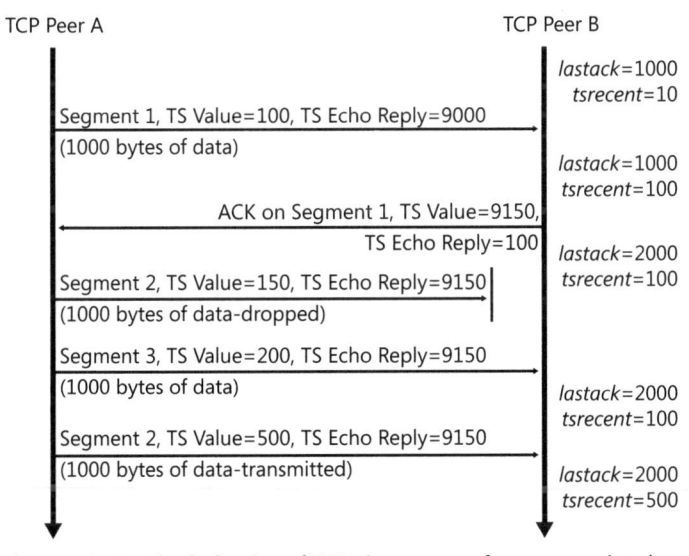

```
TCP Peer A                                              TCP Peer B
                                                        lastack=1000
                                                        tsrecent=10
      Segment 1, TS Value=100, TS Echo Reply=9000
      (1000 bytes of data)
                                                        lastack=1000
                                                        tsrecent=100
             ACK on Segment 1, TS Value=9150,
                           TS Echo Reply=100
                                                        lastack=2000
      Segment 2, TS Value=150, TS Echo Reply=9150       tsrecent=100
      (1000 bytes of data-dropped)
      Segment 3, TS Value=200, TS Echo Reply=9150
      (1000 bytes of data)
                                                        lastack=2000
                                                        tsrecent=100
      Segment 2, TS Value=500, TS Echo Reply=9150
      (1000 bytes of data-transmitted)
                                                        lastack=2000
                                                        tsrecent=500
```

Figure 13-4 The behavior of TCP timestamps for retransmitted segments

Prior to receiving any TCP segments, the value of *tsrecent* is 10 and the value of *lastack* is 1000. When TCP segment 1 arrives, it contains the *lastack* byte, and therefore, *tsrecent* is updated with the TS Value of 100. When the ACK on segment 1 is sent, the value of TS Echo Reply is set to *tsrecent*, and *lastack* is set to the value of the Acknowledgment Number field.

When TCP segment 3 arrives, it does not contain the *lastack* byte, and *tsrecent* remains at the value of 100. When the retransmitted TCP segment 2 arrives, it does contain the *lastack* byte, and the value of *tsrecent* is updated.

Karn's Algorithm

When calculating the RTT for a TCP segment being sent, the time at which the segment is sent is recorded. If the RTO expires, an exact duplicate is sent and its time is recorded. When the ACK is received, how is the RTT computed? When the TCP Timestamps option is not being used, the ACK does not distinguish between the original TCP segment and its retransmitted copy. TCP has the problem of acknowledgment ambiguity. When multiple copies of a TCP segment are sent, the ACK does not identify a specific instance of the TCP segment being acknowledged.

If we choose to calculate the RTT based on the first instance of the segment and the first instance is lost, the measured RTT is larger than the actual RTT for the connection because it includes the RTO for retransmitting the segment. The measured RTT is the difference between the time the first segment was sent and the time the ACK for the retransmitted instance was received. The new RTO grows larger than it should, resulting in lowered throughput for retransmitted segments. As more TCP segments are lost, the RTO based on this method of RTT calculation grows larger.

If we choose to calculate the RTT based on the retransmitted instance of the segment, and the RTO expired as a result of a sudden increase in the RTT, the ACK for the first instance arrives soon after the retransmitted segment is sent. The measured RTT (the difference between the time the retransmitted segment was sent and the time the ACK for the first instance was received) is now smaller than the connection's actual RTT. The updated RTO gets smaller when it should get larger, eventually resulting in unnecessary retransmissions for subsequent segments.

To prevent these conditions from incorrectly changing the RTO, RTT measurements for TCP segments that have been retransmitted are ignored. Only the RTT for ACKs that are acknowledging a single instance of a TCP segment are considered. However, ignoring the RTT for retransmitted segments introduces a new problem. When the actual RTT increases suddenly, the RTO for a TCP segment is too small and results in a retransmission. Because the RTT is not calculated for the retransmitted segment, the RTO remains at its inadequate value. Subsequent TCP segments sent would also be retransmitted.

To keep subsequent TCP segments from being sent with an inadequate RTO when the actual RTT increases suddenly, TCP/IP implementations, including TCP/IP for the Windows Server

2008 and Windows Vista, use Karn's algorithm. Karn's algorithm is named after its creator, Phil Karn, in the paper "Improving Routing-Trip Time Estimates in Reliable Transport Protocols," by Phil Karn and Craig Partridge. Karn's algorithm states that when an ACK for a retransmitted segment arrives, it should not be used to update the RTO. However, the RTO of the retransmitted segment (that has been exponentially backed off) should be used as a temporary RTO for subsequent TCP segments. When an ACK for a nonretransmitted TCP segment arrives, use its RTT to update the RTO. Then, use the updated RTO for subsequent TCP segments.

For example, if the RTO for a TCP connection is 300 ms and the actual RTT for the connection suddenly rises to 400 ms, Karn's algorithm causes the following behavior:

1. Segment A is sent, and its RTO is set to 300 ms.
2. Because the RTO for Segment A is lower than the connection's actual RTT, the RTO for Segment A expires. Segment A's RTO is set to 600 ms and retransmitted (using exponential backoff and a factor of 2).
3. The ACK for Segment A arrives (400 ms after the first instance of Segment A was sent).
4. Because the ACK is for a retransmitted segment, it is not used to update the RTO.
5. TCP temporarily sets the RTO for subsequent segments to 600 ms (the RTO of the retransmitted Segment A).
6. Segment B is transmitted and Segment B's RTO is set to 600 ms.
7. The ACK for Segment B arrives in 400 ms.
8. Because the ACK is for a segment that has not been retransmitted, its RTT is calculated and used to update the RTO.
9. Subsequent segments are sent using the updated RTO.

Karn's Algorithm and the Timestamps Option

Karn's algorithm applies when the ACKs are ambiguous—when TCP cannot distinguish the original TCP segment from a retransmitted instance. However, with the TCP Timestamps option, each TCP segment has a steadily increasing timestamp clock value (the TS Value field in the TCP Timestamps option header) and is, therefore, unique within the time that segments are being retransmitted. The ACK for different instances of a TCP segment can be distinguished from another because the ACK contains the echo of the timestamp value of the segment being acknowledged. Therefore, Karn's algorithm does not apply when TCP timestamps are being used.

If a segment is retransmitted because of a segment loss, the ACK for the retransmitted segment contains the timestamp value for the retransmitted segment, and not the original segment. Therefore, the RTT is accurately calculated as the difference in the current TCP time clock and the ACK's timestamp echo.

If a segment is retransmitted because of a sudden increase in RTT, the ACK contains the timestamp value of the first instance. Therefore, the RTT is accurately calculated as the difference in the current TCP time clock and the timestamp echo in the ACK for the first segment.

Fast Retransmit and Fast Recovery

When a TCP segment arrives and the sequence number is not the next sequence number the receiver was expecting (a noncontiguous, out-of-order segment), an immediate ACK is sent with the Acknowledgment Number field set to the next sequence number the receiver was expecting. This ACK is a duplicate of an ACK that was previously sent and is not subject to the delayed acknowledgment behavior for new contiguous data received.

After receipt of this duplicate ACK, the sender cannot determine whether the duplicate ACK was sent by the receiver because of a TCP segment that arrived out of order or because a segment was lost.

- If a TCP segment arrived out of order, the TCP segment that contains the next byte the receiver expects to receive should arrive at the receiver shortly thereafter, and a cumulative ACK is sent. Therefore, for out-of-order segments, only one or two duplicate ACKs are likely to be sent.

- If a TCP segment is lost, all of the segments beyond the contiguous segment that arrive at the receiver generate an immediate duplicate ACK. Therefore, if three or more duplicate ACKs arrive at the sender, the TCP segment containing the next byte the receiver expects is most likely lost and must be retransmitted.

Fast retransmit is the retransmission of a TCP segment before the RTO for the segment expires, based on the receipt of three duplicate ACKs where the ACK's acknowledgment number is the retransmitted segment's sequence number. The retransmitted segment is the missing segment. Fast retransmit is defined in RFC 2581.

As Figure 13-5 illustrates, TCP Peer A sends five TCP segments and the first segment is lost. As the noncontiguous segments arrive, TCP Peer B sends an immediate ACK with the ACK number it expects to receive. After the third duplicate ACK for sequence number 1000, TCP Peer A retransmits the first segment.

TCP in Windows Server 2008 and Windows Vista supports the Limited Transmit algorithm defined in RFC 3042. With Limited Transmit, TCP sends additional segments when two consecutive duplicate ACKs have been received to help ensure that fast retransmit will be used to detect a lost packet, rather than an RTO. Figure 13-6 shows an example of limited transmit behavior for the situation previously described when TCP Peer A is running Windows Server 2008 or Windows Vista.

Chapter 13: Transmission Control Protocol (TCP) Retransmission and Time-Out **287**

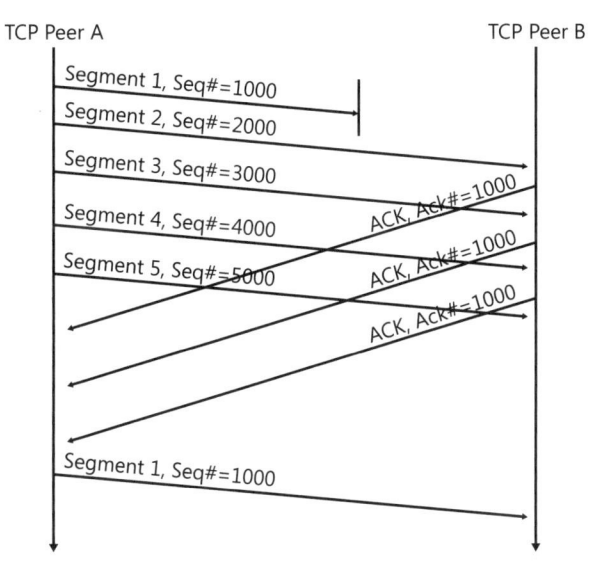

Figure 13-5 Fast retransmit behavior when the first of five segments is dropped

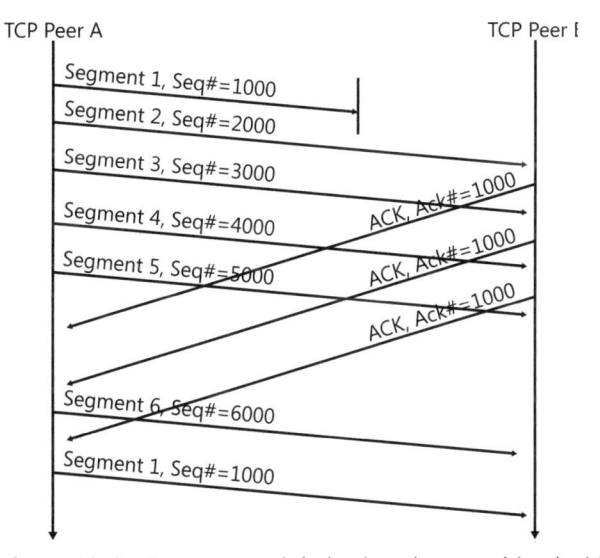

Figure 13-6 Fast retransmit behavior when combined with limited transmit

In Figure 13-6, TCP Peer A transmits Segment 6 upon receiving the first two duplicate ACKs for Segment 1. In this case, transmitting Segment 6 was not needed to detect and recover Segment 1. However, if Segment 4 and Segment 5 were lost, then only two duplicate ACKs would be received by TCP Peer A. If Segment 6 was successfully received by TCP Peer B, its duplicate ACK would allow TCP Peer A to detect that Segment 1 was lost. For more information about Limited Transmit, see Chapter 12, "Transmission Control Protocol (TCP) Data Flow."

> **Note** TCP/IP in Windows Server 2008 and Windows Vista no longer supports the TcpMaxDupAcks registry value.

Fast Recovery

Fast retransmit causes the sender to retransmit the missing TCP segment before its RTO expires. If the RTO expires, slow start and congestion avoidance algorithms are used to gradually increase the actual send window up to the advertised receive window. Because the RTO did not expire, congestion avoidance is performed, but not slow start. This behavior is known as fast recovery and is described in RFC 2581. For more information about slow start and congestion avoidance, see Chapter 12, "Transmission Control Protocol (TCP) Data Flow."

Fast recovery assumes that the arrival of duplicate ACKs indicates that segments sent before the missing TCP segment have already been received and are not adding to the internetwork congestion. Therefore, TCP can scale the congestion window faster than when using slow start.

The fast recovery algorithm is defined as follows:

1. After receipt of the third duplicate ACK, the value of the slow start threshold (*ssthresh*) is set to one half the value of the congestion window (*cwind*), with a minimum value of 2*MSS.

2. The missing segment is retransmitted and *cwind* is set to (*ssthresh* + 3*MSS). This increases *cwind* to a value that reflects the receipt of three TCP segments at the receiver (based on the receipt of three duplicate ACKs).

3. For each additional duplicate ACK, *cwind* is increased by MSS. Once again, *cwind* is being increased because of an additional segment that has arrived at the receiver.

4. If allowed by the values of *cwind* and the advertised receive window size, the next TCP segment(s) is transmitted.

5. When the ACK arrives that acknowledges the receipt of the missing new segment and all other contiguous segments, *cwind* is set to the value of *ssthresh*. At this value of *cwind*, slow start is avoided and congestion avoidance is performed.

SACK-based Loss Recovery

TCP for Windows Server 2003 and Windows XP uses SACK information only to determine which TCP segments have not arrived at the destination. TCP in Windows Server 2008 and Windows Vista supports RFC 3517, which defines a method of using SACK information to perform loss recovery when duplicate acknowledgments have been received, effectively replacing the fast recovery algorithm when SACK is enabled on a connection. TCP in Windows Server 2008 and Windows Vista keeps track of SACK information on a per-connection basis and monitors incoming acknowledgments and duplicate acknowledgments to more quickly recover when multiple segments are not received at the destination.

For details of the SACK-based loss recovery algorithm, see RFC 3517.

NewReno Support for Fast Recovery

TCP for Windows Server 2003 and Windows XP supports the Fast Recovery algorithm defined in RFC 2581, which defined the Reno algorithm. The Reno algorithm increases the amount of data that a sender can send when a segment is retransmitted due to a fast retransmit event. Although the Reno algorithm works well for single lost segments, it does not perform as well when there are multiple lost segments.

TCP for Windows Server 2008 and Windows Visa supports the NewReno algorithm defined in RFC 2582. The NewReno algorithm provides faster throughput by changing the way that senders can increase their sending rate during fast recovery when multiple segments in a window of data are lost and the sender receives a partial acknowledgment (an acknowledgment for only part of the data that has been successfully received).

For details of the NewReno algorithm, see RFC 2582.

Summary

To recover from lost TCP segments, TCP connections maintain an RTO for each segment. If the RTO expires, the segment is retransmitted, and the RTO is doubled for the retransmitted segment. After a maximum number of retransmissions, TCP abandons the connection. The RTO is based on calculations from samples of the RTT, using either a single sample per window of data or TCP timestamps. When TCP segments are sent without timestamps, TCP uses Karn's algorithm to update the RTO when an ACK for a retransmitted segment is received. Fast retransmit resends a missing segment before its RTO expires, based on the receipt of multiple duplicate ACKs. Fast recovery increases the size of the actual send window more quickly when fast retransmit occurs.

Part IV
Application Layer Protocols and Services

> **In this part:**
>
> Chapter 14: Dynamic Host Configuration Protocol (DHCP) 293
>
> Chapter 15: Domain Name System 313
>
> Chapter 16: Windows Internet Name Service 333
>
> Chapter 17 Remote Authentication Dial-In User Service (RADIUS) 353
>
> Chapter 18 Internet Protocol Security (IPsec) 373
>
> Chapter 19 Virtual Private Networks (VPNs) 407

Chapter 14
Dynamic Host Configuration Protocol (DHCP)

In this chapter:
DHCP Messages 293
DHCP Message Exchanges 301
Summary. 311

DHCP is a simple client/server protocol that simplifies the management of host computer IP addresses and other configuration settings. This chapter describes the details of DHCP messages and common DHCP message exchanges.

Note This chapter assumes prior knowledge of the benefits of DHCP, DHCP operation, the components of a DHCP infrastructure (DHCP client, DHCP server, and DHCP relay agent), and basic installation and configuration of those components provided with Microsoft Windows. For more information, see Chapter 6, "Dynamic Host Configuration Protocol," of the "TCP/IP Fundamentals for Microsoft Windows" book, located in the \Fundamentals folder on the companion CD-ROM.

DHCP Messages

DHCP clients and DHCP servers communicate by exchanging DHCP messages. There are eight types of DHCP messages, all of which are sent as User Datagram Protocol (UDP) messages. DHCP clients in the process of obtaining an IP address configuration use broadcast DHCP messages, sent to the limited broadcast IP address 255.255.255.255. DHCP clients with an IP address and a valid lease use unicast DHCP messages. DHCP clients listen on UDP port 68. DHCP servers and DHCP relay agents listen on UDP port 67.

The eight DHCP message types are the following:

- **DHCPDISCOVER** Sent by a DHCP client to locate a DHCP server.
- **DHCPOFFER** Sent by a DHCP server to a DHCP client in response to the DHCP-DISCOVER message, containing an offered IP address and other configuration settings.
- **DHCPREQUEST** Sent by the DHCP client to DHCP servers to request an offered IP address and other configuration settings from a specified DHCP server while implicitly

declining offers from other servers, or to confirm the validity of previously allocated addresses (for example, after a restart or to extend an existing DHCP lease).

- **DHCPACK** Sent by a DHCP server to a DHCP client in response to a DHCPREQUEST message to confirm an IP address and provide the client with those configuration parameters that the client has requested and the server has been configured to provide.

- **DHCPNAK** Sent by a DHCP server to a DHCP client denying the client's DHCPREQUEST. This might occur if the requested address is incorrect because the client has moved to a new subnet or because the DHCP client's lease has expired and cannot be renewed.

- **DHCPDECLINE** Sent by a DHCP client to a DHCP server, informing the server that the offered IP address is unusable because it is in use by another computer.

- **DHCPRELEASE** Sent by a DHCP client to a DHCP server, relinquishing an IP address and canceling the remaining lease.

- **DHCPINFORM** Sent from a DHCP client to a DHCP server, requesting additional configuration settings; the client already has a configured IP address. This message type is also used for rogue DHCP server detection in Windows Server 2008.

DHCP messages, options, and protocol operation are defined in RFCs 2131 and 2132.

> **More Info** All of the RFCs referenced in this chapter can be found in the \Standards\Chap14_DHCP folder on the companion CD-ROM.

DHCP Message Format

Figure 14-1 shows the structure of all DHCP messages.

The fields in the DHCP message are the following:

- **Message Op Code (Op)** A 1-byte field that indicates whether the message is a request (set to 1) or a reply (set to 2).

- **Hardware Address Type (Htype)** A 1-byte field that indicates the type of hardware being used by the DHCP client. This field uses the same values as the Hardware Type field in the Address Resolution Protocol (ARP) header. For more information, see Chapter 3, "Address Resolution Protocol (ARP)." For a complete list of ARP Hardware Type values, see http://www.iana.org/assignments/arp-parameters.

- **Hardware Address Length (Hlen)** A 1-byte field that indicates the number of high-order bytes within the fixed-length Client Hardware Address field that contains the client's hardware address. For commonly used IEEE 802-based technologies, such as Ethernet and IEEE 802.11, the value of this field is 6.

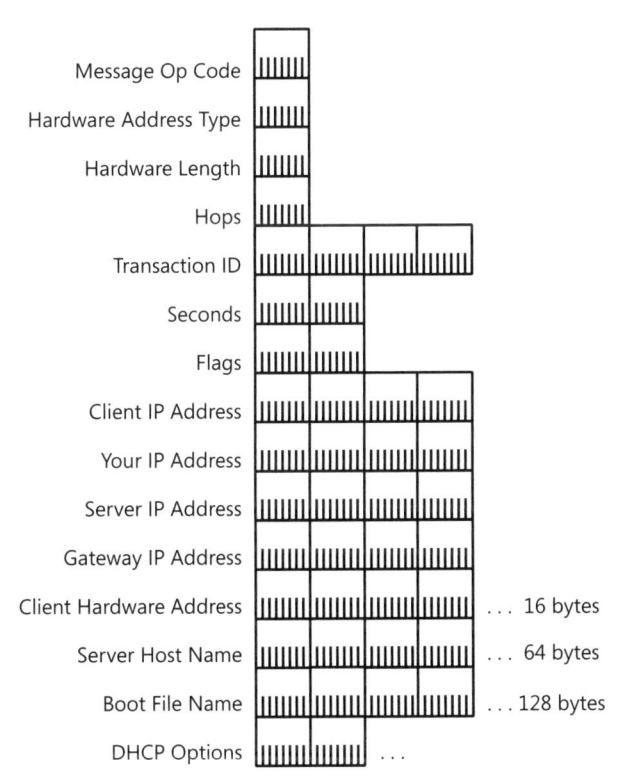

Figure 14-1 DHCP message format

- **Hops** A 1-byte field that indicates how many DHCP relay agents have forwarded the message. The initial value is 0. When a DHCP relay agent forwards a DHCP message on behalf of either a DHCP client or a DHCP server, it increments this field. The maximum number of hops in a DHCP infrastructure is 16. If the value is greater than 16, the receiving DHCP relay agent silently discards the message. DHCP relay agents can also discard DHCP messages if this field exceeds a configurable value. For example, the DHCP Relay Agent component of Routing and Remote Access in Windows Server 2008 uses a default maximum of 4 hops.

- **Transaction ID (Xid)** A 4-byte field that contains a random number derived by the DHCP client to group all of the DHCP messages of a given message exchange together, such as all of the messages for a lease acquisition.

- **Seconds (Secs)** A 2-byte field set by the DHCP client to indicate the number of seconds that have elapsed since the client began the address acquisition process.

- **Flags** A 2-byte field that indicates flags that are set by the DHCP client. RFC 2131 defines the high-order bit as the Broadcast flag. A DHCP client uses the broadcast flag to indicate that it can (set to 0) or cannot (set to 1) receive unicast IP datagrams even though it has not been configured with an IP address. Windows Server 2008 and Windows

Vista-based DHCP clients set the Broadcast flag to 1 (responses must be broadcast). If the DHCP server has been configured to process this flag, it will send its response as either a unicast (when the Broadcast flag is set to 0) or as a broadcast (when the Broadcast flag is set to 1).

- **Client IP Address (Ciaddr)** A 4-byte field that indicates a DHCP client's IP address. This field is set by the DHCP client in DHCP messages when it has been successfully configured with the IP address and can respond to ARP requests to defend the use of the address.
- **Your IP Address (Yiaddr)** A 4-byte field that indicates the IP address that is being allocated to the DHCP client by the DHCP server.
- **Server IP Address (Siaddr)** A 4-byte field that indicates the IP address of the DHCP server that is offering an IP address.
- **Gateway IP Address (Giaddr)** A 4-byte field that indicates an IP address that is assigned to the interface on the initial DHCP relay agent that received the message from the DHCP client. The initial DHCP relay agent is located on the same subnet as the DHCP client that broadcast the DHCP request message (either a DHCPDISCOVER or DHCPREQUEST message). By recording an IP address for the subnet of the DHCP client in this field, the DHCP server can determine the proper scope from which to assign an IP address to the requesting DHCP client.
- **Client Hardware Address (Chaddr)** A 16-byte field that indicates the hardware address of the DHCP client. To determine how many bytes are used for the hardware address, the DHCP server and relay agent use the value of the Hardware Address Length field. For commonly used IEEE 802-based technologies, this field contains the 6-byte media access control (MAC) address of the Ethernet or 802.11 network adapter of the DHCP client and 10 bytes set to 0.
- **Server Host Name (Sname)** A 64-byte field that indicates a name for the DHCP server. The DHCP Server service in Windows Server 2008 does not use this field.
- **Boot File Name (File)** A 128-byte field that indicates the name of the file containing a boot image for a BOOTP client. BOOTP was developed before DHCP to allow a diskless host computer to obtain an IP address configuration, the name of a boot file, and the location of a Trivial File Transfer Protocol (TFTP) server from which the computer loads the boot file. DHCP message exchanges do not use this field.
- **Options** A variable-length set of fields containing DHCP options.

Use of the Broadcast Flag

By default, the DHCP Server service in Windows Server 2008 ignores the Broadcast flag in the Flags field of broadcast-based DHCP messages received by DHCP clients. To configure the DHCP Server service to process the Broadcast flag, create and set the IgnoreBroadcastFlag registry value to 0.

```
IgnoreBroadcastFlag
Location: HKEY_LOCAL_MACHINE\SYSTEM\CurrentControlSet\Services\DhcpServer\Parameters
Data type: REG_DWORD
Valid range: 0-1
Default value: 1
Present by default: No
```

As Figure 14-1 shows, DHCP messages consist of a fixed portion 236 bytes long and a variable-length portion for DHCP options. Because DHCP messages are transmitted using UDP, all DHCP messages must fit into a UDP datagram. This limits the variable-length portion of a DHCP message to the IP maximum transmission unit (MTU) minus 264 bytes, which allows for 20 bytes for the IP header and 8 bytes for the UDP header. For Ethernet, with an IP MTU of 1500 bytes, DHCP messages can contain up to 1236 bytes of DHCP options.

DHCP Options

A DHCP option is an IP address configuration setting that is not already included in the fixed DHCP header. For example, there is no DHCP option for the IP address allocated to the DHCP client because that is already indicated in the Your IP Address field. There are DHCP options for lease management, such as the lease timeout values, and options for configuration settings explicitly requested by DHCP clients, such as the default gateway IP address.

The Windows Server 2008 DHCP Server service supports the standard DHCP option types defined in RFC 2131 and 2132 and vendor-specific DHCP options that you can use to provide Windows-based DHCP clients with additional configuration settings.

Figure 14-2 shows the format for DHCP options.

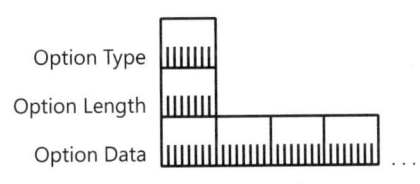

Figure 14-2 DHCP option format

The fields in a DHCP option are the following:

- **Option Type** A 1-byte field that indicates the type of DHCP option. For a complete list, see *http://www.iana.org/assignments/bootp-dhcp-parameters*.
- **Option Length** A 1-byte field that indicates the number of bytes in the DHCP option past the Option Length field.
- **Option Data** A variable-length field that contains the data for the DHCP option.

There are fixed-length options without data, fixed-length options with data, and variable-length options with data. The only fixed-length options without data are the Pad (Option Type 0) and End (Option Type 255) options.

Table 14-1 lists the set of the DHCP options that are most commonly used for Windows-based DHCP clients and servers.

Table 14-1 DHCP Options for Windows-based DHCP Clients and Servers

Option Name	Option Code (Decimal)	Option Length Value	Option Description
Pad	0	N/A	Used to cause subsequent fields to align. Can be used in any DHCP message. The Pad option consists of a single byte, the Option Code field set to 0.
Subnet Mask	1	4 bytes	Indicates the subnet mask for an offered IP address. Used in DHCPOFFER and DHCPACK messages.
Router	3	Variable; but always a multiple of 4 bytes	Indicates a list of IP addresses for routers on the client's subnet, which should be listed in order of preference. Typically, there is only one router—the default gateway—but multiple routers can be specified.
Domain Name Servers	6	Variable; but always a multiple of 4 bytes	Indicates a list of IP addresses for DNS servers.
Host Name	12	Variable length; minimum length is 1 byte	Specifies the name of the client. Used in DHCPDISCOVER, DHCPREQUEST, and DHCPNAK messages.
DNS Domain Name	15	Variable-length set of ASCII characters; minimum length is 1 byte	Specifies the DNS domain name that the DHCP client should use when resolving host names using DNS.
Perform Router Discovery	31	1 byte	Indicates whether the client should use Router Discovery to discover the routers on its subnet.
Static Route	33	Variable; but always a multiple of 8	Indicates the Internet address class-based destination IP address prefix and next-hop IP address (a router) for one or multiple static routes that the DHCP client adds to their local IP routing table.
Vendor-specific Information	43	Variable length	Used by clients and servers to exchange vendor-specific information. The definition of this information is vendor-specific and is not defined in RFC 2132.
WINS/NBNS Servers	44	Variable; but always a multiple of 4	Indicates a list of WINS server IP addresses. This is typically a primary and secondary WINS server.

Table 14-1 DHCP Options for Windows-based DHCP Clients and Servers

Option Name	Option Code (Decimal)	Option Length Value	Option Description
NetBIOS Over TCP/IP Node Type	46	1 byte	Indicates how NetBIOS names should be resolved, as follows: 1 – B-node (broadcast) 2 – P-node (point-to-point) 4 – M-node (mixed) 8 – H-node (hybrid)
NetBIOS Scope ID	47	Variable; minimum length is 1	Specifies the NetBIOS over TCP/IP scope.
Requested Address	50	4 bytes	Indicates whether the DHCP client is requesting (or declining) this address. This is used in DHCPREQUEST, DHCPDECLINE, and DHCPDISCOVER messages.
Lease Time	51	4 bytes	Indicates the length of the lease time in seconds.
DHCP Message Type	53	1 byte	Indicates the DHCP message type. The values are as follows: 1 – DHCPDISCOVER 2 – DHCPOFFER 3 – DHCPREQUEST 4 – DHCPDECLINE 5 – DHCPACK 6 – DHCPNAK 7 – DHCPRELEASE 8 – DHCPINFORM Used in all DHCP messages.
Server Identifier	54	4 bytes	Indicates the DHCP server's IP address. This is used in DHCOFFER, DHCPREQUEST, DHCPACK, DHCPDECLINE, and DHCPRELEASE messages.
Parameter Request List	55	Variable length; minimum length is 1 byte.	Indicates the list of DHCP options that a DHCP client needs. Each byte in this option is a DHCP option code value. This is used in DHCPDISCOVER, DHCPREQUEST, and DHCPINFORM messages.
Renewal Time (T1)	58	4 bytes	Indicates the length of time, in seconds, until the client enters renewal state. This is used in DHCPOFFER and DHCPACK messages.
Rebinding Time (T2)	59	4 bytes	Indicates the length of time, in seconds, until the client enters rebinding state. This is used in DHCPOFFER and DHCPACK messages.

Table 14-1 DHCP Options for Windows-based DHCP Clients and Servers

Option Name	Option Code (Decimal)	Option Length Value	Option Description
Client Identifier	61	Variable length; minimum length is 2 bytes; for Ethernet, the length is 6 bytes	Indicates a value to identify the DHCP client. For Windows-based DHCP clients, this is the client's MAC address. This is used in DHCPDISCOVER DHCPREQUEST, DHCPDECLINE, DHCPNAK, and DHCPRELEASE messages.
Dynamic DNS Update	81	Variable length	Indicates the fully qualified domain name (FQDN) of the host. The DHCP server uses the FQDN to register the name and the assigned address with a DNS server. This is used in DHCPREQUEST messages.
Classless Static Route	121	Variable, minimum length is 5 bytes.	Indicates the destination IP address prefix, subnet mask, and next-hop IP address (a router) for one or multiple static routes that the DHCP client adds to the local IP routing table. For more information, see RFC 3442.
Classless Static Route	249	Variable; minimum length is 5 bytes	Indicates the destination IP address prefix, subnet mask, and next-hop IP address (a router) for one or multiple static routes that the DHCP client adds to the local IP routing table. This is the same option as 121.
End	255	N/A	Indicates the end of the options portion of a DHCP message. This is used in all DHCP messages. The End option consists of a single byte, the Option Code field set to 255.

DHCP clients running Windows Server 2008 or Windows Vista include the following DHCP options in the Parameter Request List DHCP option (listed in requested order):

- 1 (0x01) – Subnet Mask
- 15 (0x0F) – DNS Domain Name
- 3 (0x03) – Router
- 6 (0x06) – DNS Servers
- 44 (0x2C) – WINS/NBNS Servers
- 46 (0x2E) – NetBIOS Node Type
- 47 (0x2F) – NetBIOS Scope ID
- 31 (0x1F) – Perform Router Discovery
- 33 (0x21) – Static Route
- 121 (0x79) – Classless Static Routes

- 249 (0xF9) – Classless Static Routes
- 43 (0x2B) – Vendor-Specific Information

DHCP Message Exchanges

This section describes the typical DHCP message exchanges for obtaining and renewing a DHCP-leased IP address configuration and for detecting unauthorized DHCP servers.

Obtaining an Initial Lease

Figure 14-3 shows the exchange of DHCP messages when a DHCP client and DHCP server are on the same subnet and a DHCP client acquires an initial lease.

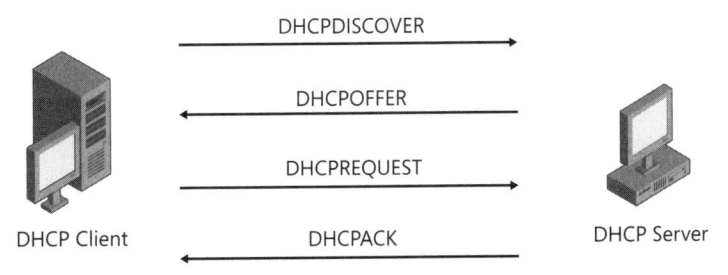

Figure 14-3 DHCP messages exchanged during initial lease acquisition

An example of this message exchange is Capture 14-01, a Network Monitor trace that is included in the \Captures folder on the companion CD-ROM. The following is the DHCPDISCOVER message (Frame 1) from Capture 14-01 as displayed with Network Monitor 3.1:

```
Frame:
- Ethernet: Etype = Internet IP (IPv4)
  + DestinationAddress: *BROADCAST
  + SourceAddress: 00123F17E0CF
    EthernetType: Internet IP (IPv4), 2048(0x800)
+ Ipv4: Next Protocol = UDP, Packet ID = 10839, Total IP Length = 328
+ Udp: SrcPort = BOOTP client(68), DstPort = BOOTP server(67), Length = 308
- Dhcp: Boot Request, MsgType = DISCOVER, TransactionID = 0xBCBCFAE3
    OpCode: Boot Request, 1(0x01)
    Hardwaretype: Ethernet
    HardwareAddressLength: 6 (0x6)
    HopCount: 0 (0x0)
    TransactionID: 3166501603 (0xBCBCFAE3)
    Seconds: 0 (0x0)
  - Flags: 32768 (0x8000)
     Broadcast: (1..............) Broadcast
     Reserved: (.000000000000000)
    ClientIP: 0.0.0.0
    YourIP: 0.0.0.0
    ServerIP: 0.0.0.0
    RelayAgentIP: 0.0.0.0
  - ClientHardwareAddress: 00-12-3F-17-E0-CF
```

```
        EthernetAddress: 00-12-3F-17-E0-CF
        ServerHostName:
        BootFileName:
        MagicCookie: 99.130.83.99
      - MessageType: DISCOVER
          Code: DHCP Message Type, 53(0x35)
          Length: 1 UINT8(s)
          Value: DISCOVER, 1(0x1)
      - AutoConfigure: Auto Configure   (1)
          Code: Auto-Configure, 116(0x74)
          Length: 1 UINT8(s)
          Value: Auto Configure   (1)
      - clientID: (Type 1)
          Code: Client-identifier, 61(0x3D)
          Length: 7 UINT8(s)
          Type: HardwareAddress(1)
          ClientID: Binary Large Object (6 Bytes)
      - RequestedIPAddress: 10.0.0.3
          Code: Requested IP Address, 50(0x32)
          Length: 4 UINT8(s)
          IpAddress: 10.0.0.3
      - HostName: VistaPC
          Code: Host Name, 12(0x0C)
          Length: 7 UINT8(s)
          Name: VistaPC
      - VendorClassIdentifier: MSFT 5.0
          Code: Class-identifier, 60(0x3C)
          Length: 8 UINT8(s)
          VendorClassIdentifier: MSFT 5.0
      - ParameterRequestList:
          Code: Parameter Request List, 55(0x37)
          Length: 12 UINT8(s)
          Parameter: Subnet Mask, 1(0x01)
          Parameter: Domain Name, 15(0x0F)
          Parameter: Router, 3(0x03)
          Parameter: Domain Name Server, 6(0x06)
          Parameter: NetBIOS over TCP/IP Name Server, 44(0x2C)
          Parameter: NetBIOS over TCP/IP Node Type, 46(0x2E)
          Parameter: NetBIOS over TCP/IP Scope, 47(0x2F)
          Parameter: Perform Router Discovery, 31(0x1F)
          Parameter: Static Route, 33(0x21)
          Parameter: Classless Static Route Option, 121(0x79)
          Parameter: Classless Static Route, 249(0xF9)
          Parameter: Vendor specific information, 43(0x2B)
      - End:
          Code: End of Options, 255(0xFF)
```

Fields or options to note are the following:

- The DHCP client is using an Ethernet network adapter. Therefore, the Hardware Type field is set to 1; the Hardware Address Length field is set to 6; and the DHCP client's MAC address is stored in the Client Hardware Address field.

- The DHCP client has chosen the transaction ID 3166501603, which is used in all of the DHCP messages of this DHCP message exchange.
- The DHCP client has set the Broadcast flag in the Flags field to 1, indicating that it must receive a reply to this message as a broadcast.
- Because this is an initial DHCP lease, all of the IP address fields (Client IP Address, Your IP Address, Server IP Address, and Gateway IP Address) are set to 0.0.0.0.
- The first option is the Magic Cookie option, set to the string 99.130.83.99. This option is included in all of these DHCP messages for BOOTP support.
- The DHCP Message Type option indicates a DHCPDISCOVER message.
- The previous IP address assigned to this DHCP client is 10.0.0.3.
- The host name of the DHCP client is VistaPC.

The following is the DHCPOFFER message (Frame 2) from Capture 14-01:

```
Frame:
- Ethernet: Etype = Internet IP (IPv4)
  + DestinationAddress: *BROADCAST
  + SourceAddress: 00123F2B3407
    EthernetType: Internet IP (IPv4), 2048(0x800)
+ Ipv4: Next Protocol = UDP, Packet ID = 572, Total IP Length = 328
+ Udp: SrcPort = BOOTP server(67), DstPort = BOOTP client(68), Length = 308
- Dhcp: Boot Reply, MsgType = OFFER, TransactionID = 0xBCBCFAE3
    OpCode: Boot Reply, 2(0x02)
    Hardwaretype: Ethernet
    HardwareAddressLength: 6 (0x6)
    HopCount: 0 (0x0)
    TransactionID: 3166501603 (0xBCBCFAE3)
    Seconds: 0 (0x0)
  - Flags: 0 (0x0)
      Broadcast: (0..............) No Broadcast
      Reserved: (.000000000000000)
    ClientIP: 10.0.0.3
    YourIP: 10.0.0.3
    ServerIP: 10.0.0.1
    RelayAgentIP: 0.0.0.0
  - ClientHardwareAddress: 00-12-3F-17-E0-CF
      EthernetAddress: 00-12-3F-17-E0-CF
    ServerHostName:
    BootFileName:
    MagicCookie: 99.130.83.99
  - MessageType: OFFER
      Code: DHCP Message Type, 53(0x35)
      Length: 1 UINT8(s)
      Value: OFFER, 2(0x2)
  - SubnetMask: 255.0.0.0
      Code: Subnet Mask, 1(0x01)
      Length: 4 UINT8(s)
      IpAddress: 255.0.0.0
```

```
      - RenewTimeValue: Subnet Mask: 4 day(s),0 hour(s) 0 minute(s) 0 second(s)
          Code: Renewal (T1) Time Value, 58(0x3A)
          Length: 4 UINT8(s)
          Timeout: 4 day(s),0 hour(s) 0 minute(s) 0 second(s)
      - RebindingTimeValue: Subnet Mask: 7 day(s),0 hour(s) 0 minute(s) 0 second(s)
          Code: Rebinding (T2) Time Value, 59(0x3B)
          Length: 4 UINT8(s)
          Timeout: 7 day(s),0 hour(s) 0 minute(s) 0 second(s)
      - IPAddressLeaseTime: Subnet Mask: 8 day(s),0 hour(s) 0 minute(s) 0 second(s)
          Code: IP Address Lease Time, 51(0x33)
          Length: 4 UINT8(s)
          Timeout: 8 day(s),0 hour(s) 0 minute(s) 0 second(s)
      - ServerIdentifier: 10.0.0.1
          Code: Server Identifier, 54(0x36)
          Length: 4 UINT8(s)
          IpAddress: 10.0.0.1
      - DomainName: contoso.com
          Code: Domain Name, 15(0x0F)
          Length: 12 UINT8(s)
          Name: contoso.com
      - DomainNameServer: 10.0.0.1
          Code: Domain Name Server, 6(0x06)
          Length: 4 UINT8(s)
          IpAddress: 10.0.0.1
      - End:
          Code: End of Options, 255(0xFF)
```

Fields or configuration items to note are the following:

- Because the Broadcast flag was set in the DHCPDISCOVER message, this message is broadcast.

- The IP address being offered to the DHCP client is 10.0.0.3.

- The IP address of the DHCP server is 10.0.0.1.

- The DHCP Message Type option indicates a DHCPOFFER message.

- The subnet mask is 255.0.0.0.

- The T1 renewal time is 4 days.

- The T2 renewal time is 7 days.

- The maximum lease time is 8 days.

- The domain name for the network adapter that is assigned this IP address is contoso.com.

- The DNS server for the network adapter that is assigned this IP address is 10.0.0.1.

The following is the DHCPREQUEST message (Frame 3) from Capture 14-01:

```
Frame:
- Ethernet: Etype = Internet IP (IPv4)
  + DestinationAddress: *BROADCAST
  + SourceAddress: 00123F17E0CF
```

```
  EthernetType: Internet IP (IPv4), 2048(0x800)
+ Ipv4: Next Protocol = UDP, Packet ID = 10840, Total IP Length = 350
+ Udp: SrcPort = BOOTP client(68), DstPort = BOOTP server(67), Length = 330
- Dhcp: Boot Request, MsgType = REQUEST, TransactionID = 0xBCBCFAE3
    OpCode: Boot Request, 1(0x01)
    Hardwaretype: Ethernet
    HardwareAddressLength: 6 (0x6)
    HopCount: 0 (0x0)
    TransactionID: 3166501603 (0xBCBCFAE3)
    Seconds: 0 (0x0)
   - Flags: 32768 (0x8000)
      Broadcast: (1..............) Broadcast
      Reserved: (.000000000000000)
    ClientIP: 0.0.0.0
    YourIP: 0.0.0.0
    ServerIP: 0.0.0.0
    RelayAgentIP: 0.0.0.0
   - ClientHardwareAddress: 00-12-3F-17-E0-CF
      EthernetAddress: 00-12-3F-17-E0-CF
    ServerHostName:
    BootFileName:
    MagicCookie: 99.130.83.99
   - MessageType: REQUEST
      Code: DHCP Message Type, 53(0x35)
      Length: 1 UINT8(s)
      Value: REQUEST, 3(0x3)
   - clientID: (Type 1)
      Code: Client-identifier, 61(0x3D)
      Length: 7 UINT8(s)
      Type: HardwareAddress(1)
      ClientID: Binary Large Object (6 Bytes)
   - RequestedIPAddress: 10.0.0.3
      Code: Requested IP Address, 50(0x32)
      Length: 4 UINT8(s)
      IpAddress: 10.0.0.3
   - ServerIdentifier: 10.0.0.1
      Code: Server Identifier, 54(0x36)
      Length: 4 UINT8(s)
      IpAddress: 10.0.0.1
   - HostName: VistaPC
      Code: Host Name, 12(0x0C)
      Length: 7 UINT8(s)
      Name: VistaPC
   - FullyQualifiedDomainName:
      Code: Fully Qualified Domain Name, 81(0x51)
      Length: 22 UINT8(s)
     - Flag: 0 (0x0)
        MBZ: (0000....) 0
        N: (....0...) SHOULD NOT perform the A RR (FQDN to address) DNS updates
        E: (.....0..) ASCII encoding of the Domain Name field (deprecated)
        O: (......0.) the server has not overridden the client's preference for the 'S' bit
        S: (.......0) SHOULD NOT perform the A RR (FQDN to address) DNS updates
      RCODE1: 0 (0x0)
      RCODE2: 0 (0x0)
      DomainName: VistaPC.contoso.com
   - VendorClassIdentifier: MSFT 5.0
```

```
            Code: Class-identifier, 60(0x3C)
            Length: 8 UINT8(s)
            VendorClassIdentifier: MSFT 5.0
          - ParameterRequestList:
            Code: Parameter Request List, 55(0x37)
            Length: 12 UINT8(s)
            Parameter: Subnet Mask, 1(0x01)
            Parameter: Domain Name, 15(0x0F)
            Parameter: Router, 3(0x03)
            Parameter: Domain Name Server, 6(0x06)
            Parameter: NetBIOS over TCP/IP Name Server, 44(0x2C)
            Parameter: NetBIOS over TCP/IP Node Type, 46(0x2E)
            Parameter: NetBIOS over TCP/IP Scope, 47(0x2F)
            Parameter: Perform Router Discovery, 31(0x1F)
            Parameter: Static Route, 33(0x21)
            Parameter: Classless Static Route Option, 121(0x79)
            Parameter: Classless Static Route, 249(0xF9)
            Parameter: Vendor specific information, 43(0x2B)
          - End:
            Code: End of Options, 255(0xFF)
```

Fields or configuration items to note are the following:

- The DHCP client has set the Broadcast flag in the Flags field, indicating that it must receive a reply to this message as a broadcast.

- The DHCP client is selecting the address offered by the DHCP server at 10.0.0.1.

- The DHCP Message Type option indicates a DHCPREQUEST message.

- The DHCP client is requesting its previous IP address of 10.0.0.3.

- The DHCP client includes its FQDN of vistapc.contoso.com, but indicates that the DHCP server not perform DNS dynamic update on its behalf.

The following is the DHCPACK message (Frame 4) from Capture 14-01:

```
    Frame:
  - Ethernet: Etype = Internet IP (IPv4)
    + DestinationAddress: *BROADCAST
    + SourceAddress: 00123F2B3407
      EthernetType: Internet IP (IPv4), 2048(0x800)
  + Ipv4: Next Protocol = UDP, Packet ID = 573, Total IP Length = 328
  + Udp: SrcPort = BOOTP server(67), DstPort = BOOTP client(68), Length = 308
  - Dhcp: Boot Reply, MsgType = ACK, TransactionID = 0xBCBCFAE3
      OpCode: Boot Reply, 2(0x02)
      Hardwaretype: Ethernet
      HardwareAddressLength: 6 (0x6)
      HopCount: 0 (0x0)
      TransactionID: 3166501603 (0xBCBCFAE3)
      Seconds: 0 (0x0)
    - Flags: 0 (0x0)
        Broadcast: (0..............) No Broadcast
        Reserved: (.000000000000000)
```

```
  ClientIP: 0.0.0.0
  YourIP: 10.0.0.3
  ServerIP: 0.0.0.0
  RelayAgentIP: 0.0.0.0
- ClientHardwareAddress: 00-12-3F-17-E0-CF
  EthernetAddress: 00-12-3F-17-E0-CF
  ServerHostName:
  BootFileName:
  MagicCookie: 99.130.83.99
- MessageType: ACK
  Code: DHCP Message Type, 53(0x35)
  Length: 1 UINT8(s)
  Value: ACK, 5(0x5)
- RenewTimeValue: Subnet Mask: 4 day(s),0 hour(s) 0 minute(s) 0 second(s)
  Code: Renewal (T1) Time Value, 58(0x3A)
  Length: 4 UINT8(s)
  Timeout: 4 day(s),0 hour(s) 0 minute(s) 0 second(s)
- RebindingTimeValue: Subnet Mask: 7 day(s),0 hour(s) 0 minute(s) 0 second(s)
  Code: Rebinding (T2) Time Value, 59(0x3B)
  Length: 4 UINT8(s)
  Timeout: 7 day(s),0 hour(s) 0 minute(s) 0 second(s)
- IPAddressLeaseTime: Subnet Mask: 8 day(s),0 hour(s) 0 minute(s) 0 second(s)
  Code: IP Address Lease Time, 51(0x33)
  Length: 4 UINT8(s)
  Timeout: 8 day(s),0 hour(s) 0 minute(s) 0 second(s)
- ServerIdentifier: 10.0.0.1
  Code: Server Identifier, 54(0x36)
  Length: 4 UINT8(s)
  IpAddress: 10.0.0.1
- SubnetMask: 255.0.0.0
  Code: Subnet Mask, 1(0x01)
  Length: 4 UINT8(s)
  IpAddress: 255.0.0.0
- FullyQualifiedDomainName:
  Code: Fully Qualified Domain Name, 81(0x51)
  Length: 3 UINT8(s)
 - Flag: 0 (0x0)
   MBZ: (0000....) 0
   N: (....0...) SHOULD NOT perform the A RR (FQDN to address) DNS updates
   E: (.....0..) ASCII encoding of the Domain Name field (deprecated)
   O: (......0.) the server has not overridden the client's preference for the 'S' bit
   S: (.......0) SHOULD NOT perform the A RR (FQDN to address) DNS updates
   RCODE1: 255 (0xFF)
   RCODE2: 255 (0xFF)
- DomainName: contoso.com
  Code: Domain Name, 15(0x0F)
  Length: 12 UINT8(s)
  Name: contoso.com
- DomainNameServer: 10.0.0.1
  Code: Domain Name Server, 6(0x06)
  Length: 4 UINT8(s)
  IpAddress: 10.0.0.1
- End:
  Code: End of Options, 255(0xFF)
```

Fields or configuration items to note are the following:

- Because the Broadcast flag was set in the DHCPREQUEST message, this message is broadcast.
- The IP address being offered to the DHCP client is 10.0.0.3.
- The DHCP Message Type option indicates a DHCPACK message.
- The DHCP server is not performing DNS dynamic update on behalf of the DHCP client.

When the DHCP client and DHCP server are separated by a DHCP relay agent, the DHCP relay agent receives the broadcast DHCPDISCOVER and DHCPREQUEST messages, increments the Hops field, records the IP address assigned to the interface on the DHCP relay agent that received the messages in the Gateway IP Address field, and then forwards them as unicast traffic to its configured DHCP servers. The DHCP servers respond with DHCPOFFER and DHCPACK messages to the unicast addresses of the DHCP relay agent. The DHCP relay agent then either unicasts (if they support the Broadcast flag and the corresponding request message has the Broadcast flag set to 0) or broadcasts these messages to the DHCP client.

Renewing a Lease

Because a typical IP address configuration lease has a finite lifetime, the client must renew the lease. A lease renewal when the DHCP client remains on the subnet involves just two DHCP messages—DHCPREQUEST and DHCPACK. If the lease renewal is made while the DHCP client is continuously on the subnet, the DHCP client and the DHCP server communicate using unicast DHCPREQUEST and DHCPACK messages. If the lease renewal is made when the DHCP client restarts on the same subnet and that IP address is available for renewal, the DHCP client and the DHCP server communicate using broadcast DHCPREQUEST and DHCPACK messages. The Network Monitor Capture 14-02, included in the \Captures folder on the companion CD-ROM, provides an example of a broadcast-based lease renewal.

Changing Subnets

If the DHCP client requests a lease through a DHCPREQUEST message that the DHCP server cannot fulfill, the DHCP server sends a DHCPNAK message to the client. This message informs the client that the requested IP address lease will not be renewed. The client then acquires a new lease using the startup DHCP message exchange previously described. A good example is when a DHCP client shuts down without releasing its address and starts up on a different subnet or when an IEEE 802.11 wireless client roams to a wireless access point that is connected to a different subnet. Figure 14-4 shows this exchange of DHCP messages.

Network Monitor Capture 14-03, included in the \Captures folder on the companion CD-ROM, provides an example of the exchange of DHCP messages when a DHCP client moves to another subnet.

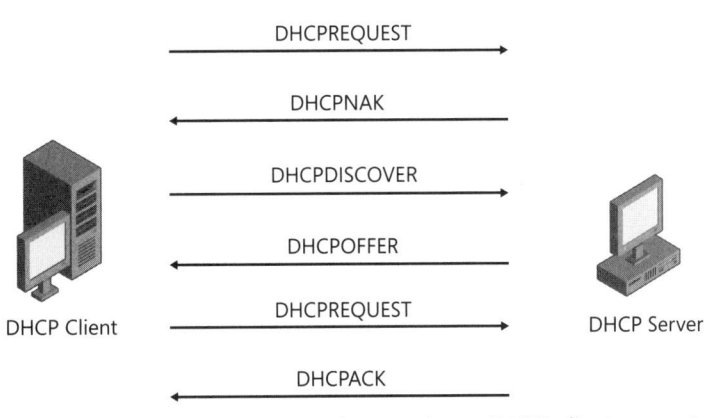

Figure 14-4 DHCP message exchange when a DHCP client moves to a different subnet

When a Windows-based DHCP client that has previously leased an address starts up, it broadcasts a DHCPREQUEST message to renew its lease. This ensures that the DHCP renewal request is sent to the DHCP server that provides DHCP addresses for the subnet the client is currently on. This could be different from the server that provided the initial lease. When the DHCP server receives the broadcast, it compares the address the DHCP client is requesting with the scopes configured on the server and the subnet the DHCPREQUEST message was received from. If it is not possible to satisfy the client request, the DHCP server issues a DHCPNAK, and the DHCP client then acquires a new lease.

If the Windows-based DHCP client is unable to locate any DHCP server, to renew its lease, it sends a broadcast ARP Request frame for the default gateway that was previously obtained, if one was provided. If the IP address of the default gateway is successfully resolved, the DHCP client assumes that it is located on the same subnet where it obtained its current lease and continues to use this lease.

If the ARP Request frame that the client sent for the default gateway receives no response, the client assumes that it has been moved to a subnet that has no DHCP services currently available (such as a home network), and it automatically configures itself using either Automatic Private IP Addressing (APIPA) or the alternate configuration. Afterward, the DHCP client tries to locate a DHCP server every 5 minutes.

Detecting Unauthorized DHCP Servers

As part of the initialization of the DHCP Server service, Windows Server 2008-based DHCP servers perform rogue server detection. If the DHCP server is a member server and is not authorized in Active Directory domain services, the DHCP Server service automatically shuts down.

If the DHCP server is a standalone server, it relies on an exchange of DHCPINFORM and DHCPACK messages for rogue server detection, as shown in Figure 14-5.

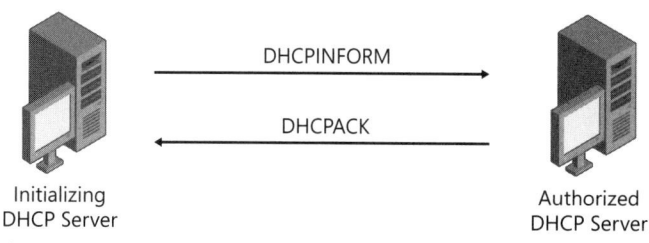

Figure 14-5 A DHCP server performing rogue server detection

Rogue server detection begins with the initializing DHCP server sending DHCPINFORM messages to determine whether there are other authorized DHCP servers on any attached subnet. Authorized servers respond with a DHCPACK message that contains the name of the domain in which they have been authorized. If authorized DHCP servers are found, the standalone DHCP server sends Lightweight Directory Access Protocol (LDAP) queries to an Active Directory domain controller to verify whether or not the found servers are authorized. If any of the found servers are authorized, the DHCP Server service shuts down.

Network Monitor Capture 14-04 (included in the \Captures folder on the companion CD-ROM) provides an example of an unauthorized server performing successful rogue server detection.

Updating DNS Entries

When a DHCP lease is allocated to an IP host, the host name and IP address mapping should be added to DNS. Traditionally, this was a manual task that involved creating the DNS forward and reverse lookup entries. Windows Server 2008 and Windows Vista support DNS dynamic update. This protocol allows computers running Windows Server 2008 or Windows Vista to automatically update DNS entries for forward and reverse lookups on the DNS server.

Each time a DHCP client receives a new lease or renews an existing lease, the client sends its FQDN to the DHCP server in the DHCPREQUEST message. The DHCPREQUEST message requests that the DHCP server register a reverse lookup mapping in the DNS server on behalf of the DHCP client. The DHCP client usually handles the forward lookup registration on its own, if it is capable.

You can configure the DHCP Server service in Windows Server 2008 to register both the forward and reverse lookup address mappings in DNS on the DHCP client's behalf. This is useful for DHCP clients that do not support DNS dynamic updates.

The Network Monitor Capture 14-05 (included in the \Captures folder on the companion CD-ROM) provides an example of a DHCP server registering both the forward and reverse lookup mappings for a new address lease. In the capture, the DHCP server queries for the DNS Start of Authority (SOA) record for the forward lookup zone and then updates the forward lookup entry for the DHCP client. The DHCP server then queries the DNS server for the reverse lookup zone and performs the update of the DHCP client's reverse lookup entry. For the dynamic updates to be successful, the DNS server must support DNS dynamic updates and have the forward and reverse lookup zones configured to allow dynamic updates.

For more information about DNS dynamic update, see Chapter 15, "Domain Name System."

Summary

DHCP has a common message format for all DHCP messages consisting of a fixed DHCP header and a variable portion that contains DHCP options. A DHCP relay agent modifies and forwards DHCP messages between DHCP clients and DHCP servers when they are not located on the same subnet. Common DHCP message exchanges allow a DHCP client to initially obtain a leased IP address configuration, renew it, and automatically obtain a new IP address configuration if it cannot renew the address previously leased. The Windows Server 2008 DHCP Server service on a standalone computer supports an additional message exchange to detect if it is in an Active Directory environment.

Chapter 15
Domain Name System

> **In this chapter:**
> DNS Messages 313
> DNS Message Exchanges 323
> Summary 331

Domain Name System (DNS) is a simple client/server protocol that provides name resolution, name registration (also known as DNS dynamic update), and zone transfers for the DNS namespace. This chapter describes the details of the DNS protocol and common DNS message exchanges between DNS clients and servers.

> **Note** This chapter assumes prior knowledge of the history and benefits of DNS, structure of the DNS namespace, DNS resource records (RRs), DNS server roles, the components of a DNS infrastructure (DNS client and DNS server), and the support, installation, and configuration of those components as supplied in Microsoft Windows. For more information, see Chapter 8, "Domain Name System Overview," and Chapter 9, "Windows Support for DNS" of the "TCP/IP Fundamentals for Microsoft Windows" book, located in the \Fundamentals folder on the companion CD-ROM.

DNS Messages

DNS clients and DNS servers communicate by exchanging DNS messages. During an iterative query or a zone transfer, a DNS server acts as a DNS client to another DNS server. There are four types of DNS messages, most of which are sent as User Datagram Protocol (UDP) messages. When a response contains more data than can be sent in a single UDP message, the responder (typically a DNS server) initially responds with a UDP message but sets a flag to indicate that the response was truncated. The DNS client or server then uses a Transmission Control Protocol (TCP) connection to obtain all of the data for the response. DNS servers listen on UDP port 53 and TCP port 53.

The different types of DNS messages described in this chapter are the following:

- **DNS Name Query Request** Sent by a DNS client or a DNS server to a DNS server to perform name resolution.

- **DNS Name Query Response** Sent by a DNS server to a DNS client or a DNS server to respond to a DNS name query request.

- **DNS Update** Sent by a DNS client to a DNS server to perform name registration.
- **DNS Update Response** Sent by a DNS server to a DNS client to respond to a DNS update.

DNS messages and protocol operation are defined in RFCs 1034, 1035, and 2136.

> **More Info** All of the RFCs referenced in this chapter can be found in the \Standards\Chap15_DNS folder on the companion CD-ROM.

DNS Name Query Request and Name Query Response Messages

DNS Name Query Request and Name Query Response messages share the same structure, as Figure 15-1 shows.

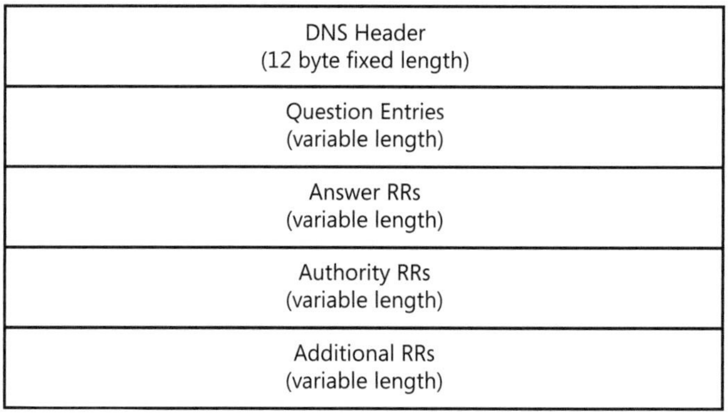

```
+---------------------------------+
|          DNS Header             |
|     (12 byte fixed length)      |
+---------------------------------+
|        Question Entries         |
|        (variable length)        |
+---------------------------------+
|          Answer RRs             |
|        (variable length)        |
+---------------------------------+
|         Authority RRs           |
|        (variable length)        |
+---------------------------------+
|         Additional RRs          |
|        (variable length)        |
+---------------------------------+
```

Figure 15-1 DNS Name Query Request and Name Query Response message structure

The DNS Name Query Request or Name Query Response messages consist of a fixed-length 12-byte header and a variable-length section containing question entries, answer RRs, authority RRs, and additional RRs.

Figure 15-2 shows the format of the 12-byte fixed DNS header for the DNS Name Query Request and Name Query Response messages.

The fields within the 12-byte fixed DNS header are the following:

- **Transaction ID** A 2-byte field that is used to identify a specific DNS transaction. The sender of the Name Query Request message creates the transaction identifier (ID), and the responder copies it into the Name Query Response message. This allows the DNS client or server to match the responses that it received from a DNS server with their requests and for the DNS server to identify duplicate requests from a DNS client.
- **Flags** A 2-byte field containing flags. For more information, see Figure 15-3.

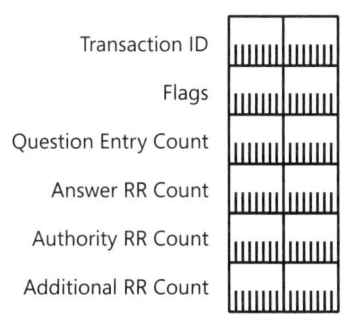

Figure 15-2 DNS Name Query Request and Name Query Response message header

- **Question Entry Count** A 2-byte field indicating the number of entries in the Question Entries section of the DNS message.

- **Answer RR Count** A 2-byte field indicating the number of RRs in the Answer RRs section of the DNS message.

- **Authority RR Count** A 2-byte field indicating the number of RRs in the Authority RRs section of the DNS message.

- **Additional RR Count** A 2-byte field indicating the number of RRs in the Additional RRs section of the DNS message.

Figure 15-3 shows the format of the Flags field in the DNS header.

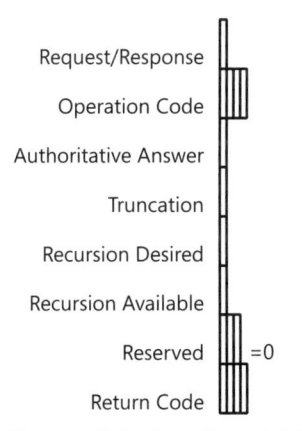

Figure 15-3 The Flags field

The fields within the Flags field are the following:

- **Request/Response** A 1-bit field that is set to 0 for a name query request and 1 for a name query response.

- **Operation Code** A 4-bit field that indicates the name service operation of the message. The Operation Code field is set to 0 for a query operation. For a complete and current list of operation code values, see *http://www.iana.org/assignments/dns-parameters*.

- **Authoritative Answer** A 1-bit field that indicates, when set to 1 in a name query response, that the responder is authoritative for the fully-qualified domain name (FQDN) in the Question RRs section of the message.

- **Truncation** A 1-bit field that indicates, when set to 1 in a name query response, that the total number of responses could not fit into the UDP-based response (for example, if the total number exceeds 512 bytes). In this case, only the first 512 bytes of the reply are returned. EDNS0 allows longer UDP-based DNS messages. EDNS0 is defined in RFC 2671.

- **Recursion Desired** A 1-bit field that indicates, when set to 1 in a name query request, that the query is recursive. When set to 0, the sender indicates an iterative query; the DNS server can return a list of other name servers that can be contacted to resolve the name.

- **Recursion Available** A 1-bit field that indicates, when set to 1 in a name query response, that the DNS server can perform recursive queries. DNS clients always set this value to zero in name query requests.

- **Reserved** A 3-bit field that is reserved and set to 0.

- **Return Code** A 4-bit field that indicates the return code in a name query response. A return code of 0 indicates a successful response; the answer to the name query is in the name query response. A return code of 2 indicates a DNS server failure because of an invalid configuration, a resource allocation error, or another critical failure. A return code of 3 indicates a name error, which is returned from an authoritative DNS server to indicate that the FQDN being queried does not exist. For a complete and current list of return code values, see *http://www.iana.org/assignments/dns-parameters*.

In a DNS name query request, the question entry contains the FQDN that is being resolved. Figure 15-4 shows the format of a question entry in the Question Entries section of a DNS name query request.

```
Question Name   |||||||||||||||||||||||   ...
Question Type   ||||||||||||||
Question Class  ||||||||||||||   =0x00-01
```

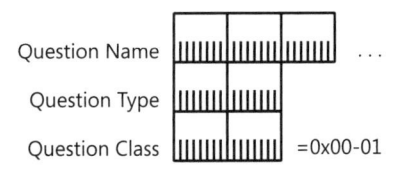

Figure 15-4 Question entry format

The fields in a question entry are the following:

- **Question Name** A variable-sized field that contains the FQDN being queried. The FQDN is expressed as a sequence of labels using a length-value format. The domain contoso.com, for example, consists of two labels (*contoso* and *com*). In the Question Name field, the domain name is encoded as a series of length-value pairs consisting of a 1-byte Length field that indicates the length of the value, followed by the value (the label). The maximum size of a label is 63 bytes. For example, the FQDN contoso.com is expressed as 0x07contoso0x03com0x00, in which the hexadecimal digits represent the 1-byte Length field of each label, the ASCII characters represent the individual labels, and the final 0x00 is a 1-byte Length field with value zero indicating the end of the FQDN.

- **Question Type** A 2-byte field that indicates the type of RRs to return in the Answer RRs section of the successful DNS name query response. Table 15-1 lists the most commonly-used record types. For a complete and current list, see *http://www.iana.org/assignments/dns-parameters*.

- **Question Class** A 2-byte field that indicates the question class. This is always set to 1 to indicate the Internet (IN) question class.

Table 15-1 The Most Common Values of the Question Type Field

Question Type Value	Record
0x01	Host address (A) record
0x02	Name server (NS) record
0x05	Alias (CNAME) record
0x06	Start of Authority (SOA) record
0x0C (12)	Reverse-lookup (PTR) record
0x0F (15)	Mail exchanger (MX) record
0x1C (28)	IPv6 host (AAAA) record
0x21 (33)	Server selection (SRV) record (also known as a Service record)
0xFB (251)	Incremental zone transfer (IXFR) record
0xFC (252)	Standard zone transfer (AXFR) record
0xFF (255)	All records

The DNS Name Query Response message can contain RRs in the Answer RRs, Authority RRs, and Additional RRs sections. These RRs can answer the question in the Question Entries section, refer the requestor to another DNS server, or include additional information. Figure 15-5 shows the format of an RR in a DNS name query response.

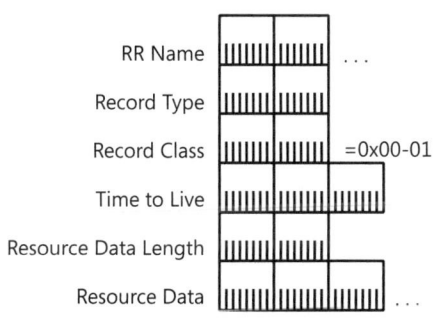

Figure 15-5 DNS RR format in a DNS name query response

The fields in an RR are the following:

- **RR Name** A variable-sized field that indicates an FQDN. This field can use the length-value encoding previously described, a 2-byte pointer value that indicates where the entire name already exists in the DNS message, or a combination of a length-value encoded name and 2-byte pointer.

- **Record Type** A 2-byte field that indicates the RR type, using the values listed in Table 15-1 (except for the value of 0xFF).

- **Record Class** A 2-byte field that indicates the record class. This is always set to 1 in current DNS implementations to indicate the Internet (IN) class.

- **Time To Live** A 4-byte field that indicates the number of seconds that the information in the RR should be considered valid and can be cached by the requestor. A value of 0 indicates the requestor should not cache the RR.

- **Resource Data Length** A 2-byte field that indicates the length of the resource data. For example, for an A record, the Resource Data Length field is set to 4 for the size of an IPv4 address. For an AAAA record, the Resource Data Length field is set to 16 for the size of an IPv6 address.

- **Resource Data** A variable-length field containing the data for the RR type. For example, for an A record, the Resource Data field contains an IPv4 address. For an AAAA record, the Resource Data field contains an IPv6 address.

If the FQDN or a portion of the FQDN is already present elsewhere in the DNS message, the RR Name field can be a 2-byte field whose value is a pointer to where the name is already present in the message. A pointer value is indicated by setting the two high-order bits in the first byte of the RR Name field to 11. If the first byte of the RR Name field is greater than or equal to 0xC0 (192), the RR Name field is a 2-byte pointer field. With the first 2 bits fixed at 11, the last 14 bits are used as a byte offset pointer (starting at 0) indicating the location of the name in the DNS message. This technique is known as message compression.

For a simple DNS Name Query Response message, the RR Name for an Answer RR is the same as the Resource Name for the Question entry, which begins in the 13th byte position from the beginning of the DNS message. But because you start counting the byte position from 0, the pointer value is set to 12. Figure 15-6 shows the Answer RR for this example.

For this example, the 2-byte RR Name field consisting of the first two bits set to 11 and the last 14 bits set to 00 0000 0000 1100 (or 12 in decimal). The resulting 2-byte field is 1100 0000 0000 1100, or 0xC0-0C. Figure 15-7 shows how this is displayed in Network Monitor 3.1.

When you click the Resource Name field in the Frame Details pane, Network Monitor 3.1 highlights the corresponding bytes in the Hex Details pane. In this example, when the Resource Name field in the Frame Details pane is selected, it corresponds to the hex digits 0xC0-0C, which indicates that the Resource Name field is pointing to the 12th byte offset (starting from 0) from the beginning of the DNS message, or the first byte of the Question Name field.

```
                    1 1 1 1 1 1
0 1 2 3 4 5 6 7 8 9 0 1 2 3 4 5
```

RR Name

| 1 | 1 | 0 | 0 | 0 | 0 | 0 | 0 | 0 | 0 | 0 | 0 | 1 | 1 | 0 | 0 |

Indicates Pointer

Indicates 12th Byte Offset (Starting at 0)

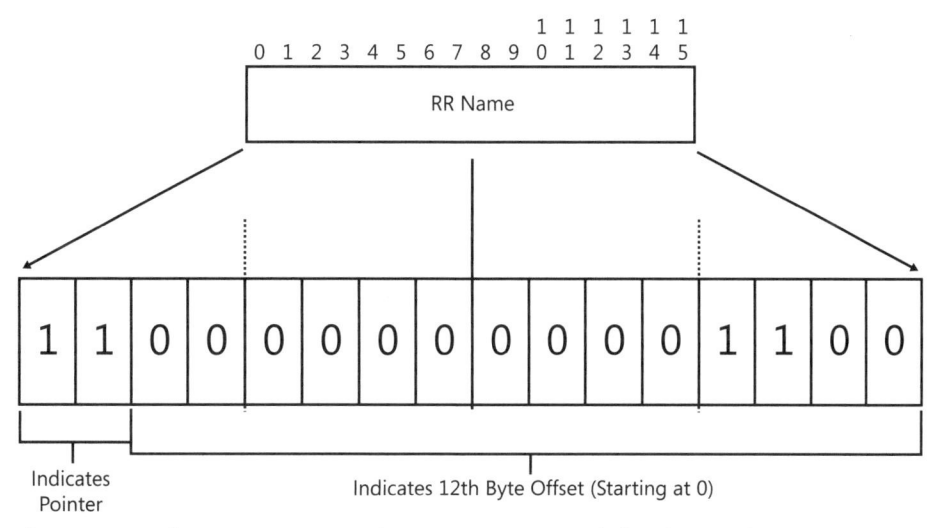

Figure 15-6 The RR Name as a pointer to a name stored elsewhere in the DNS message

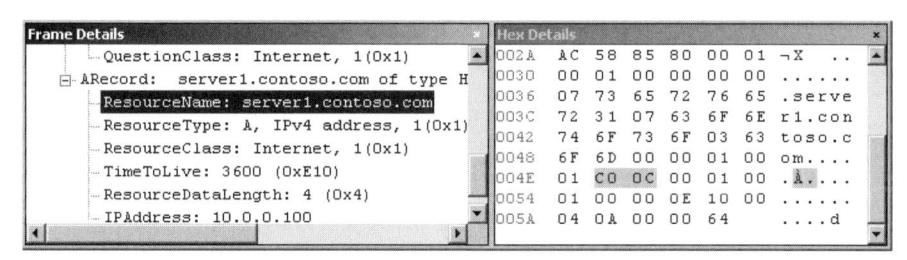

Figure 15-7 Example of a pointer value in the RR Name field in Network Monitor 3.1

DNS Update and Update Response Messages

The format of DNS Update and Update Response messages are very similar to the DNS Name Query Request and Name Query Response messages. DNS Update and Update Response messages share the same structure, as shown in Figure 15-8.

DNS Update or Update Response messages consist of a fixed-length 12-byte header and a variable-length section containing zone entries, prerequisite RRs, update RRs, and additional RRs.

Figure 15-9 shows the format of the 12-byte fixed DNS header for the DNS Update and Update Response messages.

The fields within this 12-byte fixed DNS header are the following:

- **Transaction ID** A 2-byte field used to identify a specific DNS transaction. The sender of the update message creates the identifier and the responder copies it into the update response. This field can be used by the DNS client to match replies to outstanding updates, or by the DNS server to detect duplicated updates from a DNS client.

- **Flags** A 2-byte field containing flags. For more information, see Figure 15-10.

Figure 15-8 DNS Update and Update Response message structure

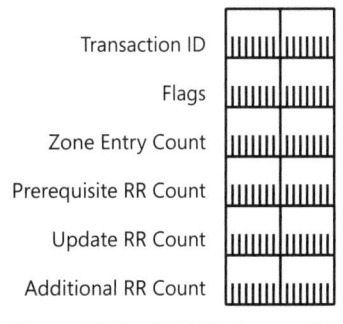

Figure 15-9 DNS Update and Update Response message header

- **Zone Entry Count** A 2-byte field indicating the number of entries in the Zone Entries section of the DNS message.

- **Prerequisite RR Count** A 2-byte field indicating the number of RRs in the Prerequisite RRs section of the DNS message.

- **Update RR Count** A 2-byte field indicating the number of RRs in the Update RRs section of the DNS message.

- **Additional RR Count** A 2-byte field indicating the number of RRs in the Additional RRs section of the DNS message.

Figure 15-10 shows the format of the Flags field for DNS Update and Update Response messages.

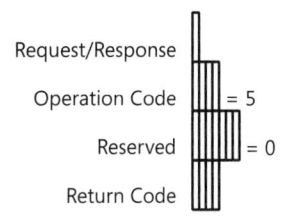

Figure 15-10 The Flags field for DNS Update and Update Response messages

The fields within the Flags field are the following:

- **Request/Response** A 1-bit field that is set to 0 for an update and 1 for an update response.
- **Operation Code** A 4-bit field that indicates the specific name service operation of the message, which is always set to 5 for DNS Update and Update Response messages.
- **Reserved** A 7-bit field that is reserved and set to 0.
- **Return Code** A 4-bit field that indicates the return code in an update response. Table 15-2 lists the Return Code values for Update Response messages.

Table 15-2 **Return Code Values for Update Response Messages**

Return Code Value	Description
0	No error; successful update.
1	Format error; the DNS server could not process the update request.
2	The DNS server encountered an internal error, such as a forwarding timeout.
3	A name that should exist does not exist.
4	The DNS server does not support the specified operation code.
5	The DNS server refuses to perform the update.
6	A name that should not exist does exist.
7	An RR set that should not exist does exist.
8	An RR set that should exist does not exist.
9	The DNS server is not authoritative for the zone named in the Zone Entries section.
10	A name used in the Prerequisite or Update sections is not within the zone specified by the Zone Entries section.

In a DNS update, a zone entry contains the FQDN for zone of the RRs that are being registered. Figure 15-11 shows the format of a zone entry in the Zone Entries section of a DNS update.

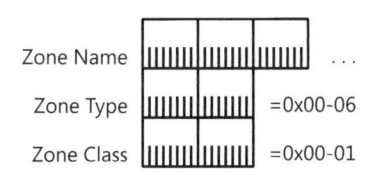

```
Zone Name  |||||||||||||||||||||||   ...
Zone Type  ||||||||||||||||  =0x00-06
Zone Class ||||||||||||||||  =0x00-01
```

Figure 15-11 Zone entry format

The fields in the zone entry are the following:

- **Zone Name** A variable-sized field that contains the FQDN of the zone, expressed as a sequence of labels using the length-value format previously described.
- **Zone Type** A 2-byte field that is set to 6 to indicate the SOA type.

- **Zone Class** A 2-byte field that indicates the zone class. This is always set to 1 in current DNS implementations to indicate the Internet (IN) zone class.

Prerequisite RRs contain a set of RR prerequisites that must be satisfied at the time the update message is received by the authoritative DNS server. The possible sets of values that can be expressed are the following:

- Resource record set exists (value independent)

    At least one RR with a specified name and type (in the zone and class specified by the Zone Entries section) must exist.

- Resource record set exists (value dependent)

    A set of RRs with the same name and type exists and has the same members with the same data as the RR set specified in this section.

- Resource record set does not exist

    No RRs with a specified name and type (in the zone and class denoted by the Zone Entries section) exist.

- Name is in use

    At least one RR with a specified name (in the zone and class specified by the Zone Entries section) exists.

- Name is not in use

    No RR of any type is owned by a specified name.

For more information about prerequisite RRs, see RFC 2136.

Update RRs contain the RRs that are to be added or deleted from the zone. The operations that can be performed during the update are the following:

- Add RRs to an RRs set.
- Delete an RRs set.
- Delete all RRs sets from a name.
- Delete an RR from an RRs set.

Additional RRs contain RRs that are related to the update or for new RRs being added by the update.

DNS clients running Windows Server 2008 or Windows Vista support secure dynamic updates. In a secure dynamic update, the DNS client and DNS server exchange a set of DNS messages to establish a security session. The subsequent update message sent by the DNS client contains a transaction signature record that validates the DNS client as the computer that sent the update. For more information, see RFC 2535.

DNS Message Exchanges

This section describes common DNS message exchanges for the following:

- Resolving names to addresses
- Resolving addresses to names
- Resolving aliases
- Dynamically updating DNS
- Transferring zone information between DNS servers

Resolving Names to Addresses

Resolving names to addresses, also known as forward name resolution, occurs when a DNS client or a DNS server sends a DNS server a DNS Name Query Request message containing an FQDN with instructions to return RRs of a specified type or all RRs. This message exchange consists of a DNS Name Query Request message and a DNS Name Query Response message.

An example of this message exchange is Capture 15-01, a Network Monitor trace that is included in the \Captures folder on the companion CD-ROM. The following is the DNS Name Query Request message from Capture 15-01 (Frame 1), as displayed with Network Monitor 3.1:

```
  Frame:
+ Ethernet: Etype = Internet IP (IPv4)
+ Ipv4: Next Protocol = UDP, Packet ID = 12998, Total IP Length = 65
- Udp: SrcPort = 53200, DstPort = DNS(53), Length = 45
    SourcePort: 53200, 53200(0xcfd0)
    DestinationPort: DNS(53), 53(0x35)
    TotalLength: 45 (0x2D)
    Checksum: 17716 (0x4534)
- Dns: QueryId = 0xAC58, QUERY (Standard query), Query  for  server1.contoso.com of type
Host Addr on class Internet
    QueryIdentifier: 44120 (0xAC58)
  - Flags:  Query, Opcode - QUERY (Standard query), RD, Rcode - Success
    QR:                (0..............) Query
    Opcode:            (.0000..........) QUERY (Standard query) 0
    AA:                (.....0.........) Not authoritative
    TC:                (......0........) Not truncated
    RD:                (.......1.......) Recursion desired
    RA:                (........0......) Recursive query support not available
    Zero:              (.........0.....) 0
    AuthenticatedData: (..........0....) Not AuthenticatedData
    CheckingDisabled:  (...........0...) Not CheckingDisabled
    Rcode:             (............0000) Success 0
    QuestionCount: 1 (0x1)
    AnswerCount: 0 (0x0)
    NameServerCount: 0 (0x0)
    AdditionalCount: 0 (0x0)
```

```
  - QRecord:  server1.contoso.com of type Host Addr on class Internet
    QuestionName: server1.contoso.com
    QuestionType: A, IPv4 address, 1(0x1)
    QuestionClass: Internet, 1(0x1)
```

In this frame, a DNS client sends a DNS Name Query Request message requesting the DNS server to return all A RRs for the FQDN server1.contoso.com. Note how the DNS client is using a dynamically allocated source UDP port and the destination UDP port of 53, which is the port on which the DNS server is listening for incoming DNS request messages. Also note that this is a recursive request (the Recursion Desired flag is set to 1).

The following is the corresponding DNS Name Query Response message from Capture 15-01 (Frame 2), as displayed with Network Monitor 3.1:

```
  Frame:
+ Ethernet: Etype = Internet IP (IPv4)
+ Ipv4: Next Protocol = UDP, Packet ID = 1212, Total IP Length = 81
- Udp: SrcPort = DNS(53), DstPort = 53200, Length = 61
    SourcePort: DNS(53), 53(0x35)
    DestinationPort: 53200, 53200(0xcfd0)
    TotalLength: 61 (0x3D)
    Checksum: 14778 (0x39BA)
- Dns: QueryId = 0xAC58, QUERY (Standard query), Response - Success
    QueryIdentifier: 44120 (0xAC58)
  - Flags:  Response, Opcode - QUERY (Standard query), AA, RD, RA, Rcode - Success
      QR:                  (1..............) Response
      Opcode:              (.0000..........) QUERY (Standard query) 0
      AA:                  (.....1..........) Is authoritative
      TC:                  (......0.........) Not truncated
      RD:                  (.......1........) Recursion desired
      RA:                  (........1.......) Recursive query support available
      Zero:                (.........0......) 0
      AuthenticatedData:   (..........0.....) Not AuthenticatedData
      CheckingDisabled:    (...........0....) Not CheckingDisabled
      Rcode:               (............0000) Success 0
    QuestionCount: 1 (0x1)
    AnswerCount: 1 (0x1)
    NameServerCount: 0 (0x0)
    AdditionalCount: 0 (0x0)
  - QRecord:  server1.contoso.com of type Host Addr on class Internet
    QuestionName: server1.contoso.com
    QuestionType: A, IPv4 address, 1(0x1)
    QuestionClass: Internet, 1(0x1)
  - ARecord:  server1.contoso.com of type Host Addr on class Internet
    ResourceName: server1.contoso.com
    ResourceType: A, IPv4 address, 1(0x1)
    ResourceClass: Internet, 1(0x1)
    TimeToLive: 3600 (0xE10)
    ResourceDataLength: 4 (0x4)
    IPAddress: 10.0.0.100
```

The name query response is sent back to the UDP port of the DNS client and contains the same Transaction ID value as the name query request (the *QueryIdentifier* field in the Network

Monitor 3.1 display). Note that the DNS server that sent this message is authoritative for the record (the Authoritative flag is set to 1) and the message contains all of the requested records (the Truncation flag is set to 0). The Question Entries portion of the message contains the original question entry from the Name Query Request message. The Answer RRs section contains a single answer RR for the IPv4 address 10.0.0.100, which the DNS client can cache for 3600 seconds (60 minutes).

Resolving Addresses to Names

Resolving addresses to names, also known as reverse name resolution, occurs when a DNS client or DNS server sends a DNS server a Name Query Request message containing an FQDN corresponding to an IPv4 address in the reverse namespace, with instructions to return all PTR RRs. For example, the FQDN corresponding to the IPv4 address 131.107.48.28 in the reverse DNS namespace is 28.48.107.131.in-addr.arpa.

An example of this message exchange is Capture 15-02, a Network Monitor trace that is included in the \Captures folder on the companion CD-ROM. The following is the DNS Name Query Request message from Capture 15-02 (Frame 1), as displayed with Network Monitor 3.1:

```
  Frame:
+ Ethernet: Etype = Internet IP (IPv4)
+ Ipv4: Next Protocol = UDP, Packet ID = 13033, Total IP Length = 69
+ Udp: SrcPort = 53206, DstPort = DNS(53), Length = 49
- Dns: QueryId = 0xB75C, QUERY (Standard query), Query  for  100.0.0.10.in-addr.arpa of type PTR on class Internet
    QueryIdentifier: 46940 (0xB75C)
  + Flags:  Query, Opcode - QUERY (Standard query), RD, Rcode - Success
    QuestionCount: 1 (0x1)
    AnswerCount: 0 (0x0)
    NameServerCount: 0 (0x0)
    AdditionalCount: 0 (0x0)
  - QRecord:  100.0.0.10.in-addr.arpa of type PTR on class Internet
     QuestionName: 100.0.0.10.in-addr.arpa
     QuestionType: PTR, Domain name pointer, 12(0xc)
     QuestionClass: Internet, 1(0x1)
```

In this frame, a DNS client is requesting that the DNS server return all PTR RRs for the FQDN 100.0.0.10.in-addr.arpa.

The following is the corresponding DNS Name Query Response message from Capture 15-02 (Frame 2), as displayed with Network Monitor 3.1:

```
  Frame:
+ Ethernet: Etype = Internet IP (IPv4)
+ Ipv4: Next Protocol = UDP, Packet ID = 1225, Total IP Length = 102
+ Udp: SrcPort = DNS(53), DstPort = 53206, Length = 82
- Dns: QueryId = 0xB75C, QUERY (Standard query), Response - Success
    QueryIdentifier: 46940 (0xB75C)
  + Flags:  Response, Opcode - QUERY (Standard query), AA, RD, RA, Rcode - Success
    QuestionCount: 1 (0x1)
```

```
    AnswerCount: 1 (0x1)
    NameServerCount: 0 (0x0)
    AdditionalCount: 0 (0x0)
 - QRecord:   100.0.0.10.in-addr.arpa of type PTR on class Internet
    QuestionName: 100.0.0.10.in-addr.arpa
    QuestionType: PTR, Domain name pointer, 12(0xc)
    QuestionClass: Internet, 1(0x1)
 - ARecord:   100.0.0.10.in-addr.arpa of type PTR on class Internet
    ResourceName: 100.0.0.10.in-addr.arpa
    ResourceType: PTR, Domain name pointer, 12(0xc)
    ResourceClass: Internet, 1(0x1)
    TimeToLive: 3600 (0xE10)
    ResourceDataLength: 21 (0x15)
    DomainNamePointer: server1.contoso.com
```

Note that the Answer RRs section in this case contains a single answer RR for the FQDN server1.contoso.com, which the DNS client can cache for 3600 seconds (60 minutes).

Resolving Aliases

The CNAME RR allows you to create an alias for an FQDN. For example, you can create an alias s1.contoso.com for the FQDN server1.contoso.com. When a DNS client performs forward name resolution and the name corresponds to a CNAME record on the DNS server, the DNS server returns multiple records in the answer section: the CNAME record and the records for the aliased name.

An example of this message exchange is Capture 15-03, a Network Monitor trace that is included in the \Captures folder on the companion CD-ROM. In Frame 1 of this exchange (not shown), a DNS client is requesting all A records for the name s1.contoso.com. On the DNS server, the s1.contoso.com FQDN corresponds to a CNAME record for the alias server1.contoso.com. The following is the DNS Name Query Response message from Capture 15-03 (Frame 2), as displayed with Network Monitor 3.1:

```
  Frame:
+ Ethernet: Etype = Internet IP (IPv4)
+ Ipv4: Next Protocol = UDP, Packet ID = 1279, Total IP Length = 98
+ Udp: SrcPort = DNS(53), DstPort = 53223, Length = 78
- Dns: QueryId = 0xBC54, QUERY (Standard query), Response - Success
    QueryIdentifier: 48212 (0xBC54)
  + Flags:  Response, Opcode - QUERY (Standard query), AA, RD, RA, Rcode - Success
    QuestionCount: 1 (0x1)
    AnswerCount: 2 (0x2)
    NameServerCount: 0 (0x0)
    AdditionalCount: 0 (0x0)
  - QRecord:   s1.contoso.com of type Host Addr on class Internet
    QuestionName: s1.contoso.com
    QuestionType: A, IPv4 address, 1(0x1)
    QuestionClass: Internet, 1(0x1)
  - ARecord:   s1.contoso.com of type CNAME on class Internet
    ResourceName: s1.contoso.com
    ResourceType: CNAME, Canonical name for an alias, 5(0x5)
    ResourceClass: Internet, 1(0x1)
```

```
            TimeToLive: 3600 (0xE10)
            ResourceDataLength: 10 (0xA)
            CName: server1.contoso.com
        - ARecord:  server1.contoso.com of type Host Addr on class Internet
            ResourceName: server1.contoso.com
            ResourceType: A, IPv4 address, 1(0x1)
            ResourceClass: Internet, 1(0x1)
            TimeToLive: 3600 (0xE10)
            ResourceDataLength: 4 (0x4)
            IPAddress: 10.0.0.100
```

Note that the first answer record is the CNAME record that maps the FQDN s1.contoso.com to the FQDN server1.contoso.com. The second answer record is an A record for the IPv4 address of the FQDN server1.contoso.com.

Dynamically Updating DNS

DNS dynamic updates, described in RFC 2136, are an exchange of DNS Update and Update Response messages that allows DNS clients to add or delete a specific RR or sets of RRs, known as RRSets, to any zone. Dynamic updates can simplify the process of managing the contents of a DNS zone, especially in an environment that uses automated configuration with the Dynamic Host Configuration Protocol (DHCP).

Dynamic update requests can also state prerequisites specified separately from update operations. These can be tested before an update can occur. When prerequisites are used with dynamic updates, the updates are said to be *atomic*; that is, all prerequisites must be satisfied for the update operation to occur.

An example of this message exchange is Capture 15-04, a Network Monitor trace that is included in the \Captures folder on the companion CD-ROM. The following is the DNS Update message from Capture 15-04 (Frame 1), as displayed with Network Monitor 3.1:

```
  Frame:
+ Ethernet: Etype = Internet IP (IPv4)
+ Ipv4: Next Protocol = UDP, Packet ID = 35, Total IP Length = 156
+ Udp: SrcPort = 53285, DstPort = DNS(53), Length = 136
- Dns: QueryId = 0x8EB7, Update, Query  for  contoso.com of type SOA on class Internet
      QueryIdentifier: 36535 (0x8EB7)
   - Flags:  Query, Opcode - Update, Rcode - Success
      QR:                (0..............) Query
      Opcode:            (.0101..........) Update 5
      AA:                (.....0..........) Not authoritative
      TC:                (......0.........) Not truncated
      RD:                (.......0........) Recursion not desired
      RA:                (........0.......) Recursive query support not available
      Zero:              (.........0......) 0
      AuthenticatedData: (..........0.....) Not AuthenticatedData
      CheckingDisabled:  (...........0....) Not CheckingDisabled
      Rcode:             (............0000) Success 0
      QuestionCount: 1 (0x1)
      AnswerCount: 1 (0x1)
```

```
            NameServerCount: 4 (0x4)
            AdditionalCount: 0 (0x0)
          - QRecord:  contoso.com of type SOA on class Internet
            QuestionName: contoso.com
            QuestionType: SOA, Marks the start of a zone of authority, 6(0x6)
            QuestionClass: Internet, 1(0x1)
          - ARecord:  VistaPC.contoso.com of type CNAME on class None
            ResourceName: VistaPC.contoso.com
            ResourceType: CNAME, Canonical name for an alias, 5(0x5)
            ResourceClass: None, 254(0xfe)
            TimeToLive: 0 (0x0)
            ResourceDataLength: 0 (0x0)
          - AuthorityRecord:  VistaPC.contoso.com of type AAAA on class Any
            ResourceName: VistaPC.contoso.com
            ResourceType: AAAA, IPv6 Address, 28(0x1c)
            ResourceClass: Any, 255(0xff)
            TimeToLive: 0 (0x0)
            ResourceDataLength: 0 (0x0)
          - AuthorityRecord:  VistaPC.contoso.com of type Host Addr on class Any
            ResourceName: VistaPC.contoso.com
            ResourceType: A, IPv4 address, 1(0x1)
            ResourceClass: Any, 255(0xff)
            TimeToLive: 0 (0x0)
            ResourceDataLength: 0 (0x0)
          - AuthorityRecord:  VistaPC.contoso.com of type AAAA on class Internet
            ResourceName: VistaPC.contoso.com
            ResourceType: AAAA, IPv6 Address, 28(0x1c)
            ResourceClass: Internet, 1(0x1)
            TimeToLive: 1200 (0x4B0)
            ResourceDataLength: 16 (0x10)
            IPv6Address: 2001:DB8:0:0:B500:734B:FE5B:3945
          - AuthorityRecord:  VistaPC.contoso.com of type Host Addr on class Internet
            ResourceName: VistaPC.contoso.com
            ResourceType: A, IPv4 address, 1(0x1)
            ResourceClass: Internet, 1(0x1)
            TimeToLive: 1200 (0x4B0)
            ResourceDataLength: 4 (0x4)
            IPAddress: 10.0.0.3
```

In this frame, a DNS client sends a DNS Update message requesting that the DNS server register an A record for the name vistapc.contoso.com with the IPv4 address 10.0.0.3 and an AAAA record for the name vistapc.contoso.com with the IPv6 address 2001:db8:0:0:b500:734b:fe5b:3945. This DNS Update message is not being sent securely. Secure DNS Update messages include a Transaction Signature record in the Additional RRs section of the message.

The following is the corresponding DNS Update Response message from Capture 15-04 (Frame 2), as displayed with Network Monitor 3.1:

```
  Frame:
+ Ethernet: Etype = Internet IP (IPv4)
+ Ipv4: Next Protocol = UDP, Packet ID = 1518, Total IP Length = 156
+ Udp: SrcPort = DNS(53), DstPort = 53285, Length = 136
- Dns: QueryId = 0x8EB7, Update, Response - Success
```

```
    QueryIdentifier: 36535 (0x8EB7)
  - Flags: Response, Opcode - Update, Rcode - Success
    QR:                       (1..............) Response
    Opcode:                   (.0101...........) Update 5
    AA:                       (.....0..........) Not authoritative
    TC:                       (......0.........) Not truncated
    RD:                       (.......0........) Recursion not desired
    RA:                       (........0.......) Recursive query support not available
    Zero:                     (.........0......) 0
    AuthenticatedData:        (..........0.....) Not AuthenticatedData
    CheckingDisabled:         (...........0....) Not CheckingDisabled
    Rcode:                    (............0000) Success 0
    QuestionCount: 1 (0x1)
    AnswerCount: 1 (0x1)
    NameServerCount: 4 (0x4)
    AdditionalCount: 0 (0x0)
  - QRecord:  contoso.com of type SOA on class Internet
    QuestionName: contoso.com
    QuestionType: SOA, Marks the start of a zone of authority, 6(0x6)
    QuestionClass: Internet, 1(0x1)
  - ARecord:  VistaPC.contoso.com of type CNAME on class None
    ResourceName: VistaPC.contoso.com
    ResourceType: CNAME, Canonical name for an alias, 5(0x5)
    ResourceClass: None, 254(0xfe)
    TimeToLive: 0 (0x0)
    ResourceDataLength: 0 (0x0)
  - AuthorityRecord:  VistaPC.contoso.com of type AAAA on class Any
    ResourceName: VistaPC.contoso.com
    ResourceType: AAAA, IPv6 Address, 28(0x1c)
    ResourceClass: Any, 255(0xff)
    TimeToLive: 0 (0x0)
    ResourceDataLength: 0 (0x0)
  - AuthorityRecord:  VistaPC.contoso.com of type Host Addr on class Any
    ResourceName: VistaPC.contoso.com
    ResourceType: A, IPv4 address, 1(0x1)
    ResourceClass: Any, 255(0xff)
    TimeToLive: 0 (0x0)
    ResourceDataLength: 0 (0x0)
  - AuthorityRecord:  VistaPC.contoso.com of type AAAA on class Internet
    ResourceName: VistaPC.contoso.com
    ResourceType: AAAA, IPv6 Address, 28(0x1c)
    ResourceClass: Internet, 1(0x1)
    TimeToLive: 1200 (0x4B0)
    ResourceDataLength: 16 (0x10)
    IPv6Address: 2001:DB8:0:0:B500:734B:FE5B:3945
  - AuthorityRecord:  VistaPC.contoso.com of type Host Addr on class Internet
    ResourceName: VistaPC.contoso.com
    ResourceType: A, IPv4 address, 1(0x1)
    ResourceClass: Internet, 1(0x1)
    TimeToLive: 1200 (0x4B0)
    ResourceDataLength: 4 (0x4)
    IPAddress: 10.0.0.3
```

The update response confirms the success of the registration and contains the records that were registered.

Transferring Zone Information Between DNS Servers

There are three methods of performing zone transfer for DNS servers running Windows Server 2008:

- **Traditional zone transfer** This method, described in RFC 1034, involves the secondary server requesting a full copy of the zone from the primary server.

- **Incremental zone transfer** This method, defined in RFC 1995, requires the DNS server hosting the primary zone to keep a record of the changes that are made between each increment of the zone's sequence number. The secondary zone can thus request only the changes that occurred since the last time the secondary zone was updated.

- **Active Directory zone transfer** In this method, Active Directory zones are replicated to all domain controllers using Active Directory replication. Active Directory replication does not use the DNS protocol.

The traditional zone transfer mechanism can be wasteful of network resources if the change in the transferred RRs is small in relation to the overall zone. In such cases, incremental zone transfer is more efficient.

The Network Monitor Capture 15-05 (included in the \Captures folder on the companion CD-ROM) provides an example of a traditional zone transfer. In the capture, a secondary DNS server for a zone creates a TCP connection with the primary DNS server and requests a zone transfer. The secondary DNS server requests the zone transfer over the TCP connection; the transfer occurs; and the secondary DNS server terminates the TCP connection.

Incremental zone transfers can be more efficient than traditional zone transfers for both large and dynamic zones. However, they place additional processing requirements on the DNS server, which needs to keep track of the zone differences and sends only the changed records. By default, the DNS Server service for Windows Server 2008 uses incremental transfers when possible.

The Network Monitor Capture 15-06 (included in the \Captures folder on the companion CD-ROM) provides an example of an incremental zone transfer. In the capture, a secondary DNS server for a zone first queries a primary DNS server for the SOA record and then requests an incremental zone transfer. For this example capture, the changed records fit within a single UDP message. Therefore, the entire incremental zone transfer is done with a single UDP-based reply message (frame 4). If the changes did not fit within a single UDP message, the reply message would have the Truncated flag set to 1. The secondary server would then create a TCP connection to the primary DNS server and request the zone transfer using TCP.

Active Directory replication is a method of zone transfer that can be used only with Windows Server 2008 or Windows Server 2003 domain controllers. Normal DNS zone transfers are pull in nature—the secondary DNS servers pull the zone or zone changes from the primary server. Active Directory replication, on the other hand, is push in nature—the directory changes are pushed from the domain controller on which the change occurred to the other domain controllers. For zones that do not change often, Active Directory replication ensures that all DNS servers storing the zone are updated quickly. For more dynamic zones this tends to smooth the replication traffic. Active Directory replication does not use the DNS protocol and is not described in this book.

Summary

DNS has a common message format for DNS Name Query Request and Name Query Response messages and a different common message format for DNS Update and Update Response messages. DNS messages have a fixed-size portion and a variable sized portion. The variable-sized portion contains entries and records to perform name resolution, registration, and zone transfers between DNS servers. DNS name resolution, either for a recursive or iterative query, consists of an exchange of DNS Name Query Request and Name Query Response messages. For successful resolution, the Name Query Response message contains the RRs for the FQDN that was requested. DNS name registration consists of an exchange of DNS Update and Update Response messages. For successful registration, the DNS Update Response message contains the data that was registered. Zone transfers between DNS servers can transfer the entire zone in a full or traditional zone transfer, or just the changes to the zone in an incremental zone transfer.

Chapter 16
Windows Internet Name Service (WINS)

In this chapter:
NetBT Name Service Messages 333
WINS Client and Server Message Exchanges. 344
Summary. 352

Network Basic Input/Output System (NetBIOS) is a protocol that provides commands and support for network name registration and verification, session establishment and termination, reliable connection-oriented session data transfer, unreliable connectionless datagram data transfer, and protocol and adapter monitoring and management. NetBIOS is also a standard application programming interface (API) so that user applications can utilize the services of installed network protocol stacks. The NetBIOS API is not discussed in this chapter.

NetBIOS over TCP/IP (NetBT) is the operation of the NetBIOS protocol over the Transmission Control Protocol (TCP) and the User Datagram Protocol (UDP) of the TCP/IP protocol stack. Windows Internet Name Service (WINS) is the Windows implementation of a NetBIOS name server (NBNS), which provides a distributed database for registering and resolving NetBIOS names to IP addresses used on your network.

This chapter describes the details of NetBT messages for WINS-based name resolution and registration and common NetBT message exchanges between WINS clients and WINS servers.

Note This chapter assumes prior knowledge of NetBT including NetBIOS names, NetBIOS name resolution, NetBIOS node types, the components of a WINS infrastructure (WINS client, WINS server, and WINS proxy), and their operation and configuration in Microsoft Windows. For more information, see Chapter 11, "NetBIOS over TCP/IP," and Chapter 12, "Windows Internet Name Service Overview," of the "TCP/IP Fundamentals for Microsoft Windows" book, located in the \Fundamentals folder on the companion CD-ROM.

NetBT Name Service Messages

WINS clients and WINS servers communicate by exchanging NetBT name service messages. NetBT messages and protocol operation are defined in RFCs 1001 and 1002. There are many types of NetBT name service messages defined in RFC 1002, which are typically sent as UDP messages. Both the WINS client and the WINS server listen on UDP port 137. The types of NetBT name service messages that are described in this chapter are the following:

- **Name Query Request**   Sent by a WINS client to a WINS server to perform NetBIOS name resolution.

- **Name Query Response**   Sent by a WINS server to a WINS client to respond to a name query request. There is a positive name query response and a negative name query response.

- **Name Registration Request**   Sent by a WINS client to a WINS server to perform name registration.

- **Name Registration Response**   Sent by a WINS server to a WINS client to respond to a name registration request. There is a positive name registration response and a negative name registration response.

- **Wait Acknowledgment**   Sent by a WINS server to a WINS client during name registration when confirming the ownership of an existing name previously registered by another client.

- **Name Refresh Request**   Sent by a WINS client to a WINS server to refresh a name that was previously registered. The response to a name refresh request is a name registration response.

- **Name Release Request**   Sent by a WINS client to a WINS server to release the registration of a name that was previously registered.

- **Name Release Response**   Sent by a WINS server to a WINS client to respond to a name release request. There is a positive name release response and a negative name release response.

More Info   All of the RFCs referenced in this chapter can be found in the \Standards\Chap16_WINS folder on the companion CD-ROM.

NetBIOS Name Service Messages

NetBIOS name service messages share a common structure, as shown in Figure 16-1.

NetBIOS name service messages consist of the following:

- **Name Service header**   Fixed length (12 bytes long), containing information about the type of name service message and the numbers of the other records in the message.

- **Question entries**   Variable length for NetBIOS Name Registration, Refresh, or Release messages. This portion of the message contains the NetBIOS name being acted on by the message.

Chapter 16: Windows Internet Name Service (WINS)

```
┌─────────────────────────────────────┐
│      Name Service Header            │
│      (12 byte fixed length)         │
├─────────────────────────────────────┤
│      Question Entries               │
│      (variable length)              │
├─────────────────────────────────────┤
│      Answer RRs                     │
│      (variable length)              │
├─────────────────────────────────────┤
│      Authority RRs                  │
│      (variable length)              │
├─────────────────────────────────────┤
│      Additional RRs                 │
│      (variable length)              │
└─────────────────────────────────────┘
```

Figure 16-1 NetBIOS name service message structure

- **Answer RRs** Variable length, containing resource records (RRs) returned in response to a question entry.

- **Authority RRs** Variable length, containing RRs used to indicate the authority for the question being asked. These are not used by the WINS Server service in Windows Server 2008.

- **Additional RRs** Variable length, containing other RRs that are not an answer to a question entry.

This is almost the same structure as Domain Name System (DNS) Name Query Request and Response messages that are described in Chapter 15, "Domain Name System."

Figure 16-2 shows the format of the 12-byte Name Service header for the NetBIOS name service messages.

```
        Transaction ID   ||||||||||||||||
                Flags    ||||||||||||||||
 Question Entry Count    ||||||||||||||||
     Answer RR Count     ||||||||||||||||
  Authority RR Count     ||||||||||||||||
 Additional RR Count     ||||||||||||||||
```

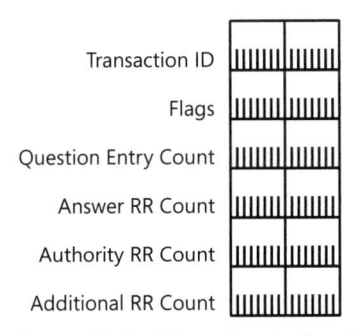

Figure 16-2 Name Service header

The fields within the 12-byte fixed Name Service header are the following:

- **Transaction ID** A 2-byte field that is used to identify a specific NetBIOS name service transaction. The sender of the request message creates the transaction ID and the responder copies it into the response message. This allows the WINS client to match the responses that it received from a WINS server with their requests. Each separate

NetBIOS name service transaction has a different transaction ID. For example, if a WINS client is registering multiple names, each Name Registration Request message has a different transaction ID.

- **Flags**   A 2-byte field containing flags. For more information, see Figure 16-3.
- **Question Entry Count**   A 2-byte field indicating the number of entries in the Question Entries section of the message. The sender of a request message always sets this value to 1 or more, although typically it is set at 1. The responder always sets this field to 0.
- **Answer RR Count**   A 2-byte field indicating the number of RRs in the Answer RRs section of the message. The sender of a request message sets this count to 0. The responder sets this to indicate the number of answers returned. This is typically 1 for unique NetBIOS name lookups and a larger number for Internet group name lookups.
- **Authority RR Count**   A 2-byte field indicating the number of RRs in the Authority RRs section of the message. Authority RRs are used for recursive NetBIOS name queries, which are not supported by the WINS Server service in Windows Server 2008. Therefore, this field is always set to 0 in NetBIOS name service messages to indicate that there are no authority RRs in the message.
- **Additional RR Count**   A 2-byte field indicating the number of RRs in the Additional RRs section of the NetBIOS name service message. These records are used when an RR needs to be included in any name service operation that is not a response to a name query request. For example, in a name release, an additional RR includes the name being released.

Figure 16-3 shows the format of the Flags field in the Name Service header.

```
Request/Response
Operation Code
Authoritative Answer
Truncation
Recursion Desired
Recursion Available
Reserved         =0
Return Code
```

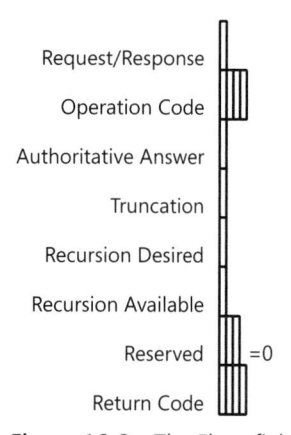

Figure 16-3   The Flags field in the Name Service header

The fields within the Flags field are the following:

- **Request/Response**   A 1-bit field that is set to 0 for a request message or 1 for a response message.
- **Operation Code**   A 4-bit field that indicates the specific name service operation of the message. See Table 16-1 for a list of Operation Code values.

- **Authoritative Answer**   A 1-bit field that indicates, when set to 1 in a name query response, that the sender is authoritative for the NetBIOS name. For name service requests, this flag is always set to 0. For name service responses, the computer responding to the request sets it to 1 if it is authoritative for a NetBIOS name.

- **Truncation**   A 1-bit field that indicates, when set to 1 in a name query response, that the message was truncated because the original datagram containing the entire message exceeded 576 bytes. Similar to DNS truncation, RFC 1001 describes the use of TCP to obtain the original datagram. Windows Server 2008 and Windows Vista do not support the use of TCP for NetBIOS name service messages. Therefore, the Truncation bit is always set to 0.

- **Recursion Desired**   A 1-bit field that indicates, when set to 1 in a name query request, that the query is recursive. When set to 0, the sender indicates an iterative query; the WINS server can return a list of other name servers that can be contacted to resolve the name. Windows Server 2008 and Windows Vista-based WINS clients set this flag to 1 for all name queries. If the flag is set to 1 in a name service message sent to a WINS server running Windows Server 2008, the WINS server sets it to 1 in the corresponding reply. Windows Server 2008 does not support iterative NetBIOS name queries.

- **Recursion Available**   A 1-bit field that indicates, when set to 1 in a name query response, that the WINS server can perform recursive queries. Set to 0 on all name request messages. The Windows Server 2008 WINS Server service sets this field to 1 in name service responses to indicate that it can perform recursive name query, name registration, and name release messages. If set to 0 in a response message, the client must iterate for name service queries and perform challenges for any name registrations.

- **Reserved**   A 2-bit field that is reserved and set to 0.

- **Broadcast**   A 1-bit field that indicates that the message is being sent as a broadcast (set to 1) or unicast (set to 0).

- **Return Code**   A 4-bit field that indicates the return code in a name query response. All name service requests set the value to 0. A return code of 0 in a name service response indicates a successful response (the answer is in the name query response message). A return code of 0 in name query responses means that the answer to the query is in the response message. A return code of 0 in name registrations means that the registration was successful.

Table 16-1   **NetBIOS Name Service Operation Codes**

Operation Code	Description
0	Name Query Request
5	Name Registration Request
6	Name Release
7	Wait Acknowledgment
8	Name Refresh

Note The field names in the NetBIOS name service message header in this chapter use the field names from the DNS message header, rather than the field names as defined in RFC 1002. Network Monitor 3.1 also uses the field names from the DNS header.

NetBIOS Name Representation

NetBIOS names in NetBIOS name service packets are encoded using a scheme that was designed to make them similar to DNS names. This was done because at the time that RFCs 1001 and 1002 were written, the DNS specifications were more restrictive in the types of characters that were allowed. For NetBIOS name service messages, the DNS form of a NetBIOS name is the concatenation of a converted NetBIOS name, the period (.) character, and the NetBIOS scope identifier (optional).

Creating the DNS form of a NetBIOS name for NetBIOS name service messages involves the following steps:

1. The 16-character NetBIOS name is converted into a 32-byte ASCII representation.
2. The period (.) character and the NetBIOS scope identifier are appended to the 32-byte ASCII representation of the NetBIOS name.
3. The resulting name is then encoded using length-value format according to the rules for fully qualified domain names (FQDNs) in DNS Name Query Request messages.

The first step involves converting the original 16-byte NetBIOS name into a 32-byte string by mapping each hexadecimal digit of the NetBIOS name to an ASCII character, as shown in Table 16-2.

Table 16-2 Converting the Hexadecimal Digit to an ASCII Character

Hexadecimal Digit	ASCII Character
0	A
1	B
2	C
3	D
4	E
5	F
6	G
7	H
8	I
9	J
A	K
B	L

Table 16-2 Converting the Hexadecimal Digit to an ASCII Character

Hexadecimal Digit	ASCII Character
C	M
D	N
E	O
F	P

This conversion results in a 32-byte string that contains only the ASCII characters A through P.

For example, consider the name of the Workstation service on the server named SERVER1. The full 16-character NetBIOS name of the Workstation service is **SERVER1   [00]**; that is, the name SERVER1 followed by eight spaces (or 0x20 in ASCII) and terminated by the hexadecimal value 0x00. When the characters of the NetBIOS name are expressed using their ASCII values and converted to hexadecimal format, the NetBIOS name becomes:

53-45-52-56-45-52-31-20-20-20-20-20-20-20-20-00

Converting this name into individual hexadecimal digits, the NetBIOS name becomes:

5-3-4-5-5-2-5-6-4-5-5-2-3-1-2-0-2-0-2-0-2-0-2-0-2-0-2-0-2-0-0-0

Converting this 32-digit hexadecimal representation of the NetBIOS name to a 32-byte ASCII string using Table 16-2, the result is the following:

FDEFFCFGEFFCDBCACACACACACACACAAA

The third step involves converting the name into the DNS length-value format. In DNS, domain names are expressed as a sequence of labels. For example, the DNS name contoso.com consists of two labels (*contoso* and *com*). Each label in a DNS message is formatted with a 1-byte-length field followed by the label. The DNS name contoso.com would be expressed as 0x07contoso0x03com0x00, in which the hexadecimal digits represent the length of each label, the ASCII characters represent the individual labels, and the final 0x00 indicates the end of the name.

To complete the DNS form of the NetBIOS name, the first label is the 32-byte converted NetBIOS name, with additional labels for the NetBIOS scope identifier (optional). If there is no NetBIOS scope identifier, the DNS form of the NetBIOS name **SERVER1   [00]** is the following:

0x20FDEFFCFGEFFCDBCACACACACACACACAAA0x00

If the NetBIOS scope identifier is contoso.com, the DNS form of the NetBIOS name **SERVER1   [00]** is the following:

0x20FDEFFCFGEFFCDBCACACACACACACACAAA0x07contoso0x03com0x00

Typical network sniffers, such as Microsoft Network Monitor, automatically interpret the DNS form of NetBIOS names. Figure 16-4 shows how a NetBIOS name within a NetBIOS name service message is displayed in Network Monitor 3.1.

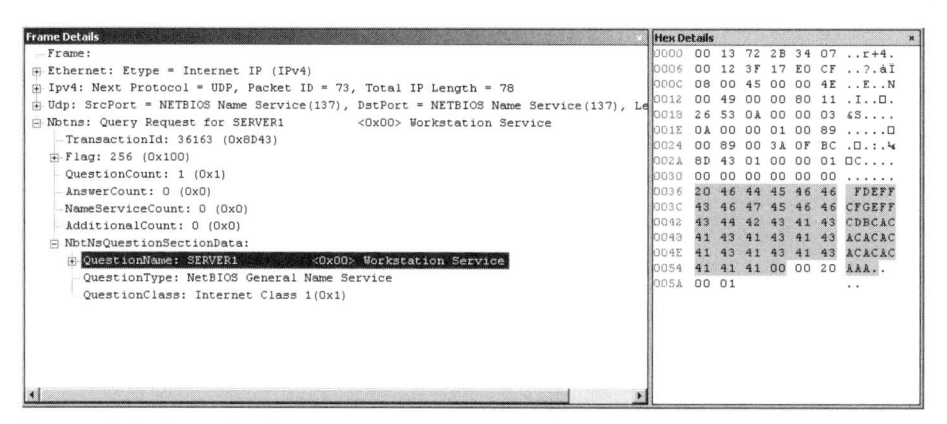

Figure 16-4 Example of a NetBIOS name in Network Monitor 3.1

When you click the Question Name field in the Frame Details pane, Network Monitor 3.1 highlights the corresponding bytes in the Hex Details pane. In this example, when the Question Name field in the Detail Frame is highlighted, it corresponds to the hexadecimal digits for the DNS form of the NetBIOS name SERVER1   [00].

Question RR Format

In a NetBIOS name service message, a question entry in the Question RR portion of the message contains the NetBIOS name that is being queried, registered, refreshed, or released. The format of a NetBIOS name service question entry is based on the DNS question entry in DNS Name Query Request and Response messages. Figure 16-5 shows the format of a Question entry.

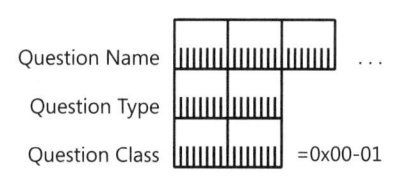

Figure 16-5 Question entry format

The fields in the question entry are the following:

- **Question Name** A variable-sized field that contains the NetBIOS name that is being queried, registered, refreshed, or released. The name is expressed using the DNS form of a NetBIOS name.

- **Question Type** A 2-byte field that indicates the type of response to return. For NetBIOS name operations, the question type is set to 0x00-20.

Chapter 16: Windows Internet Name Service (WINS)   **341**

- **Question Class** A 2-byte field that indicates the question class. This is always set to 1 to indicate the Internet (IN) question class.

The NetBIOS name service message can contain RRs in the Answer RRs and Additional RRs sections. These RRs can answer the question in the Question Entries section. Figure 16-6 shows the format of an RR in NetBIOS name service messages.

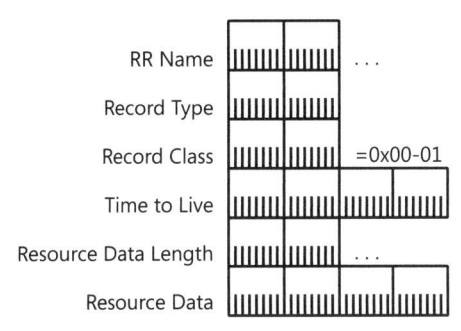

Figure 16-6 RR format in NetBIOS name service messages

The fields in an RR are the following:

- **RR Name** A variable-sized field that indicates either the DNS form of a NetBIOS name or a 2-byte pointer value that indicates where the NetBIOS name already exists in the message.
- **Record Type** A 2-byte field that indicates the RR type. See Table 16-3 for a list of record types defined in RFC 1002.
- **Record Class** A 2-byte field that indicates the record class. This is always set to 1 to indicate the Internet (IN) class.
- **Time to Live** A 4-byte field that indicates the number of seconds for the Time to Live (TTL) of the RR.
- **Resource Data Length** A 2-byte field that indicates the length of the resource data.
- **Resource Data** A variable-length field containing the data for the RR type.

Table 16-3 Values for the Record Type Field

Value	Description
0x00	IP Address RR
0x02	Name Server RR
0x0A	Null RR
0x20	NetBIOS General Name Service RR
0x21	NetBIOS Node Status RR

For NetBIOS General Name Service RRs (record type 0x20), the Resource Data field of the RR contains a 2-byte RDATA flags field and a 4-byte IP address corresponding to the name in the RR Name field. Figure 16-7 shows the format of an RR used in General Name Service RRs.

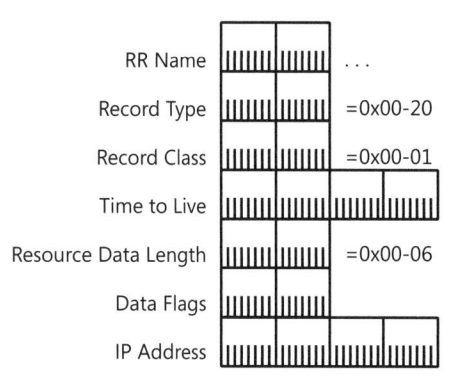

Figure 16-7 Format for General Name Service RRs

Figure 16-8 displays the format of the RDATA flags field.

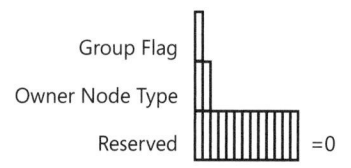

Figure 16-8 Format of the RDATA flags field

The RDATA field contains the following:

- **Group Flag**   A 1-bit field that indicates whether the name is a group name (set to 1) or a unique name (set to 0).

- **Owner Node Type**   A 2-bit field that indicates the NetBIOS node type of either the requestor or the owner of the NetBIOS name. The values for Windows Server 2008 and Windows Vista are 0 for B-Node, 1 for P-Node, 2 for M-Node, and 3 for H-Node.

- **Reserved**   A 13-bit field that is reserved and set to 0.

If the NetBIOS name is already present elsewhere in the DNS message, the RR Name field can be a 2-byte field whose value is a pointer to the NetBIOS name that is already present in the message. A pointer value is indicated by setting the two high-order bits in the first byte of the RR Name field to 11. If the first byte of the RR Name field is greater than or equal to 0xC0 (192), the RR Name field is a 2-byte pointer field. With the first 2 bits fixed at 11, the last 14 bits are used as a byte offset pointer (starting at 0) indicating the location of the NetBIOS name in the message.

For a simple Name Registration Request message, the RR Name for the Additional RR is the same as the Resource Name for the Question entry, which begins in the 13th byte position from the beginning of the message. But because we start counting the byte position from 0, the pointer value is set to 12. Figure 16-9 shows the RR Name in the Additional RR for this example.

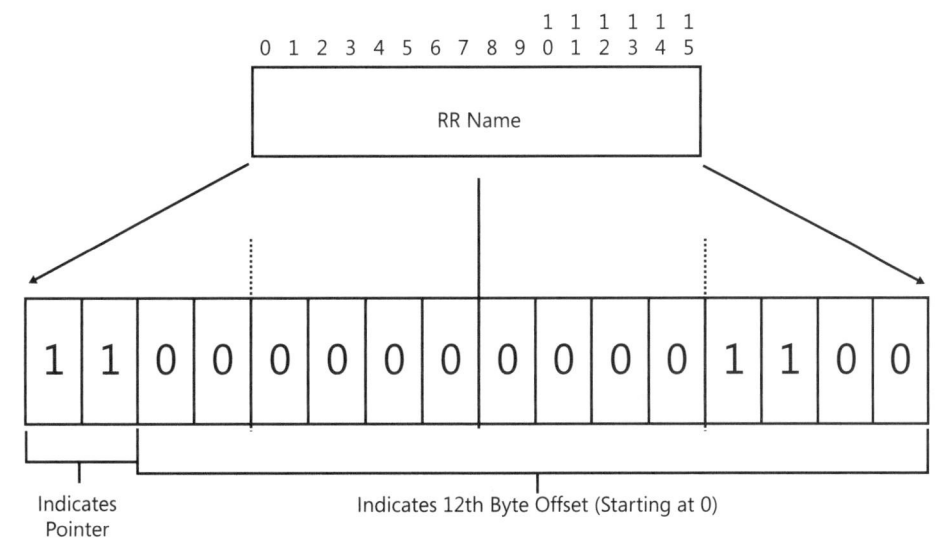

Figure 16-9 The RR Name as a pointer to a name stored elsewhere in the message

For this example, the 2-byte RR Name field consists of the first two bits set to 11 and the last 14 bits set to 00 0000 0000 1100 (or 12 in decimal). The resulting 2-byte field is 1100 0000 0000 1100, or 0xC0-0C. Figure 16-10 shows how this is displayed in Network Monitor 3.1.

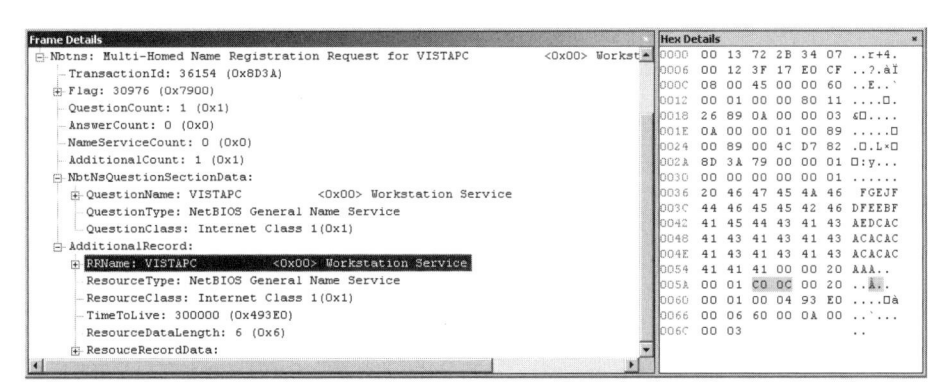

Figure 16-10 Example of a pointer value in the RR Name field in Network Monitor 3.1

When you click the Resource Name field in the Frame Details pane, Network Monitor 3.1 highlights the corresponding bytes in the Hex Details pane. In this example, when the RR Name field in the Detail Frame is highlighted, it corresponds to the hex digits 0xC0-0C, which indicates that the RR Name field is pointing to the 12th-byte offset (starting from 0) from the beginning of the message, or the first byte of the Question Name field.

WINS Client and Server Message Exchanges

This section describes common message exchanges between WINS clients and servers for the following:

- Resolving NetBIOS names to IP addresses
- Registering NetBIOS names
- Renewing NetBIOS names
- Releasing NetBIOS names

Resolving NetBIOS Names to IP Addresses

Resolving NetBIOS names to IP addresses occurs when a WINS client sends a WINS server a Name Query Request message containing a NetBIOS name. This message exchange consists of a Name Query Request message and either a Positive Name Query Response or Negative Name Query Response message.

An example of this message exchange is Capture 16-01, a Network Monitor trace that is included in the \Captures folder on the companion CD-ROM. The following is the Name Query Request message from Capture 16-01 (Frame 1), as displayed with Network Monitor 3.1:

```
  Frame:
+ Ethernet: Etype = Internet IP (IPv4)
+ Ipv4: Next Protocol = UDP, Packet ID = 73, Total IP Length = 78
- Udp: SrcPort = NETBIOS Name Service(137), DstPort = NETBIOS Name Service(137), Length = 58
    SourcePort: NETBIOS Name Service(137), 137(0x89)
    DestinationPort: NETBIOS Name Service(137), 137(0x89)
    TotalLength: 58 (0x3A)
    Checksum: 4028 (0xFBC)
- Nbtns: Query Request for SERVER1          <0x00> Workstation Service
    TransactionId: 36163 (0x8D43)
   - Flag: 256 (0x100)
      R:         (0..............) Request
      OPCode:    (.0000..........) Query
      AA:        (.....0.........) Non-authorized answer
      TC:        (......0........) Datagram not truncated
      RD:        (.......1.......) Recursion desired
      RA:        (........0......) Recursion not available
      Reserved:  (.........00....)
      B:         (...........0...) Not a broadcast packet
      RCode:     (............0000) Success
    QuestionCount: 1 (0x1)
    AnswerCount: 0 (0x0)
    NameServiceCount: 0 (0x0)
    AdditionalCount: 0 (0x0)
   - NbtNsQuestionSectionData:
    - QuestionName: SERVER1          <0x00> Workstation Service
```

```
    Name: SERVER1
    QuestionType: NetBIOS General Name Service
    QuestionClass: Internet Class 1(0x1)
```

In this frame, a WINS client sends a Name Query Request message requesting that the WINS server return an IP address for the NetBIOS name "SERVER1   [00]". Note how the WINS client is using the source and destination UDP port of 137. Also note that this is a recursive request (the Recursion Desired flag is set to 1).

The following is the corresponding Positive Name Query Response message from Capture 16-01 (Frame 2), as displayed with Network Monitor 3.1:

```
  Frame:
+ Ethernet: Etype = Internet IP (IPv4)
+ Ipv4: Next Protocol = UDP, Packet ID = 1839, Total IP Length = 90
+ Udp: SrcPort = NETBIOS Name Service(137), DstPort = NETBIOS Name Service(137), Length = 70
- Nbtns: Query Response, Success for SERVER1        <0x00> Workstation Service, 10.0.0.100
    TransactionId: 36163 (0x8D43)
  - Flag: 34176 (0x8580)
      R:         (1..............) Response
      OPCode:    (.0000...........) Query
      AA:        (.....1..........) Authorized answer
      TC:        (......0.........) Datagram not truncated
      RD:        (.......1........) Recursion desired
      RA:        (........1.......) Recursion available
      Reserved: (.........00.....)
      B:         (...........0....) Not a broadcast packet
      RCode:     (............0000) Success
    QuestionCount: 0 (0x0)
    AnswerCount: 1 (0x1)
    NameServiceCount: 0 (0x0)
    AdditionalCount: 0 (0x0)
  - AnswerRecord:
    - RRName: SERVER1        <0x00> Workstation Service
      Name: SERVER1
      ResourceType: NetBIOS General Name Service
      ResourceClass: Internet Class 1(0x1)
      TimeToLive: 0 (0x0)
      ResourceDataLength: 6 (0x6)
    - ResouceRecordData:
      - NBFlags: 0 (0x0)
        G:   (0..............) Unique NetBIOS Name
        ONT: (.00............) B node
        Rsv: (...0000000000000) Reserved
      NBAddress: 10.0.0.100
```

The positive name query response contains the same Transaction ID value as the name query request. Note that the WINS server that sent this message is authoritative for the record (the Authoritative flag is set to 1), and the message contains all of the requested records (the Truncation flag is set to 0). The Answer RRs section contains a single-answer RR for the IP address 10.0.0.100.

The following is an example of a Negative Name Query Response message from Capture 16-02 (Frame 2), as displayed with Network Monitor 3.1:

```
Frame:
+ Ethernet: Etype = Internet IP (IPv4)
+ Ipv4: Next Protocol = UDP, Packet ID = 1893, Total IP Length = 84
+ Udp: SrcPort = NETBIOS Name Service(137), DstPort = NETBIOS Name Service(137), Length = 64
- Nbtns: Query Response, Requested name doesn't exist for SERVER99          <0x00>
Workstation Service
    TransactionId: 36171 (0x8D4B)
  - Flag: 34179 (0x8583)
      R:         (1..............) Response
      OPCode:    (.0000...........) Query
      AA:        (.....1..........) Authorized answer
      TC:        (......0.........) Datagram not truncated
      RD:        (.......1........) Recursion desired
      RA:        (........1.......) Recursion available
      Reserved:  (.........00.....)
      B:         (...........0....) Not a broadcast packet
      RCode:     (............0011) Requested name doesn't exist
    QuestionCount: 0 (0x0)
    AnswerCount: 0 (0x0)
    NameServiceCount: 0 (0x0)
    AdditionalCount: 0 (0x0)
  - NegativeNMQueryRecord:
   + RRName: SERVER99           <0x00> Workstation Service
     ResourceType: Null
     ResourceClass: Internet Class 1(0x1)
     TimeToLive: 0 (0x0)
     ResourceDataLength: 0 (0x0)
```

Registering NetBIOS Names

An example of a message exchange to register a NetBIOS name with a WINS server is Capture 16-03, a Network Monitor trace that is included in the \Captures folder on the companion CD-ROM. The following is the Name Registration message from Capture 16-03 (Frame 1), as displayed with Network Monitor 3.1:

```
Frame:
+ Ethernet: Etype = Internet IP (IPv4)
+ Ipv4: Next Protocol = UDP, Packet ID = 1, Total IP Length = 96
+ Udp: SrcPort = NETBIOS Name Service(137), DstPort = NETBIOS Name Service(137), Length = 76
- Nbtns: Multi-Homed Name Registration Request for VISTAPC          <0x00>
Workstation Service, 10.0.0.3
    TransactionId: 36154 (0x8D3A)
  - Flag: 30976 (0x7900)
      R:         (0..............) Request
      OPCode:    (.1111...........) Multi-Homed Name Registration
      AA:        (.....0..........) Non-authorized answer
      TC:        (......0.........) Datagram not truncated
      RD:        (.......1........) Recursion desired
      RA:        (........0.......) Recursion not available
      Reserved:  (.........00.....)
```

```
    B:              (..........0....) Not a broadcast packet
    RCode:          (............0000) Success
  QuestionCount: 1 (0x1)
  AnswerCount: 0 (0x0)
  NameServiceCount: 0 (0x0)
  AdditionalCount: 1 (0x1)
- NbtNsQuestionSectionData:
  + QuestionName: VISTAPC          <0x00> Workstation Service
    QuestionType: NetBIOS General Name Service
    QuestionClass: Internet Class 1(0x1)
- AdditionalRecord:
  + RRName: VISTAPC                <0x00> Workstation Service
    ResourceType: NetBIOS General Name Service
    ResourceClass: Internet Class 1(0x1)
    TimeToLive: 300000 (0x493E0)
    ResourceDataLength: 6 (0x6)
  - ResouceRecordData:
    - NBFlags: 24576 (0x6000)
      G:   (0...............) Unique NetBIOS Name
      ONT: (.11.............) H node
      Rsv: (...0000000000000) Reserved
    NBAddress: 10.0.0.3
```

In this frame, a WINS client sends a Name Registration message requesting that the WINS server register the NetBIOS name **VISTAPC** <0x00> with the IP address 10.0.0.3.

The following is the corresponding Positive Name Registration Response message from Capture 16-03 (Frame 2), as displayed with Network Monitor 3.1:

```
  Frame:
+ Ethernet: Etype = Internet IP (IPv4)
+ Ipv4: Next Protocol = UDP, Packet ID = 1741, Total IP Length = 90
+ Udp: SrcPort = NETBIOS Name Service(137), DstPort = NETBIOS Name Service(137), Length = 70
- Nbtns: Registration Response, Success for VISTAPC          <0x00>
Workstation Service, 10.0.0.3
    TransactionId: 36154 (0x8D3A)
  - Flag: 44416 (0xAD80)
    R:       (1...............) Response
    OPCode:  (.0101...........) Registration
    AA:      (.....1..........) Authorized answer
    TC:      (......0.........) Datagram not truncated
    RD:      (.......1........) Recursion desired
    RA:      (........1.......) Recursion available
    Reserved: (.........00.....)
    B:       (...........0....) Not a broadcast packet
    RCode:   (............0000) Success
    QuestionCount: 0 (0x0)
    AnswerCount: 1 (0x1)
    NameServiceCount: 0 (0x0)
    AdditionalCount: 0 (0x0)
  - AnswerRecord:
  + RRName: VISTAPC               <0x00> Workstation Service
    ResourceType: NetBIOS General Name Service
    ResourceClass: Internet Class 1(0x1)
    TimeToLive: 2400 (0x960)
```

```
    ResourceDataLength: 6 (0x6)
 - ResouceRecordData:
  - NBFlags: 24576 (0x6000)
      G:   (0..............) Unique NetBIOS Name
      ONT: (.11............) H node
      Rsv: (...0000000000000) Reserved
    NBAddress: 10.0.0.3
```

The name registration response confirms the success of the registration and contains the IP address that was registered.

If the WINS server successfully registers the NetBIOS name, the return code is 0. Table 16-4 lists the return code values when the WINS server cannot register a unique name.

Table 16-4 Return Code Values for Name Registration Errors

Return Code Value	Description
1	Format error: The request was improperly formatted.
2	Server failure: There is a problem with the name server, such that it cannot process the name registration request.
4	Unsupported: The request is not supported by the NBNS.
5	Name registration request refused: For policy reasons, the NBNS could not register this name from this host. This is not used by the WINS Server service in Windows Server 2008.
6	Name active: Another node owns the name.
7	Name conflict: More than one end-node owns a unique NetBIOS name.

When a WINS server receives a request to register a unique NetBIOS name that is already registered, the WINS server verifies that the owner that originally registered the name still owns it. In this case, the WINS server sends a Wait Acknowledgment (WACK) message to the computer attempting to register the duplicate unique name. The WACK message informs the WINS client that the WINS server cannot provide a definitive positive or negative name registration response. The WINS server then sends a name query request to the owner of the registered name. Based on the response of the owner, the WINS server does one of the following:

- If the owner responds with a positive name query response, the WINS server sends the WINS client that sent the duplicate name registration request a negative name registration response.

- If the owner responds with a negative name query response or does not respond at all, the WINS server sends the WINS client that sent the duplicate name registration request a positive name registration response.

The Network Monitor trace in Capture 16-04 (included in the \Captures folder on the companion CD-ROM) shows this process.

The following is a summary of Frames 1 through 5 of Capture 16-04 in the \Captures folder on the companion CD-ROM.

```
Frame   Source           Dest             Description
1       10.10.1.52       10.152.236.200   Name Registration Request
2       10.152.236.200   10.10.1.52       WACK
3       10.152.236.200   10.152.236.212   Name Query Request
4       10.152.236.212   10.152.236.200   Positive Name Query Response
5       10.152.236.200   10.10.1.52       Negative Name Registration Response
```

In Frame 1, a WINS client (10.10.1.52) attempts to register the name JASMINE[00] with a WINS server (10.152.236.200). However, the WINS server already has a registration for that name. In Frame 2, the WINS server sends a WACK to the WINS client. In Frame 3, the WINS server queries the registered owner of the NetBIOS name JASMINE[00] (10.152.236.212). In Frame 4, the registered owner responds to the request with a positive name query response. Because the registered owner still owns the name, the WINS server sends a negative name registration response back to the WINS client with an error code set to 6, indicating that the unique name is active (Frame 5).

Refreshing NetBIOS Names

An example of a message exchange to refresh the existing registration of a NetBIOS name with a WINS server is Capture 16-05, a Network Monitor trace that is included in the \Captures folder on the companion CD-ROM. The following is the Name Refresh Request message from Capture 16-05 (Frame 1), as displayed with Network Monitor 3.1:

```
  Frame:
+ Ethernet: Etype = Internet IP (IPv4)
+ Ipv4: Next Protocol = UDP, Packet ID = 196, Total IP Length = 96
+ Udp: SrcPort = NETBIOS Name Service(137), DstPort = NETBIOS Name Service(137), Length = 76
- Nbtns: Refresh Request for VISTAPC          <0x20> File Server Service, 10.0.0.3
    TransactionId: 36176 (0x8D50)
  - Flag: 16384 (0x4000)
      R:        (0..............) Request
      OPCode:   (.1000..........) Refresh
      AA:       (.....0.........) Non-authorized answer
      TC:       (......0........) Datagram not truncated
      RD:       (.......0.......) Recursion not desired
      RA:       (........0......) Recursion not available
      Reserved: (.........00....)
      B:        (...........0...) Not a broadcast packet
      RCode:    (............0000) Success
    QuestionCount: 1 (0x1)
    AnswerCount: 0 (0x0)
    NameServiceCount: 0 (0x0)
    AdditionalCount: 1 (0x1)
  - NbtNsQuestionSectionData:
   + QuestionName: VISTAPC          <0x20> File Server Service
     QuestionType: NetBIOS General Name Service
     QuestionClass: Internet Class 1(0x1)
  - AdditionalRecord:
   + RRName: VISTAPC          <0x20> File Server Service
     ResourceType: NetBIOS General Name Service
     ResourceClass: Internet Class 1(0x1)
     TimeToLive: 300000 (0x493E0)
```

```
            ResourceDataLength: 6 (0x6)
         - ResouceRecordData:
          - NBFlags: 24576 (0x6000)
             G:    (0..............) Unique NetBIOS Name
             ONT:  (.11............) H node
             Rsv:  (...0000000000000) Reserved
             NBAddress: 10.0.0.3
```

In this frame, a WINS client sends a Name Refresh Request message requesting that the WINS server refresh the registration of the NetBIOS name **VISTAPC**   <0x20> with the IP address 10.0.0.3.

The following is the corresponding Name Registration Response message from Capture 16-05 (Frame 2), as displayed with Network Monitor 3.1:

```
  Frame:
+ Ethernet: Etype = Internet IP (IPv4)
+ Ipv4: Next Protocol = UDP, Packet ID = 1900, Total IP Length = 90
+ Udp: SrcPort = NETBIOS Name Service(137), DstPort = NETBIOS Name Service(137), Length = 70
- Nbtns: Registration Response, Success for VISTAPC          <0x20>
File Server Service, 10.0.0.3
    TransactionId: 36176 (0x8D50)
  - Flag: 44416 (0xAD80)
      R:         (1..............) Response
      OPCode:    (.0101..........) Registration
      AA:        (.....1.........) Authorized answer
      TC:        (......0........) Datagram not truncated
      RD:        (.......1.......) Recursion desired
      RA:        (........1......) Recursion available
      Reserved:  (.........00....)
      B:         (...........0...) Not a broadcast packet
      RCode:     (............0000) Success
    QuestionCount: 0 (0x0)
    AnswerCount: 1 (0x1)
    NameServiceCount: 0 (0x0)
    AdditionalCount: 0 (0x0)
  - AnswerRecord:
    - RRName: VISTAPC          <0x20> File Server Service
      Name: VISTAPC
      ResourceType: NetBIOS General Name Service
      ResourceClass: Internet Class 1(0x1)
      TimeToLive: 2400 (0x960)
      ResourceDataLength: 6 (0x6)
    - ResouceRecordData:
     - NBFlags: 24576 (0x6000)
         G:    (0..............) Unique NetBIOS Name
         ONT:  (.11............) H node
         Rsv:  (...0000000000000) Reserved
         NBAddress: 10.0.0.3
```

The name registration response confirms the success of the refresh and contains the IP address that was registered.

Releasing NetBIOS Names

An example of a message exchange to release and remove the registration of a NetBIOS name with a WINS server is Capture 16-06, a Network Monitor trace that is included in the \Captures folder on the companion CD-ROM. The following is the Name Release Request message from Capture 16-06 (Frame 1), as displayed with Network Monitor 3.1:

```
Frame:
+ Ethernet: Etype = Internet IP (IPv4)
+ Ipv4: Next Protocol = UDP, Packet ID = 57, Total IP Length = 96
+ Udp: SrcPort = NETBIOS Name Service(137), DstPort = NETBIOS Name Service(137), Length = 76
- Nbtns: Release Request for VISTAPC          <0x00> Workstation Service, 10.0.0.3
    TransactionId: 36194 (0x8D62)
  - Flag: 12288 (0x3000)
      R:         (0..............) Request
      OPCode:    (.0110..........) Release
      AA:        (.....0.........) Non-authorized answer
      TC:        (......0........) Datagram not truncated
      RD:        (.......0.......) Recursion not desired
      RA:        (........0......) Recursion not available
      Reserved:  (.........00....)
      B:         (...........0...) Not a broadcast packet
      RCode:     (............0000) Success
    QuestionCount: 1 (0x1)
    AnswerCount: 0 (0x0)
    NameServiceCount: 0 (0x0)
    AdditionalCount: 1 (0x1)
  - NbtNsQuestionSectionData:
  + QuestionName: VISTAPC          <0x00> Workstation Service
    QuestionType: NetBIOS General Name Service
    QuestionClass: Internet Class 1(0x1)
  - AdditionalRecord:
  + RRName: VISTAPC               <0x00> Workstation Service
    ResourceType: NetBIOS General Name Service
    ResourceClass: Internet Class 1(0x1)
    TimeToLive: 0 (0x0)
    ResourceDataLength: 6 (0x6)
  - ResouceRecordData:
    - NBFlags: 24576 (0x6000)
        G:    (0..............) Unique NetBIOS Name
        ONT:  (.11............) H node
        Rsv:  (...0000000000000) Reserved
      NBAddress: 10.0.0.3
```

In this frame, a WINS client sends a Name Release Request message requesting that the WINS server release and remove the registration of the NetBIOS name VISTAPC   <0x00> with the IP address 10.0.0.3.

The following is the corresponding Name Release Response message from Capture 16-06 (Frame 2), as displayed with Network Monitor 3.1:

```
  Frame:
+ Ethernet: Etype = Internet IP (IPv4)
+ Ipv4: Next Protocol = UDP, Packet ID = 1941, Total IP Length = 90
+ Udp: SrcPort = NETBIOS Name Service(137), DstPort = NETBIOS Name Service(137), Length = 70
- Nbtns: Release Response, Success for VISTAPC           <0x00> Workstation Service, 10.0.0.3
    TransactionId: 36194 (0x8D62)
  - Flag: 46080 (0xB400)
      R:          (1..............) Response
      OPCode:     (.0110..........) Release
      AA:         (.....1.........) Authorized answer
      TC:         (......0........) Datagram not truncated
      RD:         (.......0.......) Recursion not desired
      RA:         (........0......) Recursion not available
      Reserved:   (.........00....)
      B:          (...........0...) Not a broadcast packet
      RCode:      (............0000) Success
    QuestionCount: 0 (0x0)
    AnswerCount: 1 (0x1)
    NameServiceCount: 0 (0x0)
    AdditionalCount: 0 (0x0)
  - AnswerRecord:
  + RRName: VISTAPC          <0x00> Workstation Service
    ResourceType: NetBIOS General Name Service
    ResourceClass: Internet Class 1(0x1)
    TimeToLive: 0 (0x0)
    ResourceDataLength: 6 (0x6)
  - ResouceRecordData:
    - NBFlags: 24576 (0x6000)
        G:   (0..............) Unique NetBIOS Name
        ONT: (.11............) H node
        Rsv: (...0000000000000) Reserved
      NBAddress: 10.0.0.3
```

The name release response confirms the success of the release and contains the IP address that was released.

Summary

NetBT has a common message format for NetBIOS name service messages, which have a fixed-size portion and a variable-sized portion. The variable-sized portion contains entries and records to perform name resolution, registration, refresh, and release. WINS-based NetBIOS name resolution consists of an exchange of Name Query Request and Name Query Response messages. For successful resolution, the Name Query Response message contains an answer RR for the NetBIOS name that was requested. NetBIOS name registration consists of an exchange of Name Registration Request and Name Registration Response messages. If a unique NetBIOS name is already registered, the WINS server responds with a WACK message, confirms ownership of the name, and then responds with a Name Registration Response message. NetBIOS name refresh consists of an exchange of Name Refresh Request and Name Registration Response messages. NetBIOS name release consists of an exchange of Name Release Request and Name Release Response messages.

Chapter 17

Remote Authentication Dial-In User Service (RADIUS)

In this chapter:
RADIUS Messages 353
RADIUS Message Exchanges 364
Summary. 372

RADIUS is a simple client-server protocol that carries authentication, authorization, and accounting information between a network access server (NAS) and a centralized server. Examples of NASs include IEEE 802.11 wireless access points and servers that provide remote access connectivity to an organization's network or the Internet.

A RADIUS client is a NAS that initiates RADIUS message exchanges for connection requests or accounting of connections. A RADIUS server receives and evaluates connection requests for authentication and authorization or stores accounting messages. A RADIUS proxy routes RADIUS connection requests and accounting messages between RADIUS clients, RADIUS servers, or other RADIUS proxies.

This chapter describes the details of RADIUS messages and common message exchanges between RADIUS clients, RADIUS proxies, and RADIUS servers.

Note This chapter assumes prior knowledge of the components of a RADIUS infrastructure and their operation and configuration in Microsoft Windows. For more information, see Chapter 14, "Virtual Private Networking," of the "TCP/IP Fundamentals for Microsoft Windows" book, located in the \Fundamentals folder on the companion CD-ROM.

RADIUS Messages

RADIUS clients and RADIUS servers communicate by exchanging RADIUS messages. There are six types of RADIUS messages, which are sent as User Datagram Protocol (UDP) messages. A RADIUS server or RADIUS proxy listens on UDP port 1812 for incoming authentication messages and on UDP port 1813 for incoming accounting messages. RADIUS clients use a dynamically allocated UDP port for both authentication messages and accounting messages. Older versions of RADIUS used UDP port 1645 for authentication and authorization messages and UDP port 1646 for accounting messages. RADIUS does not use the Transmission Control Protocol (TCP). Most RADIUS servers, including the Network Policy Server (NPS) service in Windows Server 2008, allow you to configure the UDP ports that the RADIUS server listens on for incoming authentication and accounting messages.

The types of RADIUS messages are the following:

- **Access-Request**   Sent by a RADIUS client to request authentication and authorization for a network access connection attempt. The Access-Request also allows the RADIUS client to request whether there are any special requirements for the use of that connection. The Access-Request message contains the information needed to identify the RADIUS client, the credentials to perform the authentication, and any special requirements for the request. When the RADIUS server receives the Access-Request message, it first checks that the message came from a known RADIUS client. The server then performs the requested authentication and authorization processing and responds with an appropriate reply.

- **Access-Challenge**   Sent by a RADIUS server in response to an Access-Request message when additional information is needed to perform authentication or authorization. This message is a challenge to the RADIUS client that requires a response. The Access-Challenge message is typically used for challenge-response-based authentication protocols to verify the identity of the client. Access-Challenge messages are also used for Extensible Authentication Protocol (EAP)-based authentication methods, in which each Access-Challenge message is an EAP message from the RADIUS server to the access client.

- **Access-Accept**   Sent by a RADIUS server in response to an Access-Request message, informing the RADIUS client that the connection attempt is authenticated and authorized. The Access-Accept can also contain configuration and constraint information for the connection.

- **Access-Reject**   Sent by a RADIUS server in response to an Access-Request message, informing the RADIUS client that the connection attempt is rejected. A RADIUS server sends this message if the credentials are not authentic or the connection attempt is not authorized.

- **Accounting-Request**   Sent by a RADIUS client to specify accounting information for a connection that was accepted.

- **Accounting-Response**   Sent by the RADIUS server in response to the Accounting-Request message informing the RADIUS client that the Accounting-Request message was successfully received and processed.

RADIUS messages and protocol operation are defined in RFCs 2865 and 2866.

> **More Info** All of the RFCs referenced in this chapter can be found in the \Standards\Chap17_RADIUS folder on the companion CD-ROM.

RADIUS Message Structure

All RADIUS messages are transmitted using UDP. Each UDP message contains a single RADIUS message in its payload. All RADIUS messages have a common structure, as Figure 17-1 shows.

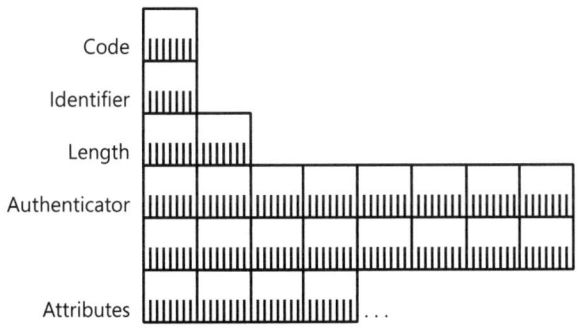

Figure 17-1 RADIUS message structure

Each RADIUS message has a common header and a variable number of attributes that comprise the data of the message. The common header consists of the following fields:

- **Code** A 1-byte field that indicates the RADIUS message type. A packet with an invalid Code field is silently discarded. The valid values for the Code field for RADIUS messages are listed in Table 17-1.

- **Identifier** A 1-byte field that is used to identify a RADIUS message exchange. The sender of the request message creates a transaction identifier value, and the responder copies it into the response message. This allows the RADIUS client or proxy to match the responses that it receives from a RADIUS server with their requests. When a RADIUS proxy sends a message to a RADIUS server, the proxy creates a new value for the Identifier field. The RADIUS proxy sends replies back to a RADIUS client with the value of the identifier corresponding to the initial request. Each proxied message has a different identifier than the initial request.

- **Length** A 2-byte field that indicates the length of the entire RADIUS message including the Code, Identifier, Length, and Authenticator fields and the RADIUS attributes. If a RADIUS message is shorter than the Length field indicates, it is silently discarded. If there are additional bytes in the RADIUS message that are beyond that indicated by the Length field, they are ignored. The Length field has a minimum value of 20 bytes and maximum value of 4096 bytes.

- **Authenticator** A 16-byte field that contains information that the RADIUS client uses to authenticate a reply message to ensure that the RADIUS client and server or RADIUS client and proxy have been configured with the same shared secret.

The Attributes section of the message is of variable-length and contains zero or more RADIUS attributes for the specific authentication, authorization, information, and configuration details for the RADIUS messages. For attributes that have multiple instances, the order of the attributes must be preserved. Otherwise, attributes do not need to have their order preserved.

Table 17-1 Values for the RADIUS Code Field

Code	Message
1	Access-Request
2	Access-Accept
3	Access-Reject
4	Accounting-Request
5	Accounting-Response
11	Access-Challenge

RADIUS Attributes

RADIUS attributes carry data values that are used in the authentication, authorization, and accounting functions carried out by RADIUS clients, servers, and proxies. These attributes can appear in network access and accounting requests and in response messages. An attribute represents a specific data item, such as a user name or the tunneling protocol in use, sent between the RADIUS client and server. Some attributes can be included more than once, the effect of which is dependent on the specific attribute. When used as a RADIUS proxy, NPS preserves the order of the attributes received from the client in messages transmitted to a RADIUS server.

There are two types of RADIUS attributes: standard attributes and vendor-specific attributes (VSAs). Standard attributes are defined in RFCs 2865 through 2869 and are used by all RADIUS clients and servers. VSAs are proprietary. Not all RADIUS clients and servers implement all VSAs. For more information, see the section "Vendor-Specific Attributes" later in this chapter.

Figure 17-2 shows the type-length-value structure of RADIUS attributes.

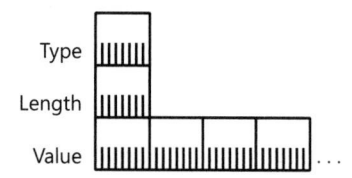

Figure 17-2 RADIUS attribute structure

The Type field is a 1-byte field that defines a specific RADIUS attribute. Table 17-2 lists and describes the purpose of common RADIUS attributes. For a complete and up-to-date list, see *http://www.iana.org/assignments/radius-types*.

Table 17-2 Common RADIUS Attributes

Attribute Type (Decimal)	Attribute Name	Purpose of Attribute
1	User-Name	Sent in Access-Request messages, this attribute indicates the name of the user that is to be authenticated.
2	User-Password	Sent in Access-Request messages, when authentication is by the Password Authentication Protocol (PAP), this field is the password to be used to authenticate the user. The password is encrypted in Access-Request messages.
3	CHAP-Password	This attribute is sent in Access-Request messages to indicate the response value provided by a Point-to-Point Protocol (PPP) Challenge Handshake Authentication Protocol (CHAP) user in response to a CHAP challenge. The value of the CHAP challenge is also included in Access-Request messages sent by the Routing and Remote Access service in Windows Server 2008.
4	NAS-IP-Address	This attribute is sent in Access-Request messages to indicate the IP address of the RADIUS client that is requesting authentication.
5	NAS-Port	This attribute is sent in Access-Request messages to indicate the physical port of the RADIUS client that is requesting authentication.
6	Service-Type	This attribute is sent in Access-Request and Access-Accept messages to indicate the type of service the RADIUS client has requested, or the type of service to be provided. The Value field is 4 bytes long and can have the following values:
	1	Login
	2	Framed
	3	Callback Login
	4	Callback Framed
	5	Outbound
	6	Administrative
	7	NAS Prompt
	8	Authenticate Only
	9	Callback NAS Prompt
	10	Call Check
	11	Callback Administrative
7	Framed-Protocol	This attribute is contained in Access-Request messages to indicate the specific framed protocol being requested. Possible values for this attribute are as follows:

Table 17-2 Common RADIUS Attributes

Attribute Type (Decimal)	Attribute Name	Purpose of Attribute
	1	PPP
	2	Serial Line Internet Protocol (SLIP)
	3	AppleTalk Remote Access Protocol (ARAP)
	4	Gandalf proprietary SingleLink/MultiLink protocol
	6	X.75 Synchronous
8	Framed-IP-Address	This attribute is included in accounting requests and indicates the IP address of the access client.
12	Framed-MTU	This attribute is included in Routing and Remote Access accounting requests and indicates the maximum transmission unit (MTU) configured for the RADIUS client.
25	Class	This attribute is available to be sent by the server to the client in an Access-Accept message and is then sent, unmodified, by the RADIUS client to the RADIUS accounting server as part of any accounting records. This attribute contains a string identifying the NAS originating the Access-Request message.
31	Calling-Station-Id	This attribute is used only in Access-Request messages. The NAS (or other device) uses this attribute to send either the phone number that the call came from for dial-up connections, or the IP address of the VPN client for VPN connections.
32	NAS-Identifier	This attribute is used only in the Access-Request message to contain a string identifying the NAS originating the Access-Request. The NAS-Identifier is not used to select the shared secret used to authenticate the request.
33	Proxy-State	This attribute is added to an Access-Request by a RADIUS proxy and is returned unmodified in the Access-Accept, Access-Reject, or Access-Challenge message. When a RADIUS proxy receives a response to its request, it removes its own Proxy-State attribute (the last Proxy-State attribute in the message) before forwarding the response to the NAS. If a Proxy-State attribute is added when forwarding a RADIUS message, the Proxy-State attribute is added after any existing Proxy-State attributes. This allows for multiple RADIUS proxies in the path between a RADIUS client and RADIUS server.
40	Acct-Status-Type	This attribute is sent in an Accounting-Request message to indicate the beginning or end of the user session or an interim update. Possible values include the following:
	1	Start
	2	Stop
	3	Interim-Update
	7	Accounting-On
	8	Accounting-Off
	9–14	Reserved for Tunnel Accounting

Table 17-2 Common RADIUS Attributes

Attribute Type (Decimal)	Attribute Name	Purpose of Attribute
	15	Failed
41	Acct-Delay-Time	This attribute is sent in an Accounting-Request message to indicate for how many seconds the RADIUS client has been trying to send this request. By subtracting this value from the time of arrival on the RADIUS server, the server can approximate the time of the event generating this Accounting-Request message.
42	Acct-Input-Octets	This attribute is sent in an Accounting-Request message in which Acct-Status-Type is set to Stop. It contains the number of data bytes that have been received from the port during the accounting session.
43	Acct-Output-Octets	This attribute is sent in an Accounting-Request message where Acct-Status-Type is set to Stop. It contains the number of data bytes that have been sent to the port during the accounting session.
44	Acct-Session-Id	This attribute is sent in Accounting Start and Accounting Stop messages and contains a unique identifier to identify a session. This makes it easier to match start and stop records in RADIUS log files, because the start and stop records for a given session have the same Acct-Session-Id. A RADIUS client can send this attribute in an Access-Request message. If so, the NAS must send the same Acct-Session-Id in Accounting-Request messages for that session.
46	Acct-Session-Time	This attribute is contained in Accounting Stop messages to indicate how many seconds the NAS has provided the service (that is, the time of the connection).
47	Acct-Input-Packets	This attribute is contained in Accounting Stop messages to indicate how many IP datagrams the NAS has received.
48	Acct-Output-Packets	This attribute is contained in Accounting Stop messages to indicate how many IP datagrams the NAS has sent.
49	Acct-Terminate-Cause	This attribute is contained in Accounting Stop messages to indicate the reason for the session being terminated. Possible values are as follows:
	1	User Request
	2	Lost Carrier
	3	Lost Service
	4	Idle Timeout
	5	Session Timeout
	6	Admin Reset
	7	Admin Reboot
	8	Port Error
	9	NAS Error

Table 17-2   Common RADIUS Attributes

Attribute Type (Decimal)	Attribute Name	Purpose of Attribute
	10	NAS Request
	11	NAS Reboot
	12	Port Unneeded
	13	Port Preempted
	14	Port Suspended
	15	Service Unavailable
	16	Callback
	17	User Error
	18	Host Request
50	Acct-Multi-Session-Id	This attribute is sent in accounting messages to enable the RADIUS accounting server to link together multiple related sessions in the RADIUS logs. Each session linked together would have a unique Acct-Session-Id but the same Acct-Multi-Session-Id.
51	Acct-Link-Count	This attribute is sent in accounting messages to enable the RADIUS accounting server to record the number of links that are used in a multilink session at the time the accounting record is generated. The NAS might include the Acct-Link-Count attribute in any Accounting-Request that might have multiple links.
55	Event-Timestamp	This attribute is included in an Accounting-Request message. It records the time that this event occurred on the NAS, in seconds since January 1, 1970, 00:00 UTC (Coordinated Universal Time).
60	CHAP-Challenge	This attribute contains the CHAP Challenge sent by the NAS to the access client. It is only used in Access-Request messages.
61	NAS-Port-Type	This attribute indicates the type of the physical port of the NAS that is authenticating the user and is contained in Access-Request packets. Possible values include the following:
	0	Async
	1	Sync
	2	Integrated Services Digital Network (ISDN) Sync
	3	ISDN Async V.120
	4	ISDN Async V.110
	5	Virtual
	6	Personal Handyphone System Internet Access Forum Standard (PIAFS)
	7	High-Level Data Link (HDLC) Clear Channel

Table 17-2 Common RADIUS Attributes

Attribute Type (Decimal)	Attribute Name	Purpose of Attribute
	8	X.25
	9	X.75
	10	G.3 Fax
	11	Symmetric DSL (SDSL)
	12	Asymmetric DSL, Carrierless Amplitude Phase (ADSL-CAP) modulation
	13	Asymmetric DSL, Discrete Multi-Tone (ADSL-DMT)
	14	ISDN Digital Subscriber Line (IDSL)
	15	Ethernet
	16	Digital Subscriber Line of unknown type (xDSL)
	17	Cable
	18	Wireless–Other
	19	Wireless–IEEE 802.11
64	Tunnel-Type	This attribute is used in Access-Request messages to indicate the type of VPN tunnel that the NAS is attempting to set up. Possible values include the following:
	1	Point-to-Point Tunneling Protocol (PPTP)
	2	Layer Two Forwarding (L2F)
	3	Layer Two Tunneling Protocol (L2TP)
	4	Ascend Tunnel Management Protocol (ATMP)
	5	Virtual Tunneling Protocol (VTP)
	6	IP Authentication Header in Tunnel-mode (AH)
	7	IP-in-IP encapsulation (IP-IP)
	8	Minimal IP-in-IP encapsulation (MIN-IP-IP)
	9	IP Encapsulating Security Payload in the Tunnel-mode (ESP)
	10	Generic Route Encapsulation (GRE)
	11	Bay Dial Virtual Services (DVS)
	12	IP-in-IP Tunneling
65	Tunnel-Medium-Type	This attribute is used when authenticating a VPN connection and indicates the transport medium that is being used when creating a tunnel for those protocols (such as L2TP) that can operate over multiple transports. Possible values are as follows:
	1	IPv4 (IP version 4)
	2	IPv6 (IP version 6)
	3	Network Service Access Point (NSAP)
	4	High-level Datalink Control (HDLC) (8-bit multidrop)
	5	Bolt, Beranek, and Neumann (BBN) 1822

Table 17-2 Common RADIUS Attributes

Attribute Type (Decimal)	Attribute Name	Purpose of Attribute
	6	802 (includes all 802 media plus Ethernet canonical format)
	7	E.163 (Plain Old Telephone Service [POTS])
	8	E.164 (Switched Multimegabit Data Service [SMDS], Frame Relay, Asynchronous Transfer Mode [ATM])
	9	F.69 (Telex)
	10	X.121 (X.25, Frame Relay)
	11	Internetwork Packet Exchange (IPX)
	12	AppleTalk
	13	Decnet IV
	14	Banyan Vines
	15	E.164 with NSAP format subaddress
66	Tunnel-Client-Endpoint	This attribute contains the address of the VPN client and can be included in both Access-Request and Access-Accept messages when a VPN tunnel is being set up.
80	Message-Authenticator	This attribute is used in RADIUS Access-Request messages to provide proof of the knowledge of the RADIUS shared secret.

Vendor-Specific Attributes

RFC 2865 defines the VSA as a mechanism to enable NAS vendors to extend the list of attributes that RADIUS messages can contain. This allows vendors to provide their own attributes for use on their hardware. VSAs are identified with the Vendor attribute (Type=26), which includes the vendor's enterprise number and the VSA data. The assigned enterprise numbers are specified at *http://www.iana.org/assignments/enterprise-numbers*. For example, Microsoft's enterprise ID is 0x137 (311 in decimal format). Microsoft-specific vendor extensions are defined in RFC 2548.

RADIUS servers ignore VSAs that they do not support. The RADIUS server can create log entries containing the ignored attribute, but this is not required. If a RADIUS client receives a VSA that is not supported, the client should attempt to work without the information, although doing so could result in degraded service for the connection because the vendor feature enabled by the VSA will not be used for the connection.

Vendor-specific attributes are encoded in RADIUS messages as normal attributes with an attribute type of 26. There are two formats for VSAs: a general structure and a recommended structure. Figure 17-3 shows the general structure for VSAs.

In the general structure, the 4-byte Vendor-ID field identifies the NAS vendor with its enterprise number. The variable-length String field contains the data for the VSA. RFC 2865 also defines a structure for the String field. Figure 17-4 shows the recommended structure for VSAs.

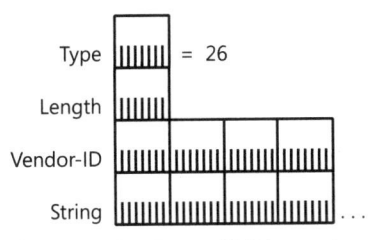

Figure 17-3 General VSA structure

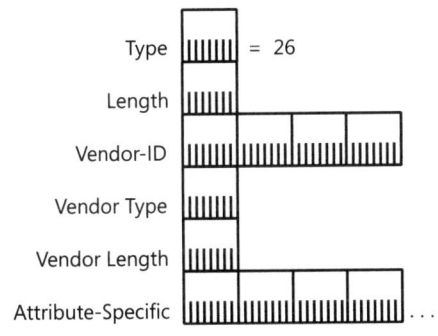

Figure 17-4 Recommended VSA structure

In the recommended structure, the String field for the general format is redefined with the following:

- A 1-byte Vendor Type field indicating the type of VSA for the vendor
- A 1-byte Vendor Length field indicating the length of the Vendor Type field, the Vendor Length field, and the new Attribute-Specific field
- An Attribute-Specific field that contains the data for the VSA

The recommended structure allows a vendor to define multiple types of VSAs.

RFC 2548 defines the Microsoft-specific attributes that are supported by the NPS and Routing and Remote Access services in Windows Server 2008. NPS and Routing and Remote Access set the Vendor-ID field of the Vendor-Specific attribute to 311 (0x0137). Table 17-3 contains the most common vendor-specific attributes that NPS and Routing and Remote Access use.

Table 17-3 Common Vendor-Specific Attributes

Vendor Type Value	Attribute Name	Description
1	MS-CHAP-Response	This attribute is sent in authentication requests that use CHAP to contain the CHAP response received from the access client.
9	MS-RAS-Vendor	This attribute is sent in authentication requests to identify the vendor (Microsoft).

Table 17-3 Common Vendor-Specific Attributes

Vendor Type Value	Attribute Name	Description
10	MS-CHAP-Domain	This attribute, which can be in both Access-Accept and Accounting-Request messages, indicates the domain in which the user has been authenticated.
11	MS-CHAP-Challenge	The CHAP challenges used in authentication requests that use CHAP, Microsoft CHAP (MS-CHAP), or MS-CHAP v2.
16	MS-MPPE-Send-Key	This attribute holds a session key for use by Microsoft Point-to-Point Encryption (MPPE). This key is intended for encrypting messages sent from the NAS to the access client and is sent only in Access-Accept messages. This attribute is encrypted using the RADIUS shared secret.
17	MS-MPPE-Recv-Key	This attribute contains a session key for use by MPPE. This key is intended for encrypting packets received by the NAS from the access client and is used only in Access-Accept messages.
18	MS-RAS-Version	The version of Routing and Remote Access sending the RADIUS message. This is sent in Access-Request and Accounting-Request messages. This attribute is encrypted using the shared secret.
25	MS-CHAP2-Response	For authentication requests that use MS-CHAP v2, the CHAP response received from the access client.
26	MS-CHAP2-Success	For authentication requests that use MS-CHAP v2, the indication that the authentication was successful.

RADIUS Message Exchanges

This section describes common RADIUS message exchanges for the following:

- Authentication of network access
- Accounting of network access
- RADIUS proxy forwarding

Authentication of Network Access

The sets of authentication messages exchanged between a RADIUS client and a RADIUS server are the following:

- **Access-Request followed by Access-Accept** This occurs when a RADIUS server successfully authenticates and authorizes a connection on behalf of a RADIUS client. The RADIUS client can commence service to an access client.

- **Access-Request followed by Access-Reject** This occurs when a RADIUS server does not successfully authenticate and authorize a connection on behalf of a RADIUS client. The

RADIUS client can then attempt to get new credentials, which it can resubmit in a new Access-Request message.

- **Access-Request followed by Access-Challenge** This occurs when a RADIUS server needs to obtain additional information. The RADIUS client submits the additional information in a new Access-Request message. There can be multiple Access-Challenge messages sent by the RADIUS server. For example, for EAP-based authentication methods, EAP messages from the access client to the RADIUS server are contained in Access-Request messages and their responses are contained in Access-Challenge messages.

After the RADIUS server receives the Access-Request, it first validates the IP address of the RADIUS client. An Access-Request message that is received from a RADIUS client for which the server is not configured is silently discarded. If the Access-Request message came from a valid RADIUS client, the server can then validate the request and return an Access-Accept or Access-Reject message, based on the success or failure of the validation. The validation of a request typically includes credential verification, but can also be based on other information included in the Access-Request message, such as the NAS port that the connection request was received on or the type of connection. There is no cryptographic verification that the Access-Request message originated from a RADIUS client with a commonly configured RADIUS shared secret unless the Access-Request includes the Message-Authenticator attribute.

When the RADIUS server returns an Access-Accept message, the server can return additional configuration information, specified as additional attributes. These can be generic RADIUS attributes or VSAs used to configure a particular vendor's NAS.

If the RADIUS server is unable to authenticate and authorize the connection, it sends an Access-Reject message back to the RADIUS client indicating that the connection request has failed. The RADIUS client could then request user identity details again or simply fail the initial service request.

When the RADIUS client receives an Access-Accept message, it matches the Identifier field with a pending Access-Request and ensures that the Response Authenticator field contains the correct response for this pending Access-Request message. Invalid messages are silently discarded.

A RADIUS client that does not support challenge and response treats the Access-Challenge as though it had received an Access-Reject message instead. This has the effect of denying the requested access. If the RADIUS client supports challenge and response, the receipt of a valid Access-Challenge message indicates that a new Access-Request is to be sent, which should contain updated request information. The RADIUS client can display a text message to the user and then prompt the user for a response. The RADIUS client then sends its original Access-Request with a new request ID and Request Authenticator, with the User-Password attribute replaced by the user's response to the challenge, suitably encrypted. If the Access-Challenge contained a State attribute from the Access-Challenge, this is also returned. Note that the Access-Request messages can contain, at most, one instance of the State attribute.

An example of an Access-Request/Access-Accept message exchange is Capture 17-01, a Network Monitor trace that is included in the \Captures folder on the companion CD-ROM. The following is the Access-Request message from Capture 17-01 (Frame 1), as displayed with Network Monitor 3.1:

```
Frame:
+ Ethernet: Etype = Internet IP (IPv4)
+ Ipv4: Next Protocol = UDP, Packet ID = 30882, Total IP Length = 277
- Udp: SrcPort = 3065, DstPort = 1812, Length = 257
    SourcePort: 3065, 3065(0xbf9)
    DestinationPort: 1812, 1812(0x714)
    TotalLength: 257 (0x101)
    Checksum: 42833 (0xA751)
- Radius: Access Request, Id = 12, Length = 249
    MessageType: Access Request, 1(0x01)
    Identifier: 12 (0xC)
    AllLength: 249 (0xF9)
    Authenticator: DB 60 44 6A  2B 19 83 57   FF 75 F1 1D   19 2C 1A 7F
  + AttributeNasIPAddress: 10.10.1.150
  + AttributeServiceType: Framed, 2(0x2)
  + AttributeFramedProtocol: PPP, 1(0x1)
  + AttributeNasPort: 128
  + AttributeVendorSpecific:
  + AttributeVendorSpecific:
  + AttributeRadiusNASPortType: Virtual, 5(0x5)
  + AttributeTunnelType: Point-to-Point Tunneling Protocol (PPTP), 1(0x1)
  + AttributeTunnelMediumType: IPv4, 1(0x1)
  + AttributeStationID: 10.10.1.62
  + AttributeTunnelClientEndpoint:
  + AttributeVendorSpecific:
  + AttributeVendorSpecific:
  + AttributeUserName: KAPOHO\tfl
  + AttributeVendorSpecific:
  + AttributeVendorSpecific:
```

In this frame, a RADIUS client sends an Access-Request message requesting authentication and authorization for a virtual private network (VPN) connection using PPTP. Note the use of a dynamically allocated source UDP port and the destination UDP port of 1812. The attributes contain information about the connection and include RADIUS attributes and VSAs.

The following is the corresponding Access-Accept message from Capture 17-01 (Frame 2), as displayed with Network Monitor 3.1:

```
Frame:
+ Ethernet: Etype = Internet IP (IPv4)
+ Ipv4: Next Protocol = UDP, Packet ID = 39615, Total IP Length = 242
+ Udp: SrcPort = 1812, DstPort = 3065, Length = 222
- Radius: Access Accept, Id = 12, Length = 214
    MessageType: Access Accept, 2(0x02)
    Identifier: 12 (0xC)
    AllLength: 214 (0xD6)
    Authenticator: 5F C7 93 40  22 EA 31 7A   A3 4F 82 B1   FA DE 15 77
  + AttributeFramedProtocol: PPP, 1(0x1)
```

```
    + AttributeServiceType: Framed, 2(0x2)
    + AttributeClass:
    + AttributeVendorSpecific:
    + AttributeVendorSpecific:
    + AttributeVendorSpecific:
    + AttributeVendorSpecific:
```

The Access-Accept contains the same Identifier field value as the Access-Request. The value of the Authenticator field allows the RADIUS client to validate that the message was sent from a RADIUS server or proxy that has been configured with a common RADIUS shared secret. The attributes contain information about the connection and include RADIUS attributes and VSAs.

An example of an Access-Request/Access-Reject message exchange is Capture 17-02, a Network Monitor trace that is included in the \Captures folder on the companion CD-ROM. The following is the Access-Reject message from Capture 17-02 (Frame 2), as displayed with Network Monitor 3.1:

```
  Frame:
+ Ethernet: Etype = Internet IP (IPv4)
+ Ipv4: Next Protocol = UDP, Packet ID = 746, Total IP Length = 70
+ Udp: SrcPort = 1812, DstPort = 2938, Length = 50
- Radius: Access Reject, Id = 7, Length = 42
    MessageType: Access Reject, 3(0x03)
    Identifier: 7 (0x7)
    AllLength: 42 (0x2A)
    Authenticator: 14 BF A3 62  F1 6C 88 42  19 A8 8C 3F  4F 83 7F 4C
  - AttributeVendorSpecific:
    Type: Vendor Specific, 26(0x1a)
    Length: 22 (0x16)
    VendorID: Microsoft, 311(0x137)
   - RadiusMSSpecificPublicTLV: MS-CHAP-Error, 1(0x1)
     VendorType: MS-CHAP-Error, 2(0x2)
     VendorLength: 16 (0x10)
    - MSCHAPError:
       Ident: 0 (0x0)
       ErrorString: E=649 R=0 V=3
```

Note how in this example the Access-Reject contains a Microsoft VSA indicating an authentication error.

Accounting of Network Access

There are two RADIUS accounting messages sent between RADIUS clients and RADIUS servers: Accounting-Request and Accounting-Response. When a connection request completes successfully, the RADIUS client sends an Accounting-Request message to a RADIUS server. This message indicates that an accounting session has started, describes the type of service being delivered, and identifies the user receiving the service. The RADIUS server responds with an Accounting-Response message indicating that the accounting start was received and recorded.

When the service being provided by the RADIUS client (for example, remote access) has been completed, the RADIUS client generates an additional Accounting-Request message called an Accounting Stop message. This describes the type of service that was delivered and statistics such as elapsed time, input and output bytes, or input and output packets, which could be used for billing or charge-back purposes. The RADIUS server then sends the RADIUS client an Accounting-Response message to indicate that the message was received and recorded.

The RADIUS client can send any valid RADIUS attribute in the Accounting-Request message, except for User-Password, CHAP-Password, Reply-Message, and State. A RADIUS client always includes either the NAS-IP-Address or NAS-Identifier attributes in the Accounting-Request. If the Accounting-Request message includes a Framed-IP-Address, this attribute contains the IP address assigned to the connection.

The RADIUS server acknowledges receipt of the Accounting Start and Accounting Stop messages by sending the RADIUS client an Accounting-Response message, which tells the RADIUS client that the Accounting-Request message has been received by the RADIUS server. Unlike the Access-Accept message, an Accounting-Response message does not normally contain attributes. If the RADIUS server cannot record the accounting information, no Accounting-Response message is sent.

When the RADIUS client receives the Accounting-Response message, it matches the response with a pending Accounting-Request to complete the accounting for this event. If no Accounting-Response is received, the RADIUS client retransmits the Accounting-Request.

As with other RADIUS messages, the Response Authenticator field in the Accounting-Response message contains the authenticator that relates to the pending Accounting-Request. Additionally, invalid packets, which can include those in which the authenticator cannot be validated, are silently discarded.

An example of an Accounting-Request/Accounting-Response message exchange is Capture 17-03, a Network Monitor trace that is included in the \Captures folder on the companion CD-ROM. The following is the Accounting-Request message from Capture 17-03 (Frame 1), as displayed with Network Monitor 3.1:

```
Frame:
+ Ethernet: Etype = Internet IP (IPv4)
+ Ipv4: Next Protocol = UDP, Packet ID = 30899, Total IP Length = 303
+ Udp: SrcPort = 3066, DstPort = 1813, Length = 283
- Radius: Accounting Request, Id = 3, Length = 275
    MessageType: Accounting Request, 4(0x04)
    Identifier: 3 (0x3)
    AllLength: 275 (0x113)
    Authenticator: EA BB 33 E2  85 8D F8 D5  A6 5C 40 76  54 73 49 09
  + AttributeAcctStatusType: Start, 1(0x1)
  + AttributeAcctDelayTime: 0
  + AttributeNasIPAddress: 10.10.1.150
```

```
  + AttributeServiceType: Framed, 2(0x2)
  + AttributeFramedProtocol: PPP, 1(0x1)
  + AttributeNasPort: 128
  + AttributeVendorSpecific:
  + AttributeVendorSpecific:
  + AttributeRadiusNASPortType: Virtual, 5(0x5)
  + AttributeTunnelType: Point-to-Point Tunneling Protocol (PPTP), 1(0x1)
  + AttributeTunnelMediumType: IPv4, 1(0x1)
  + AttributeStationID: 10.10.1.62
  + AttributeTunnelClientEndpoint:
  + AttributeVendorSpecific:
  + AttributeVendorSpecific:
  + AttributeClass:
  + AttributeVendorSpecific:
  + AttributeAcctSessionID: 4
  + AttributeUserName: KAPOHO\tfl
  + AttributeFramedIPAddress: 10.10.1.177
  + AttributeFramedMTU: 1400
  + AttributeAcctMultiSessionID: 27
  + AttributeAcctLinkCount: 1
  + AttributeEventTimestamp: 1010156648
  + AttributeAcctAuthentic: RADIUS, 1(0x1)
  + AttributeVendorSpecific:
```

In this frame, a RADIUS client sends an Accounting-Request message requesting the accounting for a VPN connection using PPTP. Note the use of a dynamically allocated source UDP port and the destination UDP port of 1813. Note that this message is an Accounting Start message (the AttributeAcctStatusType attribute). The additional attributes contain information about the connection and include RADIUS attributes and VSAs.

The following is the corresponding Accounting-Response message from Capture 17-03 (Frame 2), as displayed with Network Monitor 3.1:

```
  Frame:
+ Ethernet: Etype = Internet IP (IPv4)
+ Ipv4: Next Protocol = UDP, Packet ID = 40023, Total IP Length = 48
+ Udp: SrcPort = 1813, DstPort = 3066, Length = 28
- Radius: Accounting Response, Id = 3, Length = 20
    MessageType: Accounting Response, 5(0x05)
    Identifier: 3 (0x3)
    AllLength: 20 (0x14)
    Authenticator: F0 A9 27 34  0D 42 36 4B  7E C7 8A 83  E4 B6 98 41
```

The Accounting-Response contains the same Identifier field value as the Accounting-Request. The value of the Authenticator field allows the RADIUS client to validate that the message was sent from a RADIUS server that has been configured with a common RADIUS shared secret. Note that there are no attributes present.

Frames 3 and 4 of Capture 17-03 are for the Accounting Stop message exchange for this VPN connection.

RADIUS Proxy Forwarding

A RADIUS proxy relays authentication and accounting messages between RADIUS clients, RADIUS servers, or other RADIUS proxies. With a single RADIUS proxy between a RADIUS client and a RADIUS server, the RADIUS proxy forwards the authentication message request to a RADIUS server, receives the response from the RADIUS server, and sends that response to the RADIUS client. A RADIUS proxy can be used to route messages between RADIUS servers with different account databases or to distribute the load of RADIUS traffic among multiple RADIUS servers.

When a RADIUS proxy sends a message from a RADIUS client to a RADIUS server, it adds the Proxy-State attribute into the message, which informs the server that the RADIUS message was received from a proxy and not from the RADIUS client. When the server sends a response back to the RADIUS proxy, this attribute is copied, unmodified, into the response. The RADIUS proxy removes this attribute when sending the response back to the RADIUS client. If multiple proxies exist in the path between a RADIUS client and a RADIUS server, each RADIUS proxy adds an additional Proxy-State attribute to the RADIUS message when it is passed toward the RADIUS server and removes its Proxy-State attribute when responses are sent back to the original RADIUS client. From the RADIUS client's perspective, it sent RADIUS messages to its configured RADIUS server, which could be a RADIUS server or a RADIUS proxy. Because the Proxy-State attribute is removed in the RADIUS response messages, the RADIUS client cannot determine whether there are RADIUS proxies in the path to the RADIUS server performing the authentication and authorization.

An NPS server can function as both a RADIUS proxy and a RADIUS server; some incoming authentication requests or accounting messages are processed locally and others are forwarded to RADIUS servers. Processing of incoming requests either locally or forwarded to a RADIUS server is determined by connection request policies on the NPS server.

An example of an Access-Request message that is forwarded by a RADIUS proxy is Capture 17-04, a Network Monitor trace that is included in the \Captures folder on the companion CD-ROM. The following is the original Access-Request message from Capture 17-04 (Frame 1), as displayed with Network Monitor 3.1:

```
Frame:
+ Ethernet: Etype = Internet IP (IPv4)
- Ipv4: Next Protocol = UDP, Packet ID = 7567, Total IP Length = 278
  + Versions: IPv4, Internet Protocol; Header Length = 20
  + DifferentiatedServicesField: DSCP: 0, ECN: 0
    TotalLength: 278 (0x116)
    Identification: 7567 (0x1D8F)
  + FragmentFlags: 0 (0x0)
    TimeToLive: 128 (0x80)
    NextProtocol: UDP, 17(0x11)
    Checksum: 1238 (0x4D6)
    SourceAddress: 10.10.1.150
    DestinationAddress: 10.10.1.201
```

```
+ Udp: SrcPort = 1711, DstPort = 1812, Length = 258
- Radius: Access Request, Id = 8, Length = 250
    MessageType: Access Request, 1(0x01)
    Identifier: 8 (0x8)
    AllLength: 250 (0xFA)
    Authenticator: B2 3F 8A 21  54 25 F4 14  4C 30 08 4E  34 5A 82 27
  + AttributeNasIPAddress: 10.10.1.150
  + AttributeServiceType: Framed, 2(0x2)
  + AttributeFramedProtocol: PPP, 1(0x1)
  + AttributeNasPort: 128
  + AttributeVendorSpecific:
  + AttributeVendorSpecific:
  + AttributeRadiusNASPortType: Virtual, 5(0x5)
  + AttributeTunnelType: Point-to-Point Tunneling Protocol (PPTP), 1(0x1)
  + AttributeTunnelMediumType: IPv4, 1(0x1)
  + AttributeStationID: 10.10.1.62
  + AttributeTunnelClientEndpoint:
  + AttributeVendorSpecific:
  + AttributeVendorSpecific:
  + AttributeUserName: TCP1\rebecca
  + AttributeVendorSpecific:
  + AttributeVendorSpecific:
```

In this frame, a RADIUS client (at the IP address 10.10.1.150) sends an Access-Request message to its configured RADIUS server, which is a RADIUS proxy (at the IP address 10.10.1.201).

The following is the Access-Request message as forwarded by the RADIUS proxy to a RADIUS server (at the IP address 10.10.1.151) from Capture 17-04 (Frame 2), as displayed with Network Monitor 3.1:

```
Frame:
+ Ethernet: Etype = Internet IP (IPv4)
- Ipv4: Next Protocol = UDP, Packet ID = 2894, Total IP Length = 288
  + Versions: IPv4, Internet Protocol; Header Length = 20
  + DifferentiatedServicesField: DSCP: 0, ECN: 0
    TotalLength: 288 (0x120)
    Identification: 2894 (0xB4E)
  + FragmentFlags: 0 (0x0)
    TimeToLive: 128 (0x80)
    NextProtocol: UDP, 17(0x11)
    Checksum: 0 (0x0)
    SourceAddress: 10.10.1.201
    DestinationAddress: 10.10.1.151
+ Udp: SrcPort = 2203, DstPort = 1812, Length = 268
- Radius: Access Request, Id = 2, Length = 260
    MessageType: Access Request, 1(0x01)
    Identifier: 2 (0x2)
    AllLength: 260 (0x104)
    Authenticator: B2 3F 8A 21  54 25 F4 14  4C 30 08 4E  34 5A 82 27
  + AttributeNasIPAddress: 10.10.1.150
  + AttributeServiceType: Framed, 2(0x2)
  + AttributeFramedProtocol: PPP, 1(0x1)
  + AttributeNasPort: 128
```

```
+ AttributeRadiusNASPortType: Virtual, 5(0x5)
+ AttributeTunnelType: Point-to-Point Tunneling Protocol (PPTP), 1(0x1)
+ AttributeTunnelMediumType: IPv4, 1(0x1)
+ AttributeStationID: 10.10.1.62
+ AttributeTunnelClientEndpoint:
+ AttributeUserName: TCP1\rebecca
+ AttributeVendorSpecific:
+ AttributeVendorSpecific:
+ AttributeVendorSpecific:
+ AttributeVendorSpecific:
+ AttributeVendorSpecific:
+ AttributeVendorSpecific:
- AttributeProxyState:
    Type: Proxy State, 33(0x21)
    Length: 10 (0xA)
    ProxyState: Binary Large Object (8 Bytes)
```

Note the presence of the Proxy-State attribute at the end of the message.

The additional frames of Capture 17-03 are for the Access-Accept message (Frames 3 and 4), the Accounting Start message exchange for the connection (Frames 5 through 8), and the Accounting Stop message exchange for the connection (Frames 9 through 12).

Summary

RADIUS messages have a common structure consisting of a fixed-size portion and a variable-size portion. The fixed-size portion contains fields common to all RADIUS messages. The variable-size portion contains RADIUS attributes, which can be standard attributes or VSAs. RADIUS attributes carry data values that are used in authentication, authorization, and accounting of network access. An authentication exchange is one of the following: Access-Request/Access-Accept for a successful authentication and authorization, Access-Request/Access-Reject for an unsuccessful authentication or authorization, or Access-Request/Access-Challenge when the RADIUS server needs more information to evaluate authentication and authorization. An accounting exchange consists of an Accounting-Request and an Accounting-Response. When RADIUS proxies are between RADIUS clients and RADIUS servers, they modify RADIUS messages by adding or removing a Proxy-State attribute.

Chapter 18
Internet Protocol Security (IPsec)

In this chapter:

IPsec Headers	373
IPsec and Security Associations	383
Internet Key Exchange	385
ISAKMP Message Structure	385
Main Mode Negotiation	399
Quick Mode Negotiation	399
Authenticated Internet Protocol (AuthIP)	401
IPsec NAT Traversal	404
Summary	406

Internet Protocol security (IPsec) is a set of Internet Engineering Task Force (IETF) standards that provide protection for IP packets through the use of cryptography, security protocols, and dynamic key management. IPsec can protect IP traffic from end to end (when two IPsec peers communicate) or on an intermediate part of a network path (when IPsec routers protect traffic exchanged over the Internet). This chapter describes the details of IPsec headers and the negotiation protocols supported in Windows Server 2008 and Windows Vista.

Note This chapter assumes prior knowledge of the properties of protected communications (data origin authentication, data integrity, data confidentiality, nonrepudiation, and replay protection) and the basics of IPsec operation including IPsec protocols, modes, and negotiation phases. For more information, see Chapter 13, "Internet Protocol Security and Packet Filtering," of the "TCP/IP Fundamentals for Microsoft Windows" book, located in the \Fundamentals folder on the companion CD-ROM.

IPsec Headers

IPsec provides its protection services by wrapping the IP payload with an additional header or trailer containing information to provide data origin authentication, data integrity, data confidentiality, and replay protection. IPsec headers consist of the following:

- Authentication header (AH)

- Encapsulating Security Payload (ESP) header and trailer

The result of applying the AH or ESP to an IP datagram transforms it to a protected datagram. Consequently, AH and ESP are sometimes referred to as *transforms*.

Authentication Header

The AH is a header defined in RFC 4302 that provides data origin authentication, data integrity, and replay protection for the entire IP datagram. Figure 18-1 shows the structure of the AH and its location relative to the IP packet payload.

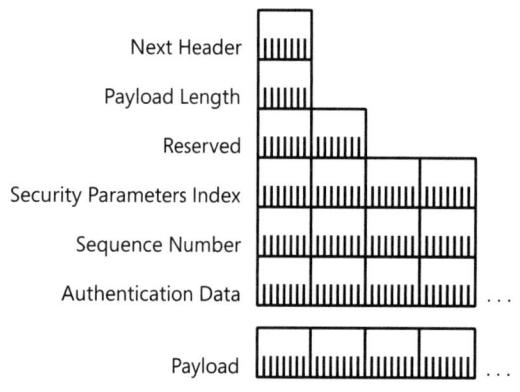

Figure 18-1 The IPsec Authentication header

The AH consists of the following fields:

- **Next Header**   A 1-byte field that is used to identify the next header in the payload. This field uses the same values as the Protocol field in the IP header.

- **Payload Length**   A 1-byte field that specifies the number of bytes in the AH past the Payload Length field in 32-bit (4-byte) blocks, not counting the first 2 blocks.

- **Reserved**   A 2-byte field that is reserved and must be set to 0. The Reserved field is included in the Authentication Data field calculation, but otherwise ignored.

- **Security Parameters Index**   A 4-byte field that identifies, when used in combination with the Destination Address field in the IP header and transform (AH), the specific security association (SA) for this datagram. For more information about SAs, see the section "IPsec and Security Associations" later in this chapter.

- **Sequence Number**   A 4-byte field that contains an incrementing counter value that starts at 0 when the SA is established. The first packet for the SA has a sequence number of 1. The Sequence Number field provides antireplay protection because its value is protected by the Integrity Check Value (ICV) calculation. When the Sequence Number counts up to its maximum value (4,294,967,295 or $2^{32} - 1$), a new IPsec SA is established to keep the Sequence Number from repeating for an SA. When the new IPsec SA is established, the Sequence Number for the new SA starts at 0. If the Sequence Number for an incoming packet is too far out of sequence or if it matches a recently received sequence number, the packet is discarded.

- **Authentication Data**   A variable-length field that contains the ICV calculation of the sender. In Windows Server 2008 and Windows Vista, this is the hash-based message authentication code (HMAC) Message Digest 5 (MD5) or HMAC Secure Hash Algorithm 1 (SHA1) keyed hash value. The Authentication Data field provides data origin authentication and data integrity security services. The size of the Authentication Data field for both the HMAC MD5 and HMAC SHA1 is 12 bytes (96 bits) long. For an arbitrary ICV algorithm, the Authentication Data field size must be an integral number of 32-bit (4-byte) blocks and will be extended with padding if needed.

> **More Info**   All of the RFCs referenced in this chapter can be found in the \Standards\Chap18_IPsec folder on the companion CD-ROM.

IPsec has two modes of protection:

- **Transport mode**   Typically used for IPsec peers doing end-to-end security. Transport mode provides protection for IP packet payloads by adding an extra header or trailer between the original IP datagram and its payload. Transport mode is typically used within an organization.

- **Tunnel mode**   Typically used by network routers to protect IP datagrams when forwarding traffic over an insecure transit network. Tunnel mode provides protection for entire IP datagrams by encapsulating the IP datagram with an IPsec header/trailer and an additional IP header. Tunnel mode is typically used outside an organization when connecting sites across a public network such as the Internet.

AH Transport Mode

Figure 18-2 shows AH Transport mode for an IP datagram.

The AH is added to the IP datagram just after the IP header. In the IP header, the Protocol field is set to 51 (0x33) to indicate that an AH is present. Normal routers forward this traffic as any other IP packet. Firewalls, on the other hand, might need to be configured to allow the forwarding of IP protocol 51 traffic. The payload is unmodified. Inserting an AH creates additional packet overhead, which lowers the effective maximum transmission unit (MTU) between the two endpoints. Calculating the ICV for the AH also imposes additional processing overhead for each protected packet. Using network adapters that can perform cryptographic calculations in hardware can minimize this overhead.

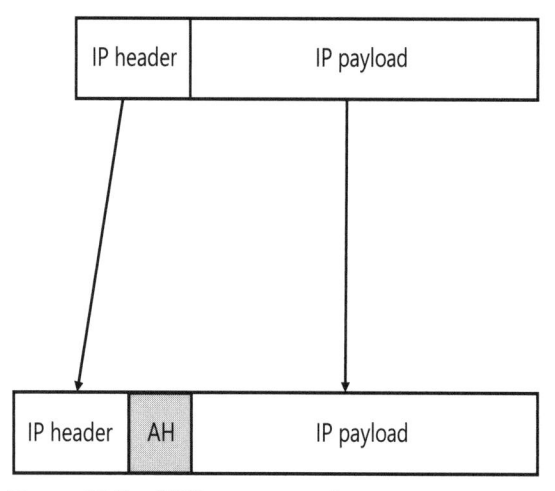

Figure 18-2 AH Transport mode

For AH Transport mode, the ICV calculation is performed over the following:

- All the fields in the IP header except those that are allowed to change in transit. These fields are the Type of Service (TOS), Flags, Fragment Offset, Time to Live (TTL), and Header Checksum, all of which are set to 0 for the ICV calculation. For source-routed IP traffic, the final destination IP address is predictable, and the appropriate fields within the Loose Source Route and Strict Source Route options are allowed to change.
- All the fields in the AH (the Authentication Data field is set to 0).
- The IP packet payload.

For AH Transport mode, the AH protects the IP header, except the fields that are allowed to change, and the payload of the original IP datagram.

The following is Frame 10 of Capture 18-01 in the \Captures folder on the companion CD-ROM, which shows an AH-protected Domain Name System (DNS) Name Query Request message, as displayed by Network Monitor 3.1:

```
Frame:
+ Ethernet: Etype = Internet IP (IPv4)
- Ipv4: Next Protocol = AH, Packet ID = 1807, Total IP Length = 86
  + Versions: IPv4, Internet Protocol; Header Length = 20
  + DifferentiatedServicesField: DSCP: 0, ECN: 0
    TotalLength: 86 (0x56)
    Identification: 1807 (0x70F)
  + FragmentFlags: 0 (0x0)
    TimeToLive: 128 (0x80)
    NextProtocol: AH, 51(0x33)
    Checksum: 11405 (0x2C8D)
    SourceAddress: 131.107.0.2
    DestinationAddress: 131.107.0.1
```

```
- Ah: Next Protocol = UDP, SPI = 0x48B7D428, Seq = 0x1
    NextHeader: UDP, 17(0x11)
    PayloadLength: 24 bytes
    Reserved: 0 (0x0)
    SecurityParametersIndex: 1220006952 (0x48B7D428)
    SequenceNumber: 1 (0x1)
    AuthenticationData: 12 UINT8(s)
+ Udp: SrcPort = 50286, DstPort = DNS(53), Length = 42
+ Dns: QueryId = 0xDE8D, QUERY (Standard query), Query  for  test.contoso.com of type Host A
ddr on class Internet
```

AH Tunnel Mode

Figure 18-3 shows AH Tunnel mode for an IP datagram.

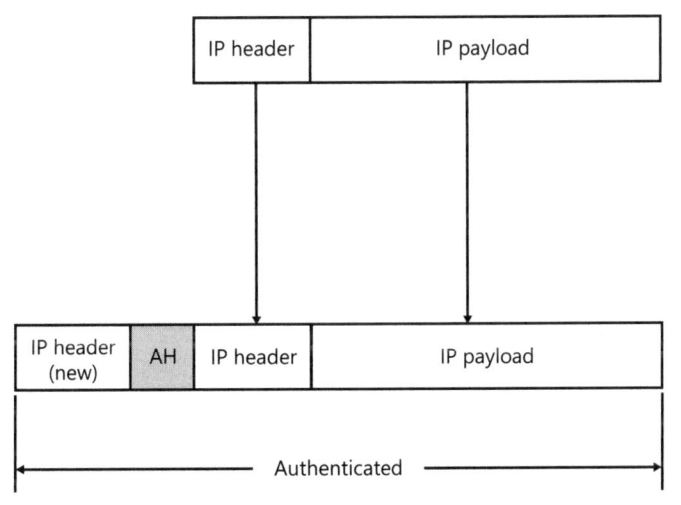

Figure 18-3 AH Tunnel mode

In AH Tunnel mode, the entire original IP datagram is encapsulated with a new (outer) IP header and an AH. In the IP header, the Protocol field is set to 51 (0x33) to indicate that an AH is present. For Tunnel mode, the original IP header and payload are unmodified.

The outer IP header is constructed from the configuration of the IPsec tunnel. The source IP address is the locally assigned IP address that is the best source to reach the tunnel destination address.

For AH Tunnel mode, the ICV calculation is performed over the following:

- All the fields in the outer IP header except those that are allowed to change in transit (TOS, Flags, Fragment Offset, TTL, Header Checksum), all of which are set to 0 for the calculation
- All the fields in the AH (the Authentication Data field is set to 0)
- The original IP packet

For AH Tunnel mode, the AH protects the entire original IP packet (both the IP header and the payload) at the expense of an additional outer IP header that is not used for AH Transport mode.

Encapsulating Security Payload (ESP)

Encapsulating Security Payload (ESP) is a header and trailer combination defined in RFC 4303 that provides data origin authentication, data integrity, replay protection, and data confidentiality for the ESP-encapsulated portion of the packet. Figure 18-4 shows the structure of the ESP header and trailer and their location relative to the IP packet payload.

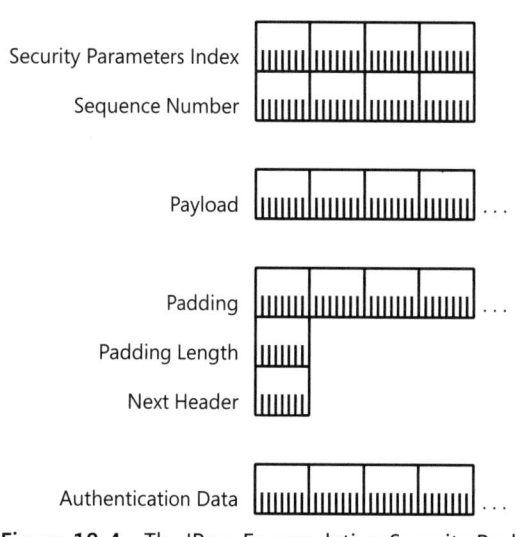

Figure 18-4 The IPsec Encapsulating Security Payload header and trailer

The ESP header consists of the following fields:

- **Security Parameters Index**   A 4-byte field that identifies, when used in combination with the Destination Address field in the IP header and transform (ESP), the specific SA for this datagram

- **Sequence Number**   A 4-byte field that is the same field as the Sequence Number field of the AH

The ESP trailer consists of the following fields:

- **Padding**   A variable-length field (0-255 bytes) that is used to pad the encrypted payload to an appropriate length (depending on the encryption algorithm used), align the ESP portion of the packet along 4-byte boundaries, or deliberately obscure the encrypted payload's length.

- **Padding Length**   A 1-byte field that specifies the number of bytes in the Padding field.

- **Next Header** A 1-byte field used to identify the next header in the payload. This field uses the same values as the Protocol field in the IP header.
- **Authentication Data** A variable-length field that contains the ICV calculation of the sender (the HMAC MD5 or HMAC SHA1 value).

Because the use of a specific ICV algorithm is negotiated before data with an ESP header and trailer is sent, each peer knows the size of the Authentication Data portion of the ESP trailer and can determine the location of the end of the ESP-encapsulated payload.

IPsec in Windows Server 2008 and Windows Vista can use the following encryption algorithms:

- Advanced Encryption Standard (AES) with a 128-bit key size (AES-128)
- AES with a 192-bit key size (AES-192)
- AES with a 256-bit key size (AES-256)
- Triple Data Encryption Standard (3DES) with three 56-bit keys
- Data Encryption Standard (DES) with a 56-bit key (not recommended)

The following is Frame 11 of Capture 18-02 in the \Captures folder on the companion CD-ROM, which shows an ESP-protected DNS Name Query Request message when using ESP and no encryption, as displayed by Network Monitor 3.1:

```
Frame:
+ Ethernet: Etype = Internet IP (IPv4)
- Ipv4: Next Protocol = ESP, Packet ID = 1542, Total IP Length = 88
  + Versions: IPv4, Internet Protocol; Header Length = 20
  + DifferentiatedServicesField: DSCP: 0, ECN: 0
    TotalLength: 88 (0x58)
    Identification: 1542 (0x606)
  + FragmentFlags: 0 (0x0)
    TimeToLive: 128 (0x80)
    NextProtocol: ESP, 50(0x32)
    Checksum: 11669 (0x2D95)
    SourceAddress: 131.107.0.2
    DestinationAddress: 131.107.0.1
- Esp: Next Protocol = UDP, SPI = 0x469021eb, Seq = 0x1
    SecurityParameterIndex: 1183850987 (0x469021EB)
    SequenceNumber: 1 (0x1)
  - Trailer:
      PaddingData: Binary Large Object (2 Bytes)
      PaddingLength: 2 (0x2)
      NextProtocol: UDP, 17(0x11)
      AuthenticationData: Binary Large Object (12 Bytes)
+ Udp: SrcPort = 50202, DstPort = DNS(53), Length = 44
+ Dns: QueryId = 0xF341, QUERY (Standard query), Query for test99.contoso.com of type Host Addr on class Internet
```

Note Network Monitor 3.1 displays the fields of the ESP trailer within the ESP header, rather than after the ESP payload.

Network Monitor 3.1 cannot interpret the encrypted portions of an ESP-protected packet.

ESP Transport Mode

Figure 18-5 shows ESP Transport mode for an IP datagram.

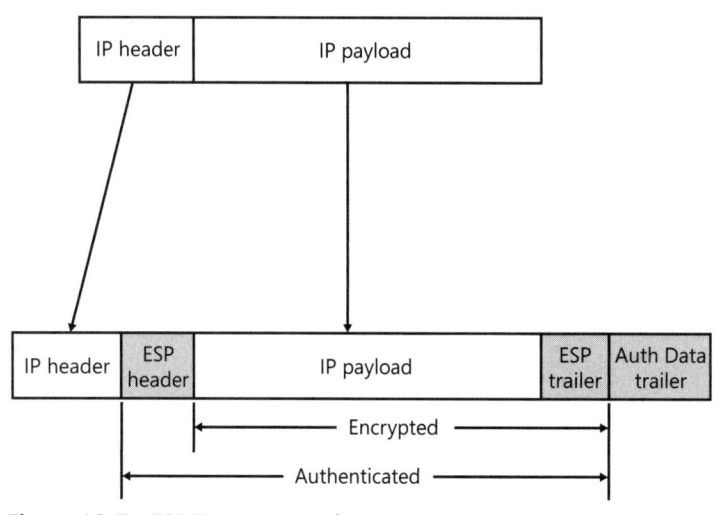

Figure 18-5 ESP Transport mode

For ESP Transport mode, the ESP header is added to the IP datagram just after the IP header and the ESP trailer is added just after the payload. In the IP header, the Protocol field is set to 50 (0x32) to indicate that an ESP header is present. Routers forward this traffic as any other IP packet. Firewalls, on the other hand, might need to be configured to allow the forwarding of IP protocol 50 traffic. The payload is unmodified.

Like AH, inserting an ESP header and trailer creates additional packet overhead, which lowers the effective MTU between the two endpoints. Performing the data encryption and calculating the ICV for the ESP trailer imposes additional processing overhead for each protected packet. Using network adapters that can perform cryptographic calculations in hardware, also known as offload adapters, can minimize this overhead.

For ESP Transport mode, the following portions of the packet are encrypted:

- The payload
- The Padding, Padding Length, and Next Header fields of the ESP trailer

For encryption algorithms that use cipher block chaining (CBC), there is an unencrypted field between the ESP header and the payload. This field is the initialization vector (IV) for the CBC calculation performed at the receiver. This field cannot be encrypted because it is used to begin the decryption process.

The inclusion of the IV as plaintext in the packet does not create a security problem. The IV does not provide additional cryptographic strength, only a way to ensure that the encryption of the same block with different IVs does not produce the same ciphertext. A malicious user might be able to view the IV, but without the encryption key, he or she cannot decrypt the ciphertext portion of the packet. To prevent a malicious user from modifying the IV and causing the receiver to produce garbled deciphered data, the IV is protected by the ICV.

For ESP Transport mode, the ICV calculation is performed over the following:

- All the fields in the ESP header
- The payload (including the plaintext IV, if needed)
- All the fields in the ESP trailer except the Authentication Data field

For ESP Transport mode, the ESP trailer does not provide protection for the IP header and the Authentication Data field of the ESP trailer. To obtain protection for these elements, use both AH and ESP, as shown in Figure 18-6.

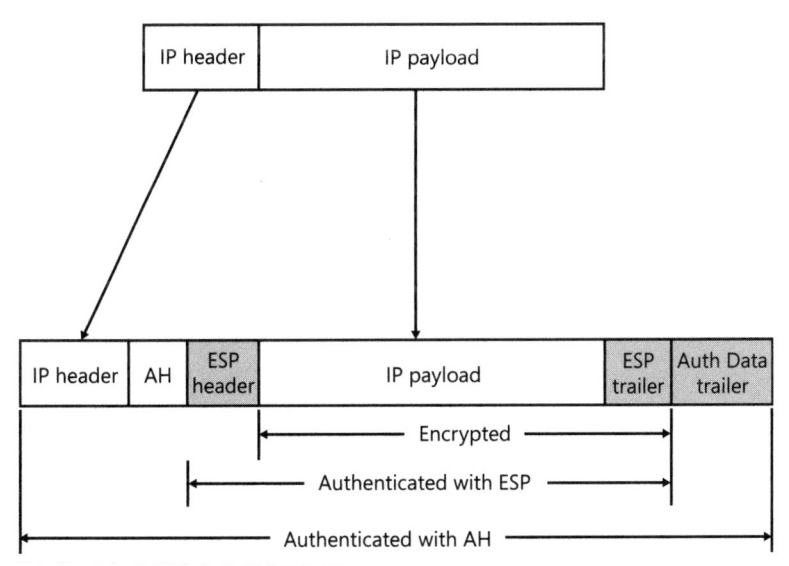

Figure 18-6 Using both AH and ESP to protect an IP packet

With AH and ESP, the ESP header and trailer wraps the payload, which then becomes the payload that is wrapped with an AH and the original IP header. Now the entire packet is protected (except the changeable fields in the IP header).

The following is Frame 10 of Capture 18-03 in the \Captures folder on the companion CD-ROM, which shows an AH- and ESP-protected IP payload with ESP encryption, as displayed by Network Monitor 3.1:

```
Frame:
+ Ethernet: Etype = Internet IP (IPv4)
- Ipv4: Next Protocol = AH, Packet ID = 1555, Total IP Length = 120
  + Versions: IPv4, Internet Protocol; Header Length = 20
  + DifferentiatedServicesField: DSCP: 0, ECN: 0
    TotalLength: 120 (0x78)
    Identification: 1555 (0x613)
  + FragmentFlags: 0 (0x0)
    TimeToLive: 128 (0x80)
    NextProtocol: AH, 51(0x33)
    Checksum: 11623 (0x2D67)
    SourceAddress: 131.107.0.2
    DestinationAddress: 131.107.0.1
- Ah: Next Protocol = ESP, SPI = 0x43E235D7, Seq = 0x1
    NextHeader: ESP, 50(0x32)
    PayloadLength: 24 bytes
    Reserved: 0 (0x0)
    SecurityParametersIndex: 1138898391 (0x43E235D7)
    SequenceNumber: 1 (0x1)
    AuthenticationData: 12 UINT8(s)
- Esp: SPI = 0x1ef5e304, Seq = 0x1
    SecurityParameterIndex: 519430916 (0x1EF5E304)
    SequenceNumber: 1 (0x1)
    EncryptedPayload: Binary Large Object (68 Bytes)
```

ESP Tunnel Mode

Figure 18-7 shows ESP Tunnel mode for an IP datagram.

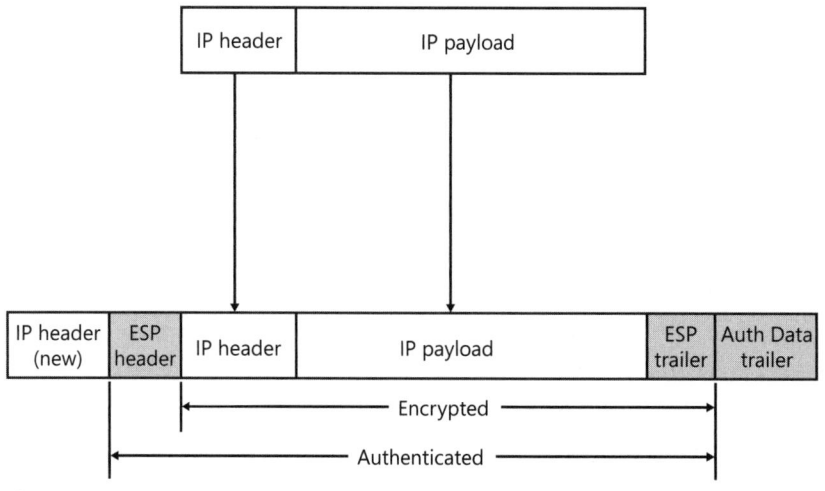

Figure 18-7 ESP Tunnel mode

In ESP Tunnel mode, the entire original IP datagram is encapsulated with a new (outer) IP header and an ESP header and trailer. In the outer IP header, the Protocol field is set to 50 (0x32) to indicate that an ESP header is present. For Tunnel mode, the original IP header and payload are unmodified. Like AH Tunnel mode, the outer IP header is constructed from the configuration of the IPsec tunnel.

For ESP Tunnel mode, the following portions of the packet are encrypted:

- The original IP datagram (IP header and payload)
- The Padding, Padding Length, and Next Header fields of the ESP trailer

For ESP Tunnel mode, the ICV calculation is performed over the following:

- All the fields in the ESP header
- The original IP datagram (IP header and payload), including the plaintext IV, if needed
- All the fields in the ESP header except the Authentication Data field

For ESP Tunnel mode, the ESP trailer provides protection for the original IP header and payload, but does not provide protection for the outer IP header and the Authentication Data field of the ESP trailer.

IPsec and Security Associations

A *security association* (SA) is the combination of security services, protection mechanisms, and cryptographic keys mutually agreed to by communicating peers. The SA contains the information needed to determine how the traffic is to be secured (the security services and protection mechanisms) and with which secret keys (cryptographic keys). There are two types of SAs that are created when IPsec peers communicate securely: the Internet Security Association and Key Management Protocol (ISAKMP) SA and the IPsec SA.

ISAKMP SA

The ISAKMP SA, also known as the main mode SA, is used to protect IPsec security negotiations. The ISAKMP SA is created by negotiating the ciphersuite used for protecting future ISAKMP traffic, exchanging key-generation material, and then identifying and authenticating each IPsec peer.

When the ISAKMP SA is complete, all future SA negotiations for IPsec SAs are protected. This is an aspect of secure communications known as *protected ciphersuite negotiation*. Not only is the data protected, but the determination of the protection algorithms negotiated by the IPsec peers is also protected. To break IPsec protection, a malicious user must first determine the ciphersuite protecting the data, which represents another cryptographic barrier. For IPsec, the exceptions to complete protected ciphersuite negotiation are the negotiations of the ciphersuites of ISAKMP SAs, which begin as plaintext.

IPsec SA

The IPsec SA, also known as the quick mode SA, is used to protect data sent between the IPsec peers. The IPsec SA ciphersuite negotiation is protected by the ISAKMP SA. No information about the type of traffic or the protection mechanisms is sent as plaintext. For a pair of IPsec peers, there are always two IPsec SAs: one is negotiated for inbound traffic and one is for outbound traffic. The inbound SA for one IPsec peer is the outbound SA for the other.

Security Parameters Index

For each IPsec session, IPsec peers must track the usage of three different SAs: the ISAKMP SA, the inbound IPsec SA, and the outbound IPsec SA. To identify a specific SA, a 32-bit pseudo-random number known as the Security Parameters Index (SPI) is used. The SPI is used for SA management at each IPsec peer and is a field in the IPsec headers protecting IPsec traffic and in the messages negotiating or managing SAs.

The node that initiates an IPsec negotiation to perform IPsec protection is known as the *initiator*. The node that responds to a request to perform IPsec protection is known as the *responder*. The initiator chooses the ISAKMP SA SPI, and each IPsec peer chooses the IPsec SA SPI for its outbound traffic.

Creating SAs

An IPsec negotiation and determination of both ISAKMP and IPsec SAs occurs in two phases: the Main mode phase (also known as Phase I) and the Quick mode phase (also known as Phase II).

Main Mode   Main mode negotiation creates the ISAKMP SA. The initiator and responder exchange a series of ISAKMP messages to negotiate the ciphersuite for the ISAKMP SA (in plaintext), exchange key determination material (in plaintext), and identify and authenticate each other (in encrypted text). For more information about the details of Main mode negotiation, see the section "Main Mode Negotiation" later in this chapter.

Quick Mode   Quick mode negotiation creates the two IPsec SAs. The initiator and responder exchange a series of ISAKMP messages to negotiate the ciphersuite for both the inbound and outbound IPsec SAs. During Quick mode negotiation, keying material is refreshed or, if necessary, new keys are generated. For more information about the details of quick mode negotiation, see the section "Quick Mode Negotiation" later in this chapter.

For IPsec for Windows Server 2008 and Windows Vista, a complete IPsec negotiation including both Main mode and Quick mode requires either 9 or 10 ISAKMP messages exchanged between IPsec peers, depending on security settings.

Internet Key Exchange

The Internet Key Exchange (IKE) is a standard that defines a mechanism to establish SAs. IKE, described in RFC 2409, combines ISAKMP and the Oakley Key Determination Protocol.

IPsec uses the ISAKMP protocol to negotiate SAs. ISAKMP includes facilities to identify and authenticate peers, manage SAs, and exchange key material. ISAKMP is a framework for negotiating secure communications independent of specific key exchange protocols, encryption and integrity algorithms, and authentication methods.

To generate secret key material for secure communications, IKE uses the Oakley Key Determination Protocol. Oakley is based on the Diffie-Hellman key exchange algorithm, which allows two peers to determine a secret key by exchanging unencrypted values over a public network. The mutually determined secret key becomes keying material from which secret keys for HMAC or encryption algorithms are derived.

> **More Info** The details of the Diffie-Hellman algorithm and the Oakley protocol are outside the scope of this book, but they are described in RFC 2412.

ISAKMP Message Structure

ISAKMP messages are sent as the payload of UDP messages using UDP port 500. Figure 18-8 shows the format of an ISAKMP message.

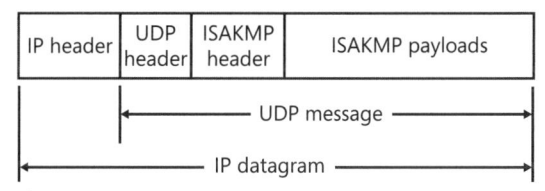

Figure 18-8 An ISAKMP message

The ISAKMP message consists of an ISAKMP header and one or more ISAKMP payloads. The ISAKMP payloads contain negotiation information and are encrypted for most ISAKMP messages. The encryption protects the negotiation from being viewed by malicious users who are capturing ISAKMP traffic. The encrypted portions of ISAKMP messages cannot be viewed with Network Monitor. ISAKMP is defined in RFC 2408.

ISAKMP Header

The ISAKMP header is a standard header that is present for all ISAKMP messages and contains information about the message, including the type of packet. Figure 18-9 shows the format of the ISAKMP header.

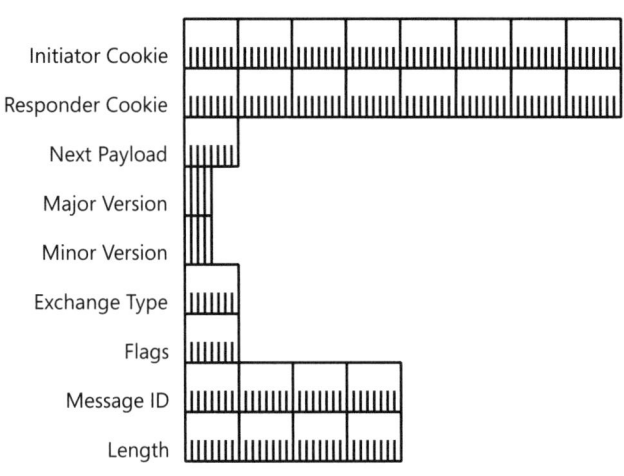

Figure 18-9 The ISAKMP header.

The fields in the ISAKMP header are defined as follows:

- **Initiator Cookie**   An 8-byte field that is set to a nonzero random number chosen by the IPsec peer that initiated the SA, is performing a notification about an existing SA, or is deleting the SA.

- **Responder Cookie**   An 8-byte field that is set to a nonzero random number chosen by the IPsec peer responding to the peer that initiated an SA.

- **Next Payload**   A 1-byte field that indicates the type of the payload that follows the ISAKMP header. Table 18-1 lists the payload types defined in RFC 2408.

Table 18-1 Values of the Next Payload Field

Next Payload Value	Next Payload Type
0	None
1	SA
2	Proposal
3	Transform
4	Key Exchange
5	Identification
6	Certificate
7	Certificate Request
8	Hash
9	Signature
10	Nonce
11	Notification
12	Delete
13	Vendor ID

Table 18-1 Values of the Next Payload Field

Next Payload Value	Next Payload Type
14–127	Reserved
128–255	Private Use

- **Major Version** A 4-bit field that indicates the major version of the ISAKMP protocol for this message. This field must be set to 1 if the implementation complies with RFC 2408. ISAKMP messages with a higher supported major version number are discarded.

- **Minor Version** A 4-bit field that indicates the minor version of the major version of the ISAKMP protocol for this message. This field must be set to 0 if the implementation complies with RFC 2408. ISAKMP messages with a higher supported minor version number are discarded, within the same supported major version.

- **Exchange Type** A 1-byte field that indicates the type of ISAKMP exchange being performed for this ISAKMP message. The type of exchange dictates the structure and the order of ISAKMP payloads. Table 18-2 lists the exchange types defined in RFC 2408.

Table 18-2 Values of the Exchange Type Field

Exchange Type Value	Exchange Type
0	None
1	Base
2	Identity Protection
3	Authentication Only
4	Aggressive
5	Informational
6–31	ISAKMP Future Use
32–239	DOI Specific Use
240–255	Private Use

- **Flags** A 1-byte field containing ISAKMP flags that are set for this ISAKMP message. There are three flags defined in RFC 2408. The low-order bit (bit 0) is the Encryption bit, which indicates the ISAKMP payloads are encrypted (when set to 1) or not encrypted (when set to 0). Encryption is done using the algorithm negotiated for the ISAKMP SA, which is identified by the combination of the Initiator Cookie and Responder Cookie fields. The next low-order bit (bit 1) is the Commit bit, which indicates that the key exchange is synchronized (when set to 1) or not synchronized (when set to 0). The Commit bit is used to ensure that the SA completes its negotiation before encrypted data is sent. The next low-order bit (bit 2) is the Authentication Only bit, which is used to indicate that the message either contains (when set to 1) or does not contain (when set to 0) the entire Notify payload of the informational exchange type and it has been authenticated but not encrypted. For more information, see the section "Notification Payload" later in this chapter.

- **Message ID**   A 4-byte field that contains a unique identifier for the message. The Message ID is used to prevent collisions due to both IPsec peers attempting to simultaneously establish an IPsec SA. The Message ID field is set to 0 for the ISAKMP SA establishment.

- **Length**   A 4-byte field that indicates the length of the entire ISAKMP message.

SA Payload

The SA payload is used to indicate the domain of interpretation (DOI) and situation for the SA negotiation. The DOI is a set of definitions for payload formats, exchange types, and naming conventions for security-related information, such as the naming of policies and cryptographic algorithms. A situation is a set of information that identifies security services in the ISAKMP message. Figure 18-10 shows the format of the SA payload.

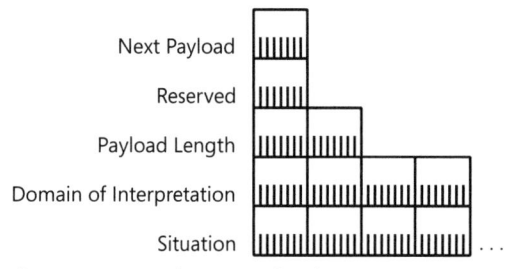

Figure 18-10   The SA payload

The fields in the SA payload are defined as follows:

- **Next Payload**   A 1-byte field that indicates the next payload in the message. Next Payload is set to 0 for the last payload in the message. For the SA payload, the Next Payload field does not indicate the Proposal or Transform payloads because they are considered part of the SA payload.

- **Reserved**   A 1-byte field set to 0.

- **Payload Length**   A 2-byte field that indicates the length of the payload. For the SA payload, the length includes the Proposal and Transform payloads.

- **Domain of Interpretation**   A 4-byte field that indicates the DOI. For IPsec and ISAKMP, the DOI field is set to 1. RFC 2407 describes the IPsec DOI for ISAKMP.

- **Situation**   A variable-length field that identifies the situation for the negotiation. For IPsec, the values of the Situation field are defined in RFC 2407. For example, the Situation field is set to 1 for SIT_IDENTITY_ONLY, a situation that specifies that the identity of the sending source is contained in an Identification payload. See section 4 of RFC 2407 for additional situation definitions.

> **Note** The Next Payload, Reserved, and Payload Length fields are common to all ISAKMP payloads. Therefore, they are not described in the payload sections that follow unless there are additional considerations for their use.

Proposal Payload

The Proposal payload contains security parameter information that is used to negotiate the security settings for either an ISAKMP or IPsec SA. The Proposal payload contains proposal settings and then a series of one or more Transform payloads that contain the specific security settings for encryption and authentication algorithms for the SA. Figure 18-11 shows the format of the Proposal payload.

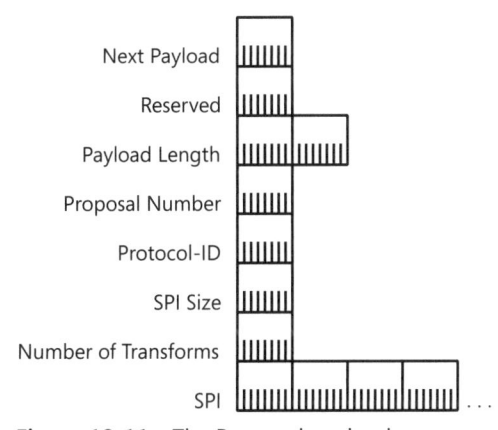

Figure 18-11 The Proposal payload

The fields in the Proposal payload are defined as follows:

- **Next Payload** For the Proposal payload, the Next Payload field must be set to either 2 for additional Proposal payloads or 0 for no more Proposal payloads.
- **Payload Length** For the Proposal payload, the Payload Length field indicates the length of the entire Proposal payload, which includes the Transform payloads for this Proposal payload.
- **Proposal Number** A 1-byte field that indicates the number of this proposal.
- **Protocol-ID** A 1-byte field that specifies the security protocol suite being negotiated, such as ISAKMP (Protocol-ID is set to 1). For a current list, see *http://www.iana.org /assignments/isakmp-registry*.
- **SPI Size** A 1-byte field that indicates the length in bytes of the optional SPI field. If the protocol indicated by the Protocol-ID field does not use a SPI, SPI size is set to 0. For example ISAKMP does not use a SPI.

- **Number of Transforms** A 1-byte field that indicates the number of Transform payloads for this proposal.
- **SPI** A variable-size field that contains the SPI. This field is only present if the SPI Size field is greater than 0.

Transform Payload

The Transform payload contains information that identifies a specific security mechanism, or *transform,* that is proposed to secure future traffic. The Transform payload also contains SA attributes, as defined in RFC 2407 for the IPsec DOI. Figure 18-12 shows the Transform payload.

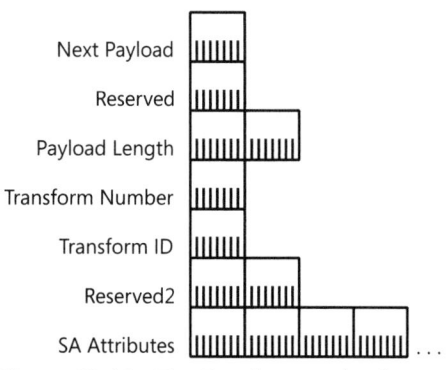

Figure 18-12 The Transform payload

The fields in the Transform payload are defined as follows:

- **Next Payload** For the Transform payload, the Next Payload field must be set to either 3 for additional Transform payloads or 0 for no more Transform payloads for this proposal.
- **Payload Length** For the Transform payload, the Payload Length field indicates the length of the entire Transform payload, which includes the SA attributes for this Transform payload.
- **Transform Number** A 1-byte field that indicates the number of this transform.
- **Transform ID** A 1-byte field that indicates the Transform identifier for the protocol of the proposal. Transform IDs are defined in RFC 2407 for the IPsec DOI.
- **Reserved2** A 2-byte field that is set to 0.
- **SA Attributes** Variable-length fields that define the SA attributes for the transform. SA attributes are either in type-value or type-length (2 bytes)-value (TLV) format. In both cases, the Type field is 2 bytes in length. To distinguish type-value from TLV format, the high-order bit of the Attribute Type field is set to 1 for type-value format and 0 for TLV format. SA attributes for the IPsec DOI are defined in section 4.5 of RFC 2407.

Chapter 18: Internet Protocol Security (IPsec)

The following is Frame 1 of Capture 18-01 in the \Captures folder on the companion CD-ROM, which shows the relationship among the SA, Proposal, and Transform payloads, and the SA attributes within a Transform payload as displayed by Network Monitor 3.1:

```
Frame:
+ Ethernet: Etype = Internet IP (IPv4)
+ Ipv4: Next Protocol = UDP, Packet ID = 1517, Total IP Length = 236
+ Udp: SrcPort = ISAKMP/IKE(500), DstPort = ISAKMP/IKE(500), Length = 216
- Ike: version = 1.0, Identity protection (Main Mode), Flags = ..., Length = 208
    InitiatorCookie: D8 22 8F 25 FE 3F DB D8
    ResponderCookie: 47 46 01 F9 67 63 0F 11
    NextPayload: Security Association (SA), 1(0x01)
  + Version: 1.0
    ExchangeType: Identity protection (Main Mode), 2(0x02)
  + FlagsVer1: ...
    MessageID: 0 (0x0)
    Length: 208 (0xD0)
  - SecurityAssociation: Next Payload = Vendor ID (VID), Length = 56
    NextPayload: Vendor ID (VID), 13(0x0D)
    Reserved: 0 (0x0)
    PayloadLength: 56 (0x38)
    DOI: IPSEC(1)
   + Situation: SIT_IDENTITY_ONLY
   - ProposalPayload: Next Payload = None, ProtocolID = ISAKMP, NumberOfTransforms = 1,
     Length = 44
     NextPayload: None, 0(0x00)
     Reserved: 0 (0x0)
     PayloadLength: 44 (0x2C)
     Proposal: 1 (0x1)
     ProtocolID: ISAKMP, 1(0x01)
     SPISize: 0 (0x0)
     NumberOfTransforms: 1 (0x1)
    - TransformPayload: Next Payload = None, TransformID = KEY_IKE, Length = 36
      NextPayload: None, 0(0x00)
      Reserved: 0 (0x0)
      PayloadLength: 36 (0x24)
      Transform: 1 (0x1)
      TransformId: KEY_IKE 1(0x01)
      RESERVED2: 0 (0x0)
     + Attribute: TV: basic Encryption algorithm = 3DES-CBC
     + Attribute: TV: basic Hash algorithm = SHA
     + Attribute: TV: basic Group description = Alternate 1024-bit MODP group
     + Attribute: TV: basic Authentication method = Pre-shared key (PSK)
     + Attribute: TV: basic Life type = seconds
     + Attribute: TLV: variable Life duration = Binary Large Object (4 Bytes)
 + VendorID: MS NT5 ISAKMPOAKLEY, Version 6, Next Payload = Vendor ID (VID), Length = 24
 + VendorID: RFC 3947 (NAT-T supported), Next Payload = Vendor ID (VID), Length = 20
 + VendorID: draft-ietf-ipsec-nat-t-ike-02, Next Payload = Vendor ID (VID), Length = 20
 + VendorID: FRAGMENTATION, Next Payload = Vendor ID (VID), Length = 20
 + VendorID: 0xfb1de3cdf341b7ea16b7e5be0855f120, Next Payload = Vendor ID (VID), Length = 20
 + VendorID: IKE CGA version 1, Next Payload = None, Length = 20
```

Vendor ID Payload

The Vendor ID payload contains a string or number that either indicates a specific capability or is defined by a vendor so that an IPsec implementation can recognize an IPsec peer running the same implementation. IPsec peers are not required to run the same implementation or support the same capabilities, so the sending of Vendor ID payloads and the actions taken when they are received are optional. If a receiver recognizes the Vendor ID, it can make use of the capability or use private payloads, which use the Payload ID numbers 128 through 255. For vendor identification, the Vendor ID value must be unique and is typically a hash of well-known text chosen by the designers of an IPsec implementation. For capability identification, the Vendor ID value must be unique and is typically chosen by the designers of the IPsec capability.

Figure 18-13 shows the format of the Vendor ID payload.

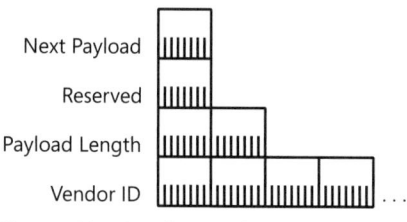

Figure 18-13 The Vendor ID payload

The only field in the Vendor ID payload (besides the Next Header, Reserved, and Payload Length fields) is the Vendor ID field, a variable-length field that contains the Vendor ID value.

IPsec for Windows Server 2008 and Windows Vista uses the following Vendor ID payloads to indicate that the IPsec peer:

- Is running a Microsoft operating system and the version of that operating system
- Supports Network Address Translator (NAT) Traversal capability based on RFC 3947
- Supports Network Address Translator (NAT) Traversal capability based on the draft-ietf-ipsec-nat-t-ike-02.txt Internet draft
- Supports fragmentation
- Supports network load balancing
- Supports Authenticated Internet Protocol (AuthIP)
- Supports Kerberos authentication using the Generic Security Services Application Programming Interface (GSSAPI)
- Supports IKE with IPv6 Cryptographically Generated Addresses (CGA)
- Supports Negotiation Discovery

Negotiation Discovery is new behavior for Windows Server 2008 and Windows Vista to automatically determine whether a potential peer supports IPsec. The Negotiation Discovery Vendor ID payload is shown in Network Monitor 3.1 as Vendor ID 0xFB1DE3CDF341B7EA16B7E5BE0855F120.

The Network Load Balancing Vendor ID payload is shown in Network Monitor 3.1 as Vendor ID Vid-Initial-Contact.

Nonce Payload

The Nonce payload contains a pseudorandom number that is used to ensure a live exchange and provide replay protection. Nonces are also used to calculate hashes in other payloads. Figure 18-14 shows the format of the Nonce payload.

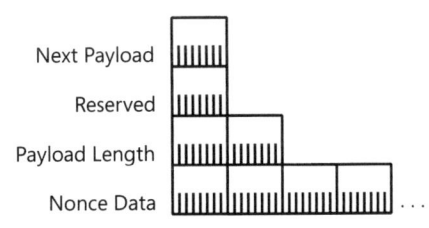

Figure 18-14 The Nonce payload

The only field in the Nonce payload (besides the Next Header, Reserved, and Payload Length fields) is the Nonce Data field, a variable-length field that contains the pseudorandom number determined by the sender of the ISAKMP message.

Key Exchange Payload

The Key Exchange payload contains information pertaining to the key exchange process. The key exchange process supported by IPsec for Windows Server 2008 and Windows Vista is Diffie-Hellman. With Diffie-Hellman, two IPsec peers exchange key values that are sent in plaintext. From the key values, each IPsec peer calculates the same private key. With the Diffie-Hellman exchange, a malicious user between the IPsec peers can view the exchanged key values but cannot easily calculate the same result as the IPsec peers. Figure 18-15 shows the format of the Key Exchange payload.

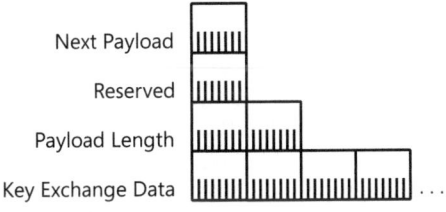

Figure 18-15 The Key Exchange payload

The only field in the Key Exchange payload (besides the Next Header, Reserved, and Payload Length fields) is the Key Exchange Data field, a variable-length field that contains the key exchange value determined by the sender of the ISAKMP message.

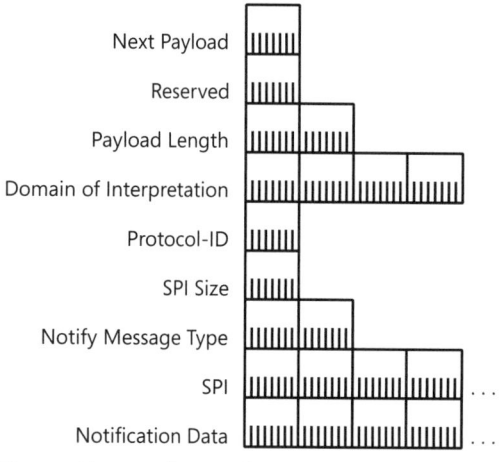

Notification Payload

The Notification payload is used to transmit control information, such as an error condition, to an IPsec peer. A single ISAKMP message can contain multiple Notification payloads. For Notification payloads within a Main mode message, the initiator and responder cookies identify the negotiation. Figure 18-16 shows the format of the Notification payload.

Figure 18-16 The Notification payload

The fields in the Notification payload are defined as follows:

- **Domain of Interpretation**   A 4-byte field that identifies the DOI for the notification. For the ISAKMP DOI, the value is 0; for the IPsec DOI, the value is 1.

- **Protocol-ID**   A 1-byte value that indicates the protocol to which the notification applies.

- **SPI Size**   A 1-byte field that indicates the length of the SPI field. For ISAKMP, the security identifier is the initiator/responder cookie pair. Therefore, the SPI Size field can be set to 0. For ISAKMP, if the SPI Size field is set to a non-zero value, the SPI field is ignored.

- **Notify Message Type**   A 2-byte field that specifies the type of notification message.

- **SPI**   A variable-length field that specifies the SPI for the notification.

- **Notification Data**   A variable-length field that contains additional information or text for the notification message indicated by the Notify Message Type field.

Table 18-3 lists some of the notification error messages specified in RFC 2408. For a complete list, see section 3.14.1 of RFC 2408.

Table 18-3 Notification Error Messages

Notification Message Type Value	Notification Message
1	INVALID-PAYLOAD-TYPE
2	DOI-NOT-SUPPORTED
3	SITUATION-NOT-SUPPORTED
4	INVALID-COOKIE
5	INVALID-MAJOR-VERSION
6	INVALID-MINOR-VERSION

Table 18-4 lists some of the notification status messages specified in RFC 2408.

Table 18-4 Notification Status Messages

Notification Message Type Value	Notification Message
16384	CONNECTED
16385–24575	RESERVED (Future Use)
24576–32767	DOI-specific codes
32768–40959	Private Use
40960–65535	RESERVED (Future Use)

Delete Payload

The Delete payload is used to inform an IPsec peer that an SA for a specific protocol has been deleted. The receiver should remove its corresponding SA. IPsec for Windows Server 2008 and Windows Vista supports verification of Delete payloads. If an ISAKMP message with a Delete payload is received, the receiver acknowledges it. If an acknowledgment is not received, the Delete payload is resent. Figure 18-17 shows the format of the Delete payload.

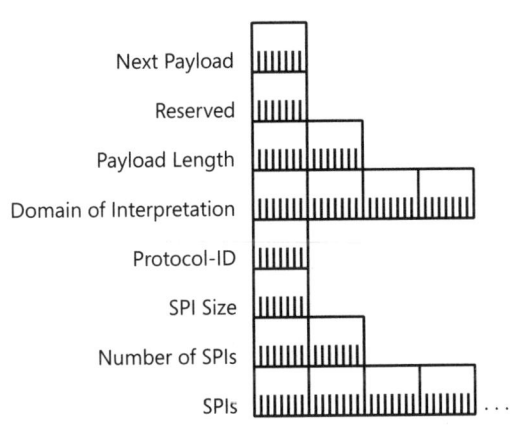

Figure 18-17 The Delete payload

The fields in the Delete payload are defined as follows:

- **Domain of Interpretation**   A 4-byte field that identifies the DOI. The DOI is 0 for ISAKMP and 1 for IPsec.
- **Protocol-ID**   A 1-byte field that identifies the protocol for the SA that was deleted. The Protocol-ID field indicates ISAKMP for main mode SA deletions and ESP or AH for Quick mode SA deletions.
- **SPI Size**   A 1-byte field that indicates the length of a SPI in the SPIs field. For the ISAKMP protocol, the SPI size is set to 16.
- **Number of SPIs**   A 2-byte field that indicates the number of SPIs in the SPIs field.
- **SPIs**   A variable-length field that identifies the SAs to delete. All of the SPIs have the same length, as indicated with the SPI Size field.

Identification Payload

The Identification payload is used to convey identification information and authenticate an IPsec peer.

Figure 18-18 shows the format of the Identification payload.

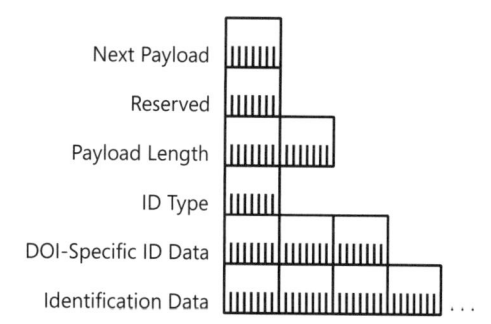

Figure 18-18   The Identification payload

The fields in the Identification payload are defined as follows:

- **ID Type**   A 1-byte field that indicates the type of identification.
- **DOI-Specific ID Data**   A 3-byte field that contains DOI-specific data. If not used, this is set to 0.
- **Identification Data**   A variable-length field that contains identity information.

Hash Payload

The Hash payload contains a hash value that is a result of a hash function computed over a set of fields or other parameters. The Hash payload can be used to provide integrity or authentication of negotiating peers. Figure 18-19 shows the format of the Hash payload.

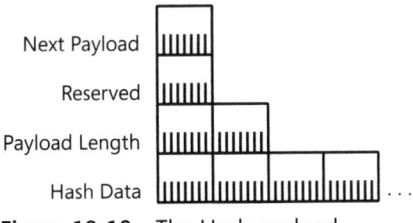

Figure 18-19 The Hash payload

The only field in the Hash payload (besides the Next Header, Reserved, and Payload Length fields) is the Hash Data field, a variable-length field that contains the hash value. Both IPsec peers must agree to the set of fields or other parameters over which the hash is calculated.

Certificate Request Payload

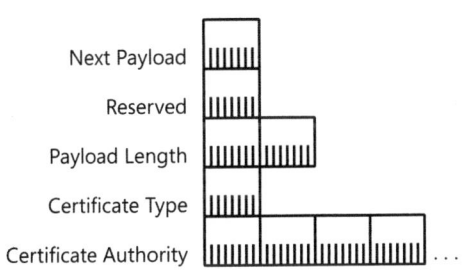

The Certificate Request payload is used to request certificates from an IPsec peer. After receipt of an ISAKMP message with a Certificate Request payload, an IPsec peer must send a certificate or certificates based on the contents of the Certificate Request payload. Figure 18-20 shows the format of the Certificate Request payload.

Figure 18-20 The Certificate Request payload

The fields in the Certificate Request payload are defined as follows:

- **Certificate Type**   A 1-byte field that indicates the type of the certificate requested. Table 18-5 lists the certificate types defined in RFC 2408.

Table 18-5 Certificate Type Values

Certificate Type Value	Certificate Type
0	None
1	Public Key Cryptography Standards (PKCS) #7 wrapped X.509 Certificate
2	Pretty Good Privacy (PGP) Certificate
3	Domain Name System (DNS) Signed Key
4	X.509 Certificate: Signature
5	X.509 Certificate: Key Exchange
6	Kerberos Tokens
7	Certificate Revocation List (CRL)

Table 18-5 Certificate Type Values

Certificate Type Value	Certificate Type
8	Authority Revocation List (ARL)
9	Simple Public Key Infrastructure (SPKI) Certificate
10	X.509 Certificate: Attribute
11–255	Reserved

- **Certificate Authority** A variable-length field that contains an acceptable certification authority (CA) for the indicated type of certificate. For example, for an X.509 certificate, the distinguished name of the issuing CA is used. If there is no specific CA required by the sending IPsec peer, this field is not present.

Certificate Payload

The Certificate payload is used by an IPsec peer when sending its certificate. This is typically done during the authentication phase of Main mode negotiation. Figure 18-21 shows the format of the Certificate payload.

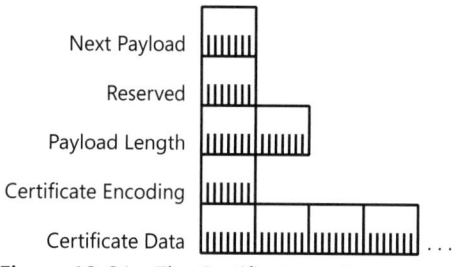

Figure 18-21 The Certificate payload

The fields in the Certificate payload are defined as follows:

- **Certificate Encoding** A 1-byte field that indicates the method for encoding the certificate information in the Certificate Data field. Table 18-5 lists the values of the Certificate Encoding field defined in RFC 2408. The same values for the Certificate Type field of the Certificate Request payload are used for the Certificate Encoding field in the Certificate payload.
- **Certificate Data** A variable-length field that contains the encoding of the certificate using the encoding method indicated in the Certificate Encoding field.

Signature Payload

The Signature payload is used to send digital signatures calculated over a set of fields or parameters. The Signature payload provides data integrity and nonrepudiation services during the authentication phase of Main mode negotiation. Figure 18-22 shows the format of the Signature payload.

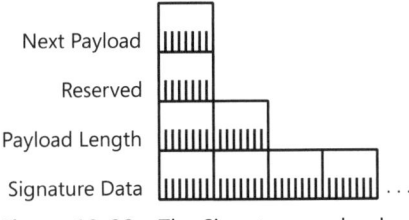

Figure 18-22 The Signature payload

The only field in the Signature payload (besides the Next Header, Reserved, and Payload Length fields) is the Signature Data field, a variable-length field that contains the digital signature value. Both IPsec peers must agree on the set of fields and parameters over which the digital signature is calculated.

Main Mode Negotiation

Main mode negotiation determines encryption key material and security protection for use in protecting subsequent Main mode or Quick mode communications. Main mode negotiation occurs in the following steps:

1. Negotiation of protection suites
2. A Diffie-Hellman exchange
3. Authentication

Main mode negotiation consists of either five or six ISAKMP messages: three sent by the initiator and two or three sent by the responder. For examples of main mode negotiation, see the following:

- Frames 1–5 of Capture 18-01 in the \Captures folder on the companion CD-ROM (Frames 4 and 5 have encrypted ISAKMP payloads)
- Frames 1–6 of Capture 18-02 (Frames 5 and 6 have encrypted ISAKMP payloads)
- Frames 1–5 of Capture 18-03 (Frames 4 and 5 have encrypted ISAKMP payloads)

Quick Mode Negotiation

When the Main mode negotiation is complete, each IPsec peer has selected a specific set of cryptographic algorithms for securing Main mode and Quick mode messages, exchanged key information to derive a shared secret key, and performed authentication. Before secure data is sent, a Quick mode negotiation must occur to determine the type of traffic to be secured and how it will be secured. A Quick mode negotiation is also done when a Quick mode SA expires. Quick mode messages are ISAKMP messages that are encrypted using the ISAKMP SA. The result of a Quick mode negotiation is two IPsec SAs: one for inbound traffic and one for outbound traffic.

Quick mode negotiation for IPsec for Windows Server 2008 and Windows Vista consists of four ISAKMP messages. The first Quick mode ISAKMP message, sent by the initiator, contains the following payloads:

- **SA** The SA payload contains a list of proposals and encryption and hashing algorithms for how to secure the traffic (AH versus ESP, AES versus 3DES, and MD5 versus SHA1) and a description of the traffic that is protected (IP addresses, IP Protocol numbers, TCP ports, UDP ports, and so on).

- **Identification** The Identification payload contains a description of the traffic to be secured.

- **Nonce** The Nonce payload contains a pseudorandom number to be used in subsequent hash calculations.

The second Quick mode ISAKMP message, sent by the responder, contains the following payloads:

- **SA** The SA payload contains a Proposal payload, which contains a single Transform payload corresponding to the protection suite that was offered by the initiator in the first Quick mode message and is acceptable to the responder for the traffic to be secured.

- **Identification** The Identification payload contains a description of the traffic to be secured.

- **Nonce** The Nonce payload contains a pseudorandom number to be used in subsequent hash calculations.

The second message has the Commit bit in the ISAKMP header set.

The third Quick mode ISAKMP message, sent by the initiator, contains the Hash payload, which contains a hash value to provide verification and replay protection.

The fourth Quick mode ISAKMP message, sent by the responder, contains the Notification payload, which contains the Notify Message Type set to 16384 (the CONNECTED status message), indicating that the SA negotiation is complete.

The setting of the Commit bit in Quick mode message 2 and the sending of the CONNECTED status message in Quick mode message 4 are not required by the ISAKMP or IKE standards. IPsec for Windows Server 2008 and Windows Vista uses this facility to prevent the initiator from sending IPsec-protected packets to the responder before the responder is ready to receive them.

For examples of quick mode negotiation, see the following:

- Frames 6–9 of Capture 18-01 in the \Captures folder on the companion CD-ROM (all of these frames have encrypted ISAKMP payloads)

- Frames 7–10 of Capture 18-02 (all of these frames have encrypted ISAKMP payloads)
- Frames 6–9 of Capture 18-03 (all of these frames have encrypted ISAKMP payloads)

Authenticated Internet Protocol (AuthIP)

In addition to IKE, Windows Server 2008 and Windows Vista support Authenticated Internet Protocol (AuthIP), an enhanced version of IKE. AuthIP supports additional authentication flexibility with support for user-level authentication, authentication with multiple credentials, improved authentication method negotiation, and asymmetric authentication.

Like IKE, AuthIP supports Main mode and Quick mode negotiation. AuthIP also supports Extended mode, a part of IPsec peer negotiation during which a second round of authentication can be performed. Extended mode, which is optional, can be used for multiple authentications. For example, with Extended mode, you can perform separate computer-level and user-level authentications.

AuthIP Messages

Both IKE and AuthIP use ISAKMP as their key exchange and SA negotiation protocol. AuthIP uses ISAKMP messages with the exchange types 243 (Main Mode), 244 (Quick Mode), 245 (Extended Mode), and 246 (Notify) in the ISAKMP header. An important difference in AuthIP-based ISAKMP messages is that they contain only one ISAKMP payload: either the Crypto payload or the Notify payload. The Crypto payload contains the embedded payloads used for the Main mode, Quick mode, or Extended mode negotiation. The Crypto payload can contain a set of plain text or encrypted payloads, depending on the Encryption bit in the Flags field of the ISAKMP header. Figure 18-23 shows the structure of AuthIP messages containing the Crypto payload.

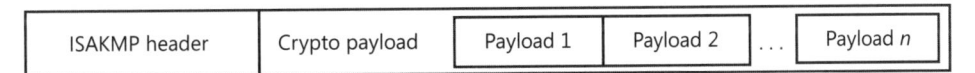

ISAKMP header	Crypto payload	Payload 1	Payload 2	...	Payload n

Figure 18-23 AuthIP messages containing the Crypto payload

> **More Info** The details of AuthIP payloads and negotiation are available through the Microsoft Communication Protocol Program (MCPP) at *http://www.microsoft.com/about/legal/intellectualproperty/protocols/mcpp.mspx*. Network Monitor 3.1 by default will not parse the payloads of AuthIP messages. To obtain Network Monitor 3.1 components to parse AuthIP messages, see *http://www.microsoft.com/about/legal/intellectualproperty/protocols/mcpp.mspx*.

AuthIP and IKE Coexistence

Windows Server 2008 and Windows Vista support both IKE and AuthIP. Windows XP and Windows Server 2003 support only IKE. An initiator that supports both AuthIP and IKE must determine whether the responder supports AuthIP or IKE and use the most appropriate protocol for negotiating IPsec protection, preferring the use of AuthIP over IKE.

To determine the negotiation protocol of the responding IPsec peer, an initiator that uses both AuthIP and IKE sends the following messages:

- Message 1: An AuthIP message initiating Main mode negotiation
- Message 2: An IKE message initiating Main mode negotiation

If the responder supports AuthIP, it must respond to Message 1 with an AuthIP message continuing the Main mode negotiation and silently discard Message 2. A responder that does not support AuthIP silently discards Message 1 because it contains a value of the Exchange Type field that the responder does not support and responds to Message 2.

To prevent IKE-based negotiation between two IPsec peers running Windows Server 2008 or Windows Vista when Message 1 is dropped from the network or arrives after Message 2, IPsec peers running Windows Server 2008 or Windows Vista send Message 2 with a vendor ID payload that indicates support for AuthIP. If an IPsec peer running Windows Server 2008 or Windows Vista receives Message 2 with the AuthIP-supported vendor ID payload, it waits for the initiating IPsec peer to retransmit Message 1 and then responds to Message 1.

The initiator keeps retransmitting both Messages 1 and 2 until it receives a response or times out. When the initiator receives a response, it determines the capability of the responder from the ISAKMP header of the received response. If the Exchange Type field is set to 243 (the exchange type for AuthIP-based Main mode negotiation), the responder is AuthIP-capable. If the Exchange Type field is set to 2 (the exchange type for Identity Protection and IKE-based Main mode negotiation), the responder is IKE-capable.

Based on the response message, the initiator responds with either the next AuthIP message for AuthIP Main mode negotiation or the next IKE message for IKE Main mode negotiation. The IPsec peers must use the same protocol that was used to negotiate the ISAKMP SA for the lifetime of the SA.

Examples of AuthIP and IKE Negotiation

The following sections describe the negotiation for the following sets of IPsec peers:

- Two Windows Vista-based IPsec peers in request communication mode (in request mode, an IPsec peer requests IPsec protection but does not require it)
- Windows Vista-based IPsec peer in request mode and a Windows XP-based IPsec peer in request mode
- Windows Vista-based IPsec peer in request mode and a Windows XP-based IPsec peer in require communication mode (in require mode, an IPsec peer requires IPsec protection and silently discards unprotected packets)

Two Windows Vista-based IPsec Peers in Request Mode Both the initiator (Peer 1) and the responder (Peer 2) are running Windows Vista. Both peers are configured with request mode for both inbound and outbound communications. The messages exchanged are the following:

1. Peer 1 sends a plaintext TCP synchronize (SYN) segment, initiating a TCP connection with Peer 2.
2. Peer 2 sends a TCP-SYN-Acknowledgment (ACK) segment.
3. Peer 1 sends a TCP-ACK segment.
4. Peer 1 sends an AuthIP-based ISAKMP message, initiating AuthIP Main mode negotiation.
5. Peer 1 sends an IKE-based ISAKMP message, initiating IKE Main mode negotiation.
6. Peer 2 responds with an AuthIP-based ISAKMP message, continuing AuthIP Main mode negotiation.
7. Peers 1 and 2 complete AuthIP Main mode, Quick mode, and Extended mode (optional) negotiation.
8. Subsequent segments sent over the TCP connection are protected with IPsec.

The exact order of Messages 1 through 5 depends on network latency. The examples described in this article are for a very low latency network, in which the TCP handshake (Messages 1 through 3) completes before Peer 1 can send the initial ISAKMP messages (Messages 4 and 5). On a higher latency network, you would see Peer 1 send the clear text TCP SYN segment, the AuthIP-based ISAKMP message, and then the IKE-based ISAKMP message as the first three messages of the message exchange.

Windows Vista-based IPsec Peer in Request Mode and a Windows XP-based IPsec Peer in Request Mode In this example, a Windows Vista-based IPsec peer (Peer 1) is the initiator and the responder is running Windows XP (Peer 2). Both peers are configured with request mode for both inbound and outbound communications. The messages exchanged are the following:

1. Peer 1 sends a plaintext TCP SYN segment, initiating a TCP connection with Peer 2.
2. Peer 2 sends a TCP-SYN-ACK segment.
3. Peer 1 sends a TCP-ACK segment.
4. Peer 1 sends an AuthIP-based ISAKMP message, initiating AuthIP Main mode negotiation.
5. Peer 1 sends an IKE-based ISAKMP message, initiating IKE Main mode negotiation.
6. Peer 2 responds with an IKE-based ISAKMP message, continuing IKE Main mode negotiation

7. Peers 1 and 2 complete IKE Main mode and Quick mode negotiation.

8. Subsequent segments sent over the TCP connection are protected with IPsec.

Windows Vista-based IPsec Peer in Request Mode and a Windows XP-based IPsec Peer in Require Mode In this example, a Windows Vista-based IPsec peer (Peer 1) is the initiator and the responder is running Windows XP (Peer 2). Peer 1 is configured with request mode for outbound communications, and Peer 2 is configured with require mode for inbound communications. The messages exchanged are the following:

1. Peer 1 sends a clear text TCP-SYN segment, initiating a TCP connection with Peer 2. Peer 2 silently discards the TCP-SYN segment.

2. Peer 1 sends an AuthIP-based ISAKMP message, initiating AuthIP Main mode negotiation.

3. Peer 1 sends an IKE-based ISAKMP message, initiating IKE Main mode negotiation.

4. Peer 2 responds with an IKE-based ISAKMP message, continuing IKE Main mode negotiation.

5. Peer 1 and Peer 2 complete IKE Main mode and Quick mode negotiation.

6. Peer 1 retransmits the TCP-SYN segment (protected with IPsec).

7. Peer 2 sends the TCP-SYN-ACK segment (protected with IPsec).

8. Peer 1 sends the TCP-ACK segment (protected with IPsec).

9. Subsequent segments sent over the TCP connection are protected with IPsec.

IPsec NAT Traversal

IPsec was designed to provide end-to-end security for two computers located in the same address domain. If two computers are located in different address domains, such as private IP addresses used on a home network and public IP addresses used on the Internet, then the addresses must be translated for communication to occur. The translation of addresses and TCP or UDP ports for network address translation to connect users to the Internet invalidates the security services of IPsec. Specifically, address and port translation causes the following problems for ESP-based IPsec traffic:

- For ESP-protected packets, the TCP and UDP ports are encrypted and, therefore, cannot be translated.

- ISAKMP messages calculate hashes and signatures based on SA information, which includes IP addresses. Translating the IP address invalidates the hash or signature.

Network Address Translators (NATs) are very prevalent in today's public address-starved Internet. To allow IKE negotiation and ESP-encapsulated packets to work over NATs, IPsec for Windows Server 2008 and Windows Vista supports IPsec NAT traversal (NAT-T) as described in RFCs 3947 and 3948. NAT-T is especially useful when making L2TP/IPsec connections from a VPN client that is behind a NAT.

NAT-T consists of the following elements used during Main mode:

- The sending of a NAT-T capability Vendor ID payload, which indicates that the IPsec peer is capable of performing NAT traversal. The NAT-T capability Vendor ID payload is sent in Main mode Messages 1 and 2.

- The sending of a NAT-Discovery (NAT-D) payload that contains a hash of the original packet's address and port number so that the receiving node can determine whether a NAT changed the IP address or port. Two separate NAT-D payloads are included in Main mode Messages 3 and 4. One NAT-D payload is for the destination address and port and the other is for the source address and port.

A receiving IPsec peer validates both NAT-D payloads. If either does not validate correctly, then an intermediate NAT is present and NAT-T Quick mode options are used. In addition, a new IKE message header format is defined that uses UDP port 4500. The NAT-T IKE header contains a new non-ESP Marker field that allows the receiver to distinguish between UDP-encapsulated ESP-protected traffic and NAT-T IKE messages.

NAT-T consists of the following elements used during Quick mode:

- The inclusion of either UDP-Encapsulated-Tunnel or UDP-Encapsulated-Transport Encapsulation mode in the proposals of the SA payload of Quick mode Message 1.

- The sending of a NAT-Original Address (NAT-OA) payload to indicate the original source address to the IPsec peer. The NAT-Original Address (NAT-OA) payload is included in Quick mode Messages 1 and 2.

NAT-T for IKE and ESP consists of the following elements used when sending data:

- The encapsulation of an ESP-protected payload with a UDP header that uses the same UDP ports as ISAKMP. By including a UDP header, the NAT can change the UDP port number and it is not part of the ESP-encrypted payload or the ISAKMP Hash or Signature payload calculation.

- If the IPsec peer is behind a NAT, it sends a periodic NAT-Keepalive packet, which is a single-byte (0xFF) UDP message that uses the ISAKMP UDP ports. The NAT-Keepalive packet is used to persist the NAT's UDP port mapping for ISAKMP and UDP-encapsulated ESP traffic. Without the use of the NAT-Keepalive packet, the UDP port mapping in the NAT eventually times out and packets from the IPsec peer are silently discarded. The IKE module on the receiving IPsec peer immediately discards the NAT-Keepalive packets.

The combination of these elements and additional processing steps allows the following:

- ISAKMP to detect a NAT-T-capable IPsec peer and the presence of NATs between the peers

- ISAKMP to complete Main mode and Quick mode negotiation despite the NAT's presence
- ESP-protected traffic to traverse a NAT

Note Windows Server 2008 and Windows Vista do not support the UDP-Encapsulated-Tunnel Encapsulation mode of NAT-T.

Summary

IPsec is the standard method of providing cryptographic protection for IP packets. The two protocols used for IP packet protection are AH and ESP. AH provides data origin authentication, data integrity, and replay protection for the entire IP packet, except for the fields in the IP header that are allowed to change in transit. ESP provides data origin authentication, data integrity, data confidentiality, and replay protection for the ESP-encapsulated payload.

To negotiate SAs for sending secure traffic, IPsec uses IKE, a combination of ISAKMP and the Oakley Key Determination Protocol. ISAKMP messages contain many types of payloads to exchange information during SA negotiation. Main mode negotiation determines the ISAKMP SA, which is used to protect all Quick mode negotiations. Quick mode negotiation determines the IPsec SAs to protect inbound and outbound data. Windows Server 2008 and Windows Vista also support AuthIP, an additional IPsec negotiation protocol that provides additional authentication flexibility.

IPsec NAT-T is a set of ISAKMP payloads, changes to the ISAKMP protocol, and a UDP-Encapsulated-Tunnel Encapsulation or UDP-Encapsulated-Transport Encapsulation mode that provides ESP protection for IPsec peers located behind a NAT.

Chapter 19
Virtual Private Networks (VPNs)

In this chapter:
PPTP 407
L2TP/IPsec 413
SSTP 418
Summary 420

A virtual private network (VPN) is the extension of a private network that encompasses links across shared or public networks. VPN connections use the connectivity of the Internet and a combination of tunneling and data encryption technologies to connect remote clients and remote offices.

Windows Server 2008 and Windows Vista with Service Pack 1 support the following VPN protocols:

- Point-to-Point Tunneling Protocol (PPTP)
- Layer Two Tunneling Protocol with Internet Protocol security (L2TP/IPsec)
- Secure Socket Tunneling Protocol (SSTP)

This chapter describes the details of the PPTP, L2TP/IPsec, and SSTP VPN protocols.

Note This chapter assumes prior knowledge of the components of a VPN and their operation and configuration in Microsoft Windows. For more information, see Chapter 14, "Virtual Private Networking," of the "TCP/IP Fundamentals for Microsoft Windows" book located in the \Fundamentals folder on the companion CD-ROM.

PPTP

PPTP is a VPN protocol that encapsulates VPN data inside PPP frames, which are then further encapsulated in IP datagrams for transmission over a transit IP internetwork such as the Internet. PPTP is defined in RFC 2637.

Creation and maintenance of a PPTP tunnel is done using a Transmission Control Protocol (TCP) connection. The VPN client uses a dynamically allocated TCP port and the PPTP server listens on TCP port 1723. Data is encapsulated using a modified Generic Routing Encapsulation (GRE) header.

PPTP Data Encapsulation

PPTP encapsulates the original IP datagram when it is transmitted between the PPTP client and PPTP server. Figure 19-1 shows the structure of a PPTP data packet.

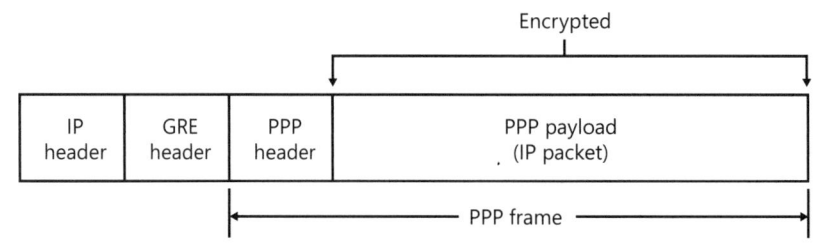

Figure 19-1 PPTP data packet structure

In Figure 19-1, the original datagram is first formatted as a PPP frame. Using PPP, this part of the datagram can be compressed using Microsoft Point-to-Point Compression (MPPC) and is typically encrypted using Microsoft Point-to-Point Encryption (MPPE). The PPP frame is encapsulated with a GRE header, which then becomes the payload of an IP packet sent between the PPTP client and server. The source and destination IP addresses of this packet correspond to the IP addresses of the PPTP client and PPTP server. After the PPTP control connection is established, data can be sent between the PPTP client and the PPTP server. The first data packets sent over a PPTP connection are used to negotiate a PPP connection.

For more information about MPPC, MPPE, and PPP negotiation, see Chapter 4, "Point-to-Point Protocol (PPP)."

PPTP uses a GRE header that is modified from the original GRE header defined in RFCs 1701 and 1702. Figure 19-2 shows the structure of the modified GRE header defined in RFC 2637.

The fields in the modified GRE header for PPTP are the following:

- **Checksum Present**   A 1-bit flag that indicates, when set to 1, that a Checksum field is present. This flag is always set to 0.
- **Routing Present**   A 1-bit flag that indicates, when set to 1, that a Routing field is present. This flag is always set to 0.
- **Key Present**   A 1-bit flag that indicates, when set to 1, that a Key field is present. This flag is always set to 1. The Key field is the combination of the Protocol Type, Payload Length, and Call ID fields.

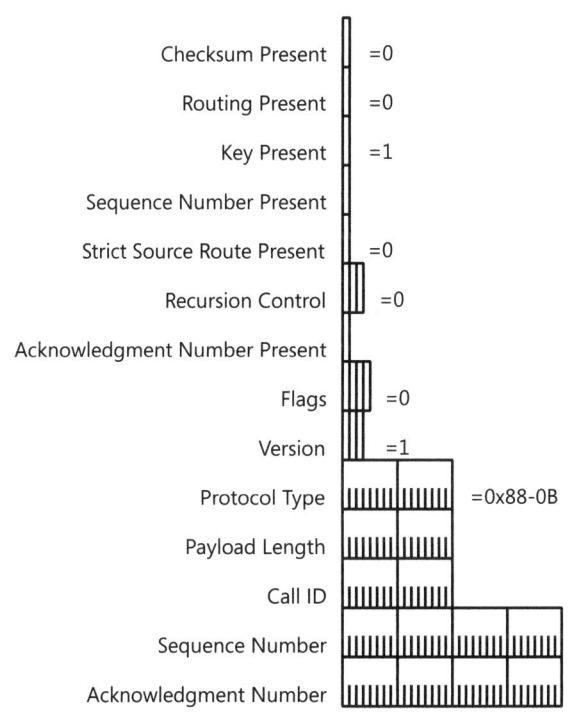

Figure 19-2 GRE header for PPTP data encapsulation

- **Sequence Number Present** A 1-bit flag that indicates, when set to 1, that the Sequence Number field is present.

- **Strict Source Route Present** A 1-bit flag that indicates, when set to 1, that a strict source route is present. This flag is always set to 0.

- **Recursion Control** A 3-bit field used for recursion. This field is always set to 0.

- **Acknowledgment Number Present** A 1-bit flag that indicates, when set to 1, that the Acknowledgment Number field is present.

- **Flags** A 4-bit field used for GRE flags. This field is always set to 0.

- **Version** A 3-bit field used to indicate the version of the GRE header. This field is always set to 1.

- **Protocol Type** A 2-byte field used to store the EtherType value for the GRE payload. This field is always set to 0x88-0B, the EtherType value for a PPP frame.

- **Payload Length** A 2-byte field used to indicate the length of the GRE payload.

- **Call ID** A 2-byte field used to indicate the PPTP tunnel for this packet. For a PPTP connection, there are two different values of the call ID. One value is used for data sent by the PPTP client and one for data sent by the PPTP server.

- **Sequence Number**   A 4-byte field used to indicate the sequence number for this packet. This field is present only when the Sequence Number Present flag is set to 1.

- **Acknowledgment Number**   A 4-byte field used to indicate the highest sequence number for a GRE-encapsulated packet received for this tunnel. This field is present only when the Acknowledgment Number Present flag is set to 1. PPTP uses the Sequence Number and Acknowledgment Number fields to detect dropped data packets.

The following is Frame 1 of Capture 19-01 in the \Captures folder on the companion CD-ROM, which shows PPTP encapsulation for an unencrypted ICMP Echo message, as displayed by Network Monitor 3.1:

```
Frame:
+ Ethernet: Etype = Internet IP (IPv4)
+ Ipv4: Next Protocol = GRE, Packet ID = 2228, Total IP Length = 93
- Gre: Protocol = PPP, Flags = ..KS............ Version 1 , Length = 0x3d , CallID = 0x752b
  - flags: ..KS............ Version 1
    - GREFlagVersion0AndVersion1:
      C:              (0..............) Checksum Absent
      R:              (.0.............) Offset Absent
      K:              (..1............) Key Present
      S:              (...1...........) Sequence Number Present
      ssr:            (....0..........) Strict Source Route Absent
      Recur:          (.....000.......) Recursion Control
      A:              (........0......) Acknowledgment sequence number Absent
      ReservedFlags:  (.........0000...)
      Version:        (............001) 1
    NextProtocol: PPP
    PayloadLength: 61 (0x3D)
    CallID: 29995 (0x752B)
    SequenceNumber: 165 (0xA5)
- Ppp: IP, Internet Protocol
    PacketType: IP, Internet Protocol, 33(0x21)
+ Ipv4: Next Protocol = ICMP, Packet ID = 2227, Total IP Length = 60
+ Icmp: Echo Request Message, From 192.168.0.2 To 192.168.0.1
```

The use of a separate mechanism for PPTP data encapsulation impacts Network Address Translators (NATs). Most NATs can translate TCP-based traffic for PPTP tunnel maintenance. However, PPTP data packets with the GRE header are not typically translated without using either a static address mapping or a PPTP NAT editor.

When a PPTP server is behind a NAT, the NAT must be configured with a static address mapping that maps all the traffic for a specific public address to a specific private address. In this case, only the addresses in the IP header are modified.

When a PPTP client is behind a NAT, a PPTP NAT editor is typically used. An NAT editor is an additional software component on the NAT that performs translation services beyond IP addresses, TCP ports, and User Datagram Protocol (UDP) ports. Although it is a simple matter for the PPTP NAT editor to monitor incoming packets for GRE payloads and translate the IP addresses in the IP header, there might be multiple PPTP clients behind the NAT. In this case, the NAT is unable to determine to which private client the incoming PPTP data packet is destined, because the same public address is being used for multiple private clients. To determine the private client to which an incoming packet is destined, the PPTP NAT editor uses the Call ID field in the GRE header. However, when two different PPTP clients use the same call ID, the NAT is unable to determine to which private client the packet is destined.

To provide correct multiplexing of GRE-encapsulated traffic to different private clients, the PTPP NAT editor monitors the PPTP control connection setup and translates both the PPTP client's Call ID field in the PPTP messages and the GRE-encapsulated data packets in the same way that it translates TCP or UDP source ports. By translating the PPTP client Call ID field, the NAT ensures that a unique call ID is used for each PPTP tunnel and for each PPTP client.

PPTP Control Connection

The PPTP control connection is a TCP connection between the VPN client and the VPN server that is used for PPTP tunnel management. There are processes for the following:

- PPTP control connection creation
- PPTP control connection maintenance
- PPTP control connection termination

PPTP control connections are managed by exchanging a series of PPTP control messages. Table 19-1 lists the PPTP control messages defined in RFC 2637, their message code (corresponding to a field in the PPTP control message), and their purpose.

Table 19-1 PPTP Control Messages

Message Name	Message Code	Purpose
Start-Control-Connection-Request	1	Control connection management
Start-Control-Connection-Reply	2	Control connection management
Stop-Control-Connection-Request	3	Control connection management
Stop-Control-Connection-Reply	4	Control connection management
Echo-Request	5	Control connection management
Echo-Reply	6	Control connection management
Outgoing-Call-Request	7	Call management
Outgoing-Call-Reply	8	Call management
Incoming-Call-Request	9	Call management
Incoming-Call-Reply	10	Call management
Incoming-Call-Connected	11	Call management
Call-Clear-Request	12	Call management
Call-Disconnect-Notify	13	Call management
WAN-Error-Notify	14	Error reporting
Set-Link-Info	15	PPP session control

Each PPTP message is the payload of a TCP segment and has a different packet structure. For the details of the packet structure of each PPTP control message, see RFC 2637.

PPTP Control Connection Creation

The creation of a PPTP control connection between a PPTP client running either Windows Server 2008 or Windows Vista and a PPTP server running either Windows Server 2008 or Windows Vista consists of the following exchange of messages:

1. The PPTP client establishes a TCP connection from a dynamically allocated port on the PPTP client to TCP port 1723 on the PPTP server.
2. The PPTP client sends a PPTP Start-Control-Connection-Request control message to initiate a PPTP control connection.
3. The PPTP server responds with a PPTP Start-Control-Connection-Reply message.
4. The PPTP client sends a PPTP Outgoing-Call-Request message and selects a call ID to identify the PPTP tunnel for data sent from the PPTP client to the PPTP server.
5. The PPTP server responds with a PPTP Outgoing-Call-Reply message and selects its own call ID to identify the PPTP tunnel for data sent from the PPTP server to the PPTP client.
6. The PPTP client sends a PPTP Set-Link-Info message to indicate PPP-negotiated options.

After the PPTP control connection is established, the PPTP client and PPTP server use the separate call IDs in the GRE header to identify data packets sent in the PPTP tunnel. The next PPTP data packets sent on the connection are typically for negotiating the PPP connection between the PPTP client and the PPTP server.

Network Monitor Capture 19-02 (in the \Captures folder on the companion CD-ROM) provides an example of the creation of a PPTP control connection and the subsequent PPP negotiation.

PPTP Control Connection Maintenance

PPTP control connections are maintained by the exchange of PPTP Echo-Request and PPTP Echo-Reply messages. Either the PPTP client or the PPTP server can send the initial PPTP Echo-Request message.

Network Monitor Capture 19-03 (in the \Captures folder on the companion CD-ROM) provides an example of PPTP control connection maintenance.

PPTP Control Connection Termination

The termination of a PPTP control connection between a PPTP client running either Windows Server 2008 or Windows Vista and a PPTP server running either Windows Server 2008 or Windows Vista consists of the following exchange of messages:

1. The PPP connection between the PPTP client and PPTP server is terminated.
2. The PPTP server sends a PPTP Call-Clear-Request message indicating that the PPTP control connection is to be terminated.
3. The PPTP client responds with a PPTP Call-Disconnect-Notify message.
4. The PPTP server sends a PPTP Stop-Control-Connection-Request message to terminate the PPTP control connection.
5. The PPTP client responds with a PPTP Stop-Control-Connection-Reply message.
6. The TCP connection is terminated in the normal way.

This example message exchange assumes that the PPTP client terminated the connection.

Network Monitor Capture 19-04 (in the \Captures folder on the companion CD-ROM) provides an example of a PPTP control connection termination.

L2TP/IPsec

L2TP is a network protocol that creates a tunnel between an L2TP client and an L2TP server and then encapsulates PPP frames to be sent over the tunnel. L2TP is defined in RFC 2661 for different types of media, such as Frame Relay, X.25, or IP. When using IP as the transport protocol, L2TP can be used as a VPN protocol over the Internet.

L2TP over IP uses UDP encapsulation for both tunnel creation and maintenance and data transmission. With L2TP, both the tunneled data and the control messages share a single UDP stream, which can simplify the passing of VPN data through corporate firewalls. L2TP traffic sent by the VPN client and server in Windows Server 2008 and Windows Vista use UDP port 1701 for both the source and destination UDP ports.

L2TP in Windows Server 2008 and Windows Vista relies on Internet Protocol security (IPsec) for encryption, and the combination of L2TP and IPsec is known as L2TP/IPsec. Both the VPN client and the VPN server must support both L2TP and IPsec. Before the first L2TP message is sent, the L2TP client and L2TP server negotiate a set of IPsec security associations (SAs) to protect L2TP traffic. By default, L2TP in Windows Server 2008 and Windows Vista uses digital certificates for IPsec peer authentication. However, both Windows Server 2008 and Windows Vista can be configured manually to use preshared keys for IPsec peer authentication.

For more information about IPsec, see Chapter 18, "Internet Protocol Security (IPsec)."

L2TP/IPsec Data Encapsulation

As with PPTP, L2TP encapsulates a PPP frame containing an IP datagram when transferred across the transit network. Because IPsec provides the encryption facilities, L2TP/IPsec encapsulation takes place in two phases. Figure 19-3 illustrates the L2TP encapsulation using UDP without IPsec encryption.

| IP header | UDP message | L2TP header | PPP header | PPP payload (IP packet) |

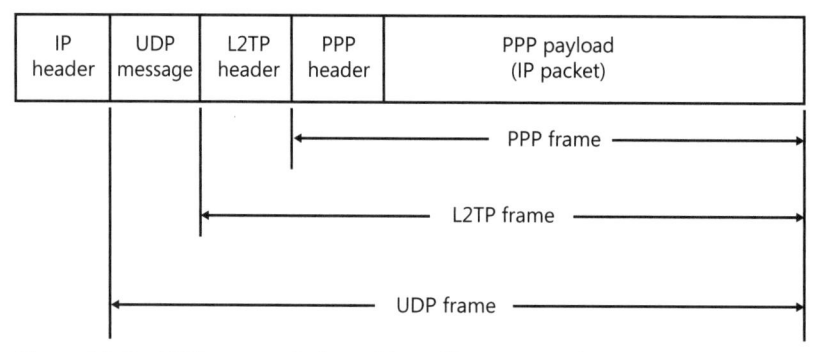

PPP frame spans from PPP header through PPP payload.
L2TP frame spans from L2TP header through PPP payload.
UDP frame spans from UDP message through PPP payload.

Figure 19-3 L2TP encapsulation without IPsec encryption

As Figure 19-3 illustrates, the L2TP encapsulation involves the original IP packet first being wrapped in a PPP frame, as with PPTP. The PPP frame is then inserted into a new IP packet with a UDP header and an L2TP header.

The resulting IP packet is then passed to the IPsec components, which add an IPsec Encapsulating Security Payload (ESP) header and trailers. ESP protection provides data integrity, data origin authentication, data confidentiality (encryption), and replay protection for the UDP message containing the L2TP frame. Figure 19-4 illustrates the L2TP encapsulation with IPsec encryption.

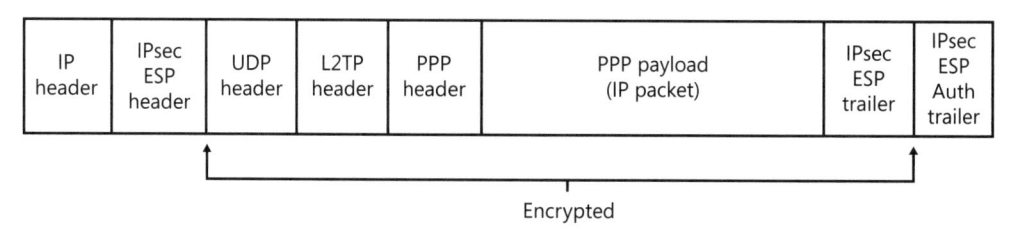

| IP header | IPsec ESP header | UDP header | L2TP header | PPP header | PPP payload (IP packet) | IPsec ESP trailer | IPsec ESP Auth trailer |

Encrypted: from UDP header through IPsec ESP trailer.

Figure 19-4 L2TP encapsulation with IPsec encryption

The outer IP header contains the source and destination IP addresses that correspond to the VPN client and server. Unlike normal IPsec policy, IPsec protection for L2TP traffic is provided by IPsec settings that are automatically created by the remote access client and the Routing and Remote Access service.

To disable the use of IPsec encryption for L2TP traffic for testing or troubleshooting purposes, use the ProhibitIPsec registry value.

ProhibitIPsec
```
Location: HKEY_LOCAL_MACHINE\System\CurrentControlSet\Services\Rasman\Parameters
Data type: REG_DWORD
Valid range: 0–1
Default value: 0
Present by default: No
```

ProhibitIPsec either disables (when set to 1) or enables (when set to 0) the use of IPsec protection for L2TP traffic.

Figure 19-5 shows the L2TP header for encapsulated data.

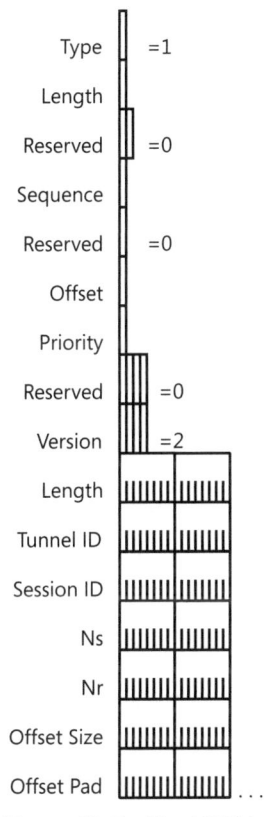

```
Type        =1
Length
Reserved    =0
Sequence
Reserved    =0
Offset
Priority
Reserved    =0
Version     =2
Length
Tunnel ID
Session ID
Ns
Nr
Offset Size
Offset Pad  ...
```

Figure 19-5 The L2TP header for encapsulated data

The fields in the L2TP header are the following:

- **Type** A 1-bit flag that indicates the type of L2TP message. The Type flag is set to 0 for a control message and 1 for a message containing data.
- **Length** A 1-bit flag that indicates, when set to 1, that the Length field is present. The Length flag is always set to 1 for control messages.
- **Reserved** A 2-bit field that is reserved for future use and set to 0.
- **Sequence** A 1-bit flag that indicates, when set to 1, that the Next Sent (Ns) and Next Received (Nr) fields are present. The Sequence flag is always set to 1 for control messages.
- **Reserved** A 1-bit field that is reserved for future use and set to 0.
- **Offset** A 1 bit flag that indicates, when set to 1, that the Offset Size field is present.

- **Priority**   A 1-bit flag that indicates, when set to 1, that the data message should be preferred. The Priority flag is always set to 0 for control messages.
- **Reserved**   A 4-bit field that is reserved for future use and set to 0.
- **Version**   A 4-bit field that indicates the version of the L2TP data message. This must be set to 2.
- **Length**   A 2-byte field that indicates the total length of the message in bytes.
- **Tunnel ID**   A 2-byte field that identifies the control connection for the receiver. Two L2TP peers can have different tunnel IDs for the same control connection.
- **Session ID**   A 2-byte field that identifies a session within a tunnel for the receiver. Two L2TP peers can have different session IDs for the same control connection.
- **Ns**   A 2-byte field that indicates the sequence number for the L2TP message being sent. Ns begins at 0 and increments for each new message sent.
- **Nr**   A 2-byte field that indicates the sequence number for the next L2TP message that is expected to be received.
- **Offset Size**   A 2-byte field that indicates where the payload data is located past the L2TP header.
- **Offset Pad**   Padding or other data between the Offset Size field and the L2TP message payload. RFC 2661 does not define the contents of the Offset Pad field

Note   Network Monitor 3.1 does not parse the L2TP header or LT2P message contents.

L2TP Control Connection

The L2TP control connection is a logical connection between the VPN client and the VPN server that is used to send UDP-encapsulated L2TP messages for L2TP tunnel management. There are processes for the following:

- L2TP control connection creation
- L2TP control connection maintenance
- L2TP control connection termination

L2TP control connections are managed by exchanging a series of L2TP messages, each of which is the payload of a UDP message.

L2TP control connections are managed by exchanging a series of L2TP control messages. Table 19-2 lists the L2TP control messages defined in RFC 2661, their message code (a field in the L2TP control message), and their purpose.

Each L2TP control message has a different packet structure. For the details of the packet structure of L2TP control messages, see RFC 2661.

Table 19-2 L2TP Control Messages

Message Name	Message Code	Purpose
Start-Control-Connection-Request	1	Control connection management
Start-Control-Connection-Reply	2	Control connection management
Start-Control-Connection-Connected	3	Control connection management
Stop-Control-Connection-Notification	4	Control connection management
Hello	6	Control connection management
Outgoing-Call-Request	7	Call management
Outgoing-Call-Reply	8	Call management
Outgoing-Call-Connected	9	Call management
Incoming-Call-Request	10	Call management
Incoming-Call-Reply	11	Call management
Incoming-Call-Connected	12	Call management
Call-Disconnect-Notify	14	Call management
WAN-Error-Notify	15	Error reporting
Set-Link-Info	16	PPP session control

Because the L2TP messages are sent over UDP, an unreliable protocol, L2TP provides its own sequencing through the Nr field, which indicates the next message number the sender is expecting to receive, and the Ns field, which indicates the message number of the sent message. The L2TP header uses a Tunnel ID field that indicates the tunnel and a Session ID field that indicates the session within the tunnel. This allows L2TP to support multiple calls, or sessions, per tunnel.

Because both L2TP-encapsulated data and L2TP control messages use an L2TP header, all L2TP control messages are encrypted with IPsec ESP for L2TP/IPsec.

L2TP Connection Creation

The creation of an L2TP control connection between an L2TP client running either Windows Server 2008 or Windows Vista and an L2TP server running either Windows Server 2008 or Windows Vista consists of the following exchange of messages:

1. The L2TP client sends an L2TP Start-Control-Connection-Request message to initiate an L2TP control connection.
2. The L2TP server responds with an L2TP Start-Control-Connection-Reply message.
3. The L2TP client sends an L2TP Start-Control-Connection-Connected message.

4. The L2TP server responds with an L2TP Incoming-Call-Request message.

5. The L2TP client sends an L2TP Incoming-Call-Connected message to indicate PPP-negotiated options.

After the L2TP control connection is established, the Tunnel ID and Session ID selected by the L2TP server in the L2TP Start-Control-Connection-Reply message is used in the L2TP header for encapsulated data to identify the L2TP session and tunnel. The next L2TP data packets sent on the connection are typically for negotiating the PPP connection between the L2TP client and the L2TP server.

L2TP Connection Maintenance

L2TP control connections are maintained by the sending of an L2TP Hello message by either the L2TP client or the L2TP server. The recipient of the L2TP Hello message sends an L2TP acknowledgment with an incremented Nr field.

L2TP Connection Termination

The termination of an L2TP control connection between an L2TP client running either Windows Server 2008 or Windows Vista and an L2TP server running either Windows Server 2008 or Windows Vista consists of the following exchange of messages:

1. The PPP connection between the L2TP client and L2TP server is terminated.

2. The L2TP client responds with an L2TP Call-Disconnect-Notify message, which contains the Tunnel ID, which identifies the L2TP tunnel, and the Session ID, which identifies the session within the L2TP tunnel.

3. The L2TP server acknowledges the receipt of the L2TP Call-Disconnect-Notify message, which includes an incremented Nr field.

4. The L2TP client sends an L2TP Stop-Control-Connection-Notification message to terminate the L2TP control connection.

5. The L2TP server acknowledges the receipt of the L2TP Stop-Control-Connection-Notification message, which includes an incremented Nr field.

This example message exchange assumes that the VPN client terminated the L2TP connection.

SSTP

VPN connections that use PPTP or L2TP/IPsec can have problems when the VPN client and VPN server are separated by firewalls, NATs, or proxy servers. For example, firewalls must support the forwarding of GRE-encapsulated PPTP traffic or ESP-protected L2TP traffic. For PPTP-based VPN clients, NATs must support a PPTP NAT editor. Proxy servers typically do not support the forwarding of PPTP or L2TP/IPsec traffic.

To address VPN connectivity issues in the presence of firewalls, NATs, and proxy servers, the Secure Socket Tunneling Protocol (SSTP) in Windows Vista with Service Pack 1 and Windows Server 2008 uses HTTP over Secure Sockets Layer (SSL) and TCP port 443. SSL is also known as Transport Layer Security (TLS). HTTP over SSL is the protocol that is typically used for Web sites when transmitting sensitive data, such as passwords and financial information. Whenever you connect to a Web address that begins with "https://", you are using HTTP over SSL. Using HTTP over SSL provides better VPN connectivity because firewalls, NATs, and Web proxies typically allow TCP port 443 traffic.

A computer running Windows Server 2008 and Routing and Remote Access is an SSTP-based VPN server. A computer running Windows Server 2008 or Windows Vista with Service Pack 1 is an SSTP-based VPN client.

Figure 19-6 shows the structure of IP packets that are sent over an SSTP-based VPN connection.

| IP header | TCP header | SSTP header | PPP header | PPP payload (IP packet) |

Encrypted by SSL session

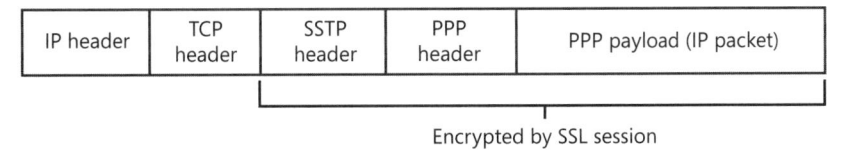

Figure 19-6 The structure of SSTP packets

An IP packet is first encapsulated with a PPP header and an SSTP header. The combination of the IP packet, the PPP header, and the SSTP header is then encrypted by the SSL session between the VPN client and VPN server, and the result is sent as the payload of a TCP segment.

More Info The details of the SSTP header, message types, and negotiation process are available through the Microsoft Communication Protocol Program (MCPP) at *http://www.microsoft.com/about/legal/intellectualproperty/protocols/mcpp.mspx*. Network Monitor 3.1, by default, will not parse the payloads of SSTP messages. To obtain Network Monitor 3.1 components to parse SSTP messages, see *http://www.microsoft.com/about/legal/intellectualproperty/protocols/mcpp.mspx*.

SSTP-based VPN Connection Creation Process

The creation of an SSTP-based VPN connection between a Windows Server 2008 or Windows Vista with Service Pack 1 SSTP client and a Windows Server 2008 SSTP server consists of the following exchange of messages:

1. The SSTP client establishes a TCP connection with the SSTP server between a dynamically allocated TCP port on the SSTP client and TCP port 443 on the SSTP server.

2. The SSTP client sends an SSL Client-Hello message, indicating that the SSTP client wants to create an SSL session with the SSTP server.

3. The SSTP server sends its digital certificate to the SSTP client.

4. The SSTP client validates the certificate, determines the encryption method for the SSL session, generates an SSL session key, and then encrypts it with the public key of the SSTP server's certificate.

5. The SSTP client sends the encrypted form of the SSL session key to the SSTP server.

6. The SSTP server decrypts the encrypted SSL session key with the private key of its certificate. All future communication between the SSTP client and the SSTP server is encrypted with the negotiated encryption method and SSL session key.

7. The SSTP client sends an HTTP over SSL request message to the SSTP server.

8. The SSTP client negotiates an SSTP tunnel with the SSTP server.

9. The SSTP client negotiates a PPP connection with the SSTP server. This negotiation includes authenticating the user's credentials with a PPP authentication method and configuring settings for IP traffic.

10. The SSTP client begins sending IP traffic over the PPP link.

Note SSTP does not support authenticated Web proxy configurations, in which the proxy requires some form of authentication during the HTTP Connect request.

Summary

Windows Server 2008 and Windows Vista with Service Pack 1 support the PPTP, L2TP/IPsec, and SSTP VPN protocols. PPTP uses a TCP control connection and PPTP control messages to maintain the tunnel and GRE encapsulation for data packets. L2TP uses UDP to encapsulate both L2TP connection control messages to maintain the tunnel and data packets. For L2TP/IPsec, IPsec provides ESP encryption for L2TP connection control messages and L2TP-encapsulated data. SSTP uses HTTP over SSL and an SSTP header for SSTP connection control messages to maintain the tunnel and data packets.

Appendix A
Internet Protocol (IP) Addressing

To successfully administer and troubleshoot IP internetworks, it is important to understand all aspects of IP addressing. One of the most important aspects of TCP/IP network administration is the assignment of unique and proper IP addresses to all the nodes of an IP internetwork. Although the concept of IP address assignment is simple, the actual mechanics of efficient IP address allocation using subnetting techniques are somewhat complicated. Additionally, it is important to understand the role of IP broadcast and multicast traffic, and how these addresses map to Network Interface Layer addresses such as Ethernet and Token Ring media access control (MAC) addresses.

Types of IP Addresses

An IP address is a 32-bit logical address that can be one of the following types:

- **Unicast**   A unicast IP address is assigned to a single network interface attached to an IP internetwork. Unicast IP addresses are used in one-to-one communications.

- **Broadcast**   A broadcast IP address is designed to be processed by every IP node on the same network segment. Broadcast IP addresses are used in one-to-everyone communications.

- **Multicast**   An IP multicast address is an address on which one or multiple nodes can be listening on the same or different network segments. IP multicast addresses are used in one-to-many communications.

Expressing IP Addresses

The IP address is a 32-bit value that computers are adept at manipulating. Humans, however, do not think in binary mode, 32 bits at a time. Because most humans are trained in the use of decimal (base 10 numbering system) rather than binary (base 2 numbering system), it is common to express IP addresses in a decimal form.

The 32-bit IP address is divided from the high-order bit to the low-order bit into four 8-bit quantities called *octets*. IP addresses are normally written as four separate decimal octets delimited by a period (a dot). This is known as dotted decimal notation.

For example, the IP address 00001010000000011111000101000011 is subdivided into four octets:

00001010 00000001 11110001 01000011

Each octet is converted to a base 10 number and separated from the others by periods:

10.1.241.67

A generalized IP address is indicated with w.x.y.z, as Figure A-1 shows.

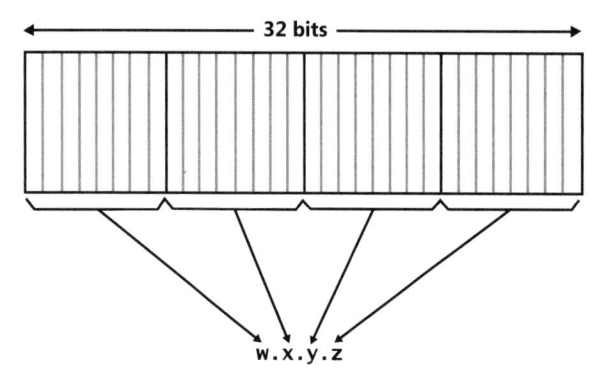

Figure A-1 The generalized IP address consisting of 32 bits expressed in dotted decimal notation.

Converting from Binary to Decimal

To convert a binary number to its decimal equivalent, add the numbers represented by the bit positions that are set to 1. Figure A-2 shows an 8-bit number and the decimal value of each position.

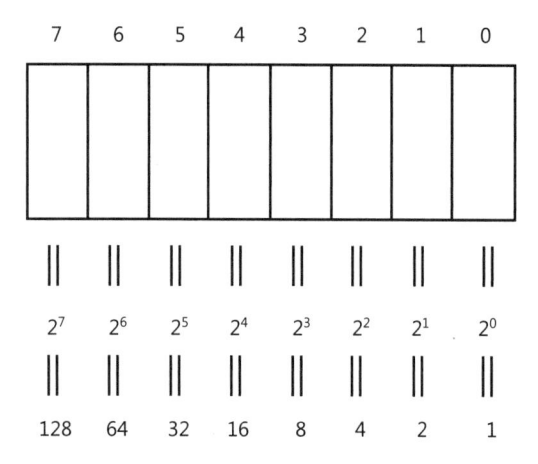

Figure A-2 An 8-bit number showing bit positions and their decimal equivalents.

For example, the 8-bit binary number 01000011 is 67 (64 + 2 + 1). The maximum number that can be expressed with an 8-bit number (11111111) is 255 (128 + 64 + 32 + 16 + 8 + 4 + 2 + 1).

Converting from Decimal to Binary

To convert from decimal to binary, analyze the decimal number to see whether it contains the quantities represented by the bit positions from the high-order bit to the low-order bit. Starting from the high-order bit quantity (128), if each quantity is present, the bit in that bit position is set to 1. For example, the decimal number 211 contains 128, 64, 16, 2, and 1. Therefore, 211 is 11010011 in binary notation.

IP Addresses in the IP Header

IP addresses are used in the IP header's Source Address and Destination Address fields.

- The IP header's Source Address field is always either a unicast address or the special address 0.0.0.0. The unspecified IP address, 0.0.0.0, is used only when the IP node is not configured with an IP address and the node is attempting to obtain an address through a configuration protocol such as Dynamic Host Configuration Protocol (DHCP).

- The IP header's Destination Address field is a unicast address, multicast address, or broadcast address.

Unicast IP Addresses

Each network interface on which TCP/IP is active must be identified by a unique, logical unicast IP address. The unicast IP address is a logical address because it is an Internet Layer address that has no direct relation to the address being used at the Network Interface Layer. For example, the unicast IP address assigned to a host on an Ethernet network has no relation to the 48-bit MAC address used by the Ethernet network adapter.

The unicast IP address is an internetwork address for IP nodes that contains a subnet prefix and a host ID.

- The subnet prefix (also known as a network address or network identifier) identifies the nodes that are located on the same logical network. In most cases, a logical network is the same as a physical network segment with boundaries that are defined by IP routers. In some cases, multiple logical networks exist on the same physical network using a practice called *multinetting*. All nodes on the same logical network share the same subnet prefix. If all nodes on the same logical network are not configured with the same subnet prefix, routing or delivery problems occur. The subnet prefix must be unique to the internetwork.

- The host ID, or host address, identifies a node within a network. A node is a router or host (a nonrouter interface such as a workstation, server, or other TCP/IP–based system). The host ID must be unique within each network segment.

Figure A-3 is an example of a unicast IP address and its subnet prefix and host ID portions.

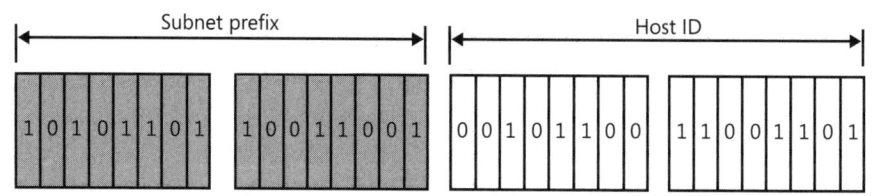

Figure A-3 The structure of an example IP address showing the subnet prefix and host ID.

A History Lesson: IP Address Classes

This section is called "A History Lesson" because modern networks are not based on the Internet address classes. Because of the Internet's recent rapid expansion, the Internet authorities saw clearly that the original class-based structure did not scale well to the size of a global internetwork. For example, if the Internet authorities were still handing out class-based addresses, there would be hundreds of thousands of routes in the routing tables of Internet backbone routers. To prevent this scaling problem, addressing on the modern Internet is classless. However, the understanding of Internet address classes is an important element in understanding IP addressing.

RFC 791 defined the unicast IP address in terms of address classes to create well-defined address prefixes for networks of various sizes. An address prefix is a generalized range of IP addresses. Address prefixes can be used as subnet prefixes when they are assigned to subnets or subdivided using subnetting techniques. The design goal was to create the following:

- A small number of large networks (networks with a large amount of nodes)
- A moderate number of moderate-sized networks
- A large number of small networks

The result was the creation of address classes, subdivisions of the 32-bit IP address space defined by setting high-order bits and dividing the remaining bits into an address prefix and host ID.

> **More Info** All of the RFCs referenced in this appendix can be found in the \Standards\APPA_IPAddr folder on the companion CD-ROM.

Class A

Class A addresses are designed for networks with a large number of hosts. The high-order bit is set to 0. The first 8 bits (the first octet) are defined as the address prefix; the last 24 bits (the last three octets) are defined as the host ID. Figure A-4 illustrates the class A address.

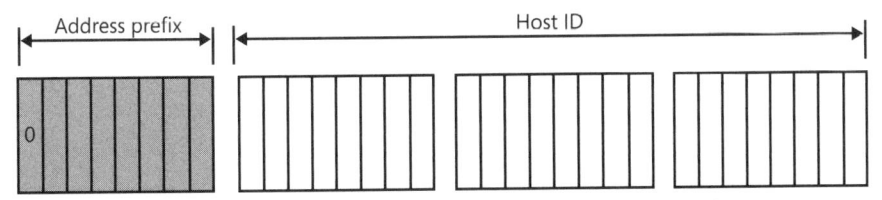

Figure A-4 The class A address showing the address prefix and the host ID.

Class B

Class B addresses are designed for moderate-sized networks with a moderate number of hosts. The two high-order bits are set to 10. The first 16 bits (the first two octets) are defined as the address prefix; the last 16 bits (the last two octets) are defined as the host ID. Figure A-5 illustrates the class B address.

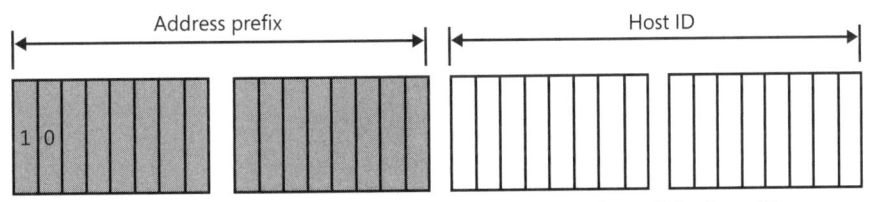

Figure A-5 The class B address showing the address prefix and the host ID.

Class C

Class C addresses are designed for small networks with a small number of hosts. The three high-order bits are set to 110. The first 24 bits (the first three octets) are defined as the address prefix; the last 8 bits (the last three octets) are defined as the host ID. Figure A-6 illustrates the class C address.

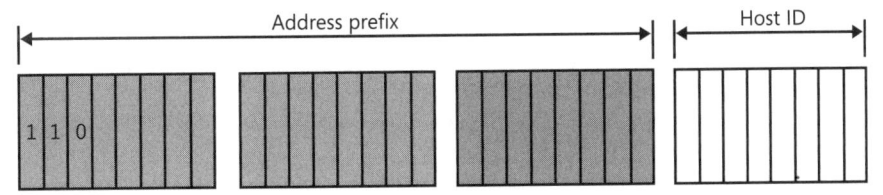

Figure A-6 The class C address showing the address prefix and the host ID.

Additional Address Classes

Class D and E addresses are defined, in addition to unicast address classes A, B, and C.

Class D Class D addresses are for IP multicast addresses. The four high-order bits are set to binary 1110. The next 28 bits are used for individual IP multicast addresses. For more information on IP multicast addresses, see the section "IP Multicast Addresses" later in this appendix. Windows Server 2008 and Windows Vista support class D addresses for IP multicast traffic.

Class E Class E addresses are experimental addresses reserved for future use. The five high-order bits in a class E address are set to 11110. Windows Server 2008 and Windows Vista do not support the use of class E addresses.

Rules for Enumerating Address Prefixes

When enumerating IP address prefixes, the following rules apply:

- **The address prefix cannot begin with 127 as the first octet** All 127.x.y.z addresses are reserved as loopback addresses.
- **All the bits in the address prefix cannot be set to 1** Address prefixes set to all 1s are reserved for broadcast addresses.
- **All the bits in the address prefix cannot be set to 0** Address prefixes set to all 0s are reserved for indicating a host on the local network.
- **The address prefix must be unique to the IP internetwork.**

Table A-1 lists the ranges of address prefixes based on the IP address classes. Class-based address prefixes are expressed by setting all host bits to 0 and expressing the result in dotted decimal notation.

Table A-1 Address Class Ranges of Address Prefixes

Address Class	First Address Prefix	Last Address Prefix	Number of Networks
Class A	1.0.0.0	126.0.0.0	126
Class B	128.0.0.0	191.255.0.0	16,384
Class C	192.0.0.0	223.255.255.0	2,097,152

Note IP address prefixes, even though expressed in dotted decimal notation, are not IP addresses assigned to network interfaces.

Rules for Enumerating Usable Host IDs

When enumerating usable IP host IDs, the following rules apply:

- **All bits in the host ID cannot be set to 1** Host IDs set to all 1s are reserved for broadcast addresses.
- **All the bits in the host ID cannot be set to 0** Host IDs set to all 0s are reserved for the expression of IP address prefixes.
- **The host ID must be unique to the network.**

Table A-2 lists the ranges of host IDs based on the IP address classes.

Table A-2 Address Class Ranges of Host IDs

Address Class	First Host ID	Last Host ID	Number of Hosts
Class A	w.0.0.1	w.255.255.254	16,777,214
Class B	w.x.0.1	w.x.255.254	65,534
Class C	w.x.y.1	w.x.y.254	254

Subnets and the Subnet Mask

Subnetting is designed to make more efficient use of a fixed address space, namely an IP address prefix. The network bits are fixed and the host bits are variable. Originally, the host bits were designed to indicate host IDs within an IP address prefix. With subnetting, host ID bits can be used to express a combination of a subnetted address prefix and a new host ID, thereby better utilizing the host bits.

Consider a class B network that has 65,534 possible hosts. A network segment of 65,534 hosts is technically possible but impractical because of the accumulation of broadcast traffic. All nodes on the same physical network segment belong to the same broadcast domain and share the same broadcast traffic. Because making all 65,534 hosts share the same broadcast traffic is not a practical configuration, most of the host IDs are not usable.

To create smaller broadcast domains and make better use of the host bits, RFC 950 defines a method of subdividing an address prefix into subnetworks—subsets of the original class-based network—by using bits in the host ID portion of the original IP address prefix. Each sub-network, or subnet, is assigned a new subnetted address prefix. Hosts on subnets are assigned host IDs from the remaining host bits in the subnetted address prefix.

Although RFC 950 discusses subnetting in terms of class-based address prefixes, subnetting is a general technique that can be used on classless address prefixes or used recursively on subnetted address prefixes. This is described in the section "Variable-Length Subnetting" later in this appendix.

The proper subnetting of an address prefix is transparent to the rest of the IP internetwork. For example, consider the class B address prefix of 131.107.0.0 (shown in Figure A-7), which is connected to the Internet. The class-based address prefix is a fixed address space. Because this class B address prefix represents an impractical broadcast domain, it is subnetted. However, in subnetting 131.107.0.0, you should not require any reconfiguration of the Internet routers.

Figure A-7 The class B address prefix 131.107.0.0 before subnetting.

From an analysis of broadcast traffic, it is determined that there should be no more than 250 nodes on each broadcast domain. Therefore, the address prefix 131.107.0.0 is subnetted to look like a class C address by using the first 8 high-order host bits (the third octet represented by y) for the subnetted address prefix. Note that before the subnetting, only the first two octets are considered the address prefix. After the subnetting, the first three octets are considered the address prefix. The new address prefixes are 131.107.1.0, 131.107.2.0, and 131.107.3.0, as Figure A-8 shows.

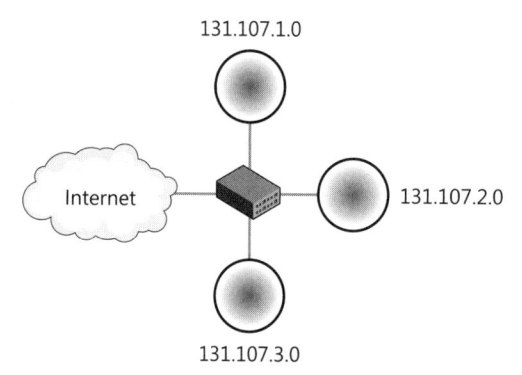

Figure A-8 The class B network 131.107.0.0 after subnetting.

The IP router connected to the Internet has an interface on each of the subnets and is aware of the new subnetting scheme. The IP router forwards IP datagrams from the Internet to the host on the appropriate subnet. The Internet routers are completely unaware of the subnetting of 131.107.0.0. They still consider all possible IP addresses in the range of 131.107.0.0 through 131.107.255.255 to be reachable through the IP router's Internet interface.

The Subnet Mask

With subnetting, a host or router can no longer assume the address prefix and host ID designations of the IP address classes. The node needs additional configuration to distinguish the address prefix and host ID portions of an IP address, whether the address prefix is class-based, classless, or subnetted.

RFC 950 defines the use of a bit mask to identify which bits in the IP address belong to the address prefix and which belong to the host ID. This bit mask, called a *subnet mask* or *address mask*, is defined by the following:

- If the bit position corresponds to a bit in the address prefix, it is set to 1.
- If the bit position corresponds to a bit in the host ID, it is set to 0.

Since the publication of RFC 950, TCP/IP nodes require a subnet mask to be configured for each IP address, even when class-based addressing is used. A default subnet mask corresponds to a class-based address prefix. A custom subnet mask corresponds to either a classless address prefix or a subnetted address prefix. The subnet mask is the definitive piece of configuration information that allows the node to determine its own subnet prefix.

Subnet Masks in Dotted Decimal Representation

Frequently, the subnet mask is expressed in dotted decimal notation. Although expressed in the same form as an IP address, the subnet mask is not an IP address. As an example of subnet masks in dotted decimal notation, default subnet masks are based on the IP address classes. Table A-3 lists the default subnet masks for class A, B, and C address prefixes in dotted decimal notation.

Table A-3 Dotted Decimal Notation for Default Subnet Masks

Address Class	Bits for Subnet Mask	Subnet Mask
Class A	11111111 00000000 00000000 00000000	255.0.0.0
Class B	11111111 11111111 00000000 00000000	255.255.0.0
Class C	11111111 11111111 11111111 00000000	255.255.255.0

A custom subnet mask is used whenever you perform nonclassful addressing. In the earlier example, the classful address prefix 131.107.0.0 is subnetted by using the third octet for subnets. The subnetted address prefix 131.107.1.0 no longer uses the default subnet mask 255.255.0.0. To express the third octet as part of the address prefix, the custom subnet mask 255.255.255.0 is used.

The subnetted address prefix and its corresponding subnet mask are expressed in dotted decimal notation as 131.107.1.0, 255.255.255.0.

Prefix Length Representation of Subnet Masks

Although it is technically possible to subnet IP address prefixes by choosing host bits in a noncontiguous fashion, it is impractical and mathematically challenging to enumerate the subnetted address prefixes and the host IDs per subnet. For this reason, you must subnet by choosing host bits in a contiguous fashion from the high-order host bit.

Because the address prefix bits are always contiguous starting from the highest order bit, an easier and more compact way of expressing the subnet mask is to indicate the number of address prefix bits using length prefix notation, or Classless Inter-Domain Routing (CIDR) notation. Prefix length notation views the IP address in terms of the prefix and the suffix (the host ID). Prefix length notation is:

/# of bits in the address prefix

Prefix length notation is commonly used with TCP/IP implementations other than Windows Server 2008 and Windows Vista, and it is an important notation to understand looking forward to IP version 6 (IPv6).

Table A-4 lists the equivalent subnet mask in prefix length notation for the IP address classes.

Table A-4 Prefix Length Notation for Default Subnet Masks

Address Class	Bits for Subnet Mask	Prefix Length
Class A	11111111 00000000 00000000 00000000	/8
Class B	11111111 11111111 00000000 00000000	/16
Class C	11111111 11111111 11111111 00000000	/24

In the earlier example, the classful address prefix 131.107.0.0, with the subnet mask of 255.255.0.0, is expressed in network prefix notation as 131.107.0.0/16. If 131.107.0.0 were subnetted by using the third octet to express subnets, a total of 24 contiguous bits would be used for the subnetted address prefix. The subnetted address prefix 131.107.1.0 and its corresponding subnet mask are expressed in network prefix notation as 131.107.1.0/24.

Expressing Address Prefixes

The fixed address prefix bits and the subnet mask define the address prefix. Therefore, address prefixes must always be expressed by the combination of the address prefix and a subnet mask. Expressing an address prefix without its subnet mask is ambiguous. For example, for the address prefix 10.16.0.0, which bits are used for the address prefix? The first 16? The first 24? The first 12?

The following are examples of properly expressed address prefixes:

- 192.168.45.0, 255.255.255.0
- 10.99.0.0/16

All hosts on the same logical network must be using the same address prefix bits and the same subnet mask. For example, 131.107.0.0/16 is not the same as 131.107.0.0/24. For the address prefix 131.107.0.0/16, the usable IP addresses range from 131.107.0.1 through 131.107.255.254. For the address prefix 131.107.0.0/24, the usable IP addresses range from 131.107.0.1 through 131.107.0.254. Clearly, 131.107.0.0/16 and 131.107.0.0/24 do not represent the same group of hosts.

Determining the Address Prefix

In earlier examples, classful address prefixes and subnetted address prefixes all fell along octet boundaries where it was easy to determine the address prefix and host ID portion of the IP address. However, real-world subnetting is not always done along octet boundaries. For example, some network administrators might determine that, for their situation, they need only three host bits for subnetting. Because subnetting can occur along nonoctet boundaries, there must be a method of determining the address prefix from an IP address with an arbitrary subnet mask. IP uses a method called a *bit-wise logical AND* to extract the address prefix.

Recall how the subnet mask is defined: 1 is used to indicate an address prefix bit, and 0 is used to indicate a host ID bit. In a logical AND comparison, the result is 1 when the value of each of the two bits being compared is 1. Otherwise, the result is 0. This comparison is done for all 32 bits of the IP address and subnet mask. The result of the bit-wise logical AND of the IP address and the subnet mask is the address prefix.

For example, what is the address prefix of the IP node 131.107.164.26 with a subnet mask of 255.255.240.0? To obtain the result in binary notation, convert both the IP address and subnet mask to binary. Then perform the logical AND comparison for each bit.

IP address	10000011 01101011 10100100 00011010
Subnet mask	11111111 11111111 11110000 00000000
Address prefix	10000011 01101011 10100000 00000000

The result of the bit-wise logical AND of the 32 bits of the IP address and the subnet mask is the address prefix 131.107.160.0 with the subnet mask of 255.255.240.0.

Notice the following:

- The bits in the address prefix portion of the IP address are copied directly to the result. A value of 1 in the address prefix portion of the IP address becomes a 1 in the result. A value of 0 in the address prefix portion of the IP address becomes a 0 in the result.

- All bits in the host ID portion of the IP address are set to 0. Because the subnet mask uses a 0 for host ID bit positions, the logical AND comparison always yields a 0.

Therefore, because the bits in the address prefix are copied and the bits in the host ID are set to 0, the result must be the address prefix.

How to Subnet

The act of subnetting an address prefix is a relatively complex procedure; although there are numerous subnet calculators available, the ability to subnet is a vital skill for any TCP/IP network administrator.

Subnetting is done in two basic steps:

1. Based on your design requirements, decide how many host bits you need for the proper balance between number of subnets and number of hosts per subnet.
2. Based on the number of host bits chosen, enumerate the subnetted address prefixes, including the ranges of usable IP addresses for each subnetted address prefix. The actual mechanics of defining the subnetted address prefixes can be done in binary or decimal notation.

There are two methods for the second step of subnetting, the enumeration of the subnetted address prefixes:

- The binary method, in which the individual bits of the subnetted address prefixes are manipulated and converted to dotted decimal notation, can be used to subnet. However, this method does not scale well to large numbers of subnets. It is described here primarily to illustrate the subnetting process in its most fundamental form.

- The decimal method, in which subnetted address prefixes are derived from calculations on decimal numbers, scales well to large numbers of subnets and lends itself well to spreadsheets and programming code.

Step 1: Determining the Number of Host Bits

To determine the number of host bits required for subnetting, perform an analysis of your internetwork. You should determine the following:

- **The number of subnets needed both now and in the future** Be sure to plan for expansion. Subnetting an existing network requires reassigning IP addresses to IP interfaces. Although DHCP can ease this burden, routers and other fixed-address types of hosts might need to be manually reconfigured. Subnetting is not something you want to do often.

- **The maximum number of hosts needed on each subnet** This number depends on how many hosts you want sharing the same broadcast traffic. In most cases, when choosing between more subnets and more hosts per subnet, the practical choice is to choose more subnets.

There is an inverse relationship between the number of subnets and the number of hosts per subnet that can be supported by a given subnetting scheme. As Figure A-9 illustrates, when you choose more high-order host bits for subnetting, the number of subnets goes up, but the number of hosts per subnet goes down by approximately a factor of 2.

If you choose one host bit when subnetting the class B address prefix 131.107.0.0, two subnets can be expressed, with 32,766 hosts per subnet. If you choose eight host bits, 256 subnets can be expressed with 254 hosts per subnet.

Determine how many subnets you need now and plan for growth by estimating how many you will need in the next five years. Each physical network segment is a subnet. Point-to-point wide area network (WAN) connections such as leased lines might need subnetted address prefixes, unless your routers support unnumbered connections. Nonbroadcast multiple access (NBMA) WAN technologies such as Frame Relay need subnetted address prefixes. Use additional bits for subnetting if the remaining host bits can express more hosts per subnet than you will need so that you have more subnets for future use.

Subnetting always starts with a fixed address space in the form of an address prefix. The address prefix to be subnetted can be a classful address prefix, a classless address prefix (as allocated using CIDR), or a previously subnetted classful or classless address prefix. The fixed address space contains a sequence of bits that are fixed (the address prefix bits) and a sequence of bits that are variable (the host ID bits).

```
     131        .        107       .         0        .         0
```

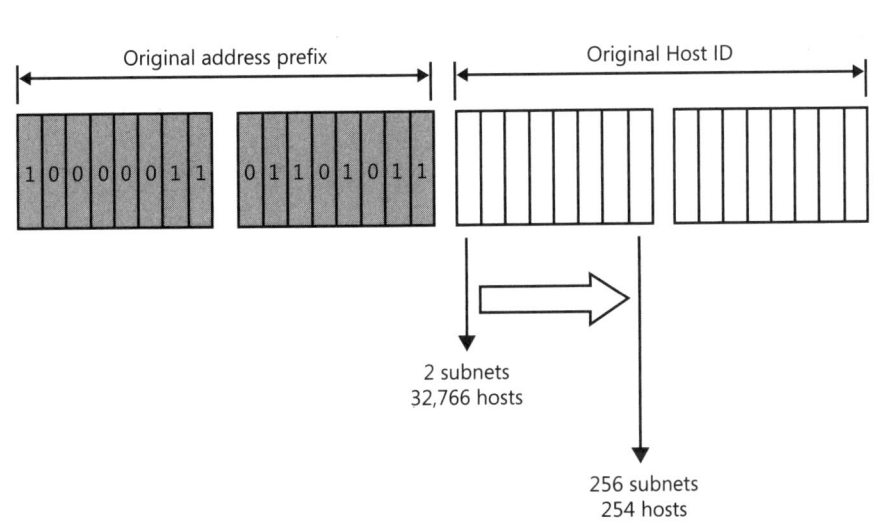

```
|←——— Original address prefix ———→|  |←————— Original Host ID —————→|
     [1 0 0 0 0 0 1 1] [0 1 1 0 1 0 1 1]  [□□□□□□□□]      [□□□□□□□□]
```

2 subnets
32,766 hosts

256 subnets
254 hosts

Figure A-9 The relationship between the number of subnets and hosts per subnet when subnetting the class B address prefix 131.107.0.0.

Based on your analysis of the desired number of subnets and number of hosts per subnet, a specific number of high-order host bits are converted from host bits into subnet bits, the bits used for subnetting. The combination of the original address prefix bits and the subnet bits becomes the new subnetted address prefix.

As you determine how many subnet bits you need, you determine the new subnet mask for your subnetted address prefixes.

Tables A-5, A-6, and A-7 list the subnetting of classful address prefixes according to the requirement of a specific number of subnets. These tables can be useful when determining a subnetting scheme for a class-based address prefix based on a required number of subnets and a desired number of hosts per subnet.

Table A-5 Subnetting of a Class A Address Prefix

Required Number of Subnets	Number of Host Bits	Subnet Mask	Number of Hosts per Subnet
1–2	1	255.128.0.0 or /9	8,388,606
3–4	2	255.192.0.0 or /10	4,194,302
5–8	3	255.224.0.0 or /11	2,097,150
9–16	4	255.240.0.0 or /12	1,048,574
17–32	5	255.248.0.0 or /13	524,286
33–64	6	255.252.0.0 or /14	262,142

Table A-5 Subnetting of a Class A Address Prefix

Required Number of Subnets	Number of Host Bits	Subnet Mask	Number of Hosts per Subnet
65–128	7	255.254.0.0 or /15	131,070
129–256	8	255.255.0.0 or /16	65,534
257–512	9	255.255.128.0 or /17	32,766
513–1024	10	255.255.192.0 or /18	16,382
1025–2048	11	255.255.224.0 or /19	8190
2049–4096	12	255.255.240.0 or /20	4094
4097–8192	13	255.255.248.0 or /21	2046
8193–16,384	14	255.255.252.0 or /22	1022
16,385–32,768	15	255.255.254.0 or /23	510
32,769–65,536	16	255.255.255.0 or /24	254
65,537–131,072	17	255.255.255.128 or /25	126
131,073–262,144	18	255.255.255.192 or /26	62
262,145–524,288	19	255.255.255.224 or /27	30
524,289–1,048,576	20	255.255.255.240 or /28	14
1,048,577–2,097,152	21	255.255.255.248 or /29	6
2,097,153–4,194,304	22	255.255.255.252 or /30	2

Table A-6 Subnetting of a Class B Address Prefix

Required Number of Subnets	Number of Host Bits	Subnet Mask	Number of Hosts per Subnet
1–2	1	255.255.128.0 or /17	32,766
3–4	2	255.255.192.0 or /18	16,382
5–8	3	255.255.224.0 or /19	8190
9–16	4	255.255.240.0 or /20	4094
17–32	5	255.255.248.0 or /21	2046
33–64	6	255.255.252.0 or /22	1022
65–128	7	255.255.254.0 or /23	510
129–256	8	255.255.255.0 or /24	254
257–512	9	255.255.255.128 or /25	126
513–1024	10	255.255.255.192 or /26	62
1025–2048	11	255.255.255.224 or /27	30
2049–4096	12	255.255.255.240 or /28	14
4097–8192	13	255.255.255.248 or /29	6
8193–16,384	14	255.255.255.252 or /30	2

Table A-7 **Subnetting of a Class C Address Prefix**

Required Number of Subnets	Number of Host Bits	Subnet Mask	Number of Hosts per Subnet
1–2	1	255.255.255.128 or /25	126
3–4	2	255.255.255.192 or /26	62
5–8	3	255.255.255.224 or /27	30
9–16	4	255.255.255.240 or /28	14
17–32	5	255.255.255.248 or /29	6
33–64	6	255.255.255.252 or /30	2

Step 2: Defining the Subnetted Address Prefixes (Binary Method)

The technique presented here describes how to subnet an arbitrary address prefix into subnets that yield both subnetted address prefixes and their corresponding range of valid IP addresses using binary analysis. There are other techniques that might seem easier, but they are typically limited in scope. This technique works for any subnetting situation.

Step 2a: Enumerating the Subnetted Address Prefixes (Binary) Create a three-column table with 2^n rows where n is the number of host bits chosen for the subnetting. The first column is used for the subnet number, the second column is for the binary representation of the subnetted address prefix, and the third column is for the dotted decimal representation of the subnetted address prefix.

For the binary representation for each entry in the table, the original address prefix bits are fixed at their original values. The host bits chosen for subnetting, hereafter known as the subnet bits, are allowed to vary over all of their possible values, and the remaining host bits are set to 0.

The table's first entry is the subnet, defined by setting all the subnet bits to 0 (also called the all-zeros subnet). The result is converted to dotted decimal notation. This subnetted address prefix does not appear to be different from the original address prefix; but remember that an address prefix is a combination of the dotted decimal notation and a subnet mask. With the new subnet mask, the subnetted address prefix is clearly different from the original address prefix.

In the following entries, treat the subnet bits as though they were distinct binary numbers. Increment the value within the subnet bits and convert the result of the entire 32-bit subnetted address prefix to dotted decimal notation.

As an example of this technique, subnet the class B address prefix 131.107.0.0 by using three bits of the classful host ID. The new subnet mask for the subnetted address prefixes is 255.255.224.0, or /19. Based on using three host bits, create a table with eight entries ($8 = 2^3$).

The first entry is the all-zeros subnet. The additional entries are increments of the binary number represented by the subnet bits (underlined). Table A-8 lists the subnetted address prefixes.

Table A-8 A 3-Bit Subnetting of 131.107.0.0 (Binary)

Subnet	Binary Representation	Subnetted Address Prefix
1	10000011.01101011.<u>000</u>00000.00000000	131.107.0.0/19
2	10000011.01101011.<u>001</u>00000.00000000	131.107.32.0/19
3	10000011.01101011.<u>010</u>00000.00000000	131.107.64.0/19
4	10000011.01101011.<u>011</u>00000.00000000	131.107.96.0/19
5	10000011.01101011.<u>100</u>00000.00000000	131.107.128.0/19
6	10000011.01101011.<u>101</u>00000.00000000	131.107.160.0/19
7	10000011.01101011.<u>110</u>00000.00000000	131.107.192.0/19
8	10000011.01101011.<u>111</u>00000.00000000	131.107.224.0/19

Step 2b: Enumerating IP Address Ranges for Each Subnetted Address Prefix (Binary)

For each subnetted address prefix, the range of valid IP addresses must be determined as follows:

1. Create a three-column table with 2^n entries where n is the number of host bits chosen for the subnetting. The first column is used for the subnet number, the second column is for the binary representation of the first and last IP address in the range, and the third column is for the dotted decimal representation of the first and last IP address in the range. Alternatively, you can extend the table created for enumerating the subnetted address prefixes by adding two columns.

2. Express the first and last IP address in the range in binary notation. The first IP address is defined by setting the remaining host bits to 0, except for the last host bit. The last IP address is defined by setting the remaining host bits to 1, except for the last host bit.

3. Convert the binary representation of the first and last IP address to dotted decimal notation.

4. Repeat steps 2 and 3 until the table is complete.

To continue the example, Table A-9 lists the enumeration of the range of valid IP addresses for the 3-bit subnetting of 131.107.0.0. The remaining host bits are underlined.

Table A-9 Enumeration of IP Addresses for the 3-Bit Subnetting of 131.107.0.0 (Binary)

Subnet	Binary Representation	Range of IP Addresses
1	10000011.01101011.000<u>00000.0000000</u>1 – 10000011.01101011.000<u>11111.1111111</u>0	131.107.0.1 – 131.107.31.254
2	10000011.01101011.001<u>00000.0000000</u>1 – 10000011.01101011.001<u>11111.1111111</u>0	131.107.32.1 – 131.107.63.254
3	10000011.01101011.010<u>00000.0000000</u>1 – 10000011.01101011.010<u>11111.1111111</u>0	131.107.64.1 – 131.107.95.254

Table A-9 Enumeration of IP Addresses for the 3-Bit Subnetting of 131.107.0.0 (Binary)

Subnet	Binary Representation	Range of IP Addresses
4	10000011.01101011.01100000.00000001 – 10000011.01101011.01111111.11111110	131.107.96.1 – 131.107.127.254
5	10000011.01101011.10000000.00000001 – 10000011.01101011.10011111.11111110	131.107.128.1 – 131.107.159.254
6	10000011.01101011.10100000.00000001 – 10000011.01101011.10111111.11111110	131.107.160.1 – 131.107.191.254
7	10000011.01101011.11000000.00000001 – 10000011.01101011.11011111.11111110	131.107.192.1 – 131.107.223.254
8	10000011.01101011.11100000.00000001 – 10000011.01101011.11111111.11111110	131.107.224.1 – 131.107.255.254

Step 3: Defining the Subnetted Address Prefixes (Decimal Method)

Although the binary subnetting method works for any valid subnetting scheme, it does not scale well. For example, if you are performing a 10-bit subnetting, you would have 1024 entries in the table. Whereas programmers are adept at binary manipulation and can create programs to automate this process, nonprogrammers find it easier to work with decimal numbers. Therefore, the following technique treats the 32-bit address prefix and IP address as a single decimal number to enumerate the subnetted address prefix and its corresponding range of IP addresses. Either technique—binary or decimal—yields the same result.

Step 3a: Enumerating the Subnetted Address Prefixes (Decimal)

1. Create a three-column table with 2^n entries where n is the number of host bits chosen for the subnetting. The first column is used for the subnet number; the second column is for the decimal representation of the subnetted address prefix; and the third column is for the dotted decimal representation of the subnetted address prefix.

2. Convert the original address prefix from dotted decimal notation ($w.x.y.z$) to N, its decimal representation:

    $N = (w \times 16777216) + (x \times 65536) + (y \times 256) + z$

3. Compute I, the increment value, based on h, the number of host bits remaining:

    $I = 2^h$

4. For the first table entry, the all-zeros subnet, the decimal representation of the subnetted address prefix is N, and the subnetted address prefix is $w.x.y.z$, with its new subnet mask.

5. For the decimal representation of the next table entry, add the increment I to the previous entry.

6. Convert the decimal representation of the subnetted address prefix to dotted decimal notation ($W.X.Y.Z$) using the following formulas (where s is the decimal representation of the subnetted address prefix):

$W = \text{int}(s/16777216)$

$X = \text{int}((s \bmod 16777216)/65536)$

$Y = \text{int}((s \bmod 65536)/256)$

$Z = s \bmod 256$

In the formulas, int ( ) denotes integer division and yields the integer multiple, and mod denotes the modulus operator and yields the remainder after division.

7. Repeat steps 5 and 6 until the table is complete.

To compare the two techniques and verify that they will both yield the same result, perform a decimal 3-bit subnetting of 131.107.0.0.

Based on n = 3, create a table with eight entries. The entry for Subnet 1 is the all-zeros subnet. N, the decimal representation of 131.107.0.0, is 2204827648 ((131 × 16777216) + (107 × 65536)). Because there are 13 remaining host bits, the increment value I is 2^{13}, or 8192. Entries for Subnets 2 through 8 are incremented by 8192.

Table A-10 lists the subnetted address prefixes of 131.107.0.0.

Table A-10 A 3-Bit Subnetting of 131.107.0.0 (Decimal)

Subnet	Decimal Representation	Subnetted Address Prefix
1	2204827648	131.107.0.0/19
2	2204835840	131.107.32.0/19
3	2204844032	131.107.64.0/19
4	2204852224	131.107.96.0/19
5	2204860416	131.107.128.0/19
6	2204868608	131.107.160.0/19
7	2204876800	131.107.192.0/19
8	2204884992	131.107.224.0/19

Step 3b: Enumerating IP Address Ranges for Each Subnetted Address Prefix (Decimal)

For each subnetted address prefix, the range of valid IP addresses must be determined as follows:

1. Create a three-column table with 2^n entries where n is the number of host bits chosen for the subnetting. The first column is used for the subnet number; the second column is for the decimal representation of the first and last IP address in the range; and the third column is for the dotted decimal representation of the first and last IP address in the range. Alternatively, you can extend the table created for enumerating the subnetted address prefixes by adding two columns.

2. Compute the increment value J based on h, the number of host bits remaining:

    $J = 2^h - 2$

3. The decimal representation of the first IP address is $N + 1$, where N is the decimal representation of the subnetted address prefix. The decimal representation of the last IP address is $N + J$.

4. Convert the decimal representation of the first and last IP address to dotted decimal notation (W.X.Y.Z) using the following formulas (where s is the decimal representation of the first or last IP address):

   W = int (s/16777216)

   X = int ((s mod 16777216)/65536)

   Y = int ((s mod 65536)/256)

   Z = s mod 256

   In the formulas, int ( ) denotes integer division and yields the integer multiple, and mod denotes the modulus operator and yields the remainder after division.

5. Repeat steps 3 and 4 until the table is complete.

To continue with the example, enumerate the range of valid IP addresses for the 3-bit subnetting of 131.107.0.0. Compute the increment value $J = 2^{13} - 2 = 8190$. Table A-11 lists the ranges of IP addresses for the eight subnetted address prefixes.

Table A-11 Enumeration of IP Addresses for the 3-Bit Subnetting of 131.107.0.0 (Decimal)

Subnet	Decimal Representation	Range of IP Addresses
1	2204827649 – 2204835838	131.107.0.1 – 131.107.31.254
2	2204835841 – 2204844030	131.107.32.1 – 131.107.63.254
3	2204844033 – 2204852222	131.107.64.1 – 131.107.95.254
4	2204852225 – 2204860414	131.107.96.1 – 131.107.127.254
5	2204860417 – 2204868606	131.107.128.1 – 131.107.159.254
6	2204868609 – 2204876798	131.107.160.1 – 131.107.131.107
7	2204876801 – 2204884990	131.107.192.1 – 131.107.223.254
8	2204884993 – 2204893182	131.107.224.1 – 131.107.255.254

All-Zeros and All-Ones Subnets

In the previous discussion's examples, the subnet where all the host bits were set to 0 (the all-zeros subnet) and the subnet where all the host bits were set to 1 (the all-ones subnet) was used. The use of these subnets is controversial.

Originally, RFC 950 forbade the use of these subnets as valid subnets because of the following:

- The all-zeros subnet caused problems for early routing protocols that did not use a subnet mask to distinguish an address prefix. Therefore, 131.107.0.0/16 was the same network to the router as 131.107.0.0/19.

- The subnet broadcast address for the all-ones subnet uses the same address as a special broadcast address, called the *all-subnets-directed broadcast address*. An IP datagram for the all-subnets-directed broadcast was designed to be forwarded by routers to all classful address prefix subnets. For more information on the all-subnets-directed broadcast address, see the section "IP Broadcast Addresses" later in this appendix.

The restriction on the use of the all-zeros and all-ones subnets is part of the legacy of classful networks. The result of this restriction is that substantial portions of a fixed address space are unusable and wasted. For example, when performing a 3-bit subnetting of 131.107.0.0 and excluding the all-zeros and all-ones subnets, only six subnets are available. The range of IP addresses 131.107.0.1 through 131.107.31.254 for the all-zeros subnet and 131.107.224.1 through 131.107.255.254 for the all-ones subnet are unusable.

RFC 1812 now allows the use of all-zeros and all-ones subnets for classless environments for the following reasons:

- Classless environments use routing protocols that advertise the subnet mask with the address prefix. Therefore, 131.107.0.0/16 is distinguishable from 131.107.0.0/19.
- The all-subnets-directed broadcast has no meaning in a classless environment.

Even though RFC 1812 now allows the use of these special subnets, there is no guarantee that all of your routers and hosts support them. It is a common default configuration for routers not to support one or the other special subnet, and they must be instructed to do so. Verify that your routers and hosts support the all-zeros and all-ones subnets before using them. Hosts and routers running Windows Server 2008 or Windows Vista support the use of the all-zeros and all-ones subnets without additional configuration.

Variable-Length Subnetting

The preceding discussion illustrates how a fixed address prefix can be subdivided into equally sized subnets. The 3-bit subnetting of the classful address prefix 131.107.0.0/16 produced eight equally sized subnets, each containing 8190 possible IP addresses. However, in the real world, network segments are not of equal sizes. Some network segments require more IP addresses than others. For example, a network segment containing hosts requires more IP addresses than a backbone network segment containing just a few routers. Point-to-point WAN connections require only two IP addresses.

If equally sized subnetting were done, it would have to be done based on the network segment that required the largest amount of hosts. All other network segments would have the same amount of IP addresses, some of which are unassigned or unusable.

To maximize the use of the fixed address space, subnetting is applied recursively to produce subnets of different sizes all derived from the same original address prefix. This is known as variable-length subnetting. Differently sized subnets use different subnet masks, or variable-length subnet masks (VLSM).

Because all of the subnets are derived from the same address prefix, if the subnets are contiguous, the routes for all the subnets can be summarized by advertising the original address prefix. Contiguous subnets are subnets of the same address prefix that are connected to each other.

When performing variable-length subnetting, care must be taken so that each subnet is unique, and with its subnet mask, can be distinguished from all other subnets of the original address prefix. Variable-length subnetting requires a careful analysis of your network segments to determine how many of each sized network you require. Then, starting from your address prefix, subnetting is performed as many times as needed to express as many subnets as desired with the proper sizes.

With variable-length subnetting, the subnetting technique is applied recursively: You subnet a previously subnetted address prefix. When subnetting a previously subnetted address prefix, the subnetted address prefix bits are fixed and an appropriate number of remaining host bits is chosen for subnetting.

Example of Variable-Length Subnetting

To expand on the earlier example, continue subnetting the classful address prefix of 131.107.0.0/16. After the 3-bit subnetting has been performed, the remaining addresses must be divided such that:

- Half of the addresses are reserved for future use.
- Three address prefixes are allocated with up to 8190 IP addresses.
- 31 address prefixes are allocated with up to 254 IP addresses.
- 64 address prefixes are allocated with only two IP addresses.

Recall that the 3-bit subnetting of 131.107.0.0/16 produced the eight address prefixes listed in Table A-12.

Table A-12 The Eight Subnets for the 3-Bit Subnetting of 131.107.0.0/16

Subnet	Subnetted Address Prefix
1	131.107.0.0/19
2	131.107.32.0/19
3	131.107.64.0/19
4	131.107.96.0/19
5	131.107.128.0/19
6	131.107.160.0/19
7	131.107.192.0/19
8	131.107.224.0/19

Reserve Half of the IP Addresses for Future Use To reserve half of the addresses for future use, set aside the first four address prefixes (131.107.0.0/19, 131.107.32.0/19, 131.107.64.0/19, 131.107.96.0/19).

Obtain Three Address Prefixes with up to 8190 IP Addresses To obtain three subnets with up to 8190 IP addresses per address prefix, choose the next three address prefixes (131.107.128.0/19, 131.107.160.0/19, 131.107.192.0/19). Each address prefix has 13 host bits, for a total of 8190 IP addresses per address prefix.

Obtain 31 Address Prefixes with up to 254 IP Addresses To obtain 31 address prefixes, each with up to 254 IP addresses, perform a 5-bit subnetting of 131.107.224.0/19. The result is 32 address prefixes (131.107.224.0/24, 131.107.225.0/24, 131.107.226.0/24 . . . 131.107.253.0/24, 131.107.254.0/24, 131.107.255.0/24). To fulfill the requirement, choose the first 31 address prefixes (131.107.224.0/24 to 131.107.254.0/24).

Obtain 64 Address Prefixes with only 2 IP Addresses To obtain 64 address prefixes with only 2 usable IP addresses, perform a 6-bit subnetting of 131.107.255.0/24. The result is 64 address prefixes (131.107.255.4/30, 131.107.255.8/30, 131.107.255.12/30 . . . 131.107.255.244/30, 131.107.255.248/30, 131.107.255.252/30).

Figure A-10 shows the variable-length subnetting of 131.107.0.0/16.

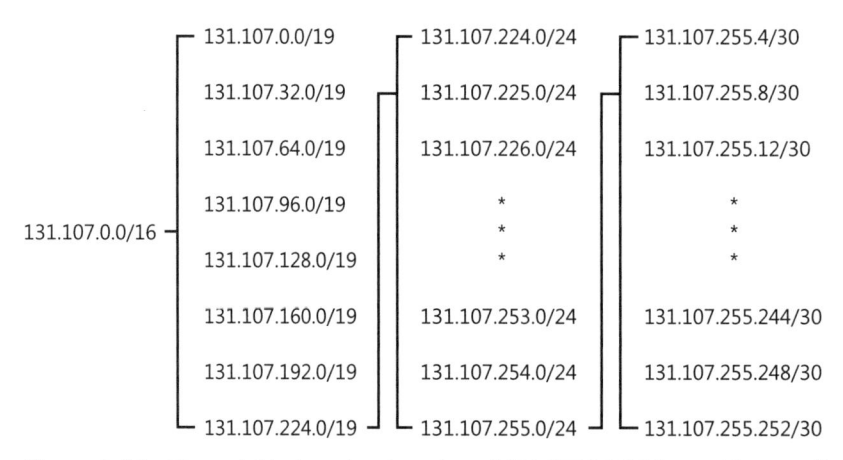

Figure A-10 The variable-length subnetting of 131.107.0.0/16 into address prefixes of different sizes.

Variable-Length Subnetting and Routing

Variable-length subnetting requires routing protocols to advertise the subnet mask with the address prefix. Routing Information Protocol (RIP) version 2, Open Shortest Path First (OSPF), and Border Gateway Protocol version 4 (BGP-v4) support variable-length subnetting environments, but RIP version 1 does not.

Supernetting and CIDR

As the Internet grew suddenly from a collection of educational institutions and government agencies to a business-oriented, pervasive global internetwork, great stress was placed on the IP address space. Assigning classful address prefixes to organizations meant a quick, wasteful depletion of the Internet address space.

For example, numerous organizations worldwide require more than 254 IP addresses. Therefore, a single class C address prefix is insufficient. A single class B address prefix, however, provides sufficient IP addresses and enough host bits to implement subnetting within the organization's internal network. Although this is good for the organization, it is bad for the Internet IP address space. Consider the smaller organization that needs only 4000 IP addresses. Assigning a class B address prefix with 65,534 possible IP addresses means that 61,534 IP addresses are unassigned and wasted.

Now, instead of an entire class B address prefix, the Internet Corporation for Assigned Names and Numbers (ICANN) assigns a range of class C address prefixes. For example, ICANN assigns 16 class C address prefixes to an organization needing 4000 IP addresses. Each class C address prefix allows for 254 IP addresses. Therefore, 16 class C address prefixes allow for 4064 IP addresses. This technique minimizes the wasting of Internet IP addresses, but it introduces a new problem. If a single class B address prefix is assigned, that single class B address prefix becomes a single route in the routing tables of the Internet backbone routers. If 16 class C address prefixes are assigned, 16 class C address prefixes become 16 routes in the routing tables of the Internet backbone routers.

Extending this example to its ultimate limits, there are more than 2 million class C address prefixes. After assigning them all, it is possible to have more than 2 million routes in the routing tables of the Internet backbone routers. Even with today's technology, it is difficult to build an IP router that can have a routing table with millions of entries, and forward IP datagrams at megabit- or gigabit-per-second speeds.

To prevent this scaling problem from overwhelming Internet routers, a route aggregation technique called Classless Inter-Domain Routing (CIDR) is used to express a range of class C address prefixes as a single route. This is the method of address allocation that the modern Internet uses. CIDR solves the scaling problem by minimizing the total number of routes that must be stored in the routing tables of Internet routers.

CIDR uses a supernetted subnet mask to express the range of class C address prefixes. A supernetted subnet mask is less specific, or contains fewer address prefix bits, than a classful subnet mask. In contrast, a subnetted subnet mask is more specific, or contains more address prefix bits, than a classful subnet mask.

Views on CIDR Allocation

The CIDR method of address allocation can be viewed in two ways:

- A range of class C address prefixes
- An address space in which multiple classful networks are combined into a single classless network

The latter perspective is more appropriate for today's Internet and for looking forward to IPv6.

A Range of Class C Address prefixes Viewed as a range of class C address prefixes, the requirement is based on the number of class C network segments needed in your organization. The following requirements are for a range of class C address prefixes to be expressible as a single route using an address prefix and a subnet mask:

- The class C address prefixes must be sequential.
- The number of allocated class C address prefixes must be expressed as a power of 2.

For example, Table A-13 lists the range (or block) of eight class C address prefixes, starting with address prefix 223.1.184.0.

Table A-13 A Block of Eight Class C Address Prefixes Starting with 223.1.184.0

Starting Address prefix	223.1.184.0	11011111 00000001 10111000 00000000
Ending Address prefix	223.1.191.0	11011111 00000001 10111111 00000000

Notice that the first 21 bits (underlined) of the range of class C address prefixes are the same. The last 3 bits of the third octet vary over all possible values from 000 through 111. This range of class C address prefixes can be aggregated with the address prefix and subnet mask listed in Table A-14.

Table A-14 The Aggregated Block of Class C Address Prefixes

Address Prefix	223.1.184.0
Subnet Mask (binary)	11111111 11111111 11111000 00000000
Subnet Mask	255.255.248.0
Prefix Length	/21

A block of class-based address prefixes, as allocated in this example, is known as a *CIDR block*.

Table A-15 lists the number of class C address prefixes and the supernetted subnet mask for a required number of hosts.

Table A-15 Supernetting and Class C Addresses

Required Hosts	Number of Class C Address Prefixes	Supernetted Subnet Mask
2–254	1	255.255.255.0 or /24
255–508	2	255.255.254.0 or /23
509–1016	4	255.255.252.0 or /22
1017–2032	8	255.255.248.0 or /21

Table A-15 Supernetting and Class C Addresses

Required Hosts	Number of Class C Address Prefixes	Supernetted Subnet Mask
2033–4064	16	255.255.240.0 or /20
4065–8128	32	255.255.224.0 or /19
8129–16,256	64	255.255.192.0 or /18
16,257–32,512	128	255.255.128.0 or /17
32,513–65,024	256	255.255.0.0 or /16

An Address Space From the perspective of an address space, CIDR blocks are no longer viewed as a range of class C address prefixes. Even though the CIDR block is obtained from the class-defined range of class C address prefixes, it does not necessarily represent a range of class C address prefixes. Viewing the CIDR block as a range of class C address prefixes implies that you will assign each class C address prefix within the block to each of your networks.

In reality, you typically want to assign address prefixes of various sizes to the networks of your intranet in a variable-length subnetting scheme. Now your requirement is based on the number of IP addresses required, rather than the number of class C subnets in your organization.

For example, to assign 4000 IP addresses to an organization, determine the number of bits required to express 4000 IP addresses. Using powers of 2, 12 bits are needed to express 4094 IP addresses. Therefore, 12 bits are used for the host ID portion, and 20 bits for the address prefix portion. The subnet mask indicates 20 bits of address prefix. For example, starting from an unassigned portion of the IP address space, ICANN allocates the 223.1.176.0 network with the subnet mask of 255.255.240.0 (or 223.1.176.0/20) address space to the organization.

The allocated address space allows the assignment of the range of IP addresses from 223.1.176.1 through 223.1.191.254. However, it is unlikely that the organization will use all 4094 IP addresses on the same network segment. Rather, the organization can use variable-length subnetting and the 12 host bits to create a series of subnetted address prefixes containing the suitable number of appropriately sized subnets.

With CIDR, IP address prefixes lose their classful heritage and become address spaces where certain bits are fixed (the address prefix bits), and certain bits are variable (the host ID bits). Using variable-length subnetting techniques, the organization's needs should determine how to best utilize the host bits.

CIDR and Routing

CIDR, like variable-length subnetting, requires routing protocols to advertise the subnet mask with the address prefix. RIP version 2, OSPF, and BGP-v4 support CIDR environments, but RIP version 1 does not.

Public and Private Addresses

When deploying an IP addressing scheme in your organization, one of the main considerations is whether your intranet is connected to the Internet:

- If your organization is not connected to the Internet, it is technically possible to choose any IP address prefixes—classful or classless—without concern for using overlapping addresses being used on the Internet. However, it is highly recommended that you choose a private address range.

- If your organization is connected to the Internet, it can be connected in one of two ways. If your organization uses a direct-routed connection using a router or firewall, you must use ICANN-compliant addresses as allocated by ICANN or an Internet service provider (ISP). If your organization uses an indirect connection using a proxy server or a Network Address Translator (NAT), you must use addresses that do not overlap with addresses that do, or might, exist on the Internet.

Organizations connected to the Internet must choose between the use of public or private addresses.

Public Addresses

ICANN assigns public addresses that are within the public address space consisting of all of the possible unicast addresses on the Internet worldwide. Historically, ICANN assigned classful address prefixes to organizations connecting to the Internet without regard to geographical location. Today, ICANN assigns CIDR blocks to ISPs based on geographical location; the ISPs then subdivide their assigned CIDR blocks to customers. Subdivision of the remaining class C address space based on geographical location was done to provide hierarchical routing and to minimize the number of routes in Internet backbone routers. Public addresses are guaranteed to be globally unique.

When an organization or an ISP is assigned a block of addresses in the public address space, a route exists in the Internet routers' routing tables so that the assigned public addresses are reachable through the ISP. Historically, a classful address prefix was added to all of the Internet routers. Today, a route consisting of the range of assigned addresses is added to the routing tables of regional and ISP Internet routers.

One or more (address prefix, mask) pairs summarize the range of public IP addresses assigned to an organization. These pairs become the routes in the ISP and Internet routers so that the IP addresses of the organization can be reached.

Illegal or Overlapping Addresses Organizations that are not connected to the Internet either directly or indirectly are free to choose any addressing scheme without regard to whether the addresses have been assigned to another ISP or organization. However, if that organization later decides to connect to the Internet, a new addressing scheme might be required.

The addresses assigned when the organization was not connected to the Internet might include public addresses that have been assigned to other organizations or ISPs by ICANN. If that is the case, these addresses are duplicates that conflict with assigned addresses. This is known as illegal, or overlapping, addressing. Internet traffic from hosts using illegal addresses is forwarded to the routers of the organization that was originally assigned those addresses. Therefore, organizations using illegal addressing are unreachable on the Internet.

For example, an organization that is not connected to the Internet decides to use the address space 207.46.130.0/24 for its intranet. As long as the organization does not connect to the Internet, the use of 207.46.130.0/24 is not an issue. If the organization then connects to the Internet using a direct routed connection, the use of 207.46.130.0/24 is illegal and no responses from hosts on the 207.46.130.0/24 network segment are received.

In this configuration, when a host sends traffic to an Internet location, it sends the traffic with the source IP address within the address space of 207.46.130.0/24. When the Internet host sends a response, it sends the response to the destination IP address within the address space of 207.46.130.0/24. ICANN assigned Microsoft Corporation the address space 207.46.130.0/24, and a route exists in Internet routers to forward traffic with the destination IP address in this range to Microsoft's routers. Therefore, the responses to traffic sent by the hosts on the illegal address space 207.46.130.0/24 are forwarded to Microsoft's routers, and not to the routers of the organization using the illegal addresses.

Note It is common practice among ISPs to discard IP packets sent from a customer site when the source IP address field is not set to a valid public address assigned to the customer. This is known as *ingress filtering*, which attempts to prevent the sending of traffic from hosts using illegal addresses and address spoofing (the sending of IP traffic from a source IP address that is not assigned to a host).

Private Addresses

As the Internet experienced exponential growth, the demand for public IP addresses increased commensurately. Because each node on an organization's intranet required a globally unique public IP address, organizations requested enough IP addresses from ICANN to assign unique IP addresses to all of the nodes within their organizations.

However, when an analysis of IP addressing within organizations was done, the Internet authorities noticed that most organizations actually needed very few public addresses. The only hosts that required public IP addresses were those that communicated directly with systems on the Internet, such as Web servers, File Transfer Protocol (FTP) servers, e-mail servers, proxy servers, and firewalls. Most of the hosts within an organization's intranet obtained access to Internet resources through Application Layer gateways such as proxy servers and e-mail servers.

For hosts within the organization's intranet that do not require direct access to the Internet, a legal IP address space must be used. For this purpose, Internet authorities created the private address space, a subset of the Internet IP address space that can be used without conflict within an organization, for hosts that do not require a direct connection to the Internet.

The private and public address spaces are separate and do not overlap. ICANN never assigns private addresses—IP addresses within the private address space—to an organization or ISP. This also means that private IP addresses are not reachable on the Internet.

Because private addresses are not reachable on the Internet, hosts on an intranet with private addressing cannot be directly connected to the Internet. Rather, they must be indirectly connected to the Internet using an NAT or an Application Layer gateway such as a proxy server.

An NAT is a router that translates between private addresses and public addresses for Internet traffic. The proxy server receives a request from a host on the intranet for Internet resources. The proxy server then sends the request to the Internet resource and the response traffic is forwarded back to the requesting host. When the proxy server sends the request to the Internet resource, it uses public addressing. Both proxy servers and NATs have private addresses on their intranet interface and public addresses on their Internet interface.

The following three address blocks define the private address space:

- **10.0.0.0/8** The 10.0.0.0/8 private network is an address space with 24 host bits that can be used for any subnetting scheme within the private organization.
- **172.16.0.0/12** The 172.16.0.0/12 private network is an address space with 20 host bits that can be used for any subnetting scheme within the private organization. From a classful perspective, the 172.16.0.0/12 private address prefix is the range of 16 class B address prefixes from 172.16.0.0/16 through 172.31.0.0/16.
- **192.168.0.0/16** The 192.168.0.0/16 private network is an address space with 16 host bits that can be used for any subnetting scheme within the private organization. From a classful perspective, the 192.168.0.0/16 private address prefix is the range of 256 class C address prefixes from 192.168.0.0/24 through 192.168.255.0/24.

Automatic Private IP Addressing

When you configure a computer running Windows Server 2008 or Windows Vista to obtain its IP address automatically and a DHCP server does not respond to the DHCPREQUEST and DHCPDISCOVER messages and there is no alternate configuration, TCP/IP for Windows Server 2008 and Windows Vista configures itself using the Automatic Private IP Addressing (APIPA) feature. Using APIPA, TCP/IP for Windows Server 2008 and Windows Vista randomly picks an IP address in the address space of 169.254.0.0/16. This address space has been reserved by the Internet Assigned Numbers Authority (IANA) and is not reachable on the Internet.

After choosing an IP address, TCP/IP for Windows Server 2008 and Windows Vista uses duplicate address detection to check for IP address uniqueness. If there is no conflict, TCP/IP for Windows Server 2008 and Windows Vista is configured for the randomly chosen IP address and the subnet mask of 255.255.0.0. If there is a conflict, TCP/IP for Windows Server 2008 and Windows Vista randomly chooses a new address in the 169.254.0.0/16 address space. After APIPA configuration, TCP/IP for Windows Server 2008 and Windows Vista continues to send DHCPDISCOVER messages every five minutes. If a DHCP server responds, TCP/IP for Windows Server 2008 and Windows Vista abandons the APIPA configuration and the DHCP-allocated address takes effect. For more information on duplicate address detection, see Chapter 3, "Address Resolution Protocol (ARP)."

APIPA was designed to simplify the configuration of a single subnet small office/home office (SOHO) network that is not connected to the Internet or any other IP internetwork. With APIPA, all the computers on a single-subnet SOHO network configure themselves and are able to communicate without manually configuring TCP/IP or setting up a DHCP server.

APIPA does not provide automatic configuration of a default gateway, the IP address of a Domain Name System (DNS) server, a DNS domain name, the IP address of a Windows Internet Name Service (WINS) server, or NetBIOS node type. A single-subnet SOHO network does not need a default gateway, and broadcast NetBIOS name queries resolve names for communication between computers.

TCP/IP for Windows Server 2008 and Windows Vista APIPA behavior is controlled by the following registry values:

IPAutoconfigurationEnabled

```
Keys: HKEY_LOCAL_MACHINE\SYSTEM\CurrentControlSet\Services\Tcpip\Parameters
and
HKEY_LOCAL_MACHINE\SYSTEM\CurrentControlSet\Services\Tcpip\Parameters\Interfaces
\InterfaceGUID
Value type: REG_DWORD
Valid range: 0 - 1
Default: 1
Present by default: No
```

IPAutoconfigurationEnabled either enables (when set to 1) or disables (when set to 0) APIPA-based IP address configuration either globally or per interface. The default is enabled both globally and per interface, and the setting for an interface overrides the global setting.

IPAutoconfigurationSubnet

```
Keys: HKEY_LOCAL_MACHINE\SYSTEM\CurrentControlSet\Services\Tcpip\Parameters
and
HKEY_LOCAL_MACHINE\SYSTEM\CurrentControlSet\Services\Tcpip\Parameters\Interfaces
\InterfaceGUID
Value type: REG_SZ (String)
Valid range: A valid IP address prefix expressed in dotted decimal notation.
Default: 169.254.0.0
Present by default: No
```

IPAutoconfigurationSubnet specifies the IP address prefix for the network prefix of APIPA-configured addresses. The default value is 169.254.0.0. IPAutoconfigurationSubnet can be specified globally or per interface, and the setting for an interface overrides the global setting.

IPAutoconfigurationMask

```
Keys: HKEY_LOCAL_MACHINE\SYSTEM\CurrentControlSet\Services\Tcpip\Parameters
and
HKEY_LOCAL_MACHINE\SYSTEM\CurrentControlSet\Services\Tcpip\Parameters\Interfaces
\InterfaceGUID
Value type: REG_SZ (String)
Valid range: A valid subnet mask expressed in dotted decimal notation.
Default: 255.255.0.0
Present by default: No
```

IPAutoconfigurationMask specifies the subnet mask for the network prefix of APIPA-configured addresses. The default value is 255.255.0.0. IPAutoconfigurationMask can be specified globally or per interface and the setting for an interface overrides the global setting.

> **Note** The address prefix specified for the IPAutoconfigurationSubnet cannot be more specific than the subnet mask specified for the IPAutoconfigurationMask. In other words, the address prefix cannot contain bits set to 1 when the corresponding bit in the mask is set to 0. An example of an incorrect address prefix and subnet mask combination is the address prefix 169.254.47.0 with the subnet mask of 255.255.0.0. The correct subnet mask for this address prefix is 255.255.255.0.

IP Broadcast Addresses

IP broadcast addresses are used for single-packet one-to-everyone delivery. A sending host addresses the IP packet using a broadcast address and every node on the sending node's network segment receives and processes the packet. IP broadcast addresses can be used only as the destination IP address.

There are four different types of IP broadcast addresses. For each type, the broadcast IP packet is addressed at the Network Interface Layer using the network technology's broadcast address. For example, for Ethernet and Token Ring networks, all IP broadcasts are sent using the Ethernet and Token Ring broadcast address 0xFF-FF-FF-FF-FF-FF.

Network Broadcast

The IP network broadcast address is the address formed by setting all the host bits to 1 for a classful address. An example of a network broadcast address for the classful address prefix 131.107.0.0/16 is 131.107.255.255. Network broadcasts are used to send packets to all hosts of a classful network, which listen for and process packets addressed to the network broadcast address. IP routers do not forward network broadcast packets.

Subnet Broadcast

The IP subnet broadcast address is the address formed by setting all the host bits to 1 for a nonclassful address. An example of a network broadcast address for the nonclassful address prefix 131.107.26.0/24 is 131.107.26.255. Subnet broadcasts are used to send packets to all hosts of a subnetted, supernetted, or otherwise nonclassful network. All hosts of a nonclassful network listen for and process packets addressed to the subnet broadcast address. IP routers do not forward subnet broadcast packets.

For a classful network, there is no subnet broadcast address, only a network broadcast address. For a nonclassful network, there is no network broadcast address, only a subnet broadcast address.

All-Subnets-Directed Broadcast

The IP all-subnets-directed broadcast address is the address formed by setting all the original classful address prefix host bits to 1 for a nonclassful network. A packet addressed to the all-subnets-directed broadcast is intended to reach all hosts on all of the subnets of a subnetted class-based address prefix. An example of an all-subnets-directed broadcast address for the subnetted address prefix 131.107.26.0/24 is 131.107.255.255. The all-subnets-directed broadcast is the network broadcast address of the original classful address prefix.

All hosts of a nonclassful network listen for and process packets addressed to the all-subnets-directed broadcast address. RFC 922 required IP routers to forward all-subnets-directed broadcast packets to all subnets of the original classful address prefix implied in the address. However, this forwarding was not widely implemented.

With the advent of classless address prefixes, the all-subnets-directed broadcast address is no longer relevant. According to RFC 1812, the use of the all-subnets-directed broadcast has been deprecated.

Notice how the all-subnets-directed address is the same as the subnet broadcast for the all-ones subnet. For example, the 8-bit subnetting of the class B address prefix 157.54.0.0 produces the subnets {157.54.0.0/24, 157.54.1.0/24 ... 157.54.254.0/24, 157.54.255.0/24}. For the last subnet, 157.54.255.0/24, the subnet broadcast is 157.54.255.255, which is the same as the all-subnets-directed broadcast address of 157.54.255.255. This address conflict is not an issue for routers that do not forward all-subnets-directed broadcast traffic.

Limited Broadcast

The limited broadcast address is the address formed by setting all 32 bits of the IP address to 1 (255.255.255.255). The limited broadcast address is used when an IP node must perform a one-to-everyone delivery on the local network but the address prefix is unknown. The limited broadcast address is typically used only by nodes during an automated configuration process such as Boot Protocol (BOOTP) or DHCP. For example, with DHCP, a DHCP client must use the limited broadcast address for all traffic sent until the DHCP server acknowledges the IP address lease.

All hosts, classful or nonclassful, listen for and process packets addressed to the limited broadcast address. Although it appears that the limited broadcast address is addressed to all nodes on all networks, it appears only on the local network and is never forwarded by routers. The limited broadcast packet is limited to the local network segment.

The following registry value controls the address of the limited broadcast address:

UseZeroBroadcast
```
Key: HKEY_LOCAL_MACHINE\SYSTEM\CurrentControlSet\Services\Tcpip\Parameters\Interface\InterfaceGUID
Value type: REG_DWORD
Valid range: 0 - 1
Default: 0
Present by default: Yes
```

UseZeroBroadcast determines whether the limited broadcast is 0.0.0.0 (when set to 1) or 255.255.255.255 (when set to 0). By default, UseZeroBroadcast is set to 0. Some implementations of TCP/IP, such as those derived from UNIX, use 0.0.0.0 as their limited broadcast address. On the same subnet, all nodes should be using the same limited broadcast address.

IP Multicast Addresses

IP multicast addresses are used for single-packet one-to-many delivery. A sending host addresses the IP packet using an IP multicast address; every node on the sending node's internetwork that is listening for the multicast traffic receives and processes the packet. Unlike broadcast packets, routers forward IP multicast packets and only the hosts listening for the IP multicast traffic are disturbed. IP multicast addresses can be used only as the destination IP address.

As RFC 1112 describes, the set of hosts listening for the traffic of a specific IP multicast address is called a *host group*. Host group members can be located anywhere on the IP internetwork. They also can join and leave the host group at any time. For routers to forward IP multicast traffic to host group members, the routers must be aware of where the members of a multicast group are located. For more information on how hosts and routers facilitate the forwarding of IP multicast traffic, see Chapter 7, "Internet Group Management Protocol (IGMP)."

Multicast IP addresses are in the class D range. Multicast IP addresses range from 224.0.0.0 through 239.255.255.255 (224.0.0.0/4). Multicast IP addresses in the range 224.0.0.0 through 224.0.0.255 (224.0.0.0/24) are reserved for local subnet traffic. Table A-16 lists some of the reserved IP addresses in this range used by Windows Server 2008. For a complete list, see *http://www.iana.org/assignments/multicast-addresses*.

Table A-16 Reserved Local Subnet IP Multicast Addresses

Multicast IP Address	Purpose
224.0.0.1	The all-hosts multicast address, designed to reach all hosts on a subnet
224.0.0.2	The all-routers multicast address, designed to reach all routers on a subnet
224.0.0.9	The RIP version 2 multicast address, designed to reach all RIP version 2 routers on a subnet

Mapping IP Multicast Addresses to MAC Addresses

To fulfill the promise of IP multicast traffic—where a single IP datagram is processed only by the host group members—IP multicast traffic must be mapped to a corresponding MAC-level multicast address. The corresponding MAC-level multicast becomes an interesting address to the network interface card (NIC), and all traffic addressed to that interesting address with a valid frame check sequence is passed up through a hardware interrupt to the operating system.

Ethernet and Fiber Distributed Data Interface

To denote a MAC-level multicast address, Ethernet network adapters set the Individual/Group (I/G) bit, the low-order bit of the first byte of the destination MAC address, to 1. For IP multicast addressing, the range of multicast MAC addresses is 0x01-00-5E-00-00-00 to 0x01-00-5E-7F-FF-FF. The high-order 25 bits are set to 0000001 00000000 01011110 0. The low-order 23 bits are available for use by IP multicast addresses.

To map an IP multicast address to an Ethernet MAC-level multicast address, the low-order 23 bits of the IP multicast address are copied to the low-order 23 bits in the Ethernet multicast address, as Figure A-11 shows.

In the high-order 9 bits of the IP multicast address, the first 4 bits are set to 1110; the next 5 bits are variable. These 5 bits do not map to the corresponding Ethernet multicast address. Therefore, up to 32 different IP multicast addresses can map to the same Ethernet MAC-level multicast address. IP multicast packets received that do not correspond to a multicast address registered by an application or another protocol are silently discarded.

A node registers interest in a specific multicast group by informing the NIC to listen for another interesting destination address for incoming frames. In Windows Server 2008 and Windows Vista, this is done through the NDISRequest( ) function. For example, by default TCP/IP for Windows Server 2008 and Windows Vista listens for all multicast traffic sent to the all-hosts multicast address 224.0.0.1. Therefore, TCP/IP informs the NIC through Network Driver Interface Specification (NDIS) to pass up frames with the destination MAC address of 0x01-00-5E-00-00-01.

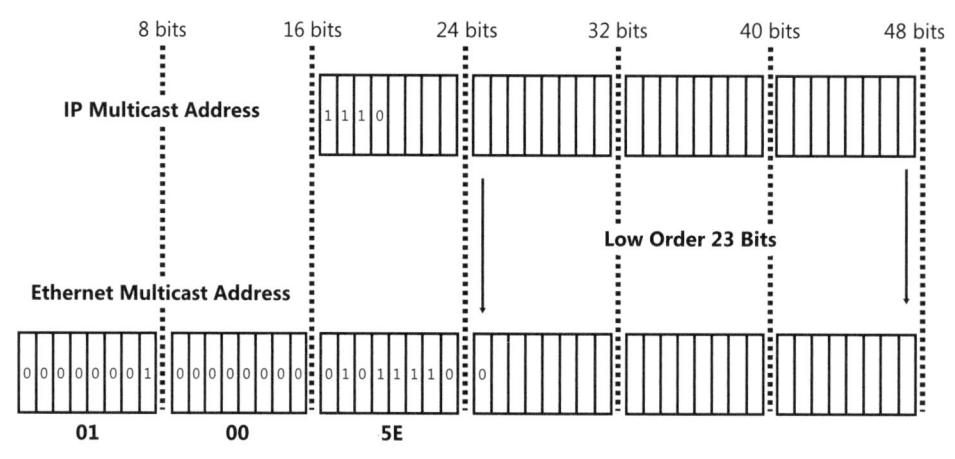

Figure A-11 The mapping of IP multicast addresses to Ethernet MAC addresses.

Token Ring

As RFC 1469 describes, Token Ring can support the same type of multicast IP-address-to-MAC mapping as Ethernet. However, because of the hardware limitations of most Token Ring network adapters, typically all IP multicast addresses are mapped to the single Token Ring functional address of 0xC0-00-00-04-00-00. This is the behavior of TCP/IP for Windows Server 2008 and Windows Vista.

> **Note** TCP/IP for Windows Server 2008 and Windows Vista no longer supports the TrFunctionalMcastAddress registry value.

Summary

IP addresses can be unicast, broadcast, or multicast. For unicast addresses, subnetting techniques allow an address prefix to be allocated, in an efficient manner, to the subnets of an IP internetwork. Internet authorities have defined public addresses that are reachable on the Internet and private addresses that are designed for use on private intranets not directly connected to the Internet. IP broadcast addresses are used to send IP datagrams to all the nodes on a physical or logical subnet. IP multicast addresses are used to send IP datagrams to all members of a multicast host group.

Glossary

Address Resolution Protocol (ARP) A protocol for resolving Internet Protocol (IP) addresses into media access control (MAC) addresses. *See also* inverse ARP (INARP) *and* reverse ARP (RARP)

AH *See* Authentication Header (AH)

APIPA *See* Automatic Private IP Addressing (APIPA)

ARP *See* Address Resolution Protocol (ARP)

ARP cache A table for each interface of static or dynamically resolved Internet Protocol (IP) addresses and their corresponding media access control (MAC) addresses. Also known as a neighbor cache.

Authenticated Internet Protocol (AuthIP) An enhanced version of the Internet Key Exchange (IKE) protocol in Windows Server 2008 and Windows Vista that supports additional authentication flexibility with support for user-level authentication, authentication with multiple credentials, improved authentication method negotiation, and asymmetric authentication.

Authentication Header (AH) An Internet Protocol security (IPsec) header that provides data origin authentication, data integrity, and replay protection for the entire IP datagram, excluding fields in the IP header that are allowed to change in transit.

AuthIP *See* Authenticated Internet Protocol (AuthIP)

Automatic Private IP Addressing (APIPA) A feature of Windows Vista, Windows Server 2008, Windows XP, and Windows Server 2003 that self-configures an Internet Protocol (IP) address and subnet mask from the range 169.254.0.0/16 when the Transmission Control Protocol/Internet Protocol (TCP/IP) protocol is configured for automatic configuration, there is no Dynamic Host Configuration Protocol (DHCP) server, and there is no alternate configuration.

Compound TCP (CTCP) A Transmission Control Protocol (TCP) performance enhancement in Windows Server 2008 and Windows Vista that provides better transmission rate recovery for connections with a large receive window size and connection capacity.

congestion avoidance A Transmission Control Protocol (TCP) algorithm that provides a linear scaling of the actual send window. The actual send window is increased by one Maximum Segment Size (MSS) for each full window of data that is acknowledged.

CTCP *See* Compound TCP (CTCP)

DHCP *See* Dynamic Host Configuration Protocol (DHCP)

DHCP Server A Windows Server 2008 service that provides Dynamic Host Configuration Protocol (DHCP)–based Internet Protocol (IP) addresses and configuration parameters to DHCP clients.

Diffie-Hellman algorithm An algorithm for determining a shared secret key by exchanging two numerical values across an insecure medium. A component of the Oakley key determination protocol.

DNS *See* Domain Name System (DNS)

Domain Name System (DNS) A set of services for storing, updating, and resolving computer names and associated Internet Protocol (IP) addresses for computers and other resources on the Internet or on private Transmission Control Protocol/Internet Protocol (TCP/IP) networks.

Dynamic Host Configuration Protocol (DHCP) A protocol for providing computers with Internet Protocol (IP) addresses and other host configuration parameters.

duplicate address detection A process to determine whether an address is already being used on a subnet.

ECN *See* Explicit Congestion Notification (ECN)

Encapsulating Security Payload (ESP) An IP security (IPsec) header and trailer combination that provides data origin authentication, data integrity, replay protection, and data confidentiality for the ESP-encapsulated portion of the packet.

ESP *See* Encapsulating Security Payload (ESP)

Explicit Congestion Notification (ECN) A set of standards for both Internet Protocol (IP) hosts and routers that enables routers to report to sending hosts that congestion is occurring, allowing the sending hosts to lower their transmission rate before the router begins dropping packets.

fast recovery A Transmission Control Protocol (TCP) algorithm that more quickly scales the TCP send window when a segment is retransmitted using fast retransmit.

fast retransmit A Transmission Control Protocol (TCP) algorithm that retransmits a segment before the retransmission time-out (RTO) expires when multiple duplicate acknowledgments of the previously received contiguous segment are received.

FDDI *See* Fiber Distributed Data Interface (FDDI)

Fiber Distributed Data Interface (FDDI) An optical fiber-based token passing ring local area network (LAN) technology with a bit rate of 100 megabits per second (Mbps).

frame relay A virtual circuit-based wide area network (WAN) technology designed for the transmission of data.

gateway A Transmission Control Protocol/Internet Protocol (TCP/IP) node that has routing capability. *See also* router

hash A one-way cryptographic algorithm that takes an input message of arbitrary length and produces a fixed-length digest. Two hash algorithms used by Windows Server 2008 and Windows Vista are Secure Hash Algorithm 1 (SHA1) and Message Digest 5 (MD5).

host A Transmission Control Protocol/Internet Protocol (TCP/IP) node that does not have routing capability.

host group The set of nodes listening for Internet Protocol (IP) multicast traffic on a specific IP multicast address.

ICMP *See* Internet Control Message Protocol (ICMP)

IETF *See* Internet Engineering Task Force (IETF)

IGMP *See* Internet Group Management Protocol (IGMP)

IKE *See* Internet Key Exchange (IKE)

INARP *See* inverse ARP (INARP)

Internet Control Message Protocol (ICMP) A protocol that works with Internet Protocol (IP) to report errors, provide diagnostics functions, and control the flow of data.

Internet Engineering Task Force (IETF) The standards body that defines the Internet Protocol (IP) and oversees the development of the Internet and the evolution of the Transmission Control Protocol/Internet Protocol (TCP/IP) protocol suite. The standards developed by the IETF and IETF working groups are published as Requests for Comments (RFCs).

Internet Group Management Protocol (IGMP) A protocol for managing multicast group membership on a subnet. There are three versions of IGMP: IGMP version 1 (IGMPv1), IGMP version 2 (IGMPv2), and IGMP version 3 (IGMPv3).

Internet Key Exchange (IKE) A standard method of negotiating security associations (SAs) used by Internet Protocol security (IPsec), based on the Internet Security Association and Key Management Protocol (ISAKMP) and the Oakley key determination protocol.

Internet Protocol (IP) An unreliable datagram delivery service that operates at the Internet layer. Also known as Internet Protocol version 4 (IPv4).

Internet Protocol version 6 (IPv6) An unreliable datagram delivery service that replaces Internet Protocol version 4 (IPv4) at the Internet layer.

Internet Security Association and Key Management Protocol (ISAKMP)   A framework for managing keys within Internet Protocol security (IPsec).

inverse ARP (INARP)   Obtains a remote system's Internet Protocol (IP) address, based on its Network Interface Layer address. Used mainly in frame relay. *See also* Address Resolution Protocol (ARP) and reverse ARP (RARP)

IP   *See* Internet Protocol (IP)

IPsec   *See* IP security (IPsec)

IP security (IPsec)   A suite of protocols and services that provide data origin authentication, data integrity, data confidentiality, and replay protection for Internet Protocol (IP) datagrams.

ISAKMP   *See* Internet Security Association and Key Management Protocol (ISAKMP)

L2TP   *See* Layer Two Tunneling Protocol (L2TP)

LAN   *See* local area network (LAN)

Layer Two Tunneling Protocol (L2TP)   A virtual private network (VPN) protocol that encapsulates VPN data inside Point-to-Point Protocol (PPP) frames, which are then further encapsulated for sending over a link layer, such as frame relay, X.25, or Internet Protocol (IP). Over IP, IP uses User Datagram Protocol (UDP) encapsulation for both tunnel creation and maintenance messages and data.

LCP   *See* Link Control Protocol (LCP)

limited transmit   A Transmission Control Protocol (TCP) performance enhancement that allows a sending TCP peer to send additional segments during fast retransmit to better detect segment losses, rather than waiting for a retransmission timeout.

Link Control Protocol (LCP)   A protocol for negotiating the Data Link Layer characteristics of a point-to-point (PPP) connection.

LLC   *See* Logical Link Control (LLC)

local area network (LAN)   A network of interconnected computers within a relatively small geographic area that typically does not use links provided by third-party telecommunications providers.

Logical Link Control (LLC)   A sublayer of the OSI Data Link Layer, as defined by the Institute of Electrical and Electronics Engineers (IEEE).

MAC   *See* media access control (MAC)

MAC address   The 48-bit address assigned to a network adapter. Also known as a physical address, an Ethernet address, a hardware address, or an Institute of Electrical and Electronics Engineers (IEEE) 802 address.

main mode   The portion of the Internet Protocol security (IPsec) negotiation that creates the Internet Security Association and Key Management Protocol (ISAKMP) security association (SA). The ISAKMP SA is used to protect future quick mode IPsec negotiations.

Maximum Receive Unit (MRU)   The maximum size of a Point-to-Point Protocol (PPP) frame.

Maximum Segment Size (MSS)   The maximum size of a Transmission Control Protocol (TCP) segment.

Maximum Transmission Unit (MTU)   The largest frame that can be sent in a packet- or frame-based network (for example, 1526 bytes for Ethernet).

media access control (MAC)   A sublayer of the OSI Data Link Layer, as defined by the Institute of Electrical and Electronics Engineers (IEEE). *See also* MAC address

MRU   *See* Maximum Receive Unit (MRU)

MSS   *See* Maximum Segment Size (MSS)

MTU   *See* Maximum Transmission Unit (MTU)

NCP   *See* Network Control Protocol (NCP)

neighbor cache   A table for each interface of static or dynamically resolved Internet Protocol (IP) addresses and their corresponding media access control (MAC) addresses. Also known as an ARP cache.

neighbor unreachability detection   A process by which an Internet Protocol (IP) node determines that the IP layer of a neighbor is no longer receiving packets.

NetBIOS   A network interface for applications and a set of network protocols providing name services, session services, and datagram services for NetBIOS applications.

NetBIOS over TCP/IP (NetBT)   The NetBIOS name, session, and datagram services operating over the Transmission Control Protocol/Internet Protocol (TCP/IP) protocol suite.

NetBT   *See* NetBIOS over TCP/IP (NetBT).

Network Control Protocol (NCP)   A protocol for configuring a Network Layer protocol over a point-to-point connection. An example of an NCP is Internet Protocol Control Protocol (IPCP), which is used to configure an IP address and other settings during the establishment of an IP-based Point-to-Point Protocol (PPP) connection.

Network Policy Server (NPS)   The Microsoft implementation of a Remote Authentication Dial-In User Service (RADIUS) server and proxy in Windows Server 2008. NPS replaces Internet Authentication Service (IAS) that was provided in Windows Server 2003.

node   A network device running the Transmission Control Protocol/Internet Protocol (TCP/IP) protocol.

NPS   *See* Network Policy Server (NPS).

Oakley   A protocol used by Internet Protocol security (IPsec) for exchanging keys securely, using the Diffie-Hellman algorithm.

Path MTU discovery (PMTU)   A method of dynamically discovering the highest Internet Protocol Maximum Transmission Unit (IP MTU) for all links between two hosts.

PDU   *See* protocol data unit (PDU).

permanent virtual circuit (PVC)   A path through a virtual circuit packet-switching network (for example, frame relay) that is statically programmed into the switches of the network.

PMTU   *See* Path MTU discovery (PMTU).

Point-to-Point Protocol (PPP)   A standard set of protocols that provide a Data Link Layer encapsulation method that supports multiple protocols simultaneously on the same link; a protocol for negotiating the Data Link Layer characteristics of the point-to-point connection called the Link Control Protocol (LCP); and a series of protocols called Network Control Protocols (NCPs) for negotiating the Network Layer properties of Network Layer protocols over the point-to-point connection.

Point-to-Point Protocol over Ethernet (PPPoE)   A standard method of encapsulating PPP frames so that they can be sent over an Ethernet network.

Point-to-Point Tunneling Protocol (PPTP)   A virtual private network (VPN) protocol that encapsulates VPN data inside Point-to-Point Protocol (PPP) frames, which are then further encapsulated in Internet Protocol (IP) datagrams for transmission over a transit IP internetwork such as the Internet.

PPP   *See* Point-to-Point Protocol (PPP).

PPPoE   *See* Point-to-Point Protocol over Ethernet (PPPoE).

PPTP   *See* Point-to-Point Tunneling Protocol (PPTP).

protocol data unit (PDU)   The unit of information that exists at any layer of a layered network architecture. The protocol data unit of layer *n* becomes the payload of layer *n*-1 (a lower layer).

PVC   *See* permanent virtual circuit (PVC).

quick mode   The portion of the Internet Protocol security (IPsec) negotiation that creates the two IPsec security associations (SAs), one for inbound traffic and one for outbound traffic. The IPsec SAs are used to protect data sent between the two IPsec peers.

RADIUS   *See* Remote Authentication Dial-In User Service (RADIUS).

RARP   *See* reverse ARP (RARP).

Receive Window Auto-Tuning   A Transmission Control Protocol (TCP) performance enhancement in Windows Server 2008 and Windows Vista that automatically determines the optimal receive window size by measuring the connection capacity and the application retrieve rate and changes the window size for ongoing transmission path and application conditions.

Remote Authentication Dial-In User Service (RADIUS)   A standard protocol that is used to provide authentication, authorization, and accounting services for network access servers (NAS) or any other similar device that needs to authenticate, authorize, and account for the usage of the device. RADIUS clients (NASs) send RADIUS requests to RADIUS servers. A RADIUS proxy can be used to route RADIUS messages between RADIUS clients and RADIUS servers.

reverse ARP (RARP)   Obtains an Internet Protocol (IP) address of a host from an RARP server, based on a media access control (MAC) address. *See also* Address Resolution Protocol (ARP) *and* inverse ARP (INARP).

Request for Comments (RFC)   A formal document or standard, developed by an individual, the Internet Engineering Task Force (IETF), or an IETF working group that defines some part of the Transmission Control Protocol/Internet Protocol (TCP/IP) protocol suite. Some RFCs are informational in nature and others are Internet standards. RFCs are never reissued, but they are superceded by new RFCs.

RFC   *See* Request for Comments (RFC)

router   A Transmission Control Protocol/Internet Protocol (TCP/IP) node that has routing capability (also called a gateway).

SA   *See* security association (SA)

Secure Socket Tunneling Protocol (SSTP)   A virtual private network (VPN) protocol in Windows Server 2008 and Windows Vista with Service Pack 1 that encapsulates VPN data using a Hypertext Transfer Protocol (HTTP) over Secure Sockets Layer (SSL) session.

security association (SA)   The combination of security services, protection mechanisms, and cryptographic keys mutually agreed to by communicating peers. The SA contains the information needed to determine how the traffic is to be secured (the security services and protection mechanisms) and with what secret keys (cryptographic keys).

slow start   A Transmission Control Protocol (TCP) algorithm that provides a quick scaling of the actual send window. The actual send window is increased by one Maximum Segment Size (MSS) for each acknowledgment segment that is received or each segment that is acknowledged.

SSTP   *See* Secure Socket Tunneling Protocol (SSTP)

SVC   *See* switched virtual circuit (SVC)

switched virtual circuit (SVC)   A path through a virtual circuit packet-switching network (for example, frame relay) that is negotiated using a signaling protocol each time a connection is initiated.

TCP   *See* Transmission Control Protocol (TCP)

TCP/IP   *See* Transmission Control Protocol/Internet Protocol (TCP/IP)

Time-To-Live (TTL)   A field in the Internet Protocol (IP) header of an IP datagram that is used to determine how many links on which the datagram can travel before being discarded by an IP router.

Token Ring   A ring access network technology specified in Institute of Electrical and Electronics Engineers (IEEE) standard 802.5.

Transmission Control Protocol (TCP)   A reliable, stream-based, full-duplex Transport Layer protocol that runs on top of the Internet Protocol (IP).

Transmission Control Protocol/Internet Protocol (TCP/IP)   An industry-standard suite of protocols designed for large internetworks. TCP/IP is the foundation of today's Internet, as well as the foundation of many private computer networks. TCP/IP includes TCP, IP, and many other protocols, such as Internet Control Message Protocol (ICMP) and User Datagram Protocol (UDP).

TTL   *See* Time-To-Live (TTL)

UDP   *See* User Datagram Protocol (UDP)

User Datagram Protocol (UDP)   An unreliable datagram-based Transport Layer protocol that runs on top of the Internet Protocol (IP). UDP provides Application Layer process identification and a checksum.

WAN   *See* wide area network (WAN)

wide area network (WAN)   A geographically dispersed network, under private control, but which typically uses network connections from third-party telecommunications vendors. *See also* local area network (LAN).

Windows Internet Name Service (WINS)   The Microsoft implementation of a NetBIOS name server (NBNS), which is used by NetBIOS over TCP/IP (NetBT) hosts to register NetBIOS names to Internet Protocol (IP) address mappings and to resolve NetBIOS names to IP addresses. WINS also refers to the name of the NBNS service in Windows Server 2003.

Windows Sockets (Winsock)   A commonly used application programming interface (API) that Windows applications utilize to transfer data using Transmission Control Protocol/Internet Protocol (TCP/IP).

WINS   *See* Windows Internet Name Service (WINS)

Winsock   *See* Windows Sockets (Winsock)

Bibliography

This bibliography provides a list of additional resources that might be helpful to readers. All these books were available for sale at the time this bibliography was written; however, some books might be out of print or might have been updated by new versions.

The books are listed by topic; within each topic, they are listed alphabetically by author.

DHCP

Droms, Ralph, and Ted Lemon. *The DHCP Handbook*. 2d ed. Indianapolis: Sams, 2002. ISBN 0672323273.

DNS

Lui, Cricket, and Paul Albitz. *DNS and BIND*. 5d ed. Sebastopol, Calif.: O'Reilly & Associates, 2006. ISBN 0596100574.

Lui, Cricket, and Matt Larson and Robbie Allen. *DNS on Windows Server 2003*. Sebastopol, Calif.: O'Reilly & Associates, 2003. ISBN 0596005628.

Liu, Cricket. *DNS and BIND Cookbook*. Sebastopol, Calif.: O'Reilly & Associates, 2002. ISBN 0596004109.

General Networking Concepts and Technologies

Stallings, William. *Data and Computer Communications*. 8d ed. Upper Saddle River, N.J.: Prentice Hall, 2006. ISBN 0132433109.

Tannenbaum, Andrew. *Computer Networks*. 4d ed. Upper Saddle River, N.J.: Prentice Hall PTR, 2002. ISBN 0130661023.

IP Security

Doraswamy, Naganand, and Dan Harkins. *IPSec: The New Security Standard for the Internet, Intranets, and Virtual Private Networks*, 2d ed. Upper Saddle River, N.J.: Prentice Hall PTR, 2003. ISBN 013046189X.

IP Version 6

Davies, Joseph. *Understanding IPv6*, 2d ed. Redmond, Wash.: Microsoft Press, 2008. ISBN 0735624461.

Hagen, Silvia. *IPv6 Essentials*, 2d ed. Sebastopol, Calif.: O'Reilly & Associates, 2006. ISBN 0596100582.

L2TP

Shea, Richard. *L2TP: Implementation and Operation*. New York: Addison-Wesley, 1999. ISBN 0201604485.

Microsoft Windows Architecture

Russinovich, Mark, and David Solomon. *Microsoft Windows Internals, Fourth Edition: Microsoft Windows Server 2003, Windows XP, and Windows 2000*. Redmond, Wash.: Microsoft Press, 2004. ISBN 0735619174.

Microsoft Windows Networking Technologies

Davies, Joseph, and Tony Northrup. *Windows Server 2008 Networking and Network Access Protection (NAP)*. Redmond, Wash.: Microsoft Press, 2008. ISBN 0735624224.

Network Security

Adams, Carlisle, and Steve Lloyd. *Understanding PKI: Concepts, Standards, and Deployment Considerations*. 2d ed. Indianapolis: Addison-Wesley Professional, 2002. ISBN 0672323915.

Burnett, Steve, and RSA Security. *RSA Security's Official Guide to Cryptography*. Berkeley, Calif.: Osborne/McGraw Hill, 2004. ISBN 0072254947.

Kaufman, Charles, Radia Perlman, and Mike Speciner. *Network Security: Private Communication in a Public World*. 2d ed. Upper Saddle River, N.J.: Prentice Hall PTR, 2002. ISBN 0130460192.

Schneier, Bruce. *Applied Cryptography: Protocols, Algorithms, and Source Code in C*. 2d ed. New York: John Wiley & Sons, 1996. ISBN 0471117099.

Stallings, William. *Cryptography and Network Security: Principles and Practices*. 4d ed. Upper Saddle River, N.J.: Prentice Hall PTR, 2005. ISBN 0131873164.

PPP

Carlson, James D. *PPP Design, Implementation, and Debugging*. 2d ed. Indianapolis: Addison-Wesley Professional, 2001. ISBN 0201700530.

Sun, Andrew. *Using and Managing PPP*. Sebastopol, Calif.: O'Reilly & Associates, 1999. ISBN 1565923219.

RADIUS

Hassell, Jonathan. *RADIUS*. Sebastopol, Calif.: O'Reilly & Associates, 2002. ISBN 0596003226.

TCP/IP

Comer, Douglas. *Internetworking with TCP/IP: Vol. 1, Principles, Protocols, and Architecture*. 5d ed. New York: Prentice Hall, 2005. ISBN 0131876716.

Stevens, W. Richard. *TCP/IP Illustrated. Volume 1: The Protocols*. Reading, Mass.: Addison-Wesley Professional, 1993. ISBN 0201633469.

Virtual Private Networks

Davies, Joseph, and Elliot Lewis. *Deploying Virtual Private Networks with Microsoft Windows Server 2003*. Redmond, Wash.: Microsoft Press, 2003. ISBN 0735615764.

Kosiur, Dave. *Building & Managing Virtual Private Networks*. New York: John Wiley and Sons, 1998. ISBN 0471295264.

Index

Symbols and Numbers
3DES (Triple Data Encryption Standard) algorithm, 379

A

ACK flag, 206
ACK segment, 228–229
ACK
    TCP Peer 1, 237–238
    TCP Peer 2, 235–236
Adams, Carlisle, 461
address resolution, ARP, 48–51
addresses
    duplicates
        defending node and, 54
        detecting, 51–54
        DHCP and, 53–54
addressing, 4
ADSL (Asymmetric Digital Subscriber Line), 34
AES (Advanced Encryption Standard) algorithm, 379
AH (Authentication Header), IPsec, 455
AH (Authentication Header), IPsec, 455
    Authentication Data field, 375
    Next Header field, 374
    Payload Length field, 374
    Reserved field, 374
    Security Parameters Index field, 374
    Sequence Number field, 374–375
    Transport mode field, 375
    Tunnel mode field, 375
AH Transport mode, 377–378
AH Tunnel mode, 377–378
Albitz, Paul, 461
ALOHA, 4
ANSI (American National Standards Institute), 21–22
APIPA (Automatic Private IP Addressing), 455
APIs (application programming interfaces), 97
Application Layer, 195
Applied Cryptography Protocols, Algorithms, and Source Code, 462
AQM (active queue management), 97
ARP (Address Resolution Protocol), 3, 31, 455
    address resolution, 48–51
    addresses:duplicate, 51–54
    ARP Cache, 45
    ARP Reply, 44
    ARP Request, 44
    Ethernet:frame padding, 50
    frames, 45–47
    header
        Hardware Address Length field, 47
        hardware Type field, 46
        Operation (Opcode) field, 47
        Protocol Address Length field, 47
        Protocol Type field, 47
        Sender Hardware Address (SHA) field, 47
        Sender Protocol Address (SPA) field, 47
        Target Hardware Address (THA) field, 47
        Target Protocol Address (TPA) field, 47
    inverse, See InARP
    MAC address and, 43
    neighbor cache, 50
        apr -s, 51
        arp -a, 51
        netsh interface ipv4 show neighbor, 51
        netsh interface ipv4 add neighbors, 51
        updating, 51
    operation values, 47
    overview, 43–45
    Proxy ARP, 58–59
    registry settings, 56
        ArpRetryCount,
        ArpUseEtherSNAP, 56–57
        EnableBcastArpReply, 57
    Reply message, reachability, 54
    Request message, reachability, 54
    Windows Server 2008, 48
    Windows Vista, 48
ARP cache, 455
ArpUseEtherSNAP, 13–14
asynchronous links:PPP on, 34–35
ATM (Asynchronous Transfer Mode), 31
atomic updates, 327
AuthIP (Authenticated Internet Protocol), 455
    IKE coexistence, 401–404
    Main mode negotiation, 401
    messages, 401
    Quick mode negotiation, 401

B

BDP (bandwidth-delay product), 255–256
bit stuffing, 35–36
bit-level integrity, 4
BRI (Basic Rate Interface), 36
Building & Managing Virtual Private Networks, 462
Burnett, Steve, 462

C

Carlson, James D., 462
CBCP (Callback Control Protocol):options, 78
CCP (Compression Control Protocol), 80–81
CDDI (Copper Data Distributed Interface), 22
CHAP (Challenge Handshake Authentication Protocol), 67
    authentication:mutual, 70–69
    Challenge message:Code field, 71
    Challenge message:Identifier field, 71
    Challenge message:Length field, 71
    Challenge message:Value Size field, 71
    Challenge message:Value field, 71

CHAP (Challenge Handshake Authentication Protocol), *(continued)*
　Challenge message:Name field, 71
　Failure message:fields, 71
　MD5, 70
　Response message:Code field, 71
　Response message:Identifier field, 71
　Response message:Length field, 71
　Response message:Value Size field, 71
　Response message:Value field, 71
　Response message:Name field, 71
　Success message:fields, 71
character stuffing, 35
ciphersuite, 383–384
CIR (committed information rate), 39
Comer, Douglas, 462
compound TCP, 264
Computer Networks, 461
Configure-Ack message, LCP, 66
Configure-Nak message, LCP, 66
Configure-Reject message, PPP, 66
Configure-Request message, 66
　LCP, 66
　responses, 66
congestion avoidance algorithm, 262–264
congestion avoidance, 455
congestion collapse, 273
congestion window (cwind), 260
congestion, explicit congestion notification, 265–267
contiguous data:cumulative for, 247–248
Cryptography and Network Security, Principles and Practices, 462
CTCP (Compound TCP), 455
cwind (congestion window), 260
CWR flag, 206

D

DARPA (Department of Defense Advanced Research Projects Agency), 89
Data and Computer Communications, 461
Data Link Layer, 3
　addressing, 4
　bit-level integrity, 4
　delimitation, 3
　protocol identification, 3
Davies, Joseph, 461, 462
defending node, 52
　duplicate address detection, 54
delimitation, 3
Deploying Virtual Private Networks with Microsoft Windows Server 2003, 462
DES (Data Encryption Standard) algorithm, 379
DHCP (Dynamic Host Configuration Protocol), 293, 455
　broadcast flag, 296
　broadcast flag:options, 297–301
　Chaddr (Client Hardware Address) field, 296
　Ciaddr (Client IP Address) field, 296
　duplicate address detection, 53–54
　File (Boot File Name) field, 296
　Flags field, 295–296
　Giaddr (Gateway IP Address) field, 296
　Hlen (Hardware Address Length) field, 294
　Hops field, 295
　Htype (Hardware Address Type) field, 294
　message exchanges
　　entries, updating, 310–311
　　initial lease, 301–308
　　renewing leases, 308
　　servers, 309–310
　　subnets, changing, 308–309
　messages, 293
　　DHCPDECLINE, 294
　　DHCPDISCOVER, 293
　　DHCPINFORM, 294
　　DHCPNAK, 294
　　DHCPOFFER, 293
　　DHCPPACK, 294
　　DHCPRELEASE, 294
　　DHCPREQUEST, 293–294
　　format, 294–296
　Op (Message Op Code) field, 294
　Options field, 296
　Secs (Seconds) field, 295
　server, 455
　Siaddr (Server IP Address) field, 296
　Sname (Server Host Name) field, 296
　Xid (Transaction ID) field, 295
　Yiaddr (Your IP Address) field, 296
Diffie-Hellman algorithm, 455
DIX frame formate, 5
DLCI (Data Link Connection Identifier), 57
DNS (Domain Name System), 455
　addresses
　　resolving names to, 323–325
　　resolving to names, 326–327
　aliases, resolving, 326–327
　dynamically updating, 327–329
　header
　　Additional RR Count field, 315, 320
　　Answer RR Count field, 315
　　Authority RR Count field, 315
　　Flags field, 314–316, 319
　　Prerequisite RR Count field, 320
　　Question Entry Count field, 315
　　Transaction ID field, 314
　　Transaction ID field, 319
　　Update RR Count field, 320
　　Zone Entry Count field, 320
　introduction, 313
　message exchanges, 323
　　resolving addresses to names, 325–326
　　resolving aliases, 326–327
　　resolving names to addresses, 323–325
　messages, 313
　　DNS Name Query Request, 313–318
　　DNS Name Query Response, 313–318
　　DNS Update Response, 314
　　DNS Update, 314, 319–322
　　UDP messages, 313
　　Update Response, 319–322

DNS (Domain Name System), (*continued*)
    question entry fields, 316–317
    RR (resource records)
        CNAME RR, 326
        Record Class field, 318
        Record Type field, 318
        Resource Data Length field, 318
        RR Name field, 318
        Time To Live field, 318
    RRSets, 327
    servers:transferring zone information between, 330–331
    zone transfers
        Active Directory, 330
        incremental, 330
        traditional, 330
DNS and BIND Cookbook, 461
DNS and BIND, 461
DNS Name Query Request, 313–314
    Additional RR Count field, 315
    Answer RR Count field, 315
    Authoritative Answer field, 316
    Authority RR Count field, 315
    Flags field, 314
    Operation Code field, 315
    Question Class field, 317
    Question Entry Count field, 315
    Question Name field, 316–317
    Question Type field, 317
    Question Type field:common values, 317
    Record Class field, 318
    Record Type field, 318
    Recursion Available field, 316
    Recursion Desired field, 316
    Request/Response field, 315
    Reserved field, 316
    Resource Data field, 318
    Resource Data Length field, 318
    Return Code field, 316
    RR Name field, 318
    Time To Live field, 318
    Transaction ID field, 314
    Truncation field, 316
DNS Name Query Response, 313
    Additional RR field, 315
    Answer RR field, 315
    Authoritative Answer field, 316
    Authority RR field, 315
    Flags field, 314
    Operation Code field, 315
    Question Class field, 317
    Question Entry Count field, 315
    Question Name field, 316–317
    Question Type field, 317
    Record Class field, 318
    Record Type field, 318
    Recursion Available field, 316
    Recursion Desired field, 316
    Request/Response field, 315
    Reserved field, 316
    Resource Data Length field, 318
    Return Code field, 316
    RR Name field, 318
    Time To Live field, 318
    Transaction ID field, 314
    Truncation field, 316
DNS on Windows Server, 461
DNS Update Response, 314
    Additional RR Count field, 320
    Flags field, 319
    Operation Code field, 321
    Prerequisite RR Count field, 320
    Request/Response field, 320
    Reserved field, 321
    Return Code field, 321
    Transaction ID field, 319
    Update RR Count field, 320
    Zone Class field, 322
    Zone Entry Count field, 320
    Zone Name field, 321
    Zone Type field, 321
DNS Update, 314
    Additional RR Count field, 320
    Flags field, 319
    Operation Code field, 321
    Prerequisite RR Count field, 320
    Request/Response field, 321
    Reserved field, 321
    Return Code field, 321
    Transaction ID field, 319
    Update RR Count field, 320
    Zone Class field, 322
    Zone Entry Count field, 320
    Zone Name field, 321
    Zone Type field, 321
DoD (Department of Defense), 89
Doraswamy, Naganand, 461
Droms, Ralph, 461
DSCP (Differentiated Services Code Point), 96
duplicate address detection, 455
DVMRP (Distance Vector Multicast Routing Protocol), 161

E

EAP, 73–74
    EAP-MSCHAP-V2, 75
    EAP-TLS, 75
    Failure message
        Code field, 76
        Identifier field, 76
        Length field, 76
    Identity, 75
    Nak, 75
    Notification, 75
    PEAP, 75
    Request message
        Code field, 75
        Identifier field, 75
        Length field, 75
        Type field, 75
        Type-Specific Data field, 75

EAP, (continued)
   Response message
      Code field, 75
      Identifier field, 75
      Length field, 75
      Type field, 75
      Type-Specific field, 75
   Success message
      Code field, 76
      Identifier field, 76
      Length field, 76
EAP-MS-CHAP v2, 76-77
EAP-TLS, 77
ECE flag, 206
ECN (Explicit Congestion Notification), 97, 455
ECP (Encryption Control Protocol), 82
encapsulation, 3-4
encryption:Main mode negotiation, 399
ephemeral ports, 195
ESP (Encapsulating Security Payload), IPsec, 456
   Authentication Data field, 379
   Next Header field, 379
   Padding field, 378
   Padding Length field, 378
   Security Parameters Index field, 378
   Sequence Number field, 378
   Transport mode, 380-382
   Tunnel mode, 382-383
Ethernet II, 4
   destination address, 5-6
   EtherType, 6
   frame check sequence, 6-7
   frame:IEEE 802.3 frame, 11
   header, 5-7
      destination address, 5-6
      EtherType, 6
      Frame Check Sequence, 6-7
      Payload, 6
      preamble, 5
      source address, 6
   payload, 6
   preamble, 5
   trailer, 5-7
      destination address, 5-6
      EtherType, 6
      Frame Check Sequence, 6-7
      Payload, 6
      preamble, 5
      source address, 6
Ethernet, 4
   ALOHA, 4
   Fast Ethernet, 4
   frame padding, 50
   frames, minimum size, 8-9
   interframe gap, 7
   MAC addresses
      Individual/Group bit, 14
      Routing Information Indicator bit, 15
      Universal/Locally Administered bit, 14-15

Node A, transmitting, 8
explicit congestion notification, 265-267

F

Fast Ethernet, 4
fast recovery, 456
fast retransmit, 456
FCS (Frame Check Sequence), 6-7
FDDI (Fiber Distributed Data Interface), 3, 21-22, 456
   frame format, 22-24
   header and trailer
      Destination Address field, 23
      End Delimiter field, 23
      Frame Check Sequence field, 23
      Frame Control field, 23
      Frame Status field, 24
      Preamble field, 22
      Source Address field, 23
      Start Delimiter field, 22-23
   IEEE 802.2 LCC header, 24
   MAC addresses, 24
   payload, 24
   SNAP, 24-25
FIN flag, 207
FIN-ACK, 234-237
FLAG character, PPP payload, 34-35
fragmentation, 103
frame format, 4
Frame Padding:Ethernet and, 50
   Frame Relay Address field, 2-byte Address field
   C/R field, 41
   DE field, 41
   DLCI field, 40
   EA field, 41
   FECN field, 41
Frame Relay DLCI, values for, 40
Frame Relay, 38-39, 456
   advantages, 38
   encapsulation, 39-41
   header and trailer
      Address field, 39
      Control field, 40
      Flag field, 39
      Frame Check Sequence field, 40
      NLPID field, 40

G

gateway, 456
GQoS (Generic QoS), 97

H

Hagen, Silvia, 461
hardware, ARP frames, 46
Harkins, Dan, 461
hash, 456
Hassell, Jonathan, 462

IEEE 802.3 467

HDLC (High-Level Data Link Control), 33
Headers, IPsec, AH (Authentication Header), 374–375
hexadecimal digits, converting to ASCII characters, 338–339
host groups, 158, 456
host, 456

I

I/G bit, 161
IANA (Internet Assigned Numbers Authority), 195
ICMP (Internet Control Message Protocol), 456
    Address Mask Reply message, 146–147
        Address Mas field, 147
        Code field, 147–151
        Identifier field, 147
        Sequence Number field, 147
        Type field, 147
    Address Mask Request message, 146–147
    Destination Unreachable message, 129–131
        Code field, 130
        IP header field, 130
        Type field, 130
        Unused field, 130
    Echo message, 127
        Code field, 127
        Identifier field, 128
        Optional Data field, 128
        Sequence Number field, 128
        Type field, 127
    Echo Reply message, 128
        Code field, 128
        Identifier field, 128
        Optional Data field, 129
        Sequence Number field, 129
        Type field, 128
    introduction, 125
    message structure, 126–127
    messages, 126
        Checksum field, 127
        Code field, 127
        common types, 127
        datagrams, 126
        IP header, 126
        Type field, 126
        Type-Specific Data field, 127
    Parameter Problem message, 145–146
        Code field, 146
        IP Header field, 146
        Pointer field, 146
        Type field, 146
        Unused field, 146
    PMTU Discovery, 133–136
    Redirect message, 137–141
    Router Advertisement message, 141
        Address Entry Size field, 142
        Code field, 141
            Lifetime field, 142
        Number Of Addresses field, 142
        Preference Level field, 142
        Router IP Address field, 142
        Type field, 141
    Router Discovery, 141–144
        Router Advertisement, 141–142
        Router Solicitation, 142–144
    Router Solicitation message, 141–142
        Code field, 143
        Reserved field, 143
        Type field, 143
    Source Quench, 136
        Code field, 137
        IP Header field, 137
        Type field, 137
        Unused field, 137
    Time Exceeded message, 144–145
        Code field, 145
        IP header field, 145
        Type field, 144
        Unused field, 145
ICMPv6, 185
IEEE 802.11, 26
    Frame Control field
        From DS field, 29
        More Data field, 29
        More Fragments field, 29
        Order field, 29
        Power Management field, 29
        Protocol Version field, 28
        Retry field, 29
        Subtype field, 29
        To DS field, 29
        Type field, 29
        WEP field, 29
    frame format, 26–29
    header and trailer
        Address 1 field, 27
        Address 2 field, 27
        Address 3 field, 27
        Address 4 field, 28
        Duration/ID field, 26
        Frame Check Sequence field, 28
        Frame Control field, 26–27
        Sequence Control field, 27
    IEEE 802.2 LLC header, 28
    payload, 28
    SNAP, 30
IEEE 802.2 LLC Header
    Control, 11
    DSAP, 10
    SSAP, 10
IEEE 802.3 Frame, Ethernet II Frame and, 11
IEEE 802.3 SNAP, 12–14
IEEE 802.3, 9–10
    header and trailer
        Destination Address field, 10
        Frame Check Sequence field, 10
        Length field, 10
        Preamble field, 10
        Source Address field, 10
        Start Delimiter field, 10

IEEE 802.5
   header and trailer
      Access Control field, 17
      Destination Address field, 17
      End Delimiter field, 18
      Frame Check Sequence field, 18
      Frame Control field, 17
      Frame Status field, 19
      Payload field, 18
      Source Address field, 18
      Start Delimiter field, 17
      trailer, 17–19
IEEE 802.5 SNAP, 19
IETF (Internet Engineering Task Force), 373, 456
IGMP (Internet Group Management Protocol), 456
   Host Membership Query messages, 160
   Host Membership Report messages, 160
   IGMPv1, 163
      Addresses, 165
      Checksum field, 164
      Group Address field, 165
      Type field, 164
      Unused field, 164
      Version field, 164
   IGMPv2
      addresses, 168
      Checksum field, 168
      Group Address field, 168
      Group-Specific Query message, 167
      Leave Group message, 166–167
      Maximum Response Time field, 168
      Type field, 168
   IGMPv3, 169–172
      Host Membership Query, 170
      Host Membership Report, 171
      Number of Sources field, 170
      Querier's Query Interval field, 170
      Querier's Robustness Variable field, 170
      Reserved field, 170
      Source Address field, 170
      Suppress Router-Side Processing field, 170
   introduction, 157
   message structure, 163
   proxy mode, 174–176
   Windows Server 2008
      Remote Access, 174–176
      Routing, 174–176
      TCPP protocol, 173
   Windows Vista
      Remote Access, 174–176
      Routing, 174–176
      TCPP protocol, 173
IKE (Internet Key Exchange), 456
   introduction, 385
   ISAKMP and, 385
   Oakley Key Determination Protocol and, 385
INARP (inverse ARP), 457
InARP, 57–58
informed discards, 125
initiator, 384
Internetworking with TCP/IP, 462

Intranet, multicast and, 161–162
IP (Internet Protocol), 456
IP address
   hop IP address, 43
   next-hop, 44
IP multicast
   host groups, 158
   host support, 158–160
   multicast groups, 158
   overview, 157–158
   permanent groups, 158
   promiscuous mode, 161
   router support, 160–161
   traffic, 159
   traffic:receiving, 160
   traffic:TTL values, 159
IP Router Alert option, 120
IP
   datagram delivery, 90
   datagram packet-switching, 91
   datagram, 92–89
      IP header, 92
      IP payload, 93
   extensibility, 91
   fragmentation, 90–91, 103
      avoiding, 109–112
      DF flag and, 109
      example, 105–107
      fields, 103–105
      fragmenting a fragment, 109
      IP payload and, 110
      reassembly example, 107–108
      source fragmentation, ping and, 110
      translational bridging, 110–112
      Windows Server 2008, 112
      Windows Vista, 112
   header, 93
      Cost field, 96
      Delay field, 95
      Destination Address, 102
      Flags field, 99
      Fragment Offset field, 99
      Header Checksum field, 101–102
      Header Length field, 94
      Indentification field, 99
      options, 102
      padding, 102
      Precedence field, 95
      Protocol field, 101
      Reliability field, 96
      Reserved field, 96
      Source Address field, 102
      Throughput field, 96
      Time-To-Live field, 99–101
      Total Length field, 98–99
      Type Of Service field, 94–97
      Version field, 93–91
   Internet Timestamp option, 121–122
   internetworking protocol, 90
   introduction, 89
   IP Router Alert option, 120

IP (*continued*)
  MTU, 91–92
  multiple client protocols, 90
  Network Interface Layer and, 90
  options, 112
    Copy field, 113
    End Of Option List, 114
    No Operation, 114
    Option Class field, 113
    Option Number field, 113
    Record Route processing, 115
    Record Route, 114–115
    Record Route, ping and, 115
  Precedence field, 95
  reassembly, 90–91
  services
    datagram delivery, 90
    datagram packet-switching technology, 91
    extensibility through IP options, 91
    fragmentation, 90–91
    internetworking protocol, 90
    multiple client protocols, 90
    Network Interface Layer independence, 90
    reassembly, 90–91
  source routing, 116–120
IPCP (Internet Protocol Control Protocol), 32, 79–80
IPsec (Internet Protocol Security), 457
  AH (Authentication Header)
    Authentication Data field, 375
    Next Header field, 374
    Payload Length field, 374
    Reserved field, 374
    Security Parameters Index field, 374
    Sequence Number field, 374–375
  ESP Encapsulating Security Payload
    Authentication Data field, 379
    Next Header field, 379
    Padding field, 378
      Padding Length field, 378
    Security Parameters Index field, 378
    Sequence Number field, 378
  ESP Transport mode, 380–382
  ESP Tunnel mode, 382–383
  headers, 373–374
  introduction, 373
  IP datagrams:AH Transport mode, 375–376
  IP datagrams:AH Tunnel mode, 377–378
  ISAKAMP:message structure, 385–399
  NATs, 404–406
  SA (Security Associations), 383
    creating, 384
  IKE (Internet Key Exchange), 385
  IPsec SA, 384
  ISAKMP SA, 383–384
  SPI (Security Parameters Index), 384
  SPI (Security Parameters Index), 384
  Transport mode, 375
  Tunnel mode, 375
  Windows Server 2008:algorithms, 379
  Windows Vista:algorithms, 379

IPSec:The New Security Standard for the Internet, Intranets, and Virtual Private Networks, 461
IPv4, 179
  disadvantages of
    address space, 179–180
    configuration, 180
    mobility, 180
    prioritized delivery, 180
    routing infrastructure, 180
    security, 180
  IPv6 comparison, 186–187
IPv6 Essentials, 461
IPv6, 456
  address space, 181
  addressing, 181–182
    syntax, 182
    types of addresses, 182–183
    Unicast addresses, 183
  configuration, 181
  DNS support, 184
  interface identifiers, 183
  IPsec headers, 181
  MLD (multicast listener discovery), 186
  mobility, 181
  prioritized delivery, 181
  protocols
    ICMPv6, 185
    IPv6 header, 184
    Neighbor Discovery, 185–186
  routing infrastructure, 181
ISAKMP (Internet Security Association and Key Management Protocol), 456–457
  Certificate Payload, 398
    Certificate Data field, 398
    Certificate Encoding field, 398
  Certificate Request Payload, 397
    Certificate Authority field, 398
    Certificate Type field, 397
    Certificate Type values, 397
  Delete Payload, 395–396
    Domain of Interpretation field, 396
    Number of SPIs field, 396
    Protocol-ID field, 396
    SPI Size field, 396
    SPIs field, 396
  Hash Payload, 396
  header
    Exchange Type field, 387
    flags field, 387
    Initiator Cookie field, 386
    Length field, 388
    Major Version field, 387
    Message ID field, 388
    Minor Version field, 387
    Next Payload field, 386
    Responder Cookie field, 386
  Identification Payload, 396
    DOI-Specific ID Data field, 396
    ID Type field, 396
    Identification Data field, 396
  Key Exchange Payload, 393–394

ISAKMP (Internet Security Association and Key Management Protocol), (*continued*)
  message structure, 385–399
  Nonce Payload, 393
  Notification Payload, 394
    Domain of Interpretation field, 394
    Notification Data field, 394
    notification error messages, 395
    notification status messages, 395
    Notify Message Type field, 394
    Protocol-ID field, 394
    SPI field, 394
    SPI Size field, 394
  Proposal Payload, 389
    Next Payload field, 389
    Number of Transforms field, 390
    Payload Length field, 389
    Proposal Number field, 389
    Protocol-ID field, 389
    SPI Size field, 389
  SA payload
    DOI (domain of interpretation), 388
    Domain of Interpretation field, 388
    Next Payload field, 388
    Payload Length field, 388
    Reserved field, 388
    Situation field, 388
  Signature Payload, 398–399
  Transform Payload
    Next Payload field, 390
    Payload Length field, 390
    Reserved2 field, 390
    SA Attributes field, 390
    Transform ID field, 390
    Transform Number field, 390
  Vendor ID Payload, 392–393
ISAKMP SA, 383–384
ISDN (Integrated Services Digital Network), 31
ISN (Initial Sequence Number), 247

K

Karn's algorithm, 284–285
Kaufman, Charles, 462
Kosiur, Dave, 462

L

L2TP (Layer Two Tunneling Protocol), 457
L2TP:Implementation and Operation, 461
LANs (local area networks), 457
Larson, Matt, 461
LCP (Link Control Protocol), 61, 63, 457
LCP (Link Control Protocol)
  Code field, 63
  Configure-Ack message, 66
  Configure-Nak message, 66
  Configure-Request message, 66
  Data field, 64
  frame types, 64

Identifier field, 63
Length field, 64
negotiation process, 66–67
options, 64–65
Lemon, Ted, 461
Lewis, Elliot, 462
limited transmit, 457
LLC (Logical Link Control), 4
LLC (Logical Link Control), 457
Lloyd, Steve, 461
Lui, Cricket, 461

M

MAC (Media Access Control), 4, 457
  addresses
    Functional Address Bit, 21
    Individual/Group bit, 14
    Individual/Group bit, 20
    Routing/Information Indicator bit, 15
    Universal/Locally Administered bit, 14–15
    Universal/Locally Administered bit, 20
MAC address, 457
MADCAP (Multicast Address Dynamic Client Allocation Protocol), 159
main mode, 457
main mode negotiation, 399
MBONE (multicast backbone), 162–163
MD5 (Message Digest 5) algorithm, 70
  messages, 70
Microsoft Windows Internals, Fourth Edition:Microsoft Windows Server 2003, Windows XP, and Windows 2000, 461
MLD (Multicast Listener Discovery), 186
MOSPF (Multicast Extensions to Open Shortest Path First), 161
MP (Multilink Protocol), 36
  Beginning Fragment Bit field, 37
  Ending Fragment Bit field, 37
  Reserved field, 37
  Sequence Number field, 37
MPPC, 80
MPPE, 80
MRU (Maximum Receive Unit), 457
MS-CHAP v2 (Microsoft Challenge Handshake Authentication Protocol version 2), 67, 71–73
  Response message
    Code field, 72
    Flags field, 73
    Identifier field, 72
    Length field, 72
    Name field, 73
    Peer Challenge field, 72
    Reserved field, 73
    Value Size field, 72
    Windows NT Response field, 73
MSS (Maximum Segment Size), 457
MTU (Maximum Transmission Unit), 210–211, 457
multicast groups, 158

N

Nagle algorithm, 257–258
name registration errors, return code values, 325
NAS (network access server), 353
NAT-D (NAT-Discovery), 405
NAT-Keepalive packet, 405
NAT-OA (NAT-Original Address), 405
NATs (Network Address Translators), 404–406
NAT-T (NAT traversal), 404–406
NCPs (Network Control Protocols), 32, 61, 458
neighbor cache, 50, 457
    arp -a, 51
    arp -s, 51
    entry states
        delay, 56
        incomplete, 55
        probe, 56
        reachable, 55–56
        stale, 56
    incorrect entries, preventing, 52
    netsh interface ipv4 add neighbors, 51
    netsh interface ipv4 show neighbors, 51
    unreachability detection, 54–56
    updating, 51
Neighbor Discovery in IPv6, 48, 185–186
    address resolution, 185
    duplicate address detection, 186
    redirect, 186
    router discovery, 186
    unreachability detection, 186
neighbor unreachability detection, 457–458
NetBIOS name representation, 338–340
NetBIOS name service messages
    Additional RR Count, 336
    Additional RRs, 335
    Answer RR Count, 336
    Answer RRs, 335
    Authoritative Answer, 337
    Authority RR Count, 336
    Authority RRs, 335
    Broadcast, 337
    Flags, 336
    Name Service header, 334
    Operation Code, 336
    Question entries, 334
    Question Entry Count, 336
    Question RR:Question Class field, 321
    Question RR:Question Name field, 321
    Question RR:Question Type field, 321
    RDATA field:Group Flag field, 322
    RDATA field:Owner Node Type field, 322
    RDATA field:Reserved field, 322
    Recursion Available, 337
    Recursion Desired, 337
    Request/Response, 336
    Reserved, 337
    Return Code, 337
    RRs:Record Class field, 321
    RRs:Record Type field, 321
    RRs:Resource Data field, 321
    RRs:Resource Data Length field, 321
    RRs:RR Name field, 321
    RRs:Time to Live field, 321
    Truncation, 337
NetBIOS, 458
    names
        refreshing, 349–350
        registering, 346–349
        releasing, 351–352
        resolving to IPv4 addresses, 344–346
NetBT (NetBIOS over TCP/IP), 333, 458
    messages
        Name Query Request, 334
        Name Query Response, 334
        Name Refresh Request, 334
        Name Registration Request, 334
        Name Registration Response, 334
        Name Release Request, 334
        Name Release Response, 334
        Wait Acknowledgment, 334
network black hole, 45
network control protocols:IPCP, 79–80
Network Security:Private Communication in a Public World, 462
network access
    accounting, 367–369
    authentication message exchanges, 364–367
next-hop IP address, 44
NLPID (Network Layer Protocol Identifier), 39
nodes, 458
noncontiguous data:selective for, 248–249
Northrup, Tony, 461
NPS (Network Policy Server), 458

O

Oakley, 458
offending node, 52
    Windows Server 2008, 52
    Windows version, 53
    Windows Vista, 52
opcodes:ARP frames, 47
Organization Code field, 12
OSI (Open Systems Interconnection), 3

P

packets, discarding, 125
packet-switching technologies
    early, 38
    frame relay, 38
PADO (PPPoE Active Discovery Offer), 84
PADR (PPPoE Active Discovery Request), 84
PADS (PPPoE Active Discovery Session-confirmation), 85
PAP (Password Authentication Protocol), 67
    Authenticate-Ack message, 68
    Authenticate-Ack message
        Code field, 69
        Identifier field, 69

PAP (Password Authentication Protocol), *(continued)*
   Authenticate-Ack message
      Length field, 69
      Message Length field, 69
      Message field, 69
   Authenticate-Nak message
      Code field, 69
      Identifier field, 69
      Length field, 69
      Message Length field, 69
      Message field, 69
   Authenticate-Request message, 68
      Code field, 68
      Identifier field, 68
      Length field, 68
      Password field, 69
      Password Length, 69
      Peer ID field, 68
      Peer ID Length field, 68
   messages, 68
Pathping.exe tool, 153–155
PDU (protocol data unit), 6, 458
PEAP (Protected EAP), 77–78
Perlman, Radia, 462
permanent groups, 158
PIM (Protocol Independent Multicast), 161
Ping.exe, 148–150
PMTU (Path MTU discovery), 458
   adjusting, 134
   black hole router, 135
   plateau values, 135
   routers not supporting, 134–136
PPP (Point-to-Point) protocol, 32–33, 458
   address, 33
   asynchronous links, 34–35
   authentication protocols, 67–68
   authentication protocols:PAP, 68–70
   bit stuffing, 35–36
   callback, 78
   CBCP, 78
   CCP (Compression Control Protocol), 80–81
   CHAP, 70
   Configure-Reject message, 66
   Configure-Request message, 66
   connection process, 62
      authentication, 62
      callback, 62
      configuration using LCP, 62
      configuration using NCPs, 63
   connection termination, 63
   control, 33
   Data Link Layers and, 61
   EAP, 73–74
   ECP, 82
   encapsulation, IP datagram, 34
   FCS (Frame Check Sequence), 33–34
   frames, HDLC encapsulation, 34
   header and trailer
      Address field, 33
      Control field, 33
      FCS (Frame Check Sequence) field, 33–34
      Flag field, 33
      Protocol field, 33
   IPCP, 79–80
   LCP (Link Control Protocol), 61
      ACCM option, 65
      Address and Control Field Compression option, 65
      Authentication Protocol option, 65
      Callback option, 65
      Code field, 63
      Code-Reject frame, 64
      Configure-Request frame, 64
      Configure-Ack frame, 64
      Configure-Nak frame, 64
      Configure-Reject frame, 64
      Configure-Nak message, 66
      Configure-Request message, 66
      Configure-Ack message, 66
      Data field, 64
      Discard-Request frame, 64
      Echo-Reject frame, 64
      Echo-Reply frame, 64
      Identifier field, 63
      Length field, 64
      Magic Number option, 65
      MRU option, 65
      negotiation process, 66–67
      options, 64–65
      Protocol Compression option, 65
      Protocol-Reject frame, 64
      Terminate-Request frame, 64
      Terminate-Ack frame, 64
   MP (Multilink Protocol), 36–37
   MPPC, 80
   MPPE, 80
   MRU (Maximum Receive Unit), 36
   MS-CHAP v2, 71–73
   NCPs (Network Control Protocols), 61
   network monitor example, 82–83
   PAP, 68
   PEAP, 77–78
   protocol, 33
   synchronous links, 35–36
PPP Design, Implementation, and Debugging, 462
PPPoE (PPP over Ethernet), 83–85, 458
   discovery stage, 84–85
   frame
      Code field, 84
      Length field, 84
      Session_ID field, 84
      Type field, 84
      Version field, 84
   PADO (PPPoE Active Discovery Offer), 84
   PADR (PPPoE Active Discovery Request), 84
   PADS (PPPoE Active Discovery Session-confirmation), 85
   phases of, 83
   session stage, 85
PPTP (Point-to-Point Tunneling Protocol), 458
propagation delay, 8–9
protected ciphersquite negotiation, 383–384
protocol identification, 3

protocols, ARP frames, 47
proxies, RADIUS, forwarding, 370-372
Proxy ARP, 58-59
PSH flag, 206-207
PSTN (Public Switched Telephone Network), 31
PVCs (permanent virtual circuits), 38-39
PVCs (permanent virtual circuits), 458

Q

Question RR format
    Question Class, 341
    Question Name, 340
    Question Type, 340
    RDATA field:Group Flag, 342
    RDATA field:Owner Node Type, 342
    RDATA field:Reserved, 342-343
    Record Class, 341
    Record Type, 341
    Resource Data, 341
    Resource Data Length, 341
    RR Name, 341
    Time To Live, 341
Quick mode negotiation, 399-400
    Identification payload, 400
    Nonce payload, 400
    SA payload, 400
quick mode, 458
qWAVE (Quality Windows Audio-Video Experience), 97

R

RADIUS, 462
RADIUS (Remote Authentication Dial-In User Service), 459
    attributes, 356-362
        vendor-specific, 362-364
    header
        Authenticator field, 356
        Code field, 355-356
        Identifier field, 355
        Length field, 355
    introduction, 353
    message exchanges, 364
        network access accounting, 367-369
        network access authentication, 364-367
    messages, 353-354
        Access-Accept, 354
        Access-Challenge, 354
        Access-Reject, 354
        Access-Request, 354
        Accounting-Request, 354
        Accounting-Response, 354
        Authenticator field, 356
        authentication, 364-367
        Code field, 355-356
        Identifier field, 355
        Length field, 355
        structure, 355-356
    proxies, forwarding, 370-372
    UDP, 353-354
RARP (reverse ARP), 459
Receive Window Auto-Tuning, 458-459
Reno algorithm, 289
responder, 384
RFC (Request for Comments), 459
routers, 459
RRs (resource records), 313
RSA Security, 462
RSA Security's Official Guide to Cryptography, 462
RST flag, 207
RSVP (ReSerVation protocol), 97
RTO (retransmission time-out), 271
    calculating, 279-280
        Karn's algorithm, 284-285
        Karn's algorithm and Timestamps, 285-286
        Timestamps option, 280-284
RTT (round-trip time), 255-256
Russinovich, Mark, 461

S

SA (Security Associations), 383, 459
    creating
        main mode, 384
        quick mode, 384
SACK-based loss recovery, 288-289
Schneier, Bruce, 462
SDLC (Synchronous Data Link Control), 33
SHA (Sender Hardware Address), ARP frames, 47
Shea, Richard, 461
short-lived ports, 195
silent discards, 125
SLIP (Serial Line Internet Protocol), 31
slot time, 8-9
slow start, 459
slow-start algorithm, 260-262
SNA (Systems Network Architecture), 33
SNAP (Sub-Network Access Protocol), 5
Soderblum, Olaf, 15-16
Solomon, David, 461
source routing
    introduction, 116
    loose, 119
        ping and, 119-120
    Strict Source Route option, 117-118
    strict:ping and, 118
SPA (Sender Protocol Address), ARP frames, 47
Speciner, Mike, 462
SPI (Security Parameters Index), 384
SRTT (smoothed round-trip time), 279
SSTP (Secure Socket Tunneling Protocol), 459
Stallings, William, 461, 462
Stevens, W. Richard, 462
Sun, Andrew, 462
SVC (switched virtual circuit), 38-39, 459
SYN attack, 231-232
SYN flag, 207
SYN segment, 225-226
SYN-ACK segment, 227-228

T

Tannenbaum, Andrew, 461
TC (Traffic Control), 97
TCB (Transmission Control Block), 231
TCP (Transmission Control Protocol), 459
    Application Layer data segmentation, 200
    byte stream, 200
    connection orientation, 199
    connection termination, 234–238
    control maintenance, 232–233
    flags, 205
        ACK, 206
        CWR, 206
        ECE, 206
        FIN, 207
        PSH, 206–207
        RST, 207
        SYN, 207
        URG, 206
    full duplex, 199
    half-open connections, 230–231
    one-to-one delivery, 200
    options, 210
        End Of Option List, 210
        Maximum Segment Size option, 210–213
        No Operation, 210
        SACK option, 217–218
        SACK permitted option, 216
        Selective Acknowledgment option, 215–216
        Timestamps option, 218–221
        Window Scale option, 213–215
    ports, 204–205
    receiver-side flow control, 200
    reliability, 200
    sender-side flow control, 200
    TCP header
        acknowledgment number, 202
        checksum, 202–203
        data offset, 202
        destination port, 201
        flags, 202
        options, 203
        reserved, 202
        sequence number, 202
        source port, 201
        urgent pointer, 203
        window, 202
    TCP pseudo header, 207–208
    TCP segment, 200
    urgent data, 208–210
TCP ACK, 246
    delayed acknowledgments, 246–247
TCP connection
    endpoints, 223
    establishing, 224–225
        ACK segment, 228–229
        results of connection, 229–230
        SYN segment, 225–226
        SYN-ACK segment, 227–228
        FIN-ACK from TCP Peer 2, 236–237
    half-open connections, 230–231
    maintenance, 232–233
    reset, 238–240
    states, 240–242
    termination, 234
        ACK from TCP Peer 1, 237–238
        ACK from TCP Peer 2, 235–236
        FIN-ACK from TCP Peer 1, 234–235
TCP data flow, 245
    acknowledgments, 245
        cumulative for contiguous data, 247–248
        delayed, 246–247
        selective for noncontiguous data, 248–249
    explicit congestion notification, 265–267
    limited transmit, 268
    Receive Window Auto-Tuning, 255–257
    send and receive windows, 245
    sender-side flow control, 245, 259–260
        compound TCP, 264
        congestion avoidance algorithm, 260
        congestion avoidance algorithm, 262–264
        cwind (congestion window), 260
        slow start algorithm, 260
        slow start algorithm, 260–262
    sliding windows, 249
        NotRcvd/Inside data, 254
        NotRcvd/Outside data, 254
        Rcvd/ACKed/NotRetr data, 254
        Rcvd/ACKed/Retr data, 253
        Rcvd/UnACKed data, 254
        receive window, 252–253
        send window, 249
        Sent/ACKed Data, 250
        Sent/UnACKed Data, 250
        shrinking window, 255
        sliding the receive window, 254–255
        sliding the send window, 251–252
        Unsent/Inside data, 250–251
        unsent/outside, 251
        zero send window, 252
    small segments, 245
        Nagle algorithm, 257–258
        SWS (silly window syndrome), 258–259
TCP header
    ACK segment, 228–229
    Acknowledgment Number field, 202, 225
    Checksum field, 202–203
    Data Offset field, 202
    Destination Port field, 201
    Destintation Port field, 225
    Flags field, 202
    MSS in the MSS TCP Option field, 226
    Options field, 203
    Reserved field, 202
    Selective Acknowledgement (SACK) Permitted TCP option, 226
    Sequence Number field, 202, 225
    Source Port field, 201, 225
    SYN flag field, 225
    SYN segment, 227
    Urgent Pointer field, 203

TCP header (*continued*)
   Window field, 202, 226
   Window scaling factor in the TCP Window Scale TCP Option field, 226
TCP MSS
   Maximum Segment Size field, 211
   Option Kind field, 211
   Option Length field, 211
TCP retransmission
   behavior, 273-274
      new connections, 275
   congestion collapse, 273
   dead gateway detection, 275-277
   fast recovery, 286-289
   fast retransmit, 286-289
   forward RTO-recovery, 277-278
   round-trip time, 271-273
   RTO (retransmission time-out), 271
      calculating, 279-286
      Karn's algorithm, 284-286
      TCP Timestamps option, 280-286
   SACK option, 278-279
   time-out, 271-273
TCP SACK option
   Left Edge of Nth Block field, 217
   Option Kind field, 217
   Option Length field, 217
   Right Edge of Nth Block field, 217
TCP Selective Acknowledgment option, 215-216
TCP Timestamps option
   Option Kind field, 219
   Option Length field, 219
   TS Echo Reply field, 219
   TS Value field, 219
TCP Window Scale option, 213-215
   Option Kind field, 214
   Option Length field, 214
   Shift Count field, 214
TCP/IP (Transmission Control Protocol/Internet Protocol), 459
TCP/IP Illustrated, 462
TcpDelAckTicks, 246-247
Telnet:TCP ACK and, 246
THA (Target Hardware Address):ARP frames, 47
The DHCP Handbook, 461
Time-To-Live field, IP, 99-101
Token Ring, 15-16
Token Ring, 459
   IEEE 802.2 LLC header, 19
   IEEE 802.5 SNAP, 19
   IEEE 802.5, header and trailer, 17-19
   MAC addresses
      Functional Address Bit, 21
      Individual/Group Bit, 20
      special bits, 20-21
      Universal/Locally Administered Bit, 20
TOS field, IP header, 94-97
   explicit congestion notification, 97-98
   RFC 2474 definition, 96-97

TPA (Target Protocol Address), ARP frames, 47
Tracert.exe tool, 150-153
transforms, 374
translational bridging, 110-112
TTL (Time-To-Live), 459

U

UDP (User Datagram Protocol), 459-460
   header, 193
      Checksum field, 194
      Destination Port field, 194
      Length field, 194
      Source Port field, 193-194
   introduction, 191-192
   messages, 193
   ports, 195-196
   pseudo header, 196-197
   uses for, 192-193
Understanding IPv6, 461
Understanding PKI:Concepts, Standards, and Deployment Considerations, 461
Unicast addresses, 183
   global, 183
   link-local, 183
   unique local, 183
updates:atomic, 327
URG flag, 206
Using and Managing PPP, 462

W

WACK (Wait Acknowledgment), 327
WAN (Wide Area Networks), 31, 460
   encapsulations
      addressing, 31
      bit-level integrity check, 32
      delimitation, 31
well-known port numbers, 195
Windows Server 2008 Networking and Network Access Protection (NAP), 461
Windows Server 2008
   fragmentation, 112
   IGMP, 173-176
   offending node, 52
Windows Vista
   fragmentation, 112
   IGMP, 173-176
   offending node, 52
WINS (Windows Internet Name Service), 460
   client/server message exchanges, 344-352
   introduction, 333
Winsock (Windows Sockets), 460

X-Y-Z

X.25 packet-switched technology, 38

Joseph Davies

Joseph Davies is a technical writer for the Microsoft Corporation. He has been a writer and instructor of TCP/IP, networking, and security topics since 1992. He started writing as a courseware developer for Microsoft Corporate Support group and then moved into the Windows group to write product help and resource kit content on networking and security technologies. Since 2001, he has been writing white papers, TechNet articles, Web sites, and Microsoft Press books for the Windows networking technology teams. He is the author of TechNet's monthly The Cable Guy column (*http://www.microsoft.com/technet/community/columns/cableguy/default.mspx*), now appearing in TechNet Magazine.

Joseph is co-author of *Windows Server 2008 Networking and Network Access Protection (NAP)* (Microsoft Press, 2008), *Deploying Virtual Private Networks with Microsoft Windows Server 2003* (Microsoft Press, 2004), *Microsoft Windows Server 2003 TCP/IP Protocols and Services Technical Reference* (Microsoft Press, 2003), and *Microsoft Windows 2000 TCP/IP Protocols and Services Technical Reference* (Microsoft Press, 2000). He is author of *Understanding IPv6, Second Edition* (Microsoft Press, 2008), *Windows Server 2008 TCP/IP Protocols and Services* (Microsoft Press, 2008), *TCP/IP Fundamentals for Microsoft Windows* (TechNet, 2006), *Deploying Secure 802.11 Wireless Networks with Microsoft Windows* (Microsoft Press, 2004), and the Puget Sound Society for Technical Communication (STC) Best of Show and International STC Distinguished Award-winning *Understanding IPv6* (Microsoft Press, 2003).

Preview Pages
Understanding IPv6, Second Edition

ISBN 978-0-7356-2446-7
Available January 2008
By Joseph Davies

Chapter 3
IPv6 Addressing

At the end of this chapter, you should be able to do the following:

- Describe the IPv6 address space, and state why the address length of 128 bits was chosen.
- Describe IPv6 address syntax, including zero suppression and compression and prefixes.
- Enumerate and describe the function of the different types of unicast IPv6 addresses.
- Describe the format of multicast IPv6 addresses.
- Describe the function of anycast IPv6 addresses.
- Describe how IPv6 interface identifiers are determined.
- Describe how to perform bit-level subnetting on the subnet identifier portion of a unicast IPv6 address prefix.
- List and compare the different addressing concepts between IPv4 addresses and IPv6 addresses.

The IPv6 Address Space

The most obvious distinguishing feature of Internet Protocol version 6 (IPv6) is its use of much larger addresses. The size of an address in IPv6 is 128 bits, a bit-string that is four times longer than the 32-bit IPv4 address. A 32-bit address space allows for 2^{32}, or 4,294,967,296, possible addresses. A 128-bit address space allows for 2^{128}, or 340,282,366,920,938,463,463,374,607,431,768,211,456 (3.4 × 10^{38} or 340 undecillion), possible addresses.

In the late 1970s, when the IPv4 address space was designed, it was unimaginable that it could ever be exhausted. However, the administrative procedures that defined address allocation did not anticipate the recent explosion of hosts on the Internet. The IPv4 address space was thus consumed to the point that, by 1992, it was clear a replacement would be necessary.

With IPv6, it is even more difficult to conceive that the IPv6 address space will ever be consumed. To help put this number in perspective, a 128-bit address space provides 6.65 × 10^{23} addresses for each square meter of the Earth's surface.

It is important to remember that the decision to make the IPv6 address 128 bits in length was not so that every square meter of the Earth could have 6.65 × 10^{23} addresses. Rather, the relatively large size of the IPv6 address is designed to be divided into hierarchical unicast routing domains that reflect the topology of the modern-day Internet. The use of 128 bits allows for multiple levels of hierarchy and flexibility in designing hierarchical unicast addressing and routing that is currently lacking on the IPv4-based Internet.

It is easy to get lost in the vastness of the IPv6 address space. As we will discover, the unthinkably large 128-bit IPv6 address that is assigned to an interface on a typical IPv6 host is composed of a 64-bit subnet prefix and a 64-bit interface identifier (a 50-50 split between subnet space and interface space). The 64 bits of subnet prefix leave enough addressing room to satisfy the addressing requirements of the levels of Internet service providers (ISPs) between your organization and the backbone of the Internet and the addressing needs of your organization. The 64 bits of interface identifier accommodate the mapping of current and future link-layer media access control (MAC) addresses.

IPv6 Address Syntax

IPv4 addresses are represented in dotted-decimal format. The 32-bit IPv4 address is divided along 8-bit boundaries. Each set of 8 bits is converted to its decimal equivalent and separated by periods. For IPv6, the 128-bit address is divided along 16-bit boundaries, and each 16-bit block is converted to a 4-digit hexadecimal number and separated by colons. The resulting representation is called *colon hexadecimal*.

The following is an IPv6 address in binary form:

0010000000000001000011011011100000000000000000000010111100111011
0000001010101010000000001111111111111000101000100111000101101010

The 128-bit address is divided along 16-bit boundaries:

0010000000000001   0000110110111000   0000000000000000   0010111100111011
0000001010101010   0000000011111111   1111111000101000   1001110001011010

Each 16-bit block is converted to hexadecimal and delimited with colons. The result is the following:

2001:0DB8:0000:2F3B:02AA:00FF:FE28:9C5A

IPv6 address representation is further simplified by suppressing the leading zeros within each 16-bit block. However, each block must have at least a single digit. With leading zero suppression, the result is the following:

2001:DB8:0:2F3B:2AA:FF:FE28:9C5A

> ### Number System Choice for IPv6
>
> IPv6 uses hexadecimal (the $Base_{16}$ numbering system), rather than decimal (the $Base_{10}$ numbering system), because it is easier to convert between hexadecimal and binary than it is to convert between decimal and binary. Each hexadecimal digit represents four binary digits.

With IPv4, decimal is used to make the IPv4 addresses more palatable for humans and a 32-bit address becomes 4 decimal numbers separated by the period (.) character. With IPv6, dotted-decimal representation would result in 16 decimal numbers separated by the period (.) character. IPv6 addresses are so large that there is no attempt to make them palatable to most humans. Configuration of typical end systems is automated, and end users will almost always use names rather than IPv6 addresses. Therefore, the addresses are expressed in a way to make them more palatable to computers and IPv6 network administrators who understand the semantics and relationship of hexadecimal and binary numbers.

Table 3-1 lists the conversion between binary, hexadecimal, and decimal numbers.

Table 3-1 Converting Between Binary, Hexadecimal, and Decimal Numbers

Binary	Hexadecimal	Decimal
0000	0	0
0001	1	1
0010	2	2
0011	3	3
0100	4	4
0101	5	5
0110	6	6
0111	7	7
1000	8	8
1001	9	9
1010	A	10
1011	B	11
1100	C	12
1101	D	13
1110	E	14
1111	F	15

Compressing Zeros

Some types of IPv6 addresses contain long sequences of zeros. To further simplify the representation of IPv6 addresses, a single contiguous sequence of 16-bit blocks set to 0 in the colon hexadecimal format can be compressed to ::, known as a *double colon*. For example, the link-local address of FE80:0:0:0:2AA:FF:FE9A:4CA2 can be compressed to FE80::2AA:FF:FE9A:4CA2. The multicast address FF02:0:0:0:0:0:0:2 can be compressed to FF02::2.

Note You cannot use zero compression to include part of a 16-bit block. For example, you cannot express FF02:30:0:0:0:0:0:5 as FF02:3::5, but FF02:30::5 is correct.

> **How Many Blocks or Bits in ::?**
>
> To determine how many 0 blocks are represented by the ::, you can count the number of blocks in the compressed address and subtract this number from 8. To determine how many 0 bits are represented by the ::, multiply the number of blocks the :: represents by 16. For example, in the address FF02::2, there are two blocks (the "FF02" block and the "2" block). The number of blocks expressed by the :: is 6 (8 − 2). The number of bits expressed by the :: is 96 (96 = 6 × 16). Zero compression can be used only once in a given address. Otherwise, you could not determine the number of 0 blocks or bits represented by each instance of ::.

IPv6 Prefixes

The prefix is the part of the address where the bits have fixed values or are the bits that define a route or subnet. Prefixes for IPv6 subnets and summarized routes are expressed in the same way as Classless Inter-Domain Routing (CIDR) notation for IPv4. An IPv6 prefix is written in *address/prefix-length* notation.

For example, 2001:DB8:2A0:2F3B::/64 is a subnet prefix and 2001:DB8:3F::/48 is a summarized route prefix. As described earlier in this chapter, the 64-bit prefix is used for individual subnets to which nodes are attached. All subnets have a 64-bit prefix. Any prefix that is less than 64 bits is a summarized route or an address range that is summarizing a portion of the IPv6 address space.

> **Note** IPv4 implementations commonly use a dotted-decimal representation of the prefix length known as the *subnet mask*. A subnet mask is not used for IPv6. Only the prefix length notation is supported.

An IPv6 prefix is relevant only for routes or address ranges, not for individual unicast addresses. In IPv4, it is common to express an IPv4 address with its prefix length. For example, 192.168.29.7/24 (equivalent to 192.168.29.7 with the subnet mask 255.255.255.0) denotes the IPv4 address 192.168.29.7 with a 24-bit subnet mask. Because IPv4 addresses are no longer class-based, you cannot assume the class-based subnet mask based on the value of the leading octet. The prefix length is included so that you can determine which bits identify the subnet and which bits identify the host on the subnet. Because the number of bits used to identify the subnet in IPv4 is variable, the prefix length is needed to separate the subnet prefix from the host ID.

In common IPv6 practice, however, there is no notion of a variable-length subnet prefix. At the individual IPv6 subnet level for currently defined unicast IPv6 addresses, the number of bits used to identify the subnet is always 64 and the number of bits used to identify the host on the subnet is always 64. Therefore, while unicast IPv6 addresses written with their prefix lengths are permitted in RFC 4291, in practice their prefix lengths are always 64 and therefore do not need to be expressed. For example, there is no need to express the IPv6 unicast address 2001:DB8::2AC4:2AA:FF:FE9A:82D4 as 2001:DB8::2AC4:2AA:FF:FE9A:82D4/64. Because of the 50-50 split of subnet prefixes and interface identifiers, the unicast IPv6 address 2001:DB8::2AC4:2AA:FF:FE9A:82D4 implies that the subnet prefix is 2001:DB8:0:0:2AC4::/64.

> **Note** Address prefixes with a prefix length longer than 64 bits can be used for point-to-point links between routers.

Types of IPv6 Addresses

There are three types of IPv6 addresses:

Unicast

A unicast address identifies a single interface within the scope of the type of address. The scope of an address is the region of the IPv6 network over which the address is unique. With the appropriate unicast routing topology, packets addressed to a unicast address are delivered to a single interface. To accommodate load-balancing systems, RFC 4291 allows for multiple interfaces to use the same address as long as they appear as a single interface to the IPv6 implementation on the host.

Multicast

A multicast address identifies zero or more interfaces on the same or different hosts. With the appropriate multicast routing topology, packets addressed to a multicast address are delivered to all interfaces identified by the address.

Anycast

An anycast address identifies multiple interfaces. With the appropriate unicast routing topology, packets addressed to an anycast address are delivered to a single interface–the nearest interface that is identified by the address. The nearest interface is defined as being the closest in terms of routing distance. A multicast address is used for one-to-many communication, with delivery to multiple interfaces. An anycast address is used for one-to-one-of-many communication, with delivery to a single interface.

In all cases, IPv6 addresses identify interfaces, not nodes. A node is identified by any unicast address assigned to any one of its interfaces.

> **Note** RFC 4291 does not define a broadcast address. All types of IPv4 broadcast addressing are performed in IPv6 using multicast addresses. For example, the subnet and limited broadcast addresses from IPv4 are replaced with the link-local scope all-nodes multicast address of FF02::1.

Unicast IPv6 Addresses

The following types of addresses are unicast IPv6 addresses:

- Global unicast addresses
- Link-local addresses
- Site-local addresses
- Unique local addresses
- Special addresses
- Transition addresses

Global Unicast Addresses

IPv6 global addresses are equivalent to public IPv4 addresses. They are globally routable and reachable on the IPv6 Internet. Global unicast addresses are designed to be aggregated or summarized for an efficient routing infrastructure. Unlike the current IPv4-based Internet, which is a mixture of both flat and hierarchical routing, the IPv6-based Internet has been designed from its foundation to support efficient, hierarchical addressing and routing. The scope of a global address is the entire IPv6 Internet.

RFC 4291 defines global addresses as all addresses that are not the unspecified, loopback, link-local unicast, or multicast addresses (described later in this chapter). However, Figure 3-1 shows the structure of global unicast addresses defined in RFC 3587 that are currently being used on the IPv6 Internet.

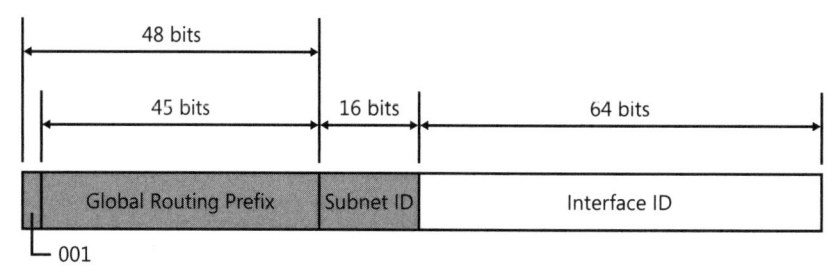

Figure 3-1 The structure of global unicast addresses defined in RFC 3587

The fields in the global unicast address are described in the following list:

- **Fixed portion set to 001** The three high-order bits are set to 001.
- **Global Routing Prefix** Indicates the global routing prefix for a specific organization's site. The combination of the three fixed bits and the 45-bit Global Routing Prefix is used to create a 48-bit site prefix, which is assigned to an individual site of an organization. A site is an autonomously operating IP-based network that is connected to the IPv6 Internet. Network architects and administrators within the site determine the addressing plan and

routing policy for the organization network. Once assigned, routers on the IPv6 Internet forward IPv6 traffic matching the 48-bit prefix to the routers of the organization's site.

- **Subnet ID**   The Subnet ID is used within an organization's site to identify subnets within its site. The size of this field is 16 bits. The organization's site can use these 16 bits within its site to create 65,536 subnets or multiple levels of addressing hierarchy and an efficient routing infrastructure. With 16 bits of subnetting flexibility, a global unicast prefix assigned to an organization site is equivalent to a public IPv4 Class A address prefix (assuming that the last octet is used for identifying nodes on subnets). The routing structure of the organization's network is not visible to the ISP.

- **Interface ID**   Indicates the interface on a specific subnet within the site. The size of this field is 64 bits. The interface ID in IPv6 is equivalent to the node ID or host ID in IPv4.

Trillions of Sites

Another way to gauge the practical size of the IPv6 address space is to examine the number of sites that can connect to the IPv6 Internet. With the current allocation practice defined in RFC 3587 of 48-bit global address prefixes, it is possible to define 2^{45} or 35,184,372,088,832 possible 48-bit prefixes to assign to sites connected to the IPv6 Internet. There are more IPv6 sites than possible IPv4 addresses. This large number of sites is possible even when we are using only one-eighth of the entire IPv6 address space.

By comparison, using the Internet address classes originally defined for IPv4, it was possible to assign 2,113,389 address prefixes to organizations connected to the Internet. The number 2,113,389 is derived from adding up all the possible Class A, Class B, and Class C address prefixes and then subtracting the prefixes used for the private address space. Even with the adoption of CIDR to make more efficient use of unassigned Class A and Class B address prefixes, the number of possible sites connected to the Internet is not substantially increased, nor does it approach the number of possible sites that can be connected to the IPv6 Internet.

Topologies Within Global Addresses

The fields within the global address create a three-level topological structure, as shown in Figure 3-2.

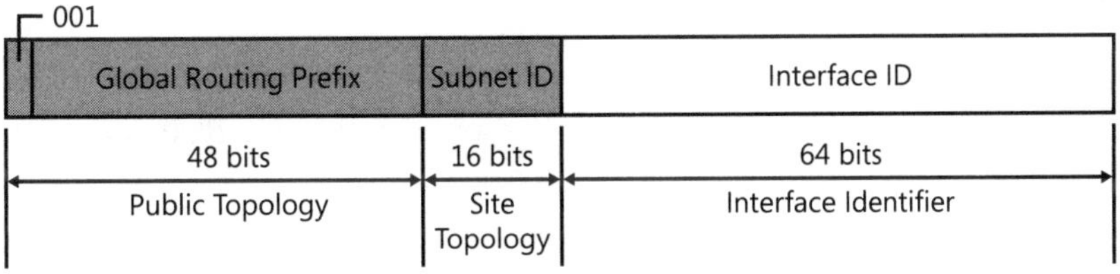

Figure 3-2   The topological structure of the global address

The public topology is the collection of larger and smaller ISPs that provide access to the IPv6 Internet. The site topology is the collection of subnets within an organization's site. The interface identifier specifies a unique interface on a subnet within an organization's site.

Local-Use Unicast Addresses

Local-use unicast addresses do not have a global scope and can be reused. There are two types of local-use unicast addresses:

1. Link-local addresses are used between on-link neighbors and for Neighbor Discovery processes.

2. Site-local addresses are used between nodes communicating with other nodes in the same organization.

Link-Local Addresses

IPv6 link-local addresses, identified by the initial 10 bits being set to 1111 1110 10 and the next 54 bits set to 0, are used by nodes when communicating with neighboring nodes on the same link. For example, on a single-link IPv6 network with no router, link-local addresses are used to communicate between hosts on the link. IPv6 link-local addresses are similar to IPv4 link-local addresses defined in RFC 3927 that use the 169.254.0.0/16 prefix. The use of IPv4 link-local addresses is known as Automatic Private IP Addressing (APIPA) in Windows Vista, Windows Server 2008, Windows Server 2003, and Windows XP. The scope of a link-local address is the local link.

Figure 3-3 shows the structure of the link-local address.

10 bits	54 bits	64 bits
1111 1110 10	000 . . . 000	Interface ID

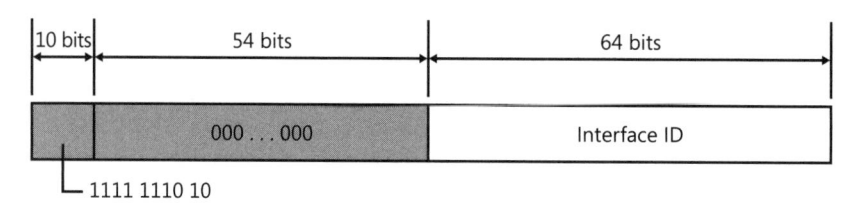

Figure 3-3 The structure of the link-local address

A link-local address is required for some Neighbor Discovery processes and is always automatically configured, even in the absence of all other unicast addresses. For more information about the address autoconfiguration process for link-local addresses, see Chapter 8, "Address Autoconfiguration."

Link-local addresses always begin with FE80. With the 64-bit interface identifier, the prefix for link-local addresses is always FE80::/64. An IPv6 router never forwards link-local traffic beyond the link.

Site-Local Addresses

Site-local addresses, identified by setting the first 10 bits to 1111 1110 11, are equivalent to the IPv4 private address space (10.0.0.0/8, 172.16.0.0/12, and 192.168.0.0/16). For example, private intranets that do not have a direct, routed connection to the IPv6 Internet can use site-local addresses without conflicting with global addresses. Site-local addresses are not reachable from other sites, and routers must not forward site-local traffic outside the site. Site-local addresses can be used in addition to global addresses. The scope of a site-local address is the site.

Figure 3-4 shows the structure of the site-local address.

10 bits	54 bits	64 bits
1111 1110 11	Subnet ID	Interface ID

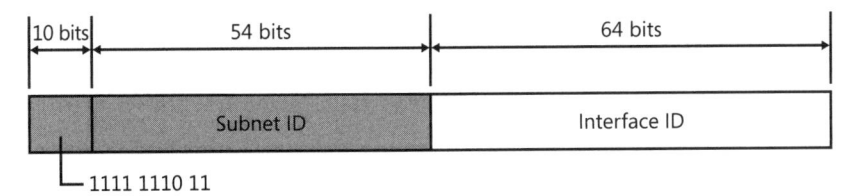

Figure 3-4 The structure of the site-local address

Unlike link-local addresses, site-local addresses are not automatically configured and must be assigned either through stateless or stateful address autoconfiguration. For more information, see Chapter 8.

The first 10 bits are always fixed for site-local addresses, beginning with FEC0::/10. After the 10 fixed bits is a 54-bit Subnet ID field that provides 54 bits with which you can create subnets within your organization. You can have a flat subnet structure, or you can divide the high-order bits of the Subnet ID field to create a hierarchical and summarizable routing infrastructure. After the Subnet ID field is a 64-bit Interface ID field that identifies a specific interface on a subnet.

Site-local addresses have been formally deprecated in RFC 3879 for future IPv6 implementations. However, existing implementations of IPv6 can continue to use site-local addresses.

Zone IDs for Local-Use Addresses

Unlike global addresses, local-use addresses (link-local and site-local addresses) can be reused. Link-local addresses are reused on each link. Site-local addresses can be reused within each site of an organization. Because of this address reuse capability, link-local and site-local addresses are ambiguous. To specify the link on which the destination is located or the site within which the destination is located, an additional identifier is needed. This additional identifier is a zone identifier (ID), also known as a scope ID, which identifies a connected portion of a network that has a specified scope.

The syntax specified in RFC 4007 for identifying the zone associated with a local-use address is *Address%zone_ID*, in which *Address* is a local-use unicast IPv6 address and *zone_ID* is an integer value representing the zone. The values of the zone ID are defined relative to the sending host. Therefore, different hosts might determine different zone ID values for the same physical zone. For example, Host A might choose 3 to represent the zone of an attached link and Host B might choose 4 to represent the same link.

For Windows-based IPv6 hosts, the zone IDs for link-local and site-local addresses are defined as follows:

- For link-local addresses, the zone ID is typically the interface index of the interface either assigned the address or to be used as the sending interface for a link-local destination. The interface index is an integer starting at 1 that is assigned to IPv6 interfaces, which include a loopback and one or multiple LAN or tunnel interfaces. Multiple interfaces can have the same link-local zone ID if they are attached to the same link. You can view the list of interface indexes from the display of the **netsh interface ipv6 show interface** command. You must include a zone ID with a link-local destination.

- For site-local addresses, the zone ID is the site ID, an integer assigned to the site of an organization. For organizations that do not reuse the site-local address prefix, the site ID is set to 1 by default and does not need to be specified. In Windows, you can view the site ID from the display of the **netsh interface ipv6 show address level=verbose** command.

The following are examples of using Windows tools and the zone ID:

- **ping fe80::2b0:d0ff:fee9:4143%3**   In this case, 3 is the interface index of the interface attached to the link containing the destination address.

- **tracert fec0::f282:2b0:d0ff:fee9:4143%2**   In this case, 2 is the site ID of the organization site containing the destination address.

In Windows Vista and Windows Server 2008, the Ipconfig.exe tool displays the zone ID of local-use IPv6 addresses. The following is an excerpt from the display of the **ipconfig** command:

```
Ethernet adapter Local Area Connection:

    Connection-specific DNS Suffix  . : ecoast.example.com
    IPv6 Address. . . . . . . . . . . : 2001:db8:21da:7:713e:a426:d167:37ab
    Temporary IPv6 Address. . . . . . : 2001:db8:21da:7:5099:ba54:9881:2e54
    Link-local IPv6 Address . . . . . : fe80::713e:a426:d167:37ab%6
    IPv4 Address. . . . . . . . . . . : 157.60.14.11
    Subnet Mask . . . . . . . . . . . : 255.255.255.0
    Default Gateway . . . . . . . . . : fe80::20a:42ff:feb0:5400%6
                                        157.60.14.1
```

For the link-local addresses in the display of the **ipconfig** command, the zone ID indicates the interface index of the interface either assigned the address (for Link-Local IPv6 Address) or the interface through which an address is reachable (for Default Gateway).

Unique Local Addresses

Site-local addresses provide a private addressing alternative to global addresses for intranet traffic. However, because the site-local address prefix can be reused to address multiple sites within an organization, a site-local address prefix can be duplicated. The ambiguity of site-local addresses in an organization adds complexity and difficulty for applications, routers, and network managers. For more information, see section 2 of RFC 3879.

To replace site-local addresses with a new type of address that is private to an organization yet unique across all the sites of the organization, RFC 4193 defines unique local IPv6 unicast addresses. Figure 3-5 shows the structure of the unique local address.

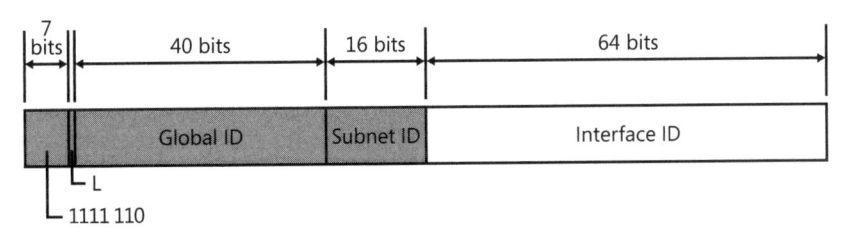

```
| 7 bits | 40 bits   | 16 bits   | 64 bits      |
|        | Global ID | Subnet ID | Interface ID |
    └ L
    └ 1111 110
```

Figure 3-5 The structure of the unique local address

The first 7 bits have the fixed binary value of 1111110. All local addresses have the address prefix FC00::/7. The Local (L) flag is set 1 to indicate that the prefix is locally assigned. The L flag value set to 0 is not defined in RFC 3879. Therefore, unique local addresses within an organization with the L flag set to 1 have the address prefix of FD00::/8. The Global ID identifies a specific site within an organization and is set to a randomly derived 40-bit value. By deriving a random value for the Global ID, an organization can have statistically unique 48-bit prefixes assigned to their sites. Additionally, two organizations that use unique local addresses that merge have a low probability of duplicating a 48-bit unique local address prefix, minimizing site renumbering. Unlike the Global Routing Prefix in global addresses, the Global IDs in unique local address prefixes are not designed to be summarized.

Unique local addresses have a global scope, but their reachability is defined by routing topology and filtering policies at Internet boundaries. Organizations will not advertise their unique local address prefixes outside of their organizations or create DNS entries with unique local addresses in the Internet DNS. Organizations can easily create filtering policies at their Internet boundaries to prevent all unique local-addressed traffic from being forwarded. Because they have a global scope, unique local addresses do not need a zone ID.

The global address and unique local address share the same structure beyond the first 48 bits of the address. In both addresses, the 16-bit Subnet ID field identifies a subnet within an organization. Because of this, you can create a subnetted routing infrastructure that is used for both local and global addresses.

For example, a specific subnet of your organization can be assigned both the global prefix 2001:DB8:4D1C:221A::/64 and the local prefix FD0E:2D:BA9:221A::/64, where the subnet is identified for both types of prefixes by the Subnet ID value of *221A*. Although the subnet identifier is the same for both prefixes, routes for both prefixes must still be propagated throughout the routing infrastructure so that addresses based on both prefixes are reachable.

Special IPv6 Addresses

The following are special IPv6 addresses:

- **Unspecified address**

    The unspecified address (0:0:0:0:0:0:0:0 or ::) is used only to indicate the absence of an address. It is equivalent to the IPv4 unspecified address of 0.0.0.0. The unspecified address is typically used as a source address when a unique address has not yet been determined. The unspecified address is never assigned to an interface or used as a destination address.

- **Loopback address**

    The loopback address (0:0:0:0:0:0:0:1 or ::1) is assigned to a loopback interface, enabling a node to send packets to itself. It is equivalent to the IPv4 loopback address of 127.0.0.1. Packets addressed to the loopback address must never be sent on a link or forwarded by an IPv6 router.

Transition Addresses

To aid in the transition from IPv4 to IPv6 and the coexistence of both types of hosts, the following addresses are defined:

- **IPv4-compatible address**

    The IPv4-compatible address, 0:0:0:0:0:0:*w.x.y.z* or ::*w.x.y.z* (where *w.x.y.z* is the dotted-decimal representation of a public IPv4 address), is used by IPv6/IPv4 nodes that are communicating with IPv6 over an IPv4 infrastructure that uses public IPv4 addresses, such as the Internet. IPv4-compatible addresses are deprecated in RFC 4291 and are not supported in IPv6 for Windows Vista and Windows Server 2008.

- **IPv4-mapped address**

    The IPv4-mapped address, 0:0:0:0:0:FFFF:*w.x.y.z* or ::FFFF: *w.x.y.z*, is used to represent an IPv4 address as a 128-bit IPv6 address.

- **6to4 address**

    An address of the type 2002:*WWXX:YYZZ:Subnet ID:Interface ID*, where *WWXX:YYZZ* is the colon hexadecimal representation of *w.x.y.z* (a public IPv4 address), is assigned a node for the 6to4 IPv6 transition technology.

- **ISATAP address**

  An address of the type *64-bit prefix*:0:5EFE:*w.x.y.z*, where *w.x.y.z* is a private IPv4 address, is assigned to a node for the Intra-Site Automatic Tunnel Addressing Protocol (ISATAP) IPv6 transition technology.

- **Teredo address**

  A global address that uses the prefix 2001::/32 and is assigned to a node for the Teredo IPv6 transition technology. Beyond the first 32 bits, Teredo addresses are used to encode the IPv4 address of a Teredo server, flags, and an obscured version of a Teredo client's external address and UDP port number.

For more information about these addresses, see Chapter 11, "IPv6 Transition Technologies."

Multicast IPv6 Addresses

In IPv6, multicast traffic operates in the same way that it does in IPv4. Arbitrarily located IPv6 nodes can listen for multicast traffic on an arbitrary IPv6 multicast address. IPv6 nodes can listen to multiple multicast addresses at the same time. Nodes can join or leave a multicast group at any time.

IPv6 multicast addresses have the first 8 bits set to 1111 1111. Therefore, an IPv6 multicast address always begins with FF. Multicast addresses cannot be used as source addresses or as intermediate destinations in a Routing extension header. Beyond the first 8 bits, multicast addresses include additional structure to identify flags, their scope, and the multicast group. Figure 3-6 shows the structure of the IPv6 multicast address.

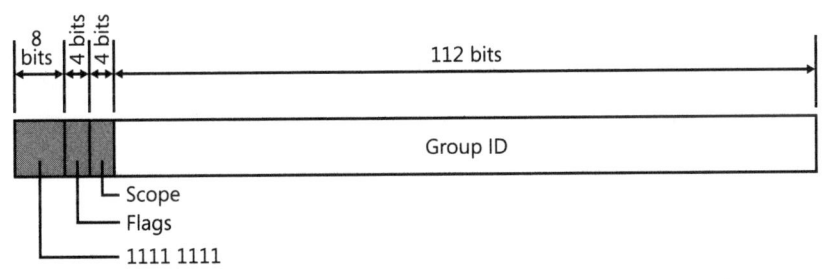

Figure 3-6 The structure of the IPv6 multicast address

The following list describes the fields in the multicast address:

- **Flags** Indicates flags set on the multicast address. The size of this field is 4 bits, consisting of three flags in the low-order bits. The first low-order bit is the Transient (T) flag. When set to 0, the T flag indicates that the multicast address is a permanently assigned (well-known) multicast address allocated by the Internet Assigned Numbers Authority (IANA). When set to 1, the T flag indicates that the multicast address is a transient (not permanently assigned) multicast address. The second low-order bit is for the Prefix (P) flag, which indicates whether the multicast address is based on a unicast address prefix.

RFC 3306 describes the P flag. The third low-order bit is for the Rendezvous Point Address (R) flag, which indicates whether the multicast address contains an embedded rendezvous point address. RFC 3956 describes the R flag.

- **Scope** Indicates the scope of the IPv6 network for which the multicast traffic is intended to be delivered. The size of this field is 4 bits. In addition to using information provided by multicast routing protocols, routers use the multicast scope to determine whether multicast traffic can be forwarded.

Table 3-2 lists the values for the Scope field assigned in RFC 4291. All other values are unassigned.

Table 3-2 Defined Values for the Scope Field

Scope Field Value	Scope
0	Reserved
1	Interface-local scope
2	Link-local scope
3	Reserved
4	Admin-local scope
5	Site-local scope
8	Organization-local scope
E	Global scope
F	Reserved

For example, traffic with the multicast address of FF02::2 has a link-local scope. An IPv6 router never forwards this traffic beyond the local link.

- **Group ID** Identifies the multicast group, and is unique within the scope. The size of this field is 112 bits. Permanently assigned group IDs are independent of the scope. Transient group IDs are relevant only to a specific scope. Multicast addresses from FF01:: through FF0F:: are reserved, well-known addresses.

To identify all nodes for the interface-local and link-local scopes, the following addresses are defined:

- FF01::1 (interface-local scope all-nodes multicast address)
- FF02::1 (link-local scope all-nodes multicast address)

To identify all routers for the interface-local, link-local, and site-local scopes, the following addresses are defined:

- FF01::2 (interface-local scope all-routers multicast address)
- FF02::2 (link-local scope all-routers multicast address)
- FF05::2 (site-local scope all-routers multicast address)

For the current list of permanently assigned IPv6 multicast addresses, see
http://www.iana.org/assignments/ipv6-multicast-addresses.

IPv6 multicast addresses replace all forms of IPv4 broadcast addresses. The IPv4 network broadcast (in which all host bits are set to 1 in a classful environment), subnet broadcast (in which all host bits are set to 1 in a non-classful environment), and limited broadcast (255.255.255.255) addresses are replaced by the link-local scope all-nodes multicast address (FF02:01) in IPv6.

Solicited-Node Address

The solicited-node address facilitates the efficient querying of network nodes during link-layer address resolution—the resolving of a link-layer address of a known IPv6 address. In IPv4, the Address Resolution Protocol (ARP) Request frame is sent to the MAC-level broadcast, disturbing all nodes on the network segment, including those that are not running IPv4. IPv6 uses the Neighbor Solicitation message to perform link-layer address resolution. However, instead of using the local-link scope all-nodes multicast address as the Neighbor Solicitation message destination, which would disturb all IPv6 nodes on the local link, the solicited-node multicast address is used. The solicited-node multicast address is constructed from the prefix FF02::1:FF00:0/104 and the last 24 bits (6 hexadecimal digits) of a unicast IPv6 address. Figure 3-7 shows the mapping of a unicast IPv6 address and its corresponding solicited-node multicast address.

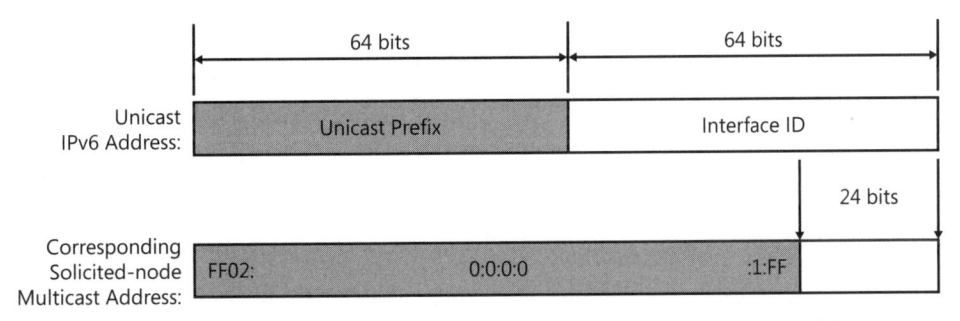

Figure 3-7 The mapping of a unicast address to its solicited-node multicast address

For example, Node A is assigned the link-local address of FE80::2AA:FF:FE28:9C5A and is also listening on the corresponding solicited-node multicast address of FF02::1:FF28:9C5A. (An underline is used to highlight the correspondence of the last six hexadecimal digits.) Node B on the local link must resolve Node A's link-local address FE80::2AA:FF:FE28:9C5A to its corresponding link-layer address. Node B sends a Neighbor Solicitation message to the solicited-node multicast address of FF02::1:FF28:9C5A. Because Node A is listening on this multicast address, it processes the Neighbor Solicitation message and sends a unicast Neighbor Advertisement message in reply.

The result of using the solicited-node multicast address is that link-layer address resolutions, a common occurrence on a link, are not using a mechanism that disturbs all network nodes. By using the solicited-node address, very few nodes are disturbed during address resolution. In practice, because of the relationship between the IPv6 interface ID and the solicited-node address, the solicited-node address acts as a pseudo-unicast address for very efficient address resolution. For more information, see the "IPv6 Interface Identifiers" section in this chapter.

Mapping IPv6 Multicast Addresses to Ethernet Addresses

When sending IPv6 multicast packets on an Ethernet link, the corresponding destination MAC address is 0x33-33-mm-mm-mm-mm, where *mm-mm-mm-mm* is a direct mapping of the last 32 bits (8 hexadecimal digits) of the IPv6 multicast address. Figure 3-8 shows the mapping of an IPv6 multicast address to an Ethernet multicast address.

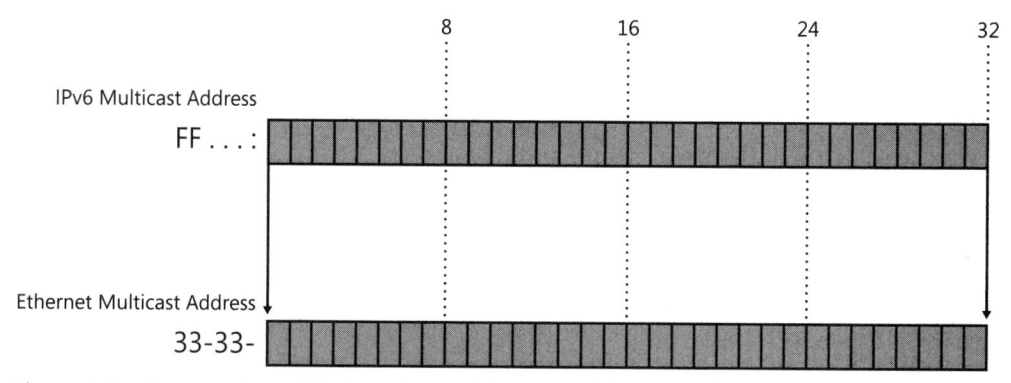

Figure 3-8 The mapping of IPv6 multicast addresses to Ethernet multicast addresses

Ethernet network adapters maintain a table of interesting destination MAC addresses. If an Ethernet frame with an interesting destination MAC address is received, it is passed to upper layers for additional processing. By default, this table contains the MAC-level broadcast address (0xFF-FF-FF-FF-FF-FF) and the unicast MAC address assigned to the adapter. To facilitate efficient delivery of multicast traffic, additional multicast destination addresses can be added or removed from the table. For every multicast address being listened to by the host, there is a corresponding entry in the table of interesting MAC addresses.

For example, an IPv6 host with the Ethernet MAC address of 00-AA-00-3F-2A-1C (link-local address of FE80::2AA:FF:FE3F:2A1C) adds the following multicast MAC addresses to the table of interesting destination MAC addresses on the Ethernet adapter:

- The address of 33-33-00-00-00-01, which corresponds to the link-local scope all-nodes multicast address of FF02::1 (fully expressed as FF02:0000:0000:0000:0000:0000:0000:0001).

- The address of 33-33-FF-3F-2A-1C, which corresponds to the solicited-node address of FF02::1:FF3F:2A1C. Remember that the solicited-node address is the prefix FF02::1:FF00:0/104 and the last 24 bits of the unicast IPv6 address.

Additional multicast addresses on which the host is listening are added and removed from the table as needed.

Anycast IPv6 Addresses

An anycast address is assigned to multiple interfaces. Packets addressed to an anycast address are forwarded by the routing infrastructure to the nearest interface to which the anycast address is assigned. To facilitate delivery, the routing infrastructure must be aware of the interfaces that have anycast addresses assigned to them and their distance in terms of routing metrics. This awareness is accomplished by the propagation of host routes throughout the routing infrastructure of the portion of the network that cannot summarize the anycast address using a route prefix.

For example, for the anycast address 3FFE:2900:D005:6187:2AA:FF:FE89:6B9A, host routes for this address are propagated within the routing infrastructure of the organization assigned the 48-bit prefix 3FFE:2900:D005::/48. Because a node assigned this anycast address can be placed anywhere on the organization's intranet, host routes for all nodes assigned this anycast address are needed in the routing tables of all routers within the organization. Outside the organization, this anycast address is summarized by the 3FFE:2900:D005::/48 prefix that is assigned to the organization. Therefore, the host routes needed to deliver IPv6 packets to the nearest anycast group member within an organization's intranet are not needed in the routing infrastructure of the IPv6 Internet.

As of RFC 4291, anycast addresses are used only as destination addresses and are assigned only to routers. Anycast addresses are assigned out of the unicast address space, and the scope of an anycast address is the scope of the type of unicast address from which the anycast address is assigned. It is not possible to determine if a given destination unicast address is also an anycast address. The only nodes that have this awareness are the routers that use host routes to forward the anycast traffic to the nearest anycast group member and the anycast group members themselves.

Subnet-Router Anycast Address

The Subnet-Router anycast address is defined in RFC 4291 and is required. It is created from the subnet prefix for a given interface. When the Subnet-Router anycast address is constructed, the bits in the subnet prefix are fixed at their appropriate values and the remaining bits are set to 0. Figure 3-9 shows the structure of the Subnet-Router anycast address.

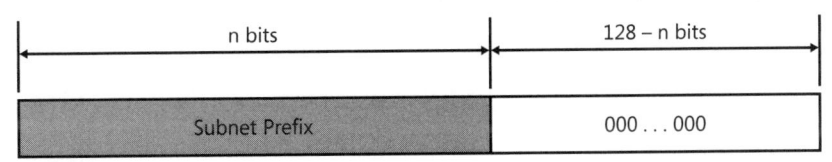

n bits	128 − n bits
Subnet Prefix	000 . . . 000

Figure 3-9 The structure of the Subnet-Router anycast address

All router interfaces attached to a subnet are assigned the Subnet-Router anycast address for that subnet. The Subnet-Router anycast address is used to communicate with the nearest router connected to a specified subnet.

IPv6 Addresses for a Host

An IPv4 host with a single network adapter typically has a single IPv4 address assigned to that adapter. An IPv6 host, however, usually has multiple IPv6 addresses assigned to each adapter. The interfaces on a typical IPv6 host are assigned the following unicast addresses:

- A link-local address for each interface
- Additional unicast addresses for each interface (which could be one or multiple unique local or global addresses)
- The loopback address (::1) for the loopback interface

Typical IPv6 hosts are always logically multihomed because they always have at least two addresses with which they can receive packets—a link-local address for local link traffic and a routable unique local or global address.

Additionally, each interface on an IPv6 host is listening for traffic on the following multicast addresses:

- The interface-local scope all-nodes multicast address (FF01::1)
- The link-local scope all-nodes multicast address (FF02::1)
- The solicited-node address for each unicast address assigned
- The multicast addresses of joined groups

IPv6 Addresses for a Router

The interfaces on an IPv6 router are assigned the following unicast addresses:

- A link-local address for each interface
- Additional unicast addresses for each interface (which could be one or multiple unique local or global addresses)
- The loopback address (::1) for the loopback interface

Additionally, the interfaces of an IPv6 router are assigned the following anycast addresses:

- A Subnet-Router anycast address for each subnet
- Additional anycast addresses (optional)

Additionally, the interfaces of an IPv6 router are listening for traffic on the following multicast addresses:

- The interface-local scope all-nodes multicast address (FF01::1)
- The interface-local scope all-routers multicast address (FF01::2)
- The link-local scope all-nodes multicast address (FF02::1)
- The link-local scope all-routers multicast address (FF02::2)
- The site-local scope all-routers multicast address (FF05::2)
- The solicited-node address for each unicast address assigned
- The multicast addresses of joined groups

Subnetting the IPv6 Address Space

Just as in IPv4, the IPv6 address space can be divided by using high-order bits that do not already have fixed values to create subnetted address prefixes. These are used either to summarize a level in the routing or addressing hierarchy (with a prefix length less than 64), or to define a specific subnet or network segment (with a prefix length of 64). IPv4 subnetting differs from IPv6 subnetting in the definition of the host ID portion of the address. In IPv4, the host ID can be of varying length, depending on the subnetting scheme. For currently defined unicast IPv6 addresses, the host ID is the interface ID portion of the IPv6 unicast address and is always a fixed size of 64 bits.

For most network administrators within an organization, subnetting the IPv6 address space consists of using subnetting techniques to divide the subnet ID portion of a global or unique local address prefix in a manner that allows for route summarization and delegation of the remaining address space to different portions of an IPv6 intranet. For both global and unique local addresses, the first 48 bits of the address are fixed. For the global address, the first 48 bits are fixed and allocated by an ISP. For the unique local address, the first 48 bits are fixed at FD00::/8 and the random 40-bit global ID assigned to a site of an organization.

Subnetting the subnet ID portion of a global or unique local address space requires a two-step procedure:

1. Determine the number of bits to be used for the subnetting.
2. Enumerate the new subnetted address prefixes.

The subnetting technique described here assumes that subnetting is done by dividing the 16-bit address space of the subnet ID using the high-order bits in the subnet ID. Although this method promotes hierarchical addressing and routing, it is not required. For example, in a small organization with a small number of subnets, you can also create a flat addressing space for the subnet ID by numbering the subnets starting at 0.

Step 1: Determining the Number of Subnetting Bits

The number of bits being used for subnetting determines the possible number of new subnetted address prefixes that can be allocated to portions of your network based on geographical or departmental divisions. In a hierarchical routing infrastructure, you need to determine how many address prefixes, and therefore how many bits, you need at each level in the hierarchy. The more bits you choose for the various levels of the hierarchy, the fewer bits you will have available to enumerate individual subnets in the last level of the hierarchy.

Depending on the needs of your organization, your subnetting scheme might be along nibble (hexadecimal digit) or bit boundaries. If you can subnet along nibble boundaries, your subnetting scheme becomes simplified and each hexadecimal digit can represent a level in the subnetting hierarchy. For example, a network administrator decides to implement a three-level hierarchy that uses the first nibble for an organization's campus, the next nibble for a building within a campus, and the last two nibbles for a subnet within a building. An example subnet ID for this scheme is 142A, which indicates campus 1, building 4, and subnet 42 (0x2A).

In some cases, bit-level subnetting is required. For example, a network administrator decides to implement a two-level hierarchy reflecting a geographical/departmental structure and uses 4 bits for the geographical level and 6 bits for the departmental level. This means that each department in each geographical location has only 6 bits of subnetting space left (16−4−6), or only 64 (= 2^6) subnets per department.

On any given level in the hierarchy, you will have a number of bits that are already fixed by the next level up in the hierarchy (f), a number of bits used for subnetting at the current level in the hierarchy (s), and a number of bits remaining for the next level down in the hierarchy (r). At all times, $f + s + r = 16$. This relationship is shown in Figure 3-10.

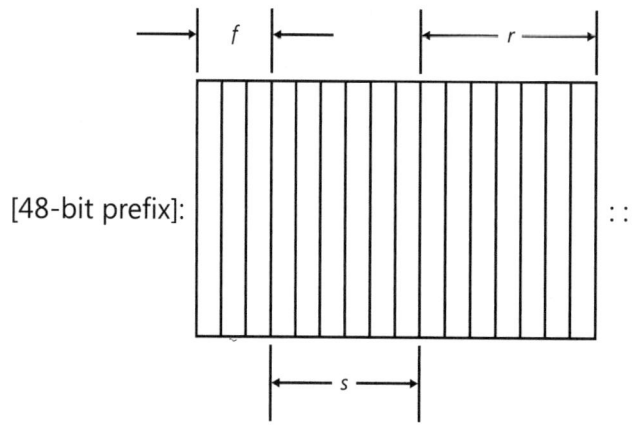

Figure 3-10 The subnetting of a subnet ID

Step 2: Enumerating Subnetted Address Prefixes

Based on the number of bits used for subnetting, you must determine the new subnetted address prefixes. There are three main approaches:

- **Binary** Enumerate new subnetted address prefixes by using binary representations of the subnet ID and converting to hexadecimal for the subnetted address prefixes.
- **Hexadecimal** Enumerate new subnetted address prefixes by using hexadecimal representations of the subnet ID and a calculated increment between successive subnetted address prefixes.
- **Decimal** Enumerate new subnetted address prefixes by using decimal representations of the subnet ID and increment.

Any of these methods produces the same result: an enumerated list of subnetted address prefixes.

Using the Binary Method

In the binary method, the 16-bit subnet ID is expressed as a 16-digit binary number. The bits within the subnet ID that are being used for subnetting are incremented for all their possible values, and for each value, the 16-digit binary number is converted to hexadecimal and combined with the 48-bit site prefix, producing the subnetted address prefixes.

1. Based on s (the number of bits chosen for subnetting), m (the prefix length of the address prefix being subnetted), and f (the number of bits already subnetted), calculate the following:

   $f = m - 48$

   f is the number of bits within the subnet ID that are already fixed.

   $n = 2^s$

   n is the number of address prefixes that are obtained.

   $l = 48 + f + s$

   l is the prefix length of the new subnetted address prefixes.

2. Create a three-column table with n entries. The first column is the address prefix number (starting with 1), the second column is the binary representation of the subnet ID portion of the new address prefix, and the third column is the subnetted address prefix (in hexadecimal), which includes the 48-bit site prefix and the subnet ID.

3. In the first table entry, set all the bits being used for subnetting to 0. Convert the resulting 16-digit binary number to hexadecimal, combine it with the 48-bit site prefix, and write the subnetted address prefix. This first subnetted address prefix is just the original address prefix with the new prefix length.

4. In the next table entry, increment the value within the subnet bits. Convert the 16-digit binary number to hexadecimal, combine it with the 48-bit site prefix, and write the resulting subnetted address prefix.

5. Repeat step 4 until the table is complete.

For example, to perform a 3-bit subnetting of the global address prefix 2001:DB8:0:C000::/51, we first calculate the values for the number of prefixes and the new prefix length. Our starting values are $s = 3$, and $f = 51 - 48 = 3$. The number of prefixes is 8 ($n = 2^3$). The new prefix length is 54 ($l = 48 + 3 + 3$). The initial value for the subnet ID in binary is 1100 0000 0000 0000 (0xC000 converted to binary).

Next, we construct a table with eight entries. The entry for the address prefix 1 is 2001:DB8:0:C000::/54. Additional entries are increments of the subnet bits in the subnet ID portion of the address prefix, as shown in Table 3-3.

Table 3-3 The Binary Subnetting Technique for Address Prefix 2001:DB8:0:C000::/51

Address Prefix Number	Binary Representation of Subnet ID	Subnetted Address Prefix
1	1100 0000 0000 0000	2001:DB8:0:C000::/54
2	1100 0100 0000 0000	2001:DB8:0:C400::/54
3	1100 1000 0000 0000	2001:DB8:0:C800::/54
4	1100 1100 0000 0000	2001:DB8:0:CC00::/54
5	1101 0000 0000 0000	2001:DB8:0:D000::/54
6	1101 0100 0000 0000	2001:DB8:0:D400::/54
7	1101 1000 0000 0000	2001:DB8:0:D800::/54
8	1101 1100 0000 0000	2001:DB8:0:DC00::/54

In Table 3-3, the underline in the second column shows the bits that are being used for subnetting.

Using the Hexadecimal Method

Although the binary method allows you to see how the subnetted address prefixes are determined at their most basic level, this method is laborious and does not scale well. For example, imagine performing an 8-bit subnetting using the binary method, producing 256 subnetted prefixes. For an arbitrary subnetting scheme, a more formulaic approach is needed. The following method uses a formula for computing the hexadecimal increment between successive subnetted address prefixes:

1. Based on s (the number of bits chosen for subnetting), m (the prefix length of the address prefix being subnetted), and F (the hexadecimal value of the subnet being subnetted), calculate the following:

    $f = m - 48$

    f is the number of bits within the subnet ID that are already fixed.

    $n = 2^s$

    n is the number of address prefixes that are obtained.

    $i = 2^{16-(f+s)}$

i is the incremental value between each successive subnet ID expressed in hexadecimal form.

$l = 48 + f + s$

l is the prefix length of the new subnetted address prefixes.

2. Create a two-column table with *n* entries. The first column is the address prefix number (starting with 1), and the second column is the new subnetted address prefix.

3. In the first table entry, based on F, the hexadecimal value of the subnet ID being subnetted, set the subnetted address prefix to *48-bit prefix:F::/l*.

4. In the next table entry, increase the value within the subnet ID portion of the site address by *i*. For example, in the second table entry, set the subnetted prefix to *48-bit prefix:F + i::/l*.

5. Repeat step 4 until the table is complete.

For example, to perform a 3-bit subnetting of the global address prefix 2001:DB8:0:C000::/51, we first calculate the values of the number of prefixes, the increment, and the new prefix length. Our starting values are $F = 0xC000$, $s = 3$, and $f = 51 - 48 = 3$. The number of prefixes is 8 ($n = 2^3$). The increment is 0x400 ($i = 2^{16-(f+s)} = 1024 = 0x400$). The new prefix length is 54 ($l = 48 + 3 + 3$).

Next, we construct a table with eight entries. The entry for the address prefix 1 is 2001:DB8:0:C000::/54. Additional entries in the table are successive increments of *i* in the subnet ID portion of the address prefix, as shown in Table 3-4.

Table 3-4 The Hexadecimal Subnetting Technique for Address Prefix 2001:DB8:0:C000::/51

Address Prefix Number	Subnetted Address Prefix
1	2001:DB8:0:C000::/54
2	2001:DB8:0:C400::/54
3	2001:DB8:0:C800::/54
4	2001:DB8:0:CC00::/54
5	2001:DB8:0:D000::/54
6	2001:DB8:0:D400::/54
7	2001:DB8:0:D800::/54
8	2001:DB8:0:DC00::/54

Using the Decimal Method

If you are more comfortable working with decimal numbers, the following formulaic procedure will produce the same results. However, there are additional steps to convert to decimal and then back to hexadecimal for the representation of the subnetted address prefix.

1. Based on s (the number of bits chosen for subnetting), m (the prefix length of the address prefix being subnetted), and F (the hexadecimal value of the subnet ID being subnetted), calculate the following:

   $f = m - 48$

   f is the number of bits within the subnet ID that are already fixed.

   $n = 2^s$

   n is the number of address prefixes that are obtained.

   $i = 2^{16-(f+s)}$

   i is the incremental value between each successive subnet ID.

   $l = 48 + f + s$

   l is the prefix length of the new subnetted address prefixes.

   $D = $ decimal representation of F

2. Create a three-column table with n entries. The first column is the address prefix number (starting with 1), the second column is the decimal representation of the subnet ID portion of the new address prefix, and the third column is the new subnetted address prefix.

3. In the first table entry, the decimal representation of the subnet ID is D and the subnetted address prefix is *48-bit prefix:F::/l*.

4. In the next table entry, for the second column, increase the value of the decimal representation of the subnet ID by i. For example, in the second table entry, the decimal representation of the subnet ID is $D + i$.

5. For the third column, convert the decimal representation of the subnet ID to hexadecimal and construct the prefix from *48-bit prefix:subnet ID::/l*. For example, in the second table entry, the subnetted address prefix is *48-bit prefix:D + i (converted to hexadecimal)::/l*.

6. Repeat steps 4 and 5 until the table is complete.

For example, to perform a 3-bit subnetting of the global address prefix 2001:DB8:0:C000::/51, we first calculate the values of the number of prefixes, the increment, the new prefix length, and the decimal representation of the starting subnet ID. Our starting values are $F = $ 0xC000, $s = 3$, and $f = 51 - 48 = 3$. The number of prefixes is 8 ($n = 2^3$). The increment is 1024 ($i = 2^{16-(f+s)}$). The new prefix length is 54 ($l = 48 + 3 + 3$). The decimal representation of the starting subnet ID is 49152 ($D = $ 0xC000 = 49152).

Next, we construct a table with eight entries. The entry for the address prefix 1 is 49152 and 2001:DB8:0:C000::/54. Additional entries in the table are successive increments of i in the subnet ID portion of the address prefix, as shown in Table 3-5.

Table 3-5 The Decimal Subnetting Technique for Address Prefix 2001:DB8:0:C000::/51

Address Prefix Number	Decimal Representation of Subnet ID	Subnetted Address Prefix
1	49152	2001:DB8:0:C000::/54
2	50176	2001:DB8:0:C400::/54
3	51200	2001:DB8:0:C800::/54
4	52224	2001:DB8:0:CC00::/54
5	53248	2001:DB8:0:D000::/54
6	54272	2001:DB8:0:D400::/54
7	55296	2001:DB8:0:D800::/54
8	56320	2001:DB8:0:DC00::/54

IPv6 Interface Identifiers

The last 64 bits of a currently defined IPv6 unicast address are for the interface identifier, which is unique for a 64-bit subnet prefix of a unicast IPv6 address. In IPv4, the host or node ID portion of an IPv4 address is a logical identifier of an interface on an IPv4 subnet. IPv4 host IDs are of variable length, depending on the subnetting scheme and how many interfaces you want to allow on a given subnet. For example, with an 8-bit host ID, there were $2^8 - 2$ or 254 possible host IDs. (The all-zeros and all-ones combinations are reserved.)

In IPv6, the interface ID is of fixed length. This length was not fixed at 64 bits to allow up to 2^{64} possible hosts on the same subnet. Rather, the IPv6 interface ID is 64 bits long to accommodate the mapping of current 48-bit MAC addresses used by many local area network (LAN) technologies such as Ethernet and the mapping of 64-bit MAC addresses of IEEE 1394 (also known as FireWire) and future LAN technologies.

The ways in which an interface identifier for a LAN interface is determined are the following:

- As defined in RFC 4291, it can be derived from the Extended Unique Identifier (EUI)-64 address. The 64-bit EUI-64 address is defined by the Institute of Electrical and Electronics Engineers (IEEE). EUI-64 addresses are either assigned to a network adapter or derived from IEEE 802 addresses. This is the default behavior for IPv6 in Windows XP and Windows Server 2003.

- As defined in RFC 4941, it might have a temporarily assigned, randomly generated interface identifier to provide a level of anonymity. For more information, see the "Temporary Address Interface Identifiers" section in this chapter.

- It is assigned during stateful address autoconfiguration—for example, via Dynamic Host Configuration Protocol for IPv6 (DHCPv6).

- As defined in RFC 5072, an interface identifier can be based on link-layer addresses or serial numbers, or it can be randomly generated when configuring a Point-to-Point Protocol (PPP) interface and an EUI-64 address is not available.

- It is assigned during manual address configuration.
- It is a permanent interface identifier that is randomly generated to mitigate address scans of unicast IPv6 addresses on a subnet. This is the default behavior for LAN interfaces for IPv6 in Windows Vista and Windows Server 2008. You can disable this behavior with the **netsh interface ipv6 set global randomizeidentifiers=disabled** command. When this behavior is disabled, IPv6 for Windows Vista and Windows Server 2008 will use EUI-64–based interface identifiers.

EUI-64 Address-Based Interface Identifiers

One way to derive an IPv6 interface identifier is through the EUI-64 address, a new type of MAC address for network adapters. To gain an understanding of EUI-64 addresses, it is useful to review the current MAC address format known as *IEEE 802 addresses*.

IEEE 802 Addresses

Network adapters for common LAN technologies such as Ethernet and IEEE 802.11 use a 48-bit address called an IEEE 802 address. It consists of a 24-bit company ID (also called the *manufacturer ID*) and a 24-bit extension ID (also called the *board ID*). The combination of the company ID, which is uniquely assigned to each manufacturer of network adapters, and the extension ID, which is uniquely assigned to each network adapter at the time of manufacture, produces a globally unique 48-bit address. This 48-bit address is also called the physical, hardware, or MAC address.

Figure 3-11 shows the structure of the 48-bit IEEE 802 address for Ethernet.

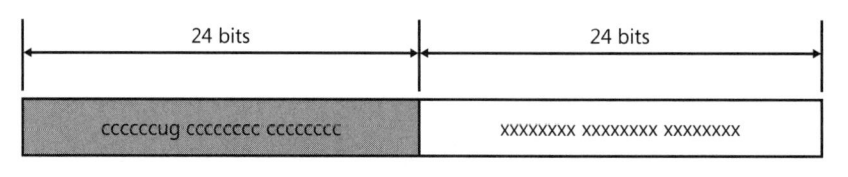

Figure 3-11   The structure of the 48-bit IEEE 802 address for Ethernet

Defined bits within the IEEE 802 address for Ethernet are as follows:

- **Universal/Local (U/L)**   The seventh bit in the first byte is used to indicate whether the address is universally or locally administered. If the U/L bit is set to 0, the IEEE (through the designation of a unique company ID) has administered the address. If the U/L bit is set to 1, the address is locally administered. In this case, the network administrator has overridden the manufactured address and specified a different address. The U/L bit is designated by the **u** in Figure 3-11.
- **Individual/Group (I/G)**   The eighth (low-order) bit of the first byte is used to indicate whether the address is an individual address (unicast) or a group address (multicast).

When set to 0, the address is a unicast address. When set to 1, the address is a multicast address. The I/G bit is designated by the **g** in Figure 3-11.

For a typical IEEE 802 address assigned to a network adapter, both the U/L and I/G bits are set to 0, corresponding to a universally administered, unicast MAC address.

IEEE EUI-64 Addresses

The IEEE EUI-64 address represents a new standard for network interface addressing. The company ID is still 24-bits long, but the extension ID is 40 bits, creating a much larger address space for a network adapter manufacturer. The EUI-64 address uses the U/L and I/G bits in the same way as the IEEE 802 address.

Figure 3-12 shows the structure of the EUI-64 address.

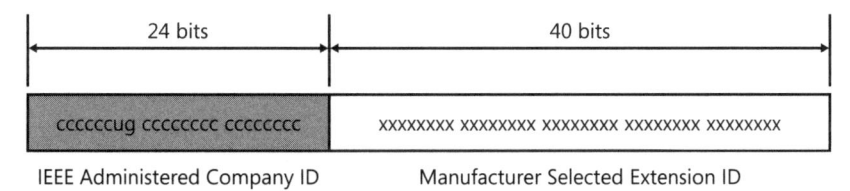

Figure 3-12 The structure of the EUI-64 address

Mapping IEEE 802 Addresses to EUI-64 Addresses   To create an EUI-64 address from an IEEE 802 address, the 16 bits of 11111111 11111110 (0xFFFE) are inserted into the IEEE 802 address between the company ID and the extension ID, as shown in Figure 3-13.

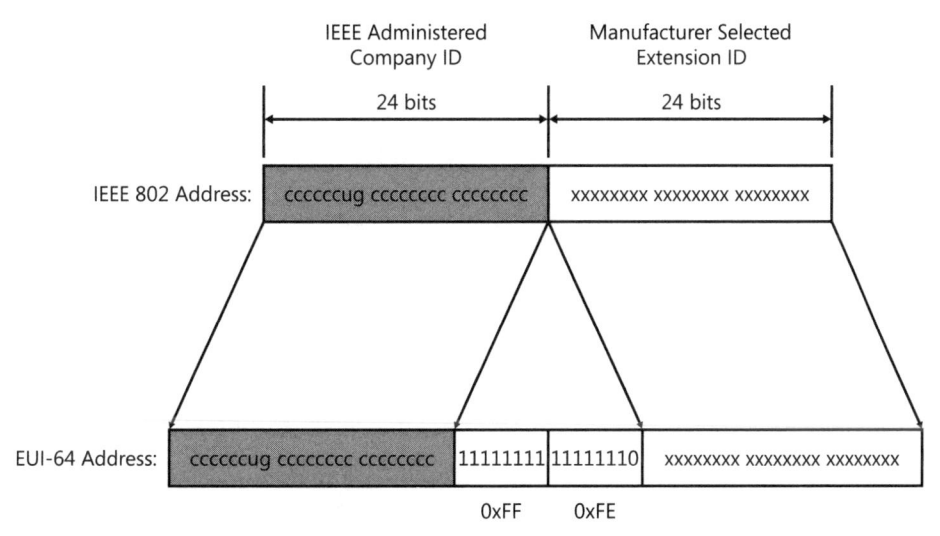

Figure 3-13 The mapping of IEEE 802 addresses to EUI-64 addresses

Obtaining Interface Identifiers for IPv6 Addresses

To obtain the 64-bit interface identifier for IPv6 unicast addresses, the U/L bit in the EUI-64 address is complemented. (If it is a 1 in the EUI-64 address, it is set to 0; and if it is a 0 in the EUI-64 address, it is set to 1.)

The main reason for complementing the U/L bit is to provide greater compressibility of locally administered EUI-64 addresses. It is common practice when assigning locally administered addresses to number them in a simple way. For example, on a point-to-point link, you can assign to one interface on the link the locally administered EUI-64 address of 02-00-00-00-00-00-00-01 and to the other interface the locally administered EUI-64 address of 02-00-00-00-00-00-00-02. If the U/L bit is not complemented, the corresponding link-local addresses for these two interfaces become FE80::200:0:0:1 and FE80::200:0:0:2. By complementing the U/L bit, the corresponding link-local addresses for these two interfaces become FE80::1 and FE80::2.

Figure 3-14 shows the conversion of an EUI-64 address to an IPv6 interface identifier.

EUI Address

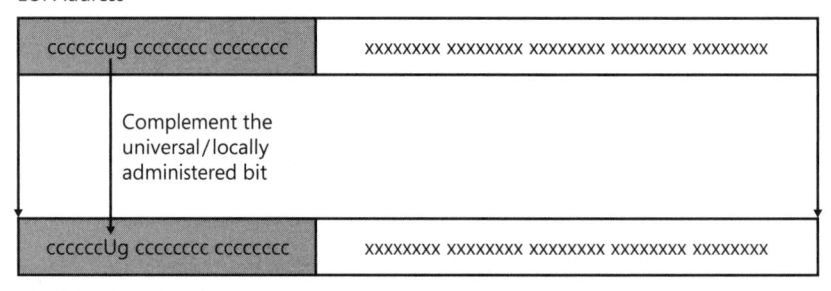

| ccccccug cccccccc cccccccc | xxxxxxxx xxxxxxxx xxxxxxxx xxxxxxxx xxxxxxxx |

Complement the universal/locally administered bit

| ccccccUg cccccccc cccccccc | xxxxxxxx xxxxxxxx xxxxxxxx xxxxxxxx xxxxxxxx |

IPv6 Interface Identifier

Figure 3-14 The conversion of an EUI-64 address to an IPv6 interface identifier

Note Because the U/L bit is complemented when converting an EUI-64 address to an IPv6 interface identifier, the resulting bit in the IPv6 interface identifier has the opposite interpretation of the IEEE-defined U/L bit. If the seventh bit of the IPv6 interface identifier is set to 0, it is locally administered. If the seventh bit of the IPv6 interface identifier is set to 1, it is universally administered.

Converting IEEE 802 Addresses to IPv6 Interface Identifiers To obtain an IPv6 interface identifier from an IEEE 802 address, you must first map the IEEE 802 address to an EUI-64 address, and then complement the U/L bit. Figure 3-15 shows this conversion process for a universally administered, unicast IEEE 802 address.

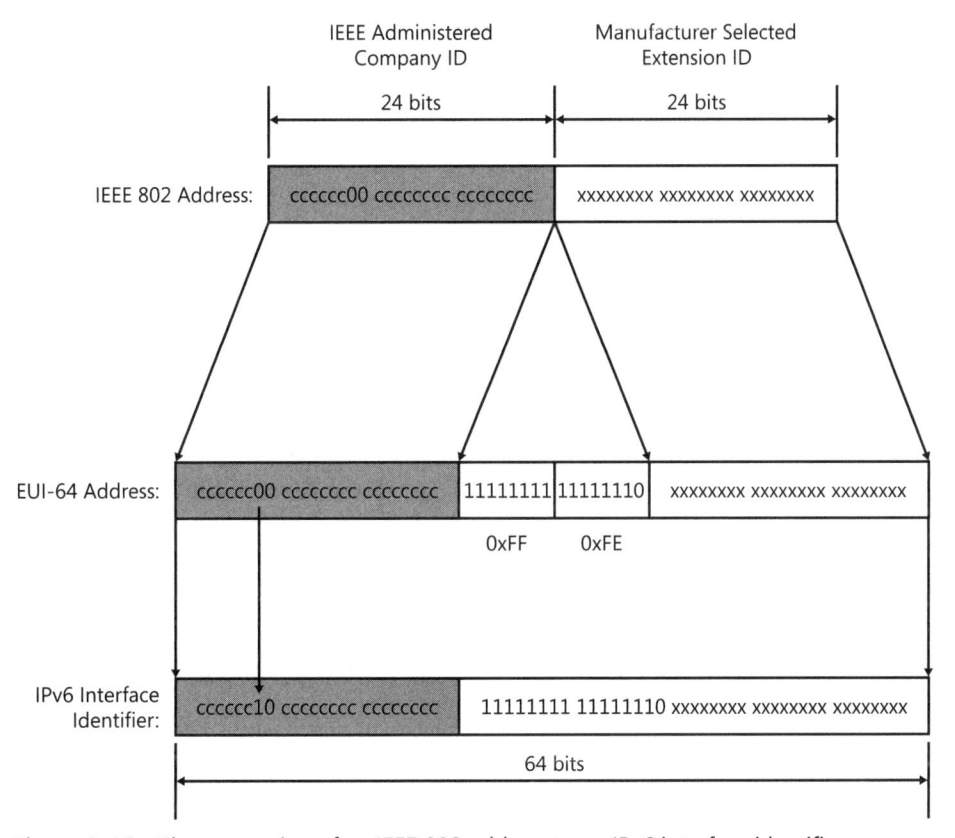

Figure 3-15 The conversion of an IEEE 802 address to an IPv6 interface identifier

IEEE 802 Address Conversion Example Host A has the Ethernet MAC address of 00-AA-00-3F-2A-1C. First, it is converted to EUI-64 format by inserting FF-FE between the third and fourth bytes, yielding 00-AA-00-FF-FE-3F-2A-1C. Then, the U/L bit, which is the seventh bit in the first byte, is complemented. The first byte in binary form is 00000000. When the seventh bit is complemented, it becomes 00000010 (0x02). The final result is 02-AA-00-FF-FE-3F-2A-1C which, when converted to colon hexadecimal notation, becomes the interface identifier 2AA:FF:FE3F:2A1C. As a result, the link-local address that corresponds to the network adapter with the MAC address of 00-AA-00-3F-2A-1C is FE80::2AA:FF:FE3F:2A1C.

> **Note** When complementing the U/L bit, add 0x2 to the first byte if the EUI-64 address is universally administered, and subtract 0x2 from the first byte if the EUI-64 address is locally administered.

Temporary Address Interface Identifiers

In today's IPv4-based Internet, a typical Internet user dials an ISP and obtains an IPv4 address using PPP and the Internet Protocol Control Protocol (IPCP). Each time the user dials, a different IPv4 address might be obtained. Therefore, it is not easy to track a dial-up user's traffic on the Internet based on the user's IPv4 address.

For IPv6-based dial-up connections, the user is assigned a 64-bit prefix, at the time of connection, by using router discovery, which consists of an exchange of Router Solicitation and Router Advertisement messages. If the interface identifier is always based on the EUI-64 address (as derived from the static IEEE 802 address), it is possible to identify the traffic of a specific node regardless of the prefix assigned at the time of connection. The use of the same 64-bit interface identifier allows identification of a user's traffic whether the user is accessing the Internet from home or from work. This makes it easy for Internet merchants and malicious users to track a specific user and his or her use of the Internet.

To address this concern and provide the same level of anonymity as that provided with IPv4, RFC 4941 describes an alternative derivation of the IPv6 interface identifier that is randomly generated and changes over time.

The initial interface identifier is generated using random number techniques. For IPv6 systems that do not have the ability to store any history information for generating future values of the interface identifier, a new random interface identifier is generated each time the IPv6 protocol is initialized. For IPv6 systems that do have storage capabilities, a history value is stored and when the IPv6 protocol is initialized, a new interface identifier is created through the following process:

1. Retrieve the history value from storage, and append the interface identifier based on the EUI-64 address of the adapter.
2. Compute the Message Digest-5 (MD5) hash over the quantity in step 1. The MD5 hash computation will produce a 128-bit value.
3. Store the low-order 64 bits of the MD5 hash computed in step 2 as the history value for the next computation of the interface identifier.
4. Take the high-order 64 bits of the MD5 hash computed in step 2 and set the seventh bit to zero. The seventh bit corresponds to the U/L bit, which, when set to 0, indicates a locally administered interface identifier. The result is the interface identifier.

The resulting IPv6 address, based on this random interface identifier, is known as a *temporary address*. Temporary addresses are generated for public address prefixes that use stateless address autoconfiguration. Temporary addresses are used for the lower of the following values of the valid and preferred lifetimes:

- The lifetimes included in the Prefix Information option in the received Router Advertisement message.
- Local default values of 1 week for valid lifetime and 1 day for preferred lifetime.

After the temporary address valid lifetime expires, a new interface identifier and temporary address is generated. For more information about router discovery, see Chapter 6, "Neighbor Discovery." For more information about stateless address autoconfiguration and valid and preferred lifetimes, see Chapter 8.

IPv4 Addresses and IPv6 Equivalents

To summarize the relationships between IPv4 addressing and IPv6 addressing, Table 3-6 lists both IPv4 addresses and addressing concepts and their IPv6 equivalents.

Table 3-6   IPv4 Addressing Concepts and Their IPv6 Equivalents

IPv4 Address	IPv6 Address
Internet address classes	Not applicable in IPv6
Multicast addresses (224.0.0.0/4)	IPv6 multicast addresses (FF00::/8)
Broadcast addresses	Not applicable in IPv6
Unspecified address is 0.0.0.0	Unspecified address is ::
Loopback address is 127.0.0.1	Loopback address is ::1
Public IP addresses	Global unicast addresses
Private IP addresses (10.0.0.0/8, 172.16.0.0/12, and 192.168.0.0/16)	Unique local (FD00::/8) or site-local addresses (FEC0::/10) (deprecated)
APIPA addresses (169.254.0.0/16)	Link-local addresses (FE80::/64)
Text representation: Dotted-decimal notation	Text representation: Colon hexadecimal format with suppression of leading zeros and zero compression.
Prefix representation: Subnet mask in dotted-decimal notation or prefix length notation	Prefix representation: Prefix length notation only

References

The following references were cited in this chapter:

- RFC 3306 – "Unicast-Prefix-based IPv6 Multicast Addresses"
- RFC 3587 – "IPv6 Global Unicast Address Format"
- RFC 3879 – "Deprecating Site Local Addresses"
- RFC 3927 – "Dynamic Configuration of IPv4 Link-Local Addresses"
- RFC 3956 – "Embedding the Rendezvous Point (RP) Address in an IPv6 Multicast Address"
- RFC 4007 – "IPv6 Scoped Address Architecture"
- RFC 4193 – "Unique Local IPv6 Unicast Addresses"

- RFC 4291 – "IP Version 6 Addressing Architecture"
- RFC 4941 – "Privacy Extensions for Stateless Address Autoconfiguration in IPv6"
- RFC 5072 – "IP Version 6 over PPP"

You can obtain these RFCs from the \RFCs_and_Drafts folder on the companion CD-ROM or from *http://www.ietf.org/rfc.html*.

Testing for Understanding

To test your understanding of IPv6 addressing, answer the following questions. See Appendix D, "Testing for Understanding Answers," to check your answers.

1. Why is the IPv6 address length 128 bits?
2. Express FEC0:0000:0000:0001:02AA:0000:0000:007A more efficiently.
3. How many blocks and bits are expressed by "::" in the addresses 2001:DB8::2AA:9FF:FE56:24DC and FF02::2?
4. Describe the difference between unicast, multicast, and anycast addresses in terms of a host sending packets to zero or more interfaces.
5. Why are no broadcast addresses defined for IPv6?
6. Define the structure, including field sizes, of the global unicast address.
7. Define the scope for each of the different types of unicast addresses.
8. Explain how global and unique local addressing can share the same subnetting infrastructure within an organization.
9. Define the structure, including field sizes, of the multicast address.
10. Explain how the solicited-node multicast address acts as a pseudo-unicast address.
11. How do routers know the nearest location of an anycast group member?
12. Perform a 4-bit subnetting on the unique local prefix FD1A:39C1:4BC2:3D80::/57.
13. What is the EUI-64–based IPv6 interface identifier for the universally administered, unicast IEEE 802 address of 0C-1C-09-A8-F9-CE? What is the corresponding link-local address? What is the corresponding solicited-node multicast address?
14. What is the IPv6 interface identifier for the locally administered, unicast EUI-64 address of 02-00-00-00-00-00-00-09? What is the corresponding link-local address?
15. For each type of address shown in the following table, identify how the address begins in colon hexadecimal notation.

Type of Address	Begins with...
Link-local unicast address	FE80
Site-local unicast address	
Unique local unicast address	
Global address (as defined by RFC 3587)	
Multicast address	
Link-local scope multicast address	
Site-local scope multicast address	
Solicited-node multicast address	
IPv4-mapped address	
6to4 address	
Teredo address	

Chapter 4
The IPv6 Header

At the end of this chapter, you should be able to do the following:

- Describe the structure of an IPv6 packet.
- List and describe the fields in the IPv4 header.
- List and describe the fields in the IPv6 header.
- Compare and contrast the fields in the IPv4 header with the fields in the IPv6 header.
- List and describe each IPv6 extension header.
- Describe the IPv6 maximum transmission unit (MTU).
- Describe the new pseudo-header used for upper-layer checksums.

Structure of an IPv6 Packet

An Internet Protocol version 6 (IPv6) packet consists of an IPv6 header, extension headers, and an upper-layer protocol data unit. Figure 4-1 shows the structure of an IPv6 packet.

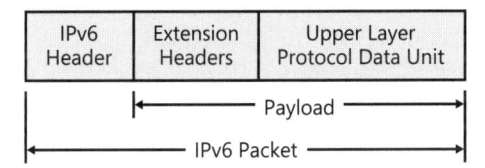

Figure 4-1 The structure of an IPv6 packet

The components of an IPv6 packet are the following:

- **IPv6 Header**   The IPv6 header is always present and is a fixed size of 40 bytes. The fields in the IPv6 header are described in the "IPv6 Header" section in this chapter.

- **Extension Headers**   Zero or more extension headers can be present and are of varying lengths. If extension headers are present, a Next Header field in the IPv6 header indicates the first extension header. Within each extension header is another Next Header field, indicating the next extension header. The last extension header indicates the header for the upper-layer protocol—such as Transmission Control Protocol (TCP), User Datagram Protocol (UDP), or Internet Control Message Protocol for version 6 (ICMPv6)—contained within the upper-layer protocol data unit.

  The IPv6 header and extension headers replace the existing IPv4 header and its options. The new extension header format allows IPv6 to be enhanced to support future needs and capabilities. Unlike options in the IPv4 header, IPv6 extension headers have no maximum size and can expand to accommodate all the extension data needed for IPv6 communication. IPv6 extension headers are described in the "IPv6 Extension Headers" section in this chapter.

- **Upper-Layer Protocol Data Unit**   The upper-layer protocol data unit (PDU) typically consists of an upper-layer protocol header and its payload (for example, an ICMPv6 message, a TCP segment, or a UDP message).

The IPv6 packet payload is the combination of the IPv6 extension headers and the upper-layer PDU. Normally, it can be up to 65,535 bytes long. IPv6 packets with payloads larger than 65,535 bytes in length, known as *jumbograms*, can also be sent.

IPv4 Header

Before examining the IPv6 header, you might find it helpful, for contrasting purposes, to review the IPv4 header shown in Figure 4-2.

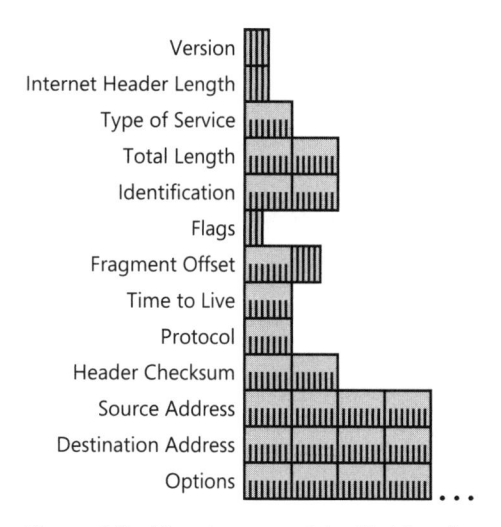

Figure 4-2   The structure of the IPv4 header

Following is a list of the fields in the IPv4 header:

- **Version**   The Version field indicates the version of IP and is set to 4. The size of this field is 4 bits.

- **Internet Header Length**   The Internet Header Length (IHL) field indicates the number of 4-byte blocks in the IPv4 header. The size of this field is 4 bits. Because an IPv4 header is a minimum of 20 bytes in size, the smallest value of the IHL field is 5. IPv4 options can extend the minimum IPv4 header size in increments of 4 bytes. If an IPv4 option is not an integral multiple of 4 bytes in length, the remaining bytes are padded with padding options, making the entire IPv4 header an integral multiple of 4 bytes. With a maximum IHL value of 0xF, the maximum size of the IPv4 header, including options, is 60 bytes (15 × 4).

- **Type of Service** The Type of Service field indicates the desired service expected by this packet for delivery through routers across the IPv4 internetwork. The size of this field is 8 bits, including bits originally defined in RFC 791 for precedence, delay, throughput, reliability, and cost characteristics. RFC 2474 provides the modern definition as the Differentiated Services (DS) field. The high-order 6 bits of the DS field comprise the DS Code Point (DSCP) field. The DSCP field allows devices in a network to mark, unmark, and classify packets for forwarding. This is usually done based on the needs of an application. For example, Voice over IP and other real-time packets take precedence over e-mail in congested areas of the network. This is commonly referred to as Quality of Service (QoS). The low-order 2 bits of the Type of Service field are used for Explicit Congestion Notification (ECN), as defined in RFC 3168.

- **Total Length** The Total Length field indicates the total length of the IPv4 packet (IPv4 header + IPv4 payload) and does not include link-layer framing. The size of this field is 16 bits, which can indicate an IPv4 packet that is up to 65,535 bytes long.

- **Identification** The Identification field identifies this specific IPv4 packet. The size of this field is 16 bits. The Identification field is selected by the source node of the IPv4 packet. If the IPv4 packet is fragmented, all the fragments retain the Identification field value so that the destination node can group the fragments for reassembly.

- **Flags** The Flags field identifies flags for the fragmentation process. The size of this field is 3 bits; however, only 2 bits are defined for current use. There are two flags—one to indicate whether the IPv4 packet can be fragmented and another to indicate whether more fragments follow the current fragment.

- **Fragment Offset** The Fragment Offset field indicates the position of the fragment relative to the beginning of the original IPv4 payload. The size of this field is 13 bits.

- **Time-to-Live** The Time-to-Live (TTL) field indicates the maximum number of links on which an IPv4 packet can travel before being discarded. The size of this field is 8 bits. The TTL field was originally defined as a time count for the number of seconds the packet could exist on the network. An IPv4 router determined the length of time required (in seconds) to forward the IPv4 packet and decremented the TTL accordingly. Modern routers almost always forward an IPv4 packet in less than a second, and they are required by RFC 791 to decrement the TTL by at least one. Therefore, the TTL becomes a maximum link count with the value set by the sending node. When the TTL equals 0, an ICMPv4 Time Exceeded-Time to Live Exceeded in Transit message is sent to the source of the packet and the packet is discarded.

- **Protocol** The Protocol field identifies the upper-layer protocol. The size of this field is 8 bits. For example, a value of 6 in this field identifies TCP as the upper-layer protocol, a decimal value of 17 identifies UDP, and a value of 1 identifies ICMPv4. The Protocol field is used to identify the upper-layer protocol that is to receive the IPv4 packet payload.

- **Header Checksum**   The Header Checksum field provides a checksum on the IPv4 header only. The size of this field is 16 bits. The IPv4 payload is not included in the checksum calculation, as the IPv4 payload usually contains its own checksum. Each IPv4 node that receives IPv4 packets verifies the IPv4 header checksum and silently discards the IPv4 packet if checksum verification fails. When a router forwards an IPv4 packet, it must decrement the TTL. Therefore, the Header Checksum value is recomputed at each hop between source and destination.
- **Source Address**   The Source Address field stores the IPv4 address of the originating host. The size of this field is 32 bits.
- **Destination Address**   The Destination Address field stores the IPv4 address of an intermediate destination (in the case of source routing) or the destination host. The size of this field is 32 bits.
- **Options**   The Options field stores one or more IPv4 options. The size of this field is a multiple of 32 bits (4 bytes). If an IPv4 option does not use all 32 bits, padding options must be added so that the IPv4 header is an integral number of 4-byte blocks that can be indicated by the IHL field.

IPv6 Header

The IPv6 header is a streamlined version of the IPv4 header. It eliminates fields that are either unneeded or rarely used, and it adds a field that provides better support for real-time traffic. Figure 4-3 shows the structure of the IPv6 header as described in RFC 2460.

Figure 4-3   The structure of the IPv6 header

The following list describes the fields in the IPv6 header:

- **Version**   The Version field indicates the version of IP and is set to 6. The size of this field is 4 bits. While the purpose of the Version field is defined in the same way for both IPv4 and IPv6, its value is not used to pass the packet to an IPv4 or IPv6 protocol layer. This identification is done through a protocol identification field in the link-layer header. For example, a common link-layer encapsulation for Ethernet, called Ethernet II, uses a

16-bit EtherType field to identify the Ethernet frame payload. For IPv4 packets, the EtherType field is set to 0x800. For IPv6 packets, the EtherType field is set to 0x86DD. Thus, the determination of the protocol of the Ethernet payload occurs before the packet is passed to the appropriate protocol layer.

- **Traffic Class**   The Traffic Class field indicates the IPv6 packet's class or priority. The size of this field is 8 bits. This field provides functionality similar to the IPv4 Type of Service field. Like the Type of Service field in the IPv4 header, the first 6 bits of the Traffic Class field are the DSCP field as defined in RFC 2474 and the last 2 bits are used for ECN as defined in RFC 3168.

- **Flow Label**   The Flow Label field indicates that this packet belongs to a specific sequence of packets between a source and destination, requiring special handling by intermediate IPv6 routers. The size of this field is 20 bits. The flow label is used for prioritized delivery, such as delivery needed by real-time data (voice and video). For default router handling, the Flow Label field is set to 0. To distinguish a given flow, an intermediate router can use the packet's source address, destination address, and flow label. Therefore, there can be multiple flows between a source and destination, as distinguished by separate non-zero flow labels. The details of the use of the Flow Label field are described in RFC 3697.

- **Payload Length**   The Payload Length field indicates the length of the IPv6 payload. The size of this field is 16 bits. The Payload Length field includes the extension headers and the upper-layer PDU. With 16 bits, an IPv6 payload of up to 65,535 bytes can be indicated. For payload lengths greater than 65,535 bytes, the Payload Length field is set to 0 and the Jumbo Payload option is used in the Hop-by-Hop Options extension header, which is described in the "Hop-by-Hop Options Header" section in this chapter.

- **Next Header**   The Next Header field indicates either the type of the first extension header (if present) or the protocol in the upper-layer PDU (such as TCP, UDP, or ICMPv6). The size of this field is 8 bits. When indicating an upper-layer protocol, the Next Header field uses the same values that are used in the IPv4 Protocol field.

- **Hop Limit**   The Hop Limit field indicates the maximum number of links over which the IPv6 packet can travel before being discarded. The size of this field is 8 bits. The Hop Limit field is similar to the IPv4 TTL field, except that there is no historical relation to the amount of time (in seconds) that the packet is queued at the router. When Hop Limit equals 0 at a router, the router sends an ICMPv6 Time Exceeded-Hop Limit Exceeded in Transit message to the source and discards the packet.

- **Source Address**   The Source Address field indicates the IPv6 address of the originating host. The size of this field is 128 bits.

- **Destination Address**   The Destination Address field indicates the IPv6 address of the current destination node. The size of this field is 128 bits. In most cases, the Destination Address field is set to the final destination address. However, if a Routing extension header is present, the Destination Address field might be set to the address of the next intermediate destination.

Network Monitor Capture

Here is an example of an IPv6 header, as displayed by Network Monitor 3.1 (capture 04_01 in the \NetworkMonitorCaptures folder on the companion CD-ROM):

```
Frame:
+ Ethernet: Etype = IPv6
- Ipv6: Next Protocol = ICMPv6, Payload Length = 40
  - Versions: IPv6, Internet Protocol, DSCP 0
    Version:    (0110..........................) IPv6, Internet Protocol, 6(0x6)
    DSCP:       (....000000....................) Differentiated services codepoint 0
    ECT:        (..........0...................) ECN-Capable Transport not set
    CE:         (...........0..................) ECN-CE not set
    FlowLabel: (............00000000000000000000) 0
    PayloadLength: 40 (0x28)
    NextProtocol: ICMPv6, 58(0x3a)
    HopLimit: 128 (0x80)
    SourceAddress: FE80:0:0:0:260:97FF:FE02:6E8F
    DestinationAddress: FE80:0:0:0:260:97FF:FE02:6D3D
+ Icmpv6: Echo request, ID = 0x0, Seq = 0x18
```

This ICMPv6 Echo Request packet uses the default Traffic Class and Flow Label and a Hop Limit of 128, and it is sent between two hosts using link-local addresses.

Values of the Next Header Field

Table 4-1 lists typical values of the Next Header field for an IPv6 header or an IPv6 extension header. Each of the IPv6 extension headers is covered later in the chapter.

Table 4-1 Typical Values of the Next Header Field

Value (Decimal)	Header
0	Hop-by-Hop Options header
6	TCP
17	UDP
41	Encapsulated IPv6 header
43	Routing header
44	Fragment header
50	Encapsulating Security Payload header
51	Authentication header
58	ICMPv6
59	No next header
60	Destination Options header

For the most current list of the reserved values for the IPv4 Protocol and IPv6 Next Header fields, see *http://www.iana.org/assignments/protocol-numbers*.

In looking at the value of the Next Header field to indicate no next header, it would seem to make more sense to set its value to 0, rather than 59. However, the designers of IPv6 wanted to optimize the processing of IPv6 packets at intermediate routers. The only extension header that must be processed at every intermediate router is the Hop-by-Hop Options header. To optimize the test of whether the Hop-by-Hop Options header is present, its Next Header value is set to 0. In router hardware, it is easier to test for a value of 0 than to test for a value of 59.

Comparing the IPv4 and IPv6 Headers

In comparing the IPv4 and IPv6 headers, you can see the following:

- The number of fields has dropped from 12 (including options) in the IPv4 header to 8 in the IPv6 header.

- The number of fields that must be processed by an intermediate router has dropped from 6 to 4, making the forwarding of normal IPv6 packets more efficient.

- Seldom-used fields such as fields supporting fragmentation and options in the IPv4 header have been moved to extension headers in the IPv6 header.

- The size of the IPv6 header has doubled from 20 bytes for a minimum-sized IPv4 header to 40 bytes. However, the new IPv6 header contains source and destination addresses that are four times longer than IPv4 source and destination addresses.

Table 4-2 lists the individual differences between the IPv4 and IPv6 header fields.

Table 4-2   IPv4 Header Fields and Corresponding IPv6 Equivalents

IPv4 Header Field	IPv6 Header Field
Version	Same field but with a different version number.
Internet Header Length	Removed in IPv6. IPv6 does not include a Header Length field because the IPv6 header is always a fixed length of 40 bytes. Each extension header is either a fixed length or indicates its own length.
Type of Service	Replaced by the IPv6 Traffic Class field.
Total Length	Replaced by the IPv6 Payload Length field, which indicates only the size of the payload.
Identification Flags Fragment Offset	Removed in IPv6. Fragmentation information is not included in the IPv6 header. It is contained in a Fragment extension header.
Time-to-Live	Replaced by the IPv6 Hop Limit field.
Protocol	Replaced by the IPv6 Next Header field.
Header Checksum	Removed in IPv6. The link layer has a checksum that performs bit-level error detection for the entire IPv6 packet.
Source Address	The field is the same except that IPv6 addresses are 128 bits in length.
Destination Address	The field is the same except that IPv6 addresses are 128 bits in length.
Options	Removed in IPv6. IPv6 extension headers replace IPv4 options.

The one new field in the IPv6 header that is not included in the IPv4 header is the Flow Label field.

The result of the new IPv6 header is a reduction in the critical router loop, the set of instructions that must be executed to determine how to forward a packet. To forward a normal IPv4 packet, a router typically performs the following in its critical router loop:

1. Verify the Header Checksum field by performing its own checksum calculation and comparing its result with the result stored in the IPv4 header. Although this step is required by RFC 1812, modern high-speed routers commonly skip it.

2. Verify the value of the Version field. Although this step is not required by RFC 791 or 1812, performing this step saves network bandwidth, as a packet containing an invalid version number is not propagated across the IPv4 internetwork only to be discarded by the destination node.

3. Decrement the value of the TTL field. If its new value is less than 1, send an ICMPv4 Time Exceeded-Time to Live Exceeded in Transit message to the source of the packet and then discard the packet. If not, place the new value in the TTL field.

4. Check for the presence of IPv4 header options. If present, process them.

5. Use the value of the Destination Address field and the contents of the local routing table to determine a forwarding interface and a next-hop IPv4 address. If a route is not found, send an ICMPv4 Destination Unreachable-Host Unreachable message to the source of the packet and discard the packet.

6. If the IPv4 MTU of the forwarding interface is less than the value of the Total Length field and the Don't Fragment (DF) flag is set to 0, perform IPv4 fragmentation. If the MTU of the forwarding interface is less than the value of the Total Length field and the DF flag is set to 1, send an ICMPv4 Destination Unreachable-Fragmentation Needed and DF Set message to the source of the packet and discard the packet.

7. Recalculate the new header checksum, and place its new value in the Header Checksum field.

8. Forward the packet by using the appropriate forwarding interface.

Note This critical router loop for IPv4 routers is a simplified list of items that an IPv4 router typically performs when forwarding. This list is not meant to imply any specific implementation nor an optimized order in which to process IPv4 packets for forwarding.

To forward a normal IPv6 packet, a router typically performs the following steps in its critical router loop:

1. Verify the value of the Version field. Although this step is not required by RFC 2460, performing it saves network bandwidth, because a packet containing an invalid version number is not propagated across the IPv6 internetwork only to be discarded by the destination node.

2. Decrement the value of the Hop Limit field. If its new value is less than 1, send an ICMPv6 Time Exceeded-Hop Limit Exceeded in Transit message to the source of the packet and discard the packet. If not, place the new value in the Hop Limit field.

3. Check the Next Header field for a value of 0. If it is 0, process the Hop-by-Hop Options header.

4. Use the value of the Destination Address field and the contents of the local routing table to determine a forwarding interface and a next-hop IPv6 address. If a route is not found, send an ICMPv6 Destination Unreachable-No Route To Destination message to the source of the packet and then discard the packet.

5. If the link MTU of the forwarding interface is less than 40 plus the value of the Payload Length field, send an ICMPv6 Packet Too Big message to the source of the packet and discard the packet.

6. Forward the packet by using the appropriate forwarding interface.

> **Note** This critical router loop for IPv6 routers is a simplified list of items that an IPv6 router typically performs when forwarding. This list is not meant to imply any specific implementation nor an optimized order in which to process packets for forwarding.

As you can see, the process to forward an IPv6 packet is much simpler than for an IPv4 packet, as it does not have to verify and recalculate a header checksum, perform fragmentation, or process options not intended for the router.

IPv6 Extension Headers

The IPv4 header includes all options. Therefore, each intermediate router must check for their existence and process them when present. This can cause performance degradation in the forwarding of IPv4 packets. With IPv6, delivery and forwarding options are moved to extension headers. The only extension header that must be processed at each intermediate router is the Hop-by-Hop Options extension header. This increases IPv6 header processing speed and improves the performance of forwarding IPv6 packets.

RFC 2460 specifies that the following IPv6 extension headers must be supported by all IPv6 nodes:

- Hop-by-Hop Options header
- Destination Options header
- Routing header
- Fragment header
- Authentication header
- Encapsulating Security Payload header

With the exception of the Authentication header and Encapsulating Security Payload header, all the IPv6 extension headers just listed are defined in RFC 2460.

In a typical IPv6 packet, no extension headers are present. If special handling is required by either intermediate routers or the destination, the sending host adds one or more extension headers.

Each extension header must fall on a 64-bit (8-byte) boundary. Extension headers of a fixed size must be an integral multiple of 8 bytes. Extension headers of variable size contain a Header Extension Length field and must use padding as needed to ensure that their size is an integral multiple of 8 bytes.

The Next Header field in the IPv6 header and zero or more extension headers form a chain of pointers. Each pointer indicates the type of header that comes after the immediate header until the upper-layer protocol is ultimately identified. Figure 4-4 shows the chain of pointers formed by the Next Header field for various IPv6 packets.

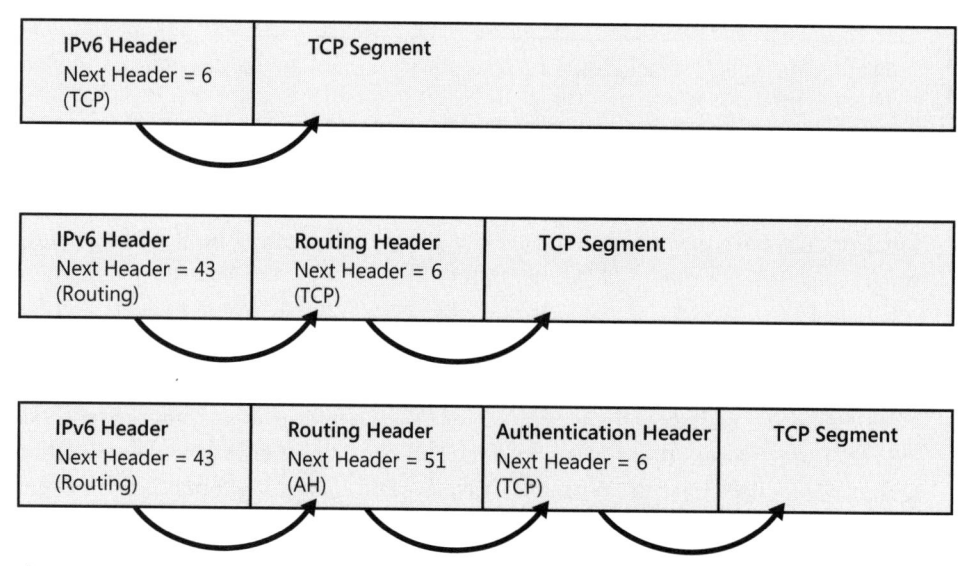

Figure 4-4 The chain of pointers formed by the Next Header field

Extension Headers Order

Extension headers are processed in the order in which they are present. Because the only extension header that is processed by every node on the path is the Hop-by-Hop Options header, it must be first. There are similar rules for other extension headers. In RFC 2460, it is recommended that extension headers be placed after the IPv6 header in the following order:

1. Hop-by-Hop Options header
2. Destination Options header (for intermediate destinations when the Routing header is present)

3. Routing header
4. Fragment header
5. Authentication header
6. Encapsulating Security Payload header
7. Destination Options header (for the final destination)

Hop-by-Hop Options Header

The Hop-by-Hop Options header is used to specify delivery parameters at each hop on the path to the destination. It is identified by the value of 0 in the IPv6 header's Next Header field. Figure 4-5 shows the structure of the Hop-by-Hop Options header.

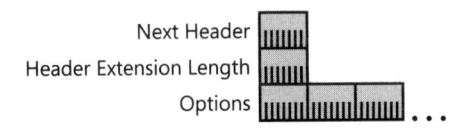

Figure 4-5 The structure of the Hop-by-Hop Options header

The Hop-by-Hop Options header consists of a Next Header field, a Header Extension Length field, and an Options field that contains one or more options. The value of the Header Extension Length field is the number of 8-byte blocks in the Hop-by-Hop Options extension header, not including the first 8 bytes. Therefore, for an 8-byte Hop-by-Hop Options header, the value of the Header Extension Length field is 0. Padding options are used to ensure 8-byte boundaries.

An IPv6 Router Optimization

The interpretation of the Header Extension Length field in the Hop-by-Hop Options header is another example of how the designers of IPv6 wanted to optimize processing of IPv6 packets at intermediate routers. For packets with a Hop-by-Hop Options header, one of the first operations is to determine the size of the header. If the Header Extension Length field were defined to be the number of 8-byte blocks in the header, its minimum value would be 1 (the minimum-sized Hop-by-Hop Options header is 8 bytes long). To ensure robustness in an IPv6 forwarding implementation, a field whose valid values begin at 1 has to be checked for the invalid value of 0 before additional processing can be done.

With the current definition of the Header Extension Length field, 0 is a valid value and no testing of invalid values needs to be done. The number of bytes in the Hop-by-Hop Options header is calculated from the following formula: (header extension length + 1) × 8.

An option is a set of fields that either describes a specific characteristic of the packet delivery or provides padding. Options are sent in the Hop-by-Hop Options header and Destination Options header (described later in this chapter). Each option is encoded in the type-length-value (TLV) format that is commonly used in TCP/IP protocols. Figure 4-6 shows the structure of an option.

```
Option Type   ▯
Option Length ▯
Option Data   ▯▯▯  . . .
```

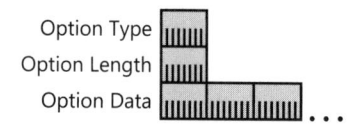

Figure 4-6 The structure of an option

The Option Type field both identifies the option and determines the way it is handled by the processing node. The Option Length field indicates the number of bytes in the option, not including the Option Type and Option Length fields. The option data is the specific data associated with the option.

An option might have an alignment requirement to ensure that specific fields within the option fall on desired boundaries. For example, it is easier to process an IPv6 address if it falls on an 8-byte boundary. Alignment requirements are expressed by using the notation $xn + y$, indicating that the option must begin at a byte boundary equal to an integral multiple of x bytes plus y bytes from the start of the header. For example, the alignment requirement $4n + 2$ indicates that the option must begin at a byte boundary of (an integral multiple of 4 bytes) + 2 bytes. In other words, the option must begin at the byte boundary of 6, 10, 14, and so on, relative to the start of the Hop-by-Hop Options or Destination Options headers. To accommodate alignment requirements, padding typically appears before an option and between each option when multiple options are present.

Option Type Field

Within the Option Type field, the two high-order bits indicate how the option is handled when the node processing the option does not recognize the option type. Table 4-3 lists the defined values of these two bits and their purpose.

Table 4-3 Values of the Two High-Order Bits in the Option Type Field

Value (Binary)	Action Taken
00	Skip the option.
01	Silently discard the packet.
10	Discard the packet, and send an ICMPv6 Parameter Problem message to the sender if the Destination Address field in the IPv6 header is a unicast or multicast address.
11	Discard the packet, and send an ICMPv6 Parameter Problem message to the sender if the Destination Address field in the IPv6 header is not a multicast address.

The third-highest-order bit of the Option Type indicates whether the option data can change (= 1) or not change (= 0) in the path to the destination.

Pad1 Option

The Pad1 option is defined in RFC 2460. It is used to insert a single byte of padding so that the Hop-by-Hop Options or Destination Options headers fall on 8-byte boundaries and to accommodate the alignment requirements of options. The Pad1 option has no alignment requirements. Figure 4-7 shows the Pad1 option.

Option Type = 0

Figure 4-7 The structure of the Pad1 option

The Pad1 option consists of a single byte; Option Type is set to 0, and it has no length or value fields. With Option Type set to 0, the option is skipped if not recognized and it is not allowed to change in transit.

PadN Option

The PadN option is defined in RFC 2460. It is used to insert two or more bytes of padding so that the Hop-by-Hop Options or Destination Options headers fall on 8-byte boundaries and to accommodate the alignment requirements of options. The PadN option has no alignment requirements. Figure 4-8 shows the PadN option.

Option Type = 1
Option Length
Option Data ...

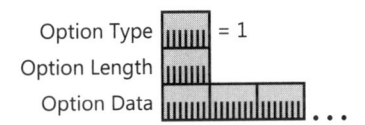

Figure 4-8 The structure of the PadN option

The PadN option consists of the Option Type field (set to 1), the Length field (set to the number of padding bytes present), and 0 or more bytes of padding. With the Option Type field set to 1, the option is skipped if not recognized and it is not allowed to change in transit.

Jumbo Payload Option

The Jumbo Payload option is defined in RFC 2675. It is used to indicate a payload size that is greater than 65,535 bytes. The Jumbo Payload option has the alignment requirement of 4n + 2. Figure 4-9 shows the Jumbo Payload option.

Option Type = 194
Option Length = 4
Jumbo Payload Length

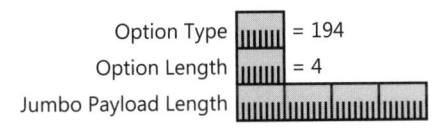

Figure 4-9 The structure of the Jumbo Payload option

With the Jumbo Payload option, the Payload Length field in the IPv6 header no longer indicates the size of the IPv6 packet payload. Instead, the Jumbo Payload Length field in the Jumbo Payload option indicates the size, in bytes, of the IPv6 packet payload. With a 32-bit Jumbo Payload Length field, payload sizes of up to 4,294,967,295 bytes can be indicated. An IPv6 packet with a payload size greater than 65,535 bytes is known as a *jumbogram*. With the Option Type field set to 194 (0xC2 hexadecimal, binary 11000010), the packet is discarded and an ICMPv6 Parameter Problem message is sent if the option is not recognized and the destination address is not a multicast address, and the option is not allowed to change in transit.

The IPv6 protocol in Windows Vista, Windows Server 2008, and Windows XP with Service Pack 2 supports incoming jumbograms at the IPv6 layer. However, there is no support in UDP or TCP for sending or receiving jumbograms.

Router Alert Option

The Router Alert option (Option Type 5) is defined in RFC 2711 and is used to indicate to a router that the contents of the packet require additional processing. The Router Alert option has the alignment requirement of 2n + 0. Figure 4-10 shows the structure of the Router Alert option.

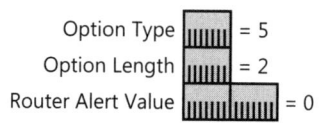

```
Option Type        = 5
Option Length      = 2
Router Alert Value = 0
```

Figure 4-10   The structure of the Router Alert option

The Router Alert option is used for Multicast Listener Discovery (MLD) and the Resource ReSerVation Protocol (RSVP). With the Option Type field set to 5, the option is skipped if not recognized and it is not allowed to change in transit.

Network Monitor Capture

Here is an example of a Hop-by-Hop Options header as displayed by Network Monitor 3.1 (capture 04_02 in the \NetworkMonitorCaptures folder on the companion CD-ROM):

```
Frame:
+ Ethernet: Etype = IPv6
- Ipv6: Next Protocol = ICMPv6, Payload Length = 32
  + Versions: IPv6, Internet Protocol, DSCP 0
    PayloadLength: 32 (0x20)
    NextProtocol: HOPOPT, IPv6 Hop-by-Hop Option, 0(0)
    HopLimit: 1 (0x1)
    SourceAddress: FE80:0:0:0:2B0:D0FF:FEE9:4143
    DestinationAddress: FF02:0:0:0:0:1:FFE9:4143
  - HopbyHopHeader:
    NextHeader: ICMPv6
    ExtHdrLen: 0(8 bytes)
   - OptionRouterAlert:
    - OptionType: Router Alert
       Action:        (00......) Skip over this option
```

```
        C:            (..0.....) Option Data does not change en-route
      OptionType:     (...00101) Router Alert
      OptDataLen: 2 bytes
      Value: Datagram contains a Multicast Listener Discovery message, 0 (0x0)
  - OptionPadN:
   - OptionType: PadN
      Action:       (00......) Skip over this option
      C:            (..0.....) Option Data does not change en-route
      OptionType:   (...00001) PadN
      OptDataLen: 0 bytes
      OptionData: 0 bytes
+ Icmpv6: Multicast Listener Report
```

Notice the use of the Router Alert option (option type 5) and the PadN option (option type 1) to pad the entire Hop-by-Hop Options header to 8 bytes (1-byte Next Header field + 1-byte Option Length field + 4-byte Router Alert option + 2-byte PadN option).

Destination Options Header

The Destination Options header is used to specify packet delivery parameters for either intermediate destinations or the final destination. This header is identified by the value of 60 in the previous header's Next Header field. The Destination Options header has the same structure as the Hop-by-Hop Options header, as shown in Figure 4-11.

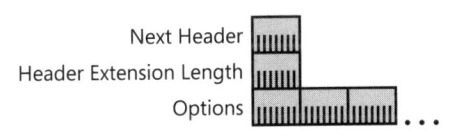

Figure 4-11 The structure of the Destination Options header

The Destination Options header is used in two ways:

1. If a Routing header is present, it specifies delivery or processing options at each intermediate destination. In this case, the Destination Options header occurs before the Routing header.

2. If no Routing header is present, or if this header occurs after the Routing header, this header specifies delivery or processing options at the final destination.

An example of a destination option is the Home Address destination option for Mobile IPv6.

Home Address Option

The Home Address destination option (Option Type 201) is defined in RFC 3775 and is used to indicate the home address of the mobile node. The home address is an address assigned to the mobile node when it is attached to the home link and through which the mobile node is always reachable, regardless of its location on an IPv6 network. For information about when the Home Address option is sent, see Appendix F, "Mobile IPv6." The Home Address option has the alignment requirement of 8n + 6. Figure 4-12 shows the structure of the Home Address option.

```
Option Type    [||||||] = 201
Option Length  [||||||] = 16
Home Address   [||||||||||||||||||||||||||||||||||||||||||||]
               [||||||||||||||||||||||||||||||||||||||||||||]
```

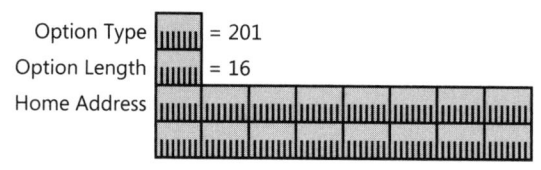

Figure 4-12 The structure of the Home Address option

The following list describes the fields in the Home Address option:

- **Option Type**   With the Option Type field set to 201 (0xC9 hexadecimal, 11001001 binary), the packet is discarded and an ICMPv6 Parameter Problem message is sent if the option is not recognized and the destination address is not a multicast address, and the option is not allowed to change in transit.

- **Option Length**   The Option Length field indicates the length of the option in bytes, not including the Option Type and Option Length fields. Because the only field past the Option Length field is the Home Address field to store an IPv6 address, the Option Length field is set to 16.

- **Home Address**   The Home Address field indicates the home address of the mobile node. The size of this field is 128 bits.

For an example of the Home Address option in the Destination Options header, see the Network Monitor Capture 04_03 in the \NetworkMonitorCaptures folder on the companion CD-ROM.

Summary of Option Types

Table 4-4 lists the different option types for options in Hop-by-Hop Options and Destination Options headers.

Table 4-4 Option Types

Option Type	Option and Where It Is Used	Alignment Requirement
0	Pad1 option: Hop-by-Hop and Destination Options headers	None
1	PadN option: Hop-by-Hop and Destination Options headers	None
194 (0xC2)	Jumbo Payload option: Hop-by-Hop Options header	4n + 2
5	Router Alert option: Hop-by-Hop Options header	2n + 0
201 (0xC9)	Home Address option: Destination Options header	8n + 6

Routing Header

IPv4 defines strict source routing, in which each intermediate destination must be only one hop away, and loose source routing, in which each intermediate destination can be one or more hops away. IPv6 source nodes can use the Routing header to specify a source route, which is a list of intermediate destinations for the packet to travel to on its path to the final destination. The Routing header is identified by the value of 43 in the previous header's Next Header field. Figure 4-13 shows the structure of the Routing header.

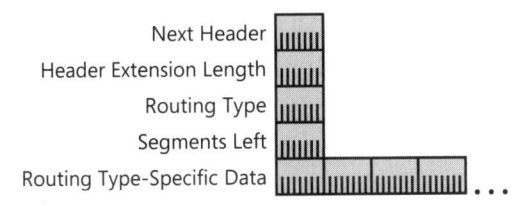

Figure 4-13 The structure of the Routing header

The Routing header consists of a Next Header field, a Header Extension Length field (defined in the same way as the Hop-by-Hop Options extension header), a Routing Type field, a Segments Left field that indicates the number of intermediate destinations that are still to be visited, and routing type-specific data.

RFC 2460 also defines Routing Type 0, used for loose source routing. Figure 4-14 shows the structure of the Routing Type 0 header.

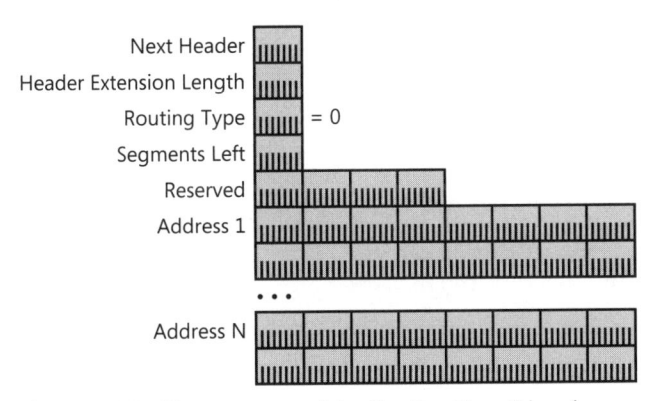

Figure 4-14 The structure of the Routing Type 0 header

For Routing Type 0, the routing type-specific data consists of a 32-bit Reserved field and a list of intermediate destination addresses, including the final destination address. When the packet is initially sent, the destination address is set to the first intermediate destination, and the routing type-specific data is the list of additional intermediate destinations and the final destination. The Segments Left field is set to the total number of addresses included in the routing type-specific data.

When the IPv6 packet reaches an intermediate destination, the Routing header is processed and the following actions are taken:

1. The current destination address and the address in the (N − Segments Left + 1) position in the list of addresses are swapped, where N is the total number of addresses in the Routing header.

2. The Segments Left field is decremented.

3. The packet is forwarded.

By the time the packet arrives at the final destination, the Segments Left field has been set to 0 and the list of intermediate addresses visited in the path to the destination is recorded in the Routing header.

IPv6 in Windows Vista will accept and process an incoming packet with a Routing Type 0 header. Because of security concerns, the Internet Engineering Task Force (IETF) is deprecating support for the Routing Type 0 header. IPv6 in Windows Server 2008 and Windows Vista Service Pack 1 will silently discard an incoming packet with a Routing Type 0 header.

Note Mobile IPv6 uses a Type 2 Routing header. For more information, see Appendix F, "Mobile IPv6."

Network Monitor Capture

Here is an example of the Routing header as displayed by Network Monitor 3.1 (capture 04_04 in the \NetworkMonitorCaptures folder on the companion CD-ROM):

```
  Frame:
+ Ethernet: Etype = IPv6
- Ipv6: Next Protocol = ICMPv6, Payload Length = 64
  + Versions: IPv6, Internet Protocol, DSCP 0
    PayloadLength: 64 (0x40)
    NextProtocol: IPv6 Routing header, 43(0x2b)
    HopLimit: 127 (0x7F)
    SourceAddress: FEC0:0:0:2:2B0:D0FF:FEE9:4143
    DestinationAddress: FEC0:0:0:2:260:97FF:FE02:6E8F
  - RoutingHeader:
    NextHeader: ICMPv6
    ExtHdrLen: 2(24 bytes)
    RoutingType: 0 (0x0)
    SegmentsLeft: 1 (0x1)
    Reserved: 0 (0x0)
    RouteAddress: FEC0:0:0:1:260:8FF:FE52:F9D8
+ Icmpv6: Echo request, ID = 0x0, Seq = 0x3d1a
```

In this simple example of the Routing header, an ICMPv6 Echo Request message is sent from the source FEC0::2:2B0:D0FF:FEE9:4143 to the destination FEC0::1:260:8FF:FE52:F9D8 using the intermediate destination of FEC0::2:260:97FF:FE02:6E8F.

Fragment Header

The Fragment header is used for IPv6 fragmentation and reassembly services. This header is identified by the value of 44 in the previous header's Next Header field. Figure 4-15 shows the structure of the Fragment header.

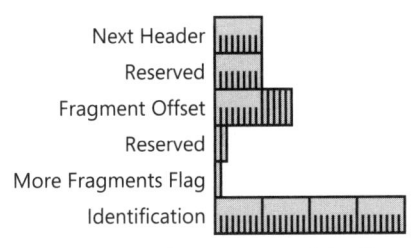

Figure 4-15 The structure of the Fragment header

The Fragment header includes a Next Header field, a 13-bit Fragment Offset field, a More Fragments flag, and a 32-bit Identification field. The Fragment Offset, More Fragments flag, and Identification fields are used in the same way as the corresponding fields in the IPv4 header. Because the use of the Fragment Offset field is defined for 8-byte fragment blocks, the Fragment header cannot be used for jumbograms. The maximum number that can be expressed with the 13-bit Fragment Offset field is 8191. Therefore, Fragment Offset can be used to indicate only a fragment data starting position of up to 8191 × 8, or 65,528.

In IPv6, only source nodes can fragment payloads. If the payload submitted by the upper-layer protocol is larger than the link or path MTU, IPv6 fragments the payload at the source and uses the Fragment header to provide reassembly information. An IPv6 router will never fragment an IPv6 packet being forwarded.

Because the IPv6 internetwork will not transparently fragment payloads, data sent from applications that do not have an awareness of the destination path MTU will not be able to sense when data needing fragmentation by the source is discarded by IPv6 routers. This can be a problem for unicast or multicast traffic sent as a UDP message or other types of message streams that do not use TCP.

> ### Differences in Fragmentation Fields
>
> There are some subtle differences between the fragmentation fields in IPv4 and IPv6. In IPv4, the fragmentation flags are the three high-order bits of the 16-bit quantity composed of the combination of the fragmentation flags and the Fragment Offset field. In IPv6, the bits used for fragmentation flags are the three low-order bits of the 16-bit quantity composed of the combination of the fragmentation flags and the Fragment Offset field. In IPv4, the Identification field is 16 bits rather than 32 bits in IPv6, and in IPv6 there is no Don't Fragment flag. Because IPv6 routers never perform fragmentation, the Don't Fragment flag is always set to 1 for all IPv6 packets and therefore does not need to be included.

IPv6 Fragmentation Process

When an IPv6 packet is fragmented, it is initially divided into unfragmentable and fragmentable parts:

- The unfragmentable part of the original IPv6 packet must be processed by intermediate nodes between the fragmenting node and the destination. This part consists of the IPv6 header, the Hop-by-Hop Options header, the Destination Options header for intermediate destinations, and the Routing header.

- The fragmentable part of the original IPv6 packet must be processed only at the final destination node. This part consists of the Authentication header, the Encapsulating Security Payload header, the Destination Options header for the final destination, and the upper-layer PDU.

Next, the IPv6 fragment packets are formed. Each fragment packet consists of the unfragmentable part, a fragment header, and a portion of the fragmentable part. Figure 4-16 shows the IPv6 fragmentation process for a packet fragmented into three fragments.

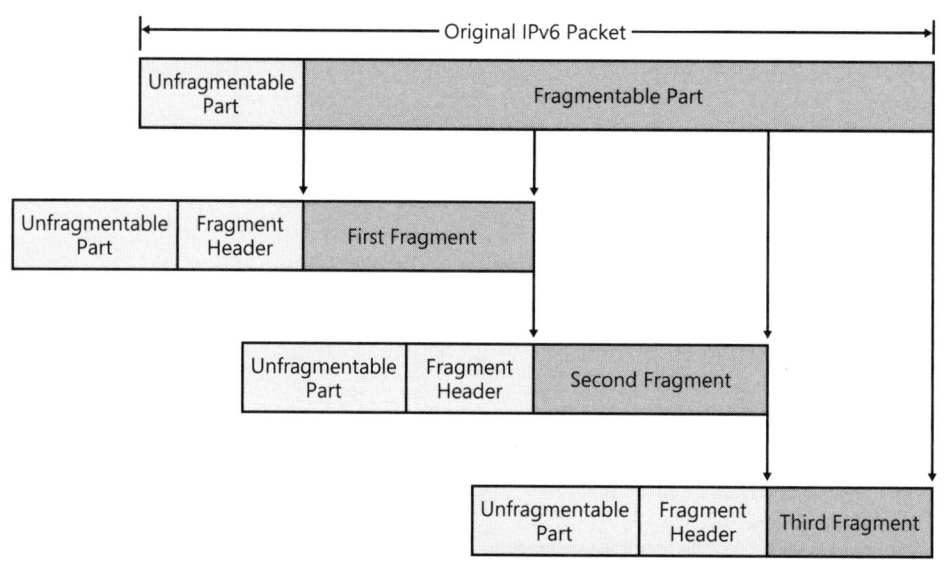

Figure 4-16 The IPv6 fragmentation process

In each fragment, the Next Header field in the Fragment header indicates the first header or the upper-layer protocol in the original fragmentable part. The Fragment Offset field in the Fragment header indicates the offset, in 8-byte units known as *fragment blocks*, of this fragment relative to the original payload. The More Fragments flag is set on all fragment packets except the last fragment packet. All fragment packets created from the same IPv6 packet must contain the same Identification field value.

Fragmentation of IPv6 packets can occur when the upper-layer protocol of the sending host submits a packet to IPv6 that is larger than the path MTU to the destination. Examples of IPv6 fragmentation are when a UDP application that is not aware of a path MTU sends large packets to a destination, or when a TCP application sends a packet before it is made aware of a path MTU update that lowers the path MTU. In this latter case, IPv6 is aware of the new path MTU, but TCP is not. TCP submits the TCP segment by using the old, larger value of the path MTU, and IPv6 fragments the TCP segment to fit the new, lower path MTU value. Once TCP is made aware of the new path MTU, subsequent TCP segments are not fragmented.

IPv6 packets sent to IPv4 destinations that undergo IPv6-to-IPv4 header translation might receive a path MTU update of less than 1280. In this case, the sending host sends IPv6 packets with a Fragment header in which the Fragment Offset field is set to 0 and the More Fragments flag is not set, and with a smaller payload size of 1272 bytes. The Fragment header is included so that the IPv6-to-IPv4 translator can use the Identification field in the Fragment header to perform IPv4 fragmentation to reach the IPv4 destination.

Network Monitor Capture

Here is an example of a Fragment header as displayed by Network Monitor 3.1 (frame 3 of capture 04_05 in the \NetworkMonitorCaptures folder on the companion CD-ROM):

```
  Frame:
+ Ethernet: Etype = IPv6
- Ipv6: Next Protocol = ICMPv6, Payload Length = 1456
  + Versions: IPv6, Internet Protocol, DSCP 0
    PayloadLength: 1456 (0x5B0)
    NextProtocol: IPv6 Fragment header, 44(0x2c)
    HopLimit: 128 (0x80)
    SourceAddress: FE80:0:0:0:210:5AFF:FEAA:20A2
    DestinationAddress: FE80:0:0:0:250:DAFF:FED8:C153
  - FragmentHeader:
      NextHeader: ICMPv6
      Reserved: 0 (0x0)
  - FragmentInfor:
      FragmentOffset: 2896(0XB50)
      Reserved: (.............00.)
      M:        (...............1) More fragments
      Identification: 5 (0x5)
      FragmentData: Binary Large Object (1448 Bytes)
```

This is a fragment of a payload that uses the identification number of 5 and starts in byte position 2896 relative to the fragmentable portion of the original IPv6 payload.

IPv6 Reassembly Process

The fragment packets are forwarded by the intermediate IPv6 router or routers to the destination IPv6 address. The fragment packets can take different paths to the destination and arrive in a different order from which they were sent. To reassemble the fragment packets into the original payload, IPv6 uses the Source Address and Destination Address fields in the IPv6 header and the Identification field in the Fragment header to group the fragments. Figure 4-17 shows the IPv6 reassembly process.

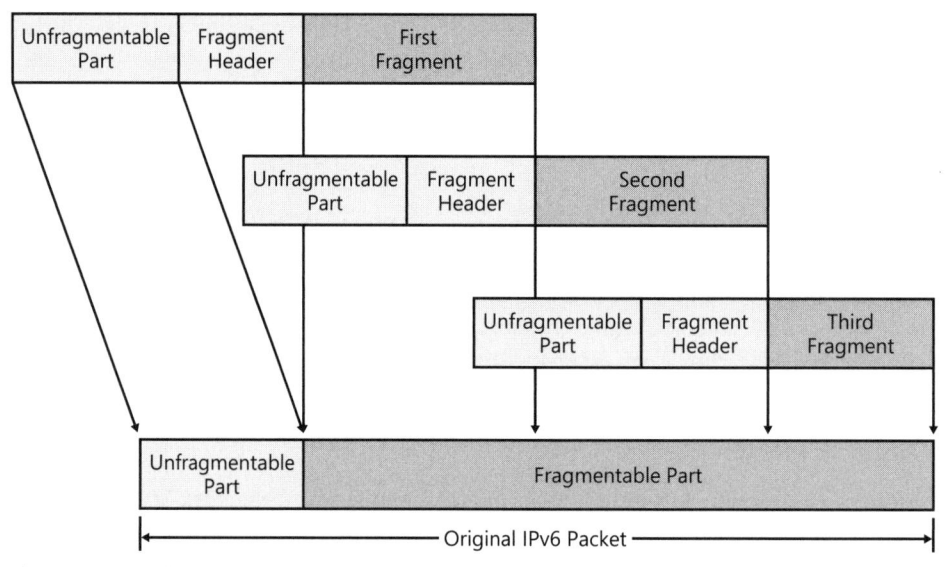

Figure 4-17 The IPv6 reassembly process

After all the fragments arrive, the original payload length is calculated and the Payload Length field in the IPv6 header for the reassembled packet is updated. Additionally, the Next Header field of the last header of the unfragmentable part is set to the Next Header field of the Fragment header of the first fragment.

RFC 2460 recommends a reassembly time of 60 seconds before abandoning reassembly and discarding the partially reassembled packet. If the first fragment has arrived and reassembly has not completed, the reassembling host sends an ICMPv6 Time Exceeded-Fragment Reassembly Time Exceeded message to the source of the fragment.

Authentication Header

The Authentication header provides data authentication (verification of the node that sent the packet), data integrity (verification that the data was not modified in transit), and antireplay protection (assurance that captured packets cannot be retransmitted and accepted as valid data) for the IPv6 packet including the fields in the IPv6 header that do not change in transit across an IPv6 internetwork. The Authentication header, described in RFC 2402, is part of the security architecture for IP, as defined in RFC 2401. The Authentication header is identified by the value of 51 in the previous header's Next Header field. Figure 4-18 shows the structure of the Authentication header.

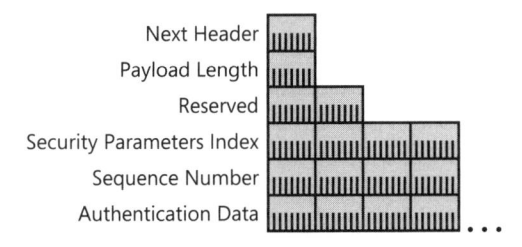

Figure 4-18 The structure of the Authentication header

The Authentication header contains a Next Header field, a Payload Length field (the number of 4-byte blocks in the Authentication header, not counting the first two), a Reserved field, a Security Parameters Index (SPI) field that helps identify a specific IP Security (IPsec) security association (SA), a Sequence Number field that provides antireplay protection, and an Authentication Data field that contains an integrity value check (ICV). The ICV provides data authentication and data integrity.

The Authentication header does not provide data confidentiality services for the upper-layer PDU by encrypting the data so that it cannot be viewed without the encryption key. To obtain data authentication and data integrity for the entire IPv6 packet and data confidentiality for the upper-layer PDU, you can use both the Authentication header and the Encapsulating Security Payload header and trailer.

Encapsulating Security Payload Header and Trailer

The Encapsulating Security Payload (ESP) header and trailer, described in RFC 2406, provide data confidentiality, data authentication, data integrity, and replay protection services to the encapsulated payload. The ESP header provides no security services for the IPv6 header or extension headers that occur before the ESP header. The ESP header and trailer are identified by the value of 50 in the previous header's Next Header field. Figure 4-19 shows the structure of the ESP header and trailer.

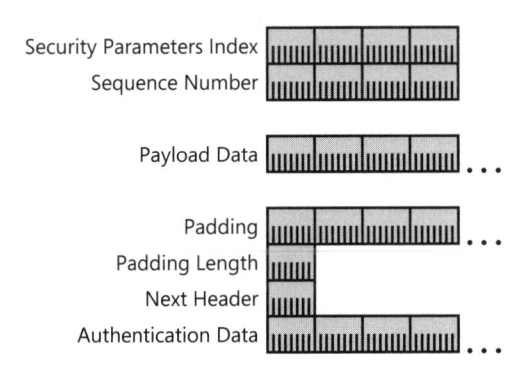

Figure 4-19 The structure of the Encapsulating Security Payload header and trailer

The ESP header contains an SPI field that helps identify the IPsec SA, and a Sequence Number field that provides antireplay protection. The ESP trailer contains the Padding, Padding Length, Next Header, and Authentication Data fields. The Padding field is used to ensure 4-byte boundaries for the ESP payload and appropriate data-block boundaries for encryption algorithms. The Padding Length field indicates the size of the Padding field in bytes. The Authentication Data field contains the ICV.

Details about how the ESP header and trailer provide data confidentiality, authentication, and integrity through cryptographic techniques are beyond the scope of this book.

IPv6 MTU

IPv6 requires that the link layer support a minimum MTU size of 1280 bytes. Link layers that do not support this MTU size must provide a link-layer fragmentation and reassembly scheme that is transparent to IPv6. For link layers that can support a configurable MTU size, RFC 2460 recommends that they be configured with an MTU size of at least 1500 bytes (the IPv6 MTU for Ethernet II encapsulation). An example of a configurable MTU is the Maximum Receive Unit (MRU) of a Point-to-Point Protocol (PPP) link.

Like IPv4, IPv6 provides a Path MTU Discovery process that uses the ICMPv6 Packet Too Big message described in the "Path MTU Discovery" section of Chapter 5, "ICMPv6." Path MTU Discovery allows the transmission of IPv6 packets that are larger than 1280 bytes.

IPv6 source hosts can fragment payloads of upper-layer protocols that are larger than the path MTU by using the process and Fragment header previously described. However, the use of IPv6 fragmentation is highly discouraged. An IPv6 node must be able to reassemble a fragmented packet that is at least 1500 bytes in size.

Table 4-5 lists commonly used local area network (LAN) and wide area network (WAN) technologies and their defined IPv6 MTUs.

Table 4-5   IPv6 MTUs for Common LAN and WAN Technologies

LAN or WAN Technology	IPv6 MTU
Ethernet (Ethernet II encapsulation)	1500
Ethernet (IEEE 802.3 SubNetwork Access Protocol [SNAP] encapsulation)	1492
IEEE 802.11	2312
Token Ring	Varies
Fiber Distributed Data Interface (FDDI)	4352
Attached Resource Computer Network (ARCNet)	9072
PPP	1500
X.25	1280
Frame Relay	1592
Asynchronous Transfer Mode (ATM) (Null or SNAP encapsulation)	9180

For more information about LAN and WAN encapsulations for IPv6 packets, see Appendix A, "Link-Layer Support for IPv6."

Upper-Layer Checksums

The current implementation of TCP, UDP, and ICMP for IPv4 incorporates into their checksum calculation a pseudo-header that includes both the IPv4 Source Address and Destination Address fields. This checksum calculation must be modified for TCP, UDP, and ICMPv6 traffic sent over IPv6 to include IPv6 addresses. Figure 4-20 shows the structure of the new IPv6 pseudo-header that must be used by TCP, UDP, and ICMPv6 checksum calculations. IPv6 uses the same algorithm as IPv4 for computing the checksum value.

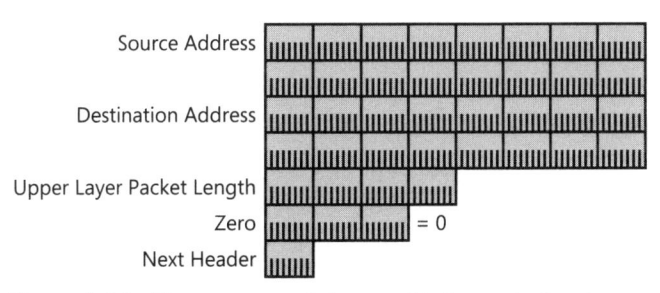

Figure 4-20 The structure of the new IPv6 pseudo-header

The IPv6 pseudo-header includes the Source Address field, the Destination Address field, an Upper Layer Packet Length field that indicates the length of the upper-layer PDU, and a Next Header field that indicates the upper-layer protocol for which the checksum is being calculated.

References

The following references were cited in this chapter:

- RFC 791 – "Internet Protocol"
- RFC 1812 – "Requirements for IP Version 4 Routers"
- RFC 2401 – "Security Architecture for the Internet Protocol"
- RFC 2402 – "IP Authentication Header"
- RFC 2406 – "IP Encapsulating Security Payload (ESP)"
- RFC 2460 – "Internet Protocol, Version 6 (IPv6)"
- RFC 2474 – "Definition of the Differentiated Services Field (DS Field)"
- RFC 2675 – "IPv6 Jumbograms"
- RFC 2711 – "IPv6 Router Alert Option"

- RFC 3168 – "The Addition of Explicit Congestion Notification (ECN) to IP"
- RFC 3697 – "IPv6 Flow Label Specification"
- RFC 3775 – "Mobility Support in IPv6"

You can obtain these RFCs from the \RFCs_and_Drafts folder on the companion CD-ROM or from *http://www.ietf.org/rfc.html*.

Testing for Understanding

To test your understanding of the IPv6 header, answer the following questions. See Appendix D, "Testing for Understanding Answers," to check your answers.

1. Why does the IPv6 header not include a checksum?
2. What is the IPv6 equivalent to the IHL field in the IPv4 header?
3. How does the combination of the Traffic Class and Flow Label fields provide better support for prioritized traffic delivery?
4. Which extension headers are fragmentable and why? Which extension headers are not fragmentable and why?
5. Describe a situation that results in an IPv6 packet that contains a Fragment Header in which the Fragment Offset field is set to 0 and the More Fragments flag is not set to 1.
6. Describe how the new upper-layer checksum calculation affects transport layer protocols such as TCP and UDP.
7. If the minimum MTU for IPv6 packets is 1280 bytes, how are 1280-byte packets sent on a link that supports only 512-byte frames?

Chapter 6
Neighbor Discovery

At the end of this chapter, you should be able to do the following:

- Describe the functions of the Neighbor Discovery (ND) protocol.
- List and describe the function and format of ND options.
- List and describe the function and format of ND messages.
- Describe which ND messages use which ND options.
- Describe the details of the address resolution, neighbor unreachability detection, duplicate address detection, router discovery, and redirect processes.
- Describe the host sending algorithm in terms of host data structures and ND messages.

Neighbor Discovery Overview

Internet Protocol version 6 (IPv6) Neighbor Discovery (ND) is a set of messages and processes defined in RFC 4861 that determine relationships between neighboring nodes. ND replaces Address Resolution Protocol (ARP), Internet Control Message Protocol (ICMP) router discovery, and the ICMP Redirect message used in IPv4. ND also provides additional functionality.

ND is used by nodes to do the following:

- Resolve the link-layer address of a neighboring node to which an IPv6 packet is being forwarded.
- Determine when the link-layer address of a neighboring node has changed.
- Determine whether a neighbor is still reachable.

ND is used by hosts to do the following:

- Discover neighboring routers.
- Autoconfigure addresses, address prefixes, routes, and other configuration parameters.

ND is used by routers to do the following:

- Advertise their presence, host configuration parameters, routes, and on-link prefixes.
- Inform hosts of a better next-hop address to forward packets for a specific destination.

IPv6 ND processes include the following:

- **Router discovery**   During router discovery, a host discovers the local routers on an attached link. This process is equivalent to ICMPv4 router discovery. For more information, see the "Router Discovery" section in this chapter.

- **Prefix discovery**   Prefix discovery is the process by which hosts discover the network prefixes for local link destinations. This is similar to the exchange of the ICMPv4 Address Mask Request and Address Mask Reply messages. For more information, see the "Router Discovery" section in this chapter.

- **Parameter discovery**   The parameter discovery process enables hosts to discover additional operating parameters, including the link maximum transmission unit (MTU) and the default hop limit for outgoing packets. For more information, see the "Router Discovery" section in this chapter.

- **Address autoconfiguration**   During address autoconfiguration, IP addresses are configured for interfaces in either the presence or absence of an address configuration server, such as a Dynamic Host Configuration Protocol for IPv6 (DHCPv6) server. For more information, see Chapter 8, "Address Autoconfiguration."

- **Address resolution**   Address resolution is the process by which nodes resolve a neighbor's IPv6 address to its link-layer address. It is equivalent to ARP in IPv4. For more information, see the "Address Resolution" section in this chapter.

- **Next-hop determination**   During next-hop determination, a node determines the IPv6 address of the neighbor to which a packet is being forwarded, based on the destination address. The next-hop address is either the destination address or the address of an on-link default router. For more information, see "Host Sending Algorithm" in this chapter.

- **Neighbor unreachability detection**   The neighbor unreachability detection process is the means by which a node determines that the IPv6 layer of a neighbor is no longer receiving packets or that an IPv6 address has moved to a different physical interface. For more information, see the "Neighbor Unreachability Detection" section in this chapter.

- **Duplicate address detection**   During duplicate address detection, a node determines that an address considered for use is not already in use by a neighboring node. This process is equivalent to using gratuitous ARP frames in IPv4. For more information, see the "Duplicate Address Detection" section in this chapter.

- **Redirect function**   The redirect function is the process of informing a host of a better first-hop IPv6 address to reach a destination. It is equivalent to the use of the ICMPv4 Redirect message. For more information, see the "Redirect Function" section in this chapter.

Neighbor Discovery Message Format

ND messages use the ICMPv6 message structure and ICMPv6 types 133 through 137. ND messages consist of an ND message header, composed of an ICMPv6 header and ND message-specific data, and zero or more ND options. Figure 6-1 shows the format of an ND message.

Figure 6-1 The format of an ND message

There are five different ND messages:

- Router Solicitation (ICMPv6 type 133)
- Router Advertisement (ICMPv6 type 134)
- Neighbor Solicitation (ICMPv6 type 135)
- Neighbor Advertisement (ICMPv6 type 136)
- Redirect (ICMPv6 type 137)

ND message options provide additional information, indicating MAC addresses, on-link network prefixes, on-link MTU information, redirection data, mobility information, and specific routes.

To ensure that ND messages that are received have originated from a node on the local link (either a physical link or a tunnel), all ND messages are sent with a hop limit of 255. When an ND message is received, the Hop Limit field in the IPv6 header is checked. If it is not set to 255, the message is silently discarded. Verifying that the ND message has a hop limit of 255 provides protection from ND-based network attacks that are launched from off-link nodes. With a hop limit of 255, a router could not have forwarded the ND message from an off-link node.

Neighbor Discovery Options

ND options are formatted in type-length-value (TLV) format. Figure 6-2 shows the TLV format.

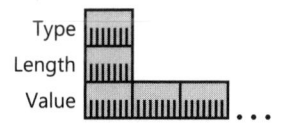

Figure 6-2 The TLV format for ND options

The 8-bit Type field indicates the type of ND option. Table 6-1 lists the ND option types defined in RFC 4861, RFC 3775, and RFC 4191.

Table 6-1 IPv6 ND Option Types

Type	Option Name	Source Document
1	Source Link-Layer Address	RFC 4861 (Neighbor Discovery for IPv6)
2	Target Link-Layer Address	RFC 4861
3	Prefix Information	RFC 4861
4	Redirected Header	RFC 4861
5	MTU	RFC 4861
7	Advertisement Interval	RFC 3775 (Mobile IPv6)
8	Home Agent Information	RFC 3775
24	Route Information	RFC 4191 (Default Router Preferences and More-Specific Routes)

The 8-bit Length field indicates the length of the entire option in 8-byte blocks. All ND options must fall on 8-byte boundaries. The variable length Value field contains the data for the option.

The Advertisement Interval and Home Agent Information options are described in Appendix F, "Mobile IPv6."

Source and Target Link-Layer Address Options

The Source Link-Layer Address option indicates the link-layer address of the ND message sender. The Source Link-Layer Address option is included in the Neighbor Solicitation, Router Solicitation, and Router Advertisement messages. The Source Link-Layer Address option is not included when the source address of the ND message is the unspecified address (::).

Figure 6-3 shows the structure of the Source Link-Layer Address option.

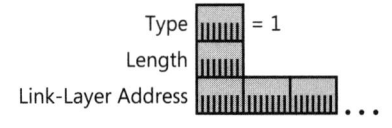

```
         Type  ||||||| = 1
       Length  |||||||
Link-Layer Address  |||||||||||||||||||  . . .
```

Figure 6-3 The structure of the Source Link-Layer Address option

The Target Link-Layer Address option indicates the link-layer address of the neighboring node to which IPv6 packets should be directed. The Target Link-Layer Address option is included in the Neighbor Advertisement and Redirect messages.

Figure 6-4 shows the structure of the Target Link-Layer Address option.

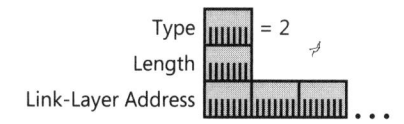

Figure 6-4 The structure of the Target Link-Layer Address option

The Source Link-Layer Address option and the Target Link-Layer Address option have the same format.

The Type field is set to 1 for a Source Link-Layer Address option and 2 for a Target Link-Layer Address option. The Length field is set to the number of 8-byte blocks in the entire option. The Link-Layer Address field is a variable-length field that contains the link-layer address of the source or target. Each link layer defined for IPv6 must specify the way in which the link-layer address is formatted in the Source and Target Link-Layer Address options.

For example, RFC 2464 defines how IPv6 packets are sent over Ethernet networks. It also includes the format of the Source and Target Link-Layer Address ND options. For Ethernet, the link-layer address is 48 bits (6 bytes) in length. Figure 6-5 shows the Target Link-Layer Address option for Ethernet.

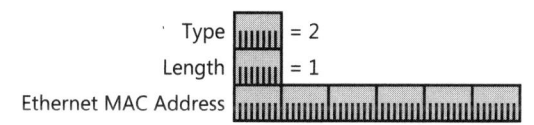

Figure 6-5 The Target Link-Layer Address option for Ethernet

Network Monitor Capture

Here is an example of a Source Link-Layer Address option used in a Neighbor Solicitation message as displayed by Network Monitor 3.1 (frame 1 of capture 06_01 in the \Network-MonitorCaptures folder on the companion CD-ROM):

```
  Frame:
+ Ethernet: Etype = IPv6
+ Ipv6: Next Protocol = ICMPv6, Payload Length = 32
- Icmpv6: Neighbor Solicitation, Target = FE80:0:0:0:260:97FF:FE02:6EA5
    MessageType: Neighbor Solicitation, 135(0x87)
  - NeighborSolicitation:
    Code: 0 (0x0)
    Checksum: 3893 (0xF35)
    Reserved: 0 (0x0)
    TargetAddress: FE80:0:0:0:260:97FF:FE02:6EA5
  - SourceLinkLayerAddress:
    Type: Source Link-Layer Address, 1(0x1)
    Length: 1, in unit of 8 octets
    Address: 00-10-5A-AA-20-A2
```

Prefix Information Option

The Prefix Information option is sent in Router Advertisement messages to indicate both address prefixes and information about address autoconfiguration. There can be multiple Prefix Information options included in a Router Advertisement message, indicating multiple address prefixes.

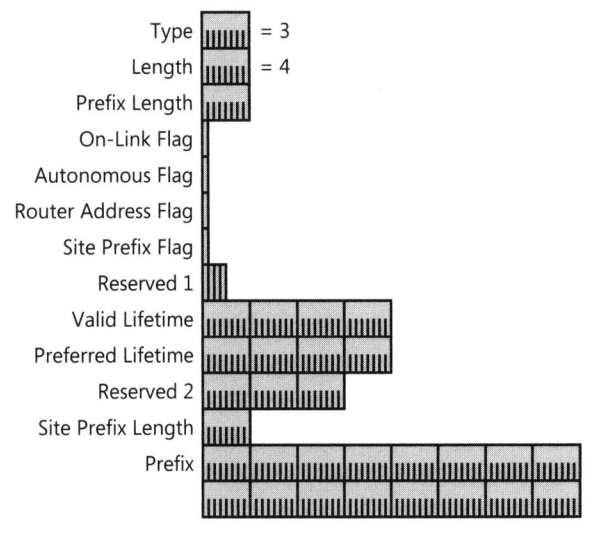

Figure 6-6 shows the structure of the Prefix Information option.

Figure 6-6 The structure of the Prefix Information option

The fields in the Prefix Information option are as follows:

- **Type** The value of this field is 3.
- **Length** The value of this field is 4. (The entire option is 32 bytes in length.)
- **Prefix Length** The Prefix Length field indicates the number of leading bits in the Prefix field that make up the address prefix. The size of this field is 8 bits. The Prefix Length field has a value from 0 through 128. Because typical prefixes advertised are for subnet identifiers, the Prefix Length field is usually set to 64.
- **On-Link flag** The On-Link flag indicates, when set to 1, that the addresses implied by the included prefix are available on the link on which this Router Advertisement message was received. When this flag is set to 0, it is not assumed that the addresses that match the prefix are available on-link. The size of this field is 1 bit.
- **Autonomous flag** The Autonomous flag indicates, when set to 1, that the included prefix is used to create an autonomous (or stateless) address configuration. When this flag is set to 0, the included prefix is not used to create a stateless address configuration. The size of this field is 1 bit.
- **Router Address flag** The Router Address flag is defined in RFC 3775 for Mobile IPv6. For more information, see Appendix F.

- **Site Prefix flag** The Site Prefix flag indicates, when set to 1, that the site prefix defined by the Prefix field and the Site Prefix Length field be used to update the site prefix table. The site prefix table is maintained by the host and is utilized to prefer the use of site-local addresses when a global address matches a site prefix. This flag is described in the Internet draft titled "Site Prefixes in Neighbor Discovery."
- **Reserved1** The Reserved1 field is a 4-bit field reserved for future use and set to 0.
- **Valid Lifetime** The Valid Lifetime field indicates the number of seconds that an address, based on the included prefix and using stateless address configuration, remains valid. The size of this field is 32 bits. The Valid Lifetime field also indicates the number of seconds that the included prefix is valid for on-link determination. For an infinite valid lifetime, the Valid Lifetime field is set to 0xFFFFFFFF.
- **Preferred Lifetime** The Preferred Lifetime field indicates the number of seconds that an address, based on the included prefix and using stateless address autoconfiguration, remains in a preferred state. The size of this field is 32 bits. Stateless autoconfiguration addresses that are still valid are either in a preferred or deprecated state. In the preferred state, the address can be used for unrestricted communication. In the deprecated state, the use of the address is not recommended for new communications. However, existing communications using a deprecated address can continue. An address goes from the preferred state to the deprecated state when its preferred lifetime expires. For an infinite preferred lifetime, the Preferred Lifetime field is set to 0xFFFFFFFF.
- **Reserved2** The Reserved2 field is a 24-bit field reserved for future use and set to 0.
- **Site Prefix Length** The Site Prefix Length field indicates the number of leading bits in the Prefix field that define a site prefix. The length of this field is 8 bits. This field is significant only if the Site Prefix flag is set to 1. This field is described in the Internet draft titled "Site Prefixes in Neighbor Discovery."
- **Prefix** The Prefix field indicates the prefix for the IPv6 address derived through stateless autoconfiguration. The size of this field is 128 bits. Bits in the Prefix field—up to a count equaling the value of the Prefix Length field—are significant for creating the prefix. The combination of the Prefix Length field and the Prefix field unambiguously defines the prefix which, when combined with the interface identifier for the node, creates an IPv6 address. The link-local prefix should not be sent and is ignored by the receiving host.

Network Monitor Capture

Here is an example of a Prefix Information option used in a Router Advertisement message as displayed by Network Monitor 3.1 (capture 06_02 in the \NetworkMonitorCaptures folder on the companion CD-ROM):

```
Frame:
+ Ethernet: Etype = IPv6
+ Ipv6: Next Protocol = ICMPv6, Payload Length = 96
- Icmpv6: Router Advertisement
    MessageType: Router Advertisement, 134(0x86)
```

```
+ RouterAdvertisement:
- SourceLinkLayerAddress:
    Type: Source Link-Layer Address, 1(0x1)
    Length: 1, in unit of 8 octets
    Address: 00-B0-D0-23-47-33
+ MTU:
+ PrefixInformation:
- PrefixInformation:
    Type: Prefix Information, 3(0x3)
    Length: 4, in unit of 8 octets
    PrefixLength: 64 (0x40)
  - Flags: 192 (0xC0)
      L:   (1.......) On-Link determination allowed
      A:   (.1......) Autonomous address-configuration
      R:   (..0.....) Not router Address
      S:   (...0....) Not a site prefix
      P:   (....0...) Not a router prefix
      Rsv: (.....000)
    ValidLifetime: 4294967295 (0xFFFFFFFF)
    PreferredLifetime: 4294967295 (0xFFFFFFFF)
    Reserved: 0 (0x0)
    Prefix: FD43:2DA1:3FE9:2:0:0:0:0
```

Redirected Header Option

The Redirected Header option is sent in Redirect messages to specify the IPv6 packet that caused the router to send a Redirect message. It can contain all or part of the redirected IPv6 packet, depending on the size of the IPv6 packet that was initially sent.

Figure 6-7 shows the structure of the Redirected Header option.

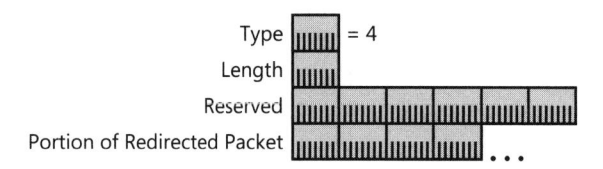

Figure 6-7 The structure of the Redirected Header option

The following list describes the fields in the Redirected Header option:

- **Type**   The value of this field is 4.

- **Length**   The value of this field is the number of 8-byte blocks in the entire option.

- **Reserved**   The Reserved field is a 48-bit field reserved for future use and set to 0.

- **Portion of redirected packet**   This field contains either the IPv6 packet or a portion of the IPv6 packet that caused the Redirect message to be sent. The amount of the original packet that is included is the leading portion of the packet so that the entire Redirect message is no more than 1280 bytes in length.

Network Monitor Capture

Here is an example of a Redirected Header option used in a Redirect message as displayed by Network Monitor 3.1 (capture 06_03 in the \NetworkMonitorCaptures folder on the companion CD-ROM):

```
Frame:
+ Ethernet: Etype = IPv6
+ Ipv6: Next Protocol = ICMPv6, Payload Length = 128
- Icmpv6: Redirect, Target = FE80:0:0:0:2B0:D0FF:FE23:4735
    MessageType: Redirect, 137(0x89)
  - Redirect:
    Code: 0 (0x0)
    Checksum: 31003 (0x791B)
    Reserved: 0 (0x0)
    TargetAddress: FE80:0:0:0:2B0:D0FF:FE23:4735
    DestAddress: 2001:DB8:0:0:0:0:0:1
  - RedirectedHeader:
    Type: Redirected Header, 4(0x4)
    Length: 11, in unit of 8 octets
    Reserved: 0 (0x0)
   - InvokingPacket: Next Protocol = ICMPv6, Payload Length = 40
    - Versions: IPv6, Internet Protocol, DSCP 0
      Version:    (0110...........................) IPv6, Internet Protocol,
         6(0x6)
      DSCP:       (....000000.....................) Differentiated services
         codepoint 0
      ECT:        (..........0....................) ECN-Capable Transport not
         set
      CE:         (...........0...................) ECN-CE not set
      FlowLabe:   (............00000000000000000000) 0
      PayloadLength: 40 (0x28)
      NextProtocol: ICMPv6, 58(0x3a)
      HopLimit: 128 (0x80)
      SourceAddress: FE80:0:0:0:260:8FF:FE52:F9D8
      DestinationAddress: 3000:0:0:0:0:0:0:1
      OriginalIPPayload: Binary Large Object (40 Bytes)
```

MTU Option

The MTU option is sent in Router Advertisement messages to indicate the IPv6 MTU of the link. This option is typically used when the IPv6 MTU for a link is not well known or needs to be set because of a translational or mixed-media bridging configuration. The MTU option overrides the IPv6 MTU reported by the interface hardware.

In bridged or Layer-2 switched environments, it is possible to have different link-layer technologies with different link-layer MTUs on the same link. In this case, differences in IPv6 MTUs between nodes on the same link are not detected through Path MTU Discovery. The MTU option is used to indicate the highest IPv6 MTU supported by all link-layer technologies on the link.

Figure 6-8 shows a switched configuration where the MTU option is used to solve a mixed-media problem.

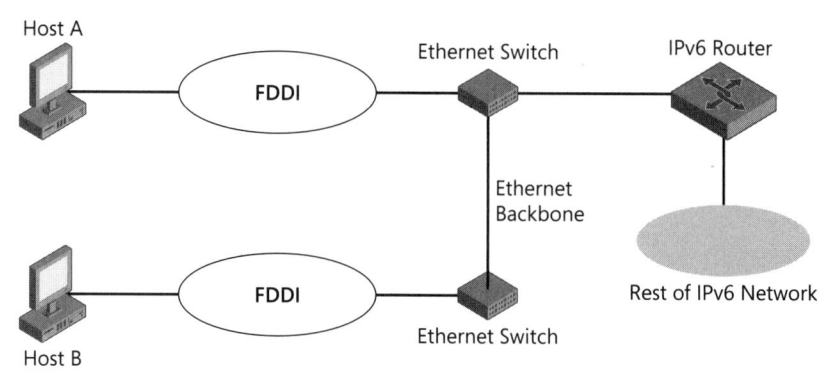

Figure 6-8 A mixed-media configuration

Two IPv6 hosts, Host A and Host B, are connected to two different Ethernet (Layer 2) switches using Fiber Distributed Data Interface (FDDI) ports. The two switches are connected by an Ethernet backbone. When Host A and Host B negotiate a TCP connection, each reports a TCP maximum segment size of 4312 (the FDDI IPv6 MTU of 4352, minus 40 bytes of the IPv6 header). However, when TCP data on the connection begins to flow, the switches silently discard IPv6 packets larger than 1500 bytes that are sent between Host A and Host B.

With the MTU option, the IPv6 router for the subnet reports an IPv6 MTU of 1500 in the Router Advertisement message for all hosts on the link. When both Host A and Host B adjust their IPv6 MTU from 4352 to 1500, maximum-sized TCP segments sent between them are not discarded by the intermediate switches.

Note FDDI is an older technology whose use has been made obsolete by 100-Mbps Ethernet. This configuration is unlikely to be used on modern networks and serves only as an example of a mixed-media subnet.

Figure 6-9 shows the structure of the MTU option.

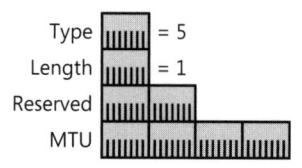

Figure 6-9 The structure of the MTU option

The following list describes the fields in the MTU option:

- **Type** The value of this field is 5.
- **Length** The value of this field is 1. (There are 8 bytes in the entire option.)

- **Reserved** The Reserved field is a 16-bit field reserved for future use and set to 0.
- **MTU** The MTU field indicates the IPv6 MTU that should be used by the host for the link on which the Router Advertisement was received. The size of this field is 32 bits. The value in the MTU field is ignored if it is larger than the link MTU.

Network Monitor Capture

Here is an example of an MTU option used in a Router Advertisement message as displayed by Network Monitor 3.1 (capture 06_02 in the \NetworkMonitorCaptures folder on the companion CD-ROM):

```
Frame:
+ Ethernet: Etype = IPv6
+ Ipv6: Next Protocol = ICMPv6, Payload Length = 96
- Icmpv6: Router Advertisement
    MessageType: Router Advertisement, 134(0x86)
  + RouterAdvertisement:
  - SourceLinkLayerAddress:
    Type: Source Link-Layer Address, 1(0x1)
    Length: 1, in unit of 8 octets
    Address: 00-B0-D0-23-47-33
  - MTU:
    Type: MTU, 5(0x5)
    Length: 1, in unit of 8 octets
    Reserved: 0 (0x0)
    MTU: 1500 (0x5DC)
  + PrefixInformation:
  + PrefixInformation:
```

Route Information Option

The Route Information option is sent in Router Advertisement messages to specify individual routes for receiving hosts to add to their local routing table. The Route Information option is described in RFC 4191.

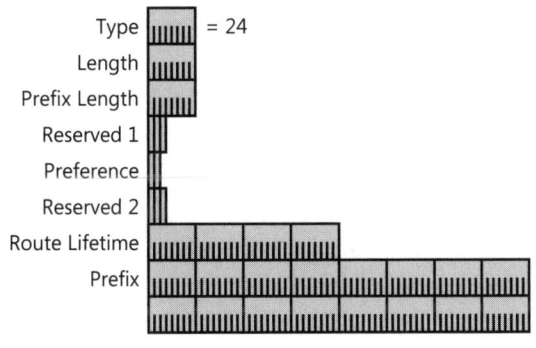

Figure 6-10 shows the structure of the Route Information option.

Figure 6-10 The structure of the Route Information option

The fields in the Route Information option are as follows:

- **Type**   The value of this field is 24.
- **Length**   The value of the Length field depends on the prefix length of the route and the corresponding size of the Prefix field. If the prefix length is 0 (and there is no Prefix field), the value of the Length field is 1. If the prefix length is greater than 0 and less than 65, the length of the Prefix field is 64 bits and the value of the Length field is 2. If the prefix length is greater than 64, the length of the Prefix field is 128 bits and the value of the Length field is 3.
- **Prefix Length**   The Prefix Length field indicates the number of leading bits in the Prefix field that are significant for the route. Valid values range from 0 through 128. The size of this field is 8 bits.
- **Reserved1**   The Reserved1 field is a 3-bit field reserved for future use and set to 0.
- **Preference**   The Preference field indicates the level of preference for this route as sent from the advertising router. If multiple routers advertise the same prefix using a Route Information option, you can configure the routers so that they advertise the route with different preference levels. Valid values in binary are 01 (High), 00 (Medium), and 11 (Low). The size of this field is 2 bits.
- **Reserved2**   The Reserved2 field is a 3-bit field reserved for future use and set to 0.
- **Route Lifetime**   The Route Lifetime field indicates the amount of time in seconds that the prefix is valid for route determination. The size of this field is 32 bits. For an infinite route lifetime, the Route Lifetime field is set to 0xFFFFFFFF.
- **Prefix**   The Prefix field indicates the route prefix. The size of the Prefix field can be 0, 64, or 128 bits, depending on the value of the Prefix Length field. If the prefix length is 0, the size of the Prefix field is 0. If the prefix length is greater than 0 and less than 65, the size of the Prefix field is 64 bits. If the prefix length is greater than 64, the size of the Prefix field is 128 bits. The prefix length indicates the number of high-order bits in the prefix that are relevant for route determination. All bits in the Prefix field past the prefix length must be set to 0.

A typical use of the Route Information option is to enable hosts to make better forwarding decisions when sending data. Figure 6-11 shows a simple network configuration where the Route Information option can be useful.

Without the Route Information option, you would typically configure the routers so that only Router 1 advertises itself as a default router on Subnet 1. Hosts on Subnet 1 sending traffic to hosts on Subnet 2 would have to rely on Redirect messages from Router 1 to inform them that the best next-hop address to reach hosts on Subnet 2 is actually Router 2. For more information, see the "Redirect Function" section in this chapter.

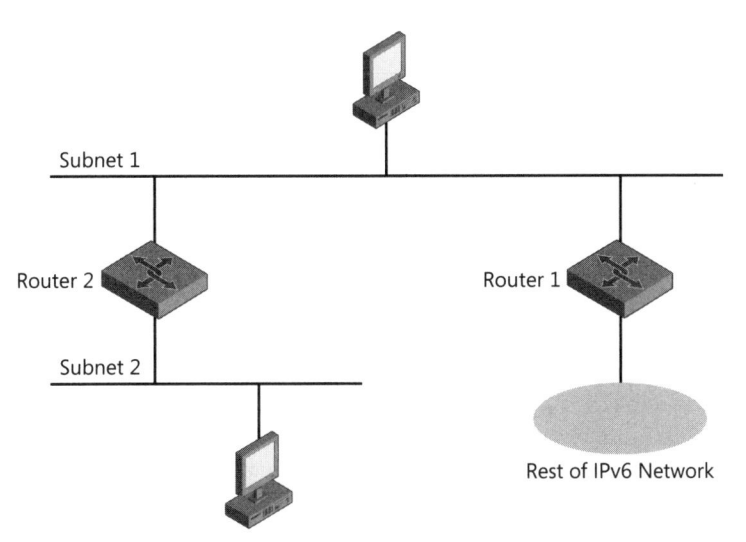

Figure 6-11 An example configuration in which the Route Information option is used

Using the Route Information option, Router 2 is configured to advertise the prefix of Subnet 2. Upon receipt of router advertisements from both routers, hosts on Subnet 1 automatically add a default route with Router 1 as its next-hop address and a specific route for the Subnet 2 prefix with Router 2 as its next-hop address. Now all the hosts on Subnet 2 are reachable by hosts on Subnet 1 without having to rely on redirects from Router 1.

A computer running Windows Server 2008, Windows Vista, Windows XP, or Windows Server 2003, acting as an IPv6 router that does not have a default route that is configured to be published, will send Route Information options in Router Advertisements to inform hosts of the subnet prefixes of the other subnets to which the IPv6 router is attached.

Neighbor Discovery Messages

All the functions of IPv6 ND are performed with the following messages:

- Router Solicitation
- Router Advertisement
- Neighbor Solicitation
- Neighbor Advertisement
- Redirect

Router Solicitation

The Router Solicitation message is sent by IPv6 hosts to discover the presence of IPv6 routers on the link. A host sends a multicast Router Solicitation message to prompt IPv6 routers to respond immediately, rather than waiting for an unsolicited Router Advertisement message.

For example, assuming that the local link is Ethernet, in the Ethernet header of the Router Solicitation message you will find these settings:

- The Source Address field is set to the MAC address of the sending network adapter.
- The Destination Address field is set to 33-33-00-00-00-02.

In the IPv6 header of the Router Solicitation message, you will find the following settings:

- The Source Address field is set to either a link-local IPv6 address assigned to the sending interface or the IPv6 unspecified address (::).
- The Destination Address field is set to the link-local scope all-routers multicast address (FF02::2).
- The Hop Limit field is set to 255.

Figure 6-12 shows the structure of the Router Solicitation message.

```
Type       = 133
Code       = 0
Checksum
Reserved
Options    ...
```

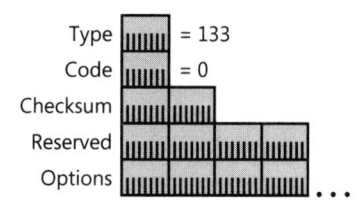

Figure 6-12 The structure of the Router Solicitation message

The following list describes the fields in the Router Solicitation message:

- **Type** The value of this field is 133.
- **Code** The value of this field is 0.
- **Checksum** The value of this field is the ICMPv6 checksum.
- **Reserved** This is a 32-bit field reserved for future use and set to 0.
- **Source Link-Layer Address option** When present, the Source Link-Layer Address option contains the link-layer address of the sender. For an Ethernet node, the Source Link-Layer Address option contains the Ethernet MAC address of the sending host. The address in the Source Link-Layer Address option is used by the receiving router to determine the unicast MAC address of the host to which the corresponding unicast Router Advertisement is sent.

Network Monitor Capture

Here is an example of a Router Solicitation message as displayed by Network Monitor 3.1 (capture 06_04 in the \NetworkMonitorCaptures folder on the companion CD-ROM):

```
Frame:
+ Ethernet: Etype = IPv6
+ Ipv6: Next Protocol = ICMPv6, Payload Length = 16
- Icmpv6: Router Solicitation
    MessageType: Router Solicitation, 133(0x85)
  - RouterSolicitation:
    Code: 0 (0x0)
    Checksum: 19232 (0x4B20)
    Reserved: 0 (0x0)
  - SourceLinkLayerAddress:
    Type: Source Link-Layer Address, 1(0x1)
    Length: 1, in unit of 8 octets
    Address: 00-B0-D0-23-47-33
```

Router Advertisement

IPv6 routers send unsolicited Router Advertisement messages pseudo-periodically—that is, the interval between unsolicited advertisements is randomized to reduce synchronization issues when there are multiple advertising routers on a link—and solicited Router Advertisement messages in response to the receipt of a Router Solicitation message. The Router Advertisement message contains the information required by hosts to determine the link prefixes, the link MTU, specific routes, whether or not to use address autoconfiguration, and the duration for which addresses created through address autoconfiguration are valid and preferred.

For example, assuming that the local link is Ethernet, in the Ethernet header of the Router Advertisement message, you will find these settings:

- The Source Address field is set to the MAC address of the sending network adapter.
- The Destination Address field is set to either 33-33-00-00-00-01 or the unicast MAC address of the host that sent a Router Solicitation from a unicast address.

In the IPv6 header of the Router Advertisement message, you will find the following settings:

- The Source Address field is set to the link-local address assigned to the sending interface.
- The Destination Address field is set to either the link-local scope all-nodes multicast address (FF02::1) or the unicast IPv6 address of the host that sent the Router Solicitation message from a unicast address.
- The Hop Limit field is set to 255.

Figure 6-13 shows the structure of the Router Advertisement message.

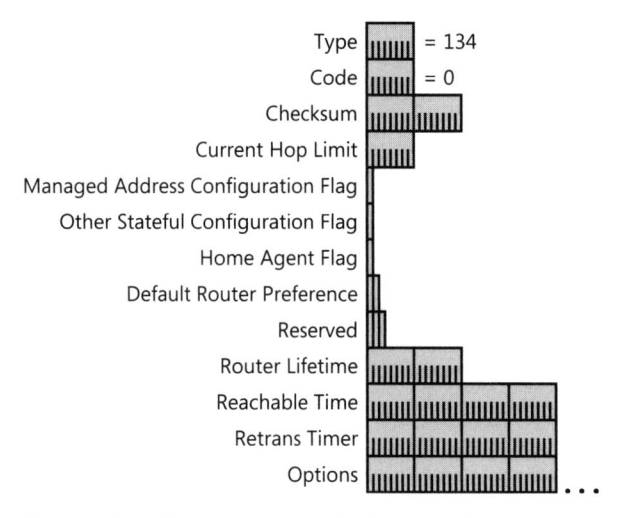

```
                         Type |IIIIII| = 134
                         Code |IIIIII| = 0
                     Checksum |IIIIII|IIIIII|
             Current Hop Limit |IIIIII|
  Managed Address Configuration Flag |
    Other Stateful Configuration Flag |
               Home Agent Flag |
        Default Router Preference |
                     Reserved ||
               Router Lifetime |IIIIII|IIIIII|
               Reachable Time |IIIIII|IIIIII|IIIIII|IIIIII|
                 Retrans Timer |IIIIII|IIIIII|IIIIII|IIIIII|
                      Options |IIIIII|IIIIII|IIIIII|IIIIII| . . .
```

Figure 6-13 The structure of the Router Advertisement message

The fields in the Router Advertisement message are as follows:

- **Type**   The value of this field is 134.

- **Code**   The value of this field is 0.

- **Checksum**   The value of this field is the ICMPv6 checksum.

- **Current Hop Limit**   The Current Hop Limit field indicates the default value of the Hop Limit field in the IPv6 header for packets sent by hosts that receive this Router Advertisement message. The size of this field is 8 bits. A current hop limit of 0 indicates that the default value of the Hop Limit field is not specified by the router.

- **Managed Address Configuration flag**   The Managed Address Configuration flag indicates, when set to 1, that hosts receiving this Router Advertisement message must use an address configuration protocol such as DHCPv6 to obtain addresses in addition to the addresses that might be derived from stateless address autoconfiguration. The size of this field is 1 bit.

- **Other Stateful Configuration flag**   The Other Stateful Configuration flag indicates, when set to 1, that hosts receiving this Router Advertisement message must use an address configuration protocol (for example, DHCPv6) to obtain non-address configuration information. The size of this field is 1 bit.

- **Home Agent flag**   The Home Agent flag is defined in RFC 3775 for Mobile IPv6. For more information, see Appendix F.

- **Default Router Preference**   The Default Router Preference field indicates the level of preference for this router as the default router. If multiple routers advertise themselves as default routers, you can configure the routers so that they advertise with different preference levels. Valid values in binary are 01 (High), 00 (Medium), and 11 (Low). If the preference is set to 10, the receiving host should assume a value of 0 for the Router Lifetime field, effectively disabling the advertising router as a default router. The size of this field is 2 bits. This field is described in RFC 4191.

A typical configuration that can use the default router preference is a subnet that has two routers connected to the Internet or an organization intranet—one router is the primary router, and another router is a slower, secondary router intended to provide fault tolerance for the primary router. Both routers advertise themselves as default routers; however, the primary router advertises a default router preference of 01 (High) and the secondary router advertises a default router preference of 00 (Medium). If the primary router becomes unavailable, the hosts on the subnet will use the secondary router until the primary router becomes available.

- **Reserved**   This is a 3-bit field reserved for future use and set to 0.
- **Router Lifetime**   The Router Lifetime field indicates the lifetime (in seconds) of the router as the default router. The size of this field is 16 bits. The maximum Router Lifetime value is 65,535 seconds (about 18.2 hours). A value of 0 indicates that the router cannot be considered a default router; however, all other information contained in the Router Advertisement is still valid. A computer running Windows Server 2008, Windows Vista, Windows XP, or Windows Server 2003 acting as an IPv6 router that does not have a default route that is configured to be published sets the Router Lifetime field to 0.
- **Reachable Time**   The Reachable Time field indicates the amount of time (in milliseconds) that a node can consider a neighboring node reachable after receiving a reachability confirmation. The size of this field is 32 bits. A value of 0 indicates that the router does not specify the reachable time. For more information, see the "Neighbor Unreachability Detection" section in this chapter.
- **Retransmission Timer**   The Retransmission Timer field indicates the amount of time (in milliseconds) between retransmissions of Neighbor Solicitation messages. The size of this field is 32 bits. The retransmission timer is used during neighbor unreachability detection. A value of 0 indicates that the router does not specify the retransmission timer value.

The options that can be present in a Router Advertisement message are the following:

- **Source Link-Layer Address option**   When present, the Source Link-Layer Address option contains the link-layer address of the interface on which the Router Advertisement message was sent. This option can be omitted when the router is load-balancing across multiple link-layer addresses.
- **MTU option**   When present, the MTU option contains the MTU of the link. It is typically sent on links that have a variable MTU or in switched environments that have multiple link-layer technologies on the same link.

- **Prefix Information options**   When present, Prefix Information options contain the on-link prefixes that are used for address autoconfiguration. The link-local prefix is never sent as a Prefix Information option.
- **Advertisement Interval option**   For more information, see Appendix F.
- **Home Agent Information option**   For more information, see Appendix F.
- **Route Information options**   When present, Route Information options contain routes to add to the local routing table for more efficient host forwarding decisions.

Network Monitor Capture

Here is an example of a Router Advertisement message as displayed by Network Monitor 3.1 (capture 06_02 in the \NetworkMonitorCaptures folder on the companion CD-ROM):

```
Frame:
+ Ethernet: Etype = IPv6
+ Ipv6: Next Protocol = ICMPv6, Payload Length = 96
- Icmpv6: Router Advertisement
    MessageType: Router Advertisement, 134(0x86)
  - RouterAdvertisement:
    Code: 0 (0x0)
    Checksum: 8095 (0x1F9F)
    CurHopLimit: 0 (0x0)
   - RouterAdvertisementFlag:
    M:                 (0.......) Not managed address configuration
    O:                 (.0......) Not other stateful configuration
    A:                 (..0.....) Not a Mobile IP Home Agent
    RouterPreference:  (...00...) Medium,0(0x0)
    Reserved:          (.....000)
    RouterLifetime: 0 (0x0)
    ReachableTime: 0 (0x0)
    RetransTimer: 0 (0x0)
+ SourceLinkLayerAddress:
+ MTU:
+ PrefixInformation:
+ PrefixInformation:
```

Neighbor Solicitation

IPv6 nodes send the Neighbor Solicitation message to discover the link-layer address of an on-link IPv6 node or to confirm a previously determined link-layer address. It typically includes the link-layer address of the sender. Typical Neighbor Solicitation messages are multicast for address resolution and unicast when the reachability of a neighboring node is being verified.

For example, assuming that the local link is Ethernet, in the Ethernet header of the Neighbor Solicitation message, you will find the following settings:

- The Source Address field is set to the MAC address of the sending network adapter.

- For a multicast Neighbor Solicitation message, the Destination Address field is set to the Ethernet MAC address that corresponds to the solicited-node address of the target. For a unicast Neighbor Solicitation message, the Destination Address field is set to the unicast MAC address of the neighbor.

In the IPv6 header of the Neighbor Solicitation message, you will find these settings:

- The Source Address field is set to either a unicast IPv6 address assigned to the sending interface or, during duplicate address detection, the unspecified address (::).
- For a multicast Neighbor Solicitation, the Destination Address field is set to the solicited-node address of the target. For a unicast Neighbor Solicitation, the Destination Address field is set to the unicast address of the target.
- The Hop Limit field is set to 255.

Figure 6-14 shows the structure of the Neighbor Solicitation message.

```
        Type  |||||| = 135
        Code  |||||| = 0
    Checksum  ||||||||||||
    Reserved  ||||||||||||||||||||||||
Target Address |||||||||||||||||||||||||||||||||||||||||||||||
               |||||||||||||||||||||||||||||||||||||||||||||||
     Options  |||||||||||||||||||| . . .
```

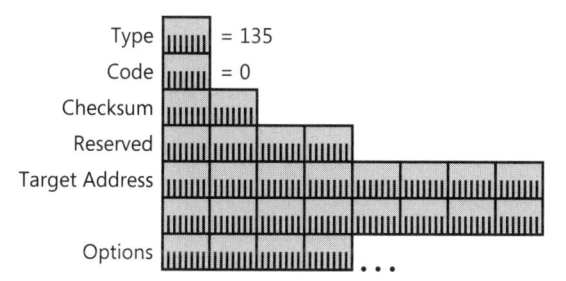

Figure 6-14 The structure of the Neighbor Solicitation message

The fields in the Neighbor Solicitation message are as follows:

- **Type**   The value of this field is 135.
- **Code**   The value of this field is 0.
- **Checksum**   The value of this field is the ICMPv6 checksum.
- **Reserved**   This is a 32-bit field reserved for future use and set to 0.
- **Target Address**   The Target Address field indicates the IP address of the target. The size of this field is 128 bits.
- **Source Link-Layer Address option**   When present, the Source Link-Layer Address option contains the link-layer address of the sender. For an Ethernet node, the Source Link-Layer Address option contains the Ethernet MAC address of the sending node. The receiving node uses the address in the Source Link-Layer Address option to determine the unicast MAC address of the node to which the corresponding Neighbor Advertisement is sent. During duplicate address detection, when the source IPv6 address is the unspecified address (::), the Source Link-Layer Address option is not included.

Network Monitor Capture

Here is an example of a Neighbor Solicitation message as displayed by Network Monitor 3.1 (frame 1 of capture 06_01 in the \NetworkMonitorCaptures folder on the companion CD-ROM):

```
Frame:
- Ethernet: Etype = IPv6
  + DestinationAddress: 3333FF 026EA5
  + SourceAddress: 00105A AA20A2
    EthernetType: IPv6, 34525(0x86dd)
- Ipv6: Next Protocol = ICMPv6, Payload Length = 32
  + Versions: IPv6, Internet Protocol, DSCP 0
    PayloadLength: 32 (0x20)
    NextProtocol: ICMPv6, 58(0x3a)
    HopLimit: 255 (0xFF)
    SourceAddress: FE80:0:0:0:210:5AFF:FEAA:20A2
    DestinationAddress: FF02:0:0:0:0:1:FF02:6EA5
- Icmpv6: Neighbor Solicitation, Target = FE80:0:0:0:260:97FF:FE02:6EA5
    MessageType: Neighbor Solicitation, 135(0x87)
  - NeighborSolicitation:
    Code: 0 (0x0)
    Checksum: 3893 (0xF35)
    Reserved: 0 (0x0)
    TargetAddress: FE80:0:0:0:260:97FF:FE02:6EA5
  - SourceLinkLayerAddress:
    Type: Source Link-Layer Address, 1(0x1)
    Length: 1, in unit of 8 octets
    Address: 00-10-5A-AA-20-A2
```

Notice how the last 24 bits of the target address (FE80::260:97FF:FE02:6EA5) correspond to the last 24 bits of the solicited-node destination address (FF02::1:FF02:6EA5) (corresponding bits underlined). Also notice how the last 32 bits of the solicited-node destination address (FF02::1:FF02:6EA5) correspond to the last 32 bits of the Ethernet destination address (3333FF026EA5) (corresponding bits underlined).

Neighbor Advertisement

An IPv6 node sends the Neighbor Advertisement message in response to a Neighbor Solicitation message. An IPv6 node also sends unsolicited Neighbor Advertisements to inform neighboring nodes of changes in link-layer addresses or the node's role. The Neighbor Advertisement contains information required by nodes to determine the type of Neighbor Advertisement message, the sender's role on the network, and typically the link-layer address of the sender.

For example, assuming that the local link is Ethernet, in the Ethernet header of the Neighbor Advertisement message, you will find the following settings:

- The Source Address field is set to the MAC address of the sending network adapter.
- The Destination Address field is set, for a solicited Neighbor Advertisement, to the unicast MAC address of the initial Neighbor Solicitation sender. For an unsolicited Neighbor

Advertisement, the Destination Address field is set to 33-33-00-00-00-01, which is the Ethernet MAC address corresponding to the link-local scope all-nodes multicast address.

In the IPv6 header of the Neighbor Advertisement message, you will find these settings:

- The Source Address field is set to a unicast address assigned to the sending interface.
- The Destination Address field is set, for a solicited Neighbor Advertisement, to the unicast IP address of the sender of the initial Neighbor Solicitation. For an unsolicited Neighbor Advertisement, the Destination Address field is set to the link-local scope all-nodes multicast address (FF02::1).
- The Hop Limit field is set to 255.

Figure 6-15 shows the structure of the Neighbor Advertisement message.

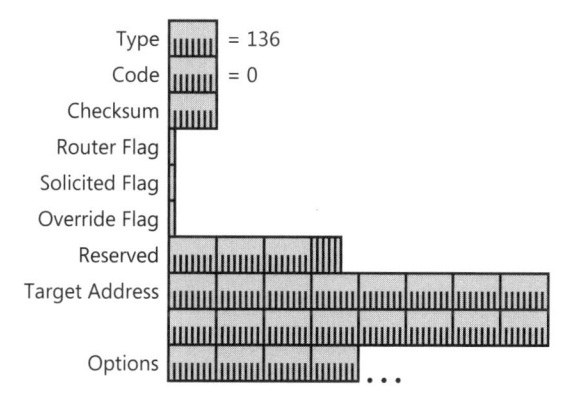

Figure 6-15 The structure of the Neighbor Advertisement message

The following list describes the fields in the Neighbor Advertisement message:

- **Type**   The value of this field is 136.
- **Code**   The value of this field is 0.
- **Checksum**   The value of this field is the ICMPv6 checksum.
- **Router flag**   The Router flag indicates the role of the sender of the Neighbor Advertisement message. The size of this field is 1 bit. The Router flag is set to 1 when the sender is a router and 0 when the sender is not. The Router flag is used by the neighbor unreachability detection process to determine when a router changes to a host.
- **Solicited flag**   The Solicited flag indicates, when set to 1, that the Neighbor Advertisement message was sent in response to a Neighbor Solicitation message. The size of this field is 1 bit. The Solicited flag is used as a reachability confirmation during neighbor unreachability detection. The Solicited flag is set to 0 for both multicast Neighbor Advertisements and unsolicited unicast Neighbor Advertisements.
- **Override flag**   The Override flag indicates, when set to 1, that the link-layer address in the included Target Link-Layer Address option should override the link-layer address

in the existing neighbor cache entry. The size of this field is 1 bit. If the Override flag is set to 0, the enclosed link-layer address updates a neighbor cache entry only if the link-layer address is not known. The Override flag is set to 0 for a solicited anycast address or a proxied advertisement. The Override flag is set to 1 in other solicited and unsolicited advertisements. For more information about the neighbor cache, see the "Neighbor Discovery Processes" section in this chapter.

- **Reserved**   This is a 29-bit field reserved for future use and set to 0.
- **Target Address**   The Target Address field indicates the address being advertised. The size of this field is 128 bits. For solicited Neighbor Advertisement messages, the target address is set to the value of the Target Address field in the corresponding Neighbor Solicitation. For unsolicited Neighbor Advertisement messages, the target address is the address whose link-layer address or role has changed.
- **Target Link-Layer Address option**   When present, the Target Link-Layer Address option contains the link-layer address of the target, which is the sender of the Neighbor Advertisement. For an Ethernet node, the Target Link-Layer Address option contains the Ethernet MAC address of the sending node. The address in the Target Link-Layer Address option is used by receiving nodes to determine the unicast MAC address of the advertising node.

Network Monitor Capture

Here is an example of a solicited Neighbor Advertisement message as displayed by Network Monitor 3.1 (frame 2 of capture 06_01 in the \NetworkMonitorCaptures folder on the companion CD-ROM):

```
  Frame:
+ Ethernet: Etype = IPv6
- Ipv6: Next Protocol = ICMPv6, Payload Length = 32
  + Versions: IPv6, Internet Protocol, DSCP 0
    PayloadLength: 32 (0x20)
    NextProtocol: ICMPv6, 58(0x3a)
    HopLimit: 255 (0xFF)
    SourceAddress: FE80:0:0:0:260:97FF:FE02:6EA5
    DestinationAddress: FE80:0:0:0:210:5AFF:FEAA:20A2
- Icmpv6: Neighbor Advertisement, Target = FE80:0:0:0:260:97FF:FE02:6EA5
    MessageType: Neighbor Advertisement, 136(0x88)
  - NeighborAdvertisement:
    Code: 0 (0x0)
    Checksum: 35244 (0x89AC)
  - NeighborAdvertisementFlag: 1610612736 (0x60000000)
      R:    (0............................) Not router
      S:    (.1...........................) Solicited
      O:    (..1..........................) Override
      Rsv:  (...00000000000000000000000000000)
    TargetAddress: FE80:0:0:0:260:97FF:FE02:6EA5
  + TargetLinkLayerAddress:
```

Redirect

The Redirect message is sent by an IPv6 router to inform an originating host of a better first-hop address for a specific destination. Redirect messages are sent only by routers for unicast traffic, are unicast only to originating hosts, and are processed only by hosts.

For example, assuming that the local link is Ethernet, in the Ethernet header of the Redirect message, you will find the following settings:

- The Source Address field is set to the MAC address of the sending network adapter.
- The Destination Address field is set to the unicast MAC address of the originating sender.

In the IPv6 header of the Redirect message, you will find these settings:

- The Source Address field is set to a unicast address that is assigned to the sending interface.
- The Destination Address field is set to the unicast IP address of the originating host.
- The Hop Limit field is set to 255.

Figure 6-16 shows the structure of the Redirect message.

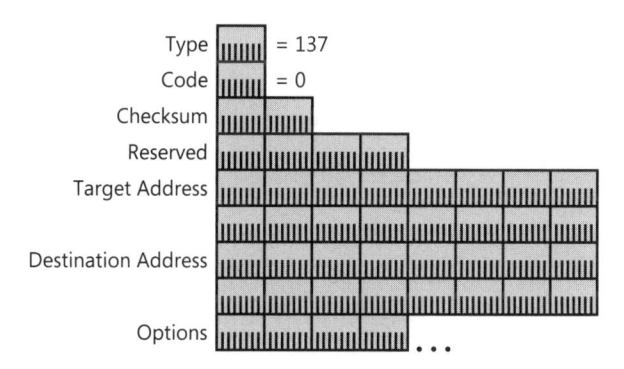

Figure 6-16 The structure of the Redirect message

The following list describes the fields in the Redirect message:

- **Type** The value of this field is 137.
- **Code** The value of this field is 0.
- **Checksum** The value of this field is the ICMPv6 checksum.
- **Reserved** This is a 32-bit field reserved for the future and set to 0.
- **Target Address** The Target Address field indicates the better next-hop address for packets addressed to the node in the Destination Address field. The size of this field is 128 bits. For off-link traffic, the Target Address field is set to the link-local address of a

local router. For on-link traffic, the Target Address field is set to the Destination Address field in the Redirect message.

- **Destination Address**   The Destination Address field contains the destination address of the packet that caused the router to send the Redirect message. The size of this field is 128 bits. Upon receipt at the originating host, the Target Address and Destination Address fields are used to update forwarding information for the destination. Subsequent packets sent to the destination by the host are forwarded to the address in the Target Address field.

The options that can be present in a Redirect message are the following:

- **Target Link-Layer Address option**   The Target Link-Layer Address option contains the link-layer address of the target (the node to which subsequent packets should be sent). The Target Link-Layer Address option can be included when known by the router, although it is not typically sent.
- **Redirected Header option**   The Redirected Header option includes the leading portion of the original packet that caused the Redirect message to be sent, sized so that the entire IPv6 packet containing the Redirect message is no larger than 1280 bytes.

Network Monitor Capture

Here is an example of a Redirect message as displayed by Network Monitor 3.1 (capture 06_03 in the \NetworkMonitorCaptures folder on the companion CD-ROM):

```
  Frame:
+ Ethernet: Etype = IPv6
+ Ipv6: Next Protocol = ICMPv6, Payload Length = 128
- Icmpv6: Redirect, Target = FE80:0:0:0:2B0:D0FF:FE23:4735
    MessageType: Redirect, 137(0x89)
  - Redirect:
    Code: 0 (0x0)
    Checksum: 31003 (0x791B)
    Reserved: 0 (0x0)
    TargetAddress: FE80:0:0:0:2B0:D0FF:FE23:4735
    DestAddress: 2001:DB8:0:0:0:0:0:1
  - RedirectedHeader:
    Type: Redirected Header, 4(0x4)
    Length: 11, in unit of 8 octets
    Reserved: 0 (0x0)
  + InvokingPacket: Next Protocol = ICMPv6, Payload Length = 40
```

Summary of Neighbor Discovery Messages and Options

Table 6-2 lists each ND message and the options that might be included with the message.

Table 6-2 ND Messages and the Options That Might Be Included

ND Message	ND Options that Might Be Included
Router Solicitation	Source Link-Layer Address option: Used to inform the router of the link-layer address of the host for the unicast Router Advertisement response.
Router Advertisement	Source Link-Layer Address option: Used to inform the receiving host(s) of the link-layer address of the router.
	Prefix Information option(s): Used to inform the receiving host(s) of on-link prefixes and whether to autoconfigure stateless addresses.
	MTU option: Used to inform the receiving host(s) of the IPv6 MTU of the link.
	Advertisement Interval option: Used to inform the receiving host how often the router (the home agent) is sending unsolicited multicast router advertisements.
	Home Agent Information option: Used to advertise the home agent's preference and lifetime.
	Route Information option(s): Used to inform the receiving host(s) of specific routes to add to a local routing table.
Neighbor Solicitation	Source Link-Layer Address option: Used to inform the receiving node of the link-layer address of the sender.
Neighbor Advertisement	Target Link-Layer Address option: Used to inform the receiving node(s) of the link-layer address corresponding to the Target Address field.
Redirect	Redirected Header option: Used to include all or a portion of the packet that was redirected.
	Target Link-Layer Address option: Used to inform the receiving node(s) of the link-layer address corresponding to the Target Address field.

Neighbor Discovery Processes

The ND protocol provides message exchanges for the following processes:

- Address resolution (including duplicate address detection)
- Router discovery (includes prefix and parameter discovery)
- Neighbor unreachability detection
- Redirect function

For information about address autoconfiguration, see Chapter 8. For information about next-hop determination, see the "Host Sending Algorithm" section in this chapter.

Conceptual Host Data Structures

To facilitate interactions between neighboring nodes, RFC 4861 defines the following conceptual host data structures as an example of how to store information for ND processes:

- **Neighbor cache** The neighbor cache stores the on-link IP address of each neighbor, its corresponding link-layer address, and an indication of the neighbor's reachability state. The neighbor cache is equivalent to the ARP cache in IPv4.

- **Destination cache** The destination cache stores information on next-hop IP addresses for destinations to which traffic has recently been sent. Each entry in the destination cache contains the destination IP address (either local or remote), the previously resolved next-hop IP address, and the path MTU for the destination.

- **Prefix list** The prefix list contains on-link prefixes. Each entry in the prefix list defines a range of IP addresses for destinations that are directly reachable (neighbors). This list is populated from prefixes advertised by routers using the Router Advertisement message.

- **Default router list** IP addresses corresponding to on-link routers that have sent Router Advertisement messages and are eligible to be default routers are included in the default router list.

Figure 6-17 shows the conceptual host data structures defined in RFC 4861.

Destination Cache		
Destination	Next-Hop Address	PMTU

Neighbor Cache		
Next-Hop Address	Link-Layer Address	PMTU

Prefix List

Default Router List

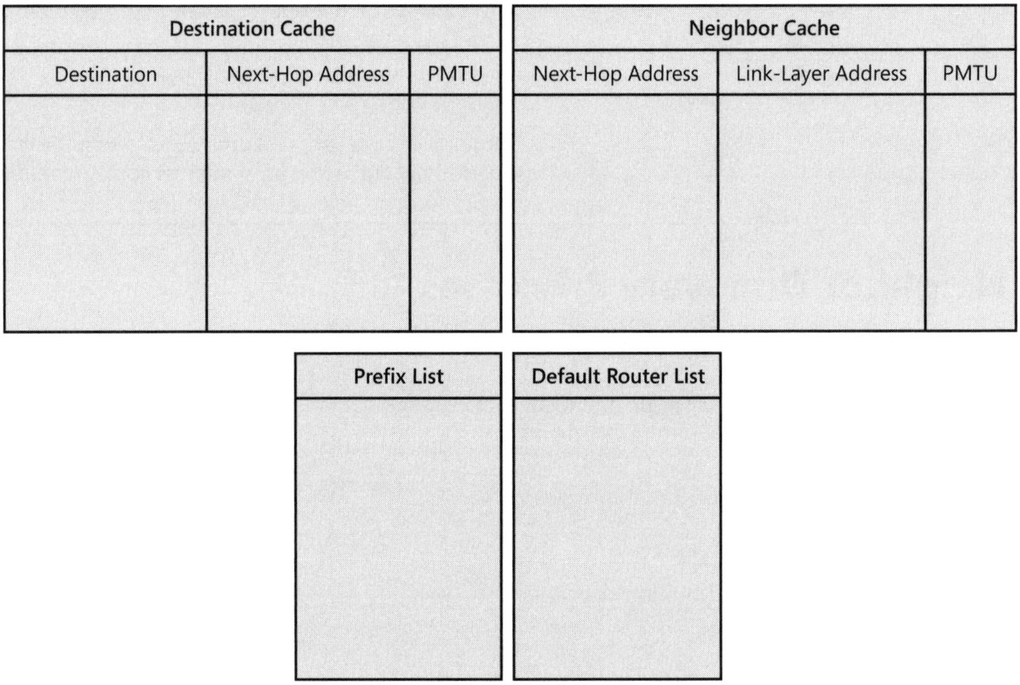

Figure 6-17 The conceptual host data structures defined in RFC 4861

RFC 4861 defines these data structures as an example of an IPv6 host conceptual model. An IPv6 implementation is not required to create these exact data structures as long as the external behavior of the host is consistent with RFC 4861. For example, the IPv6 protocol for Windows Server 2008 and Windows Vista uses a destination cache and neighbor cache. However, to determine the next-hop address for a given destination, the IPv6 protocol for Windows Server 2008 and Windows Vista uses a routing table rather than a prefix list and default router list. For more information about the IPv6 routing table, see Chapter 10, "IPv6 Routing." For more information about how IPv6 determines the next-hop address using the conceptual RFC 4861 data structures, see the "Host Sending Algorithm" section in this chapter.

To view the destination cache on a computer running Windows Server 2008 or Windows Vista, type **netsh interface ipv6 show destinationcache** at a command prompt. To view the neighbor cache, type **netsh interface ipv6 show neighbors** at a command prompt. To view the routing table, type **netsh interface ipv6 show routes** at a command prompt.

Address Resolution

The address resolution process for IPv6 nodes consists of an exchange of Neighbor Solicitation and Neighbor Advertisement messages to resolve the link-layer address of the on-link next-hop address for a given destination. The sending host sends a multicast Neighbor Solicitation message on the appropriate interface. The multicast address of the Neighbor Solicitation message is the solicited-node multicast address derived from the target IP address. The Neighbor Solicitation message includes the link-layer address of the sending host in the Source Link-Layer Address option. For information about how a host determines the next-hop address for a destination, see "Host Sending Algorithm" in this chapter.

When the target host receives the Neighbor Solicitation message, it updates its own neighbor cache based on the source address of the Neighbor Solicitation message and the link-layer address in the Source Link-Layer Address option. Next, the target node sends a unicast Neighbor Advertisement to the Neighbor Solicitation sender. The Neighbor Advertisement includes the Target Link-Layer Address option.

After receiving the Neighbor Advertisement from the target, the sending host updates its neighbor cache with an entry for the target based on the information in the Target Link-Layer Address option. At this point, unicast IPv6 traffic between the sending host and the target of the Neighbor Solicitation can be sent.

Address Resolution Example—Part 1

Host A has an Ethernet MAC address of 00-10-5A-AA-20-A2 and a corresponding link-local address of FE80::210:5AFF:FEAA:20A2. Host B has an Ethernet MAC address of 00-60-97-02-6E-A5 and a corresponding link-local address of FE80::260:97FF:FE02:6EA5. To send a packet to Host B, Host A must first use address resolution to resolve Host B's link-layer address.

Based on Host B's IP address, Host A sends a multicast Neighbor Solicitation message to the solicited-node address of FF02::1:FF02:6EA5, as shown in Figure 6-18.

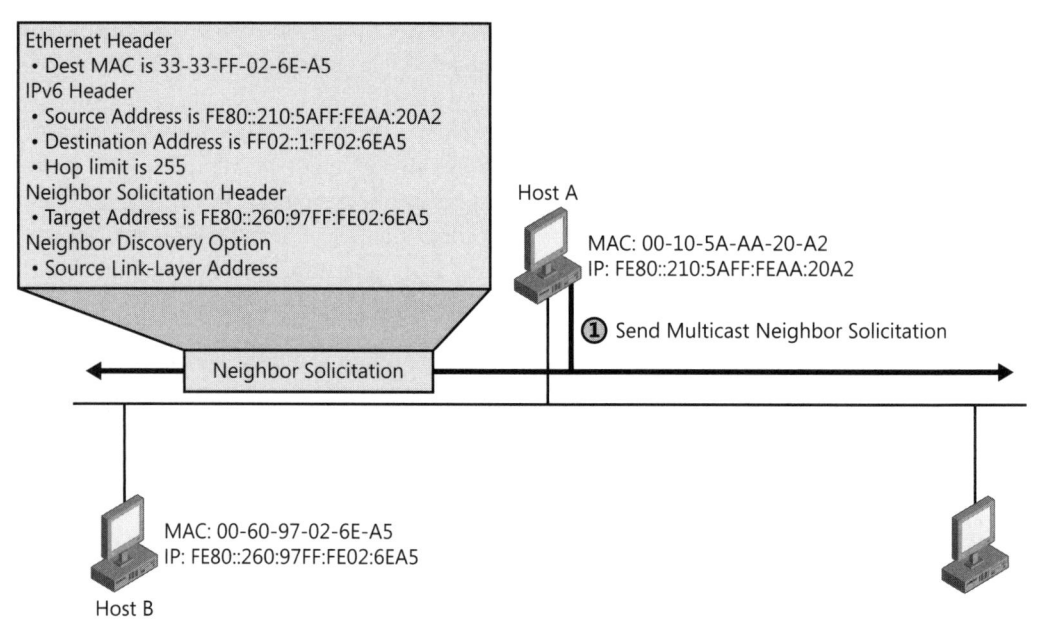

Figure 6-18 The multicast Neighbor Solicitation message

Network Monitor Capture

Here is the Neighbor Solicitation message for this example as displayed by Network Monitor 3.1 (frame 1 of capture 06_01 in the \NetworkMonitorCaptures folder on the companion CD-ROM):

```
Frame:
- Ethernet: Etype = IPv6
  + DestinationAddress: 3333FF 026EA5
  + SourceAddress: 00105A AA20A2
    EthernetType: IPv6, 34525(0x86dd)
- Ipv6: Next Protocol = ICMPv6, Payload Length = 32
  + Versions: IPv6, Internet Protocol, DSCP 0
    PayloadLength: 32 (0x20)
    NextProtocol: ICMPv6, 58(0x3a)
    HopLimit: 255 (0xFF)
    SourceAddress: FE80:0:0:0:210:5AFF:FEAA:20A2
    DestinationAddress: FF02:0:0:0:0:1:FF02:6EA5
- Icmpv6: Neighbor Solicitation, Target = FE80:0:0:0:260:97FF:FE02:6EA5
    MessageType: Neighbor Solicitation, 135(0x87)
  - NeighborSolicitation:
    Code: 0 (0x0)
    Checksum: 3893 (0xF35)
    Reserved: 0 (0x0)
    TargetAddress: FE80:0:0:0:260:97FF:FE02:6EA5
  - SourceLinkLayerAddress:
    Type: Source Link-Layer Address, 1(0x1)
    Length: 1, in unit of 8 octets
    Address: 00-10-5A-AA-20-A2
```

Address Resolution Example—Part 2

Host B, having registered the multicast MAC address of 33-33-FF-02-6E-A5 with its Ethernet adapter, receives and processes the Neighbor Solicitation message. Host B responds with a unicast Neighbor Advertisement message, as shown in Figure 6-19.

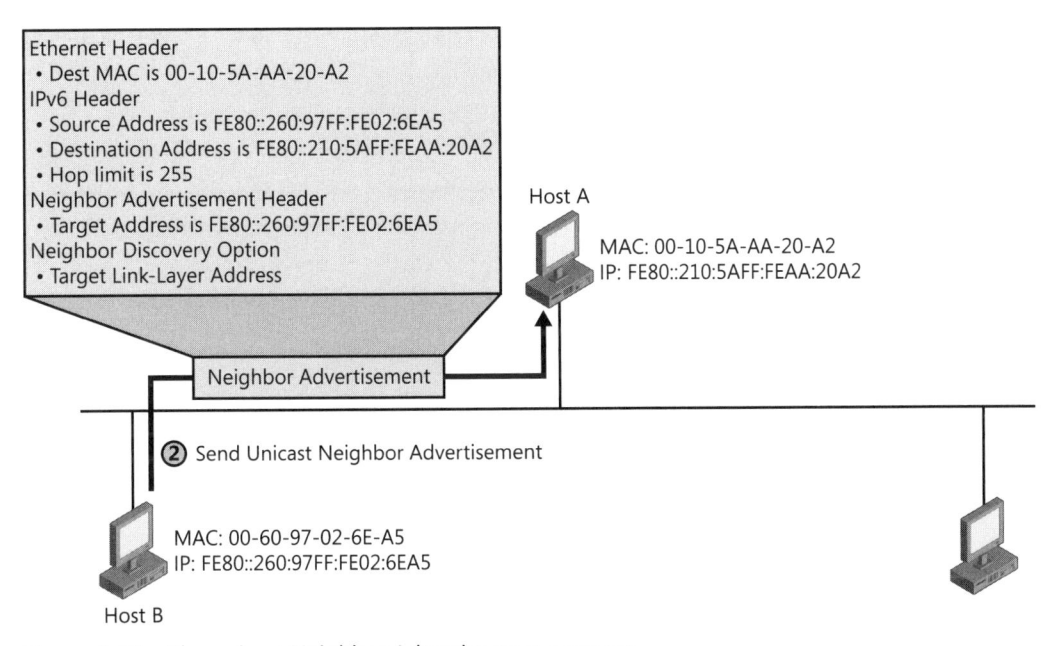

```
Ethernet Header
 • Dest MAC is 00-10-5A-AA-20-A2
IPv6 Header
 • Source Address is FE80::260:97FF:FE02:6EA5
 • Destination Address is FE80::210:5AFF:FEAA:20A2
 • Hop limit is 255
Neighbor Advertisement Header
 • Target Address is FE80::260:97FF:FE02:6EA5
Neighbor Discovery Option
 • Target Link-Layer Address
```

Host A
MAC: 00-10-5A-AA-20-A2
IP: FE80::210:5AFF:FEAA:20A2

Neighbor Advertisement

② Send Unicast Neighbor Advertisement

MAC: 00-60-97-02-6E-A5
IP: FE80::260:97FF:FE02:6EA5

Host B

Figure 6-19 The unicast Neighbor Advertisement message

Network Monitor Capture

Here is the Neighbor Advertisement message for this example as displayed by Network Monitor 3.1 (frame 2 of capture 06_01 in the \NetworkMonitorCaptures folder on the companion CD-ROM):

```
Frame:
- Ethernet: Etype = IPv6
  + DestinationAddress: 00105A AA20A2
  + SourceAddress: 00105A 026EA5
    EthernetType: IPv6, 34525(0x86dd)
- Ipv6: Next Protocol = ICMPv6, Payload Length = 32
  + Versions: IPv6, Internet Protocol, DSCP 0
    PayloadLength: 32 (0x20)
    NextProtocol: ICMPv6, 58(0x3a)
    HopLimit: 255 (0xFF)
    SourceAddress: FE80:0:0:0:260:97FF:FE02:6EA5
    DestinationAddress: FE80:0:0:0:210:5AFF:FEAA:20A2
- Icmpv6: Neighbor Advertisement, Target = FE80:0:0:0:260:97FF:FE02:6EA5
    MessageType: Neighbor Advertisement, 136(0x88)
  - NeighborAdvertisement:
    Code: 0 (0x0)
    Checksum: 35244 (0x89AC)
   - NeighborAdvertisementFlag: 1610612736 (0x60000000)
```

```
            R:       (0............................) Not router
            S:       (.1...........................) Solicited
            O:       (..1..........................) Override
            Rsv:     (...00000000000000000000000000000)
        TargetAddress: FE80:0:0:0:260:97FF:FE02:6EA5
    - TargetLinkLayerAddress:
        Type: Target Link-Layer Address, 2(0x2)
        Length: 1, in unit of 8 octets
        Address: 00-60-97-02-6E-A5
```

Neighbor Unreachability Detection

A neighboring node is reachable if there has been a recent confirmation that IPv6 packets sent to the neighboring node were received and processed by the neighboring node. Neighbor unreachability does not necessarily verify the end-to-end reachability of the destination. Because a neighboring node can be a host or router, the neighboring node might not be the final destination of the packet. Neighbor unreachability verifies only the reachability of the first hop to the destination.

One of the ways that reachability is confirmed is through the sending of a unicast Neighbor Solicitation message and the receipt of a solicited Neighbor Advertisement message. A solicited Neighbor Advertisement message, which has its Solicited flag set to 1, is sent only in response to a Neighbor Solicitation message. Unsolicited Neighbor Advertisement or Router Advertisement messages are not considered proof of reachability. The exchange of Neighbor Solicitation and Neighbor Advertisement messages confirms only the reachability of the node that sent the Neighbor Advertisement from the node that sent the Neighbor Solicitation. It does not confirm the reachability of the node that sent the Neighbor Solicitation from the node that sent the Neighbor Advertisement.

For example, if Host A sends a unicast Neighbor Solicitation to Host B and Host B sends a solicited unicast Neighbor Advertisement to Host A, Host A considers Host B reachable. Because there is no confirmation in this exchange that Host A actually received the Neighbor Advertisement, Host B does not consider Host A reachable. To confirm reachability of Host A from Host B, Host B must send its own unicast Neighbor Solicitation to Host A and receive a solicited unicast Neighbor Advertisement from Host A.

Here is an example of an exchange of ND messages to establish neighbor reachability by two nodes (HOST_A and HOST_B) for each other as displayed by Network Monitor 3.1 (capture 06_05 in the \NetworkMonitorCaptures folder on the companion CD-ROM):

```
1       8.356000        HOST_A      HOST_B          ICMP6
        Neighbor Solicitation; Target = fe80::210:5aff:feaa:20a2
2       8.357000        HOST_B      HOST_A          ICMP6
        Neighbor Advertisement; Target = fe80::210:5aff:feaa:20a2
3       8.527000        HOST_B      HOST_A          ICMP6
        Neighbor Solicitation; Target = fe80::250:daff:fed8:c153
4       8.527000        HOST_A      HOST_B          ICMP6
        Neighbor Advertisement; Target = fe80::250:daff:fed8:c153
```

In frames 1 and 2, HOST_A establishes the reachability of HOST_B. In frames 3 and 4, HOST_B establishes the reachability of HOST_A.

> **Note** The Network Monitor frame summary lines have been wrapped for improved readability.

Another method of determining reachability is when upper-layer protocols indicate that the communication using the next-hop address is making forward progress. For TCP traffic, forward progress is determined when acknowledgement segments for sent data are received. The end-to-end reachability confirmed by the receipt of TCP acknowledgments implies the reachability of the first hop to the destination. The TCP module provides these indications to the IPv6 module on an ongoing basis.

Other protocols, such as UDP, might not have a method of determining or indicating the forward progress of communication. In this case, the exchange of Neighbor Solicitation and Neighbor Advertisement messages is used to confirm reachability.

Neighbor Cache Entry States

The reachability of a neighboring node is determined by monitoring the state of the neighboring node's entry in the neighbor cache.

Figure 6-20 shows the states of a neighbor cache entry.

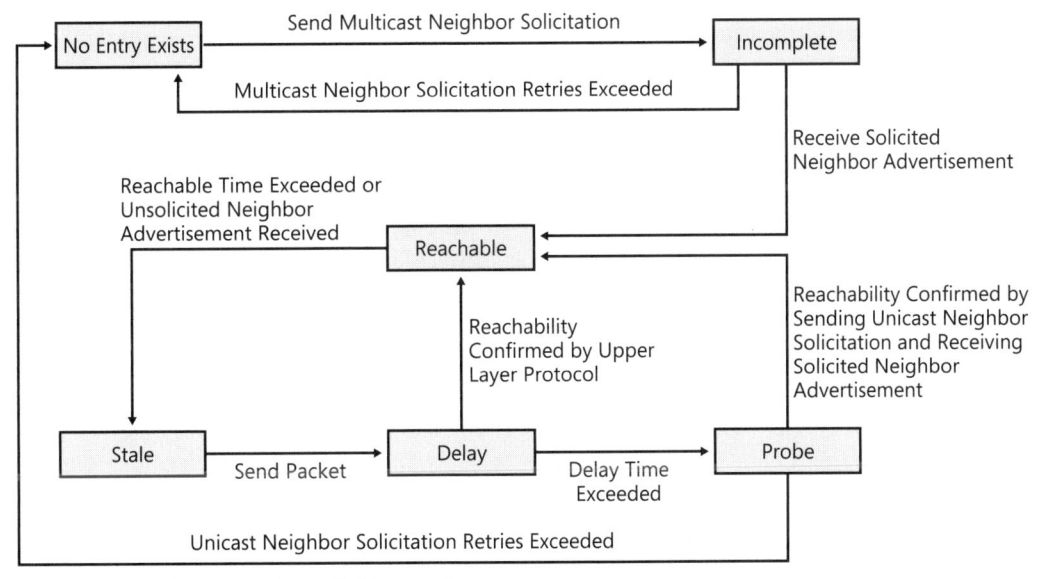

Figure 6-20 The states of a neighbor cache entry

RFC 4861 defines the following states for a neighbor cache entry:

- **INCOMPLETE** IPv6 address resolution, which uses a solicited-node multicast Neighbor Solicitation message, is in progress. The INCOMPLETE state is entered when a new neighbor cache entry is created but does not yet have the node's corresponding link-layer address. The number of multicast neighbor solicitations sent before abandoning the address resolution process and removing the neighbor cache entry is set by a configurable variable. RFC 4861 uses the variable name of MAX_MULTICAST_SOLICIT and recommends a value of 3.

- **REACHABLE** Reachability has been confirmed by receipt of a solicited unicast Neighbor Advertisement message by an indication from an upper-layer protocol. The neighbor cache entry stays in the REACHABLE state until the number of milliseconds indicated in the Reachable Time field in the Router Advertisement message (or a host default value) elapses. As long as upper-layer protocols such as TCP indicate that communication is making forward progress, the entry stays in the REACHABLE state. Each time an indication of forward progress is made, the reachable time for the entry is refreshed.

- **STALE** Reachable time (the duration since the last reachability confirmation was received) has elapsed. The neighbor cache entry goes into the STALE state after the value (milliseconds) in the Reachable Time field in the Router Advertisement message (or a host default value) elapses, and it remains in this state until a packet is sent to the neighbor. The STALE state is also entered when an unsolicited neighbor advertisement that advertises the link-layer address is received.

- **DELAY** To allow time for upper-layer protocols to provide reachability confirmation before sending Neighbor Solicitation messages, the neighbor cache entry enters the DELAY state and waits a configurable period of time. RFC 4861 uses the variable name of DELAY_FIRST_PROBE_TIME and recommends a value of 5 seconds. If no reachability confirmation is received by the delay time, the entry enters the PROBE state and a unicast Neighbor Solicitation message is sent.

- **PROBE** Reachability confirmation is in progress for a neighbor cache entry that was in either the STALE state or the DELAY state. Unicast Neighbor Solicitation messages are sent at intervals corresponding to the Retransmission Timer field in the Router Advertisement message received by this host (or a default host value). The number of Neighbor Solicitations sent before abandoning the reachability detection process and removing the neighbor cache entry is set by a configurable variable. RFC 4861 uses the variable name of MAX_UNICAST_SOLICITS and recommends a value of 3.

Depending on the IPv6 implementation, any entry can go from any state to the NO ENTRY EXISTS state at any time (not shown in Figure 6-20).

If the unreachable neighbor is a router, the host chooses another router from the default router list and performs both address resolution and neighbor unreachability detection on it.

If a router becomes a host, it should send a multicast Neighbor Advertisement message with the Router flag set to 0. If a host receives a Neighbor Advertisement message from a router where the Router flag is set to 0, the host removes that router from the default router list and, if necessary, chooses another router.

Neighbor Unreachability Detection and Dead Gateway Detection

The TCP/IP (IPv4) protocol for Windows Server 2008 and Windows Vista supports an algorithm known as *dead gateway detection*. Dead gateway detection detects the failure of the current default gateway by monitoring the number of failing TCP connections. When 25 percent of the active TCP connections have failed and have been switched to another default gateway, the default gateway of the host is switched to another default gateway.

Dead gateway detection provides some default gateway fault tolerance for hosts on subnets containing multiple default routers. However, dead gateway detection has the following limitations:

- Monitors only TCP traffic. If connectivity fails for other types of traffic, the default gateway is not switched.

- Can cause the default gateway configuration to change when a remote router fails. Remote routers in the path between the host and the destination that fail might also cause TCP connections forwarded along that path to fail and for the host to switch its default gateway. Because dead gateway detection relies on an end-to-end protocol (such as TCP), a host can switch its default gateway even when the current default gateway is fully operational.

Neighbor unreachability detection is an improvement over dead gateway detection because it does the following:

- Provides for host-based default router fault tolerance for all types of traffic, not just TCP. Although forward progress indicators are used for TCP traffic, other protocols can rely on an exchange of Neighbor Solicitation and Neighbor Advertisement messages to determine reachability.

- Detects whether the neighboring default router is operational. Neighbor unreachability detection will not cause the default router configuration to change because of a failing remote router.

Duplicate Address Detection

IPv4 nodes use ARP Request messages and a method called *gratuitous ARP* to detect a duplicate unicast IPv4 address on the local link. Similarly, IPv6 nodes use the Neighbor Solicitation message to detect duplicate address use on the local link in a process known as duplicate address detection that is described in RFC 4862.

With IPv4 gratuitous ARP, the Source Protocol Address and Target Protocol Address fields in the ARP Request message header are set to the IPv4 address for which duplication is being detected. In IPv6 duplicate address detection, the Target Address field in the Neighbor Solicitation message is set to the IPv6 address for which duplication is being detected.

Duplicate address detection differs from address resolution in the following ways:

- In the duplicate address detection Neighbor Solicitation message, the Source Address field in the IPv6 header is set to the unspecified address (::). The address being queried for duplication cannot be used until it is determined that there are no duplicates.

- In the Neighbor Advertisement reply to a duplicate address detection Neighbor Solicitation message, the Destination Address in the IPv6 header is set to the link-local scope all-nodes multicast address (FF02::1). The Solicited flag in the Neighbor Advertisement message is set to 0. Because the sender of the duplicate address detection Neighbor Solicitation message is not using the desired IP address, it cannot receive unicast Neighbor Advertisements. Therefore, the Neighbor Advertisement is multicast.

Upon receipt of the multicast Neighbor Advertisement with the Target Address field set to the IP address for which duplication is being detected, the node disables the use of the duplicate IP address on the interface. If the node does not receive a Neighbor Advertisement that defends the use of the address, it initializes the address on the interface.

An IPv6 node does not perform duplicate address detection for anycast addresses. Anycast addresses are not unique to a node.

Duplicate Address Detection Example—Part 1

Host B has a global address of 2001:DB8::2:260:8FF:FE52:F9D8. Host A is attempting to use the global address of 2001:DB8::2:260:8FF:FE52:F9D8. However, before Host A can use this address, it must verify its uniqueness through duplicate address detection.

Host A sends a Neighbor Solicitation message to the solicited-node multicast address FF02::1:FF52:F9D8, as shown in Figure 6-21.

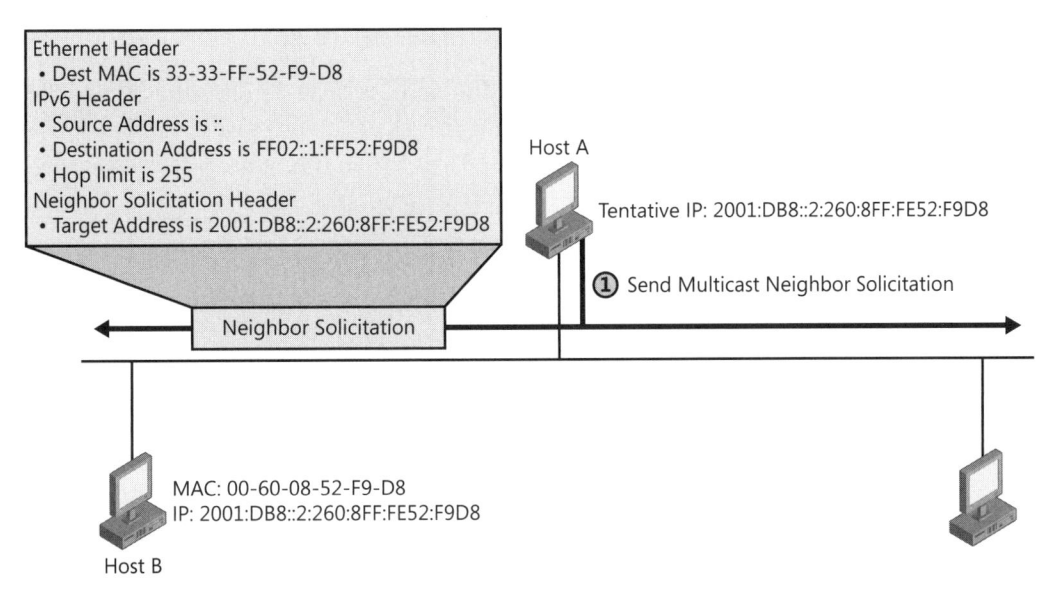

Figure 6-21 A multicast Neighbor Solicitation message for duplicate address detection

Network Monitor Capture

Here is the Neighbor Solicitation message for this example as displayed by Network Monitor 3.1 (frame 1 of capture 06_06 in the \NetworkMonitorCaptures folder on the companion CD-ROM):

```
Frame:
- Ethernet: Etype = IPv6
  + DestinationAddress: 3333FF 52F9D8
  + SourceAddress: 00B0D0 234733
    EthernetType: IPv6, 34525(0x86dd)
- Ipv6: Next Protocol = ICMPv6, Payload Length = 24
  + Versions: IPv6, Internet Protocol, DSCP 0
    PayloadLength: 24 (0x18)
    NextProtocol: ICMPv6, 58(0x3a)
    HopLimit: 255 (0xFF)
  + SourceAddress: 0:0:0:0:0:0:0:0
    DestinationAddress: FF02:0:0:0:0:1:FF52:F9D8
- Icmpv6: Neighbor Solicitation, Target = 2001:DB8:0:2:260:8FF:FE52:F9D8
    MessageType: Neighbor Solicitation, 135(0x87)
  - NeighborSolicitation:
    Code: 0 (0x0)
    Checksum: 20279 (0x4F37)
    Reserved: 0 (0x0)
    TargetAddress: 2001:DB8:0:2:260:8FF:FE52:F9D8
```

Notice the use of the unspecified address (::) in the Source Address field in the IPv6 header and the lack of the Source Link-Layer Address option.

Duplicate Address Detection Example—Part 2

Host B, having registered the multicast MAC address of 33-33-FF-52-F9-D8 with its Ethernet adapter, receives and processes the Neighbor Solicitation message. Host B notes that the source address is the unspecified address. Host B then responds with a multicast Neighbor Advertisement message, as shown in Figure 6-22.

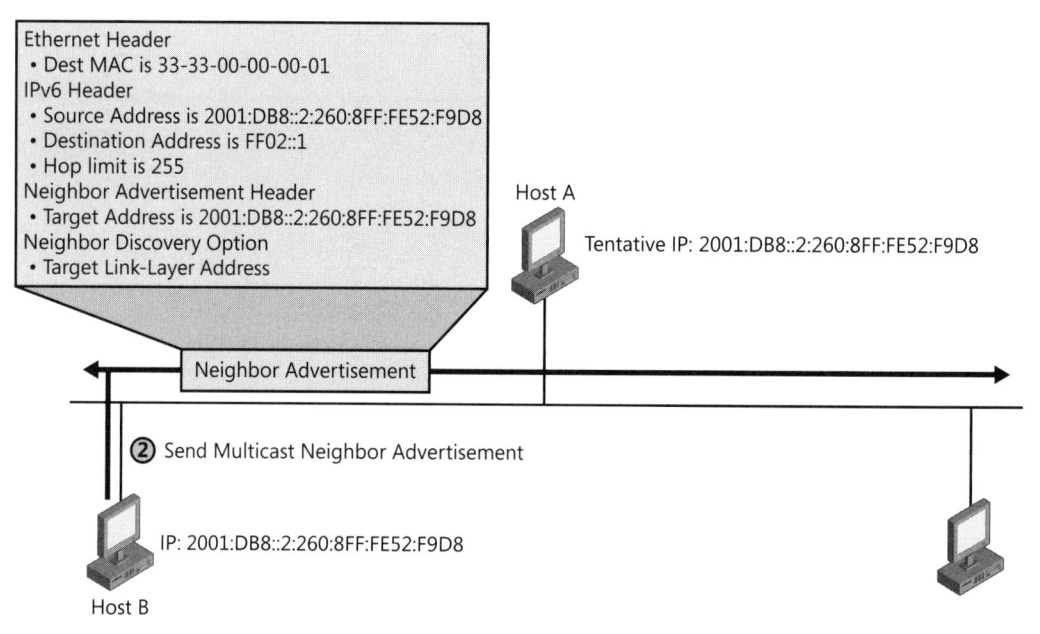

Ethernet Header
- Dest MAC is 33-33-00-00-00-01

IPv6 Header
- Source Address is 2001:DB8::2:260:8FF:FE52:F9D8
- Destination Address is FF02::1
- Hop limit is 255

Neighbor Advertisement Header
- Target Address is 2001:DB8::2:260:8FF:FE52:F9D8

Neighbor Discovery Option
- Target Link-Layer Address

Host A — Tentative IP: 2001:DB8::2:260:8FF:FE52:F9D8

Neighbor Advertisement

② Send Multicast Neighbor Advertisement

Host B — IP: 2001:DB8::2:260:8FF:FE52:F9D8

Figure 6-22 The multicast Neighbor Advertisement message

Network Monitor Capture

Here is the Neighbor Advertisement message for this example as displayed by Network Monitor 3.1 (frame 2 of capture 06_06 in the \NetworkMonitorCaptures folder on the companion CD-ROM):

```
Frame:
- Ethernet: Etype = IPv6
  + DestinationAddress: 333300 000001
  + SourceAddress: 006008 52F9D8
    EthernetType: IPv6, 34525(0x86dd)
- Ipv6: Next Protocol = ICMPv6, Payload Length = 32
  + Versions: IPv6, Internet Protocol, DSCP 0
    PayloadLength: 32 (0x20)
    NextProtocol: ICMPv6, 58(0x3a)
    HopLimit: 255 (0xFF)
    SourceAddress: 2001:DB8:0:2:260:8FF:FE52:F9D8
    DestinationAddress: FF02:0:0:0:0:0:0:1
- Icmpv6: Neighbor Advertisement, Target = 2001:DB8:0:2:260:8FF:FE52:F9D8
    MessageType: Neighbor Advertisement, 136(0x88)
  - NeighborAdvertisement:
```

```
      Code: 0 (0x0)
      Checksum: 61832 (0xF188)
    - NeighborAdvertisementFlag: 536870912 (0x20000000)
      R:   (0............................) Not router
      S:   (.0...........................) Not solicited
      O:   (..1..........................) Override
      Rsv: (...00000000000000000000000000000)
      TargetAddress: 2001:DB8:0:2:260:8FF:FE52:F9D8
    - TargetLinkLayerAddress:
      Type: Target Link-Layer Address, 2(0x2)
      Length: 1, in unit of 8 octets
      Address: 00-60-08-52-F9-D8
```

Notice the use of the link-local scope all-nodes multicast address as the destination address and the values of the Solicited and Override flags.

Router Discovery

Router discovery is the process through which nodes attempt to discover the set of routers on the local link. Router discovery in IPv6 is similar to ICMP router discovery for IPv4 described in RFC 1256. ICMP router discovery is a set of ICMP messages that allow IPv4 hosts to determine the presence of local routers, determine which local router is automatically configured as a default gateway, and automatically switch to a different router as their default gateway when the current default gateway becomes unavailable.

An important difference between ICMPv4 router discovery and IPv6 router discovery is the mechanism through which a new default router is selected when the current one becomes unavailable. In ICMPv4 router discovery, the Router Advertisement message includes an Advertisement Lifetime field. Advertisement Lifetime is the time after which the router can be considered unavailable. In the worst case, a router can become unavailable and hosts will not attempt to discover a new default router until the Router Advertisement time has elapsed.

IPv6 has a Router Lifetime field in the Router Advertisement message. This field indicates the length of time that the router can be considered a default router. However, if the current default router becomes unavailable, the condition is detected through neighbor unreachability detection instead of the Router Lifetime field in the Router Advertisement message. Because neighbor unreachability detection determines that the router is no longer reachable, a new router is chosen immediately from the default router list or the host sends a Router Solicitation message to determine if additional default routers are present on the link. For more information, see the "Neighbor Unreachability Detection" section in this chapter.

In addition to configuring a default router, IPv6 router discovery also configures the following:

- The default setting for the Hop Limit field in the IPv6 header.
- A determination of whether the node should use an address protocol, such as Dynamic Host Configuration Protocol for IPv6 (DHCPv6), for addresses and other configuration parameters.

- The timers used in neighbor unreachability detection and the retransmission of Neighbor Solicitations.

- The list of network prefixes defined for the link. Each network prefix contains both the IPv6 network prefix and its valid and preferred lifetimes. If indicated, a network prefix combined with the interface identifier creates a stateless IP address configuration for the receiving interface. A network prefix also defines the range of addresses for nodes on the local link.

- The MTU of the local link.

- Specific routes to add to the routing table.

The IPv6 router discovery processes are the following:

- IPv6 routers pseudo-periodically send a Router Advertisement message on the local link advertising their existence as routers. They also provide configuration parameters such as default hop limit, MTU, prefixes, and routes. For more information about how often routers send pseudo-periodic router advertisements, see section 6.2.4 of RFC 4861.

- Active IPv6 hosts on the local link receive the Router Advertisement messages and use the contents to maintain the default router and prefix lists, autoconfigure addresses, add routes, and configure other parameters.

- A host that is starting sends a Router Solicitation message to the link-local scope all-routers multicast address (FF02::2). If the starting host is already configured with a unicast address, the Router Solicitation is sent with a unicast source address. Otherwise, the Router Solicitation is sent with an unspecified source address (::). Upon receipt of a Router Solicitation message, all routers on the local link send a Router Advertisement message to either the unicast address of the host that sent the Router Solicitation (if the source address of the Router Solicitation is a unicast address), or to the link-local scope all-nodes multicast address (FF02::1) (if the source address of the Router Solicitation message is unspecified). The host receives the Router Advertisement messages and uses their contents to build the default router and prefix lists and set other configuration parameters. The number of Router Solicitations sent before abandoning the router discovery process is set by a configurable variable. RFC 4861 uses the variable name of MAX_RTR_SOLICITATIONS and recommends a value of 3.

Router Discovery Example—Part 1

Host A has the Ethernet MAC address of 00-B0-D0-E9-41-43. The router has an Ethernet MAC address of 00-10-FF-D6-58-C0 and a corresponding link-local address of FE80::210:FFFF:FED6:58C0. To forward packets to off-link destinations, Host A must discover the presence of the router.

As part of the startup process, Host A sends a multicast Router Solicitation message to the address FF02::2 before it has confirmed the use of its corresponding link-local address, as shown in Figure 6-23.

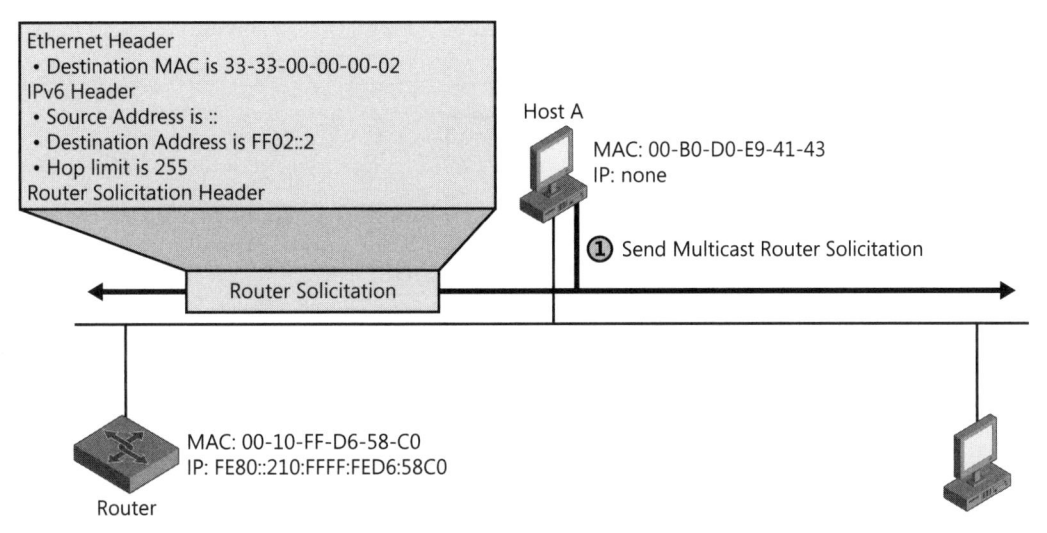

Figure 6-23 The multicast Router Solicitation message

Network Monitor Capture

Here is the Router Solicitation message for this example as displayed by Network Monitor 3.1 (frame 1 of capture 06_07 in the \NetworkMonitorCaptures folder on the companion CD-ROM):

```
Frame:
- Ethernet: Etype = IPv6
  + DestinationAddress: 333300 000002
  + SourceAddress: 00B0D0 E94143
    EthernetType: IPv6, 34525(0x86dd)
- Ipv6: Next Protocol = ICMPv6, Payload Length = 8
  + Versions: IPv6, Internet Protocol, DSCP 0
    PayloadLength: 8 (0x8)
    NextProtocol: ICMPv6, 58(0x3a)
    HopLimit: 255 (0xFF)
  + SourceAddress: 0:0:0:0:0:0:0:0
    DestinationAddress: FF02:0:0:0:0:0:0:2
- Icmpv6: Router Solicitation
    MessageType: Router Solicitation, 133(0x85)
  - RouterSolicitation:
    Code: 0 (0x0)
    Checksum: 31672 (0x7BB8)
    Reserved: 0 (0x0)
```

Notice the use of the unspecified address (::) as the source and that the Source Link-Layer Address option is not included.

Router Discovery Example—Part 2

The router, having registered the multicast MAC address of 33-33-00-00-00-02 with its Ethernet adapter, receives and processes the Router Solicitation. The router responds with a multicast Router Advertisement message containing configuration parameters and local link prefixes, as shown in Figure 6-24.

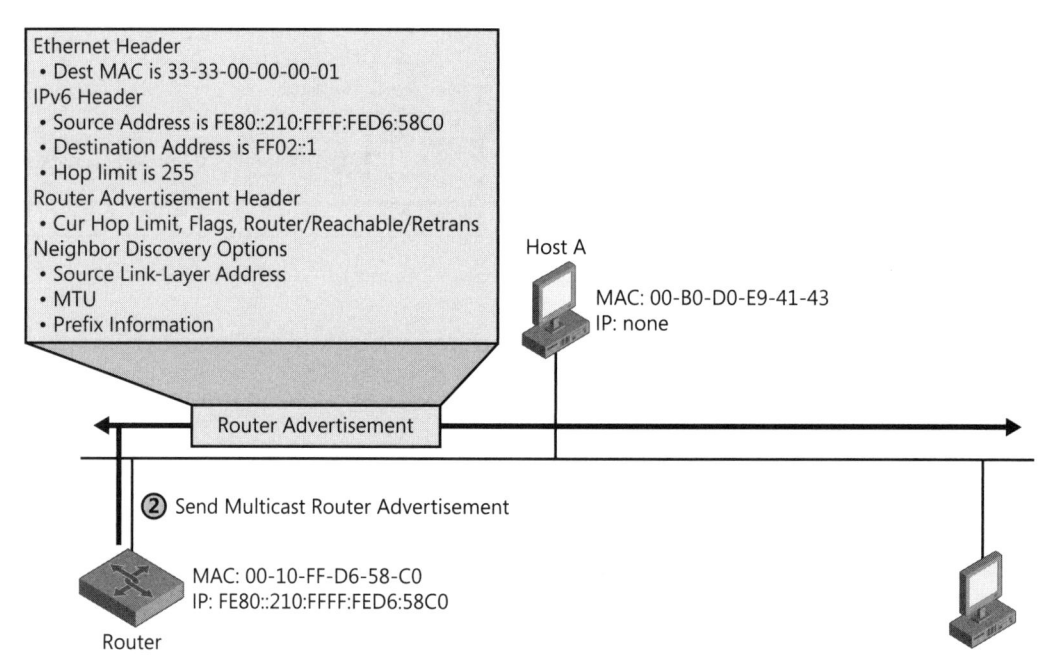

Figure 6-24 The unicast Router Advertisement message

Network Monitor Capture

Here is the Router Advertisement message for this example as displayed by Network Monitor 3.1 (frame 2 of capture 06_07 in the \NetworkMonitorCaptures folder on the companion CD-ROM):

```
  Frame:
- Ethernet: Etype = IPv6
  + DestinationAddress: 333300 000001
  + SourceAddress: 0010FF D658C0
    EthernetType: IPv6, 34525(0x86dd)
- Ipv6: Next Protocol = ICMPv6, Payload Length = 88
  + Versions: IPv6, Internet Protocol, DSCP 28
    PayloadLength: 88 (0x58)
    NextProtocol: ICMPv6, 58(0x3a)
    HopLimit: 255 (0xFF)
    SourceAddress: FE80:0:0:0:210:FFFF:FED6:58C0
    DestinationAddress: FF02:0:0:0:0:0:0:1
- Icmpv6: Router Advertisement
    MessageType: Router Advertisement, 134(0x86)
```

```
- RouterAdvertisement:
  Code: 0 (0x0)
  Checksum: 24725 (0x6095)
  CurHopLimit: 64 (0x40)
  - RouterAdvertisementFlag:
    M:                      (0.......) Not managed address configuration
    O:                      (.0......) Not other stateful configuration
    A:                      (..0.....) Not a Mobile IP Home Agent
    RouterPreference: (...00...) Medium,0(0x0)
    Reserved:               (.....000)
  RouterLifetime: 1800 (0x708)
  ReachableTime: 0 (0x0)
  RetransTimer: 0 (0x0)
- SourceLinkLayerAddress:
  Type: Source Link-Layer Address, 1(0x1)
  Length: 1, in unit of 8 octets
  Address: 00-10-FF-D6-58-C0
- PrefixInformation:
  Type: Prefix Information, 3(0x3)
  Length: 4, in unit of 8 octets
  PrefixLength: 64 (0x40)
  - Flags: 192 (0xC0)
    L:   (1.......) On-Link determination allowed
    A:   (.1......) Autonomous address-configuration
    R:   (..0.....) Not router Address
    S:   (...0....) Not a site prefix
    P:   (....0...) Not a router prefix
    Rsv: (.....000)
  ValidLifetime: 2592000 (0x278D00)
  PreferredLifetime: 604800 (0x93A80)
  Reserved: 0 (0x0)
  Prefix: 2001:DB8:0:F282:0:0:0:0
- PrefixInformation:
  Type: Prefix Information, 3(0x3)
  Length: 4, in unit of 8 octets
  PrefixLength: 64 (0x40)
  - Flags: 192 (0xC0)
    L:   (1.......) On-Link determination allowed
    A:   (.1......) Autonomous address-configuration
    R:   (..0.....) Not router Address
    S:   (...0....) Not a site prefix
    P:   (....0...) Not a router prefix
    Rsv: (.....000)
  ValidLifetime: 2592000 (0x278D00)
  PreferredLifetime: 604800 (0x93A80)
  Reserved: 0 (0x0)
  Prefix: FD5A:29F1:D005:F282:0:0:0:0
```

This Router Advertisement contains two prefixes—one for 2001:DB8:0:F282::/64 and one for FD5A:29F1:D005:F282::/64. Notice how both the global prefix and the unique local prefix use the same subnet identifier (F282).

Redirect Function

Routers use the redirect function to inform originating hosts of a better first-hop neighbor to which traffic should be forwarded for a specific destination. There are two instances where redirect is used:

1. A router informs an originating host of the IP address of a router available on the local link that is "closer" to the destination. "Closer" is a routing metric function used to reach the destination network segment. This condition can occur when there are multiple routers on a network segment, and the originating host chooses a default router and it is not the better ("closer") one to use to reach the destination.

2. A router informs an originating host that the destination is a neighbor (that is, it is on the same link as the originating host). This condition can occur when the prefix list of a host does not include the prefix of the destination. Because the destination does not match a prefix in the list, the originating host forwards the packet to its default router.

The following steps occur in the IPv6 redirect process:

1. The originating host forwards a unicast packet to its default router.

2. The router processes the packet and notes that the address of the originating host is a neighbor. Additionally, it notes that both the originating host's address and the next-hop address are on the same link.

3. The router sends the originating host a Redirect message. In the Target Address field of the Redirect message is the next-hop address of the node to which the originating host should send subsequent packets addressed to the destination.

4. The router forwards the packet to the appropriate next-hop address, using address resolution if needed to obtain the link-layer address of the next hop.

    For packets redirected to a router, the Target Address field is set to the link-local address of the router. For packets redirected to a host, the Target Address field is set to the destination address of the packet originally sent.

    The Redirect message includes the Redirected Header option. It might also include the Target Link-Layer Address option.

5. Upon receipt of the Redirect message, the originating host updates the destination address entry in the destination cache with the address in the Target Address field. If the Target Link-Layer Address option is included in the Redirect message, its contents are used to create or update the corresponding neighbor cache entry.

Redirect messages are sent only by the first router in the path between the originating host and the destination. Hosts never send Redirect messages and routers never update routing tables based on the receipt of a Redirect message. Like ICMPv6 error messages, Redirect messages are rate limited.

Redirect Example—Part 1

Host A has the Ethernet MAC address of 00-AA-00-11-11-11 and a corresponding link-local address of FE80::2AA:FF:FE11:1111. Host A also has the global address of 2001:DB8::1:2AA:FF:FE11:1111. Router 2 has the Ethernet MAC address of 00-AA-00-22-22-22 and a corresponding link-local address of FE80::2AA:FF:FE22:2222. Router 2 also has the site-local address of 2001:DB8::1:2AA:FF:FE22:2222. Router 3 has the Ethernet MAC address of 00-AA-00-33-33-33 and a corresponding link-local address of FE80::2AA:FF:FE33:3333. Router 3 also has the site-local address of 2001:DB8::1:2AA:FF:FE33:3333. Host A sends a packet to an off-link host at 2001:DB8::2:2AA:FF:FE99:9999 (not shown in Figure 6-25) and uses Router 2 as its current default router. However, Router 3 is the better router to use to reach this destination.

Host A performs address resolution if needed and sends the packet destined to 2001:DB8::2:2AA:FF:FE99:9999 to Router 2, as shown in Figure 6-25.

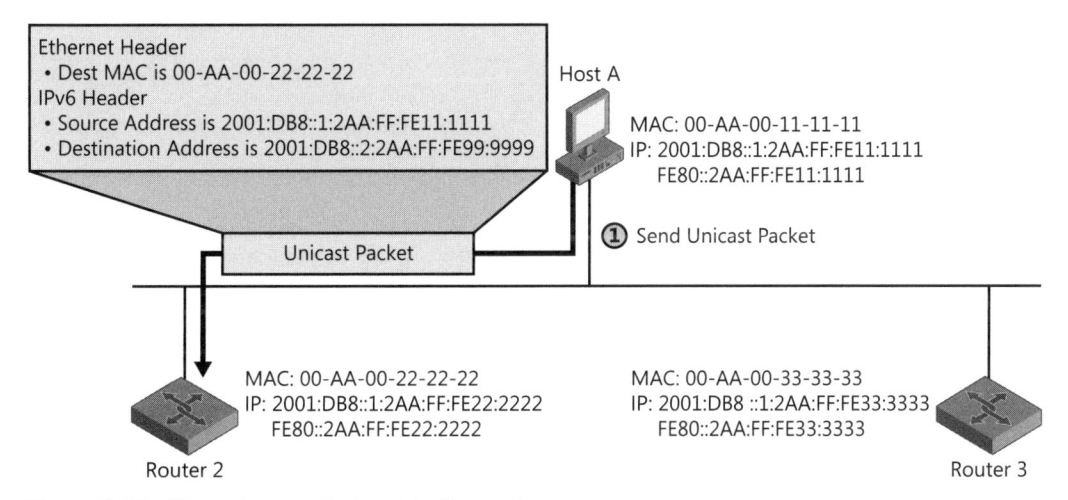

Figure 6-25 The unicast packet sent to the router

Redirect Example—Part 2

Router 2 receives the packet from Host A and notes that Host A is a neighbor. It also notes that Host A and the next-hop address for the destination are on the same link. To inform Host A that subsequent packets to the destination of 2001:DB8::2:2AA:EE:FE99:9999 should be sent to Router 3, Router 2 performs address resolution if needed and sends a Redirect message to Host A, as shown in Figure 6-26.

Ethernet Header
- Dest MAC is 00-AA-00-11-11-11

IPv6 Header
- Source Address is FE80::2AA:FF:FE22:2222
- Destination Address is 2001:DB8::1:2AA:FF:FE11:1111
- Hop limit is 255

Redirect Header
- Target Address is FE80::2AA:FF:FE33:3333
- Destination Address is 2001:DB8::2:2AA:FF:FE99:9999

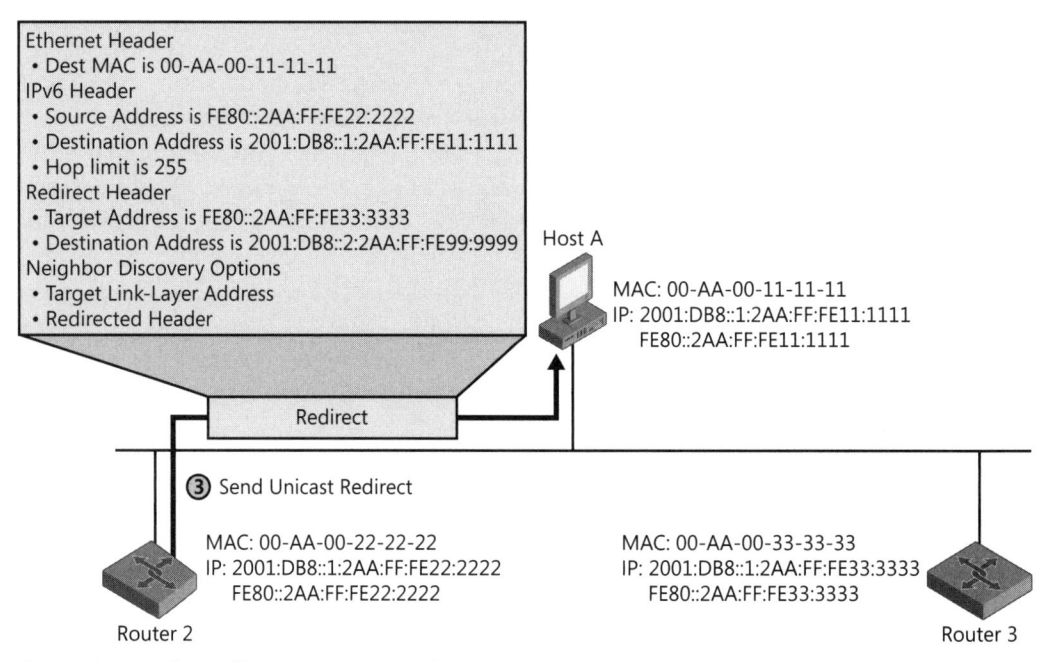

Neighbor Discovery Options
- Target Link-Layer Address
- Redirected Header

Figure 6-26 The Redirect message sent by the router

Redirect Example—Part 3

Based on the contents of its local routing table, Router 2 performs address resolution if needed and forwards the unicast packet received from Host A to Router 3, as shown in Figure 6-27.

Ethernet Header
- Dest MAC is 00-AA-00-33-33-33

IPv6 Header
- Source Address is 2001:DB8::1:2AA:FF:FE11:1111
- Destination Address is 2001:DB8::2:2AA:FF:FE99:9999

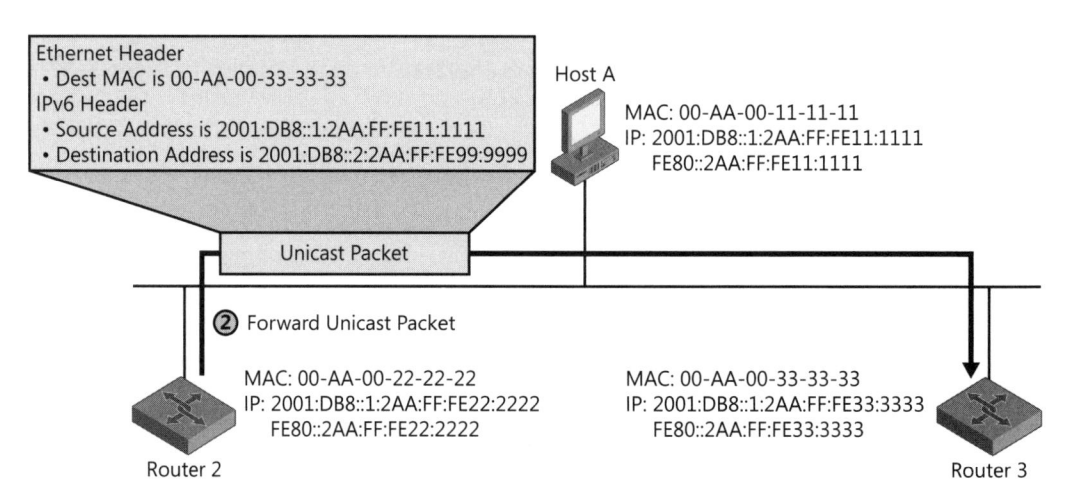

Figure 6-27 The unicast packet forwarded by the router

Host Sending Algorithm

The process by which an IPv6 host sends a unicast IPv6 packet uses a combination of the local host's conceptual data structures and the ND protocol. Based on RFC 4861, an IPv6 host uses the following algorithm when sending a unicast packet to an arbitrary destination:

1. Check the destination cache for an entry matching the destination address.

2. If an entry matching the destination address is found in the destination cache, obtain the next-hop address from the destination cache entry. If the destination is a Mobile IPv6 node, the destination cache entry might contain a pointer to a care-of destination cache entry. If so, the next-hop address is obtained from the care-of destination cache entry. For more information about Mobile IPv6, see Appendix F. Go to step 4.

   If an entry matching the destination address is not found in the destination cache, determine if the destination address matches a prefix in the prefix list:

   - If the destination address matches a prefix in the prefix list, the next-hop address is set to the destination address. Go to step 3.
   - If the destination address does not match a prefix in the prefix list, a default router is chosen from the default router list and the next-hop address is set to the default router address.

3. Update the destination cache.

4. Check the neighbor cache for an entry matching the next-hop address.

5. If an entry matching the next-hop address is found in the neighbor cache, use the link-layer address of the matching entry.

   If an entry matching the next-hop address is not found in the neighbor cache, use address resolution to obtain the link-layer address for the next-hop address.

   If address resolution fails, indicate an error.

6. Send the packet by using the link-layer address of the neighbor cache entry.

Figure 6-28 shows the host sending algorithm in flowchart form.

Because the IPv6 protocol for Windows Server 2008 and Windows Vista uses a routing table in place of a prefix list and default router list, the host-sending algorithm uses a different method to determine the next-hop address for the destination. For more information, see the "End-to-End IPv6 Delivery Process" section in Chapter 10.

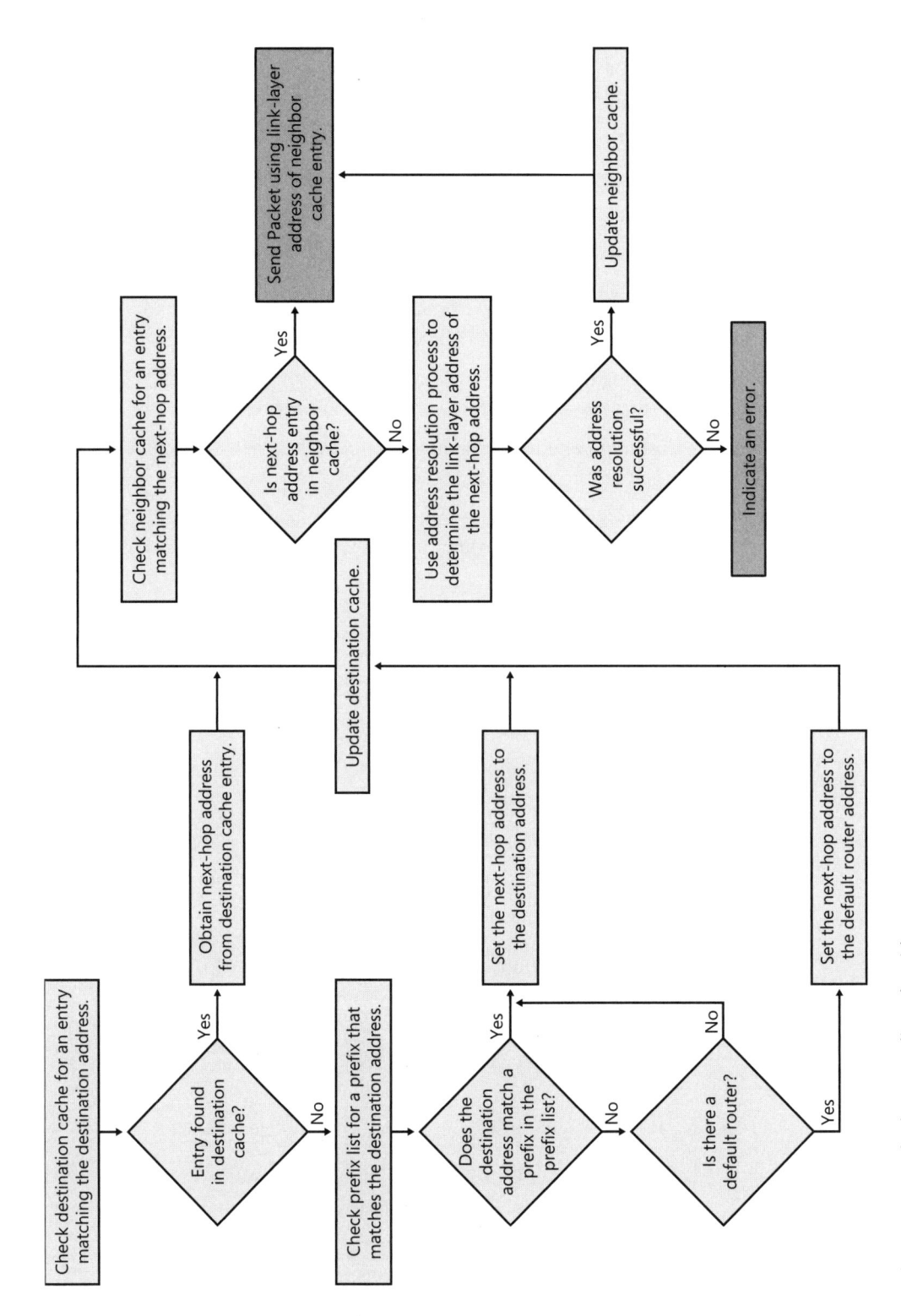

Figure 6-28 The host sending algorithm

IPv4 Neighbor Messages and Functions and IPv6 Equivalents

Table 6-3 lists IPv4 neighbor messages, components, and functions and their IPv6 equivalents.

Table 6-3 IPv4 Neighbor Messages, Components, and Functions and Their IPv6 Equivalents

IPv4	IPv6
ARP Request message	Neighbor Solicitation message
ARP Reply message	Neighbor Advertisement message
ARP cache	Neighbor cache
Gratuitous ARP	Duplicate address detection
Router Solicitation message (optional)	Router Solicitation message (required)
Router Advertisement message (optional)	Router Advertisement message (required)
Redirect message	Redirect message

References

The following references were cited in this chapter:

- RFC 1256 – "ICMP Router Discovery Messages"
- RFC 2464 – "Transmission of IPv6 Packets over Ethernet Networks"
- RFC 3775 – "Mobile IPv6"
- RFC 4191 – "Default Router Preferences and More-Specific Routes"
- RFC 4861 – "Neighbor Discovery for IP Version 6 (IPv6)"
- RFC 4862 – "IPv6 Stateless Address Autoconfiguration"
- Internet Draft – "Site Prefixes in Neighbor Discovery"

You can obtain these RFCs from the \RFCs_and_Drafts folder on the companion CD-ROM or from *http://www.ietf.org/rfc.html*.

Testing for Understanding

To test your understanding of IPv6 ND, answer the following questions. See Appendix D, "Testing for Understanding Answers," to check your answers.

1. List the IPv4 facilities that are replaced by the IPv6 ND protocol.
2. List the capabilities of the IPv6 ND protocol that are not present in IPv4.
3. List the five different ND messages and the options that can be included with them.

4. Describe the interpretation of the Length field in ND options.

5. What is the value of the Length field for a maximum-sized Redirected Header option (assuming no IPv6 extension headers are present)?

6. Describe how you would use the MTU option to provide seamless connectivity between Ethernet nodes and Asynchronous Transfer Mode (ATM) nodes on a transparently bridged link.

7. Why is the Source Link-Layer Address option not included in the Neighbor Solicitation message sent during duplicate address detection?

8. Describe the configuration parameters and their corresponding fields sent in the Router Advertisement message (not including options). Describe the configuration parameters and their corresponding fields sent in the Prefix Information option.

9. Under what circumstances is an unsolicited Neighbor Advertisement message sent?

10. What are the differences in address resolution and duplicate address detection node behavior for anycast addresses?

11. Why is the response to a duplicate address detection sent as multicast? Who sends the response, the offending or defending node?

12. Why is the value of the Hop Limit field set to 255 for all ND messages?

13. Describe the purpose of each of the host data structures described in RFC 4861.

14. What field in the Redirect message contains the next-hop address of the better router to use for packets addressed to a specific destination? Describe how the contents of that field are used to update the conceptual host data structures for subsequent data sent to the destination.

15. Under what circumstances does a router send a Router Advertisement?

16. For Host A and Host B on the same link, why is the exchange of a Neighbor Solicitation message (sent by Host A to Host B) and a Neighbor Advertisement message (sent by Host B to Host A) not considered by Host B as proof that Host A is reachable?

System Requirements

To use this book's companion CD-ROM, you need a computer equipped with the following minimum configuration:

- Microsoft Windows Server 2008, Windows Vista, Windows Server 2003, or Windows XP
- 1 GHz 32-bit (x86) or 64-bit (x64) processor (depending on the minimum requirements of the operating system)
- 1 GB of system memory (depending on the minimum requirements of the operating system)
- A hard disk partition with at least 1 GB of available space
- Support for DirectX 9 graphics and 32 MB of graphics memory (depending on the minimum requirements of the operating system)
- Appropriate video monitor
- Keyboard
- Mouse or other pointing device
- CD-ROM drive

To view the online version of this book and the *TCP/IP Fundamentals for Microsoft Windows* online book, you will need the Adobe Systems, Inc. Adobe Reader. See *http://www.adobe.com* for information about disk space requirements for the Adobe Reader.

To install Microsoft Network Monitor 3.1 from *http://go.microsoft.com/fwlink/?LinkID=92844* or a link on the companion CD-ROM, you need the following additional minimum configuration:

- A hard disk partition with approximately 25 MB of free disk space

To install the Microsoft PowerPoint Viewer from *http://go.microsoft.com/fwlink/?LinkID=59771* or a link on the companion CD-ROM, you need the following additional minimum configuration:

- A hard disk partition with approximately 4 MB of free disk space

What do you think of this book?

We want to hear from you!

Do you have a few minutes to participate in a brief online survey?

Microsoft is interested in hearing your feedback so we can continually improve our books and learning resources for you.

To participate in our survey, please visit:

www.microsoft.com/learning/booksurvey/

...and enter this book's ISBN-10 or ISBN-13 number (located above barcode on back cover*). As a thank-you to survey participants in the United States and Canada, each month we'll randomly select five respondents to win one of five $100 gift certificates from a leading online merchant. At the conclusion of the survey, you can enter the drawing by providing your e-mail address, which will be used for prize notification only.

Thanks in advance for your input. Your opinion counts!

*Where to find the ISBN on back cover

ISBN-13: 000-0-0000-0000-0
ISBN-10: 0-0000-0000-0

Example only. Each book has unique ISBN.

Microsoft® Press

No purchase necessary. Void where prohibited. Open only to residents of the 50 United States (includes District of Columbia) and Canada (void in Quebec). For official rules and entry dates see:

www.microsoft.com/learning/booksurvey/